Handbook of Enterprise Systems Architecture in Practice

Pallab Saha
National University of Singapore
Institute of Systems Science, Singapore

 **INFORMATION SCIENCE REFERENCE**

Hershey · London · Melbourne · Singapore

Acquisitions Editor:	Kristin Klinger
Development Editor:	Kristin Roth
Senior Managing Editor:	Jennifer Neidig
Managing Editor:	Sara Reed
Assistant Managing Editor:	Sharon Berger
Copy Editor:	Larissa Vinci
Typesetter:	Jamie Snavely
Cover Design:	Lisa Tosheff
Printed at:	Yurchak Printing Inc.

Published in the United States of America by
Information Science Reference (an imprint of Idea Group Inc.)
701 E. Chocolate Avenue, Suite 200
Hershey PA 17033
Tel: 717-533-8845
Fax: 717-533-8661
E-mail: cust@idea-group.com
Web site: http://www.info-sci-ref.com

and in the United Kingdom by
Information Science Reference (an imprint of Idea Group Inc.)
3 Henrietta Street
Covent Garden
London WC2E 8LU
Tel: 44 20 7240 0856
Fax: 44 20 7379 0609
Web site: http://www.eurospanonline.com

Library of Congress Cataloging-in-Publication Data

Enterprise systems architecture in practice / Pallab Saha, editor.

p. cm.

Summary: "This book is a valuable addition to the reading list of executives, managers, and staff in business, government, and other sectors who seek to keep their enterprises agile and efficient as they manage change, implement new business processes and supporting technologies, and pursue important strategic goals"--Provided by publisher.

Includes bibliographical references and index.

ISBN 978-1-59904-189-6 (hardcover) -- ISBN 978--59904-191-9 (ebook)

1. Management—Data processing. 2. Business enterprises—Communication systems—Management. 3. Computer architecture. 4. Management information systems. I. Saha, Pallab, 1970-

HD30.2.E58 2007

658.4'038011--dc22

2006033766

British Cataloguing in Publication Data
A Cataloguing in Publication record for this book is available from the British Library.

All work contributed to this book set is new, previously-unpublished material. The views expressed in this book are those of the authors, but not necessarily of the publisher.

Table of Contents

Section I
Frameworks and Methodologies

Section V
Technology and Service-Oriented Architecture

Detailed Table of Contents

Section I
Frameworks and Methodologies

Chapter I

The federal enterprise architecture framework (FEAF) is perhaps the most adopted EA framework, especially within the U.S. Government agencies. Either FEAF has been adopted as-is or other frameworks derived from FEAF have been used. FEAF today continues to be the most comprehensive framework available for guidance by agencies. It consists of a full-fledged methodology, several reference models, target architectures, and even a toolkit that facilitates adoption across all agencies. Chapter I evaluates synergies between the comprehensive FEAF against the Generalized Enterprise Reference Architecture and Methodology (GERAM) framework. The chapter discusses the level of completeness in the FEAF based on GERAM requirements and additionally areas where the FEAF goes well beyond GERAM requirements.

Chapter II

Enterprise architecture is a non-trivial initiative. Organizations usually face difficulty in understanding which of the organization elements they need to be aware of and which of them would be relevant to CIOs and IT managers. Chapter II presents an EA framework that is lightweight and selective to meet the needs of the organization. The chapter uses the "agile" approach to develop architectural artifacts. It starts with the need for frameworks and some of the currently popular frameworks. Then it argues why interoperability both at systems and human level is critical followed by a discussion on the relevant architectural views that is derived from the XAF matrix and elements that need to be created. The chapter concludes with a comparison of the proposed framework with other established frameworks from the point of view of simplicity and ease of use.

Chapter III

Organizations are usually unclear about the activities and deliverables of an EA program. This situation is further exacerbated by the fact that some of the more popular and emerging architecture frameworks tend to be proprietary. There are open frameworks that often provide a long list of artifacts that are required as part of EA, but do not make any mention under what circumstances, which artifacts are relevant. Chapter III provides a meta-methodology based on existing architecture frameworks that facilitates organizations assess and select architectural elements and artifacts within the context of specific EA program requirements. The proposed approach in the chapter allows organizations to configure their EA programme, instead of "doing the whole nine yards" for every situation. The chapter illustrates the proposed approach with a real-life case study.

Chapter IV

With the intent of being more competitive and agile, organizations are now collaborating at the level of value chains. This entails end-to-end business processes that span multiple organizations. This move toward a new operating model is giving rise to the concept of virtual enterprises (VE). Given the absence of any current architecture methodology, Chapter IV presents a modeling framework that business architects and domain specialists can use to build and configure architectural elements and models specifically for VEs. The chapter uses and improves upon existing modeling standards and practices (like BPMN, UML, MDA) and applies concepts of service-oriented architecture (SOA) to make organizations more responsive to change.

Chapter V

The Department of Defense Architecture Framework (DODAF) provides guidelines to DOD commands, services, and agencies in developing their EA both for war fighting operations and business processes. The DODAF is a structured approach that defines architecture views, perspectives, artifacts, reference models, and deliverables. Chapter V presents the DOD defined methodology that uses DODAF to create architecture outputs. Activity-based methodology (ABM) discussed in this chapter is presented as a step-by-step approach that allows a common reference point for all architectural assets in terms of scope, breadth, depth, and intensity. Several DOD entities have adopted or are in the process of adopting ABM, thereby providing credence to its applicability in practice.

Chapter VI

Business architecture is a key component of EA and without doubt drives the rest of the sub-architectures. Target business architecture definition typically consists of target outcomes (i.e., business metrics representing the ends) and target business processes (i.e., representing the means). Thus, process modeling is a critical activity in developing business architecture. Chapter VI presents a Petri-net based methodology, transaction-oriented Petri-nets (TOP) to enterprise process modeling. The chapter starts with a brief background of existing architecture frameworks and discusses the role of business architecture. Then it presents the details of the TOP notation, following which the complete TOP methodology framework is discussed in a step-by-step manner, with examples provided to illustrate each step and their respective output.

Chapter VII

In almost all countries, government is the biggest organization. This is associated with multiplicity of factors that add to the complexity of the operations of any government. Singapore has traditionally ranked very high on e-government readiness and usually within the global top 5. Chapter VII is a discussion of the role of enterprise architecture in the Singapore's e-government programmes. The chapter discusses the evolution of the country's e-government action plans and policies and examines the linkages and roles that EA plays including IT governance and investment planning. The chapter briefly presents the currently ongoing efforts within the government to define reference models that are intended for use by agencies to develop their own EA in alignment with the overall government-wide EA. Within the current e-government plan, the iGOV 2010, EA is one the three key pillars of programme success.

Section II
Governance and Management

Chapter VIII

One of the critical success factors in EA programmes is the need to disseminate the EA blueprint within the enterprise. Often EA blueprints are defined and developed by corporate IT departments, but the same is not adequately communicated to the rest of the organization. This creates problems in governing the architecture with the individual locations and business units typically failing to appreciate the need for an organization-wide EA and the need to comply with the same. Chapter VIII discusses current best practices and provides guidelines in communicating EA to the users. The recommended approaches and practices presented in the chapter are derived from the United States National Institutes of Health (NIH) EA programmes. The intent of this chapter is to educate CIOs and chief architects about the need to communicate EA, recommended approaches, and its key benefits to the EA programme.

Chapter IX continues on the theme of architecture governance and management. This chapter begins with a discussion on the need to improve stakeholder communications and enhance engagement with the users in an EA programme. The chapter presents five steps to involve stakeholders in EA programmes, followed by ten strategies and mechanisms to institutionalize stakeholder involvement. The application of the steps, strategies, and mechanisms presented in the chapter are illustrated through a detailed case study of United States Federal Deposit Insurance Corporation (FDIC). The chapter concludes with a set of lessons learned that organizations can refer to.

Often IT systems implementations fail to adequately account for transition management. Given the fact that enterprise systems inevitably lead to redesign and digitization of business processes and associated business rules, it has the capability to trigger large-scale organizational change. As a result, IT implementation programmes must incorporate transition management as a key activity often as a critical success factor. Chapter X presents an integrated holistic approach to IT systems implementation called the better enterprise systems implementation (BEST). The chapter treats IT systems implementation as an organizational development issue and positions the BEST methodology as an approach to manage IT driven organizational change. The chapter then illustrates the application of the methodology through three case studies in Norway and Israel.

Chapter XI is a description of an approach that allows organizations to simulate, predict, and control the emergent properties of enterprise systems from an architectural perspective. The chapter argues that existing methodologies and toolsets are by nature bottom-up and often fail to take into consideration the non-functional requirements of the IT systems from an architectural viewpoint. The chapter begins with a brief discussion of the key non-functional requirements that most IT systems are expected to fulfill. It then presents a five-step methodology that organizations can use to build and evolve their architectures. The chapter concludes with the benefits of the proposed methodology.

Section III
Transformation and Value Realization

Chapter XII

Chapter XII presents an approach where EA is viewed as a business issue. The chapter starts with a discussion on business transformation that is triggered through EA. The chapter argues that EA is an imperative irrespective of the business condition that an organization might be in and places forth business diagnostics as a key element of any architectural initiative. The chapter illustrates the application of the proposed approach in a financial services organization and discusses business process driven business transformation. The chapter then concludes with a discussion on non-process driven business transformation and why process architecture-based transformation was used as an example.

Chapter XIII

Most large IT system implementation initiatives are plagued by several factors that often make implementations less than desirable. While factors leading to failure for large IT implementations have been documented and analyzed, the intriguing issue is that organizations seem to repeat the same mistakes over and over again. This necessitates the need for a mechanism that allows planners and managers to evaluate the start-up situation in such projects, including capturing the project dynamics in a coherent manner. Chapter XIII presents such an approach based on better enterprise systems implementation (BEST). In doing this, the two key questions addressed are what problems can be pre-empted and what can be done about them. The chapter then continues to illustrate the proposed approach through several mini-cases derived out of real-life scenarios. The chapter concludes with a discussion on areas for further research.

Chapter XIV

Organizations typically tend to consider and implement EA in isolation. However, in reality, EA has the capability to impact several other activities within the enterprise. Chapter XIV explores and discusses the linkages that EA has with IT investment management and system development processes and hence the need for a holistic approach. In doing so, it proposes an integrated enterprise lifecycle (IELC). The chapter starts with a discussion of the IELC and its various components. The chapter positions IELC as a key IT governance mechanism and presents several governance archetypes that are part of the IELC. It concludes with a brief discussion on the proposed move towards IELC by the U.S. Office of Management and Budget (OMB) and U.S. General Accounting Office (GAO) under the Federal Enterprise Architecture (FEA) program.

Chapter XV presents U.S. Department of Defense (DOD)'s goal of net-centric transformation as an implementation of EA. The chapter argues that to achieve net-centricity, the existence of an integrated architecture provided by the DOD global information Grid (GIG) is a key imperative. The chapter then provides an overview of the key performance parameters to support net readiness (NR-KPP). It details the adoption of net-centric transformation through the use of net-centric data strategy, net-centric IA strategy, service-oriented architecture (SOA), and communications transport strategy. The chapter concludes with a discussion on upcoming and future trends to enable DOD's move towards net-centricity.

Section IV
Implementation and Deployment

Chapter XVI is a case study on application of EA to develop an efficient and effective e-governance system for citizen services administration by the Government of India. The chapter starts with a background on various e-government initiatives, including a brief discussion on the administrative structure in India. The chapter then puts forth key imperatives that are required for successful e-government programs keeping in mind the Indian context. EA is then presented as one the critical success factors. The chapter continues with a detailed discussion of a proposed framework (derived from the Zachman framework) that facilitates the application of EA in the context of e-government in India. The chapter concludes with a mapping of the earlier presented imperatives to the key elements of the proposed framework.

Chapter XVII presents enterprise resource planning (ERP) system architecture that makes individual business modules reusable through the use of Web services-based shared and non-monolithic architecture. The chapter is based on a practical challenge that enterprises currently face, wherein systems (especially the ERP tools) have proprietary data models, thus limiting their usage and in conflict to their claim of being positioned as "enterprise systems." This leads to vendor lock-in. The chapter begins with a background on existing ERP systems with a discussion of their limitations as real enterprise systems. The chapter then presents the federated ERP system approach and discusses how the federated approach addresses the shortcomings of existing siloed ERP systems. The chapter concludes with a discussion on the kind of adoption challenges that the federated approach might face along with a short brief on future trends and research.

Chapter XVIII

This chapter moves away from the traditional four sub-architecture-based view of EA and takes a network-based view that is based on understanding and capturing the dependencies between the elements of the EA. The proposed approach asserts that such dependencies are a factor of time and typically emerge as the architecture evolves. Dependencies that emerge during the design, deployment, and operations of the EA are based on both technical and social factors. The chapter presents a case study of the application of the proposed approach in a financial services company. The chapter concludes with a discussion of the limitations of the proposed approach and presents pointers to how the limitations can be addressed.

Chapter XIX

Typically, EA programmes tend to consist of large teams that develop and implement the target architecture for a single organization or company. Chapter XIX presents experiences and best practices in developing EA by a small team for a federated organization. A federated structure is typical in many governments where the administrative structure is organized into national/federal entities followed by states, districts, or provinces. Given the federated structure, developing EA presents several practical challenges. The chapter discusses factors to be considered in such a scenario when developing EA in terms of scope, intensity, use of tools, open standards, shared business services and programme governance.

Chapter XX

Chapter XX presents the experiences of development and evolution of EA at Syngenta. The key drivers in Syngenta's architecture programme are business efficiency, growth, and innovation. The chapter shares the experiences and insights from several business areas. The case studies presented in the chapter include EA initiatives like server rationalization and development of global infrastructure services, integrated "go-to-market" platform, providing an unified research platform, and building an enterprise-wide business intelligence. The chapter then presents a simple framework for EA and discusses the case studies in the context of the framework. The chapter concludes with future trends and discusses a few plausible areas of research.

Chapter XXI

Chapter XXI describes the application of the generalized enterprise reference architecture and methodology (GERAM) in analyzing the ANZAC ship alliance (ASA). The chapter discusses the details of the use of GERA in developing and studying a virtual enterprise, especially issues relating to logistics and information architecture management needed to support the operations of ASA as a virtual enterprise. The chapter starts with a brief overview of the GERAM including the key reasons of why it was selected for use. The chapter then describes ASA as a virtual enterprise including the peculiarities and nuances of a virtual enterprise. The chapter concludes with a description of enterprise engineering programme at ASA, the artifacts, and models developed based on GERAM requirements.

Chapter XXII is a description of business process modeling capabilities within the CIMOSA application server (CAS). The CAS is an information system for enterprise modeling and designing. The chapter starts with a brief overview of the problems that are faced by organizations in integrating their disparate systems. Then it describes the CAS project, its goals and objectives, and the primary reason for selecting CIMOSA as the reference architecture. Following this, the chapter describes the CIMOSA modeling framework and conceptual model. The chapter then describes the business process modeling aspects with an example of a manufacturing organization including the views and artifacts needed to support the requirements of enterprise systems.   .

Chapter XXIII elaborates the role of EA in a service-oriented enterprise (SOE). Driven by the need to be adaptable, agile, and responsive to change, organizations are now adopting the SOE paradigm where organizations view themselves as a bundle of services that are available for use through technology enablement. The chapter begins with the issues that enterprise architects need to grapple with, namely, business services, service-oriented solutions, infrastructure services, and IT organization changes. It goes on to compare a traditional enterprise with a SOE. The chapter then discusses the development of strategy in a SOE and its peculiarities. The chapter provides real-life examples on various aspects of service orientation adopted by various organizations.

Chapter XXIV is a case study of the re-establishment of EA for the local government following Hurricane Katrina in Louisiana. The chapter presents an approach to address areas in EA that have not received much attention as part of preparedness, response, and recovery phases. The chapter proposes the use of service-oriented architecture (SOA) paradigm to address some of the key issues. The chapter starts with a brief background of the underlying EA framework that was used in the given situation, followed by a detailed description of the conceptual data model and how a critical portion of the EA was developed. The chapter concludes with a discussion on other technologies that can be used to extend the current solution.

Integration technologies to support and enable business-to-business collaborations have been around for some time now. However, all existing approaches overly focus on the operational transaction portion of the overall collaboration mechanism. Chapter XXV proposes to use the Web services paradigm as a way to deal with all aspects of business collaborations. The chapter starts with an overview of Web services as an integration platform, followed by a description of the criticality of the life cycle approach in integration. The chapter demonstrates with examples the use of Web services in extending its support of operational aspects alone to the full life cycle of business collaborations, thereby enabling seamless e-business collaborations and trading.

Most organizations are now characterized by end-to-end cross enterprise business processes that aim to enable value chain integration. Although organizations recognize the need for integration both at the business process and at the system level, very few utilize formal approaches in designing and implementing business rules that are needed to govern cross-enterprise processes. The criticality of the managing business rules in cross enterprise business processes is further driven by the fact that business partners tend to have their own agendas and goals in partnering. Chapter XXVI presents a rule-based enterprise integration approach enabled through messaging technology. The chapter begins with the challenges of large-scale collaborative systems and the evolution of technology solutions to address some of the challenges. The chapter then presents the proposed enterprise integration architecture and an overview of related technologies. Following this, the chapter elaborates the steps in rule design, validation, and deployment and its adoption within the proposed integration architecture. The chapter concludes with a discussion on future developments in the proposed area.

Foreword

Historically, enterprise architecture has been a non-issue because in the industrial age, it was the industrial products that were growing in complexity and changing and the concept of the enterprise was relatively simple: create a good product and then find a lot of people to sell it to. As we approximate the realities of information age, major changes are taking place in the global marketplace. It is the enterprise that is growing in complexity and the enterprise that is changing. No longer is business as simple as "get yourself a good product and then find a lot of customers to sell it to." That is, historically, from the perspective of the enterprise, the market (the customers) is integrated. Increasingly, the concept is, find yourself a good customer and then you (the enterprise) identify the range of products (or services) required to keep that customer a good customer. That is, from the perspective of the customer, the product and/or the enterprise must be integrated to the customer's requirement.

If the enterprise has to treat each customer as a unique requirement and customize every product or service of the enterprise to the perspective of each customer, it will drive the complexity of the enterprise out of sight and I would suggest that this information age characteristic is quite independent of whether it is the enterprise or the enterprise's product or whether the enterprise is public sector or private sector or how big or small the enterprise is.

Integration is where the complexity lies. Increasingly, all the parts of the enterprise have to be engineered to fit together to the specification of the customer… enterprise-wide. Furthermore, to create complex industrial products that are economically viable, as many parts as possible must be engineered as standard, interchangeable parts, reusable, or "normalized." That is, in the information age, the enterprise is going to have to be engineered such that all of the "parts" fit together enterprise-wide and that everything possible is engineered to be standard and interchangeable (reusable) and that, in order to be "lean," no concept should recur, (everything (not only the data) will have to be "normalized").

A second characteristic of the changing global marketplace is dramatic escalation of the rate of change. The way that dramatic escalation of the rate of change affects products (or enterprises) is in reducing the time-to-market, that is, reducing the time it takes from the point in time an order is placed for a new product until a finished good is produced, in the case of enterprises until a new enterprise-wide, integrated, implemented enterprise, is produced. The information age customer demand is for custom products (integrated to the specification of the customer requirement), mass-produced in quantities of one for immediate delivery, that is, a time-to-market of virtually zero. You might recognize this as the present definition of "mass-customization."

In short, the known characteristics of the information age are extreme complexity and dramatic escalation of the rate of change. There is a plethora of business and academic literature that argues this case.

A survey of 7,000 years of history of human kind would conclude that the only known strategy for accommodating extreme complexity and high rates of change is *architecture*. If you can't describe something, you can't create it, whether it is an airplane, a hundred storey building, a computer, an automobile… or an enterprise. Once you get a complex product created and you want to change it, the basis for change is its descriptive representations. I would suggest that architecture is the total set of descriptive representations relevant for describing something, anything complex you want to create, which serves as the baseline for change if you ever want to change the thing you have created. You don't need architecture if you want to create a simple object. For example, if all you want is a log cabin, chop down trees and build a log cabin. You don't need architecture. You can see and understand everything all at the same time. On the other hand, if you want a hundred storey building, you cannot see and understand everything all at the same time and you are going to have to have architecture and the architectural representations will be the basis for changing it once it is built.

If you want to reduce the time-to-market for creating a complex product, you could engineer the parts, prefabricate them, have them in inventory long before you ever get the order. Then you could reduce the time to market to just the time it takes to assemble the product. If you cleverly engineered the parts such that they could be assembled into more than one finished good, you could build a virtually infinite number of custom finished goods from the same set of prefabricated parts. In other words, you could manufacture custom products, mass-produced in quantities of one for immediate delivery. I might observe that although there is no manufacturer that has completely perfected the concepts of mass-customization, the Japanese taught the western manufactures a lot of hard lessons in the last 25 or 30 years and anymore, to get into or stay in a complex industrial product manufacturing business, mass-customization is fundamental and integral to survival.

Clearly, my argument is, we will have to apply the same kind of concepts to the enterprise in the information age that we have applied to the industrial products of the industrial age. We will have to produce different, custom manifestations (or implementations) of the enterprise, enterprise-wide, on demand.

By mixing the metaphor (industrial products and enterprises), I have tried to encapsulate in a few short paragraphs the underlying argument for enterprise architecture. In the information age, I am quite certain that the question to the enterprise is, "how do you intend to deal with extreme complexity and dramatic escalation of the rate of change?" I would submit, if the enterprise does not have an enterprise architecture strategy, they are neither going to accommodate extreme complexity nor the escalating rate of change and therefore, I would suggest, it is questionable whether they are going to be able to exist. My opinion is enterprise architecture is the most profound, significant, issue of the information age.

The next question is, "what is enterprise architecture, what does it look like?" We know what architecture is for airplanes. We know what architecture is for buildings. We know what architecture is for computers. We know what architecture is for industrial products because in the industrial age, it was the industrial product that was increasing in complexity and changing. If we hadn't figured out what architecture is for industrial products, we would not have Boeing 747s (airplanes), hundred storey buildings, computers, ocean liners, or Acura Legends (automobiles). We would not have complex industrial products.

An observation of architecture for industrial products shows that architecture is architecture is architecture. All industrial products have bills-of-materials. They all have functional specs, they all have drawings, they all of operating instructions, they all have timing diagrams, and they all have engineering design objectives. Each of these sets of descriptions is completely different and varies independently from one another. However, they are all related to one another. Generically, they describe WHAT the product is made of, HOW the product works, WHERE the components are located, WHO is responsible for operation, WHEN do things happen, and WHY do they happen. This classification of descriptive representations has been employed by humanity for thousands of years. It is universal.

There is another dimension of classification of descriptions that have to do with the audiences for which the descriptions are prepared and employed. Very complex products will have some scoping or bounding expression for the originators. They all have concept definitions (requirements) for the end owners. They all have logic representations (schematics) for the designers. They all have technology constructs (blueprints) for the builders. They all have production tool configurations for the implementers.

These two classifications for descriptive representations are orthogonal and constitute a structured order or schema for descriptions, that is, a "framework for architecture," which classifies and defines the set of descriptive representations for anything.

I spent something over 40 years of my professional life trying to find an answer to the question, "What does architecture look like for enterprises?" If I have done anything of any value, my contribution has been in the form of a framework, a framework for enterprise architecture, which simply puts some definition around the set of descriptive representations that are relevant for describing enterprises. Anyone who has followed my work would recognize my framework in the previous description of the architecture schema. I simply put enterprise names on the same engineering design artifacts that constitute architecture for industrial products. In 2006, the time of writing this foreword, we do not have experience with producing all of the descriptions (models) for an enterprise that are prescribed by this framework, in fact, we don't even have formalisms for many of them. There is a lot of room for creativity, research and development, and collaboration.

Which brings me to Pallab Saha's book… this is a very timely and important book. Pallab Saha has assembled substantive discussions about all of the known architecture-related subjects of which we are aware at the moment. The subjects are wide and varied and clearly, there is a lot of creativity and work that needs to be done. I do not think that we will have several hundred years to accumulate experience, develop formalisms, and do all the architectural instantiations that will be required to operate enterprises in the information age. In fact, we may only have several decades to make major progress because at the point in time that the enterprise finds itself in extremis, unable to accommodate any more complexity and unable to cope with the escalating rate of change, that is, at the point in time the enterprise discovers it is imperative to have enterprise architecture to survive, it is going to be to late to start working on it. Pallab's book is timely because tomorrow morning is not too early to start working on enterprise architecture!

I hope Pallab Saha starts working on the next book immediately. The next book must integrate and normalize all the subjects of the first book. He would likely find my framework for enterprise architecture helpful if he actually undertook this next endeavor. However, the present book is a good place to start. It is a book that not only systems people should read, but enterprise business people should read as well. In fact, I hope in my brief foreword, I have sufficiently argued that enterprise architecture is an ENTERPRISE issue, not simply a systems issue. Maybe, by the time the next book is ready for publication, the urgency of complexity and change will be so apparent to the business world, they will be more prepared to read it.

John A. Zachman
Glendale, California 2006

John A. Zachman is the originator of the Framework for Enterprise Architecture, which has received broad acceptance around the world as an integrative framework, or "periodic table" of descriptive representations for enterprises. Dr. Zachman is not only known for his work on this book, but is also known for his early contributions to IBM's information strategy methodology (business systems planning) as well as to their executive team planning techniques (intensive planning).

Dr. Zachman retired from IBM in 1990, having served them for 26 years. He is chief executive officer of the Zachman Institute for Framework Advancement (ZIFA), an organization dedicated to advancing the conceptual and implementation states of the art in enterprise architecture. Dr. Zachman serves on the executive council for information management and technology of the United States General Accounting Office. He is a fellow for the College of Business Administration of the University of North Texas. He serves on the advisory board for the Data Resource Management Program at the University of Washington and on the advisory board of the Data Administration Management Association International (DAMA-I) from whom he was awarded the 2002 Lifetime Achievement Award. He was awarded the 2004 Oakland University, Applied Technology in Business (ATIB), and the Award for IS Excellence and Innovation. Dr. Zachman has been focusing on enterprise architecture since 1970 and has written extensively on the subject. He is the author of the e-book. "The Zachman Framework for Enterprise Architecture: A Primer on Enterprise Engineering and Manufacturing." He has facilitated innumerable executive team planning sessions. He travels nationally and internationally, teaching and consulting, and is a popular conference speaker known for his motivating messages on enterprise architecture issues. He has spoken to many thousands of enterprise managers and information professionals on every continent. Prior to joining IBM, Dr. Zachman served as a line officer in the United States Navy and is a retired Commander in the U.S. Naval Reserve. He chaired a panel on "Planning, Development, and Maintenance Tools and Methods Integration" for the U.S. National Institute of Standards and Technology. He holds a degree in chemistry from Northwestern University, has taught at Tufts University, has served on the board of councilors for the School of Library and Information Management at the University of

Southern California as a special advisor to the School of Library and Information Management at Emporia State University, and on the advisory council to the School of Library and Information Management at Dominican University.

***

I congratulate Dr. Pallab Saha and the authors who have contributed to the *Handbook of Enterprise Systems Architecture in Practice*. This book covers a wide range of enterprise architecture (EA) issues in a way that reflects many aspects of a global EA discussion that has been going on for nearly 20 years. You will find some variance in the approach and lexicon that contributing authors use in many of the chapters, but you will also find a number of common threads that are an indication of both the richness and diversity of thought in the EA community and of the continuing maturity of EA as a management best practice and a career field for business and technology professionals. As such, the *Handbook of Enterprise Systems Architecture in Practice* is a valuable addition to the reading list of executives, managers, and staff in business, government, and other sectors who seek to keep their enterprises agile and efficient as they manage change, implement new business processes and supporting technologies, and pursue important strategic goals.

EA is distinguished from, and yet encompasses, other forms of business, service, systems, data, and technology architecture. EA seeks to be the over-arching framework and methodology for integrating strategic, business, and technology planning across the entire enterprise. In so doing, EA claims to be the highest level of all meta-concepts that guide the analysis, design, and ongoing improvement of enterprises in the public, private, military, academic, and non-profit sectors. This expanded claim arises not from ego, but from necessity, as CEOs, CFOs, CIOs, and COOs seek new ways to envision and transform the enterprises they lead. Architectures exist in the mind of every executive and manager, yet these architectures are mostly held within, as executives are not familiar with EA methods and frameworks that offer ways to take abstract mental images and transform them into a sharable model of the enterprise. The CEO is the ultimate owner of the EA, yet that too is not fully realized. When it is, EA will further contribute to the ongoing success of enterprises in all sectors.

This book presents over two dozen articles by leading authors, researchers, and practitioners, who cover various aspects of implementing systems architecture in the context of solving enterprise-level business problems.

The approach to EA that I have written about previously centers on a framework with five hierarchical levels (strategic goals, business services, information flows, systems, and infrastructure) and three threads that pervade all levels of the architecture (security, standards, and training). In teaching this and other approaches to EA, I have had the privilege of helping to create several training programs and have delivered EA courses and seminars all over the world. To convey the essential and unique aspects of EA as it is most effectively practiced, I start my lectures with a simple equation: EA = S+B+T that stands for "EA equals strategy + business + technology." This is meant to differentiate EA from early stand-alone forms of business architecture, data architecture, systems architecture, and network architecture… all of which are active and relevant sub-architectures within an integrated EA. This equation also indicates that strategic priorities drive business requirements, which drive technology solutions… including the design, implementation, and operation of information technology systems. EA is not just about technology, it is about designing and improving enterprises in all aspects, doing so through a repeatable and increasingly effective and mature methodology.

My next lecture point is to usually say that a complete approach to EA must include an interlocking set of elements, including (1) a detailed step-by-step *methodology* for establishing the EA program and documenting current and future versions of the EA on an ongoing basis; (2) an analysis and documentation *framework* that establishes the scope and relationship of the EA; (3) a set of EA documentation *artifacts* (also known as work products) that cover all areas of the EA as defined by the framework; (4) the selection of a set of proven *best practices* for doing EA analysis, design, and documentation work, and which cover all areas of the framework; and (5) an online *repository* for archiving EA artifacts that incorporates automated documentation and analysis tools to the maximum extent possible. Unfortunately, many current approaches to EA do not have all of these elements, and/or the elements are not designed to work together. Examples include a lack of a complete set of artifacts to cover all areas of the EA framework; artifacts that are not derived from proven best practices, best practices that do not map to all levels of the framework, and a repository design that does not reflect the underlying analysis and design framework and is therefore difficult to understand, navigate, and use.

I also point out how EA is but one of a number of areas of business and technology governance that must work together to be effective. These areas of governance include the decision-making processes, standards and policy for strategic planning, capital planning, enterprise architecture, workforce planning, program management, records management, security, systems development, and operations.

The final lecture point that I usually present at the beginning of an EA seminar or class is to talk about five areas of value that EA creates for the enterprise: (1) increased alignment of business and technology programs with strategic goals; (2) increased business agility through improved decision-making and reduced cycle time in conducting workflow/dataflow/systems analysis, design, and implementation; (3) the ability to embark on business transformation initiatives and the improved management of change through the visualization of the entire enterprise in the strategic, business, and technology dimensions; (4) increased success in implementing or changing technologies that support key business processes and service/product delivery; and (5) increased ability to control otherwise escalating technology costs through the avoidance of duplication, and better matches between business requirements and technology solutions that extend across more lines of business.

While these lecture points and lists are not all-inclusive, they hopefully address important points for students who are first being exposed to the multitude of concepts that EA encompasses. By being "the" meta-concept for enterprise analysis, design, and improvement, EA has become a rich, complex set of methods that must be effectively integrated and explained to those who sponsor and implement architectures in equally complex and dynamic enterprises. Fortunately, EA has itself become agile and purposeful as it matures and systems architecture is an essential part of this.

Again, I congratulate Dr. Pallab and the other authors on the publication of this important contribution to the global EA discourse. I recently had the opportunity to talk with Dr. Pallab while on a teaching trip to Singapore and I can tell you that he not only understands all aspects of EA and systems architecture, but he is a thought leader in business and technology governance as well. His talk with my students about the integration of architecture and investment planning was very informative. I also know that many of the authors are active EA practitioners, teachers, researchers, or consultants and I especially value the opportunity that the *Handbook of Enterprise Systems Architecture in Practice* has given me to stay current in our evolving discipline through the sharing of their thoughts and best practices.

Scott A. Bernard, PhD
August 2006

Scott A. Bernard currently serves as the deputy chief information officer and chief enterprise architect of the Federal Railroad Administration in Washington, DC. He is also an assistant professor for the School of Information Studies at Syracuse University, and a senior lecturer in the Executive Program of the Institute for Software Research International at Carnegie Mellon University's Computer Science Department. Dr. Bernard founded and currently serves as president of the Association of Enterprise Architects and is chief editor of the Journal of Enterprise Architecture. *Dr. Bernard has nearly 20 years of experience as an information technology (IT) executive and manager including work in the academic, federal government, military, and private sectors. He has held positions as a chief information officer (CIO), senior management consultant, line-of-business manager, network operations manager, telecommunications manager, and project manager for several major systems installations. Dr. Bernard's areas of current research, teaching, and consulting include IT-related leadership, e-government policy development, strategic planning, enterprise architecture, systems analysis and design, project management, and capital planning.*

Preface

I am not sure exactly when the importance of enterprise architecture (EA) dawned on me. What is clear is that it wasn't a "one fine day" realization, rather a result of numerous conversations with CIOs, IT managers, CFOs, process managers, and multiple research studies that convinced me that EA is perhaps the most important and the most misunderstood idea in information technology (IT) and a critical emerging discipline to elevate the role of IT organizations in enterprises. Metaphorically, an EA is to an organization's operations and systems as a set of blueprints is to a building. This handbook, unlike any other available today, aims:

- To provide a comprehensive and unified overview of practical aspects of EA.
- To integrate EA theory and concepts to field-tested methods, practical strategic issues, and implementation challenges.
- To illustrate development methods and the process cycle through case studies and detailed examples.
- To provide insights into the impact of effective EA on IT governance, IT portfolio management, IT risks, and IT outsourcing.
- To demonstrate the criticality of EA economics and its role in the strategic value of IT

This handbook is a compilation of 26 chapters on enterprise architecture written by practitioners and practicing academics from countries including Australia, France, Germany, India, Israel, Norway, Netherlands, Singapore, South Africa, South Korea, Switzerland, Portugal, United Kingdom, and the United States of America. The authors of these chapters were included in the review process in addition to having their submissions reviewed by a panel of independent reviewers. The handbook has been "foreworded" by John Zachman, the "father" of the Zachman Framework; undoubtedly the first formal framework in the discipline of EA and Dr. Scott Bernard, an accomplished EA practitioner who is now also an academic being associated with the Carnegie Mellon University.

The chapters in the handbook have been selected with the intention to address professionals with a wide variety of interests and with different levels of EA knowledge. The handbook has a very strong practical orientation and is primarily targeted at:

- CIOs, IT/IS managers, architects, analysts, and designers seeking better, quicker, and easier approaches to respond to needs of their internal and external customers.
- Line-of-Business managers concerned with maximizing business value of IT and business competitiveness.
- CTOs of business software companies interested in incorporating EA to differentiate their products and services and increasing the value proposition to their customers.
- Consultants and practitioners desirous of new solutions and technologies to improve the productivity of their corporate clients.
- MIS and IT educators interested in imparting knowledge about this vital discipline.
- Researchers looking to uncover and characterize new research problems and programs. IT professionals involved with organizational technology strategic planning, technology procurement, management of technology projects, consulting and advising on technology issues, and management of total cost of IT ownership.

The handbook is structured logically into five parts. Section I on frameworks and methodologies focuses on approaches and mechanisms that organizations use to develop their architecture blueprints. Section II on governance and management shows how organizations initiate and sustain their EA practices. Section III provides insights into how organizations employ EA to drive their transformation programs, gain tighter business-IT alignment, and realize business value out of their IT investments. Section IV consists of descriptions of the adoption of EA in large and small organizations with insights on key practical challenges they face and how the whole EA programmes are sustained. Finally, Section V demonstrates the role of technology, especially service-oriented architecture (SOA) in EA implementation.

Section I: Frameworks and Methodologies
Section I is a collection of chapters describing approaches and methods used by organizations to plan and develop their EA blueprints.

Chapter I: A Synergistic Assessment of the Federal Enterprise Architecture Framework against GERAM (ISO15704:2000), by Pallab Saha of the National University of Singapore, evaluates synergies between the comprehensive FEAF against the generalized enterprise reference architecture and methodology (GERAM) framework. The federal enterprise architecture framework (FEAF) is perhaps the most adopted EA framework, especially within the U.S. Government agencies. Either FEAF has been adopted as-is or other frameworks derived from FEAF have been used. FEAF today continues to be the most comprehensive framework available for guidance by agencies. It consists of a full-fledged methodology, several reference models, target architectures, and even a toolkit that facilitates adoption across all agencies. The chapter discusses the level of completeness in the FEAF based on GERAM requirements and additionally identifies areas where the FEAF goes well beyond GERAM requirements.

Chapter II: Extreme Architecture Framework: A Minimalist Framework for Modern Times, by Phil Robinson of Lonsdale Systems, Australia and Floris Gout, an Independent Consultant based in Australia, presents an EA framework that is lightweight and selective to meet the needs of the organization. The chapter uses the "agile" approach to develop architectural artifacts. It starts with the need for frameworks and some of the currently popular frameworks. Then it argues why interoperability both at systems and human level is critical followed by a discussion on the relevant architectural views that is derived from the XAF matrix and elements that need to be created. The chapter concludes with a comparison of the proposed framework with other established frameworks from the point of view of simplicity and ease of use.

Chapter III: Discovering and Modelling Enterprise Engineering Project Processes, by Ovidiu Noran from Griffith University, Australia, provides a meta-methodology based on existing architecture frameworks that facilitates organizations to assess and select architectural elements and artifacts within the context of specific EA program requirements. The proposed approach in the chapter allows organizations to configure their EA programme, instead of "doing the whole nine yards" for every situation. The chapter illustrates the proposed approach with a real-life case study.

Chapter IV: Enterprise Architecture Framework for Agile and Interoperable Virtual Enterprises, by Tae-Young Kim, Sunjae Lee, Jeong-Soo Lee, and Kwangsoo Kim of the Pohang University of Science and Technology, South Korea and Cheol-Han Kim from Daejeon University, South Korea, presents a modeling framework that business architects and domain specialists can use to build and configure architectural elements and models specifically for virtual enterprises (VE). The chapter uses and improves upon existing modeling standards and practices (like BPMN, UML, MDA) and applies concepts of service-oriented architecture (SOA) to make organizations more responsive to change.

Chapter V: Activity-Based Methodology for Development and Analysis of Integrated DoD Architectures, by Steven J. Ring and Dave Nicholson from the MITRE Corporation, USA and Stanley Harris, Lockheed Martin Corporation, USA, presents the DOD defined methodology that uses DODAF to create architecture outputs. Activity-based methodology (ABM) discussed in this chapter is presented as a step-by-step approach that allows a common reference point for all architectural assets in terms of scope, breadth, depth and intensity. Several DOD entities have adopted or are in the process of adopting ABM, thereby providing credence to its applicability in practice.

Chapter VI: Business Process Modeling as a Blueprint for Enterprise Architecture by Joseph Barjis of Georgia Southern University, USA and Isaac Barjis of City University of New York, USA, presents a Petri-net-based methodology, transaction-oriented Petri-nets (TOP), to enterprise process modeling. The chapter starts with a brief background of existing architecture frameworks and discusses the role of business architecture. Then it presents the details of the TOP notation, following which the complete TOP methodology framework is discussed in a step-by-step manner with examples provided to illustrate each step and their respective output.

Chapter VII: Enterprise Architecture in the Singapore Government by Tan Eng Pheng and Gan Wei Boon from Infocomm Development Authority of Singapore, Singapore, is a discussion of the role of enterprise architecture in the Singapore's e-government programmes. The chapter discusses the evolution of the country's e-government action plans and policies and examines the linkages and role that EA plays including IT governance and investment planning. The chapter briefly presents the currently ongoing efforts within the government to define reference models that are intended for use by agencies to develop their own EA in alignment with the overall Government-wide EA. Within the current e-government plan, the iGOV 2010, EA is one the three key pillars of programme success.

Section II: Governance and Management
Section II of the handbook comprises of chapters that are useful to institute and sustain the EA practice within the organization.

Chapter VIII: Understanding and Communicating with Enterprise Architecture Users, by Steven Thornton from the National Institutes of Health, USA, discusses current best practices and provides guidelines in communicating EA to the users. The recommended approaches and practices presented in the chapter are derived from the United States National Institutes of Health (NIH) EA programmes. The intent of this chapter is to educate CIOs and chief architects about the need to communicate EA, recommended approaches, and its key benefits to the EA programme.

Chapter IX: Improving Stakeholder Communications and IT Engagement: A Case Study Perspective, by Gail L. Verley of the Federal Deposit Insurance Corporation, USA, continues on the theme of architecture governance and management. This chapter begins with a discussion on the need to improve stakeholder communications and enhance engagement with the users in an EA programme. The chapter presents five steps to involve stakeholders in EA programmes, followed by ten strategies and mechanisms to institutionalize stakeholder involvement. The application of the steps, strategies, and mechanisms presented in the chapter are illustrated through a detailed case study of United States Federal Deposit Insurance Corporation (FDIC). The chapter concludes with a set of lessons learned that organizations can refer to.

Chapter X: The Role of Change Management in IT Systems Implementation, by Ron S. Kenett of KPA Limited, Israel and Sebastiano Lombardo from the Foundation for Scientific and Industrial Research at the Norwegian Institute of Technology (NTH), Norway, presents an integrated holistic approach to IT systems implementation called the better enterprise systems implementation (BEST). The chapter treats IT systems implementation as an organizational development issue and positions the BEST methodology as an approach to manage IT driven organizational change. The chapter then illustrates the application of the methodology through three case studies in Norway and Israel.

Chapter XI: Managing Enterprise Architecture Change, by Tim O'Neill, Mark Denford, and John Leaney of the University of Technology Sydney, Australia and Kyle Dunsire from Avolution Pty. Limited, Australia, is a description of an approach that allows organizations to simulate, predict, and control the emergent properties of enterprise systems from an architectural perspective. The chapter argues that existing methodologies and toolsets are by nature bottom-up and often fail to take into consideration the non-functional requirements of the IT systems from an architectural viewpoint. The chapter begins with a brief discussion of the key non-functional requirements that most IT systems are expected to fulfill. It then presents a five-step methodology that organizations can use to build and evolve their architectures. The chapter concludes with the benefits of the proposed methodology.

Section III: Transformation and Value Realization

This section of the handbook focuses on how organizations use EA to facilitate and drive their organizational transformation objectives seeking to enhance alignment between their business and IT functions. Business value of IT being a key point in today's IT organizations is covered in this part by way of how EA is used to realize economic value.

Chapter XII: Architecture Driven Business Transformation, by Chris Lawrence of Old Mutual South Africa, South Africa, presents an approach where EA is viewed as a business issue. The chapter starts with a discussion on business transformation that is triggered through EA. The chapter argues that EA is an imperative irrespective of the business condition that an organization might be in and places forth business diagnostics as a key element of any architectural initiative. The chapter illustrates the application of the proposed approach in a financial services organization and discusses process driven business transformation. The chapter then concludes with a discussion on non-process driven business transformation and why process architecture based transformation was used as an example.

Chapter XIII: Maturity of IT-Business Alignment: An Assessment Tool, by Nel Wognum of the University of Twente, The Netherlands and Fan Ip-Shing from Cranfield University, United Kingdom, presents such an approach based on better enterprise systems implementation (BEST). In doing this, the two key questions addressed are what problems can be pre-empted and what can be done about them. The chapter then continues to illustrate the proposed approach through several mini-cases derived out of real-life scenarios. The chapter concludes with a discussion on areas for further research. Most large IT system implementation initiatives are plagued by several factors that often make implementations less than desirable. While factors leading to failure for large IT implementations have been documented and analyzed, the intriguing issue is that organizations seem to repeat the same mistakes over and over again. This necessitates the need for a mechanism that allows planners and managers to evaluate the start-up situation in such projects, including capturing the project dynamics in a coherent manner.

Chapter XIV: The Integrated Enterprise Life Cycle: Enterprise Architecture, Investment Management, and System Development, by Frank J. Armour from Armour LLC, USA, Chris Emery and Jonathan Houk of the U.S. Architect of Capitol, USA, Stephen H. Kaisler from SET Associates, USA, and John S. "Stan" Kirk from the U.S. National Science Foundation, USA, explores and discusses the linkages that EA has with IT investment management and system development processes and hence the need for a holistic approach. In doing so, it proposes an integrated enterprise life cycle (IELC). The chapter starts with a discussion of the IELC and its various components. The chapter positions IELC as a key IT governance mechanism and presents several governance archetypes that are part of the IELC. The chapter concludes with a brief discussion on the proposed move towards IELC by the U.S. Office of Management and Budget (OMB) and U.S. General Accounting Office (GAO) under the Federal Enterprise Architecture (FEA) program.

Chapter XV: Promoting Netcentricity through the Use of Enterprise Architecture, by Supriya Ghosh from Lockheed Martin Corporation, USA, presents U.S. Department of Defense (DOD)'s goal of net-centric transformation as an implementation of EA. The chapter argues that to achieve net-centricity the existence of an integrated architecture provided by the DOD Global Information Grid (GIG) is a key imperative. The chapter then provides an overview of the key performance parameters to support net readiness. It details the adoption of net-centric transformation through the use of net-centric data strategy, net-centric IA strategy, service-oriented architecture (SOA), and communications transport strategy. The chapter concludes with a discussion on upcoming and future trends to enable DOD's move towards net-centricity.

Section IV: Implementation and Deployment
Section IV of the handbook looks at EA from an ongoing implementation and transition perspective through cases both in large and small organization scenarios.

Chapter XVI: Enterprise Architecture as an Enabler for E-Governance: An Indian Perspective, by Raghunath Mahapatra of Ernst & Young India, India and Sinnakkrishnan Perumal from the Indian Institute of Management Calcutta, India, is a case study on application of EA to develop an efficient and effective e-governance system for citizen services administration by the Government of India. The chapter starts with a background on various e-government initiatives, including a brief discussion on the administrative structure in India. The chapter then puts forth key imperatives that are required for successful e-government programs, keeping in mind the Indian context. EA is then presented as one the critical success factors. The chapter continues with a detailed discussion of a proposed framework (derived from the Zachman Framework) that facilitates the application of EA in the context of e-government in India. The chapter concludes with a mapping of the earlier presented imperatives to the key elements of the proposed framework.

Chapter XVII: Federated Enterprise Resource Planning Systems, by Nico Brehm from the Carl-von-Ossietzky-Universität Oldenburg, Germany, Daniel Lübke from the University Hannover, Germany, and Jorge Marx Gómez from the Carl-von-Ossietzky-Universität Oldenburg, Germany, presents enterprise resource planning (ERP) system architecture that makes individual business modules reusable through the use of Web services based on shared and non-monolithic architecture. The chapter is based on a practical challenge that enterprises currently face wherein systems (especially the ERP tools) have proprietary data models, thus limiting their usage and in conflict to their claim of being positioned as "enterprise systems." This leads to vendor lock-in. The chapter begins with a background on existing ERP systems with a discussion of their limitations as real enterprise systems. The chapter then presents the federated ERP system approach and discusses how the federated approach addresses the shortcomings of existing "siloed" ERP systems. The chapter concludes with a discussion on the kind of adoption challenges that the federated approach might face along with a short brief on future trends and research.

Chapter XVIII: A Network Based View of Enterprise Architecture, by Bala Iyer of Babson College and David Dreyfus of Boston University, USA and Per Gyllstrom, PFPC Worldwide Inc., USA, moves away from the traditional four sub-architecture-based view of EA and takes a network-based view that is based on understanding and capturing the dependencies between the elements of the EA. The proposed approach asserts that such dependencies are a factor of time and typically emerge as the architecture evolves. Dependencies that emerge during the design, deployment, and operations of the EA are based on both technical and social factors. The chapter presents a case study of the application of the proposed approach in a financial services company. The chapter concludes with a discussion of the limitations of the proposed approach and presents pointers to how the limitations can be addressed.

Chapter XIX: Enterprise Architecture by a Small Unit in a Federated Organization, by Roger Sliva from the State of Nevada, USA, presents experiences and best practices in developing EA by a small team for a federated organization. A federated structure is typical in many governments where the administrative structure is organized into national/federal entities followed by states, districts, or provinces. Given the federated structure, developing EA presents several practical challenges. The chapter discusses factors to be considered in such a scenario when developing EA in terms of scope, intensity, use of tools, open standards, shared business services, and programme governance.

Chapter XX: The Syngenta Architecture Story, by Peter Hungerford from Syngenta AG., Switzerland, presents the experiences of development and evolution of EA at Syngenta. The key drivers in Syngenta's architecture programme are business efficiency, growth, and innovation. The chapter shares the experiences and insights from several business areas. The case studies presented in the chapter includes EA initiatives like server rationalization and development of global infrastructure services, integrated "go-to-market" platform, providing an unified research platform, and building an enterprise-wide business intelligence. The chapter then presents a simple framework for EA and discusses the case studies in the context of the framework. The chapter concludes with future trends and discusses a few plausible areas of research.

Chapter XXI: The Use of GERAM for Design of a Virtual Enterprise for a Ship Maintenance Consortium, by John Mo from the Commonwealth Scientific and Industrial Research Organization, Australia, describes the application of the generalized enterprise reference architecture and methodology (GERAM) in analyzing the ANZAC ship alliance (ASA). The chapter discusses the details of the use of GERA in developing and studying a virtual enterprise, especially issues relating to logistics and information architecture management needed to support the operations of ASA as a virtual enterprise. The chapter starts with a brief overview of the GERAM including the key reasons of why it was selected for use. The chapter then describes ASA as a virtual enterprise including the peculiarities and nuances of a virtual enterprise. The chapter concludes with a description of enterprise engineering programme at ASA, the artifacts and models developed based on GERAM requirements.

Chapter XXII: Information Systems Architecture for Business Process Modelling, by Michel Spadoni of the Ecole Nationale d'Ingénieurs de Metz & Laboratory for Industrial and Mechanical Engineering, France and Anis Abdmouleh from Metz University and Laboratory for Industrial and Mechanical Engineering, France, is a description of business process modeling capabilities within the CIMOSA application server (CAS). The CAS is an information system for enterprise modeling and designing. The chapter starts with a brief overview of the problems that is faced by organizations in integrating their disparate systems. Then it describes the CAS project, its goals and objectives and the primary reason for selecting CIMOSA as the reference architecture. Following this, the chapter describes the CIMOSA modeling framework and conceptual model. The chapter then describes the business process modeling aspects with an example of a manufacturing organization including the views and artifacts needed to support the requirements of enterprise systems.

Section V: Technology and Service-Oriented Architecture
This section of the handbook is a compilation of chapters on the role technology plays in an architectural initiative.

Chapter XXIII: Enterprise Architecture within the Service-Oriented Enterprise, by Scott J. Dowell of Shirnia & Dowell LLC, USA, elaborates the role of EA in a service-oriented enterprise (SOE). Driven by the need to the adaptable, agile, and responsive to change, organizations are now adopting the SOE paradigm where organizations view themselves as a bundle of services that are available for use through technology enablement. The chapter begins with the issues that enterprise architects need to grapple with, namely, business services, service-oriented solutions, infrastructure services, and IT organization changes. It goes on to compare a traditional enterprise with a SOE. The chapter then discusses the development of strategy in a SOE and its peculiarities. The chapter provides real-life examples on various aspects of service orientation adopted by various organizations.

Chapter XXIV: A Fundamental SOA Approach to Rebuilding Enterprise Architecture for a Local Government after a Disaster, by Zachary B. Wheeler of SDDM Technology, USA, is a case study of the reestablishment of EA for the local Government following Hurricane Katrina in Louisiana. The chapter presents an approach to address areas in EA that have not received much attention as part of preparedness, response, and recovery phases. The chapter proposes the use of SOA paradigm to address some the key issues. The chapter starts with a brief background of the underlying EA framework that was used in the given situation, followed by a detailed description of the conceptual data model and how a critical portion of the EA was developed. The chapter concludes with a discussion on other technologies that can be used to extend the current solution.

Chapter XXV: Business Networking with Web Services—Supporting the Full Life Cycle of Business Collaborations, by Diogo R. Ferreira from the Technical University of Lisbon, Portugal, proposes to use the Web services paradigm as a way to deal with all aspects of business collaborations. The chapter starts with an overview of Web services as an integration platform, followed by a description of the criticality of the life cycle approach in integration. The chapter demonstrates with examples the use of Web services in extending its support of operational aspects alone to the full life cycle of business collaborations, thereby enabling seamless e-business collaborations and trading.

Chapter XXVI: Enterprise Integration Architecture for Harmonized Messaging, by Dat Cao Ma, Belinda Carter, Shazia W. Sadiq, and Maria E. Orlowska, University of Queensland, Australia, presents a rule-based enterprise integration approach enabled through messaging technology. The chapter begins with the challenges of large-scale collaborative systems and the evolution of technology solutions to address some of the challenges. The chapter then presents the proposed enterprise integration architecture and an overview of related technologies. Following this, the chapter elaborates the steps in rule design, validation, and deployment and its adoption within the proposed integration architecture. The chapter concludes with a discussion on future developments in the proposed area.

In conclusion, I hope that this handbook makes its contribution to the emerging discipline of EA, which is only going to gain importance in organizations. I would like to invite readers to share their comments about the handbook in addition to their success stories that may well spawn of future editions of this Handbook.

Dr. Pallab Saha
National University of Singapore
December 2006

Acknowledgments

This handbook is a result of the efforts and support of many people. Without their advice, assistance, and deep involvement, the handbook would not have achieved its current form. I would like to express my gratitude and thank all involved in the collation and review process of this reference book on enterprise architecture.

I would like to start with IGI who gave me the opportunity to realize my cherished dream. This handbook allowed me to make significant contributions to an emerging and timely discipline. A special word of thanks to **Kristin Roth** of IGI who guided me with numerous e-mails and to **Dr. Mehdi Khosrow-Pour** who motivated me to initially accept his invitation for taking on this project.

I would like to specially acknowledge the contribution of the independent reviewers of the chapters, who readily agreed to review despite their own busy schedules, often working on very tight deadlines given by me. Herein goes my sincere thanks to **Dr. Hoe Siu Loon** of Singapore Telecommunications, **Rina Levy** of The Mitre Corporation, and **Dr. Sam Chung** of the University Of Washington (Tacoma). Representing both industry and academia points of view, they provided excellent review comments that improved the overall submission quality.

An important part of this handbook is the chapter authors. I appreciate their excellent contributions and want to thank them for assisting me in the review process.

Last but not the least, this handbook would not have become a reality without the support of my mother **Shrimati Anima Saha**, my wife **Neeta,** and our adorable daughter **Anushka** (who was born last year as I conceived this book). Above all, I would like to dedicate this book to my father, the late **Shri Jagatbandhu Saha**.

Dr. Pallab Saha
Singapore
December 2006

Section I
Frameworks and Methodologies

Chapter I

A Synergistic Assessment of the Federal Enterprise Architecture Framework against GERAM (ISO15704:2000)

Pallab Saha
Institute of Systems Science, Singapore

ABSTRACT

The federal enterprise architecture framework (FEAF) is perhaps the most adopted EA framework, especially within the U.S. Government agencies. Either the FEAF has been adopted as-is or other frameworks derived from the FEAF have been used. The FEAF today continues to be the most comprehensive framework available for guidance by agencies. It consists of a full-fledged methodology, several reference models, target architectures, and even a toolkit that facilitates adoption across all agencies. This chapter evaluates the synergies between the comprehensive FEAF against the generalized enterprise reference architecture and methodology (GERAM) framework. The intent of the evaluation is to present the level of completeness in the FEAF based on GERAM requirements and additionally discuss areas where the FEAF goes well beyond ISO15704:2000 requirements leading to improvement opportunities in GERAM.

INTRODUCTION

Enterprise architecture (EA) is the discipline of designing enterprises guided with principles, frameworks, methodologies, requirements, tools, reference models, and standards. Managers are becoming architects. Their new roles include designing structure, engineering processes, developing people, leveraging technology, facilitating learning, and changing the whole (Morabito, Sack, & Bhate, 1999). The manager-architect must design across enterprise boundaries, engineer processes into strategic capabilities, align information technology and business strategies, and integrate the enterprise. In order for the manager to achieve all these, several contending architecture frameworks are available (Bernus, Nemes, & Schmidt, 2003; Chen & Doumeingts, 1996; Chen, Vallespir, & Doumeingts, 1997). Of the several contending architecture frameworks, this chapter analyzes the federal enterprise architecture framework (FEAF) approach to EA against the generalized enterprise reference architecture and methodology (GERAM) / ISO15704:2000 requirements. The objective of this detailed analysis is to provide prospective users of the FEAF, an understanding of GERAM/ISO15704:2000 requirements, and the extent to which the FEAF-based approach meets these requirements.

Several other frameworks have been analyzed against the GERAM/ISO15704:2000 requirements (Noran, 2003, 2005; Saha, 2004a), currently there is no mapping between the FEAF and GERAM and the chapter attempts to address this gap. The key objectives of the analysis presented in this chapter include: (1) map and compare the FEAF-based approach to a common set of EA requirements as specified in GERAM; and (2) identify areas where the FEAF is richer/weaker, with the aim that managers and researchers can take benefit in practice and in identification of newer areas for research, including enhancement of existing frameworks.

The key motivations for selecting FEAF for this assessment include:

- The FEAF is perhaps most implemented either as-is or in derived form. It may be argued that FEAF is relevant only in the context of United States Federal Government agencies. However, in reality, all of the FEAF documentation is available in public domain and many EA programs around the world take cue from FEAF (localized for specific needs).
- The FEAF is an embodiment of best practices and guidelines. An assessment actually has the capability to further the EA discipline and its practice.

- The FEAF by design is generic and applicable to all agencies, irrespective of the industry they operate in. This makes FEAF application non-industry specific and broad.

BACKGROUND

Short Overview of GERAM

Existence of several architecture frameworks provides a recipe for confusion. The overriding goal of the generalized enterprise reference architecture and methodology (GERAM) is to encompass and generalize the common requirements of various EA frameworks and EA reference architectures (Bernus, 2001; IFIP-IFAC Task Force, 1999). The GERAM is not another EA framework or EA reference architecture. GERAM aims to classify prevalent EA frameworks and their associated artifact types (methodologies, reference models, ontologies, etc.). The scope of GERAM (depicted in Figure 1 of Chapter XXI of this handbook) encompasses all knowledge required for enterprise engineering and enterprise integration with the intention of unifying several disciplines such as industrial engineering, management science, control engineering, and information and communication technology to build a coherent organizational design (Bernus et al., 2003).

The central component in the GERAM framework is generalized enterprise reference architecture (GERA), which specifies the basic/core concepts to be utilized in an EA initiative. Besides GERA, other components in GERAM identify requirements regarding process methodologies, modeling languages, tools, and enterprise models necessary for architecting the enterprise. The GERAM framework components would form the basis for mapping and analysis of the FEAF-based approach in this chapter.

Short Overview of the FEAF

Mandated by the Clinger-Cohen Act of 1996, the office of management and budget (OMB) along with the Federal CIO Council developed the federal enterprise architecture framework, which is a business-based framework for government-wide improvement envisioned to facilitate efforts in transforming the U.S. Federal Government to one that is citizen-centered, results-oriented, and market-based (CIO Council, 1999). The framework provides an approach to identify, develop, and specify architecture descriptions of high priority areas that in built on common business areas and designs that span multiple organizations, not limited by organizational boundaries (CIO Council, 1999). The FEAF provides a structured approach to federal organizations to integrate their respective architectures into the federal enterprise architecture (FEA). The federal enterprise architecture (FEA) was commissioned in 2002. According to the CIO Council, the primary objectives of developing the FEAF was to organize federal information on a government-wide scale, promote information sharing among federal organizations, facilitate federal organizations develop their respective architectures, facilitate federal organizations develop their IT investment processes, and serve customer needs better, faster, and cost effectively.

In designing the FEAF, eight core components were taken into consideration and elaborated. These components deemed essential to develop and maintain the FEA were *architecture drivers, strategic direction, current architecture, target architecture, transitional processes, architectural segments, architectural models,* and *standards.* The scope of the FEAF encompasses all aspects of enterprise architecture development. The *business architecture* specifies an organization's business strategies, goals, and objectives and links these to business processes that are required to execute the identified strategies. The *data architecture* describes the structure of an organization's logical and physical data resources and management of such resources. The *technology architecture* describes the information technology infrastructure required to support the organization's business processes and information architecture. The *application architecture* describes the software applications needed to deploy organization's business processes governed by business rules (CIO Council, 1999).

ASSESSMENT APPROACH

The analysis attempts to assess the FEAF in meeting GERAM requirements. In case of the FEAF lacking in certain areas, this chapter provides guidance toward ensuring common understanding of deliverables, and ways to complete it using GERAM requirements as the reference. With this aim, the analysis centers on several aspects, each discussed in detail in subsequent sections.

LIFE CYCLE PHASES

Current literature in EA points to two main perspectives in architectural framework specification: the *static* perspective representing the structural aspects at a specified point in time and the *dynamic* perspective capturing the various stages that architecture development goes through (Noran, 2003). An architecture life cycle phase in GERAM usually represents activities and tasks performed during the architecture development process, the inputs and outputs of each activity, and the artifacts (or deliverables) that are developed as part of phase realization. While it is possible to represent phases in a sequential manner, in reality, organizations prefer to develop EA iteratively. The crucial point is that life cycle phases in GERA represent logical groupings of activities performed and artifacts produced, and not the temporal aspects in EA development (IFIP-IFAC Task Force, 1999).

The FEAF Life Cycle Aspect

While an EA framework like the FEAF provides valuable guidance on the content of enterprise architectures, however, in order for organizations to successfully manage the process of envisioning, developing, deploying, using, and maintaining the EA, the CIO Council in 2001 provided a step-by-step process guide. The processes described represent principles of good EA. The mapping is largely direct. The *identification* and *concept* phases in GERA map to *obtain executive buy-in & support* and *establish management structure & control* stages in the FEAF process. This is where the EA program is initiated in the organization and the overall EA policy is developed based on the organization's architectural principles. The EA policy (at the least) addresses issues like: purpose and value of the EA, relationship between EA and organization's strategic goals, transformation of business strategies into EA goals, and objectives and establishment of the EA program office and core team with roles and responsibilities. The EA core team is responsible for all activities involving development, implementation, deployment, and maintenance of the EA. The *requirements* phase in GERA maps to *define an architecture process and approach* activity. In this phase, the organization elaborates the scope and intended use of the architecture. Besides, the overall intent of early GERA phases is also reflected in the way reference models are sequenced in the FEAF, where upstream activities like *performance* and *business reference models* influence and drive the development of the remaining reference models downstream. To summarize, this phase sets the tone for the rest of the EA development process.

GERA splits the actual EA design into two phases that are *preliminary design* and *detailed design*. These two phases directly map to the FEAF *develop baseline architecture* and *develop target architecture* stages. In building the EA, the first logical step is to understand the "as-is" state. This is crucial as it enables future progress to be measured against a reference or baseline. As baseline architectures focus on capturing the current state, organizations usually decide on the level of details and complexity desired. This phase of developing the baseline architecture takes and provides critical input to the requirements phase. Once the organization documents the current architecture and requirements for the future "to-be" architecture, it is ready to undertake the development of the target architecture, which primarily is the process of addressing gaps between the "as-is" and "to-be" states. The next phase in GERA is *implementation* of the EA and this maps to *develop the sequencing plan* in the FEAF. This process focuses in developing a transition/migration plan for the organization to move from the "as-is" state to the "to-be" state. In this, phase organizations usually take inputs from industry specific standards that may be available. The primary goal of this stage is that the organization starts operating with the new EA in place. The next GERA phase of *operation* maps directly to *use the enterprise architecture* process in the FEAF. The focus here is to ensure the target EA is implemented and good EA management practices enforced leading to continuous governance. *Decommissioning* the EA at the end of its useful life is the last phase in GERA; the FEAF specifies *maintain the enterprise architecture* as its last process step. The objective of this phase is to establish a process to ensure that the baseline architecture accurately reflects the current state and the target architecture correctly represents the future business vision.

Concluding Remarks on Life Cycle Phases

The common underlying premise that evolution of enterprises, represented as enterprise life cycle consisting of progressive stages like conception, design, deployment, operation and maintenance, and retirement, is an iterative process that incorporates new business processes, new technology, and new capabilities is evident in both GERA and the FEAF. While the EA process specified by the CIO Council is not specific to the FEAF, its application in the FEAF context is well accepted.

TEMPORALITY AND SUCCESSION

The development and maintenance of architecture is a continuous process that includes assessment of current business conditions and exploration for target solutions. In addition to the logical groupings of activities and tasks represented earlier as life cycle phases in the EA process, the development of EA also progresses in time and detail. Hence, timeline related aspects form a crucial portion of the GERAM requirements. A separate and explicit temporal aspect allows organizations to evolve and adapt to changing business environment during the progress of the enterprise architecture development. This is made possible by the fact that an organization may necessarily not delve into details at the initiation stage of EA development, but has the flexibility to add increasing details over time.

Temporality and Succession in the FEAF

The FEAF explicitly specifies timeline- and succession-based approaches to architecture development. Temporality and succession in the FEAF is realized through successive levels of decomposition and drill-down on each core component. The decomposition process is a basis for a four-level framework, with each level providing a frame of reference for the next. The four levels represent a continuum that captures progression, evolution, and adaptation in time. The first three levels represent the progression of eight increasingly detailed components leading to a logical structure for classifying and organizing the organization specific descriptive representa-

tions of the Federal EA at Level IV. The temporal aspect is tightly integrated to the FEAF EA process, providing time-based anchors during the architecture life cycle to represent various forms that the EA takes.

Level I is the highest level of the FEAF that introduces the eight core components and interplay between them in developing and maintaining the architecture. Level II depicts the business and design elements and the relationships between them. At this level, the business of the enterprise along with the architectural design needed to support the business is represented. The relationship is push-pull, where the business pushes the design and the design pulls the business to higher levels of capability and service delivery. Level II further elaborates on the migration processes that facilitates the movement of the enterprise from the baseline to the target architecture adhering to the architecture standards. A critical activity in Level II is the development of the *business architecture*.

Level III expands on the design elements that are needed to support the business architecture. This includes development of the *data, technology,* and *applications architecture.* Application of design standards like data standards, security standards, applications standards, and technology standards is a critical activity at this level.

Level IV identifies the specific kinds of models that specify the business architecture along with the design architectures (data, technology, and applications). At this level, the mechanism for design architectures to support the business architecture is made explicit. Additionally EA planning takes place at this level. The models to specify the business and design architectures and the architecture planning that occur at Level IV are based on the Zachman Framework for EA (Zachman, 2000) and Spewak's EA Planning Methodology (Spewak, 1993). In its current form, the FEAF Level IV incorporates only three of the six columns from the Zachman Framework (i.e., what, how, and where). The "who, when, and why" columns will be considered for incorporation in future.

Concluding Remarks on Temporality and Succession

Time-based progression and succession in levels of details is critical in GERAM, and the FEAF explicitly addresses this with a four-level architecture framework. As an organization progresses through the architecture development process, the level of details specified increases leading to a "generic-to-specific" continuum that ensures bidirectional traceability between enterprise entities. The architecture reference models elaborated subsequently form the initial basis and a starting point for successive architecture specifications in increasing levels of details.

MODELING FRAMEWORK

The GERA modeling framework is included as a core component in the GERA reference architecture. In specifying the scope and type of enterprise models that need to be developed and maintained as part of the architecture development process, the modeling framework plays a crucial role. The analysis of the FEAF against GERAM modeling requirements incorporates two critical issues, which are: (1) the richness of guidance provided in the FEAF with regard to the scope and types of models to be created and maintained; and (2) the ability of the FEAF to accommodate the complete scope of modeling framework as in the GERA specifications.

The FEAF Modeling Framework

The FEA framework at Level IV is based on the Zachman Framework and so is its modeling framework. The FEAF modeling framework is anchored around three dimensions:

1. The *life cycle* dimension,
2. The *life history* dimension, and
3. The *perspective* dimension.

The coverage and mapping of the first two dimensions by the FEAF has already been discussed. With regard to the perspective dimension, the FEAF explicitly mentions the existence of multiple perspectives and their mapping to the various architectures that are developed to build the overall EA. Each row (perspective) represents a holistic view of the architecture from a particular perspective. Each row represents a unique perspective; however, the model for each perspective provide necessary details to specify the solution at the level of the perspective and translates to the next lower row explicitly. The FEAF recommends five perspectives/views. The *planner's view* specifies the overall scope of the architecture, while the *owner's, designer's, builder's,* and the *subcontractor's views* specify the enterprise, information systems, technology, and detailed specification models, respectively. Each column represents a specific area of focus and this drives the way the overall architecture is partitioned. In summary, each column poses a fundamental question (i.e., what, how, and where), while the way these fundamental questions are answered depend on the viewpoints of the stakeholders in architecture development. The intersections of the rows and columns specify the models that need to be developed. The FEAF specification provides fairly detailed descriptions of the models that are to be developed and further enriched with illustrations. With the same intention of reducing complexity and providing a structuring mechanism, GERA also supports multiple views that accommodate viewpoints of different stakeholders. While GERA is not normative about the actual views, it explicitly identifies two areas for conformance by candidate architectures, which are: (1) the overall intent of the four GERA views must be covered; and (2) the views should be subdivisions of an integrated metamodel such that the combined scope of the modeling framework is complete.

The mapping between GERA and the FEAF views is a little convoluted. GERA *model content views* with focus on user-oriented process representation of the enterprise entity descriptions maps to the FEAF *planner's* and *owner's view* but largely along the *activities* column. GERA *purpose views* with focus on mission of the enterprise entity and products and services required to support the enterprise objectives roughly map to the FEAF *planner's* and *owner's view* mostly along the *entities* column. GERA *implementation views* focusing on tasks that are/are not to be automated roughly maps to the FEAF *designer's view*. Lastly, GERA *physical manifestation views* with focus on software and hardware required to realize the architecture maps to both the FEAF *builder's* and *subcontractor's view*.

Concluding Remarks on Modeling Framework

In mapping the FEAF against GERA modeling views, it is to be noted that even within the same column, each intersecting cell in the FEAF covers GERA views to a different extent, depending on the perspective (row) containing them. A modeling framework is a structure specifying the artifacts (deliverables) required to accomplish the architecture development. From the modeling framework point of view, in line with GERA requirements, the FEAF has a direct mapping vis-à-vis GERA life cycle and temporality dimensions. On the view dimension, while there are areas where the mapping is not direct, the point to be noted is that the FEAF taxonomy of recommended views largely covers the entire intent of GERA view concepts. This is made possible as the FEAF Level IV is based on Zachman framework, which has been analyzed against GERAM (Noran, 2003). The FEAF specifications do not limit the modeling framework to just models, but also include other construct types like the technical reference model

(TRM), business reference model (BRM), performance reference model (PRM), service component reference model (SRM), and the data reference model (DRM). Additionally, it is believed that as and when the FEAF specifications include the remaining three columns (i.e., who, when, and why) addressing three more fundamental questions, the mapping with GERA would become tighter.

MODELING LANGUAGES

Enterprise architecture involves creation of several models governed by a modeling framework and influenced by a modeling methodology. GERAM recognizes that any enterprise architecture initiative is a large and complex undertaking and thus, would require potentially multiple modeling languages (IFIP-IFAC Task Force, 1999). GERAM specified requirements for modeling languages include:

1. The (set of) modeling language(s) must be able to represent every modeling view/viewpoint for every enterprise architecture artifact in the development methodology and extent of specificity.
2. Models developed for one view must be linkable with models in other views as such linkages are a logical requirement for a coherent enterprise architecture view.
3. Modeling languages must be based on reliable ontologies (metamodels with semantic rules).

Modeling Language(s) for the FEAF

The FEAF, while explicitly specifying the models and architecture products required to be developed and when and how they are to be developed, does not define any dedicated architecture development language. However, as guide to organizations implementing the FEAF, it does recommend third-party modeling languages that might be appropriate in developing critical EA products (CIO Council, 2001). Enterprise architects selecting the FEAF must utilize several proprietary and third-party modeling languages in order to accomplish all architectural activities and products. Lack of the single/unified set of modeling language(s) for EA, based on a single underlying metamodel, creates the risk of low consistency and interoperability between various models and products, and it is upon the architect to impose discipline in this regard. The EA tool selected by the organization further influences the selection of modeling language(s) depending on the languages supported. In summary, the FEAF is open and non-prescriptive about any specific modeling language, as long as the architect's goal is accomplished.

Concluding Remarks on Modeling Languages

The FEAF does not recommend/specify any language. Currently, there is no single modeling language capable of modeling all aspects of an enterprise. Hence, meaningful and complete enterprise model development needs several languages (Bernus et al., 2003; Vernadat, 1998). Several general-purpose languages currently available are candidates. Using several languages not belonging to the same family (and not having the same underlying metamodel) creates challenges in maintaining consistency and interoperability. One potential solution currently under development is the proposed unified enterprise modeling language (UEML), which would be based on a common integrated set of metamodels, semantic rules, and language constructs (Vernadat, 1998). This initiative is still in its infancy and the hope to find "a language" that is able to accomplish all of EA modeling objectives is still farfetched. The architect must therefore choose language(s) appropriate to project requirements. Several general-purpose languages currently available are candidates and they include:

- Unified modeling language (UML) for application architecture,
- Entity-relationship (ER) data model using IDEF 1x for information architecture,
- Object-role modeling (ORM) and object constraint language (OCL) for specifying business rules,
- Event driven process chain (EPC) and business process modeling notation (BPMN) for specifying business process view, among others.

Table 1 provides an indicative list of notations and languages that could be used in the different stages of the EA development.

METHODOLOGIES

A formal methodology seeking to fulfill GERA requirements must:

1. Identify and elaborate the phases involved in the architectural development life cycle,
2. Specify the scope and intent of each phase,
3. Describe the required inputs and expected outputs of each phase,
4. Include activity and task level elaborations of each phase,
5. Provide guidance to progress through the phases, and
6. Furnish any supporting materials that may be useful in the EA pursuit.

In addition, GERA has several requirements for modeling methodologies, which include:

1. The criticality of human involvement in architecture development for overall program success.
2. The need to differentiate between user-oriented and technology-oriented design,

impacting the extent of automation required by the enterprise.

3. The need to utilize and imbibe accepted project management techniques and practices leading to increase in the extent of management and control.

4. The need to provide due consideration to economic and performance factors to facilitate justification of the initiative and alignment with business objectives.

The FEAF Methodology

The FEAF EA process is a detailed architecture development methodology that fulfills all requirements of a comprehensive and guided step-by-step approach as mandated by GERAM. While

the FEA framework provides valuable inputs on the content of enterprise architectures, a federal level guidance specifically addressing issues like conceptualizing, realizing, implementing, operating, and maintaining an EA is also available to interested organizations (CIO Council, 2001). This treats an EA program as a project with specific activities and deliverables in each phase, allowing enterprises to follow a disciplined and structured approach to architecture development.

The EA process is not a framework specific EA methodology. The decision to choose the specific framework for implementation is left to the organization. Besides the methodology, the FEAF also recognizes and recommends the establishment of EA governance structure for overall success. The recommended governance

Table 1. Partial list of candidate modeling languages for FEAF documentation

Architectural Phases	Key Phase Artifacts	Proposed Modeling Languages
Architecture visioning	• Request for architecture work. • Initial statement of architecture work. • Architecture principles. • Architecture vision. • Baseline architectures.	• Rich pictures / English.
Business architecture	• Statement of architecture work. • Business principles. • Target business architecture. • Business architecture views. • Gap analysis report.	• Rich pictures / English. • UML. • System dynamics. • BPMN/BPML. • OCL. • Structured English. • IDEF 0 & IDEF 3. • ORM. • EPC.
Information architecture	• Target information architecture. • Information architecture views. • Gap analysis report. • Impact analysis report.	• IDEF 1. • UML. • ERM. • ORM.
Application architecture	• Target application architecture. • Application architecture views. • Gap analysis report. • Impact analysis report.	• UML. • Structured English.
Technology architecture	• Technology baseline description. • Technology principles. • Target technology architecture. • Gap analysis report. • Impact analysis report. • Technology architecture views.	• FEAF format. • Rich pictures / English.

structure is in the form of: (1) setting an *executive steering committee*, providing management oversight and sponsorship to the EA initiative and (2) forming an *EA program management office* to manage, monitor, and control development and maintenance of the EA. Investment management is closely associated with the EA processes. Within the context of FEA, organizations are required to configure investments that make the organizations move toward the target architecture and these investment decisions should comply with the sequencing plan. The CIO Council recommends the use of General accounting office's *information technology investment management framework* in this regard (United States General Accounting Office, 2004). At Level IV, the FEAF is based on the Zachman framework. Various tool vendors have developed proprietary methodologies for the Zachman framework.

The NASCIO EA Toolkit

To facilitate EA adoption, the National Association of State Chief Information Officers (NASCIO) provides an enterprise architecture development toolkit (NASCIO, 2004). The toolkit organizes the complete EA into four sub-architecture sections, namely: business architecture, information architecture, technology architecture, and solution architecture. In addition, it also has a section on architecture governance and management. Each section consists of a glossary of relevant terms, the detailed development process represented as workflow activities, including roles expected to perform specific activities, input and outputs items produced, templates and facilitation guides to derive the blueprint items, complete with examples and illustrations. Used in conjunction with the FEAF methodology, the toolkit is a rich source of guidance for all adopting agencies and meets GERA requirements and expectations.

Concluding Remarks on Methodologies

The FEAF, while providing guidance to EA development, still maintains its generosity, allowing enterprises to choose appropriate methodologies. Integration with investment management framework further facilitates monitoring and control of EA initiative's financial goals and objectives. Mandating a strong management structure and control enables organizations to make informed and reasoned decisions and enforces discipline. Agencies can further monitor the efficacy of their methodologies by assessing the EA program using the five-level *enterprise architecture management maturity model* (EAMMF) on *completion, use,* and *results* dimensions, thus improving overall architectural practices (United States General Accounting Office, 2003).

REFERENCE MODELS

Well-developed enterprise architectures have the capability to capture, classify, and encapsulate enterprise knowledge. *Complete* or *partial* reuse is the only reason to justify management of enterprise knowledge. In the case of enterprise architectures, *reference models* (also called *partial enterprise models*) facilitate such reuse. Applicability of reference models becomes narrow and focused as their specificity increases. Hence, the extent of reuse depends on the depth of reuse and the breadth of reuse. Reference models are used to increase overall modeling efficiencies, requiring enterprise specific adaptation. Partial enterprise models in the GERA sense may capture some common part of a class of enterprises; represent prototypes or abstract models that require specialization and adaptation before being realized as enterprise specific models. GERA categorizes partial models into four groups, which are:

1. Partial human role models focusing on organization and responsibilities,
2. Partial process models with focus on business processes and services,
3. Partial technology models providing industry specific common description of resources and their aggregations, and
4. Partial models of IT systems describing the components needed communications and information processing to enable enterprise integration.

The FEAF Reference Models

The FEAF explicitly defines the notion of reference models by specifying several reference models to facilitate cross organization analysis and improvement (CIO Council, 1999). From a business perspective, the FEAF specifies two reference models. The *performance reference model* (PRM) provides a common set of generic performance measures for organizations to achieve business goals and objectives (FEAPMO CRM, 2006). The PRM is designed for three main purposes:

1. Facilitate enhanced IT performance information to improve strategic and operational decision making.
2. Improve business-IT alignment, thereby creating a clear "line-of-sight" to desired results.
3. Identify performance improvement opportunities spanning organizational structures and boundaries.

The *business reference model* (BRM) on the other hand describes the business operations and services of the enterprise (in this case the federal government) independent of the specific organizations that perform them, including services performed by state and local government (FEAPMO CRM, 2006). The BRM, which forms a critical component in specifying the overall services blueprint of the enterprise, is organized

into four business areas, 39 lines of business, and 153 sub-functions. Together the PRM and the BRM owned by line of business owners, map to GERAM *partial process* and *partial human model* requirements. While the mapping to *partial process model* requirements against BRM is direct, the intent of the *partial human model* requirements is covered by the PRM through identification of organizational inputs, outputs, and outcomes along with key performance indicators. These can be mapped to organization and responsibilities as required by GERAM.

From a technology perspective, the FEAF specifies three reference models. The *service component reference model* (SRM) identifies and classifies application components that support the organizations and facilitate reuse of these components (FEAPMO CRM, 2006). The SRM is categorized into seven service domains differentiated by business-oriented capability they represent. The *data reference model* (DRM) describes at an aggregate level, the type of data and information along with their relationships required for supporting program and business line operations (FEAPMO DRM, 2006). The *technical reference model* (TRM) describes the use of technology in delivering business services and relevant standards for implementing the technology (FEAPMO CRM, 2006). The TRM is comprised of four core service areas that include: service access and delivery, service platform and infrastructure, component framework, and service interface and integration. The TRM can be mapped to GERAM *partial technology model* requirements as the TRM focuses on the technology infrastructure required for delivery of business services identified in the BRM. The SRM and DRM together cover the requirements of GERAM *partial models of IT systems*. A study of the FEAF reference models reveals that the intent of GERAM *partial enterprise models* is covered in totality, though as expected the approaches taken to categorize the models and their intent differ.

Concluding Remarks on Reference Models

An architecture framework like FEAF must provide constructs, frameworks, and guidelines to develop these models to be GERAM compliant. By providing templates, reference models play a significant role in reducing this complexity and accelerating the architecture initiative. Reference models are created either by specializing generic models or generalizing specific models, thus requiring a strong validation process. The FEAF largely meets the GERA *partial enterprise model* requirements, though mechanism to create executable partial models would greatly enhance ease of implementation (Noran, 2003).

TOOLS FOR ARCHITECTING ENTERPRISES

There can potentially be a large number of requirements for EA tools; GERAM identifies a few vital high-level requirements in this respect and expects organizations to select appropriate tools based on their requirements. GERAM is not normative in recommending tool selection criteria. The core requirements specified by GERAM are:

1. Support for analysis and evaluation of enterprise models allowing model enactment through simulation.
2. Comprehensive user guidance and embedded architecture development process.
3. Support for collaborative as well as individual design and engineering activities.
4. Provision of shared repository of all reference models, informal design descriptions and patterns, document, etc.
5. Ability to incorporate engineering of both products and enterprises.
6. Forward and reverse engineering capabilities.

Tools for the FEAF

In the current state of affairs, there is no single toolset that meets all requirements of an EA project in general and an EA project using the FEAF in specific. The situation is further exacerbated by: (1) existence of several competing architecture frameworks that are available for organization to adopt and (2) non-availability of a comprehensive EA language based on a common underlying metamodel. These factors encourage EA tool vendors to support multiple architecture frameworks and myriads of languages, lest they reduce tool marketability and acceptance. The FEAF is not prescriptive about any specific toolset, but explicitly includes "tool selection" as a mandatory activity in the architecture development life cycle. It further provides criteria that can be used to make such a selection. Table 2 provides a summary of tools and their generic enterprise architecture capabilities (Arbab et al., 2002). Note that "++" depicts primary functionality and "+" depicts secondary functionality.

Concluding Remarks on Enterprise Architecture Tools

In the absence of a single EA modeling language and existence of several architecture frameworks, it is challenging to find a tool that is sufficient to complete all aspects of architecture development. Organizations thus need to use multiple languages and tools to accomplish the stated objectives of an EA initiative. Use of multiple languages and tools creates challenges in model interoperability and integration.

ADDITIONAL ASPECTS OF ANALYSIS

This section aims to cover the remaining GERAM components and also identify areas where the

Table 2. Partial list of enterprise architecture tools and their capabilities

	Process & organization modeling	Software & system modeling	Information management modeling	Repository	Management
Aris Toolset	++				
Asg-rochade				++	
Enterprise Architect	+	++			
Front Arena Enterprise				+	++
Troux	++	+	+	+	
Microsoft Visio		++	+		
Ms Visual Studio .net		++			
Ptech Framework	++	+	+	+	
IBM Rational Rose		++			
Select Enterprise	+	++		+	
System Architect	++	++			
Tivoli Enterprise					++

FEAF goes beyond GERAM specifications. Aspects analyzed in this section include:

- **Entity types and their recursivity:** The GERAM explicitly states that the life cycle of more than one entity may be related to each other. GERA incorporates the concept of entity types and identifies five recursive entity types, which are: (1) strategic enterprise management entity, (2) enterprise engineering entity, (3) enterprise entity, (4) product entity, and (5) methodology entity.
- **Enterprise modules:** Similar to component based software engineering, GERAM also recommends the use of pre-built "components/modules" and incorporate an assembly based approach to enterprise architecture.
- **Areas for improvement in GERAM:** This chapter assesses the FEAF against GERAM requirements. However, the assessment also

reveals at least three critical areas where GERAM is found to be weak and these have been discussed briefly.

RECURSIVITY OF ENTITY TYPES IN THE FEAF

The FEAF does not explicitly mention the concept of entity types, though the four levels of succession in the FEAF recognize the notion of entity types, as each level could ideally be performed by a different entity and involves activities in increasing details and granularity. However, the framework is compatible with GERAM requirements on recursion. This is evident in the way the FEA reference models are sequenced (CIO Council, 1999). This allows organizations to progress through the architecture development in a continuum through time, where different groups (entities) perform different activities, but maintaining bidirectional traceability along the reference model continuum.

ENTERPRISE MODULES IN THE FEAF

In the FEAF, a component is defined as:

A self contained business process or service with predetermined functionality that may be exposed through a business or technology interface (FEAPMO CRM, 2006).

Components as architecture building blocks are clearly evident and explicit in the FEAF. The FEAF specifies components at increasing levels of granularity that include: federated component, business component system, business component, and distributed component. The SRM, which is the base reference model recommending a component-based approach, is organized into three levels with *service domains* followed by *service types* and *components*. There are seven service domains that categorize service capabilities from a business perspective. The 29 service types elaborate and categorize service capabilities within a specific service domain. Lastly, the 168 components are the building blocks with their interface specifications of a business or application service component (FEAPMO CRM, 2006). Thus, the concept of enterprise modules as architecture building blocks is directly compatible with the FEA components.

AREAS FOR IMPROVEMENT IN GERAM

Interestingly, the assessment presented in this chapter revealed three areas where there is scope for improvement in the GERAM. From the author's experience, these have been found to be critical to the overall success of the EA program.

Architecture Governance and Management

This involves specifying the decision rights and the accountability framework required to encourage the desirable use of the EA. From a practical perspective, this entails establishing a control mechanism over the development, implementation, and continued evolution of all EA elements and components. A key requirement for any EA program (and also in the FEAF) is compliance to the EA (CIO Council, 2001). Practice has revealed that if individual IT initiatives within the enterprise are not required to comply with the EA, then the EA program itself faces the danger of irrelevancy. To address such issues, the FEAF strongly recommends the establishment of a central EA office within the organization. From this point of view, GERAM is found to be weak. Key governance mechanisms recommended within the FEAF include:

1. Conducting architecture readiness assessment at the start of the EA program.
2. Setting up the architecture program management office and other roles like the architecture review board.
3. Establishing architecture principles.
4. Defining architecture compliance review process.
5. Defining architecture life cycle processes.

Architecture Effectiveness Assessment

EA, when treated as a program as suggested by the FEAF (CIO Council, 2001), is a long-term and an ongoing effort. The challenge thus is to create and sustain senior management and stakeholder interest. In this regard, one of the key components of the EA program is to establish a set of metrics early in the program life cycle that can be used: (1) as a way to manage stakeholder expectations from the EA program, and (2) as a mechanism to evaluate and communicate the success and effectiveness of the EA program. GERAM makes no mention of such metrics, while this is a key component within the FEAF driven initiatives (NASCIO, 2004). The FEAF recommends that agencies identify EA effectiveness metrics to support their architecture goals and objectives. Typical architecture objectives include, but are not limited to:

1. Cost reduction,
2. Higher business value of IT,
3. Flexible IT,
4. Cheaper and faster solutions/acquisitions,
5. Reduction in project failures,
6. Integration and interoperability of information services,

7. Adoption of service-oriented architecture (SOA),
8. Service quality guarantee,
9. Compliance,
10. Efficient portfolio management, and
11. Risk reduction.

Touch-Points with Organization's Other Activities

EA provides several benefits to the agencies, especially on issues concerning procurement and decommissioning of IT solutions. Hence, it is critical for the agencies to understand and acknowledge the fact that EA has very logical touch-points with

Table 3. Linkages of agency EA program to other activities

Activity	Nature of linkage from the EA program
IT governance	IT governance is "the process of specifying the decision rights and the accountability framework to encourage desirable behavior in the use of IT." The linkage between EA and IT governance is most extensive in architecture governance as this is derived from IT governance. Agencies can benefit from key IT governance mechanisms (like IT leadership committee, IT investment evaluation board, architecture committee, chargeback agreements, etc.) in utilizing them as architecture governance mechanisms. Another area where the linkage is strong is IT policies. When defining architecture principles, agencies must strive to derive them from the agency's IT policies.
IT portfolio management	Typically, an EA blueprint results in identifying IT projects and initiatives that help an organization transition toward the target architecture. The identified IT projects and initiatives lend themselves very well to populating the organization's IT portfolio. In other words, the IT projects in the EA programs feeds into the IT portfolio, which can then be categorized and administered as a portfolio asset mix to balance risks and returns (Saha, 2004b).
IT project anagement	EA is a more upstream activity, while IT project management represents downstream activity. The linkage between EA and project management happens through the fact that IT project management facilitates the agency's transition to the target architecture using a series of IT projects and initiatives. Individual projects should utilize the EA blueprint as the main source of their business requirements, business case development, and for understanding the interdependencies between the various projects. The EA blueprint provides the big-picture view. From a governance perspective as each executed project takes the agency toward the target architecture, it must also demonstrate compliance to the agency blueprint at all times. This is accomplished through conducting regular architecture compliance reviews.
Strategic IT planning	An agency's strategic IT plan represents its long term IT plan and projects usually in-line with its strategic business plan. EA provides a very disciplined approach to identifying and prioritizing IT projects and initiatives, which can then become part of the strategic IT plan for a specific period of time (usually 3 or 5 years).
IT performance management	The linkage in this case is in the area of EA effectiveness metrics. Organizations usually derive their IT scorecard from their balanced scorecard (BSC). IT scorecard metrics can be categorized into four perspectives, namely, corporate contribution, customer orientation, operational excellence, and future readiness. The EA program plays a critical role in positively impacting IT scorecard metrics across all perspectives.
Strategic planning	While there is no direct impact of the EA into the strategic planning exercise, it has been noticed that successful EA programs usually elevate the role of the IT department within the organization. As a result organizations with mature EA programs tend to include IT as a key resource and asset in executing business strategies through a series of strategic programs and initiatives.

other key organizational activities. GERAM does not make any explicit mention about the type and intensity of impact the EA program can have on some of the organization's other activities. The FEAF on the other hand recognizes these. Table 3 lists the organizational activities that the EA programs has linkages to and also briefly describes the nature of such linkages.

FINAL CONCLUSION

Reducing complexities, enhancing standardization, and disseminating best practices are some of the crucial recurring themes in EA practice. Standardization helps an organization to ultimately reap the benefits of economies of scale and scope. This is one of the critical goals of the FEAF. However, the advancement of practice in EA by the FEAF is limited due to the absence of a single unified architecture development language based on a common underlying metamodel. Using GERAM as a meta-framework, the assessment revealed that FEAF largely fulfills all the key GERAM concepts. By providing a generalized set of requirements, GERAM / ISO15704:2000 is an excellent baseline to map and assess candidate architecture frameworks like the FEAF. GERAM is not to be viewed as a competitor to the FEAF or any other framework. Rather, it represents a minimum set of requirements that constitute enterprise architecture practice. Such a baseline allows enterprises and architects to assess various candidate reference architectures and choose the most appropriate one based on their specific business needs. This makes the rationale for choosing a specific framework correct and reasoned and not impulsive and swayed by hype. It is clearly evident from the analysis in this chapter that the FEAF largely meets GERAM requirements and also exceeds them in a few areas. The few areas where the FEAF is found to be 'deficient' are limited to guidance and specifications only and

not in concepts. In this regard, two points to be noted are:

- The FEAF is still evolving and it is highly likely that eventually it would map to GERAM even further, as a common set of requirements also has the potential to assist in the evolution of enterprise architecture practice.
- The discipline and practice of enterprise architecture is also evolving, hence every architecture framework "hopes" to set trends rather than follow it, in order to maintain its comparative advantage.

GERAM at this instance is found weak in areas of (1) architecture governance and management, (2) architecture effectiveness metrics, and (3) linkages that a typical EA program might have on the organizations' other related activities. From a practical perspective, these are critical to sustain the EA practice within an organization. Similarly, it is near impossible to get key stakeholder buy-in in the absence of metrics that can be used by organizations to demonstrate and communicate the effectiveness of the EA program. Nonetheless, an assessment of this nature is beneficial to ensure the continued relevancy of GERAM as a meta-framework for EA.

REFERENCES

Arbab, F., Bonsangue, M., Scholten, J. G., Iacob, M. E., Jonkers, H., Lankhorst, M., Proper, E., & Stam, A. (2002). *State of the art in architecture framework and tools*. Telematica Institut Version 1.2.

Bernus, P. (2001). Some thoughts on enterprise modeling. *International Journal of Production Planning and Control, 12*(2), 110-118.

Bernus, P., Nemes, L., & Schmidt, G. (2003). *Handbook on enterprise architecture.* Berlin-Heidelberg: Springer-Verlag.

Bernus, P., Nemes, L., & Williams, T. J. (1996). *Architectures for enterprise integration.* London: Chapman & Hall.

Chen, D., & Doumeingts, G. (1996). *T*he GRAI-GIM reference model, architecture, and methodology. In P. Bernus, L. Nemes, & T. J. Williams (Eds.), *Architectures for enterprise integration.* London: Chapman & Hall.

Chen, D., Vallespir, B., & Doumeingts, G. (1997). GRAI integrated methodology and its mapping onto generic enterprise reference architecture and methodology. *Computers in Industry, 33*(3), 387-394.

CIO Council. (1999). *Federal enterprise architecture framework, Version 1.1.* Retrieved from http://www.whitehouse.gov/omb/egov/a-1-fea. html

CIO Council. (2001). *A practical guide to federal enterprise architecture, Version 1.1.* Retrieved from http://www.gao.gov/bestpractices/bpea-guide.pdf

FEAPMO DRM. (2005). *The data reference model, Version 2.0.* Retrieved from http://www. whitehouse.gov/omb/egov/a-1-fea.html

FEAPMO CRM. (2006). *FEA consolidated reference model, Version 2.0.* Retrieved from http:// www.whitehouse.gov/omb/egov/a-1-fea.html

IFIP-IFAC Task Force. (1999). *GERAM: Generalized enterprise reference architecture and methodology.* IFIP-IFAC Task Force on Architectures for Enterprise Integration, Version 1.6.3, (March).

Morabito, J., Sack, I., & Bhate, A. (1999). *Organization modeling: innovative architectures for the 21ˢᵗ century.* Upper Saddle River, NJ: Prentice Hall PTR.

NASCIO. (2004). *Enterprise architecture development toolkit Version 3.0.* Retrieved from http://www.nascio.org

Noran, O. (2003). An analysis of the Zachman framework for enterprise architecture from the GERAM perspective. *Annual Reviews in Control, 27,* 163-183.

Noran, O. (2005). A systematic evaluation of the C4ISR AF Using ISO 15704 Annex A (GERAM). *Computers in Industry, 56*(2005), 407-427.

Saha, P. (2004a). *Analyzing the open group architecture framework (TOGAF) from the GERAM perspective.* The open group architecture forum, TOGAF White Papers, (October). Retrieved from http://www.opengroup.org/architecture/wp/

Saha, P. (2004b). *A real options perspective to enterprise architecture as an investment activity.* The Open Group Architecture Forum, TOGAF White Papers, (November). Retrieved from http://www.opengroup.org/architecture/wp/

Spewak, S. H. (2002). *Enterprise architecture planning* (2ⁿᵈ ed.). NY: John Wiley & Sons.

United States General Accounting Office. (2003). *A framework for assessing & improving enterprise architecture management, Version 1.1.* Retrieved from http://www.gao.gov/new.items/d03584g. pdf

United States General Accounting Office. (2004). *Information technology investment management: A framework for assessing process maturity, Version 1.1.* Retrieved from http://www.gao.gov/new. items/d04394g.pdf

Vernadat, F. B. (1998). The CIMOSA languages. In P. Bernus, K. Mertins, & G. Schmidt (Eds.), *Handbook of information systems* (pp. 243-263). Berli-Heidelberg: Springer-Verlag.

Zachman, J. A. (2000). *Enterprise architecture: A framework.* Retrieved from http://www.zifa. com

Chapter II
Extreme Architecture Framework:
A Minimalist Framework for Modern Times

Phil Robinson
Lonsdale Systems, Australia

Floris Gout
Independent Consultant, Australia

ABSTRACT

As consultant-educators, the authors created the extreme architecture framework (XAF) in order to quickly grasp an understanding of an organisation's architecture from different perspectives. The framework is presented as a matrix of system types and architectural perspectives that is described by a single uncluttered diagram. Elements within the framework are defined along with the content that can include architectural representations, planning, and governance information. A discussion follows to show the relationship of the framework to planning, development, and governance activities. The minimalist framework presents a consolidated view of both human activity and software systems and can also help to foster a shared understanding between IT groups and business areas.
It has been designed to answer a manager's questions:

- *Which elements of the enterprise do I need to be aware of and understand; and*
- *Which elements am I responsible for and need to manage?*

INTRODUCTION

The enterprise architecture framework described here evolved slowly over a period of time. It has been heavily influenced by the assignments un-dertaken by the authors who consult to a variety of clients across a range of industry sectors. In presenting "yet another framework," it is not the authors' intention to "reinvent the wheel" but rather to synthesise some of the best ideas in the field of enterprise architecture and inject a healthy dose of experience in order to create an enterprise architecture framework that has strong conceptual foundations but can also be applied to practical situations.

Early in the evolution of the framework, both authors were introduced to the ideas advocated by the extreme programming (XP) community (Beck, 2000). XP is a lightweight but highly rigorous approach to software development that the authors originally sought to emulate in their architecture framework. The "extreme" in XP refers to the way in which well-established best practices have been taken to the "extreme."

In the area of enterprise architecture, there is less consensus on what represents best practice. This also means that there is less opportunity to develop "extreme" practices. In fact, as the extreme architecture framework (XAF) evolved, it became obvious that the "extreme" in XAF was in fact a pun. The XAF is best described as a "lightweight" pragmatic approach to enterprise architecture that avoids the "extremes" of perfection and chaos.

In contrast to other architecture frameworks the XAF:

- Is easy to describe.
- Encourages an agile approach to architectural work products.
- Unifies a number of disparate disciplines.
- Offers a simple, consistent view to the various parties involved in the management of enterprise resources.

Above all, the XAF can be used to answer the two questions most often asked by the authors' clients (frequently IT managers and chief information officers):

- "Which elements of the enterprise do I need to be aware of and understand; and
- Which elements am I responsible for and need to manage?"

The remainder of this chapter describes how the XAF attempts to present a unified view of human activity and software systems from the three perspectives of business processes, information systems, and technology infrastructure. The unified view attempts to strike a balance between architectural perfection and the inevitable chaos when there is an absence of architecture.

The XAF embodies three guiding principles:

1. The contribution of frameworks themselves.
2. The need for interoperability between systems whether they be human or software systems.
3. The various different architectural perspectives that are required to be managed (IEEE Computer Society, 2000).

The chapter concludes with a description of how elements of the enterprise can be organised into groupings that reflect the disciplines responsible for building and managing the enterprise. The XAF is a perfect mechanism for highlighting these grouping and revealing the nature of the relationship between them.

BUILDINGS, URBAN DISTRICTS, SOFTWARE, AND ARCHITECTURE

A clear and simple definition of what constitutes architecture can be difficult to achieve. The authors like this definition of building architecture that was provided by Ean MacDonald, a retired architect (e-mail communication October 5, 2003).

"Architectural design is the simultaneous resolution and solution of the various architectural problems including location, aspect, and prospect, sun, wind, and weather, materials and method, finance, function, and form, to which may be added a dash of flair that can make a structure work of art."

Surprisingly, the view that architecture can be both a science and an art is shared by some software architects. Roger Pressman describes architecture as representations of a software system that allow software engineers,

... to (1) analyse the effectiveness of the design in meeting its stated requirements, (2) consider architectural alternatives at a stage when making design changes is still relatively easy, and (3) reduce risks associated with the construction of the software. (Pressman, 2005, p. 288)

At the same time, he unashamedly notes that architecture is an art (Pressman, 2005, p. 287).

Based on the opinions of these two architects working in different fields, it seems that architecture is intended to provide both functional design and aesthetic appeal.

Before presenting the XAF in detail, it is useful to further explore a metaphor that equates buildings with software systems and the urban landscape with enterprises.

In his well-known essay on software architecture, Brooks (1995, p. 42) cites the building of the cathedral at Reims as a triumph of architectural vision. According to Brooks, eight generations of highly skilled builders sacrificed their own

ideas in order to maintain the design integrity of the cathedral. In describing the cathedral, Brooks states:

...the joy that stirs the beholder comes as much from the integrity of the design as from any particular excellences.

Brooks offers the triumph of Reims as a sort of Holy Grail for software developers.

In stark contrast, the authors of the "Big Ball of Mud Pattern" describe what they claim is the most frequently adopted software systems architecture. They use the metaphor of a "shantytown" structure to describe the software architecture and point out that the buildings are:

...built from common, inexpensive materials and simple tools...using relatively unskilled labor. (Foote & Yoder, 1999, p. 7)

Figure 2. The shantytown

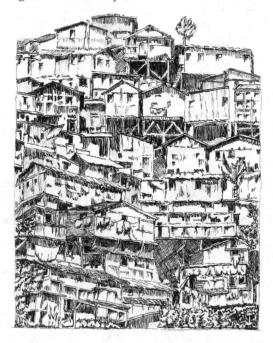

Figure 1. The cathedral

Foote et al. argue that there are a number of reasons why the big ball of mud is common:

- Pressure on project schedules and costs.
- Inexperience, lack of skills and high staff turnover.
- The complexity and rate of change of the software requirements.

Care must be taken not to mix metaphors. The Reims metaphor is based on the architecture of a single building while the shantytown metaphor is simultaneously based on the architecture of

buildings and a chronic lack of urban planning. Urban planning involves laying out the streets and amenities for a suburb and planning the provision of services such as water, electricity, and telephone. Individual residents of the suburb are free to build whatever style of house they desire providing it conforms to the building standards and guidelines laid down for the suburb.

An example of urban planning that equates to the construction of Reims is the planning of Canberra, Australia's national capital, by Walter Burley-Griffin. It is true that modern-day Canberra does not have the casino, trams, or sole

Figure 3. The 1912 plan of Canberra

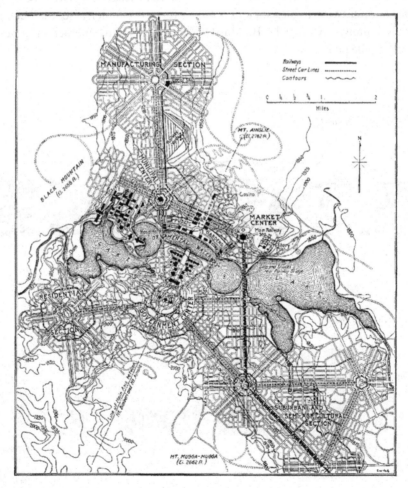

residential centre envisaged by Griffin. However, the overall layout of Canberra and its capital is instantly recognisable in the original 1912 plan.

In contrast to Canberra, a shantytown represents an extreme lack of urban design resulting in opportunistic utilisation of space that has adverse affects on land use and the shantytown's residents.

These metaphors provided the starting point for the XAF. Reims and Canberra reflect the extremes of "architecture as art." Reims was built as a symbol of glorification and Canberra as a symbol of national pride. At the opposite extreme, a shantytown suffers from a complete absence of urban planning and is built from whatever comes to hand. The result is misery for the town's inhabitants and degradation of the environment.

Confronted by these two extremes, the authors found themselves drawn to what the Buddhist faith calls the "middle path."

...avoiding the extremes gives vision and knowledge and leads to calm, realization, enlightenment. (Thera, 1958)

It is a fact that most architects and urban planners spend the majority of their time following the "middle path." Few are involved in the planning of entire cities or the design of cathedrals. Instead, the majority of architects and planners spend their time designing suburban houses and planning the layout of residential suburbs. This simple reality offers the perfect metaphor of a suburban house in a residential suburb sitting between the two extremes of perfection (Reims, Canberra) and chaos (shantytown).

The precise choice of architectural elements used to describe an enterprise provides the structure of an enterprise architecture. The selected elements must interact with each other in a con-

Figure 4. The suburban house

Figure 5. The "middle path"

sistent manner in order to provide a holistic view of the enterprise.

An enterprise architecture framework provides support by serving as a checklist to identify the actual enterprise elements[1] that describe an enterprise.

The structural integrity of an enterprise architecture is maintained by carefully defining the relationships between architectural elements and ensuring that framework will highlight the impact of change.

THE NEED FOR FRAMEWORKS

The use of frameworks to provide structure and support is a common practice in many disciplines. The role of frameworks can be illustrated by returning once more to the building metaphor. There is a style of building that involves first constructing a steel or wooden frame and then "cladding" it with a suitable material. The frame defines the structure of the building and provides

support while the cladding provides shelter and aesthetic appeal. Maintaining the exterior of such a building is a simple matter of replacing worn or damaged sections of the external cladding. When required, the appearance of a building can be completely renovated by simply replacing the cladding. Maintaining or renovating the exterior of a building with a frame has no impact on the structural integrity of the building. To summarise, the role of a building's frame is to provide structure and support while maintaining structural integrity in the face of change.

Enterprise architecture frameworks provide structure, support, and integrity in much the same manner as the frame of a building:

There are a plethora of enterprise architecture frameworks. For those interested, Shekkerman (2004) offers a useful inventory of the more important frameworks. The three frameworks that have had the greatest influence on the XAF are listed next:

Figure 6. A building framework

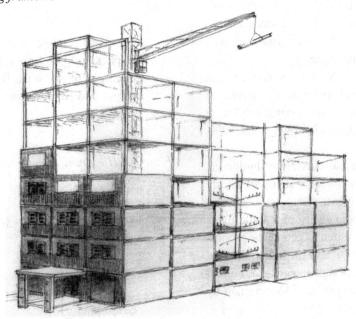

- The Zachman framework (Zachman, 1987) is perhaps the best-known enterprise architecture framework. The presentation of the XAF as a matrix reflects the influence of this framework.
- The NIST framework (Fong & Goldfine 1989) is one of the earliest enterprise architecture frameworks and has had a strong influenced on many subsequent frameworks. The architectural views adopted by the XAF as matrix columns, reflect the influence of this framework.
- The TOGAF framework (The Open Group, 2003) is a comprehensive enterprise architecture methodology that places great emphasis on interoperability between systems. The influence of this framework on the XAF is reflected in the choice of systems as matrix rows.

SYSTEMS AND INTEROPERABILITY

Although useful at a superficial level, the building and urban planning metaphors for enterprise architecture have quite important limitations. Buildings are static structures that interact minimally with their environment. Services such as water, gas, electricity, and access roads are well defined and change infrequently.

Fundamental to the XAF is the concept that an enterprise can be regarded as a collection of human activity and software systems exhibiting "purposeful design" (Checkland & Scholes, 1990, p. 21-22).

In contrast to the static nature of buildings, human activity, and software systems are highly dynamic and interactive.

While the design integrity of a building is determined by factors such as geometric proportion, structural strength, and the materials used for construction, the design integrity of human activity and software systems is determined by factors that are far more abstract and often quite difficult to measure.

Figure 7 shows the classification of human activity and software systems on which the XAF is based. There are three categories of human activity system:

1. An industry sector is a system of interacting enterprises that are all engaged in a similar type of activity. Travel, banking, and education are all examples of industry sectors.
2. An enterprise is a collection of individuals performing systematic and purposeful activities in support of a well-defined mission. Travel agents, airlines, banks, and educational institutions are all examples of enterprises.
3. A business process has been defined as "a sequence of activities that produce outputs of value to the customers of the process" (Hammer & Champy, 2003). Hotel or airline reservations, funds transfer, and student enrolments are all examples of business processes.

There are two categories of software system:

1. A software application is a mechanism for packaging and physically deploying a collection of software functions that are designed to support one or more business processes.

Figure 7. Hierarchy of enterprise systems

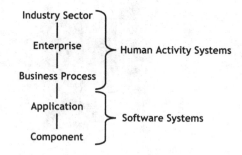

2. A software component is a piece of software that can be easily replaced by another piece of software and can potentially be reused in a number of different applications. A reservations Web service provided by an airline, a calendar visual component, a banking database, and a reusable computer-based training module are all examples of components.

The enterprise systems shown in Figure 7 are organised into a hierarchy. This is a common representation of enterprise systems that emphasises their composition. The hierarchy of systems suggests that industry sectors are composed from a number of enterprises, enterprises are composed from a number of business processes, and software applications are composed from a number of software components.

Another common representation of enterprise systems is to show them "nested" one inside the other. This perspective suggests that an individual system can only interact with the system that contains it or the other systems sharing the same container. This implies that a business processes may not interact with the business processes of

another enterprise or that a software application may only support a single business process.

While the hierarchical and nested representations of enterprise systems may have been convenient in the past, there are a number of factors in the modern business environment that now make this perspective somewhat less valid:

*   It is common for business processes to be outsourced. This means that more than one enterprise can have responsibility for a business process and invalidates the notion of a business process being nested inside a single containing system.
*   It is now normal practice for people outside an enterprise, such as customers, agents, and suppliers, to interact directly with the enterprise's software applications. This invalidates the notion that software applications are nested inside business processes that are in turn nested inside an enterprise.
*   Modern software development techniques emphasise the creation of reusable software components. This invalidates the notion that a software component is nested inside a

Figure 8. Independent and overlapping nature of enterprise systems

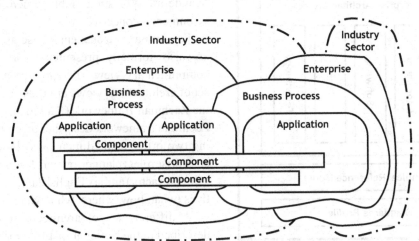

single software application since the goal is to reuse a component many times in order to construct a variety of software applications. In addition, the recent trend toward internet Web services means that an entire industry sector can use the services provided by a single software component thus invalidating the entire hierarchy of systems.

For these reasons, the authors believe that it is more realistic to view the human activity and software systems of an enterprise as a number of "independent" and "overlapping" systems. This representation is shown in Figure 8.

Independent, overlapping systems are able to interact with each other in an unrestricted manner. For example:

- A single software applications may support a number of disparate business processes.
- A single business processes may extend across a number of different enterprises.
- A single software application may support the business process of a number of different, unrelated enterprises.

Figure 9. The OMB architecture framework

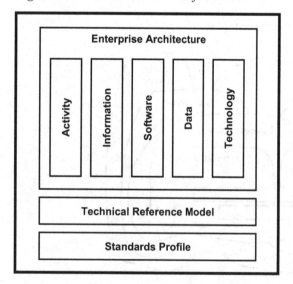

- A software component may be designed to provide a suite of generic services that are used by one or more industry sectors.

Regarding human activity and software systems as independent and overlapping leads to an overriding requirement for interoperability between the individual systems. Interoperability can be defined as the ability of a system to successfully interact with other specified systems.

ARCHITECTURAL VIEWS

High levels of interoperability are unlikely to be found in enterprises that resemble a shantytown. Interoperability requires a high level of structural integrity in the interfaces between enterprise systems. As the builders of Reims and Canberra knew only too well, it is necessary to develop a detailed architectural plan and stick to it in order to achieve a high level of structural integrity.

Describing a large building, town, or city is a complex task and for this reason architects and urban planners present their plans using a number of complimentary "views." An urban planner might create one view to show the proposed subdivision of land. Another view might show the routing of services such as electricity, gas, water, and sewage. Additional views might include transportation, public amenities, or environmental concerns.

For similar reasons, enterprise architectures are also normally presented as a number of complimentary views. Perhaps the best-known set of architectural views are those described in the Zachman framework (Zachman, 1987). The Zachman framework describes an enterprise using two orthogonal "dimensions" based on five enterprise roles (planner, owner, designer, builder, sub-contractor) and six English language imperatives (what, how, where, who, when, why).

A different set of architectural views are described in the National Institute for Standards and Technology (NIST) architecture framework (Fong et al., 1989). Following the enactment of the Clinger-Cohen Act in the United States, the NIST architectural views were endorsed by the Office of Management and Budget (OMB), which issued a directive requiring government agencies to develop enterprise architectures. The directive included an architecture framework based on the NIST framework.

Since the enactment of the Clinger-Cohen Act, the U.S. government has unveiled a number of electronic government initiatives. To support these initiatives, the OMB has developed and published its federal enterprise architecture (FEA). In contrast to the original OMB reference architecture, FEA is more complex and closely aligned with the specific needs of the U.S. government.

One of the attractions of the original OMB reference architecture is its simplicity. It has just three major components:

1. Enterprise architecture.
2. Technical reference model.
3. Standards profile.

The enterprise architecture consists of five architectural views that together describe the enterprise:

1. **Activity architecture**[2]: Describes an enterprise's high-level business activities and workflows.
2. **Information architecture**[3]: Describes the information required to support the business activities described in the activity architecture.
3. **Software architecture**[4]: Describes the software that is required to support the Activity and Information Architectures.
4. **Data architecture**[5]: Describes the logical and physical structure of the enterprise's software-maintained data stores.
5. **Technology architecture**[6]: Describes the

technical environment in which software executes.

The technical reference model is a comprehensive list of the generic services provided by the enterprise's technology infrastructure. The list includes items such as:

- Data interchange services
- Data management services
- Graphics services
- Directory management services
- Network services
- Operating system services

The technical reference model groups the services into logical classifications rather than identifying specific products or solutions The TOGAF framework (The Open Group, 2003) includes a detailed example of a technical reference model.

The standards profile is a collection of standards that fully specify the generic services identified in the technical reference model. Standards are fundamental to the achievement of interoperability between systems. Internally developed guidelines, de facto standards, and formal international standards may all be included in the standards profile.

It should be briefly noted that the reference architecture described in the OMB directive does not exhaustively define an enterprise. A full understanding of an enterprise must include elements such as business strategy, culture, and values. These elements will influence the architecture in much the same way that financial, political, and social factors influence urban planning.

The architectural views from the OMB enterprise architecture have been chosen as the basis for architectural views in the XAF because of their ease of understanding when compared to the architectural views presented in the Zachman framework. In the authors' experience, most people readily understand the Zachman framework views that are based on the six English language imperatives. However, many people struggle with the Zachman framework views that are based on the five enterprise roles.

THE EXTREME ARCHITECTURE FRAMEWORK

It is now time to introduce the complete XAF. The framework is presented as a matrix, which maps the orthogonal enterprise architecture dimensions of systems and architectural views. A matrix format was chosen because the Zachman framework has demonstrated the power of mapping orthogonal dimensions coupled with the simplicity and universal appeal of presenting an architecture framework as a matrix.

The rows of the XAF matrix are labelled with the five independent, overlapping systems previously described. The columns of the matrix are labelled with the five architectural views from the OMB reference architecture.

The individual cells of the matrix are used to organise architectural content. The labels of the

Figure 10. The extreme architecture framework presented as a matrix

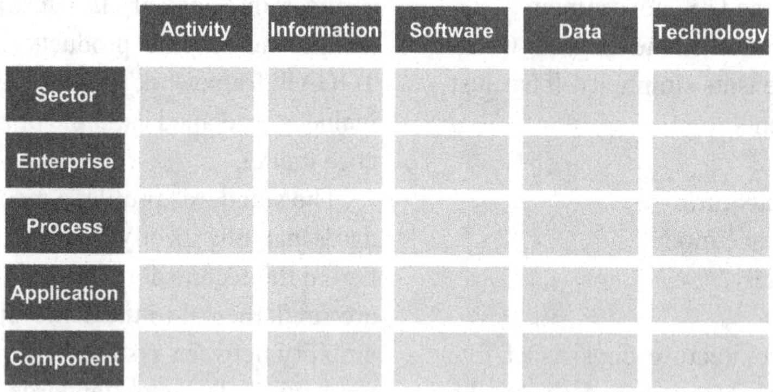

Figure 4. The extreme architecture framework

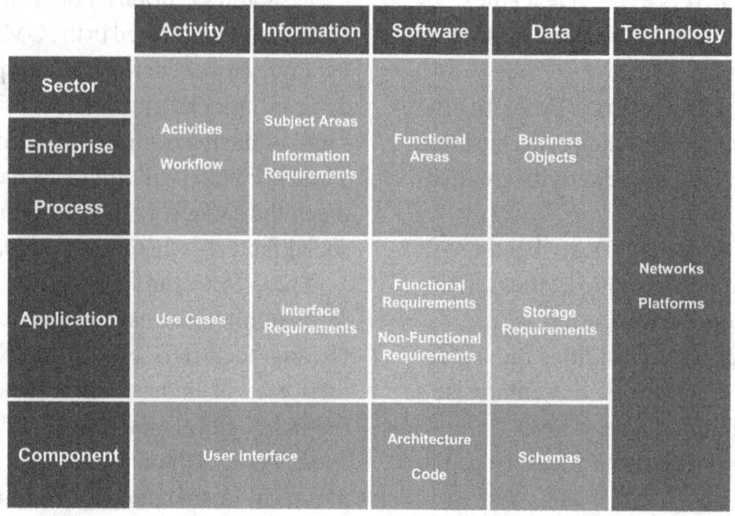

intersecting row and column classify the content of each cell. For example:

- The cell at the intersection of the sector row and the activity column contains content that describes the activities performed within an industry sector.
- The cell at the intersection of the process row and data column contains content that describes the data associated with a business process.
- The cell at the intersection of the application row and software column contains content that describes the requirements for an individual software application.

ARCHITECTURAL ELEMENTS

Each cell in the matrix contains a number of architectural elements that further refine the coarse classification scheme provided by the rows and columns of the matrix.

Figure 4 shows the complete XAF with the 18 architectural elements added to the framework. Notice how some of the cells have been grouped together when they share similar content across a number of rows of columns. The most obvious examples are the grouping of sector, enterprise, and process into a single row representing human activity systems and the grouping of the entire technology column into a single cell.

A necessarily brief description of the 18 architectural elements is given next. The descriptions are deliberately presented at a fairly high level of detail in order to facilitate the mapping of the XAF to other standards such as the unified modelling language (UML) or the integrated definition methods (IDEF) series of standards.

- **Activities:** Describe the business activities performed within a sector, enterprise, or business process.

- **Workflows:** Describe the flow of physical objects and information between business activities.
- **Subject areas:** Classify and group information requirements having a common theme, subject areas can also be used to group businesses objects and storage requirements. A database[7] is a special case of subject area that is actually implemented and physically deployed.
- **Information requirements:** Identify and describe the information required in order to successfully perform an activity as well as any information that is produced as an outcome of the activity.
- **Functional areas:** Used to classify and group functional requirements that have a common purpose. Functional areas can also used to group non-functional requirements, interface requirements, and use cases.
- **Business objects[8]:** Represent the concepts of interest within the sector, enterprise, or process. A useful scheme for classifying concepts of interest can be found in Peter Coad's work which identifies the following categories (Coad et al., 1999, pp. 3-6):
  - Business-related events and time periods.
  - The roles of people, organisations, places, and things.
  - The actual people, organisations, places, and things.
  - Classifications of any of the above.
- **Use cases:** Describe the usage of a software application by identifying interactions between an actor (user) and the software (Jacobson, 1992). Each step in the interaction either provides some direct value to the actor or indirect value to the application's stakeholders. Use case steps provide value by:
  - Enforcing business rules.
  - Controlling a hardware device.
  - Storing data.
  - Presenting information to the actor.

- **Interface requirements:** Provides a detailed description of either a user or software interface. Interface requirements may include detailed definitions for each of the data elements included in the interface.
- **Functional requirements:** Describe the mandatory capabilities, actions, and behaviour of a proposed software application.
- **Non-functional requirements:** Describes the requirements of a proposed software application that are not related to its capabilities, actions, or behaviour. Non-functional requirements include:
  - Quality attributes of an application such as performance, usability, security, reliability, recovery, audit, and archiving.
  - Application constraints relating to the software platform, the stakeholders, the external environment, the application's life cycle, and its design.
- **Storage requirements:** Describe data that will be permanently stored (persistent data). Storage requirements may include detailed definitions for each of the data elements included in the requirements.
- **User interfaces:** The physical screens reports and Web pages that a user interacts with.
- **Architecture:** Various high-level views of a software application. A useful scheme for classifying architectural views can be found in Hofmeister et al. (1999), which identifies the following views:
  - Underlying conceptual organization of the software.
  - The individual modules from which the software constructed.
  - The organisation of the source code.
  - The run-time deployment of the software.
- **Code:** The human readable source code that defines the software and the binary code that is executed.

- **Schemas:** Defines an electronic data store in terms of the records (or tables) and the relationships between the records.
- **Networks:** The mechanisms that are used to interconnect hardware and software platforms to permit the transfer of data and invocation of remote of services.
- **Platforms:** The hardware, firmware, system software, and middleware required to deploy and execute a software application.
- **Frameworks:** Standard component models and/or reference software architectures such as J2EE or .Net.

ENTERPRISE ELEMENTS

The XAF architectural elements offer a checklist that can be used to identify the elements that actually describe a specific enterprise. The XAF uses the term "enterprise elements" to differentiate these elements from the architectural elements previously described.

The following enterprise elements might be used to describe part of an enterprise architecture for a hotel:

- **Activities:**
  - Accept reservations
  - Check in guest
  - Provide room service
  - Provide laundry
  - Check out guest
- **Information Requirements:**
  - Guest details
  - Room types
  - Room availability
  - Room maintenance schedule
  - Room utilisation rate
- **Functional Requirements:**
  - The system shall allow reservations to be created from guest history.
  - The system shall allow reservations to be created for individuals or groups.

- The system shall allow reservations for more than one room to be created.
- The system shall record the guest's arrival date, time, and flight number.

ARCHITECTURE CONTENT

The XAF architectural elements also provide a classification scheme for architecture content. Each cell (or group of cells) in the framework matrix can contain different types of content.

The content can be further classified into content that describes architectural elements or enterprise elements.

ARCHITECTURAL ELEMENT CONTENT

Content for architectural elements define the vision, principles, and strategies that guide the current functioning and future evolution of an enterprise.

Typical content for this category of elements include:

- **A vision of some desirable, future state of an architectural element and its associated enterprise elements:** The vision should describe how the future state will contribute to business strategies and goals. For example, a vision that data will be seamlessly transferred between different business activities. This vision would apply equally to all business activities.
- **An underlying principle associated with an architectural element:** A principle is a short statement that guides or constrains some aspect of the architectural element. Principles tend to define fundamental aspects of an architecture that are infrequently changed or amended. Principles that actually guide the development and implementation

of the architecture itself can also be defined. For example, the principles of minimising data redundancy and duplication or the principle of performing data entry at the first point of data capture. Again this principle would apply equally to all information and storage requirements.

- **A strategy or course of action to achieve a desirable, future state of an architectural element:** For example, a strategy to facilitate transfer of data between business activities by integrating software applications using a "hub and spoke" architecture.

Content for architectural elements is normally associated with planning. It would also be possible to extend this area of the framework to incorporate balanced scorecard techniques (Kaplan & Norton 1990, 2004) as well as the planning models described by the Business Rules Group (Hall, Healy, & Ross, 2005, p. 1-2). The authors have experimented with synthesising the ideas from these thinkers into the framework.

ENTERPRISE ELEMENT CONTENT

Content for enterprise elements describes the detail of the enterprise. Typical content for this category of elements include:

- **A model, list, or definition describing enterprise elements:** For example, a list of the core business activities performed by a hotel, a glossary defining the key business objects that are relevant to the hospitality sector, or a UML model describing a hotel management application.
- **An assessment or SWOT analysis of the current state of an enterprise element:** For example, an assessment of data quality associated with hotel reservation data, or a SWOT analysis of the user interface of an existing hotel management application. As-

sessments might also refer to potential risks and rewards associated with the current state of the enterprise element.

- **A potential risk associated with an enterprise element:** For example, low customer satisfaction associated with the check in process at a hotel.
- **A potential reward associated with an enterprise element:** For example, a reduction in staff costs associated with an internet-based guest reservation system.

GROUPING FRAMEWORK CELLS

Although this chapter does not deal with the governance or development tasks associated with an enterprise architecture, the authors have found that the framework reflects aspects of both tasks. In addition to what can be regarded as the "standard" grouping of cells shown in the framework diagram above, cells of the matrix can be grouped in a number of other ways. Grouping cells is the main technique used to highlight focus areas of the framework.

ROWS

Partitioning the cells of the framework into rows and attempting to name them offers a major insight into the framework. The most obvious choice of names for the rows tends to reflect the major disciplines associated with the systems development life cycle.

The "business modeling" row describes "what" the enterprise does and how its activities are supported by its software systems. The row includes the activities performed, workflows between activities, information requirements, business objects, a high-level grouping of software functions into a number of functional areas, and the technology platforms and networks used to support business activity. This row provides the

context for the individual software applications of the enterprise.

The "requirements definition" row defines the requirements for a single software application. The row includes the application's use cases, interface requirements, functional and non-functional requirements, data storage requirements, and an elaboration of technology requirements documents. It should be obvious that the content of this row also reflects the typical content of a requirement definition document.

The "software construction" row describes the physical artefacts that together implement a single software application. Here are found the artefacts of software development such as user interfaces, software architecture, program code, and database schemas. Notice how a part of the technology column is included in all three of the rows. This would appear to reflect that the appropriate use of technology needs to be considered at all three levels.

COLUMNS

Partitioning the framework into columns also provides a major insight into the framework. The logical choice of names for the columns tends to reflect the management disciplines frequently tasked with the governance of the enterprise architecture.

The "process improvement" column includes the elements that are the focus of business process reengineering projects or continuous improvement initiatives. Activities define the scope of the improvement while workflows define the improved processes. Use cases and user interfaces describe how a software application will support the improved process.

The "information management" column includes the elements that need to be properly managed in order for an organisation to make effective use of information. It includes the grouping of information requirements into subject

Figure 11. Partitioning into life cycle disciplines

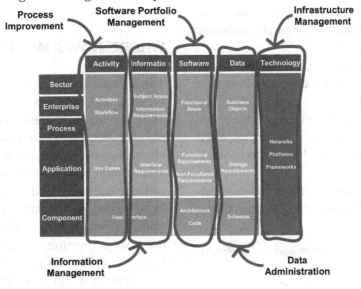

Figure 12. Partitioning into management disciplines

areas that are independent of business processes and the management of all electronic and paper-based records.

The "software portfolio management" column includes the elements that define an organisation's software portfolio. The portfolio is likely to a mixture of bought-in packaged software and custom in-house developed software. A major concern of those who focus on this column is the integration of disparate software.

The "data administration" column includes the elements that define an organisation's electronic databases. While data administration is often regarded as an on-going function, it should not be forgotten that this is also the discipline that drives data quality improvement and data integration projects.

The "infrastructure management" column is often viewed as the "operations" domain. The elements in this column represent the organisation's hardware and software platforms together with the networks that interconnect them. The "operations" group also manages the technical frameworks underlying the technology. While the discipline is mainly concerned with guaranteeing "the smooth running" of technology, infrastructure projects such as the technology conversion, standard operating environments, or rationalisation of networks and technology also fall into this domain.

BUSINESS AND IT RESPONSIBILITIES

Considering the columns of the XAF offers one further insight into the governance of enterprise architecture. Frequently tension develops between business and IT groups.

The reason for the tension becomes clearer when the responsibility for different columns is highlighted on the XAF—business groups are usually responsible for the elements in the activity and information columns while IT groups are usually responsible for the data and technology columns.

Many would include the software column as an IT responsibility. It is true that IT areas actually

Figure 13. The "axis of joy or sorrow" business and IT ownership

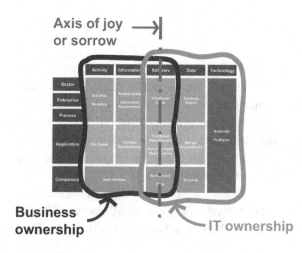

construct the software portfolio by identifying the functional requirements, designing databases, and writing program code. However, it can be argued that business groups must be actively involved in the management of the software portfolio if it is to meet their needs and be properly aligned to the goals of the enterprise.

The authors' conclusion is that both groups must share responsibility for the software portfolio. This column represents the "boundary" between the two groups; it is where most benefit will be gained from collaboration and joint responsibility. For many enterprises, this column will come to represent what the authors call an "axis of joy" or an "axis of sorrow."

WHERE ROWS MEET COLUMNS

The individual cells of the XAF are where the life cycle and management disciplines intersect. They also highlight areas where cooperation is required and conflict is common. For example, the intersection between the component row and the data column could involve interaction between the software developers and the data administrator. Many readers will be familiar with situations in which software developers design a data structure that does not conform to enterprise standards. Often the developers have compelling reasons to do this but it will inevitably bring them into conflict with the data administrator.

The XAF offers a way out by providing a platform for both parties to present their arguments while at the same time offering an opportunity to acknowledge the importance of the opposing point of view.

ARBITRARY AREAS

As well as the rows and columns previously described, the cells of the XAF can be grouped into any number of arbitrary areas. This approach

Figure 14. Where disciplines intersect

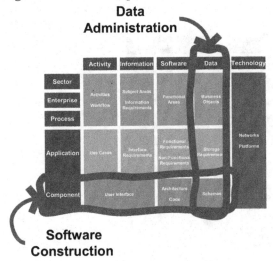

can be very useful for scoping areas of special interest.

As an example, the authors will briefly discuss how they have used the framework to scope consultancy projects.

In one project, the framework was used to plan the development of a "requirements traceability matrix." The client wanted to be certain that the software application they had acquired satisfied their documented requirements and would successfully integrate with other applications. The basic question they wanted to answer was, "Have we covered everything?"

To determine the scope of the assignment, the authors presented the framework using a colourful laminated card. As well as helping to explain the nature of the XAF, the reference card served as a focal point for negotiating the scope of the assignment.

A number of possible boundaries for the assignment were physically sketched on the reference card. Presentation of the XAF in this manner assisted the client to articulate what they wanted at the authors to cover. The final sketch became the scope of the assignment and the basis of the project charter.

To summarise the various groupings of the XAF previously discussed:

- The horizontal rows describe the disciplines associated with projects and are applied to various phases of the system development life cycle.
- The vertical columns represent the management disciplines that are required for proper governance of the enterprise architecture.
- Groupings of vertical columns represent the responsibilities of business and IT groups with the software column representing an area of joint responsibility.
- Individual cells represent areas of potential conflict (or cooperation) between the needs of projects and good governance.
- Arbitrary areas represent the scope of unique types of work; typically project assignments.

WHO OWNS THE FRAMEWORK?

Using groupings of framework cells to highlight the responsibilities of business and IT groups raises the question "Who is responsible for the framework itself?" The author's initial reaction to this question is that the framework is simple enough not to require an owner! However, it is a fact that the successful development of an enterprise architecture will require firm leadership and the allocation of appropriate resources. With this in mind, the authors envisage that an enterprise architect role will be required and that this role will serve as the "custodian" (rather than owner) of the framework.

The responsibilities of the enterprise architect role would include:

- Facilitating the population of the framework with a variety of content.

Figure 9. Defining the scope of a consultancy project

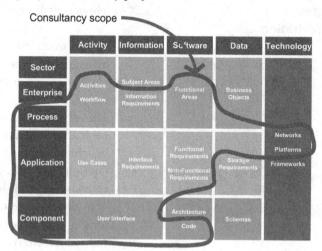

- Coordinating activities performed by the life cycle disciplines and management disciplines.
- Arbitrating in conflicts between the life cycle and management disciplines.

WHY EXTREME?

How can an architecture framework that evolved out of a search for the "middle path" be called extreme?

Firstly, enterprise architecture is beset by extremes. At one extreme, the would-be builders of corporate cathedrals will settle for nothing less than perfection. At the other extreme, the builders of chaotic shantytowns grab the first solution that comes to hand. As we have seen earlier, when the image of a modest suburban house is placed between the images of a cathedral and a shantytown it becomes obvious that the "middle path" is in fact an attractive alternative to the two extremes. However, it is important to emphasise that following the "middle path" is not the same as sitting on the fence.

The suburban house as a metaphor for self-reliance, affordability, and pragmatism has a much greater relevance to the modern enterprise than the abundance, privilege, and order of Reims cathedral or the disenfranchisement, poverty, and chaos found in a shantytown.

Secondly, the XAF is extreme because it exaggerates the best aspects of other architecture frameworks.

- **Like the Zachman framework, the XAF is easy to describe:** It is based on a simple five by five matrix. The body of the matrix is populated with just 18 architectural elements. The authors present the framework using a single, colourful reference card that everyone seems to want.

  The use of a matrix provides a simple structuring mechanism for the architecture. The relationship and interaction between elements in adjacent cells is easy to understand and the impact of change is easy to see. The complete matrix offers a holistic view of the enterprise as a whole. In contrast, many architecture frameworks are complex and difficult to describe. The documentation for TOGAF Version 8 runs to 313 pages and includes many complex diagrams.

- **The XAF encourages an agile approach to architecture work products:** The 18 architectural elements serve as a comprehensive but manageable checklist for many different types of architectural content. This versatility supports the development of many different styles of enterprise content. In contrast, many architecture frameworks advocate the creation of a large number of elaborate and detailed models. For example, the Zachman framework identifies no less that 36 "primitive" models.

- **The XAF unifies a number of disparate disciplines:** We know of architecture groups that work in splendid isolation. Their elaborate models never make one iota of difference to the business managers, business analysts, software developers, or IT infrastructure groups. In our framework, the 19 architectural elements can be grouped into four different areas. Each area is focused on a particular group but retains the context of its relationship to the other elements.

- **The XAF offers a simple, consistent view to the various parties involved in the management of enterprise resources:** This encourages shared understanding between disparate groups by presenting an area of "common ground" that can be understood by everyone. This leads to increased participation and ownership by all parties. In contrast, some frameworks organise models according to various roles and disciplines. This tends to encourage redundant descriptions of architectural elements at different levels of detail. For example, the Zachman framework answers the questions what, why, when, how, where, and who from the perspective of five different roles.

- **The framework can provide a means to explicitly acknowledge the responsibility that some groups have for certain architectural elements:** From the opposite perspective, it also serves as an encouragement for people to acknowledge the responsibility that others have for architectural elements.

Above all, the XAF is a middle of the road vehicle for those businesses and IT groups who cannot afford the comprehensive nature of some published frameworks and who wish to avoid the chaos of not having one at all.

REFERENCES

Beck, K. (2000). *Extreme programming explained: Embrace change.* Upper Saddle River, NJ: Addison Wesley.

Brooks, F. P., Jr. (1995). *The mythical man-month: essays on software engineering.* Reading, MA: Addison-Wesley.

Checkland, P., & Scholes, J. (1990). *Soft systems methodology in action.* Chichester, UK: John Wiley.

Coad, P., et al. (1999). *Java modelling in color with UML: Enterprise components and processes.* Upper Saddle River, NJ: Prentice Hall.

Fong, E. N., & Goldfine, A. H. (1989). *Information management directions: The integration challenge.* National Institute for Standards and Technology (NIST).

Foote, B., & Yoder, J. (1999). *Big ball of mud: Pattern languages of program design 4.* Addison-Wesley.

Hall, J., Healy, K., & Ross, R. G. (2005). *The business motivation model—Business governance in a volatile world.* Business Rules Group. Hammer, M., & Champy, J. (2003). *Reengineering the corporation: A manifesto for business change.* HarperCollins.

Hofmeister, C., et al. (1999). *Applied software architecture.* Addison Wesley.

IEEE Computer Society. (2000). *Recommended practice for architectural description of software-intensive systems*, Std 1471-2000 IEEE.

Pressman, R. (2005). *Software engineering: A practitioner's approach* (6th ed.). New York: McGraw-Hill.

The Open Group. (2003). *The Open Group architecture framework* (TOGAF), Version 8, Enterprise Edition, San Francisco, California: The Open Group. Retrieved July 18, 2003, from http://www.opengroup.org/architecture/togaf8-doc/arch/

Thera, V. P. (1958). *The Buddha: His life and teachings. Kandy, Sri Lanka: Buddhist Publication Society.* Retrieved January 2006 http://www.buddhanet.net/e-learning/buddhism/bud_lt11.htm

Zachman, J. A. (1987). A framework for information systems architecture. *IBM Systems J., 26*(3).

ENDNOTES

[1]   Enterprise elements can be regarded as "instances" of architectural elements. For example, a framework might include business objects as one of its architectural elements. The corresponding enterprise elements would include the actual business objects such customer, supplier, product, and purchase that are relevant to a specific enterprise.

[2]   In the OMB memorandum, this architecture is called the business process architecture. We have changed the name because we have already used the phrase business process to describe a type of system.

[3]   It is common practice to either combine the information architecture with the activity architecture and call it a business architecture or to include information requirements in the data architecture. We do not like the first approach, as the phrase business architecture sounds rather vague and nebulous. As far as the second approach is concerned, we feel it does not highlight the fact that information is related to business activity while data is more closely related to information technology. In addition, there are issues associated with an information architecture such as the management of non-electronic records that are not accommodated well in the data architecture.

[4]   In the OBM memorandum, this architecture is called an applications architecture. We have changed the name because we have already used the word application to describe a type of system. The change of name also allows for a more service-oriented view of software.

[5]   The software architecture and data architecture together could be viewed as the definition of an information systems architecture. In fact, this composite architecture would appear to be a much better candidate to be named applications architecture.

[6]   The technology architecture includes components such as hardware platforms, operating systems, database management systems, networking software, and the communications infrastructure.

[7]   Terms used in the database world can be mapped to those used in the framework. A logical data model is equivalent to the business objects. A physical data model (or database design) is equivalent to storage requirements. Data manipulation language (DML) is code. Data definition language (DDL) defines a database schema. A DBMS such as Oracle is technology.

[8]   Strictly speaking, the objects of object-orientation have relevance in three places in the framework; The persistent business objects described here belong in the data column; business objects that have behaviour (as well as state) belong in the activity column (we actually don't recommend that activities are modelled in this way but some users of the framework may prefer this approach); and software classes and components belong in the component row.

Chapter III
Discovering and Modelling Enterprise Engineering Project Processes

Ovidiu Noran
Griffith University, Australia

ABSTRACT

Often, in an enterprise engineering (EE) project, it is quite difficult to figure out what exactly needs to be done due to the rather generic (and often proprietary) character of the EE methods available. In addition, selecting appropriate elements from the multitude of available and emerging architecture frameworks (AFs) in order to model and manage the given EE undertaking is a non-trivial task. This chapter proposes a way to assist the inference of processes and to facilitate the selection and use of AF elements needed to accomplish EE projects. This is accomplished by assessing and organising AF elements into a structured repository (SR) using a generalised architecture framework (ISO15704:2000 Annex A) and by providing a "method to create methods" (a meta-methodology) for specific EE tasks that also guides the selection of AF elements from the SR. A brief introduction outlining the previously mentioned EE problems is followed by the description of the meta-methodology principle and of the assessment reference used. Next, a case study presents a sample application of the meta-methodology for a real EE project. The chapter closes with conclusions on the presented approach and a description of further work to refine and enrich the meta-methodology.

INTRODUCTION

Typically, the scope of enterprise engineering (EE) projects requires significant resources and involves large turn-around periods. Therefore, such projects should be approached using suitable and mature methods, modelling constructs, and tools. EE practice in the virtual enterprise (VE) domain (Globemen, 2000-2002) has shown that often, the initial problem in an EE project is the lack of a clear image of the activities that need to be performed to manage and execute that project. The currently available public and proprietary EE methods are quite generic, resembling reference models that need to be customised for specific projects; this typically requires knowledge of those methods (Noran, 2003a).

EE artefacts typically required by EE projects, such as modelling frameworks (MFs), reference models (RMs), modelling constructs (languages), and tools, etc., can be provided in an integrated manner by architecture frameworks (AFs). Note that the term "architecture framework" is understood in this chapter as an artefact defining the types of elements needed to support the creation of an object from the identification of the need to create that object through to its decommissioning. However, often the artefacts composing a single AF do not provide sufficient coverage for a specific EE project and thus, a combination of elements from several AFs is necessary. The complexity involved in most EE tasks makes the selection of AF elements a non-trivial task, usually requiring knowledge of the elements' outcomes, prerequisites, and dependencies on other AF elements.

This chapter proposes a basic method to guide the creation of a set of activity type descriptions expressing what needs to be done in a particular EE project, based on *domain* knowledge (i.e., based on project stakeholder/champion knowledge about the participating entities and their relations). The proposed method also assists in the selection of suitable AF elements for the specific needs of the particular EE project, based on their capabilities assessed in relation to a reference AF.

Note that the method and the reference AF used in this example do *not* prescribe the use of any specific AF or AF elements; they provide a way to assess AF element capabilities, to present a set of steps that specify types of activities needed to accomplish specific EE tasks and to

recommend sets of AF elements suitable for those tasks; it is then up to the user to select specific AF elements out of ranked lists, or override the recommendations. Therefore, this approach could be reused by EA practitioners to evaluate and select their preferred AF elements and to assess other methods for applicability to their specific EE project(s).

BACKGROUND: ISSUES IN ENTERPRISE ENGINEERING PRACTICE

The critical review of several mainstream AFs described in (Noran, 2003a, 2004a) has identified some of the problems associated with the use of AF elements in EE practice. The reviewed AFs were Purdue enterprise reference architecture (PERA) (Williams, 1994), GRAI (graphs with results and activities inter-related) (Doumeingts, 1984), computer integrated manufacturing–open system architecture (CIMOSA) (CIMOSA Association, 1996), the Zachman framework (Zachman, 1987), command, control, communications, computers, intelligence, surveillance, and reconnaissance (C4ISR) (C4ISR architectures working group, 1997), and architecture for information systems (ARIS) (Scheer, 1992).

Note that subsequently, several other AFs such as TOGAF (the Open Group architecture framework) (The Open Group, 2006), FEAF (Federal enterprise architecture framework) (U.S. Federal CIO Council), Department of Defence architecture framework (DODAF) (Department of Defence Architecture Framework Working Group, 2003), and TEAF (Treasury Enterprise architecture framework) (Department of the Treasury CIO Council, 2000) have also been examined and found to be related to, and/or display similar main problems to the first six AFs. These problems are summarized next.

Methods: Generality

Several methodologies associated with, or relating to AFs have been reviewed in Noran (2003a), such as the Purdue methodology, (published as a "Handbook for Master Planning" (Williams, Rathwell, & Li, 2001)), the structured approach of the GRAI integrated methodology (Doumeingts, Vallespir, Zanettin, & Chen, 1992), the CIMOSA methodology (Zelm, Vernadat, & Kosanke, 1995), Zachman foresight (Zachman, 2000), and Popkin process (Popkin Software, 2001), the six-step C4ISR process (C4ISR Architectures Working Group, 1997), and ARIS house/house of business engineering (Scheer, 1998a, 1998b).

The review has found that all methods display various degrees of generality, reflecting the parent AFs' aim to have broad applicability. However, for this reason the available methods are rather *reference models of methods* that need to be customised for each particular EE project. It has also been found that knowledge of these methods is required in order to decide on their selection and to subsequently customise them for the specific EE task.

Models: Consistency

A given EE task typically requires several enterprise models focusing on specific aspects. This creates the issue of consistency between the models created. For example, if the functionality of the enterprise is expressed in an activity/process model, the inputs/outputs, resources, and controls of the activities represented in that model could also be described in information, resources, and organisational models. In that case, it is imperative that the various descriptions of the same artefact are kept in agreement. Typically, this is no easy task and can be enforced by the users via policies (weak), triggers, and procedures (medium), or through more formal means such as meta-models underlying modelling constructs (strong). Some of the reviewed AFs aim to ensure such consis-

tency by integrating the views contained in their MFs (e.g., C4ISR's core architecture data model, Zachman's metamodel (Sowa & Zachman, 1992), and ARIS high-level metamodel (Scheer, 1999).

Languages: Integration, Complexity, Control

Some reviewed AFs such as PERA and Zachman aim not to prescribe a complete set of languages, instead arguing that the given engineering domain already has adequate means to describe any deliverable, and the architecture is only there to create a checklist of deliverables and to make their relationships explicit. Such AFs only give examples of typical modelling languages. However, the choice of modelling languages is paramount for the user/ stakeholder support and thus ultimately, for the success of an EE task. Thus, modelling languages can provide a degree of inter-model consistency by being part of a set/"family" (e.g., IDEF (Menzel & Mayer, 1998) or UML (Rumbaugh, Jacobson, & Booch, 1999)), ideally integrated through a set of metamodels (e.g., UML, but not IDEF (Noran, 2003b)). Layering and complexity hiding abilities of a language allow parts of the same model to be developed and used simultaneously by several user groups while maintaining overall model consistency. It also allows presenting the model to various audiences, from technical personnel to upper management/CEO.

Reference Models: Generality vs. Specialisation

The review undertaken has found that RMs provided by some AFs, such as the Purdue CIM reference model (Williams, 1988), the GRAI Grid reference model (Doumeingts, Vallespir, & Chen, 1998), the CIMOSA integration infrastructure services, the C4ISR universal reference resources, and the ARIS Y-CIM model (Scheer, 1994) come in various degrees of specialisation. A specialised RM has a narrow area of application, while a more generic RM needs to be customised before being used for a specific EE task. Knowledge of the RM is needed, either to be able to use a specialised RM, or to customise a generic one. RMs also vary greatly in their ability and efficiency to cover various life cycle phases.

Tools: Awareness, Integration

Effective enterprise modelling tools have to be "aware" of the languages they support (i.e., support their syntax at a minimum). Noran (2004a) has reviewed several tools, including FirstStep (Levi & Klapsis, 1999), IMAGIM (GRAISoft, 2002), and system architect (Popkin Software, 2001). It has been found that tools belonging to a "suite" and/or based on a shared repository and supporting languages belonging to a set can provide a degree of integration of the models produced. Existing/legacy modelling tools and staff skills may constitute deciding factors in modelling tools selection for an EE task.

Proposed Solution

The previously described issues can be addressed in two main steps. First, evaluate and organise AF elements in respect to a *generalised reference* AF. Second, develop a method guiding the discovery of the processes involved in accomplishing EE tasks and supporting the user in selecting suitable AF elements for those tasks. These two steps have been addressed in the *meta-methodology* (method to create methods) research described by Noran (2004a). Thus, one of the main meta-methodology components is a *structured repository* containing elements of several AFs assessed in respect to ISO15704:2000 Annex A (ISO/TC184, 2000) as a common reference. The other major component is a set of steps assisting the inference of activity types that need to be undertaken for specific EE tasks. The meta-methodology steps use the repository content to build ranked lists of AF elements recommended to the user for each

step, taking into account the applicable aspects and life cycle phases.

EVALUATION AND SELECTION OF ARCHITECTURE FRAMEWORK ELEMENTS

The Architecture Framework Assessment Reference

The ISO15704:2000 standard, "Requirements for enterprise reference architectures and methodologies," has been developed to supply a generic set of criteria to test the ability of existing AFs to provide relevant assistance for EA tasks. Annex A of the standard, the generalised enterprise reference architecture and methodology (GERAM, see Figure 1) is a generic AF compliant with ISO15704, obtained by generalising concepts present in several mainstream AFs and in EA best-practice. Note that GERAM only specifies *requirements* for tools, methods, and models; it does not enforce any particular choices to satisfy these requirements.

GERAM Components

A main component of GERAM is its reference architecture (GERA), whose MF features a three-dimensional structure containing several views that may be used to structure the knowledge in various *interrelated* models (refer Figure 2). GERA does not enforce the presence of all views; also, other view types can be added if necessary. The condition however is that the views that *are* present must together cover the necessary aspects of the specific EE task. Thus, the user is presented with a list of possible views and must make informed decisions as to which views are indeed necessary for the task at hand. GERA is further described in the next section.

ISO15704:2000 specifies a requirement for compliant AFs to have associated methods (ex-

Figure 1. A GERAM metamodel

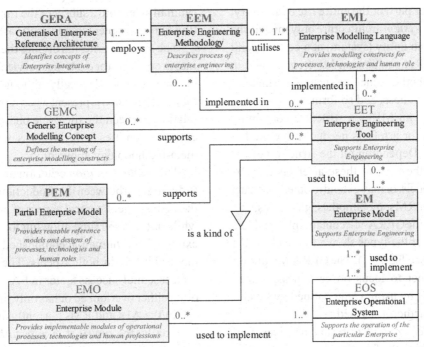

emplified in GERAM by enterprise engineering methodologies (EEMs)) guiding the user in utilising their elements. The level of specialisation of such methods can be assessed by using GERA's MF Instantiation dimension (see next section).

Enterprise modelling languages (EMLs) provide the necessary constructs to describe the various artefacts present within GERAM. For example, EEMs represent the models of engineering processes by means of EMLs. Typically, a combination of EMLs has to be used to describe all necessary modelling aspects (information, function, organisation, behaviour, etc.) of an EE project.

GERAM calls RMs *partial enterprise models* (PEMs)—reusable templates for human roles (organisational), processes (common functionality), or technology (e.g., IT resources).

Enterprise models (EMs) are the main vehicle for structuring the knowledge existent in the enterprise (e.g., by modelling the AS-IS state) but are

also essential enablers of the change processes that may have prompted their creation (by modelling TO-BE states). A typical set of EMs as required by ISO15704:2000 and described by GERAM should include enterprise operations, organisation, IS and resources, and clearly show the human role within the control and production systems. Further detail, such as hardware/software may also be required depending on models' intended use (see the GERA views in Figure 2).

Enterprise modules (EMOs) are implemented RMs, usable as trusted "plug-and-play" components. For example, if a design has used certain RMs, the EMOs corresponding to those RMs can be directly used in the implementation of that design.

GERA Structure

GERA is a *life cycle* reference architecture (i.e., an architecture that can specify types of activities involved in the implementation of a project spanning over part, or the entire life of an entity; in contrast, a *system* architecture only models the structure of an entity (system) at a certain point in time). GERA contains an MF (represented in Figure 2) and other concepts such as life history, entity recursiveness, and so forth.

Generally, an MF is a structure containing placeholders for artefacts needed in the modelling process. Depending on the structure of the framework, the type of these artefacts may be limited to models, or may extend to other construct types such as RMs, metamodels, glossaries, etc. For example, the GERA MF contains placeholders for artefacts of the types shown in the GERAM metamodel (see Figure 1). The GERA MF allows the practitioner to focus on certain aspects of complex EMs by using *views* defined by several criteria, as further described.

The *model content* criterion provides four views describing the functional, information, resource, and organisation aspects of an enterprise. It is to be noted that the organisation view may

be obtained by mapping part of the resource view (human side) onto a subset of the functional view (the human-implemented functions).

The *purpose* criterion divides the EE artefacts into production (or customer service) and control (or management). Typically (although not mandatory), this division is present when representing the relation between the life cycle phases of various enterprise entities in the business models used in meta-methodology application.

The *implementation* criterion provides a way to distinguish between the production/service and the management/control aspect of an enterprise, while at the same time allowing to represent the extent of the human-accomplished tasks ("humanisability") in both aspects. The human role is an essential success factor in EA, although it is often either overlooked or has only limited coverage in the AFs and RMs currently available.

Finally, the *physical manifestation* criterion provides a finer subdivision, setting apart hardware and software aspects of EA artefacts. It is mostly used to scope views derived from other criteria.

The second dimension of the GERA MF contains the concept of *specialisation*, which allows it to represent all of the previous aspects at the generic, partial, and particular levels (see Figure 2). For example, the partial level of GERA can be used to assess the coverage and degree of specialisation of RMs (PEMs) or methods (EEMs).

Life cycle represents the third dimension of the GERA MF, allowing it to represent (and assess) the applicability of AF elements to various life cycle phases of the modelled entity. For example, this dimension enables the creation of business models in the context of the life cycles of the participating entities, which is an essential meta-methodology requirement.

Several other GERA artefacts reside outside its MF. For example, the concept of life *history* can be used to model process concurrency. In GERA, life "history" implies a time dimension and represents the collection of life cycle phases

Figure 2. The modelling framework of GERA (ISO/TC184, 2000)

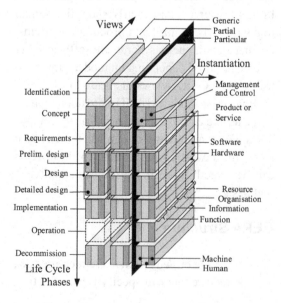

that the entity has gone (or *will* go) through during its life. In contrast, life *cycle* abstracts from time and is a collection of life cycle phases that the entity *could* go through during its life.

In conclusion, GERAM provides a suitable reference for assessing the pool of AF elements needed to construct a repository and support the meta-methodology application.

Architecture Framework Element Assessment and Organisation into a Knowledge Base

In addition to identifying problems in EE practice, the critical literature review described in (Noran, 2003a) has also mapped the reviewed AFs against GERAM, attempting to identify relevant components such as MFs, RMs, generic modelling concepts (such as metamodels, ontologies, etc), modelling methods, languages, tools, etc. The MF of GERA has then been used to *scope* the identified AF elements in order to check their intended coverage and determine

Figure 3. Knowledge base showing AF elements and selection/ordering rules

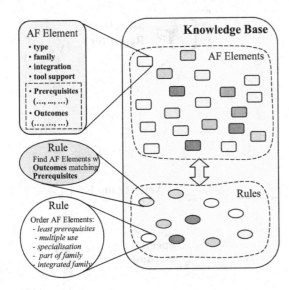

their *potential* applicability domain(s) in terms of views, life cycle, and specialisation. The assessed and mapped AF elements have then been stored in a knowledge base (KB) organising AF elements by name, type, family, integration, tools, and importantly, associating *prerequisites* and *outcomes* to each AF element. The KB has then been added rules for the selection of the AF elements and their ordering in ranked lists, resulting in the rule-based KB shown in Figure 3. The subsequent addition of an inference engine to the KB has resulted in the structured repository (SR) currently used by the meta-methodology concept (see Figure 5, left).

For example, the representation of a GRAI Grid decisional RM (explained elsewhere in this chapter) includes its name (="GRAI Grid"), type (="Reference Model"), whether it belongs to a set of reference models (YES, ="GRAI"), if the set is integrated (NO – not formally), and whether the RM is supported by any available tools (YES, ="IMAGIM"). The main outcome of the GRAI Grid RM representation in the KB would be "decisional modelling." However, GRAI Grid RMs can be also used for organisational modelling *if* the human resources have been previously mapped. Therefore, this GRAI Grid RM could also have an "organisational modelling" outcome, however associated with a "resource modelling" prerequisite.

The mapping of the AF elements on GERAM and GERA has revealed that typically, elements of several AFs can cover a particular area of an EE project. However, their *efficiency* in modelling the area in question may vary greatly in respect to various aspects and life cycle phases. For example, GRAI Grid would be quite efficient in modelling the decisional/organisational structure for the concept, requirements, and architectural design of an entity, but less efficient for the detailed design, implementation, or operation of that entity. Therefore, the inference engine would create *ranked lists* of matching AF elements for the specific task; the user can then accept or override recommended choices and thus test various scenarios.

GUIDANCE FOR PROCESS DISCOVERY

In response to the methodological problem identified in the Background section, a basic procedure ("meta-methodology") has been developed to guide the development of methods (sets of activity/process types) for specific EE tasks. This method is based on the concept of "reading" the life cycle phases of the target entity (here, one or more enterprises) in the context of its relations with other entities, using a life cycle-based business model, and, based on domain knowledge, inferring the necessary activities for each life cycle phase. The meta-methodology contains the following main steps (see Figure 4):

1. Identify a list of entities relevant to the EE project. If one or more projects are set up to build the target entity (entities), consider including them as target entities as well.
2. Create a business model showing the relations between the life cycles of the identified

entities, while re-assessing the need for the presence of each entity in the diagram, and the extent of life cycle set to be represented for each entity (e.g., full set, single phase, etc).

3. Reading the life cycle diagram of the target entity, phase by phase, infer a set of activities describing the creation of the entity and the roles played by other entities. For several target entities, determine the order in which they are influenced (from the relations in the diagram) and create the activity model in that order. Detail the activities to the necessary level using the aspects adopted and, if applicable, the views of a suitable MF.

The sub-steps relating to all the main steps are as follows:

a. Identify a suitable MF if applicable. Choose the aspects to model, depending on the meta-methodology step. Resolve any aspect dependencies.

Figure 4. The meta-methodology concept (Noran, 2004a)

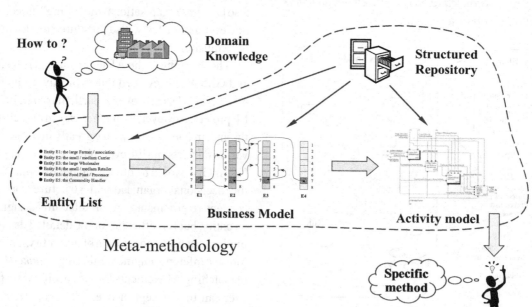

b.   Choose whether to represent only the present (AS-IS), future (TO-BE), or both states. If both, choose whether to represent them separately or combined.

c.   Choose modelling formalism(s) depending on the aspect(s) selected and on modelling best-practice criteria, such as: previously used in the modelling, specialisation in those aspects, potential multiple use, part of a family, family integration. Choose modelling tool depending on formalism and other factors (such as belonging to a suite, availability, etc).

The application of these steps is illustrated in a case study presented further in this Chapter.

In building the activity model (step 3), a "sufficient" level of detail is reached when the processes can be directly executed by the envisaged resources.

Note that the main aim of this chapter is to incite reader interest in the potential meta-methodology reuse and application to other EE tasks, rather than to provide a full description of the meta-methodology development and use. The interested reader is invited to get further meta-methodology details from (Noran, 2004a).

Note on the Meta-Methodology Capabilities

The meta-methodology provides guidance and assistance, but it does *not* infer the activities for the user. This is because as shown in Figure 4, the domain knowledge required to deduce such activities is quite specific and owned by the specific project's stakeholders. The meta-methodology user (typically the enterprise architect) has to elicit this knowledge from the stakeholders or otherwise acquire it by immersing in the participating organisation(s).

For example, step 3 tells the user how to elicit the activities from the business model. The sub-steps applied to step 3 assist and prompt the user to select appropriate aspects and modelling formalisms in order to enforce a degree of coherence to the activity inference process. However, specific conclusions and insights gained by the user in steps 1 and 2 should also be used to select and (if warranted) even override step 3 recommendations.

In conclusion, the meta-methodology concept implies *constructive assistance*, rather than blindly following a set of fixed steps that automatically lead to a unique, "best" solution.

INTEGRATION OF THE META-METHODOLOGY STEPS AND THE STRUCTURED REPOSITORY

As can be seen in Figure 4, there is a close relationship between the SR and the meta-methodology steps. This connection is further detailed in Figure 5. The SR (containing the KB) is integrated with the meta-methodology steps in a *meta-methodology environment*. Thus, the search/inference engine (or an artefact with similar functionality, depending on the implementation) within the SR selects AF elements at the request of the meta-methodology steps and sub-steps and arranges them in ranked lists using the KB matching and ordering rules. The engine also attempts to resolve dependencies and prerequisites (i.e., if the chosen AF elements require other elements in the KB, they are also added as ranked lists to the proposed solution). The user is notified of any unsatisfied prerequisites.

Another aspect of the previously mentioned integration is the implementation of meta-methodology step logic in the KB rules. For example, the main aspect recommended for modelling in sub-step a can be supplied by a rule in the KB of the SR (e.g., on the basis of the step number); subsequently, the engine would also resolve any aspect dependencies by recommending additional aspects if applicable.

Figure 5. *Meta-methodology steps interaction with the structured repository*

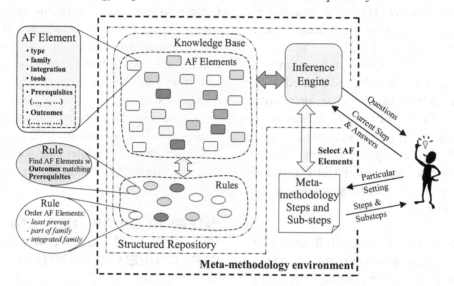

Dynamic facts (specific to the particular setting) that cannot be stored in the KB, such as staff proficiency in particular modelling languages and modelling tools, available/legacy systems, and other relevant constraints within the participating organisations are gathered from the user at runtime and are used in ranking the AF element lists.

CASE STUDY: THE FORMATION OF A VIRTUAL ORGANISATION

This section provides an example of using the previously described meta-methodology environment to infer the types of activities needed to accomplish a concrete EE task, namely the creation of a *virtual organisation* in the higher education sector. AF elements needed to model and manage the virtual organisation creation process are also suggested. Note that the presented example is also applicable to the creation of other VO types in other areas.

Collaborative Networks and Virtual Organisations in the Industry

In the current global market, enterprises worldwide must often come together for the purpose of tendering, executing, and servicing large-scale projects requiring competencies and resources beyond their individual capabilities. The resulting organisations, although composed of various participants, appear as an indivisible entity to the outside environment (service providers, clients, etc.)—hence their name of *virtual* organisations (VOs). VOs exist as separate entities for legal and commercial purposes although in fact, most of their resources belong to the participant organisations.

Usually, the formation of VOs takes time, due to potentially lengthy processes such as trust building, obtaining commitment from management, agreement on a stable common ICT infrastructure, establishment of commonly understood RMs, etc. Typically, however, the time available to react to a business opportunity (such as a large project) is limited. Therefore, enterprises aiming to successfully tender for such projects often become collaborative networked organisations (CNO) forming a *collaborative network* (Camarinha-Matos, 2004) or a *company network* (CN) (Globemen, 2000-2002) (see Figure 6). Such a CN provides a "breeding environment" where the participants can accomplish the previously described processes in advance and thus improve their *preparedness* to quickly form VOs as required.

A Virtual Organisation for the Tertiary Education Sector

Faculty FAC within University U contains several schools (A to D), with schools A and B having the same profile. School A is based in two campuses, situated at locations L1 and L2, while school B is based on single campus, situated at location L3 (AS-IS state in Figure 7). Although of the same profile, and belonging to the same FAC and U, Schools A and B are confronted with a lack of consistency in their products and resources, such as the programs and courses offered, allocated budget, academic profile, and availability of teaching staff, etc. This situation causes negative effects such as additional costs in student administration and in course/program design/maintenance and staff perceptions of unequal academic and professional standing between campuses, all of which are detrimental to the entire faculty.

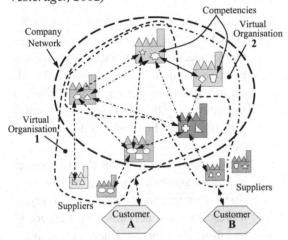

Figure 6. Company network and virtual organisation concepts (Globemen, 2000-2002; Tølle & Vesterager, 2002)

Figure 7. AS-IS and possible TO-BE state (organisational scenarios also shown)

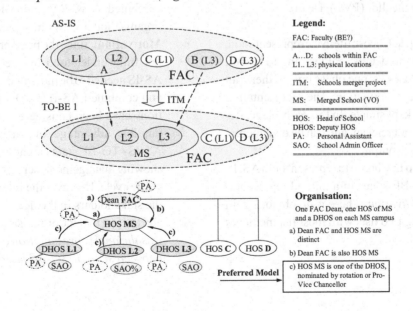

49

The problems previously described could be resolved by Schools A and B forming a VO (called *merged school* (MS) in the TO-BE state in Figure 7) with cross-campus management and policies ensuring inherent consistency in the strategy regarding the products delivered and the resources allocated to future VO campuses at L1, L2, and L3. The individual campuses are set to retain most of their internal decisional and organisational structure except for the highest layer, which will be replaced by the VO governance structure.

In view of the CN/VO model previously explained, in this case study the CN function is performed by FAC, which contains several schools forming VOs as necessary. The "partners" (i.e., schools) A and B within the CN come together at the initiative of U to form an *on-going* VO project. Importantly, the partners cease to operate independently during the life of MS.

Meta-Methodology Application

Step 1: Identification of the Entities Relevant to the EE Project

The list of entities has been built according to the domain knowledge elicited from, and checked with the stakeholders and the project champions (Pro-Vice-Chancellor (PVC), Dean).

- **Sub-step a:** Choose life cycle representation, however no details: only stating to be full set of phases vs. one phase only. Others not necessary. *Motivation:* The representation must be kept simple. In this early stage, details are not relevant and can be detrimental to creative output.
- **Sub-step b:** Choose to represent both AS-IS and TO-BE states in a unified representation. *Motivation:* There is no obvious gain in having two lists with most list members identical.

- **Sub-step c:** Choose text representation as modelling formalism. Choose a plain text editor or whiteboard as "tool." *Motivation:* Formalism and tool must preserve simplicity (see a above).

The list of entities constructed in this step is shown in the legend of Figure 10.

Step 2: A Business Model Expressing Entity Roles in a Life Cycle Context

- **Sub-step a:** Adopt GERA as an MF. Using GERA as a checklist, it has been established that management vs. product/service aspects and also decisional and organisational models of the entities participating in the VO formation may be necessary. These representations must be shown in the context of life cycle.
- **Motivation:** The scope of this EE project includes management, product/service, decisional structure, and organisation. Life cycle representation is necessary for the second and third main meta-methodology steps.
- **Sub-step b:** Represent both AS-IS and TO-BE states. For management/service and life cycle, represent AS-IS and TO-BE in a combined view. Represent decisional and organisational views in separate models.
- **Motivation:** Since the present situation was not fully understood by the stakeholders, AS-IS needed to be modelled. Both separate and combined AS-IS / TO-BE representations have been considered. There was no tangible advantage in showing separate AS-IS / TO-BE states in the business model showing management / service in the context of life cycle. However the interest shown by the stakeholders in the decisional structure and the fact that the organisational structure *was the only representation able to discern between several TO-BE states* have deter-

mined the choice of separate AS-IS and TO-BE representations.

• **Sub-step c:** Choose modelling formalisms ranking highest in efficiency for the aspects selected in sub-step a. For life cycle and management/service, choose a "chocolate bar" formalism derived from GERA as shown in Figure 8.

Choose the GRAI Grid formalism (Figure 9) for decisional and organisational aspects. GRAI Grid ranks high in respect to other candidate languages due to its specialisation for the decisional aspect, potential multiple use (e.g., for organisational aspect), and no prerequisites.

Next, construct the business model (Figure 10) illustrating entity roles in accomplishing the

Figure 8. Modelling formalism used for the life cycle and management vs. service/product views of the business model

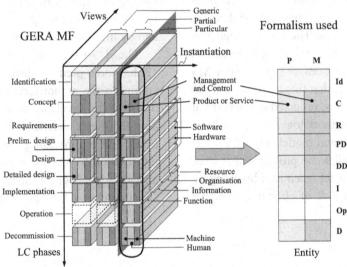

Figure 9. GRAI Grid modelling formalism for decisional aspects (mapped organisational roles show possible use for organisational modelling)

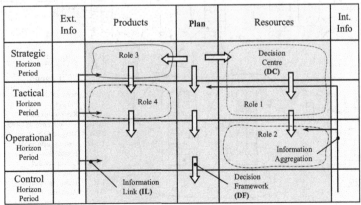

EE project in the context of their life cycles and management vs. production/service aspects.

The only candidate specialised tool for decisional/organisational models is IMAGIM. Due to costs and availability, a simple graphical editor has been used, thus, the consistency of entities showing in both decisional and organisational models had to be ensured by the user.

The business model in Figure 10 allows a bird's eye view on the entities involved in the target entities' life cycle phases and has been constructed using the domain knowledge of the stakeholders as elicited by the user. Several entities influence various life cycle phases of MS directly, or through other entities. The main influence is exercised by ITM, which is in fact a project set up to build the VO and ceases to exist after MS starts operating. Note that this is a common occurrence in EE projects, reflected in the body of step 1 of the meta-methodology.

The AS-IS decisional model (Figure 11) has shown in more detail some problems that have triggered the EE project, such as a high degree of turbulence and a lack of clear and effective strategy within the organisation. Thus, the Head of School (HOS) in the role of planner had to put out "fires" (product/resource discrepancies requiring immediate reconciliation) on a short-term basis, rather than having strategies in place to *avoid the cause* of such problems. This can be seen in Figure 11 in the form of decisional frameworks (DFs) flowing from planning toward products and resources at *all* horizons. The AS-IS decisional model has also shown a lack of sufficient financial and decisional independence of the schools A and B and a shortage of information crucial to long-term strategy making (shown in Figure 11 by several DFs coming from outside the School and by limited external information flow).

The TO-BE decisional model (see Figure 12) has attempted to address these problems by confining the authoritarian role of the HOS to the strategic level, by increasing the financial and decisional independence of the target VO (MS), and by providing the necessary external information to MS for the purpose of strategy making and self-governance. This is reflected in a lesser number of horizontal DFs originating from

Figure 10. Business model expressing entity roles in accomplishing the EE project

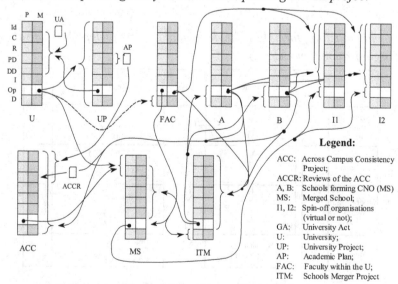

Legend:

ACC: Across Campus Consistency Project;
ACCR: Reviews of the ACC
A, B: Schools forming CNO (MS)
MS: Merged School;
I1, I2: Spin-off organisations (virtual or not);
GA: University Act
U: University;
UP: University Project;
AP: Academic Plan;
FAC: Faculty within the U;
ITM: Schools Merger Project

Figure 11. AS-IS decisional/organisational situation (GRAI Grid model)

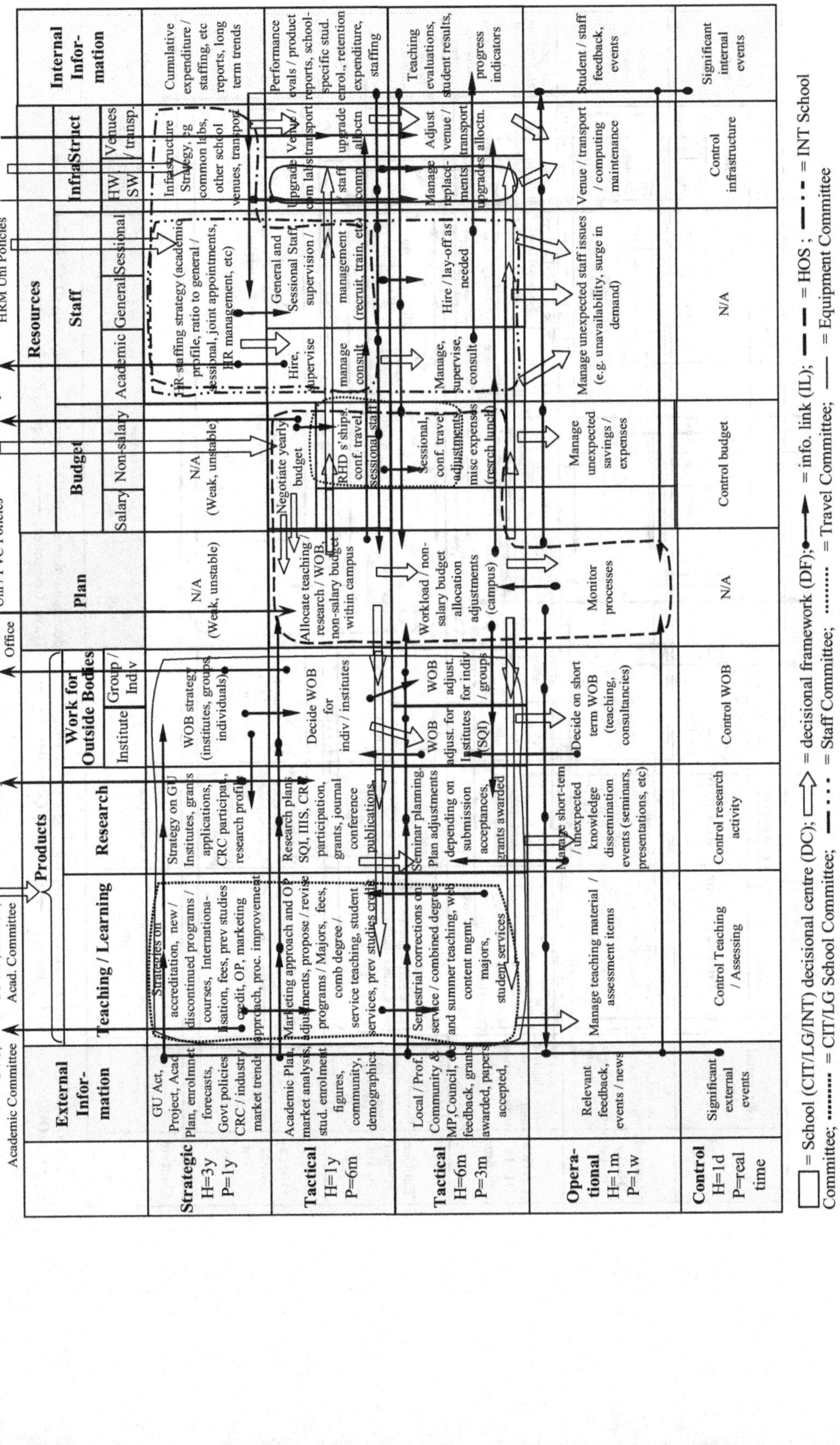

Figure 12. Preferred TO-BE decisional and organisational situation (GRAI Grid model)

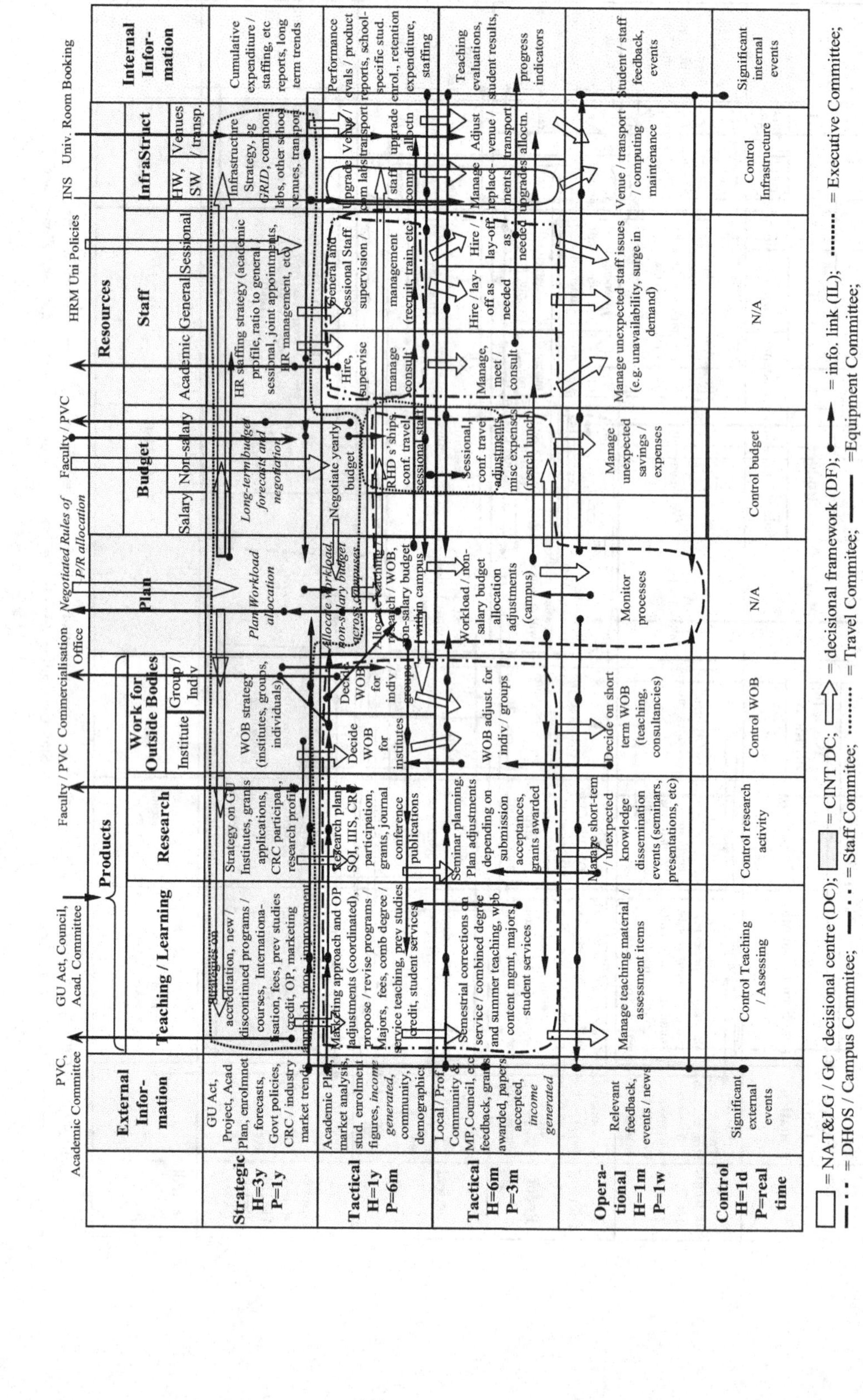

planning, less DFs coming from U and increased number of information flows in Figure 12. Also, some existing external DFs have been relocated so as to minimise the negative impact on MS.

Figure 11 and Figure 12 show the AS-IS and TO-BE decisional and organisational models.

Interestingly, the TO-BE decisional model has been found to match all potential scenarios, with differences only obvious in the *organisational* structure derived from the decisional model (i.e., the allocation of the various human resource groups to the decision centres [e.g., see areas defined as "committees" in Figure 12]). Therefore, modelling the organisational structure was instrumental in distinguishing between the available TO-BE options.

Step 3: The Set of Activities describing the EE Project Accomplishment

This step represents the main purpose of the meta-methodology, resulting in a set of activities describing *how to* accomplish the EE project (here, the VO creation and partly operation). The step is accomplished by "reading" the life cycle diagram of the entity to be designed (MS) and its relations with the other entities shown in Figure 10. The set of activities obtained is then refined and decomposed into sub-activities, using views of the selected MF (GERA).

Figure 13. IDEF0 modelling formalism (1ˢᵗ, or "context" level shown)

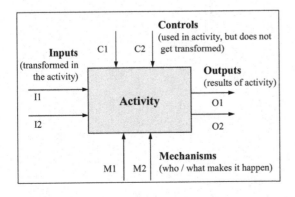

- **Sub-step a:** Aspects: functional and life cycle, but use other categories to detail activities. *Motivation:* The main deliverable is an activity model, hence functional. However, the activities must be detailed using aspect from the SR and views from the selected AF, in this case management/service with human vs. machine and software vs. hardware aspects.
- **Sub-step b:** Choose to represent both AS-IS and TO-BE states in a unified representation. *Motivation:* The activity model is expressing the transition from AS-IS to TO-BE, thus both states should be represented; here, separate views did not justify the consistency overhead.
- **Sub-step c:** Choose IDEF0 (NIST, 1993) functional modelling formalism (see Figure 13 for a basic explanation of its elements). Select AI0Win tool by Knowledge-Based Systems, Inc. *Motivations:* UML and IDEF0 are both suitable; UML ranks higher than IDEF0, due to integrated metamodel present and wider tool support. However, the available (AI0Win) modelling tool and necessary skills were an overriding factor. AI0Win is also semi-integrated with information/resources modelling ("SmartER") and behaviour modelling ("ProSIM") tools, similar to a "suite," thus ensuring some degree of model consistency. Therefore, overall IDEF0 and AI0Win were considered a suitable choice in this particular case.

Creating the Activity Types in Step 3

A set of activities must be inferred for each life cycle phase represented in the business model. Thus, the functional model can be initiated by creating one main activity for each life cycle phase identified in the business model (such as shown in Figure 14). The modelling formalism chosen to represent the model will assist in developing the model. For example, IDEF0 requires that inputs,

Figure 14. IDEF0 Activity model for the VO creation and operation (2ⁿᵈ level shown)

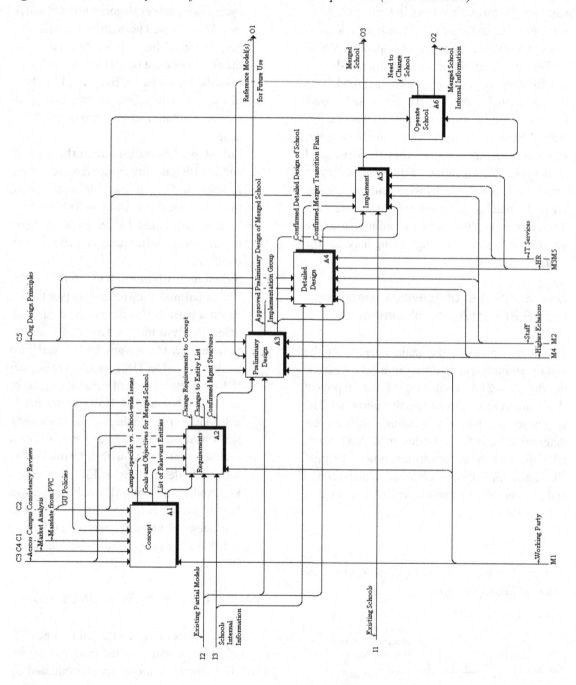

controls, outputs, and mechanisms (ICOMs) are defined for these activities (see Figure 13, where inputs can be omitted if justified). Therefore, the user has to give consideration to what (if anything) is used in the activity, what controls it, what is produced by the activity and who/what executes it. This information can be construed from the roles shown in the business model and further domain knowledge.

Each activity must be recursively decomposed down to a level where it can be directly executed; this can be assisted by a "checklist" of views used in previous steps and/or the chosen MF (if any) and/or available in the MFs contained in the SR. For example, if GERA's MF is chosen, the checklist contains function, information, resources, organisation, management vs. production/service, human roles, and hardware/software. For example, in Figure 16, management vs. production/service and human role views have been used to decompose the detailed design activity.

Note that not all aspects are relevant to all life cycle phases. For example, early life cycles (e.g., identification, concept) require few or no aspects, and the human aspect may only be visible/relevant in the preliminary/detailed design phases, such as illustrated in Figure 2.

Example: Creating the Second Level of the Functional Model

Figure 10 shows that the MS entity is influenced by the University U, across campus consistency (ACC), project and by the project that builds it, namely ITM.

The first phase in the life cycle of MS is the identification of the need for this artefact. However, in this case, domain knowledge obtained from stakeholders has established that this phase has already been accomplished by U (i.e., the PVC has determined the need for an MS and *mandated* its creation) thus, identification does

Figure 15. Decomposition of the requirements activity (3rd level IDEF0 model)

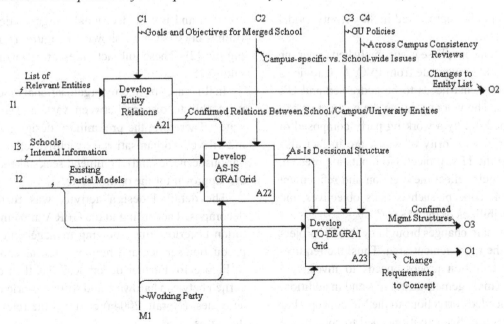

Figure 16. Decomposition of the detailed design activity (3rd level IDEF0 model)

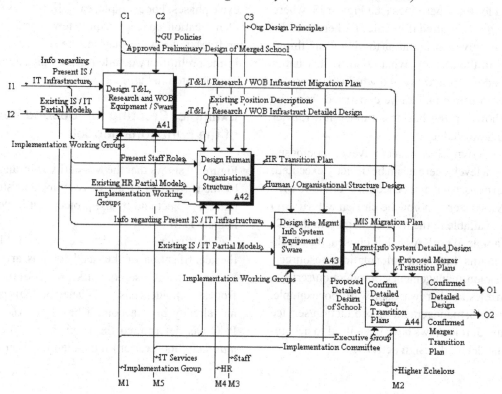

not need to be represented in the activity model in this case.

The concept phase is accomplished under the control of the mandate from PVC, ACC reviews that show what needs to be addressed and U's policies. The work to define the concept of MS is carried out by a working party composed of U staff, the majority of which are in fact also staffing the ITM project. No inputs are present. The outputs reflect the creation and refinement of the MS concept, such as goals, objectives, and responsibilities of the MS.

The main changes brought by this EE project are in the management area. Thus, the requirements definition process needs to investigate suitable management structures and in addition, make needed corrections to the MS concept. For this purpose this activity needed to contain the

creation and use of decisional / organisational frameworks (such as shown in Figure 11 and Figure 12). These sub-activities are shown in Figure 15.

In this case study, only organisational models were able to discern between various TO-BE states. Therefore, the preliminary design phase must develop organisational structures reflecting various scenarios and recommend/seek stakeholders' approval for the optimal one.

The detailed design activity was further decomposed according to the GERA implementation criterion, thus showing management vs. production/service and human roles, as shown in Figure 16. Further decompositions then discerned between hardware and software-oriented activities. (Noran, 2004a) contains the relevant diagrams.

The VO implementation process must set up the transition process and then implement the detailed specifications produced by the detailed design sub-activities (thus some of its decomposition was similar to detailed design activity).

In this case, the operation process of the School can be decomposed in operation and monitoring (producing internal information for the management and requests for change that cannot be handled at operational level). The EE project did not include a detailed operation of the VO, thus no decompositions below level three have been produced for this activity.

A full description of the activity model creation and structure (which is beyond the purpose of this chapter) is contained in Noran (2004b). Note that the activity model created represents only one of the many possible suitable solutions to this EE problem.

CONCLUSION AND FURTHER WORK

A practical problem in EE projects is not knowing what *exactly* needs to be done since potentially usable methods, reference models, modelling frameworks, etc., are rather general in nature. Furthermore, *several* such AF elements are often suitable for any given area of the project in question, although their modelling efficiency varies greatly depending on aspect, life cycle phase, and specialisation required. Selecting and customising suitable AF elements requires knowledge of such artefacts, which is not normally available. However, *domain* knowledge describing the problems that triggered the project, specific features, and relations between project participants, etc., is typically available within stakeholders and/or project champion(s), even if often in a tacit form needing to be elicited.

In conclusion, help is needed to discover and model what needs to be done for a specific EE project and to select AF elements that suit the particular project but also the host organisation's specific proficiencies, legacies, and culture.

This chapter has described a method aiming to assist the discovery of activity types involved in accomplishing specific EE tasks and to provide guidance for the selection of AF elements needed to model and manage those tasks. The proposed meta-methodology achieves these goals through a *meta-methodology environment* comprising a set of steps and an SR containing AF elements assessed and organised in respect to a suitable reference (GERAM).

Research currently in progress aims to implement the KB and SR in a Web-based, open source expert system for possible use as a decision support system for upper/middle management. Future research efforts in this area will be focused toward formalising the meta-methodology environment and enriching the content of the KB by mapping additional AF elements against the chosen reference. Further field-testing and refinement of the KB rules and meta-methodology steps is also needed in order to improve its accuracy and usefulness.

REFERENCES

C4ISR Architectures Working Group. (1997). *Command, control, communications, computers, intelligence, surveillance, and reconnaissance—C4ISR*. Retrieved 2004, from http://www.cisa.osd.mil

Camarinha-Matos, L. M. (2004). Virtual enterprises and collaborative networks. *Proceedings of IFIP 18th World Congress—TC5/WG5.5 (PROVE 04): 5th IFIP Working Conference on Virtual Enterprises)*. Toulouse/France: Kluwer Academic Publishers.

CIMOSA Association. (1996). CIMOSA—Open system architecture for CIM. Technical Baseline, ver 3.2. Private Publication.

Department of Defence Architecture Framework Working Group. (2003). *DoD architecture framework*. Retrieved 2004, from http://aitc.aitcnet.org/dodfw/

Department of the Treasury CIO Council. (2000). *Treasury enterprise architecture framework (v.1)*. Washington, DC: Department of Treasury.

Doumeingts, G. (1984). *La Methode GRAI*. Unpublished Doctoral Thesis, University of Bordeaux I, Bordeaux, France.

Doumeingts, G., Vallespir, B., & Chen, D. (1998). GRAI Grid decisional modelling. In P. Bernus, K. Mertins, & G. Schmidt (Eds.), *Handbook on architectures of information systems* (pp. 313-339). Heidelberg: Springer Verlag.

Doumeingts, G., Vallespir, B., Zanettin, M., & Chen, D. (1992). *GIM-GRAI integrated methodology—A methodology for designing CIM systems*. Bordeaux: Version 1.0, Unnumbered Report, LAP/GRAI, University Bordeaux 1.

Globemen. (2000-2002). *Global engineering and manufacturing in enterprise networks (IMS project no. 99004 / IST-1999-60002)*. Retrieved from http://globemen.vtt.fi/

GRAISoft. (2002). *IMAGIM software product*. Retrieved August 2002, from http://www.graisoft.com

ISO/TC184. (2000). Annex A: GERAM. In *ISO/IS 15704: Industrial automation systems - Requirements for enterprise-reference architectures and methodologies*.

Levi, M. H., & Klapsis, M. P. (1999). FirstSTEP process modeler—A CIMOSA-compliant modeling tool. *Computers in Industry, 40,* 267-277.

Menzel, C., & Mayer, R. J. (1998). The IDEF family of languages. In P. Bernus, K. Mertins, & G. Schmidt (Eds.), *Handbook on architectures of*

information systems (pp. 209-241). Heidelberg: Springer Verlag Berlin.

NIST. (1993). *Integration definition for function modelling (IDEF0)* (No. 183: Federal Information Processing Standards Publication): Computer Systems Laboratory, National Institute of Standards and Technology.

Noran, O. (2003a). A mapping of individual architecture frameworks (GRAI, PERA, C4ISR, CIMOSA, Zachman, ARIS) onto GERAM. In P. Bernus, L. Nemes, & G. Schmidt (Eds.), *Handbook of enterprise architecture* (pp. 65-210). Heidelberg: Springer Verlag.

Noran, O. (2003b). UML vs. IDEF: An ontology-oriented comparative study in view of business modelling. In I. Seruca, J. Filipe, S. Hammoudi, & J. Cordeiro (Eds.), *6th International Conference on Enterprise Information Systems (ICEIS 2004)* (Vol. 3, pp. 674-682). Porto / Portugal: ICEIS.

Noran, O. (2004a). *A meta-methodology for collaborative networked organisations*. Unpublished Doctoral Thesis, School of CIT, Griffith University.

Noran, O. (2004b). A meta-methodology for collaborative networked organisations: A case study and reflections. In P. Bernus, M. Fox, & J. B. M. Goossenaerts (Eds.), *Knowledge sharing in the integrated enterprise: Interoperability strategies for the enterprise architect (Proceedings of International Conference on Enterprise Integration Modelling and Technology—ICEIMT'04)*. Toronto, Canada: Kluwer Academic Publishers.

Popkin Software. (2001). *Building an enterprise architecture: The Popkin process*. Retrieved October 2002, from www.popkin.com

Rumbaugh, J., Jacobson, I., & Booch, G. (1999). *The unified modelling language reference manual*. Reading, MA: Addison-Wesley.

Scheer, A. W. (1992). *Architecture for integrated information systems*. Berlin: Springer-Verlag.

Scheer, A. W. (1994). *Business process engineering—Reference models for industrial enterprises*. Berlin: Springer-Verlag.

Scheer, A. W. (1998a). ARIS—House of business engineering. In A. Molina, A. Kusiak, & J. Sanchez (Eds.), *Handbook of life cycle engineering—Concepts, models, and technologies*. Dordrecht: Kluwer Academic Publishers.

Scheer, A. W. (1998b). *ARIS—Business process modeling* (2nd ed.). Berlin: Springer-Verlag.

Scheer, A. W. (1999). *ARIS—Business process frameworks* (3rd ed.). Berlin: Springer-Verlag.

Sowa, J. F., & Zachman, J. A. (1992). Extending and formalizing the framework for information systems architecture. *IBM Systems Journal, 31*(3), 590-616.

The Open Group. (2006). *The open group architecture framework (TOGAF)*. Retrieved Mar 2006, from http://www.opengroup.org/togaf/

Tølle, M., & Vesterager, J. (2002). VEM: Virtual enterprise methodology. In I. Karvoinen, R. van den Berg, P. Bernus, Y. Fukuda, M. Hannus, I. Hartel, & J. Vesterager (Eds.), *Global engineering and manufacturing in enterprise networks (Globemen). VTT Symposium 224*. Helsinki, Finland.

U.S. Federal CIO Council. (2006). *Federal enterprise architecture framework (FEAF)*. Retrieved March 2006, from http://www.itpolicy.gsa.gov/mke/archplus/fedarch1.pdf

Williams, T. J. (1994). The Purdue enterprise reference architecture. *Computers in Industry, 24*(2-3), 141-158.

Williams, T. J. (1988). *CIM reference model committee: A reference model for computer integrated manufacturing (CIM)—A description from the viewpoint of industrial automation* (2nd ed.). Research Triangle Park, NC: Instrument Society of America.

Williams, T. J., Rathwell, G. A., & Li, H. (2001). *A handbook on master planning and implementation* (No. Report 160). West Lafayette, IN: Purdue Laboratory for Applied Industrial Control.

Zachman, J. A. (1987). A framework for information systems architecture. *IBM Systems Journal, 26*(3), 276-292.

Zachman, J. A. (2000). *Zachman framework definition and enterprise architecture quick start*. Retrieved June 2002, from www.zifa.com

Zelm, M., Vernadat, F., & Kosanke, K. (1995). The CIMOSA modelling process. *Computers in Industry, 27*(2), 123-142.

Chapter IV
Enterprise Architecture Framework for Agile and Interoperable Virtual Enterprises

Tae-Young Kim
Pohang University of Science and Technology, South Korea

Sunjae Lee
Pohang University of Science and Technology, South Korea

Jeong-Soo Lee
Pohang University of Science and Technology, South Korea

Kwangsoo Kim
Pohang University of Science and Technology, South Korea

Cheol-Han Kim
Daejeon University, South Korea

ABSTRACT

Virtual enterprise (VE) has become a prime candidate to survive under the increasingly turbulent and competitive business environment. In order to quickly respond to the rapidly changing business environment, the agility and interoperability are regarded as the core requirements for the VEs. Unfortunately, there is no previous approach to fully support configurations of the agile and interoperable VE. The systematic modeling framework based on the meta-model driven approach could be used for business domain experts and developers to construct VE models quickly and systematically with insights. It should be noted that this chapter aims to present a systematic modeling framework itself, not to generate only instances of VE models. Based on the proposed framework, business domain experts and developers would configure all of VE models such as VE architectures, modeling languages, model transformations, and deployment models, as well as instances of VE models.

INTRODUCTION

Today, enterprises are facing a rapidly changing business environment and can no longer make predictable long-term provisions. Moreover, business competition is no longer enterprise to enterprise, but value chain to value chain (Cadence Design Systems, 2003). In order to respond to these business environments, most competitive enterprises seek to enhance competitive performance by closely integrating internal operations and effectively linking them with the external operations of suppliers, customers, and other business partners. As each enterprise operates as a node in the network composed of suppliers, customers, engineers, and other specialized service providers, collaborations among multiple business partners are becoming important (Barnett, Presley, & Liles, 1994; Camarinha-Matos & Afsarmanesh, 2003; Jagdev & Thoben, 2001). The virtual enterprise (VE), which is a collaborative network across the value chains, has become a key factor to survive under the competitive business environment. For efficient collaborations among the business partners of the VE, the agility and interoperability among heterogeneous enterprise models in different business domains of interests is required. The agility is the capability to flexibly adapt enterprise models of VE in order to cope with unanticipated business environments. The interoperability means seamless communications among enterprise models, which can be shared and exchanged. To guarantee the agility and the interoperability, participants of the VE must understand each other through EA of participant enterprise. The EA mean business components and their relationships that are required for business activities. Business components are things such as application, data, technology, and business architecture that require enterprise business. Hence, EA of VE describes business components and their relationship that are required by business partners.

In order to establish and manage an agile and interoperable VE, it is keenly necessary to develop a systematic methodology for configuration of a VE based on the collaborative business processes. It should be noted that the configuration of a VE in this chapter means not only the designing instances of VE models, but also the designing VE architecture, modeling languages, and deployed models.

The goal of this chapter is to introduce a new systematic modeling framework that can be used for designing and managing the agile and interoperable VEs. The systematic modeling framework has a hybrid approach that harmonizes the up-to-date technologies such as enterprise architecture (EA), model driven architecture (MDA), meta-modeling approach, domain specific methodology (DSM), model transformation, framework-based development, and so on. It combines the advantages of the heterogeneous technologies so that it can produce integrated synergy effects, as well as it can take individual advantages of each technology. This proposed modeling framework provides modeling concepts that underpin the representation of all of the VE from different viewpoints, at different levels of granularity, generality, and abstraction during different life cycle of a VE. It would be used systematically by business domain experts and developers who want to design and manage a VE quickly and effectively.

The rest of this chapter is organized as follows. Requirements of VE to Support the Agility and Interoperability Section, describes the requirements of the VE to support the agility and interoperability. Literature Review Section, reviews the related researches. In Systematic Modeling Framework for the Agile and Interoperable VE Section, we introduce our systematic modeling framework for the agile and interoperable VEs. Finally, Discussion and Conclusion Section, provides some conclusions and gives some suggestions for future work.

REQUIREMENTS OF VE TO SUPPORT THE AGILITY AND INTEROPERABILITY

Definition of VE

Since the advent of the concept of the VE in the 1990s, many studies have progressed. The interest of a researcher is generally given to the development of models, protocols, infrastructures, and mechanisms for VE interoperation (Camarinha-Matos et al., 2003; Gou, Huang, Liu, & Li, 2003; NIIP). Nevertheless, the definition and features of the VE have not even been prescribed completely yet. A variety of terms and definitions have been used in various ways by scholars with different viewpoints.

Carmrinha-Matos et al. summarize the common keywords from several definitions of the VE as follows:

- Cooperation and complementarities.
- Networked or distributed organization.
- Temporary organization.
- Infrastructure supporting interoperation.

From the several previous definitions and keywords, the VE is considered as a temporary organization in which various distributed business partners form a cooperative network on the value chain. Therefore, it is important to establish a value chain systematically and quickly with core competitive functionalities that are the business processes in the form of the set of the service components of the business partners.

Consequently, we re-define the following terminologies, the VE and the value chain, as follows:

- **Virtual enterprise (VE):** *"In order to realize the common business goal which is to secure business opportunity, the VE is an active collaborative organization structure which is temporarily made up of value chains."*
- **Value chain:** *"A value chain is a comprehensive collection of all of the loosely-coupled business processes of distributed business partners who offer the core complementary functionality and resources."*

Figure 1. Concept of VE

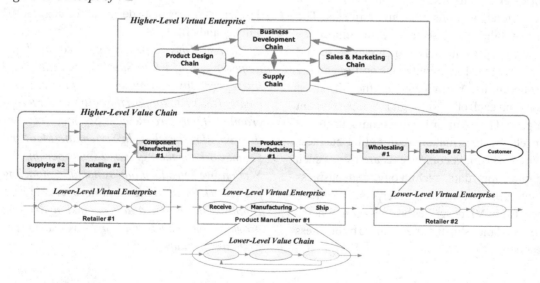

According to these definitions, it is possible to understand the concept of the VE as Figure 1. The VE is made up of the hierarchical value chains and each value chain is recursively made up of the collaborative business processes, the lower-level VE, and the lower-level value chains. This composition manner among the VEs, the value chains, and the collaborative business processes is repeated recursively until these cannot be divided any more.

Requirements for VE

It has not been easy to develop and realize the VE due to several obstacles. Firstly, real business processes of VE are diverse and complex. Because their business processes are very context-dependent and resource-dependent, it is not suitable to apply a specific traditional methodology. The traditional methodology is too generic to be utilized for the specific type of business processes of a specific business domain (Harmon, 2003a). Secondly, VE has multiple stakeholders who are interested in different aspects of the enterprise models. In most cases, a number of the enterprise

models are distinguished separately, such as different perspectives and different views. But there is no comprehensive approach that enables the integrated enterprise modeling. Thirdly, business processes of VE are very distributed and heterogeneous across value chains. The applications in VE should be performed on distributed and heterogeneous platforms with different types of information and different levels of functionality (Zarli & Richaud, 1999). However, there is a lack of standard definitions and effective mechanisms, which are guaranteed the agility and interoperability of VE models.

Therefore, it is necessary to develop a common modeling framework to settle the previously mentioned obstacles. It should provide a narrow-focused modeling approach for representing a specific business domain. On the other hand, it should also provide a coherent modeling approach that supports the representation of VE models from different viewpoints, at different perspectives during the life cycle of the VE, and it should provide a standard mechanism that supports the agility and interoperability of VE models on the heterogeneous platforms in the distributed network.

Figure 2. Technology architecture

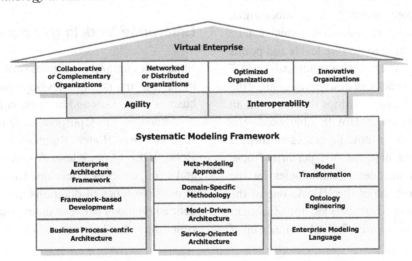

LITERATURE REVIEW

There is a research area for the integration of all knowledge that is needed to support the enterprise development, the enterprise management, and the enterprise integration. This research area is called enterprise engineering. Enterprise engineering can be used to support the life cycle of the VE (Vernadat, 1996). Each technology has been dealt in different interests and developed independently to address its own purpose. Even if they have the advantages in their own viewpoints, they have not provided a complete solution to support all aspects of the VE configuration. Therefore, it is keenly to develop a well-established common methodology to completely support the configuration of the agile and interoperable VEs through the VE life cycle.

Focusing on the agility and interoperability of VE, we present a technology architecture that includes several technologies of enterprise engineering as illustrated in Figure 2. In this chapter, we consider that these relevant technologies play important roles in developing the systematic modeling framework for the agile and interoperable VEs.

EA Framework

A VE consists of business processes and various business components such as information, systems, organizations, and so on, which can be classified according to diverse levels and points of view. The term "enterprise architecture (EA)" refers to a comprehensive description of all of the key elements and relationships that make up an enterprise (Harmon, 2003b). In other words, the EA identifies the essential processes performed by the VE, and how the VE performs these processes, and includes methodologies for the rapid reconfiguration of the VE. As one of the earliest systematic frameworks, the Zachman framework (Zachman, 1987; ZIFA) is made up of

a number of other architectures that are focusing on different, specific areas of concern.

The most extensive efforts in the development of reference architecture for a single enterprise have been undertaken by the generalised enterprise reference architecture and methodology (GERAM) (IFIP-IFAC Task Force, 1999). The GERAM framework includes harmonization with software engineering, system engineering, and the developments of frameworks such as Perdue enterprise reference architecture (PERA) (Williams, 1993), computer integrated manufacturing open systems architecture (CIMOSA) (Vernadat, 1993), GRAI integrated methodology (GIM), Zachman framework, and so on. Based on GERAM, virtual enterprise reference architecture (VERA) and its methodology is developed to enable rapid formation of customer-focused and customer-tailored VEs by taking advantages of information technology (IT) (Vesterager, Tolle, & Bernus, 2002).

Although current EAs provide approaches to generations of EA models and products and to management procedure of EA models, they are missing the big picture. It means that they have no concept to inter-relate the relevant elements and have no integration mechanism for different views and different perspectives. Also, they have no collaboration mechanism for different value chains.

Enterprise Modeling Language

Enterprise engineering applies various enterprise modeling languages to develop and manage the business processes and business components.

Although generic purpose modeling languages such as UML (Booch, Rumbaugh, & Jacobson, 1999), IDEF (Ang, Khoo, & Gay, 1999) series, and so on, have been developed as the collection of multiple types of diagrams they have poorly defined relations between them. This may cause either the redundancy or the loss of some subset models. Another restriction is that generic purpose modeling languages are too general to correctly design the specific models of a specific business domain.

As the business process-centric approach is becoming a major topic for all kinds of businesses, some of the following languages are emerging: the business process definition meta-model (BPDM) (Object Management Group, 2003a), business process modeling notation (BPMN) (Business Process Management Initiative, 2003), business process execution language for Web service (BPEL4WS) (Andrews et al., 2003), Web services description language (WSDL) (W3C, 2001), and business process modeling language (BPML) (Arkin, 2002). BPEL4WS, WSDL, and BPML are XML-based languages for modeling the business processes that are originated from platform specific process language. Recently, UML 2.0 has been developed and addresses many issues to make strides toward becoming the standard notation for depicting architectures (Object Management Group, 2003b, 2003c).

DSM

Since the VE models have the characteristics of complexity and diversity, as well as context-dependency and resource-dependency on the business domains, it is difficult to use the generic purpose modeling languages as it is.

The DSM intends to freely develop abstract graphic languages that business domain experts or developers can easily and accurately use in a specific business domain in order to design and manage a model through shifting the modeling concept from code levels to design levels (Frankel, 2004; MetaCase, 2005). Consequently, the DSM lets developers use the knowledge and skills of business domain experts to design VE models easier.

DSM is similar to model driven architecture (MDA), as they intend to design and manage a model itself in the business domain through

shifting the modeling concept from code levels to design levels. However, while MDA emphasizes presenting the architecture and the guideline for the meta-modeling, DSM emphasizes freely developing an abstract graphic language, which developers can use easily and accurately in the specific business domain.

As DSM lacks integration mechanism currently, DSM can't provide really linking mechanism among narrowly domain-focused languages. DSM has a limitation to design, not only domain specific VE models, but also domain integrated VE models in order to support a coherent modeling.

Meta-Modeling Approach

As a meta-model means the rendering of a language definition as an object model, the meta-modeling approach is becoming a standard way of defining and managing the meta-models that is used for designing the VE models. Therefore, it can be used for enabling the designed models and the defined meta-models to have the interoperability with each other.

Recently, it has been demonstrated that the meta-modeling can be used to define concrete syntax and abstract syntax, as well as semantics. OMG has suggested the concept of UML profiles in the form of the extended UML meta-model to make good use of the particular domains (Object Management Group, 2003b, 2003c, 2004a). It has been discussed how a UML profile can be defined for specific domains that require a specialization of the general UML mete-model in order to focus UML to more precisely describe the domain.

MDA

As the technology platforms of the VE continue changing quickly and the demands of integrating the heterogeneous legacy systems continue to grow, the MDA has created a buzz of interest by promising to increase the productivity, flexibility, and portability of VE models (Object Management Group, 2002a).

The MDA defines an approach that separates the specification of system functionality from the specification of the implementation of that functionality on a specific technology platform, and it also defines an approach for software development based on modeling and automated mapping of models to implementations. The MDA makes a distinction among the computation independent model (CIM), the platform independent model (PIM), and the platform specific model (PSM). According to this, it provides an open and technology-neutral approach to the challenge of business and technology change (Miller & Mukerji, 2003). The MDA also defines the 4-layer architecture for structuring the meta-modeling. It would be a sound foundation for this meta-modeling approach in this chapter. Therefore, we define a meta-model in the form of UML profile at M2 (meta-model) layer.

Although MDA is in the limelight of software engineering, there is no well-established concrete methodology for realizing MDA. To give an example, model transformation between PIM and PSM is indispensable in MDA. However, the mechanism or implementation for the model transformation is not thoroughgoing enough up to now.

Framework-Based Development

The framework-based development is usually said to be the second generation business process methodology (Harmon, 2003a). Important efforts are dedicated to exploiting the best practices and the design patterns of the business processes, the business components, and the architectural frameworks for the coherent design and implementation.

Since many quality properties such as the maintainability, portability, efficiency, reusability, etc., rely on framework-based development, it is essential to establish agile and interoperable VEs and

their loosely coupled integration. Consequently, the framework-based development allows improving and accelerating the development of enterprise models in VE.

The Supply Chain Council (SCC) established the supply chain operations reference model (SCOR) for the supply chain management domain (Supply Chain Council, 2003). In the domain of telecommunication, the next generation operations systems and software (NGOSS) are proposed by telemanagement forum (TeleManagement Forum, 2002). The instrumentation, systems, and automation society (ISA) have tried to standardize the processes in manufacturing execution system (MES) domain (Instrumentation, Systems, and Automation Society, 2004).

However, as the current framework-based development does not separate each element of enterprise models such as business process, application, information, etc., they are too mixed-up and complex to assure agility and flexibility of the VE models. Thus, in this chapter, we bring component-based architecture and service-oriented architecture in the framework-based development in order to manage independently the elements of enterprise models.

Business Process-Centric Architecture

According to Smith and Fingar (2003), the business process management will be the heart of the future business systems and will support the dynamic integration and collaboration of all participants in the value chain.

In the context of this chapter, the basis of the collaboration in a VE has evolved from the data-centric enterprise integration into the process-centric enterprise integration (CSC, 2002). In consequence, the VE is more focused on what can be done to achieve the common goal, and it has to be more dynamic and loosely-coupled with the value chains. The value chain of VE is defined as a set of linked business processes that are distributed at business partners. And these business processes should be managed and controlled autonomously and in a distributed manner because each business partners can be in different places and different time zones.

Ontology Engineering

It is even the case that the business functionalities and information of the VE are not properly understood yet. In other words, the VEs usually have some problems related to the interoperability of vocabularies for the enterprise models in different business domains because they are just temporary and distributed organizations across several business boundaries. In order to achieve interoperability regardless of the heterogeneities of business domains, it is needed to define the ontology and semantics with standardized mechanisms.

Although the importance of ontology engineering is well understood, it is also known that building a good ontology is a hard task. There are some approaches that present the procedure and the guidelines for ontology development (de Falbo, de Menezes, & da Rocha, 1998). Uschold, King, Moralee, and Zorgios (1997) aim to provide an environment for integrating and capturing key aspects of an enterprise based on ontology. There is another big project for enterprise ontology development: Toronto virtual enterprise (TOVE) project whose goal is to create generic and reusable enterprise ontology (Fox & Gruninger, 1998).

The semantic Web movement also discusses the importance of ontology engineering. In order to realize the semantic Web, Berners-Lee defined three distinct levels that incrementally introduce expressive primitives: meta-data layer, schema layer and logical layer (Berners-Lee, 1998). Based on the Berners-Lee's levels, Web ontology languages built on uniform resource identifier (URI) and XML (extensible markup language) technology, such as resource description framework (RDF) and RDF schema, are used

for representing information and for the defining semantics of terminology. Recently, Web ontology language (OWL) that is built on top of RDF/RDF schema became a standard recommended by the World Wide Web Consortium (W3C) (W3C, 2004).

In this chapter, the ontology engineering is associated with the systematic modeling framework for the agile and interoperable VEs. It offers the basis for the model transformation and the model synchronization in a general open universe of businesses.

Model Transformation

As the model transformation is the process of converting one model to another model, it is of interest for defining synchronization among the models within or across VEs. Therefore, it is undoubtedly considered as a major matter that plays a vital role in our systematic modeling framework for the agile and interoperable VEs.

As research area on model transformation is a relatively new area, its taxonomy is defined lately. Some researches have tried to classify and analyze various model transformation techniques in different domains in order to provide an insight into this new area (Czarnecki & Helsen, 2003; Prakash, Srivastava, & Sabharwal, 2006; Sendall & Kozaczynski, 2003). Currently, several researches are performed in the direction of how to express the transformation between models. Gerber, Lawley, Raymond, Steel, and Wood (2002) have indicated that the model transformation is the missing link of MDA. They have tried to express mapping from the enterprise distributed object computing (EDOC) business process model to the breeze workflow model using a number of different model transformation technologies.

SOA and Web Service

Contrary to the conventional tightly coupled object-oriented paradigm, service oriented architecture (SOA) is the new emerging paradigm for building the agile networks of collaborating business applications distributed within and across business boundaries.

As the SOA separates the service interface from the service implementation, it enables service components to be fine-grained and isolated. This separation produces an architecture style that promotes the collaborations among the VE models to be extremely loose and easily reconfigured at the enterprise application level. The SOA serves as glue between well integrated IT systems and well-defined business processes. It encourages the definition and the deployment of the business processes.

Although Web service is not the only way to accomplish the SOA, it is usually considered as the ideal candidate for collaboration among the models of the virtual enterprises on the open and loosely coupled platform. The SOA and Web service can bridge the gap between diverse applications and address the increasing need for the agility and interoperability of the VE models.

However, current SOA focuses on collaborations at the enterprise application level. As this chapter promotes the concept of the SOA to higher types of VE collaboration, it applies the SOA into the designing of VE architecture, modeling languages, and VE models, as well as the deployment of VE models.

SYSTEMATIC MODELING FRAMEWORK FOR THE AGILE AND INTEROPERABLE VE

These mentioned technologies have their own advantages, but they are dealt in separate interests and were developed independently to address their own purpose. Therefore, it is necessary to develop a common modeling framework that integrates these up-to-date technologies in order to configure the agile and interoperable VEs. In order to establish this systematic modeling framework, this

chapter proposes a synthesized architecture and a procedural framework. We combine all relevant technologies into the synthesized architecture. Based on this synthesized architecture, we guide business domain experts and developers through the procedural framework to the entire VE modeling.

Synthesized Architecture

Figure 3 represents diagrammatically the synthesized architecture. First of all, the synthesized architecture is based on EA because EA is usually considered as a systematic approach to configuration and analysis of enterprises or enterprise systems. Our synthesized architecture is based on the original Zachman framework. In our framework, we substitute two dimensions with the perspective layers and the modeling domains, respectively. The shown EA in Figure 3 is just only an example for understanding. It can be extended or modified flexibly according to the characteristics of a VE or the interests of business domain experts.

Based on the EA, we combine several technologies such as the MDA, the model transformation, the ontology engineering, and the SOA for the perspective layer integration. Applying the MDA, we regard contextual and conceptual layers as CIM of the MDA. In the same way, we regard logical layer and physical layer as PIM and PSM of the MDA, respectively. In the context of this chapter, these presumptions are sufficient to represent all of the "who? (perspective)" on VE models. In the relationship between logical layer and physical layer, we apply the model transformation and the ontology engineering in order to transform PIM to PSM. The Web services based on the SOA particularly is applied to PSM of the MDA, because it is considered as a suitable technology on the loosely coupled platform.

For the modeling domain integration, we combine the business process-centric architecture

Figure 3. Synthesized architecture

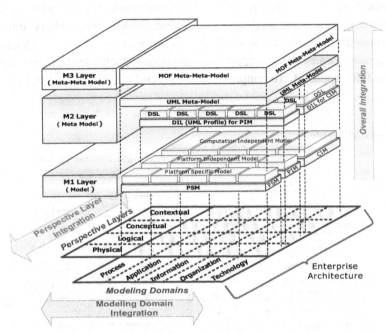

and the SOA. According to the VE definition, we declare that a VE is made up of value chains with collaborative business processes. In consequence, the process domain is a main interest of the modeling domains and other modeling domains do a role to support the process domain. To realize it, we also apply the SOA, which means the component-based architecture for each modeling domains.

In order to support the integration of VE modeling, we combine the meta-modeling approach and the MDA's 4-layer meta-modeling architecture. The componentized CIM, PIM, and PSM at the M1 (model) layer are built in the EA as shown in Figure 3. Above the M1 layer, there is the M2 (meta-model) layer where the modeling languages are defined to describe each model. Above the M2 layer, there is the M3 (meta-meta-model) layer, which is the top layer in the MDA architecture. We introduce the idea of a family of inter-related, but individually specialized,

modeling language which is based on the DSM. In other words, we apply the DSM into the M2 layer in order to freely develop modeling languages, which developers can use easily and accurately in their specific business domains.

Procedural Framework

In order to support the entire VE modeling, our systematic modeling framework is organized as shown in Figure 4.

The left side of Figure 4 shows the procedure for the configuration of the VE. It contains four phases focusing on details of the configuration. These phases will be described in detail in the following sections. The right side of Figure 4 briefly shows the facilities supporting each phase. There are several facilities that support each phase. Each modeling facility such as *EA designer*, *DSL/DIL designers*, *CIM/PIM modelers*, and *PSM mapper* is associated with its relevant reference repository, ontology repository, and local instance repository. To increase portability, agility, and interoperability of the models, each modeling facility enables to reuse the best practices stored in each reference repository under the concept of the framework-based development. To support

the communication and the comprehension for retrieval and use, each modeling facility is also connected with the ontology repository.

The procedure of the entire VE modeling under the systematic modeling framework is described with IDEF0 model as shown in Figure 5.

Figure 4. Procedural framework

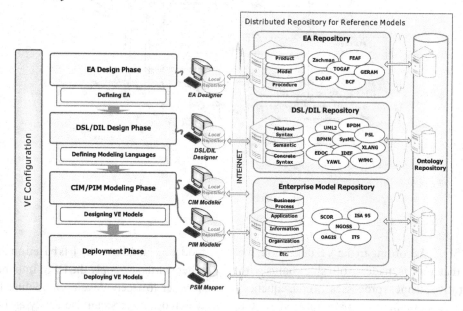

Figure 5. Procedure of entire VE modeling

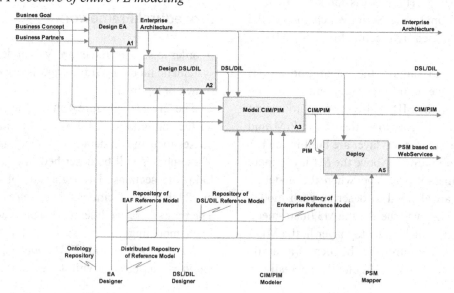

EA Design Phase

First of all, the standardized collaborative models of the VE are established through the EA. It is for that reason that an EA defines all the business components and business processes of a VE and explains how all the enterprise components work together as a whole. It is important that formal EA specification should ideally capture all the aspects that are unique to the enterprise system and also help in making various architecture decisions.

The procedure to establish the EA is described as follow:

- **Determining the organizational structure of the VE:** The organizational structure of the VE is determined.
- **Assigning the roles of each major partner:** The roles are assigned to the selected major partners
- **Decomposing views and perspectives:** Because the VE models can be understood in a broad sense, from a number of different

views at different abstract levels, the process of decomposing and separating concerns of various participants is performed.

- **Establishing EA:** Through the process of decomposing and separating concerns of various stakeholders, an EA can be built to support these different views and different abstract levels.
- **Fulfilling EA:** Once we have established an EA, we begin to collect everything that fulfills it such as business process models, information models, resource models, etc., from the suitable reference repositories.

For EA of VE, we suggest a meta-model of the EA as illustrated in Figure 6. Basically, the EA has several perspective layers and some views. Each EA cell that is produced by a pair of a perspective and a view provides a container of the cell content lists, the modeling language, and the enterprise models. The perspectives correspond to the MDA models and the views correspond to the modeling domains. In addition, Figure 6 also

Figure 6. Meta-model of EA

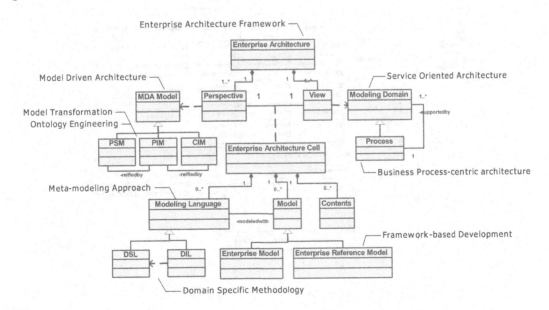

shows how the relevant technologies are reflected in the meta-model of the EA.

To define EA for VE, we introduce two assumptions into the EA: One is that each view of the EA corresponds to one modeling domain. The other is that each perspective of the EA refers to the models of MDA such as CIM, PIM, and PSM (Frankel et al., 2003). In the context of this chapter, these assumptions are sufficient to represent all of the "who? (perspective)" and "what? (view)" on the VE models.

Modeling Domains: "What?"

According to our definition of the VE, EA design is usually based on efforts to divide all work of the VE into value chains, which are repeatedly subdivided into the business processes. Therefore, it is natural that our EA seems to be a process-centric framework.

For example, we can divide the views of the EA into the following 5 modeling domains.

1. **Process domain:** Focusing on the business processes, which are the core of the EA.
2. **Application domain:** Focusing on the business applications supporting the business processes.
3. **Information domain:** Focusing on the business information or system information supporting the business processes and applications respectively.
4. **Organization domain:** Focusing on the participants responsible for the supporting and execution of the business processes.
5. **Technology domain:** Focusing on the technology environment and infrastructures supporting the business applications.

Figure 7. EA designer

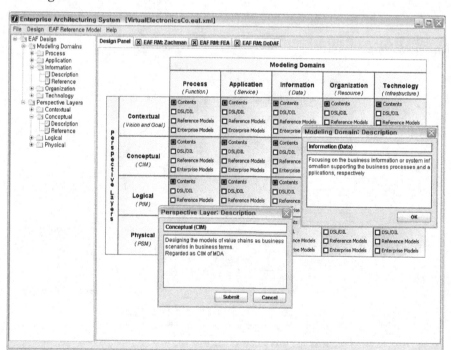

Perspective Layers: "Who?"

Meanwhile, the rows of the EA are made for the different perspectives. For example, the perspectives can be the contextual layer, conceptual layer, logical layer and physical layer.

- **Contextual layer:** Defining the goal, purpose, and visions of the VE, which restrict the business boundaries. Regarded as CIM in the MDA.
- **Conceptual layer:** Designing the models of value chains as business scenarios in business terms. Regarded as CIM in the MDA.
- **Logical layer:** Designing the models of the business processes and the business components in more rigorous terms than conceptual layer. Regarded as PIM in the MDA.
- **Physical layer:** Designing the deployed models related with specific technology. Regarded as PSM in the MDA.

Figure 7 illustrates the implemented *EA designer* for this EA design phase. As previously described, *EA designer* generates 2D-matrix EA in which each EA cell provides a container of the content lists, the DSL/DIL, the reference models and the enterprise models of VE.

DSL/DIL Design Phase

In this phase, the modeling languages are developed to describe the VE models. The modeling languages, which are domain specific language (DSL) or domain integrated language (DIL) in this chapter, are designed based on the synthesized architecture in Figure 3. As this chapter, as well as MDA, assumes that PSM can be generated from PIM through the model transformation, we focus on the VE modeling at the business logic level. Therefore, we concentrate on designing

the modeling languages within CIM and PIM of the MDA at the M2 layer. More information about the generation of PSM is described in the deployment phase of Section 4.6.

The DSL/DIL design proceeds on a two-step development. The two steps to design DSLs and DILs are briefly summarized as follows: Firstly, DSLs for CIM and DSLs for PIM are designed for each EA cell. Secondly, DSLs for CIM and DSLs for PIM are simply assembled into DIL for CIM and DIL for PIM, respectively. As this DSL/DIL design phase is based on the meta-modeling approach, each DSL/DIL is developed in the form of UML profile and is composed of abstract syntax, semantics, and concrete syntaxes.

DSL Design

Standing on the basis of the DSM and the meta-modeling approach, this session uses the idea of a family of inter-related, but individually specialized, modeling languages, namely DSL. Each narrowly focused DSL can be very effective at describing the VE models in each modeling domain. Therefore, we intend to freely develop the most suitable language and to use it correctly and effectively for the business domain of the VE. As each EA cell has its own DSL, it is natural that DSLs have to be suitable to the contexts of each EA cell and to be inter-related with each other.

It has been stated that UML extension mechanism of UML profile is very useful to defining a suite of modeling languages. Thus, DSLs are developed in the form of UML profiles, which is MOF-compliant at M2 layer in Figure 3. To explain the DSL design more easily, the M2 layer of Figure 3 is scaled up in Figure 8, which illustrates some fragments of the example DSL. It shows three EA cells, which are produced by the pairs of logical layer and process domain/information domain/application domain. Based on the characteristics of each EA cell, each DSL is defined with abstract syntax, semantics, and concrete syntaxes.

Figure 8. Fragments of DSL and DIL

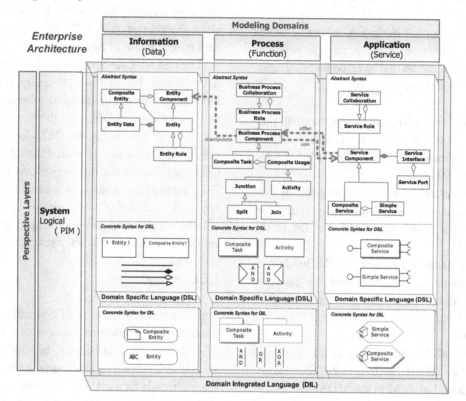

DIL Design

DSLs are isolated from each other so that each DSL is expressible enough to design the models of corresponding EA cells. However, there is also a need for a coherent modeling language that provides the ability to design and integrate the inter-related models and their relationships across several EA cells. This coherent modeling language can provide insights and enable communication among different stakeholders.

As integrating DSLs, DIL are to bridge the gaps between these modeling domains and to integrate the models of the heterogeneous modeling domains. While DSLs are used to design the models that are restricted within each EA cell, DIL is used to design the integrated models that support multiple EA cells throughout CIM

and PIM modeling. Therefore, DSLs provide the easiest and most correct way to establish specific domain models that correspond to requirements of various stakeholders. In addition, the usage of DILs enables different stakeholders to readily understand the enterprise model as a whole.

To support it, like the links expressed as dotted bold lines in Figure 8, the related modeling elements among DSLs of different EA cells can be connected. MOF-compliant UML profile of the MDA provides the base to manage different DSLs in an integrated fashion and to knit these isolated DSLs together. DIL is not completely independent of DSL because DIL is a type of meta-model (UML profile) assembling several DSLs. Therefore, the model based on a DSL and the model based on a DIL can be interchanged with and converted to each other easily.

Figure 9. DSL designer

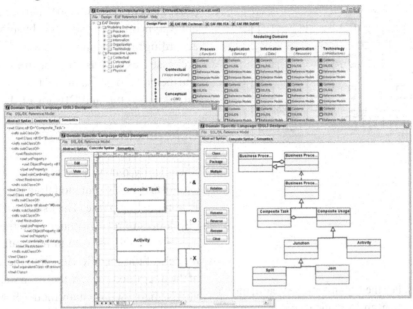

The facility, which supports the DSL/DIL design phase is implemented in the previously mentioned *EA designer*. Figure 9 shows *DSL designer* of the implemented *DSL/DIL designers*. The designed elements of DSL such as abstract syntax, concrete syntax, and semantics are packed in the EA cell.

CIM/PIM Modeling Phase

The business components including the business processes of the VE are modeled at the M1 layer using the EA and the DSL/DIL for CIM/PIM.

The modeling process for the VE proceeds on each perspective of the EA. This process is based on a top-down modeling paradigm in which more concrete models are created from abstract models. Therefore, the business list, the business purpose, the vision, and the boundaries of the VE are described at the contextual layer, and the value chains of the VE are modeled as CIM at the conceptual layer. Then, the detailed business components composing CIM are modeled as PIM at the Logical layer.

As the VE is considered as a set of the value chains made up of collaborative business processes, it is natural that the VE can be modeled with the process-centric approach. A generalized and process-centric representation for business partners was presented and implemented in our previous research (Kim, Son, Kim, Kim, & Baik, 2005; Kim, Kim, Lee, & Kim, 2005). As this CIM/PIM modeling phase is based on the modeling philosophy of our previous research, CIM and PIM for the VE are regarded as the business scenarios and the collaborative business processes, respectively, as illustrated in Figure 10.

In CIM modeling for the business scenarios, functional areas and organizations of each business partner are determined using the function-organization matrix that describes the process stream and organization stream of the VE. With respect to the process stream, the units of enterprise activities are logically and temporally ordered to

Figure 10. Modeling CIM and PIM

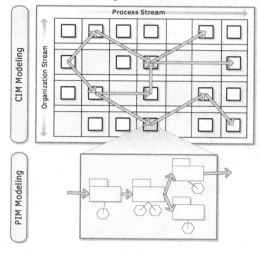

In PIM modeling for the collaborative business processes, we recommend to perform a top-down analysis primarily to show the business processes according to the business scenario. These business processes, as well as other business components and their relationships, are systematically modeled through the DSL and DIL for PIM.

Coherent Modeling

Specifically, our systematic modeling framework supports the coherent modeling using DIL in the PIM modeling phase. The usage of DILs enables developers to readily understand the VE models as a whole. DIL is used to integrate the domain models of the specific view into the entire model of the integrated view, so that each stakeholder can verify their own domain model from the entire model through view navigation. The integrated view using DIL is useful when different stake-

realize products. For the organization stream, the organization, human, and technical resources are systematically and repetitively assigned.

Figure 11. Coherent modeling

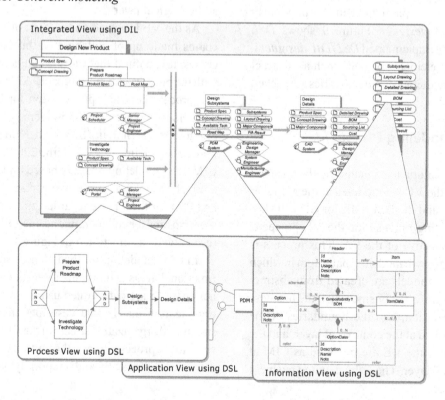

holders design an integrated model and evaluate the relationships among the individual domain models and integrated models. An example of the coherent modeling is represented in Figure 11.

The facility, which supports the CIM/PIM modeling phase is also implemented in the previously mentioned *EA designer*. Figure 12 shows the implemented *CIM/PIM modelers*. The implemented *CIM/PIM modelers* also provides the coherent modeling functionality in order to design and integrate the inter-related models and their relationships across several EA cells. The designed VE models such as CIM and PIM are packed in the EA cell.

Deployment Phase

In this deployment phase, the designed VE models are deployed into PSM for actual execution so as to be suitable for specific technology platform.

In order to deploy the designed VE models into PSMs, the model transformation through

meta-model mapping can be introduced. It is obvious that business domain experts can not define DSL/DIL, which provides the executable ability in the DSL/DIL design phase. Thus, it is better to transform the VE models to the execution models through the model transformation.

As briefly shown in Figure 13, a meta-model of PSM, that is Web service language, is developed as a UML profile. And then, it is mapped from the DSL/DIL. Such meta-model mapping at the M2 layer enables to transform the CIM/PIM into PSM, namely Web service models.

In this chapter, Web service is considered to be the best solution for PSM. Web service is a way to implement the SOA, which is intended to enable developers to create the service components that can be assembled and deployed in a distributed environment. Therefore, Web service is a useful candidate for integrating the enterprise application and setting up the open and loosely coupled information platform for the VE.

Figure 12. CIM/PIM modelers

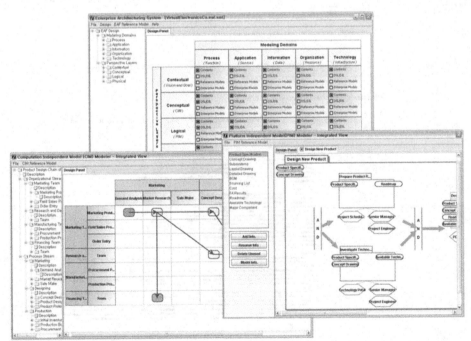

Figure 13. Model transformation for deployment

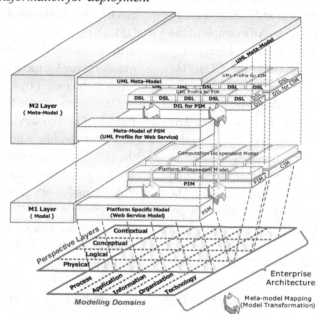

Figure 14. Deployment of VE models

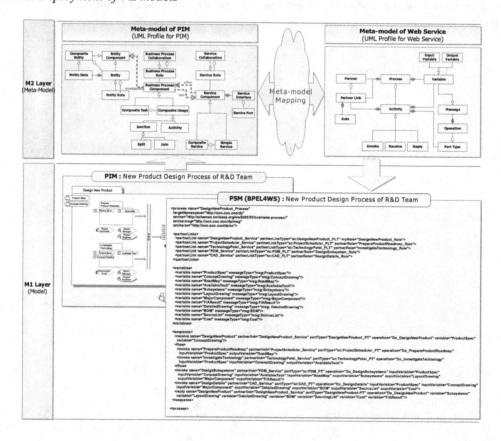

As represented diagrammatically in Figure 14, PIM, which are modeled in Figure 11, can be transformed into BPEL4WS model via the meta-model mapping between DSL/DIL into the meta-model of BPEL4WS. And the generated BPEL4WS model is expected to be possibly executed through the existing commercial Web server systems, such as WebSphere or WebLogic.

DISCUSSION AND CONCLUSION

The VE based on the process-centric loosely coupled integration has become a key for survival in the competitive business environment. In order to establish this VE models quickly and systematically, it is necessary to develop a systematic modeling framework for supporting the entire VE modeling such as VE architectures, the modeling languages, VE models, and deployment.

Unfortunately, existing technologies in enterprise engineering doesn't fully support the design and management of the VE. Although they have their own advantages, the review of current technologies reveals that none support all aspects of the VE model because each technology deals with diverse domains in different ways and has been developed independently to address its own purpose. This observation has motivated the development of a systematic modeling framework for the agile and interoperable VE based on a hybrid approach. It harmonizes the up-to-date approaches in order to not only utilize the individual advantages of each approach, but also to produce integrated synergy effects.

In this chapter, we aim to suggest a systematic modeling framework itself, not to propose an EA, modeling languages, or VE model instances. Based on our modeling framework, business domain experts and developers of VE can design their own EA, DSLs/DILs, and deployed models, as well as VE models. In order to establish the systematic modeling framework, we propose the synthesized architecture, which combines all relevant technologies. Based on the synthesized architecture, we also propose the procedural framework, which guides the enterprise configuration to support the entire VE.

The proposed systematic modeling framework could be used by business domain experts and developers to build an agile and interoperable VE quickly and systematically by composing business partners and by designing the collaborative business processes and the business components across the value chains of the VE. For communications among the different stakeholders, it also supports the coherent enterprise modeling in which various stakeholders, having their own aspects and methodology, such as an IT manager and a business manager, can communicate effectively. Consequently, this systematic modeling framework could contribute significantly to the configuration of agile and interoperable VEs.

Although the modeling framework is developed in this chapter, works are currently underway to enrich it as yet. The in-depth meta-models for specific business domains have not been covered in this chapter because they are too complicated to be described in detail. Through gathering industrial data and cases, the meta-models, which are applicable to real industrial example, should be constructed and proved by experiments. We have implemented a modeling system supporting the proposed modeling framework. Nevertheless, because there is much room for improvement as ever, we are under discussion on better and more robust system implementations.

REFERENCES

Andrews, T., Curbera, F., Dholakia, H., Goland, Y., Klein, J., Leymann, F., et al. (2003). *Business process execution language for web services version 1.1*. Retrieved from http://www-106.ibm.com/developerworks/Webservices/library/ws-bpel/

Ang, C. L., Khoo, L. P., & Gay, R. K. L. (1999). IDEF*: A comprehensive modeling methodology for development of manufacturing enterprise system. *International Journal of Production Research, 37*(17), 3839-3858.

Arkin, A. (2002). *Business process modeling language.* Retrieved from http://www.bpmi.org/downloads/BPML1.0.zip

Barnett, W., Presley, M. J., & Liles, D. (1994). *An architecture for the virtual enterprise.* Paper presented at the IEEE International Conference on Systems, Man, and Cybernetics, San Antonio.

Berners-Lee, T. (1998). *Semantic Web road map.* Retrieved from http://w3.org/DisignIssues/Semantic.html

Booch, G., Rumbaugh, J., & Jacobson, I. (1999). *The unified modeling language user guide.* Addison-Wesley.

Business Process Management Initiative. (2003). *Business process modeling natation working draft 1.0.* Retrieved from http://www.bpmi.org/downloads/BPMN-V1.0.pdf

Cadence Design Systems. (2003). *Design chain optimization: Competing in the disaggregated electronic industry.* Cadence Design Systems, Whitepaper.

Camarinha-Matos, L. M., & Afsarmanesh, H. (2003). Elements of a base VE infrastructure. *Computers in Industry, 51*, 139-163

CIO Council. (2001). *A practical guide to federal enterprise architecture version 1.0.* Retrieved from http://www.cio.gov

CSC. (2002). *The emergence of business process management version 1.0.* A Report by CSC's Research Services

Czarnecki, K., & Helsen, S. (2003). *Classification of model transformation approaches.* Paper presented at the OOPSLA'03 Workshop on Generative Techniques in the Context of Model-Driven Architecture. Retrieved from http://www.softmetaware.com/oopsla2003/mda-workshop.html

DoDAF Working Group. (2003). *DoD architecture framework version 1.0:* Volume I: Definition and guidelines.

de Falbo, R. A., de Menezes, C. S., & da Rocha, A. R. C. (1998). A systematic approach for building ontologies. *IBERAMIA'98, LNAI 1484.*

Fox, M. S., & Gruninger, M. (1998). Enterprise modeling. *AI Magazine,* American Association for Artificial Intelligence Press.

Frankel, D. S., et al. (2003). *The Zachman framework and the OMG's model driven architecture.* Business process Trends: Whitepaper.

Frankel, D. S. (2004). Domain-specific modeling and model driven architecture. *Business Process Trends: MDA Journal.*

Gerber, A., Lawley, M., Raymond, K., Steel, J., & Wood, A. (2002). Transformation: The missing link of MDA. In *Proceedings of International Conference on Graph Transformation (ICGT),* Barcelona, Spain.

Gou, H., Huang, B., Liu, W., & Li, X. (2003). A framework for virtual enterprise operation management. *Computers in Industry, 50*, 333-352

Harmon, P. (2003a). Second generation business process methodologies. *Business Process Trends: Newsletter, 1*(5).

Harmon, P. (2003b). *Developing an enterprise architecture.* Business process Trends: Whitepaper.

IFIP-IFAC Task Force. (1999). *GERAM: Generalised enterprise reference architecture and methodology version 1.6.3.* Retrieved from http://www.cit.gu.edu.au/~bernus/taskforce/geram/versions/geram1-6-3/GERAMv1.6.3.pdf

The Instrumentation, Systems, and Automation Society. (2004). Enterprise-control system integration—Part 3: Models of manufacturing operations management, ISA Draft 95.00.03.

Jagdev, H. S., & Thoben, K. D. (2001). Anatomy of enterprise collaborations. *Production Planning & Control, 12*(5), 437-451

Kim, C. H., Son, Y. J., Kim, T. Y., Kim, K., & Baik, K. (2005). A modeling approach for designing a value chain of virtual enterprise. *International Journal of Advanced Manufacturing Technology.* Online first retrieved http://dx.doi.org/10.1007/s00170-004-2445-4

Kim, T. Y., Kim, C. H., Lee, J. S., & Kim, K. (2005). Enterprise architecture framework based on MDA to support virtual enterprise modeling. In *Proceedings of the 9th International IEEE EDOC Workshop on VORTE (Vocabularies, Ontologies, and Rules for The Enterprise)*, Enschede, Netherlands.

MetaCase. (2005). *Domain-specific modelling, application development advisor.* Retrieved from http://www.appdevadvisor.co.uk/express/vendor/domain.html

Miller, J., & Mukerji, J. (2003). *MDA guide version 1.0.1.* Retrieved from http://www.omg.org/docs/omg/03-06-01.pdf

NIIIP. Retrieved from http://www.niiip.org

Object Management Group. (2002). *Model driven architecture (MDA).* Retrieved from http://www.omg.org/mda/

Object Management Group. (2003a). *Request for proposal: business process definition metamodel RFP.* Retrieved from http://www.omg.org/docs/bei/03-01-06.pdf

Object Management Group. (2003b). *UML 2.0 infrastructure specification: Final adopted specification.* Retrieved from http://www.omg.org/docs/ptc/03-09-15.pdf

Object Management Group. (2003c). *UML 2.0 superstructure specification: Final adopted specification.* Retrieved from http://www.omg.org/docs/ptc/03-08-02.pdf

Object Management Group. (2004). *UML profile for enterprise collaboration architecture specification version 1.0.* Retrieved from http://www.omg.org/docs/formal/04-02-05.pdf

Prakash, N., Srivastava, S., & Sabharwal, S. (2006). The classification framework for model transformation. *Journal of Computer Science, 2*(2), 166-170.

Supply Chain Council. (2003). S*upply chain operations reference model—SCOR version 6.0.* Supply Chain Council, Inc.

Sendall, S., & Kozaczynski, W. (2003). Model transformation: The heart and soul of model-driven software development. *IEEE Software*, Special Issue on Model Driven Software Development, Sep./Oct.

Smith, H., & Fingar, P. (2003). *Business process management: The third wave.* Meghan-Kiffer Press.

TeleManagement Forum. (2002). Enhanced telecom operations MapTM (eTOM): The business process framework version 3.0, GB921.

Uschold, M., King, M., Moralee, S., & Zorgios, Y. (1997). The enterprise ontology. *Knowledge Engineering Review, 13.*

Vernadat, F. B. (1993). *CIMOSA: Enterprise modeling and enterprise integration using a process-based approach.* Paper presented at the Workshop on the Design of Information Infrastructure Systems for Manufacturing, The Japan Society for Precision Engineering.

Vernadat, F. B. (1996). *Enterprise modeling and integration: Principles and applications.* Chapman and Hall.

Vesterager, J., Tolle, M., & Bernus, P. (2002). VERA: Virtual enterprise reference architecture. Paper presented at the Blobeman Plenary Conference, Helsinki.

W3C. (2001). *Web services description language (WSDL) 1.1, W3C Notes*. Retrieved from http://www.w3.org/TR/wsdl/

W3C. (2004). *OWL Web ontology language guide, W3C Recommendation*. Retrieved from http://www.w3.org/TR/owl-guide/

Williams, T. J. (1993). *The Perdue enterprise reference architecture*. Paper presented at the Workshop on the Design of Information Infrastructure Systems for Manufacturing, The Japan Society for Precision Engineering.

Zachman, J. A. (1987). A framework for information systems architecture. *IBM Systems Journal, 26*(3).

Zarli, A., & Richaud, O. (1999). Requirements and technology integration for IT-based business-oriented frameworks in building and construction. *Electronic Journal of Information Technology in Construction, 4*.

ZIFA. Retrieved from http://www.zifa.com

Chapter V
Activity–Based Methodology for Development and Analysis of Integrated DoD Architectures

Steven J. Ring
The MITRE Corporation, USA

Dave Nicholson
The MITRE Corporation, USA

ABSTRACT

This chapter describes the activity-based methodology (ABM), an efficient and effective approach toward development and analysis of DoD integrated architectures that will enable them to align with and fully support decision-making processes and mission outcomes. ABM consists of a tool-independent disciplined approach to developing fully integrated, unambiguous, and consistent DODAF Operational, System, and Technical views in supporting both "as-is" architectures (where all current elements are known) and "to-be" architectures (where not all future elements are known). ABM enables architects to concentrate on the Art and Science of architectures—that is identifying core architecture elements, their views, how they are related together, and the resulting analysis used for decision-making purposes. ABM delivers significant architecture development productivity and quality gains by generating several DoDAF products and their elements from the core architecture elements. ABM facilitates the transition from integrated "static" architectures to executable "dynamic" process models for time-dependent assessments of complex operations and resource usage. Workflow steps for creating integrated architecture are detailed. Numerous architecture analysis strategies are presented that show the value of integrated architectures to decision makers and mission outcomes.

INTRODUCTION

This document provides guidance in developing fully integrated, unambiguous, and consistent DoD architecture framework (DoDAF) and architecture descriptions in supporting both "as-is" domains (where all current elements are known) and "to-be" domains (where not all future elements are known). It presents a disciplined approach in identifying core architecture data elements, their views, how they are related together, and how they compare with other architectures developed according to this guidance. The resulting analysis based on common, integrated architecture data can then be used for decision-making purposes. The associations between these core elements form the basis of an integrated architecture data model. Using these core architecture data elements and their associations, significant architecture development productivity and quality gains can be obtained by providing a standard means for comparing and relating architecture descriptions. Workflow steps in creating an integrated architecture are detailed.

Architectures are a means to an end and not an end to themselves. They need to be aligned with and support the decision-making process and ultimately mission outcomes and objectives. Figure 1 depicts this process where mission outcomes are determined by mission decisions, chosen from among a set of courses of actions, based on analysis and assessments of architecture

data, coming from both integrated and executable architectures. Having a disciplined process that ensures quality architectures raises the potential for quality and consistency in their descriptions and minimizes discrepancies. Consequently, the analytics will produce quality results, not be prone to misinterpretations, and thus, be of high value to decision makers and mission outcomes.

BACKGROUND

The DoD architecture framework (DoDAF) provides DoD commands, services, and agencies with the rules and guidance for describing architectures for both warfighting operations and business processes (DoDAF, 2003). DoDAF's purpose is to ensure that the architecture descriptions contain related architecture entities and relationships that can be used (1) for understanding, comparing, and integrating families of systems (FOSs) and systems of systems (SoSs) and (2) to enable in-

Figure 1. Role of architectures in the decision-making and mission outcome processes

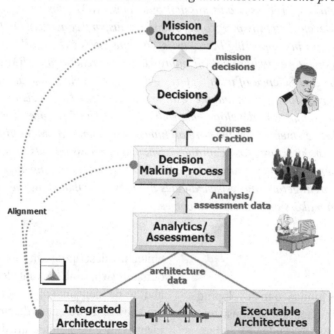

teroperating and interacting architectures within and across organizational boundaries, including joint and multi-national.

DoDAF is not an architecture by itself. DoDAF is an *architecture framework* that provides structured guidance and rules for classifying and organizing architectures within an enterprise. It represents approaches, standards, concepts, descriptions, views, visualizations, products, and architecture artifacts in a single framework.

An *architecture* is a representation of a defined domain as of a current or future point in time. The term is generally used both to refer to an *architecture description* and an *architecture implementation*. In this document, the term *architecture* will be used as a shortened reference to *architecture description*. An *architecture description*, then, is a representation of a defined domain as of a current or future point in time, in terms of its component parts, what those parts do, how the parts relate to each other, and the rules and constraints under which the parts function.

What constitutes domains and components depends on the degree of detail of interest. For example, domains can be at any level, from DoD as a whole down to individual functional areas or groups of functional areas. Component parts can be anything from "U.S. Air Force" as a component of DoD, down to a "satellite ground station" as a component part of a communications network, or a UAV operator as a component part of a reconnaissance system. What those parts do can be as general as their high-level operational concept or as specific as the lowest-level action they perform. How the parts relate to each other can be as general as how organizations fit into a very high-level command structure or as specific as what frequency one unit uses in communicating with another. The rules and constraints under which they work can be as general as high-level doctrine or as specific as the e-mail standard they must use. An *architecture description* can represent requirements without a specific implementation or it can represent both requirements and their implementation.

An *architecture description* consists of integrated *architecture perspectives* (or *views*). Architecture *descriptions* and *views* help communicate domain complexity and aid in its understanding. *Architecture perspectives* are logical perspectives used to separate components into unique viewpoints or frames of reference. Each *architecture view*, by itself, consists of one or more related "real-world" *models* (*or products*) of processes, resources, rules, and relationships for a specific viewpoint. These *products* are graphical, textual, or tabular related representations of *architecture artifacts (elements)*. At the lowest level, *architecture artifacts* are instances of activities, nodes, organizational elements, organizations, systems, networks, interfaces, etc.

DOD ARCHITECTURE FRAMEWORK

DoDAF defines four *perspectives* (i.e., three of the four views are shown in Figure 3) that logically combine to form an *architecture description*: Operational View (OV), System View (SV), and Technical Standards View (TSV). OV is a de-

Figure 2. Architecture framework hierarchy

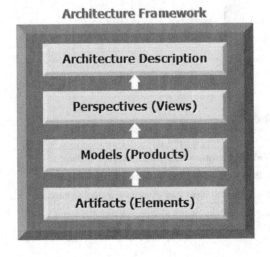

scription of an enterprise's operational elements required to accomplish DoD missions. SV is a refinement of the OV that describes system elements, their functions and interfaces, and their exchanges supporting operational missions. TSV is the set of standards to be applied to the elements and their relationships in the OV and SV.

A fourth view, All-Views (AV), relates overarching aspects of OV, SV, and TSV. AV products provide information pertinent to the entire architecture but do not represent a distinct view of the architecture. AV products set the scope and context of the architecture to include (i) subject area and timeframe for the architecture, (ii) setting in which the architecture exists, (iii) interrelated conditions such as doctrine, tactics, techniques, and procedures that compose the context for the

architecture, (iv) relevant goals and vision statements, (v) concepts of operations, scenarios, and environmental conditions.

Each view is composed of sets of architecture elements that are depicted via a baseline set of 26 graphic, tabular, and textual architecture products. It is important to distinguish between an architecture *view* and an *architecture product*. As stated earlier, an *architecture view* represents a given perspective of an architecture, while an *architecture product* is a specific representation of a particular aspect of that perspective. At the lowest level, these *architecture artifacts* are data instances of activities, nodes, organizational elements, organizations, systems, networks, interfaces, etc.

Figure 3. Linkages among OV, SV, and TSV Views

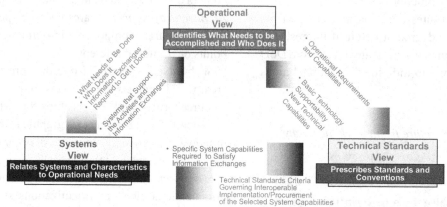

Table 1. All views and technical architecture view products

Product	Product Name	General Description
AV-1	Overview and Summary Information	Scope, purpose, intended users, environment depicted, analytical findings
AV-2	Integrated Dictionary	Architecture data repository with definitions of all terms used in all products
TV-1	Technical Standards Profile	Listing of standards that apply to Systems View elements in a given architecture
TV-2	Technical Standards Forecast	Description of emerging standards and potential impact on current Systems View elements, within a set of time frames

Table 2. Operational View products

Product	Product Name	General Description
OV-1	High-Level Operational Concept Graphic	High-level graphical/textual description of operational concept
OV-2	Operational Node Connectivity Description	Operational nodes, connectivity, and information exchange need lines between nodes
OV-3	Operational Information Exchange Matrix	Information exchanged between nodes and the relevant attributes of that exchange
OV-4	Organizational Relationships Chart	Organizational, role, or other relationships among organizations
OV-5	Operational Activity Model	Capabilities, operational activities, relationships among activities, inputs, and outputs; overlays can show cost, performing nodes, or other pertinent information
OV-6a	Operational Rules Model	One of three products used to describe operational activity—identifies business rules that constrain operation
OV-6b	Operational State Transition Description	One of three products used to describe operational activity—identifies business process responses to events
OV-6c	Operational Event-Trace Description	One of three products used to describe operational activity—traces actions in a scenario or sequence of events
OV-7	Logical Data Model	Documentation of the system data requirements and structural business process rules of the operational view

Table 3. System View products

Product	Product Name	General Description
SV-1	Systems Interface Description	Identification of systems nodes, systems, and system items and their interconnections, within and between nodes
SV-2	Systems Communications Description	Systems nodes, systems, and system items, and their related communications laydowns
SV-3	Systems-Systems Matrix	Relationships among systems in a given architecture; can be designed to show relationships of interest (e.g., system-type interfaces, planned vs. existing interfaces, etc).
SV-4	Systems Functionality Description	Functions performed by systems and the system data flows among system functions
SV-5	Operational Activity to Systems Function Traceability Matrix	Mapping of systems back to capabilities or of system functions back to operational activities
SV-6	Systems Data Exchange Matrix	Provides details of system data elements being exchanged between systems and the attributes of that exchange
SV-7	Systems Performance Parameters Matrix	Performance characteristics of systems view elements for the appropriate time frame(s)
SV-8	Systems Evolution Description	Planned incremental steps toward migrating a suite of systems to a more efficient suite, or toward evolving a current system to a future implementation
SV-9	Systems Technology Forecast	Emerging technologies and software/hardware products that are expected to be available in a given set of time frames and that will affect future development of the architecture
SV-10a	Systems Rules Model	One of three products used to describe system functionality—identifies constraints that are imposed on systems functionality due to some aspect of systems design or implementation
SV-10b	Systems State Transition Description	One of three products used to describe system functionality—identifies responses of a system to events
SV-10c	Systems Event-Trace Description	One of three products used to describe system functionality—identifies system-specific refinements of critical sequences of events described in the operational view
SV-11	Physical Schema	Physical implementation of the logical data model entities (e.g., message formats, file structures, physical schema)

CURRENT STATE OF DoD ARCHITECTING

As we near the end of the first generation of DoD architecting, differing interpretations and definitions of DoDAF concepts within the architecture community combined with variations in architecture development workflow processes, practices, and results have, in almost all cases, led to architectures that cannot be federated, compared, analyzed, or assessed (Nicholson, Mercer, & Ang, 2005). While there are "pockets of good architecture practice," too often applying DoDAF in any consistent and repeatable way is improbable and difficult. Architects are unsure of how to apply DoDAF and wind up practicing "check the box" architecting just to get to the next program/project development stage.

Although DoD architects have produced thousands of architecture descriptions, they generally have not produced actionable decision information in support of core organizational processes, yet, the purpose of DoD architecting has always been to support the development of such actionable information. These core organizational processes include joint capabilities integration and development system (JCIDS, 2005) process, information technology portfolio management (ITPM) (DoDI 8115.bb, 2006) process of managing investments as portfolios, and a capabilities-based planning process that provides useful architecture descriptions expressed as the full range of military Doctrine, Organization, Material, Training, Leadership, Personnel and Facilities (DOTMLPF) alternatives.

The ability to develop integrated architectures that produce actionable information to support these core processes results in the need for a conceptual architecture model that meets the following requirements:

- Provides a data-centric (not product-centric) approach to integrated architecting.

- Is unambiguous and semantically rich: eliminate semantic overloading of architecture data elements.
- Identifies a set of core architecture elements.
- Ensures DoDAF architectures do not become dis-integrated.
- Supports executable architecture development and analysis.
- Enables linking ("federating") producing and consuming architectures.
- Captures sufficient architectural detail for full DOTMLPF analysis (not just material).

Provides a Data-Centric (Not Product-Centric) Approach to Integrated Architecting

The current emphasis on discrete DoDAF product development obscures the real purpose in describing architectures—i.e., producing *actionable architectures* that can be used for decision and mission outcome objectives. The lack of a single holistic model of architecture concepts as the underlying foundation of the 26 DoDAF products characterizes DoDAF as product-centric rather than data-centric. A more appropriate approach begins with the descriptive concepts employed in DoD architecting that leads to a holistic collection of the descriptive concepts, in the form of data types, as the foundation of architecture descriptions. This is the basis of the data-centric ABM approach to architecture development.

Is Unambiguous and Semantically Rich: Eliminate Semantic Overloading of Architecture Data Elements

Semantic overloading is where one descriptive element conveys more than one semantic concept. This results in definitions of architecture elements being "subject-to-differing-interpretations" by architects and creates ambiguity that may or may not be resolved through examination, on an individual basis, of the context in which the element is used. It is primarily DoDAF's inconsistent expression of semantics that characterizes it as semantically incomplete. Most notably, an "Operational Node" is defined (and has been since the original 1997 C4ISR Framework (C4ISR AF, 1997, pp. 4-11)) to be an element that represents *"Organizations, Organization Types, and Occupational Specialties"* (DoDAF, Vol II, pp. 3-10), while at the same time is defined to be an element that *"produces, consumes, or processes information"* (DoDAF, Vol II, pp. 4-7). Operational nodes have also been increasingly interpreted as platforms (ground, air, and sea), facilities, and systems in many OV architectures. Thus, what constitutes an operational node can vary among architectures, including, but not limited to, an operational/human role, an organization, organization type, and so on. Another example is the semantic overloading of the Operational View (OV). Current OV describes both (1) a human performer-only view and (2) an undifferentiated logical view that treats performers as neither human nor machine, but instead as resources composed of both. Again, only by examining the context of each OV can one resolve the intention of the architecture. To eliminate any ambiguity and semantic overloading, an architecture taxonomy, at the highest level, must be based on the six "interrogatives"—WHO, WHERE, WHAT, WHY, WHEN, and HOW. This eliminates the case where "WHO" and "WHERE" are combined into a single element ("Operational Node").

Identifies a Set of Core Architecture Elements

While DoDAF defines a set of products that make up an integrated architecture, it doesn't identify any architecture elements within those products as being core building block foundations of integrated architecture. Without defining any specific core

set of architecture elements and their respective framework products that are the sources of those elements, integrated architectures may not always be produced. For example, while an OV-3 is part of the integrated product set, some architectures that only consist of an OV-3 are declared to be integrated without one ever producing an OV-2 or OV-5. A set of four core architecture elements from the six interrogatives—nodes (WHERE), resources (WHO), products (WHAT), functions (HOW) serve as the foundation of an integrated architecture.

Ensures DODAF Architectures do not become Dis-Integrated

Because there is no identification of core integrated architecture data elements, there is no consistent workflow process ordering of framework product development. In a recent DoD enterprise architecture survey (Ring & Johnson, 2005), not having a consistent workflow process was highlighted as a major concern. It is precisely because one can start anywhere, that DoDAF architectures can become dis-integrated and inconsistent over time. For example, one could start with an OV-3, jump to the OV-2, and then develop an OV-5. However, because an OV-3 is made up of activities and nodes coming from an OV-2 and OV-5, one could define activities and nodes in an OV-3 that never appear in OV-2 and OV-5. Conversely, one could create activities and nodes on OV-2 and OV-5 that are never entered in an OV-3. This results in an architecture that is dis-integrated, out of sync, and not useful for any purpose. If the OV-2, 3, 5 are independently developed, then one must continuously manually ensure that they are always in sync and consistent to ensure an integrated architecture. A workflow procedure, associated with the capture of four core architecture elements, can be established to provide a consistent, repeatable, ordering of framework product development. A major benefit from defining a set of four core elements and this standard workflow procedure is that two exchange products, OV-3 and SV-6, can automatically be generated from their constituent core elements as defined in their respective framework products (OV-2, OV-5, SV-1, and SV-4). This eliminates any manual synchronization by architects and improves and accelerates the entire development process.

Supports Executable Architecture Development and Analysis

A majority of the current 26 DoDAF products capture only "static" information for their Operational and System views. Several products (OV-6 and SV-10) provide for "dynamic" views of operations. However, these products do not adequately address how to capture time dependencies and organizational resource (human and system) responsibilities. These dependencies and resource allocations are needed to analyze and assess operational and system dynamic "behavior" of how organizations and resources interact with each over time as part of DOTMLPF analysis. DoDAF architectures need to be able to capture sufficient details that will enable them to be transitioned and transformed from static to dynamic architectures.

Enables Linking ("Federating") Producing and Consuming Architectures

DoDAF does not provide for separate producing and consuming architectures to be linked and federated. This can be accomplished by (1) explicitly defining new "external" core architecture elements (i.e., NODES, FUNCTIONS, RESOURCES) that are outside the scope, "external," of one producing architecture but that are inside the scope, "internal," of a second consuming architecture and then (2) extending the exchange definitions (OV-3, SV-6) to include these producing and consuming external core elements.

Captures Sufficient Architectural Detail for Full DOTMLPF Analysis

DoDAF does not capture sufficient architectural detail needed for full DOTMLPF analysis. For example, in the framework products identified as making up an integrated architecture, OV-4 is missing. OV-4 is fundamental to providing architecture detail for organizations and people which are the "(O)rganization" and "(P)ersonnel" of DOTMLPF. In addition, there is no current way to define "(T)raining" and "(L)eadership" aspects. This can be accomplished by basing an architectural taxonomy on the six interrogatives which, in turn, can then be mapped to full range of DOTMLPF.

Summary of Current State

We must evolve and mature DoD architecting to address these issues and to meet new requirements and demands on future integrated architecture usage such as: JCIDS, capabilities-based planning processes with useful integrated architecture descriptions expressed in the full range of DOTMLPF architecture alternatives; systems acquisition and portfolio planning/ investment processes based on integrated architectures with an unambiguous way to compare architecture alternatives; and linking integrated architectures with enterprise systems engineering processes by providing information to support requirements development and analysis.

What is needed, then, is a small yet powerful set of DoD architecture description principles and concepts, as provided by ABM, that provides a semantically shared vocabulary for the DoD architecting community. Descriptive concepts can, in turn, serve as a formal foundation for development of the next-generation DoD architecture framework that will support interoperability between DoD architecting practices and also architecture-based analysis in support of DoD core processes.

INTEGRATED ARCHITECTURES

Before one can use architecture descriptions for any analysis, decision-making, and mission outcome purposes, one must first start with an architecture that is integrated, unambiguous, and consistent. There are two definitions of an integrated architecture. The first comes from DoDAF and is considered as a top down "product" perspective. The second is described by ABM here and is considered as a bottom up "data" perspective. For both definitions, integrated architectures facilitate integration and promote interoperability across family-of-systems and system-of-systems and compatibility among related mission area architectures.

From a top down "product" perspective, DoDAF defines a single architecture description to be an *integrated architecture* "when products and their constituent architecture data elements are developed such that architecture data elements defined in one view are the same (i.e., same names, definitions, and values) as architecture data elements referenced in another view." A subset of DoDAF products make up the foundation of an *integrated architecture* and consists of AV-1, AV-2, OV-2, OV-3, OV-5, SV-1, and TV-1 at a minimum (DoDAF, Vol I, p. 1-5). From a bottom up "data" perspective, ABM defines an integrated architecture description to be when *architecture data elements* are defined based on a methodology-independent, semantically complete model of the concepts used in understanding and describing integrated architectures.

Integrated architectures usually have associated with them a time frame, whether by specific years (e.g., 2005-2010) or by designations such as "as-is," "to-be," "transitional," "objective," "epoch," etc. In all cases, this reduces to either inventories of current capability ("as-is") or blueprints of future capability ("to-be"). Domain experts, program managers, and decision-makers need to be able to analyze these architectures to locate, identify, and resolve definitions, properties, facts,

constraints, inferences, and issues both within and across architectural boundaries that are redundant, conflicting, missing, and/or obsolete. The analysis must also be able to determine the effect and impact of change ("what if") when something is redefined, redeployed, deleted, moved, delayed, accelerated, or defunded. In most "as-is" architectures, details about architecture elements are fully known and architectures analysis can be readily accomplished.

The present DoDAF approach to developing *"to-be"* integrated architectures and their analysis does not fully enable them to be used for true system engineering purposes to discover future enterprise rules, patterns, practices, relationships, and system and organizational requirements. That is because not all architecture details are known resulting in architecture descriptions that are based on unknowns and abstract elements. However, with ABM and by examining aggregations and clusters of architecture elements and by performing gap analysis and assessments, new system and organizational requirements can be derived. This would support justifications for future funding decisions of new systems, their elements, components, and supporting operational organizations.

It is assumed that any architecture project begins with an effort to identify the architecture's intended purpose, its scope, and level of detail that follows the six-step process detailed in (DoDAF Vol. I, pp. 5-4).

ACTIVITY-BASED METHODOLOGY

ABM presents a holistic approach for architecture development (Ring, Nicholson, Thilenius, & Harris, 2005). It establishes a common means to express integrated architecture data consistent with intent of DoDAF, JCIDS, ITPM, and the Clinger-Cohen Act (CCA, 1996). ABM provides a rigorous, disciplined, and structured approach to integrated architecture development and analysis that is lacking today. It consists of a tool-independent methodology that enables fully integrated, unambiguous, and consistent DODAF views to be developed in supporting both "as-is" architectures and their analysis as well as "to-be" architecture and their analysis to include future gap-analysis.

The Zachman framework (Zachman, 1987) describes a structure for defining and capturing architecture descriptions. It is arranged as a matrix where the columns represent six logical interrogative abstractions or aspects—*WHAT (Product), HOW (Function), WHERE (Node), WHO (Resourse), WHEN (Event), WHY (Rule)*—and the rows represent unique viewpoint perspectives

or frames of reference (O'Rourke, Fishman, & Selkow, 2003). ABM *architecture descriptions* are based on this Zachman framework matrix with the six columns representing *architecture elements* and three *architecture view* row perspectives representing the three DoDAF views—OV, SV, and TSV. Grouping of *architecture elements* into the six interrogatives ensures consistency in their meaning and eliminates any possible conflicting and/or misinterpretation of their definitions. Figure 4 illustrates DoDAF with ABM based on this matrix.

ABM does not impact the DoDAF All View (AV) or Technical Standards View (TSV). However, the Operational View (OV) and System

Figure 4. DoDAF with ABM

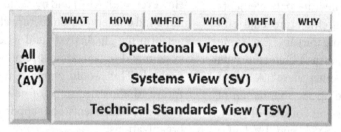

Figure 5. Five pillars of an integrated architecture

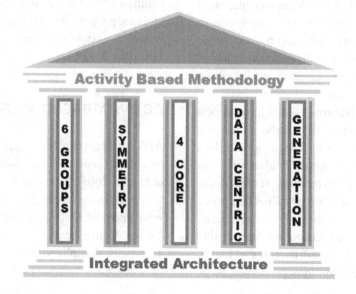

View (SV) are directly impacted. ABM uses a data centric approach that supports cross-product relationships based on an integrated symmetric set of architecture building block elements. These enable several architecture elements and architecture products to be automatically generated.

An integrated architecture, based on ABM, is built on a foundation of five pillars (Figure 5):

1. Separation of architecture elements into six interrogative groupings.
2. Symmetric alignment of architecture elements.
3. Four core architecture elements.
4. Data-centric architecture data model.
5. Generation of DoDAF elements and products.

Pillar 1: Separation of Architecture Elements into Six Interrogative Groupings

The development of ABM began with a fundament architecture principle that architectural elements should be grouped according to the six interrogatives. From this fundamental architecture principle, the three-way association between three of the column interrogatives, *HOW* at *WHERE* by *WHO*, was observed (Figure 6).

In the triple association, one can see in Figure 7 that the intersection of any two is the third.

Figure 8 shows how DoDAF associates its constituent architecture elements to each of the six interrogatives within the three DoDAF perspective views (*Operational, System, Technical*).

Pillar 2: Symmetric Alignment of Architecture Elements

The development of ABM led to a second observation that there are symmetrically aligned patterns of Operational and System *architecture elements* within each of the six interrogatives. By symmetric alignment, we mean that Operational and System *architecture elements* have similar meanings, associations/relationships, properties, and characteristics. For example, in the HOW aspect, *activities* within the Operational View are aligned with and correspond to *system functions* within the System View. The recognition of these DoDAF symmetric elements was a guiding principle in the development of ABM.

These symmetrically aligned elements are divided into three object classes: entities, relationships, and attributes. In following an E-R-A approach to architecture objects, entity objects are the objects about which architecture data is collected, Relationship objects are the associations between entity objects, and attribute objects identify characteristics of entity and relationship objects. This symmetry and alignment is shown in Figure 9.

Figure 6. Three-way associations of the six interrogatives

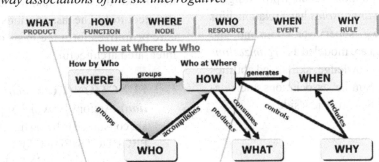

Figure 7. Intersections of HOW at WHERE by WHO

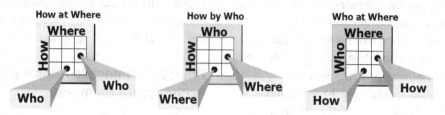

Figure 8. Mapping of DoDAF architecture elements to the six interrogatives

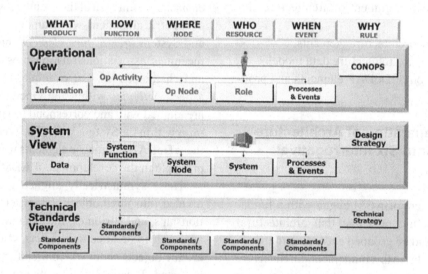

On the Operational View side, *concept of operations* (CONOPS), *information*, *activities*, *nodes*, *roles*, and *processes* represent the primary architecture objects. *Need lines* represent associations between *information*, *activities* and *node* entities with the *information exchange* providing the attributes of *need lines*. *Roles* have relationships with each other (e.g., supervisor, command, and coordinate), which are modeled as *organizations* and they possess knowledge, skills, and abilities (*KSA*) attributes. Similar associations and relations exist on the System View side.

Pillar 3: Four Core Architecture Elements

Four primary objects within each view are considered *core* (i.e., those building block primitives that make up the foundation of an integrated architecture). The associations between these core primitives form the basis of a data-centric integrated architecture.

1. **FUNCTION (HOW: *activity, system function*):** Actions by which input PRODUCTS are consumed in being transformed to output PRODUCTS. FUNCTIONS are usually decomposed to sub-FUNCTIONS. They carry

Figure 9. Symmetrically aligned architecture objects

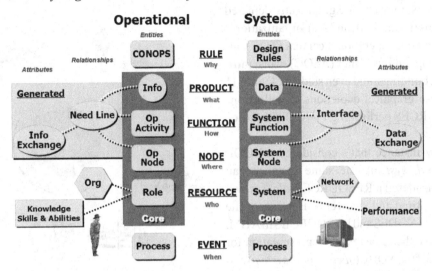

dynamic time and costs properties needed in an executable architecture.

2. **RESOURCE (WHO:** *role, system*): Means by which a FUNCTION is performed, processed, or executed. *Roles* are human resources, characterized by a set of knowledge, skills and abilities (*KSA*) assigned to humans and are analogous to job titles or job responsibilities. *Systems* are machine resources and are described in terms of their performance characteristics. *Roles* and *systems* can be structurally composed into organizations and networks. They each carry dynamic time and costs properties needed in an executable architecture.

3. **PRODUCT (WHAT:** *information, data*): Formalized representations of data subject to a transformation process. They are the inputs and outputs of FUNCTIONS. PRODUCTS can be decomposed into their component items so that, at higher levels of a FUNCTION model, an input/output can be considered as a "bundle" while at

the lower levels the input/outputs consists of the "unbundled" component items. For example, "weather" could be made up of "temperature" and "humidity" so that "weather" is produced/consumed at the higher FUNCTION levels but "temperature" and "humidity" are separate inputs and outputs at the lower FUNCTION levels. Bundled information is usually graphically depicted as "branchs/joins." PRODUCTS do not have time properties—their e*xchanges* do.

4. **NODE (WHERE:** *operational node, system node*): Logical or functional encapsulations (i.e., groupings or collections) of (1) RESOURCES (if known) performing FUNCTIONS and (2) FUNCTIONS alone when RESOURCES are unknown (see Figure 10). NODES are usually where RESOURCES are located in performing FUNCTIONS. NODES can be decomposed to sub-NODES. They carry no dynamic time properties but carry cost properties.

Since NODES are considered as encapsulations or collections, they may be graphically depicted as platforms (ground, air, and sea), organizations, facilities, tactical operational centers (TOC), air and space operations center (ASOC), vans, military units, buildings, and even soldiers. Figure 11 shows these graphical depictions of collections of RESOURCES performing FUNCTIONS (i.e., NODES).

For any instance that's considered a NODE (*operational, system*), the same instance can also be considered a RESOURCE (*role, system*) at the same time and vice versa. Because of the separation of NODES and RESOURCES in ABM, one can have the same textual representation for both—once for a NODE (*operational, system*) and once for a RESOURCE (*role, system*). Having the same textual representation for both NODE and RESOURCE has no impact because they separately exist. Note that a NODE could also have been considered an *organization* and an *organization* also considered as a NODE. Again, with the separation in ABM, one can have the same textual representation for both concepts in the same architecture. This separation eliminates any semantic overloading of the NODE definition.

Figure 10. NODES as collections of RESOURCES performing FUNCTIONS

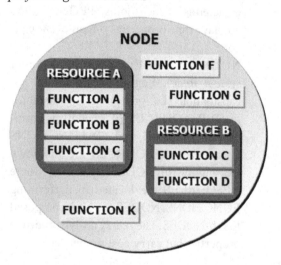

Figure 11. Graphical examples of nodes

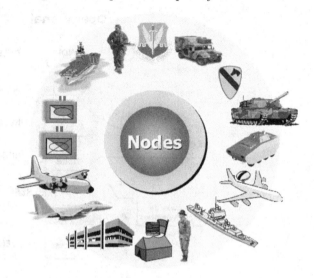

For example, lets say an architect views a military unit organization as a *role* and creates the "1-8 Armor Battalion" *role*. If in the same architecture, the same military unit organization is considered as a *node*, then the architect creates the "1-8 Armor Battalion" *node*. Because of the separation of the two *node* and *role* definitions in ABM, *information exchanges* and *need lines* will be consistent. That is, some *activity* is performed by the "1-8 Armor Battalion" *role* at the "1-8 Armor Battalion" *node*. In addition, when the OV-2 node diagram is viewed, the architecture will see the "1-8 Armor Battalion" as a *node* item which is entirely consistent with the architect's view of the architecture. Similarly, when the OV-4 organization diagram is viewed, the architect will see the "1-8 Armor Battalion" as a *role* item—again entirely consistent with architect's view of the architecture.

In all cases, the consistency of the three-way association between NODE, FUNCTION, and RESOURCE is always maintained allowing complete flexibility in creating architectures. The benefit to the architect is that the architecture diagrams and models are consistent with

Figure 12. Three-way associations of core architecture objects

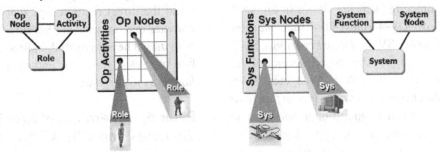

Figure 13. Visualization of three-way associations

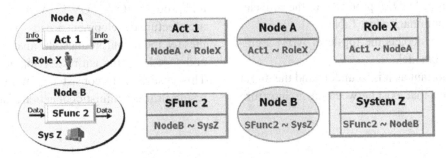

the manner in which they are defined, viewed, and intended.

The core elements relate to each other such that:

- Each (*activity, system function*) that produces and consumes (*information, data*) is performed at an (*operational node, system node*) by a (*role, system*)

- Each (*operational node, system node*) contains a (*role, system*) that performs an (*activity, system function*) that produces and consumes (*information, data*)

- Each (*role, system*) in an (*operational node, system node*) performs an (*activity, system function*) that produces and consumes (*information, data*)

- (*information, data*) is produced from and consumed by an (*activity, system function*)

performed by (*role, system*) at a (*operational node, system node*)

This is the foundation for the dual set of three-way relationships as shown in Figure 12. The intersection of the association between an a*ctivity* and a *node* is a *role* and, likewise, the intersection of the association between a *system function* and a *system node* is a *system*.

Figure 13 shows how the three-way associations can be visualized by having each FUNCTION, NODE, and RESOURCE core element graphic object display its respective associations with the other two core elements.

Pillar 4: Data-Centric Architecture Data Model

Figure 14 shows how the core architecture elements are related and their source DoDAF products. Because of the symmetrically aligned set of architecture elements shown in Figure 9, ABM added—OV-4 (*roles*), OV-7 (*information*), SV-2 (*Networks*), SV-4 (*system Functions*), SV-5, and SV-11 (*Data*)—to the original seven DoDAF integrated product set (AV-1, AV-2, etc.). SV-5, in particular, maps *activities* to *system functions* enabling integrated Operational and System views within a single architecture. The four core elements come together to form *information exchanges* and *system data exchanges* from which *need lines* and *interfaces* are extracted.

The source DoDAF products for the core elements are summarized in Table 4.

Figure 15 depicts the top-level ABM architecture data model.

As important as it is to understand the direct relationships that exist between the architecture data elements, it is equally important to understand the direct relationships that do not exist. For example, *systems* are not directly related to *activities*. They are related, indirectly (via SV-5), first to *system functions* and then from *system functions* to *activities*.

Pillar 5: Generation of Architecture Elements and DODAF Products

ABM introduces generation of several architecture elements (*exchanges, need lines,* and *interfaces*) and products (OV-2, OV-3, SV-1, SV-6) into the architecture development process. Generation of these elements and products eliminates user inputs and speeds up the entire development process. This ensures data consistency and quality and results in a deterministic collection of architecture

Figure 14. Core architecture element associations

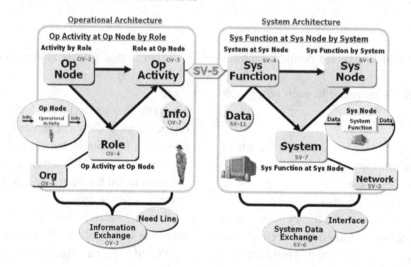

Table 4. Core architecture element source products

CORE	SOURCE OV	SOURCE SV
Function	OV-5 *activities*	SV-4 *system function*
Product	OV-7 *information*	SV-11 *data*
Node	OV-2 *operational node*	SV-1 *system node*
Resource	OV-4 *role*	SV-1 *system*

Figure 15. Top level ABM architecture data model

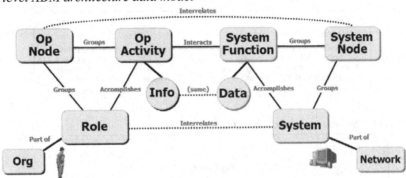

artifacts that can be repeatedly regenerated as the architecture evolves and matures.

To enable valid generation of these elements and products, ABM introduces *external* FUNC-TIONS as high level context FUNCTIONS in the FUNCTION model. They are perfomed by *external RESOURCES* at *external NODES* in producing and consuming PRODUCTS (*information, data*) to/from the highest level context FUNCTION. E*xternal FUNCTIONS, External RESOURCES, and External NODES* are all considered outside the scope of the context FUNCTION model. They provide producing and consuming ending FUNCTIONS when generating *operational/ system exchanges* between themselves and leaf FUNCTIONS.

Figure 16 shows an Operational View example where two *external activities* are each associated with their own *external nodes* and *external roles* in providing the source of an input and the destination of an output into and out of the context *activity*. Defining *external* (producing and consuming) elements enables ABM-based integrated architectures to be federated together. This is because the consuming *external* elements of one architecture are the producing *external* elements of a second "federated" architecture. Conversely, the producing *external* elements of one architecuere are the consuming *external* elements of a second "federated" architecture.

Need lines (Operational) and *interfaces* (System) document the requirement to exchange (1) PRODUCTS between NODES and (2) PROD-UCTS between RESOURCES. *Exchanges* identify *who* exchanges *what* products, with *whom*, *why* the information is necessary, and *how* the information exchange must occur.

Exchanges and their *need lines/interfaces* are generated from their four producing and consuming core elements—leaf FUNCTIONS (including *external activities*), their input and output PRODUCTS (*information, data*), and their associations to NODES (including *external nodes*) and to RESOURCES (including external *roles and systems*). FUNCTION models are decomposed down to the appropriate level for the purposes of the architecture. Leaf FUNCTIONS are at the lowest decomposition level. Usually, this would be to the level where a FUNCTION is capable of being (i) associated with a single NODE and/or (ii) assigned to an individual RESOURCE, and/or (iii) has a single input or single output PRODUCT. Usually leaf FUNCTIONS are some combination of these three and subject to judgment calls by the architect.

Figure 17 graphically illustrates how NODE *need lines/interfaces* (between two NODES) contain collections of RESOURCE *need lines/ interfaces* (between two RESOURCES within each NODE) which, in turn, contain the entire

Figure 16. Context activity model with two external activities

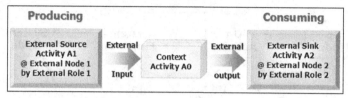

Figure 17. Need lines/interfaces and exchanges

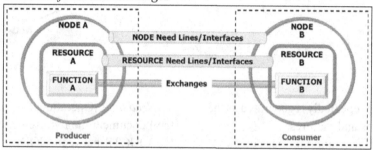

collection of the individual *exchanges* (between two functions performed by the two RESOURCES at the two NODES).

Need lines/interfaces can be alternatively be visualized (Figure 18) where a single NODE *need line/interface* pipeline consists of one or more RESOURCE *need line/interface* pipelines each consisting of one or more exchanges.

OV-3 *information exchanges* and OV-2 *need lines* are generated from their four producing and consuming core elements—leaf *activities*, their *information* inputs and outputs, and their associations to *nodes* and to *roles* as shown in Figure 19.

Figure 18. Need line/interface collections

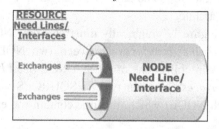

Likewise, the SV-6 *system data exchanges* and SV-1 *interfaces* are generated from their four producing and consuming core elements—leaf *system functions*, their *data* inputs and outputs, and their associations to *system nodes* and to *systems* as show in Figure 20.

Information exchanges are always generated between producing and consuming leaf *activities* and their associated *op nodes*. However, valid and consistent *need lines* on OV-2 diagrams are only obtained when *information exchanges* are formed from leaf *activities* at different *nodes*. Likewise, *system data exchanges* are always generated between producing and consuming leaf *system functions* and their associated *system nodes*. However, valid and consistent *interfaces* on SV-1 diagrams are only obtained when *system data exchanges* are formed from leaf *system functions* at different *system nodes*.

While *exchanges* can be generated, their DoDAF properties (transport times, security classification, etc.) can not be automatically filled in and, therefore, must be defined manually. This makes *exchanges* persistent architecture data in

Figure 19. Operational Exchanges and need lines

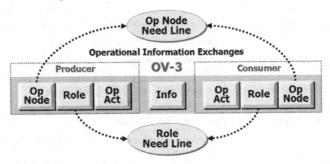

Figure 20. System Exchanges and interfaces

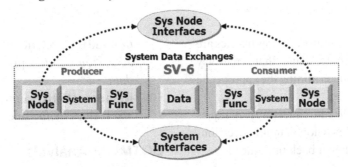

that, once generated and their properties defined, they should not be deleted because their DoDAF property attributes will be lost. *Need lines* and *interfaces*, on the other hand, carry no properties and can be deleted and regenerated again as the (*activity, system function*) model grows and contracts with additional (or subtractive) (*activities, system functions*), (*information, data*) inputs/outputs, *nodes*, and (*roles, systems*).

In ABM, because *need lines* and *interfaces* have been identified from the generation of *exchanges*, both OV-2 and SV-1 diagrams can be graphically populated with *nodes* and their corresponding *need lines* and *interfaces*. In fact, as many individual node-centric OV-2 and SV-1 diagrams can be graphically populated as there are *operational* and *system nodes*. This makes OV-2 and SV-1 expendable because they can always be repopulated with *nodes* and (*need lines, interfaces*) and their associated *exchanges* as the architecture model changes and matures.

The OV-3 product is, essentially, a spreadsheet document since it consists of the entire collection of *information exchanges* (and their properties) within an architecture model. Likewise, SV-6 product is a spreadsheet document since it consists of the entire collection of *system data exchanges* and their properties.

ANALYSIS (STATIC)

From the top level ABM architecture data model in Figure 15, it can be seen that the basic triple association is very simple and elegant yet very powerful. From this model, one can obtain a more detailed and complete analysis of complex architectures. In fact, one could say that all the

Table 5. DOTMLPF analysis

Doctrine	Activities, roles, nodes	Examine tactics, techniques, and procedures
Organization	Org units	Examine organizational structure
Training	Activities, roles, systems	Train personnel on their activities and any systems they use in performing those activities
Material	System functions, systems, system nodes	Examine materiel solutions—a new system
Leadership	Org units, roles, systems	Examine leadership issues
Personnel	Roles	Examine personnel solutions—new personnel or personnel with better qualifications
Facilities	Operational nodes, system nodes	Examine fixing, building, or modifying facilities

answers to static architecture analysis queries are already in the architecture data—that is the easy part. The hard part is determining the appropriate analysis queries.

Four unique but related architecture techniques support the eventual mission outcome decision-making process as shown back in Figure 1.

- Core integrated architecture analysis.
- DOTMLPF analysis.
- Gap analysis of "to-be" architectures.
- Architect data mining of *exchanges*.

Core Integrated Architecture Analysis

By examining different sets of relationships between and among the four core architect elements, various types of integrated architecture analyses can be obtained:

- **Functional (HOW) analysis:** *Activities* and their related *system functions*.
- **Nodal (WHERE) analysis:** *Activities* and their *op nodes* and their relationships to *system functions* and their *system nodes*.
- **Product (WHAT) analysis:** *Activities* at *op nodes* producing/consuming *informa-*

tion and their relations to *system functions* at *system nodes* producing/consuming *data*.

- **Resource (WHO) analysis:** *Roles, systems* and their *activities* and *system functions*.

DOTMLPF Analysis

DOTMLPF analysis leads to better definitions of warfighting capabilities by being able to anticipate effects and assess impact of change on domains and by examining usage (who/what affects something) and references (who/what is affected by something). DOTMLPF domains map to ABM architecture element analysis as shown in Table 5.

Gap Analysis of *"To-Be"* Architectures

For *"to-be"* architectures, where not all elements are known, gap-analysis can discover those unknowns. Usually, in *"as-is"* and *"to-be"* architectures, both *activities* (*system functions*) and *nodes* (*operational* and *system*) are usually known. Also, in *"as-is"* architectures, *roles* (*systems*) are usually known. However, for *"to-be"* architectures, in most cases *roles* (*systems*) may or may not be known. Figure 21 shows how gap-analysis of *"to-be"* architectures reveals:

- **Orphaned activities:** *Activities* at *nodes* without *roles*.
- **Orphaned systems:** *System functions* at *system nodes* without *systems*.

By clustering and aggregating these orphaned elements and by performing gap analysis and assessments, new system and organizational requirements can be derived. This would support justifications for future funding decisions of new systems, components, and supporting operational organizations.

ARCHITECTURE DATA MINING ANALYSIS OF EXCHANGES

Mining architecture data reveals and helps discover hidden patterns, rules, practices, gaps, overlaps, redundancies, relationships, and require-

ments on how an enterprise operates. OV-3, SV-6 *exchanges* together with SV-5, as show in Figure 22, identify connections between producers and consumers at the functional leaf level.

This is essential for "what if" and "if what" impact assessments between what is required and what is delivered. For example, one could assess the impact of losing a *system* or a *system node* on operations (*activities, nodes, roles*, etc). In addition, one could obtain a set of hidden requirements for an *operational node* and a *role* where such requirements would be derived from the indirect relationship between *nodes* and *roles* to *systems, system nodes*, and to *system functions*.

DYNAMIC ANALYSIS AND TRANSITION TO EXECUTABLE ARCHITECTURES

Static operational models only show that operational *activities* "must be capable of" producing and consuming *information*. They do not provide

Figure 21. "To-be" gap analysis

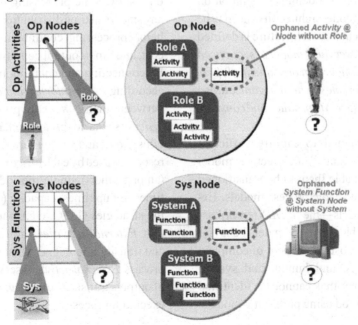

Figure 22. Architecture data mining with OV-3/SV-6 exchanges

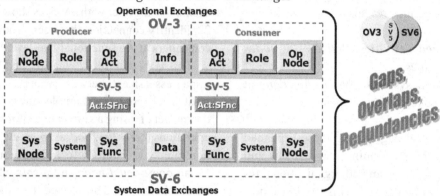

details on how or under what input/output conditions *PRODUCT (information, data)* is produced/consumed. They also do not explicitly identify, for each *activity*, the timing details or the number (capacity) of *RESOURCES (roles, systems)* needed or their ordering for the case when multiple *roles* perform the same *activity* (who operates on the first input, who operates on the second, etc).

To appropriately assess measures of performance and effectiveness in an operational environment, "dynamic" modeling and simulation executable process model architectures need to be developed. An executable architecture is defined here as a *dynamic (over time) model of sequenced processes/events (concurrent or sequential) performed at a node by roles (within organizations) using resources (systems) to produce and consume information (data)*.

ABM was designed to capture sufficient representations of "static" architecture model descriptions that enable them to be transitioned into "dynamic" executable process models. Executable process models—the *"WHEN (event)"* aspect analysis—enables time-dependent behavior analysis and dollar cost assessment of complex, dynamic operations, and human and system resource interactions that cannot be identified or properly understood using pure static models.

Dynamic executable process models go beyond "must be capable of" and define precisely under what conditions information and data is actually produced/consumed and the exact number and ordering of *roles*. It can be used to show how to transform and evolve organizations, processes, and modes of operation to adapt to new roles, relationships, technologies, and threats.

The transition is accomplished by starting with the extracted set of leaf *activities* to which (among others) dynamic processing time (duration) and any statistical time distribution, average wait time before processing, continuation strategy, activity cost, and input/output conditions are all defined. By connecting and chaining these leaf *activities* according to the *information exchanges* defined between them, we can produce "candidate" *process* scenario thread models of sequenced actions. *Roles* and *systems* are the human/machine resources used by each *process* and they may have (among others) single/periodic (un)availability times, set up times, capacity (quantity), processing strategies (FIFO, etc.), and hourly and fixed cost. *External activities* serve as sources of inputs and transition to *triggers* that start the execution process. *External activities* serving as destinations of outputs transition to *outputs* that terminate the execution process.

Executable Architecture Methodology for Analysis (EAMA)

In a MITRE research effort, a federation of executable architecture simulations were linked, within the context of a mission thread, to dynamically access and measure process performance and force effectiveness, organizational work efforts, resource allocation, communication capability, and ultimately, mission success (Pawlowski, Barr, & Ring, 2004). The federation consisted of a three-way link (via HLA) between an executable operational architecture model of processes and organizations, an executable network and communications model of exchanges and information flow, and a combat simulation model that provided the operational context and warfighting environment for the mission thread.

Lockheed-Martin used the EAMA approach in building their Federated Executable Architecture Technology (FEAT) demonstration for the Air Force Agency for Modeling and Simulation (AFAMS) (Harrison, Benjamin, Elliot, Hutt, & Kern, 2005). FEAT is an enabling technology that supplies architecture verification and optimization, multi-resolution distributed simulation, and hybrid simulation of architected scenarios.

Portfolio Investment Analysis

At present, architecture-based portfolio investment decisions are not prevalent in the DoD. Another MITRE research effort showed that linking integrated and executable architectures with portfolio investment analysis tools and techniques provides a robust analytical foundation for capability and architecture-based investment decisions that fully supports critical DoD transformation goals, guidelines, and policies (Ring, Lamar, Heim, & Goyette 2005). A portfolio investment analysis helps decision-makers select the "best" combination (or portfolio) of investments from a set of potential investment options to achieve mission-level objectives and outcomes in a cost-effective manner.

WORKFLOW STEPS TO AN INTEGRATED ARCHITECTURE: THE *ART OF ARCHITECTURE*

ABM architecture development workflow consists of seven steps—three modeling steps, one association step, and three automated steps. This ensures a consistent ordering of framework product development associated with the four core architecture elements.

The first step in the ABM workflow creates a FUNCTION model together with a PRODUCT model for the two of the core architecture objects. The next step creates the third core object, NODES, and the fourth, RESOURCES. At this point, the core objects have been defined and they can be associated together. ABM considers these first four workflow steps the *Art of Architecture* (i.e., understanding and identifying the core architecture objects and how they are related). If one considers the FUNCTION, RESOURCE, NODE, and PRODUCT models as an artists' canvas and the core architecture elements as a set of paints and paintbrushes, then an architect developing an architecture is similar to an artist creating a masterpiece painting.

From this point on, there is sufficient architecture data for automation to take over—generating *exchanges (information, system data)* and their related *need lines* and *interfaces*. The NODE products, OV-2 and SV-1, can now be graphically completed by auto-connecting each *node* pair with their corresponding *need lines* and *interfaces*. The various DoDAF *exchange* properties can now be defined. *Exchanges,* together with their property values, become the OV-3/ SV-6 product. ABM considers the analysis of architectures (as discussed in earlier in the chapter) as the *science of architecture*. Table 6 and Figure 23 summarize the ABM workflow steps.

Workflow Steps to an Integrated Operational Architecture

The Operational View workflow steps follow the basic ABM workflow steps.

Table 7 and Figure 24 illustrates these steps. An OV-5 activity model should consist of a well-formed, balanced, and consistent set of *activities*, their sub-*activities, external (activities, roles, and nodes)* and their various inputs and outputs.

Workflow Steps to an Integrated System Architecture

The System View workflow adds two more steps to the workflow for SV-3 and SV-5. Figure 25 and Table 8 illustrates these steps. Like an OV-5 activity model, an SV-4 *system function* model should consist of a well formed, balanced, and consistent set of *system functions*, their sub-*system function*, *external (system functions, system nodes,* and *systems)* and their various inputs and outputs.

Table 6. AMB workflow steps and Summary of integrated product set

	Steps	OV	SV
Model	1a) Create FUNCTION Model	*Activities - OV-5*	*System Function – SV-4*
	1b) Create PRODUCT Model	*Information – OV-7*	*Data – SV-11*
	2) Create NODES	*Operational Node – OV-2*	*System Node – SV-1*
	3) Create RESOURCES	*Role - OV-4*	*System – SV-1*
Associate	4) Associate FUNCTIONS with NODES with RESOURCES	1) *Activities* with *Op Nodes* with *Roles*	1) *System Functions* with *System Nodes* with *Systems* 2) *Activities* with *System Functions – SV-5*
Automate	5) Generate *EXCHANGES* and fill in properties 6) Complete NODE products – OV2, SV-1, with *Need Lines* and *Interfaces* 7) Generate *EXCHANGE Products – OV3/SV6*	1) Generate *Information Exchanges and Need Lines* 2) Complete OV-2 with *Need Lines* 3) Generate OV3	1) Generate *System Data Exchanges* 2) Complete SV-1 with *Interfaces* 3) Generate SV-3 *Systems-Systems Matrix* 4) Generate SV-6

Figure 23. ABM workflow

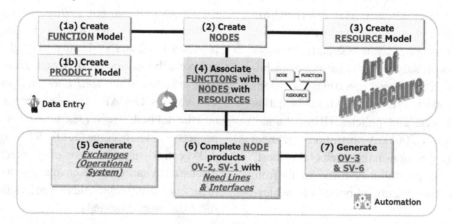

COMPARING ABM WITH IDEF0

ABM uses some of the IDEF0 (FIPS 183, 1994) modeling conventions (e.g., parent/child activity decomposition hierarchy) but does not use others (mechanisms and controls). This is because some IDEF0 conventions are incompatible with building consistent DODAF data-centric integrated architectures (e.g., mechanisms can be systems) and other conventions (e.g., outputs as controls, etc.) are incompatible with generating *exchanges*. Building integrated architectures and generating *exchanges* are more important and take precedence over adherence to strict IDEF0 modeling conventions and rules.

For example, ABM does not use mechanism or control arrows per se with *activities*. For mechanisms, a different approach was taken based on the three-way association between FUNCTIONS, NODES, and RESOURCES. Because of the separation of RESOURCES into *roles* and *system, systems* can only be only indirectly associated with *activities* though SV-5. That is, *systems* are associated with *system functions*, which in turn, are associated with *activities* via SV-5. This is incompatible with the IDEF0 definition of a mechanism of an *activity* as being a *system*.

For controls, a different approach was taken by defining an association between *activities* (*system functions*) and *standards. Standards* (from the DoDAF Technical Standards View) take the

Table 7. Operational View workflow steps

	1a. Create OV-5 *activity* model. 1b. Create OV-7 *information* model. 2. Create OV-2 *nodes*. 3. Create OV-4 *roles* and *organizational units*.
	4. Associate *activities* with *nodes* with *roles*.
	5. Generate *information exchanges* and fill in properties. 6. Complete OV2 with *need lines*. 7. Generate OV3 operational information exchange matrix.

Figure 24. Operational workflow

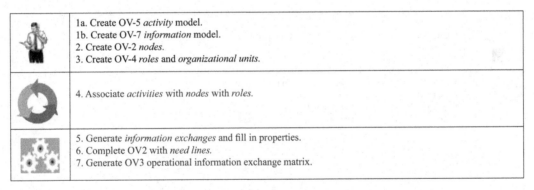

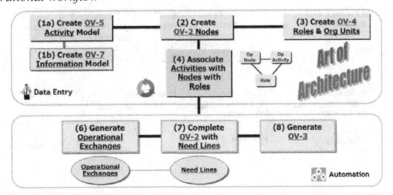

place of controls and can be associated with both *activities* and *system functions*. Figure 26 shows an example of this 2-way association. Again, consistency of building integrated architectures and generating *exchanges* is more important and takes precedence over adherence to strict IDEF0 modeling rules.

ABM SYNTAX RULES

ABM syntax rules ensure (i) accurate generation of *exchanges* between any two functions (*activities, system functions*) and (ii) consistency in node and resource models.

- **Rule #1:** FUNCTION models must include at least two *external* FUNCTIONS (*activities, system functions*).

Table 8. System View workflow steps

	1a. Create SV-4 *system function* model. 1b. Create SV-11 *data* model. 2. Create SV-1 *system nodes*. 3. Create SV-1 *systems*.
	4. Associate *system function* with *system nodes* with *systems*.
	5. Create SV-5--associate *system function* with *activities*
	6. Generate *system data exchanges* and fill in properties. 7. Complete SV-1 with *interfaces*. 8. Generate SV-3 systems-systems matrix product. 9. Generate SV-6 systems data exchange matrix product.

Figure 25. System view workflow

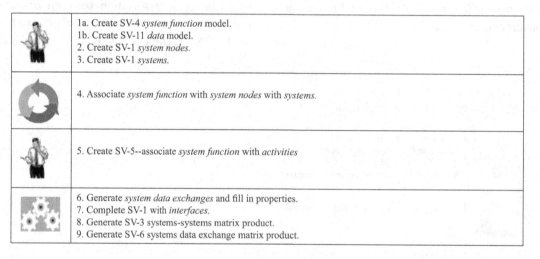

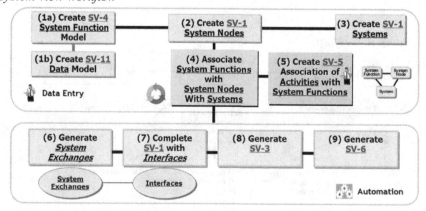

- **Rule #2:** Leaf FUNCTIONS (*activities, system functions*) must have at least one input and at least one output (different from each other) from/to either another FUNCTION (*activity, system function*) or an *external* FUNCTION (*activity, system function*).

- **Rule #3:** (*Need lines, interfaces*) within the same NODE (*operational, system*) or RESOURCE (*role, system*): one must first decompose the NODE or RESOURCE into sub-NODES and/or sub-RESOURCES and then reassocciate the appropriate FUNCTIONS (*activities, system Functions*) to the appropriate sub-NODES and or sub-RESOURCES.

Figure 26. Activity to standard associations

	STD 01	STD-02
Act A	X	
Act B		X

SUMMARY AND CONCLUSION

This chapter presented the activity-based methodology, a rigorous, disciplined, and structured approach to the *Art and Science of architectures*. A set of architecture requirements showed how *actionable information* can be produced from *actionable architectures* that supports a set of core organizational processes. Five pillars of ABM were defined as the foundation of integrated architectures with the fundamental principle that architectural elements should be grouped according to the six interrogatives. The four core architecture elements, how they are symmetrically aligned, and related together in a data-centric architecture description model were explained. How ABM delivers significant architecture development productivity and quality gains was shown. Numerous static and dynamic analysis techniques and strategies were presented to show the value of integrated architectures to decision makers and mission outcomes. Workflow steps for creating integrated architecture were detailed.

Architectures are not just paper models to be hung on walls and admired. They are living electronic documents evolving and maturing over

Figure 27. Decision-making roadmap

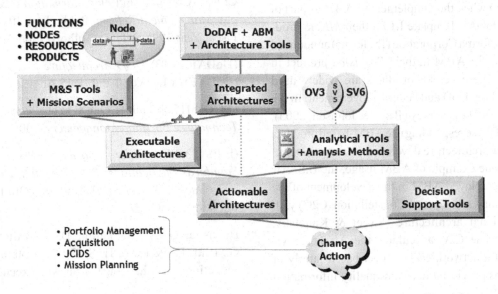

time that, through various analysis and assessment techniques, provide real value to an organization, to an enterprise and, ultimately, to a decision maker and mission outcomes and objectives.

In conclusion, the roadmap in Figure 27 validates the original premise from Figure 1. Architecture development guidance combined with compliant architecture tools and the activity-based methodology makes possible integrated architectures. Integrated architectures combined with simulation tools and scenarios render executable architectures. Integrated architectures, executable architectures, analytical tools, and methods render quantitative actionable architectures, which, in turns supports such decision-making processes as portfolio management, acquisition, JCIDS, and mission planning in support of mission outcomes.

AVAILABILITY OF ABM

ABM is in the public domain and is commercially available. Three major enterprise architecture technology companies have implemented ABM. Telelogic Corporation (Telelogic) has supported ABM in their *System Architect* product since 2004. This was followed in 2005 by Troux Technologies (Troux) when they implemented ABM as part of their DoDAF Template 1.1 for their *METIS* product. Proforma Corporation (Proforma) announced support for ABM in their *ProVision* product in 2006. These vendor products are widely used throughout DoD and Federal Government. In the recent DoD EA survey (Ring, & Johnson, 2005), 25% of those responding use ABM-based products in their architecture development environment.

In one example of ABM usage, the U.S. Air Force employed ABM in the development of the Command and Control Constellation (C2C) v2.0 operational architecture (Sweet & Kanefsky, 2004). The C2C articulates the Air Force vision of a network-centric, peer-based family of systems providing decision-quality information

to warfighters. The C2C architecture was the best true OV-5 representation of Constellation processes and was widely distributed to the C2 community. The architecture was published as part of the U.S. Air Force's Warfighting enterprise architecture (AF EA, 2005).

ACKNOWLEDGMENTS

The authors would like to acknowledge the United States Air Force Deputy Chief of Staff Office, Warfighting Integration (AF/XI), and United States Air Force Chief Architect's Office (AF CIO/A) for their support in the development of ABM.

The authors would also like to acknowledge the effort of Stanley Harris (of Lockheed-Martin Corporation) for his guidance, assistance, and contributions that made the activity-based methodology possible.

REFERENCES

C4ISR Architecture Framework, v2.0 (1997). December 18.

Clinger-Cohen Act of 1996: *Information Technology Management Reform*, Public Law 104-106, Fiscal Year 1996 Defense Authorization Act.

(DoDAF, 2003) *DOD Architecture Framework (DoDAF)*, V1.0, Vol. I and II, 15 August 2003

(DODI 8115.bb, 2006) DODI 8115.bb, *Information Technology Portfolio Management*, 2006

(FIPS 183, 1994) *Federal information Processing Standards Publications 183, Integration Definition Function Modeling* (IDEF0), June 30, 1994. www.idef.com

Harrison, G. A., Benjamin, D. C., Elliot, L. G., Hutt, R., & Kern, H. S. (2005, September). Modeling and enhancing C4ISR with executable architectures. *The 2005 Fall Simulation Interoperability Workshop*, sponsored by Simulation Interoperability Standards Organization, Orlando, FL (pp. 18-23).

(JCIDS, 2005) *Joint Capabilities Integration And Development system* (JCIDS), CJCSI 3170.01, 11 May 2005

Nicholson, D., Mercer, B., & Ang, H. (2005). Addressing conceptual deficiencies in DoDAF through an architecture specification model—ASM. In *Proceedings of Conference on Defense Transformation and Network-Centric Systems* (Vol. 5820), SPIE, Orlando, FL.

O'Rourke, C., Fishman, N., & Selkow, W. (2003). *Enterprise architecture using the Zachman framework*. Thomson Course Technology Publishing.

Pawlowski, T., Barr, P., & Ring, S. J. (2004). *Applying executable architectures to support dynamic analysis of C2 systems, #113, 2004*. Command and Control Research and Technology Symposium, San Diego, CA.

(Proforma) *Proforma Corporation*, http://www.proformacorp.com/

Ring, S. J., & Johnson, M. (2005). *State of DoD Architecting*. Command Information Superiority Architectures (CISA) Worldwide Conference, Omaha, NE, December 1, 2005

Ring, S. J., Lamar, B., Heim, J., & Goyette, E., (2005). *Integrated architecture-based portfolio investment strategies*. The 10th International Command and Control Research and Technology (ICCRTS) Symposium, McLean, VA.

Ring, S. J., Nicholson, D., Thilenius, J., & Harris, S., (2005), *An activity-based methodology for development and analysis of integrated DoD architectures*. 2004 Command and Control Research and Technology Symposium, San Diego, CA.

Sweet, N., & Kanefsky, S. (2004). *The C2 constellation: A US Air Force network centric warfare program network centric applications and C4ISR architecture*. 2004 Command and Control Research and Technology Symposium, San Diego, CA.

Telelogic Corporation. www.telelogic.com

Troux Technologies, www.troux.com

U.S. Air Force Chief Architect's Office (2005, May 31). *United States Air Force Enterprise Architecture*, CD-ROM.

Zachman, J. A. (1987), A framework for information systems architecture. *IBM System Journal, 26*(3). Retrieved from www.zifa.com

Chapter VI
Business Process Modeling as a Blueprint for Enterprise Architecture

Joseph Barjis
Georgia Southern University, USA

Isaac Barjis
City University of New York, USA

ABSTRACT

For a successful study, design and development of the enterprise architecture, a thorough insight into the essence of the work and operation of an enterprise, is a crucial factor. As the well-known Zachman and other modern frameworks illustrate, enterprise processes and process modeling are one of the fundamental components of enterprise architecture for providing such an insight. Like building construction in which construction drawings or blueprints play crucial roles, enterprise process models are critical in developing enterprise architecture. Moreover, one may argue that the role of business process modeling in enterprise architecture is similar to the floor plan that defines the boundaries of a building to be constructed. Therefore, a suitable enterprise process modeling approach that could capture the essential operations and reflect the cross-enterprise (cross-departmental) processes is a needed component to complement enterprise architecture. In this chapter, authors study, discuss, and review the practical role of enterprise process modeling in enterprise architecture using a real life organization-based case study. Authors introduce a modeling methodology that captures essential activities not only within a process but also from the enterprise perspective where cross departmental or enterprise processes are represented.

INTRODUCTION

For developing business goals-oriented enterprise architecture, system designers need to seriously focus on enterprise process perspective in such a task. This stand will not only allow organizations to achieve their business goals, but also enable them to better reconcile business and IT that consumes millions of dollars invested into the enterprise IT infrastructure. In fact, enterprise architecture provides a high-level description and view of the primary resources of any enterprise (Anaya & Ortiz 2005). These primary resources include users (users), processes (business processes), and technology (hardware and software). However, the process or business process component of enterprise architecture represents the most central and fundamental, because it connects the other two resources (users and technology). Poor definition of business processes in an enterprise architecture leads to a number of problems such as "business and IT gap."

A number of tools, techniques, and methodologies are developed to support enterprise business process modeling that could ensure a well-developed enterprise architecture that guarantees achievement of business goals. According to Dalal, Kamath, Kolarik, and Sivaraman (2004), among multiple tools are data flow diagrams (DFDs), integration definition for function modeling (IDEF0), and activity diagrams in the unified modeling language that all have their roots in process modeling for software development. Similarly, a number of methodologies for enterprise business process modeling were developed, each taking a different philosophical stand such as organizational semiotics by Stamper (1988, 1997) and DEMO (Design & Engineering Methodology for Organizations) methodology by Dietz (2006). In this chapter, we use the language action perspective paradigm supported by a rigorous modeling technique based on Petri nets. The methodology is illustrated on a case study conducted in a small enterprise. Petri nets have been tested and used in enterprise process modeling and workflow management by many authors (van der Aalst & van Hee, 2002; Deiters, 1998; Jensen, 1997a, 1997b); however, in this chapter we discuss application of Petri nets based on the language action perspective. The main motive on using and adopting Petri nets in enterprise business process

modeling is their capability to model and analyze concurrency, choice, asynchronous completion, as well as their ability to visualize and simulate the modeled process. The type of Petri net introduced in this chapter is based on the language action perspective, or more precisely, on the transaction concept introduced in Dietz (1999).

The transaction concept provides a transparent insight into the essence of enterprise processing irrespective of its realization or technical aspects. The concept is based on the notion that an enterprise is a network of business transactions that are exchanged daily while carrying out the mission of the enterprise and interacting with the environment (customers, partners).

The remainder of this chapter provides an introduction to Petri nets, the transaction concept, and its underlying paradigm—language action perspective. The proposed methodology is illustrated on a case study conducted in a small enterprise. For those readers not familiar with the language action perspective, the background section contains a brief overview of this framework.

Business Architecture

The business architecture component (domain, level, or subset) of the enterprise architecture (EA) framework represents an essential component and, therefore, in all different EA Frameworks it is given an important emphasis. In the well-known Zachman framework for enterprise architecture, business architecture is identified as "business model." In the open group architecture framework (TOGAF), which provides a comprehensive approach to the planning, design, implementation, and governance of enterprise information architecture, business architecture is called "business." Within the TOGAF, there are four types of architecture that are commonly accepted as subsets of an overall enterprise architecture. These subsets or components are:

- A "business (or business process) architecture" that in particular defines key business processes.
- An "applications architecture" that provides a blueprint for the individual application systems to be deployed, their interactions, and their relationships to the core business processes of the organization.
- A "data architecture" that describes the structure of an organization's logical and physical data assets and data management resources.
- A "technology architecture" that describes the software infrastructure intended to support the deployment of core, mission-critical applications. This type of software is sometimes referred to as "middleware."

The third framework that is noteworthy is the one derived from a practical project and a real life system within the U.S. National Institutes of Health (NIH). National Institutes of Health is the part of the U.S. Department of Health and Human Services that serves as a primary Federal agency for conducting and supporting medical research. The enterprise architecture framework of NIH, which is based on the Federal enterprise architecture, consists of three distinct architecture areas: business architecture, information architecture, and technology architecture.

The intention of this brief introduction of a few EA frameworks, which resulted from research studies as well as specific projects, is to highlight the critical and strategic place of business architecture within the EA framework. Furthermore, it is important to stress the importance of business process, the need for holistic approach in business process, and detailed level analysis of business process. Since business processes constitute the foundation in a business architecture (Herman, 2001), in this chapter the main emphasis is put on business processes and the use of modeling for process elicitation. Also, it should be noted that in order to develop enterprise architecture, busi-

ness process requires a more holistic (integrated) approach rather then an isolated approach (Lopez & Genovese, 2004; Taft, 1996). In developing realistic and accurate enterprise architecture, the modeled business process should be capable of dealing with a very detailed level of analysis. In this respect, McDavid (1999) refers to an old saying "the devil is in the details." He suggests that for a useful architectural approach, analysts need to be able to represent and organize the complete range of details relevant to the business processes. Thus, this chapter is an attempt to tackle the details of business processes relevant to the overall objective of a business architecture and enterprise architecture.

BACKGROUND

The increasing interest in studies on enterprise architecture and its components is a clear manifest of considering business process management as a backbone of enterprise architecture. Advocates of business process management, within the enterprise context, claim that accurate incorporation of business processes into enterprise architecture development prevent disastrous IT failures. A significant portion of enterprise budgets is consumed by IT (Carr, 2003), that is, IT failure exposes ever-increasing consequences and disaster for businesses. Thus, the inclusion of enterprise business process into enterprise architecture development should be considered of vital importance for success. One of the challenges in enterprise business process study is the adequacy, simplicity, integrity, and computer support of methodologies and tools used for this purpose. The difficulty arises from the fact that different methodologies and tools came out of experiences and expertise of authors with certain predetermined scope. While some methodologies are well zoomed and focused on one aspect, they lack strength in another aspect; for instance, a methodology may provide a profound theoretical concept but lack clear diagrammatic notations or computer support.

In this chapter, the transaction concept and Petri nets are integrated to furnish enterprise systems designers and developers with better tools. This arsenal is further complemented by rigorous graphical notations of Petri nets extended for the language action perspective.

The transaction concept, authored and introduced by Dietz (1994, 1999, 2002), is based on the language action perspective looking at communication as a representation of actions. The transaction concept, that will be discussed later, is about how communication leads to actions and can serve as a basis for capturing essential business processes within an enterprise.

It is very natural that people describe their work and activities in a natural language. People use natural language to communicate while conducting business and carrying out tasks, therefore, the transaction concept is a profound tool to watch and observe communication in an organization in order to identify patterns of action. In order to put these patterns of action in a meaningful order, visualize these patterns, build a complete model of these patterns, analyze the model, and communicate the results back to the users, clear and readable graphical notations are needed. For this purpose, the rich graphical notations of Petri nets are combined with the transaction concept that resulted in transaction-oriented Petri nets methodology, or TOP methodology for short.

The concept of language action perspective traces its origins to the speech act theory stating that language is not only a means of exchanging information but also a means of social activities or actions (Austin, 1962). Austin's historic work, "How to do things with word," paved a profound road for extensive research interest resulting into what is now known as the language action perspective and communication modeling. The Austin theory was further advanced and complemented in the works of Searle (1969), who presents a theory

of speech acts relying on the notion of constitutive rules (Habermas, 1984; Medina-Mora, Winograd, Flores, & Flores, 1992; Winograd & Flores, 1986). The work of Winograd and Flores introduced a modeling approach that illustrates "conversation for action" as sequences of communicative acts involving two actors. Their schema "conversation for action" was further developed by Dietz (1999) in the concept of business transaction, the core concept of the DEMO methodology. This chapter is based on the transaction concept as introduced within the DEMO framework and using Petri nets as a modeling technique.

PETRI NETS (PN)

Since its introduction in 1962 by Carl Adam Petri in his PhD dissertation, Petri nets have been applied to a variety of application domains such as communications networks, transportation systems, manufacturing systems, defense systems, and biological systems, just to name a few. Its comprehensive graphical notations, powerful formal specification tool, and executable technique for specification, analysis, and design of systems secured a distinguished place among other conventional techniques, methods, and methodologies. Apart from these features, Petri nets are one of the well computer supported tools including free and commercially available software for supporting Petri nets.

The application of Petri nets to systems design and modeling has driven tremendous interest among researchers and practitioners, and a huge number of papers, theses, and projects were devoted to this issue. As a result, Petri nets have been extended to various domains, resulting in different types of Petri nets; however, the basic principles of Petri nets and graphical notations remain almost the same. For interested readers, some references on Petri nets include:

- Standard (or elementary/classic/low level) Petri nets (Peterson, 1981) in which token are identical or indistinguishable.
- Colored Petri nets in which each token has value, thus tokens are different or distinguishable (Jensen, 1997a, 1997b).
- Hierarchical Petri nets in which certain elements (e.g., a transition) of Petri nets encompasses a subnet or entire Petri nets.
- High level Petri nets usually represent colored and hierarchical Petri nets (Reisig & Rozenberg, 1998).
- Stochastic Petri nets add non deterministic time (Haas, 2002).
- Timed Petri Nets in which transitions are assigned duration weight.
- Predict/transition nets (Pr/T-nets).
- Workflow Petri nets (van der Aalst et al., 2002), etc.

- **Definition:** Petri nets are a graphical and mathematical modeling tool that is particularly well suited for discrete event systems. The Petri nets diagrammatic structure consists of *places*, *transitions*, and *directed arcs* as depicted in Figure 1. Places can contain tokens (one or more). Graphically, places are represented by circles (or ellipses), transitions by rectangles (or bars), and tokens by black dots (or numbers).
- **Place:** (two types) Input place and output place: an input place may represent input data, condition, command, request, or material; an output place may represent a state or a result achieved after its corresponding

Figure 1. Graphical notations of Petri nets

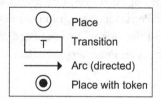

activity (transition) takes place. Places can contain tokens that illustrate the current state of the modeled system (*the marking*). The marking used to describe the initial state of the system is called the *initial marking*.
- **Transition:** A transition represents an action, process, operation, or any activity that changes the state of the system or causes advances and progress in a process.
- **Arc:** In its common role, an arc illustrates the course of actions, the flow of processes, or the sequence of operations.
- **Token:** Tokens are indicators of the system's state. Thus, an overall distribution of tokens represents the overall state of the system at a given time. The current state of the modeled system is given by the number of tokens in each place or by type if the tokens are colored (distinguishable).

THE TRANSACTION CONCEPT

As we previously mentioned, the transaction (or business transaction) concept used in this chapter, originated from the DEMO methodology authored and developed by Dietz (1999, 2002). The concept is based on the idea that an organization and its underlying business processes are a network of business transactions that constitutes the essence of this organization. This concept looks at communication, more precisely, business communication as a tool to capture underlying action patterns that represent the business processes. In this context, the notion of communication is not an exchange of information (words and sentences), but the negotiation, coordination, agreement, and commitment that lead to certain actions. In turn, these actions create new facts, deliver results, and accomplish the mission of an organization. This way of looking at communication became known as the Language-Action Perspective (Dietz, 1999; Goldkuhl, 2005; Goldkuhl, Lind, & Seigerroth, 1998). Thus, the Language-Action Perspective considers communication as a way of acting and carrying out certain tasks.

Each business transaction encompasses *action* and *interaction* as illustrated in Figure 2. The *action* is the core of a business transaction; it represents an activity that changes the state of the world or creates a new fact. The *interaction* is either for initiation of an action or communication of a fact as the result of the action. For example, an interaction can be a request made by one actor toward another actor that leads to creation of a new fact; an interaction can be also click of "apply" button or "submit" in an electronic form; or inserting debit card into the ATM's card reader to withdraw cash.

- **Example 1a:** A customer applies for a home mortgage to a loan officer in a bank. The first *interaction* takes place when the customer communicates with the officer to request a loan and submits an application. Then the officer processes the application, checks the documents, and makes a decision, that is, takes an *action*. The second *interaction* takes place when the officer, after processing the application, communicates the decision to the customer.

As the "mortgage" example shows, the process has three stages: the first *interaction*, the *action*, and the second *interaction*. Accordingly, as illustrated in Figure 3, the transaction concept states that each business transaction consists of three phases called the *order, execution*, and *result phases*. The order phase is the first interaction, the result phase is the second interaction, and the execution phase is where the action takes

place; these phases are abbreviated as O, E, and R correspondingly. They are also referred to as OER concept illustrated in Figure 3 using Petri net notations. The order (O) and result (R) phases are interactions and the execution (E) phase is an action. In order to distinguish between *action* and *interaction*, the action (execution phase) is represented by a different color. This differentiation makes more meaningful sense when conducting modeling.

On the left side of Figure 3, a transaction is represented as a sequence of the three phases, while for compactness, the right side of the figure compresses the three phases into one box called a *transaction* (T). The need of decomposing a transaction into three phases or compressing them into one box arises when modeling complex enterprise processes, in which numerous transactions are chained together and nested into each other. A simple transaction is carried out in a straightforward manner without involving (triggering or causing) another transaction (or transactions) during its entire execution. Thus, it is unnecessary to split a simple transaction into three phases, and therefore a compact notation is used. Using the compressed notation will help to build more compact models of enterprise processes, while the expanded notation will help

Figure 3. The transaction structure using Petri nets diagram (detailed and compact notations)

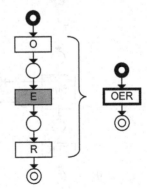

Figure 2. The business transaction concept

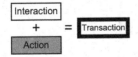

to show if a transaction is nesting other transaction(-s) within it.

- **Example 1b:** In the "requesting mortgage" transaction, the application processing triggers another transaction "checking credit." In order for the officer to approve or decline the application, he or she needs to check the customer's credit history with an authorized credit reporting agency. It means the "requesting mortgage" transaction is a composite transaction that nests the "checking credit" transaction. Thus, the "requesting mortgage" transaction starts first and the "checking credit" transaction starts afterward, but the "requesting mortgage" transaction cannot be completed until the result of the "checking credit" transaction is not known.

Based on the previously modified description of the "mortgage" process, the following is a business process model using the transaction concept:

Transaction 1: 'requesting mortgage'
    Initiator: 'customer'

    Executor: 'officer'
    Result: 'mortgage is approved'

Transaction 2: 'checking credit'
    Initiator: 'officer'
    Executor: 'credit agency'
    Result: 'credit report is generated'

From the two previous transactions, Transaction T2 must be initiated and executed during Transaction T1, as depicted in Figure 4. Thus, initiation, execution, or completion of a business transaction may lead to initiation and execution of new transactions. In this way, transactions are chained into arbitrarily large structures, called *business processes* (Dietz, 1999).

The actual sequence of actions is shown Figure 4b. According to this diagram, the execution of Transaction 2 takes place as part of the execution phase of Transaction 1.

This simple model should be read in the following manner: Transaction T1 starts with order phase (T1/O); the execution phase of this transaction (T1/E) nests Transaction T2, that is, the execution phase of Transaction T1 starts and then it triggers Transaction T2 that should be completely executed and the result should be

Figure 4. (a) A composite transaction; (b) A composite transaction indicating the action flow and process boundary

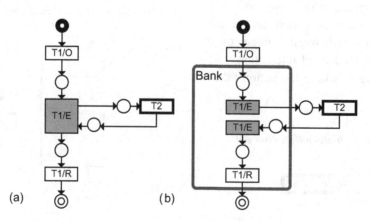

(a)   (b)

returned back to T1/E in order to complete T1/E. Once the result of Transaction T2 is returned and the execution phase of Transaction T1 (T1/E) is also completed, it proceeds to the result phase (T1/R). The result phase of Transaction T1 means that the mortgage decision is communicated to the customer.

In real life, enterprise processes are more complex than the "mortgage" example that is intentionally simplified in order to evade an in-depth discussion at this stage.

Now that the transaction structure is explained, it is necessary to look at the roles of the actors involved in a business transaction. As is apparent from the "mortgage" example, each transaction involves two actors. The actor that initiates the transaction is called the *initiator* of the transaction (e.g., customer, client, consumer, submitter of electronic form), while the actor that executes the transaction is called the *executor* of the transaction (e.g., supplier, server, provider, IT application). Actors can be humans, software agents, or machines. For example, if the mortgage application is submitted online, a software agent will collect data and process the application instead of the loan officer and make preliminary estimates for later approval by a human actor (the loan officer).

Now that the transaction concept is introduced, it is appropriate to give a definition of business transaction used in this chapter.

• **Definition:** A *business transaction* is a generic pattern of activity carried out in a close interaction between two distinct actors called the initiator and executor. The activity is carried out in three phases, called the order phase (O), execution phase (E), and result phase (R), that create a new fact or change the state of the world. These three phases are made up of interaction and action, in which the order and result phases represent the interaction and the execution phase represents the action.

The following is a definition of enterprise process in the framework of the methodology that is applied in this chapter based on the transaction concept.

• **Definition:** An enterprise business process is a network of interrelated business transactions that delivers value (good or service) to a customer having one start point and one end point. It starts with a request by an actor and ends with a result communicated to the same actor. Usually a business process is one super transaction that nests multiple transactions in it.

TRANSACTION-ORIENTED PETRI NETS

In order to use Petri nets for enterprise process modeling based on the language action perspective, a few minor extensions to the graphical notations of the standard Petri nets are suggested in this chapter. These extensions add important modeling features such as capabilities depicting process boundary, distinguishing between intra- and inter-departmental, intra- and inter-organizational levels of interaction, and indicating the start and the end points of certain processes. These extensions make the models easily understandable, intuitively readable, and a straightforward input for further analysis, simulation, verification, or comparison of different model scenarios.

As the notations in Table 1 illustrate, there are distinct graphical elements for *action* (rectangle with plain line filled in grey), *interaction* (rectangle with plain line), a complete *transaction* where action and interaction are represented together (rectangle with a bold line), and *composite transaction* where a transaction is nesting one or more transactions (multiple rectangles with a plain line). A transaction is called composite if its completion requires execution of another transaction(s). In terms of the Petri nets concept, all these elements are transitions and thus represented by different types of rectangles.

Further, the proposed extensions suggest two places, a *start place* and an *end place* that indicate where a process starts and where it eventually ends. These two new places are used along with the standard Petri nets element called *state* that shows the intermediate states of processes (transactions). Again, in terms of the Petri nets concept, all these elements are places and thus represented by different types of circle.

For distinguishing between intra-organizational and inter-organizational processes, the process *boundary* element is added. Introduction of this element helps when analysts need to model or illustrate the interaction of one process with another process within an organization or with the environment. This interaction can be modeled with a set of places between the process boundaries.

The final extension concerns the introduction of an *optional link*. In standard Petri nets, all input places must hold in order for a transition to be executed, that is, execution of a transition is guaranteed only whenever all its input places have a token in them. Optional links weaken this assumption and therefore allow the analyst to represent situations where the transition is executed, even when a state represented by its input places does not hold. For instance, prior to applying for a policy, customers usually request a quote. However, it is entirely possible for customers to apply for a policy without first requesting a quote. Thus, the relationship between requesting a quote and applying for a policy is an optional one.

THE TOP METHODOLOGY FRAMEWORK

For a successful enterprise processes study, a practitioner needs to follow some formal framework (steps) that would help to determine where to look for pieces of essential or business related information. Since we are applying the TOP methodology, this methodology suggests that first an organization is described in terms of major business processes (order processing, customer

Table 1. Notations of the TOP methodology

Element	Notation	Description
Start	●	A start represents a starting point for a process that leads to the creation of a new result or a previously unknown fact.
Interaction	▭	An interaction represents the transfer of some information from one actor to another, e.g. a request to perform some action, or a communication of the result of some action. In terms of the OER model, both the Order and the Result phases are interactions.
Action	▬	An action represents a production act when a certain result is created. The Execution phase in the OER model is an action.
Transaction	▭	A transaction encompasses the entire OER cycle. The introduction of a symbol for an entire transaction shows that our notation is an example of a hierarchical Petri net. The reason for the introduction is that it allows the modeler to abstract away from certain details that he or she considers irrelevant to the model.
Composite Transaction	▭	A composite transaction is a set of transactions, and thus summarizes a sub-net. It is useful if the modeler wants to hide certain details.
Sequence Flow	→	A sequence flow indicates the order in which interactions and actions are initiated and performed.
Optional	- - - →	An optional link represents a link that is neither a condition for proceeding nor essential, but one that usually takes place. E.g., before applying for a policy, customers usually request a quote, but customers can apply for a policy without first requesting a quote.
Boundary	▭	A boundary illustrates the boundary of a business process (department or organization). It is this feature that allows the modeling of intra- and inter-departmental and intra- and inter-organizational processes.
Intermediate state	○	An intermediate state represents a result or state achieved after an interaction or action.
End	◎	An end notation represents a termination point for a process, and thus represents the final result of the process.

call processing, inventory control, admission to hospital, new member enrollment, insurance claim processing, etc.). Then each of these major business processes is studied and described as a network of business transactions (essential activities), in which each transaction involves two actors, one initiator of the activity and one executor of it. According to the transaction concept, an activity is considered as a business transaction if it creates a new fact, changes the status of the system, or brings results. Now having this in mind, the following is a high-level framework to follow:

- **Definition of major business processes:** This step is a high-level definition of major processes that can be done by reading the documentation of an organization. Examples of a major process can be "order processing," "goods delivery," "procurement," "restocking," etc. Usually, these major processes are interrelated and all together constitute the mission of the organization.
- **Description of each major business process:** This step is either based on documentation of an organization where processes and procedures are described, or such a description can be prepared through interviews with the manager of a specific business process. Experience shows that even if a written documentation is available, interviews still need to be conducted for clarification and further information.
- **Identification of business transactions (core activities or key processes) and relevant actors for each major business process:** In this step, identify transactions (main activities) that cause changes in the states of the process and advance the process. Identify who is the initiator and who is the executor for each transaction. According to the transaction concept, the initiator and the executor are two distinct actors.
- **Construction of model(s) of each major business process:** In this step, using the

notations of the TOP methodology, all the identified transactions are put together in sequential order.

These steps and the TOP methodology are applied and tested through a series of case studies. The following section will discuss one of these case examples.

APPLICATION OF THE TOP METHODOLOGY

This section represents a case study conducted in a multinational insurance company identified by a fictitious name "SSM Insurance" company. As one of the world's largest financial institutions, SSM currently includes approximately 80,200 employees and 17,000 agents servicing more than 70 million policies in the United States and Canada.

Business Architecture of SSM

For the application of the TOP methodology to a specific business process, it is essential to first draw the big picture in the form of capturing the SSM Business Architecture that reflects essential major processes. The SSM Business Architecture comprises major business processes such as *reviewing new applicants*, *generating contracts*, *reviewing claims,* and *reviewing current applicants*, as depicted in Figure 5. By decomposing each of these major processes, it will reveal more detailed business activities in SSM.

The SSM business architecture is an essential component or subset of the SSM enterprise architecture in general. Although enterprise business processes would be completely studied only if all the models are developed and the interactions between the models are identified and illustrated, in the following sections, we focus on the details of business processes relevant to a new policy issuance.

Figure 5. SSM business architecture

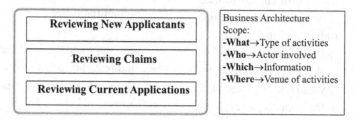

Major Business Processes

As depicted in the SSM business architecture, the major business processes within SSM insurance excluding the agents are *reviewing new applicants*, *generating contracts*, *reviewing claims*, *reviewing current applicants*, and *serving customers daily*. The first two actually comprise the policy issuance process studied in the next subsection. The agent is a part of the insurance company in that they are the face of the company. They are the ones that directly and personally interact with customers.

Description: Applying for Insurance Process

If a person wants SSM insurance company to be his or her insurance agency, he or she contacts an SSM insurance company agent. These agents then offer plans and the prices to best fit the person. The premium offered is based on the customer's driving record (number of tickets and accidents), age, marital status, residence, car type, etc. Also, the premium is based on customer claims, which are obtained from a consumer reporting agency. If the person wishes to purchase the insurance, then an application may be filed with the insurance agent. The agent then sends the application to one of the regional offices. The regional office checks the background of the applicant. The background check consists of traffic tickets and claims made. Claims typically made are any type that have been requested by that customer in the past. Claims can

consist of auto claims and homeowner claims. If approved, the regional office notifies the agent and the agent tells the client that they are approved and a contract is generated. All contracts are pre-made by the system with added information about the customer and car. The contracts are produced at the regional office and sent to the customer's agent who adds the type of coverage the customer has. The agent then explains what is and is not covered under the plan and asks the client to sign the contract. By signing the contract, the customer pays an initial payment to start the coverage when approved. The customer is issued a temporary insurance card, and the official card is mailed to the customer at a later date. If the client is not approved by the regional office, the agent notifies the client and all transactions between the client and agent end there.

SSM insurance company's regional office does not deal with customers directly. The agents are the primary contact for customers.

Identification of Business Transactions and Actors

Now, based on the description of the business process in regard to the policy issuance, business transactions and their relevant actors are identified using the transaction concept. As mentioned, each business transaction should have two distinct actors and create a new result or fact.

Following this concept, the first business transaction can be identified as "obtaining a quote" or "requesting a quote."

T1: Requesting for a quote
    Initiator: customer
    Executor: agent
    Result: a quote is given

After completion of this transaction, the customer may decline or consider applying for an insurance policy. If the customer decides to apply for a policy, this will constitute the second transaction:

T2: Applying for a policy
    Initiator: customer
    Executor: agent
    Result: a policy is issued

In order for the agent to proceed, the agent must request approval of the regional office, which checks the customer's background:

T3: Requesting regional approval
    Initiator: agent
    Executor: regional office
    Result: approved/declined

If the approval is given, the agent asks the regional office to generate a contract based on the inputs of the customer:

T4: Generating a contract
    Initiator: agent
    Executor: regional office
    Result: a contract is generated

Now the agent reviews and explains the prepared contract to the customer (agent and customer). If the customer agrees to the terms and conditions of the contract, the agent requests the customer to sign the contract and make the initial payment:

T5: Paying for the policy
    Initiator: agent

    Executor: customer
    Result: policy is paid

Developing an Enterprise Process Model of SSM Insurance

After having all the business transactions identified, the TOP graphical elements are applied to construct an enterprise process model based on the identified transactions by first grouping and drawing the boundary of the two departments, the agent office and the regional office. Second, transactions that are executed with the agent's office, regional office, and environment are grouped. Figure 6 shows all the transactions in sequential order and their relation in regard to the organization's boundaries.

In the Figure 6, the organization boundary is represented by the thick gray rectangle with rounded angles (e.g., agent office, regional office).

The figure should be read in the following manner: The two circles with black dots (tokens) represent the start point; correspondingly, the two circles with the holes represent the end point of the processes, where the processes terminate. Transaction T1 starts in the environment and the result is also communicated to the environment. This is a simple transaction and is, therefore, executed completely at once. Its result can serve as a conditional link for the initiation of Transaction T2; therefore, the dotted arrow connects the result of transaction T1 to Transaction T2; therefore, a dotted arrow is drawn between T1 and T2. Now, Transaction T2 is a composite transaction that nests Transactions T3, T4, and T5; therefore, this transaction is split into three phases showing that for the completion of Transaction T2, Transactions T3, T4, and T5 are initiated and should be completed before proceeding with Transaction T2. As for Transactions T3 and T4, they are initiated in the agent office, executed in the regional office, and the results are communicated back to the agent office. Transaction T5, payment for the policy, is

Figure 6. Transactional model of "policy issuing process"

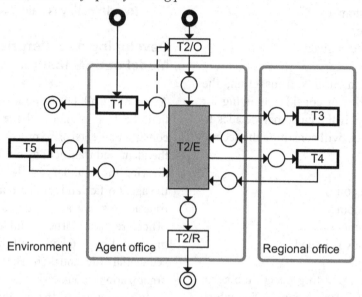

initiated in the agent office, executed in the environment, and the result is communicated back to the agent office. Finally, the circles positioned between the agent office and the regional office models intra-organizational processes. One more aspect of the Figure 6 is the distinction between intra-organizational and inter-organizational processes. For example, Transactions T3 and T4 are inter-organizational processes. In this case, the actors involved are not persons but rather organizations; however, detailed discussion of this matter will be left for a future opportunity.

In Figure 6, focus is placed on the insurance policy issuance process; therefore, the other processes such as "reviewing claims" and "reviewing current members" are not discussed; however, their analysis and modeling should not be difficult following the same manner as with the "policy issuance process."

Back to Business Architecture and EA Framework

The studied example and the methodology illustrate how enterprise processes can be modeled for incorporation into the EA development process. Although the studied example is only one of the few major business processes of SSM, for real projects, the ultimate goal should be the development of a series of such models that capture all essential processes that support the mission of an enterprise. Next to the modeling part, it should be studied how to align the process models to the supporting IT components or how to build a one-to-one accordance between the business processes and IT functionalities.

In concluding the chapter, it should be stated that a strategic factor in the success of enterprise architecture is the degree to which the enterprise architecture is based and linked to business requirements, and demonstrably supporting and facilitating the enterprise to achieve its business objectives.

CONCLUSION

This chapter discussed both the role of business architecture as a subset of enterprise architecture framework and business processes as the foundation of business architecture. The discussion opened with consideration of enterprise process modeling as a crucial component in developing adequate enterprise architecture. In order to study, model, and visualize enterprise processes, the chapter introduced a comprehensive methodology based on language action perspective. The applicability of the methodology is tested on a small case study demonstrating that enterprise processes are cross departmental and cross organizational by nature.

Although more complex examples and case studies are needed to explore the full benefit of process modeling in developing detailed enterprise architecture, it is not difficult to draw some conclusions based on the enterprise case study discussed. Enterprise processes are cross departmental with interaction with the business environment. Transactions exchanged between different actors may cross boundaries of a single process and expect results from other processes. Thus, enterprise processes are truly a collaborative network of business transactions.

Revelation of these characteristics of enterprise processes greatly help system designers, especially enterprise architectures, to define the boundaries and underlying IT infrastructure more precisely in order to support the enterprise processes. Therefore, definition of enterprise processes may serve as a blueprint in developing enterprise architecture.

REFERENCES

Anaya, V., & Ortiz, A. (2005). How enterprise architectures can support integration. In *Proceedings of the 1ˢᵗ International Workshop on Interoperability of Heterogeneous Information systems*.

Austin, J. L. (1962). *How to do things with words.* Cambridge, MA: Harvard University Press.

Carr, N. G. (2003). IT doesn't matter. *Harvard Business Review, 81*(5).

Dalal, N. P., Kamath, M., Kolarik, W. J., & Sivaraman, E. (2004). Toward an integrated framework for modeling enterprise processes. *Communications of the ACM, 47*(3).

Deiters, W. (1998). Information gathering and process modeling in a Petri net-based approach. In W. van der Aalst, J. Desel, & A. Oberweis (Eds.), *Business process management: Models, techniques, and empirical studies.* Berlin; Heidelberg; New York: Springer-Verlag.

Dietz, J. L. G. (1994). Business modeling for business redesign. In *Proceedings of the 27ᵗʰ Hawaii International Conference on System Sciences* (pp. 723-732). Los Alamitos; IEEE Computer Society Press.

Dietz, J. L. G. (1999, November). Understanding and modelling business processes with DEMO. In *Proceedings of the Annual International Conference on Conceptual Modelling (ER'99)*, Paris.

Dietz, J. L. G. (2002). The atoms, molecules, and matter of organizations. In *Proceedings of the 7ᵗʰ International Workshop on the LAP*, Delft, The Netherlands.

Dietz, J. L. G. (2006). *Enterprise ontology—Theory and methodology.* Springer.

Goldkuhl, G. (2005, June). Beyond communication loops—Articulating the principle of multi-responsiveness. In *Proceedings of the 10th International Working Conference on the Language Action Perspective on Communication Modeling.* Kiruna, Sweden.

Goldkuhl, G., Lind, M., & Seigerroth, U. (1998). The language action perspective on communication modelling. In *Proceedings of the 3rd International Workshop on LAP*, Department of Informatics, Jönköping International Business School, Sweden.

Haas, P. (2002). *Stochastic Petri nets: Modelling, stability, simulation.* New York: Springer-Verlag.

Habermas, J. (1984). *The theory of communicative action: Reason and rationalization of society.* Cambridge: Polity Press.

Herman, J. (2001). *Creating a business architecture. Business Communication Review*, 22-23, December.

Jensen, K. (1997a). *Coloured Petri nets. Basic concepts, analysis methods and practical use. Volume 1, Basic Concepts.* Monographs in Theoretical Computer Science, Springer-Verlag, 2nd ed. ISBN: 3-540-60943-1.

Jensen, K. (1997b). *Coloured Petri nets. Basic concepts, analysis methods and practical use. Volume 2, Analysis Methods.* Monographs in Theoretical Computer Science, Springer-Verlag, 2nd ed. ISBN: 3-540-58276-2.

Lopez, J., & Genovese, Y. (2004). *Shift to integrated business architecture.* Gartner, Inc.

McDavid, D. W. (1999). A standard for business architecture description. *IBM Systems Journal, 38*(1), 12.

Medina-Mora, R., Winograd, T., Flores, R., & Flores, F. (1992). The action workflow approach to workflow management technology. In J. Turner, & R. Kraut (Eds.), In *Proceedings of the Conference on Computer-Supported Cooperative Work, CSCW'92.* New York: ACM Press

Peterson, J. L. (1981) *Petri net theory and the modelling of systems.* Englewood Cliffs, NJ: Prentice-Hall, Inc..

Reisig, W., & Rozenberg, G. (1998). Lectures on Petri nets I: Basic models. *Advances in Petri Nets, Lecture Notes in Computer Science, Vol. 1491.* Springer-Verlag.

Searle, J. (1969). *Speech acts: An essay in the philosophy of language.* Cambridge: Cambridge University Press.

Stamper, R. K. (1988). *MEASUR.* University of Twente, Enschede, The Netherlands.

Stamper, R. K. (1997). Organizational semiotics. In J. Mingers, & F. Stowell (Eds.), *Information systems: An emerging discipline.* London: McGraw Hill.

Taft, D. K. (1996, October). Anderson sets enterprise blueprint. *Computer Reseller News*, October 28, p. 132.

van der Aalst, W., & van Hee, K. (2002). *Workflow management: Models, methods, and systems.* MIT Press.

Winograd, T., & Flores, F. (1986). *Understanding computers and cognition: A new foundation for design.* Ablex, Norwood.

Chapter VII
Enterprise Architecture in the Singapore Government

Tan Eng Pheng
Infocomm Development Authority of Singapore, Singapore

Gan Wei Boon
Infocomm Development Authority of Singapore, Singapore

ABSTRACT

The Singapore government enterprise architecture is a blueprint that will provide a holistic view of business functions, supporting data standards, and IT systems and services, regardless of the organisational structure and ownership of these functions and systems. The blueprint will also enable analysis of IT investments and their alignment to business functions, as well as facilitate collaboration among government agencies. When implemented, the Singapore government enterprise architecture will help bring about transformation in public sector by yielding optimised end-to-end business processes and system capabilities in alignment with government enterprise needs and missions. This chapter presents the considerations and approach taken to develop the Singapore government enterprise architecture. It examines the linkages of enterprise architecture with other initiatives such as the e-government action plans, policies, and processes related to IT governance, as well as summaries of lessons learned.

INTRODUCTION

The Singapore government enterprise architecture is a blueprint that will provide a holistic view of business functions, supporting data standards, and information technology (IT) systems and services, regardless of the organisational structure and ownership of these functions and systems. It comprises four elements and reference models for the business, information, solution, and technical architectures. Of the four elements, the technical architecture has been developed in 2002 while the other three are currently being developed.

The Singapore government enterprise architecture is to support e-government, and in particular, realise the outcomes of networked government where many agencies integrate across organisational boundaries to provide citizen-centric services.

SINGAPORE E-GOVERNMENT

E-government is about enabling our government to harness info-communications technology (ICT) to better serve our citizens and businesses, and to deliver public services with greater convenience, effectiveness, and efficiency. For the Singapore public service, our e-government journey started in 1980 with the launch of the Civil Service Computerisation Programme.

1980-1999: Civil Service Computerisation Programme (CSCP)

The Civil Service Computerisation Programme (CSCP) was conceived with a clear direction of turning the Singapore government into a world-class exploiter of IT. It marked the beginning of computerisation in the Singapore public sector that focused on improving internal operational efficiencies through the automation of traditional work functions and reducing paperwork. In the 20-year period, we evolved from using IT as a tool to improve productivity to leveraging the Internet to deliver 24×7 electronic services to our customers. By the late 1990s, the convergence of IT and telecommunications transformed the concept of service delivery. This required a paradigm shift in the way government services were delivered and the first e-government action plan was born.

2000-2003: E-Government Action Plan I (eGAP I)

The e-government action plan (eGAP) is the primary vehicle for a strategic transformation of the public sector in the delivery of public services by harnessing ICT technology. Launched in June 2000, the vision of the first eGAP was to be a leading e-government to better serve Singapore and Singaporeans in the new knowledge-based economy. The objective was to foster a shared vision of a leading e-government in the new millennium, develop a public sector that could contribute positively and work actively at propelling Singapore forward in the new economy, and provide a framework for informed, coordinated, and flexible ICT deployment. To move businesses, citizens, public officers, and the government toward the e-government vision, the first eGAP prescribed the broad directions of ICT deployment with five strategic thrusts and six programmes.

The five strategic thrusts of the first eGAP were:

1. Re-inventing government in the digital economy.
2. Delivering integrated electronic service delivery.
3. Being proactive and responsive.
4. Using infocomm technologies to build new capabilities and capacities.
5. Innovating with infocomm technologies.

The six programmes identified to drive the strategic thrusts in the first eGAP include:

1. Knowledge-based workplace.
2. Electronic services delivery.
3. Technology experimentation.
4. Operational efficiency improvement.
5. Adaptive and robust infocomm infrastructure.
6. Infocomm education.

The key focus of the first eGAP was transforming the way the public sector interacts with its customers. Primarily, all public services deemed feasible for electronic delivery were designated for this transformation. The public sector would need to better understand the impact of ICT, continually innovating and adapting business and operational processes to re-engineer, and totally transform the way things were done. In line with Singapore's vision for service excellence, this plan would see an increase in the number of electronic services or e-service provisions to customers in three fronts—citizens, businesses, and within the public service.

The first eGAP covered the period 2000 to 2003. By the time it concluded in 2003, its achievements and accolades include the following:

1. One of the most advanced e-governments in the world as reflected in international benchmark studies by third parties. Singapore was ranked among the top leading e-governments by both accenture and the world economic forum, and also won several international e-government awards.

2. Over 1,600 public e-services have been implemented. In a study of e-governments worldwide, Singapore was ranked second by Brown University at putting public services and information online.

3. Our citizens are generally satisfied with e-government and with the quality of our e-services.

While the first eGAP had provided the common vision for agencies in their ICT deployment, it was important to continue to engage all agencies in the conceptualisation and implementation of common systems, especially with gradual decentralisation of budgets as well as ICT deployment decisions to these agencies. Continual efforts would have to be put in to encourage and ensure that agencies pool their resources in the development of ICT applications with similar functionalities. Such engagement and customer-centric approach to delivering public services from the foundation laid by first eGAP would continue into the second eGAP.

Figure 1. E-government action plan II (2002-2006) outcomes

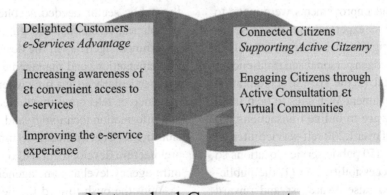

E-Government Strategic Framework
Strategies To Realise The Vision & Outcomes

Delighted Customers
e-Services Advantage

Increasing awareness of & convenient access to e-services

Improving the e-service experience

Connected Citizens
Supporting Active Citzenry

Engaging Citizens through Active Consultation & Virtual Communities

Networked Government
Fostering Inter-Agency Collaboration

2003-2006: E-Government Action Plan II (eGAP II)

The focus of the e-government action plan II (GAP II) covering 2003 to 2006 was to transform the public service into a networked government that delivers accessible, integrated, and value-adding e-services to our customers and helps bring citizens closer together. The eGAP II was to achieve three distinct outcomes: (1) Delighted customers, (2) Connected citizens, and (3) Networked government as shown in Figure 1.

To enable the two desired outcomes of "delighted customers" and "connected citizens" in e-GAP II, the "networked government" outcome must first be realised. A networked government is one where our many agencies move beyond seeing themselves as separate and distinct entities to "one government." That is, one that collaborates, shares information, and leverages on its collective knowledge enabled by infocomm, to serve the public seamlessly and effectively.

E-government's contribution toward building a networked government is in the interconnection of our government agencies through common infrastructure, information management, and technical standards, as well as collaborative undertakings to deliver citizen-centric services.

At the close of eGAP II in 2006, at least 10 new cross-agency integrated e-services were implemented, and improvements were made to customer's e-service experience and their ease-of-use. Some of the significant initiatives were: (1) an enhanced My.eCitizen personalised front-end for the eCitizen portal, (2) the TrustSg accreditation scheme for government Web sites to help instil customer confidence in online transactions, (3) the installation of over 1,200 self-service internet terminals across 150 public service locations so as to increase accessibility, and (4) the publicity campaigns to raise awareness and reward citizens who transacted electronically with the government.

Our efforts in implementing e-services have been recognised internationally as well. Notably, we received the United Nations Public Service Award 2005 for the Online Business Licensing Service (www.business.gov.sg), an integrated e-service, which offers businesses a total of 69 licenses from 19 government agencies and allows 80% of all start-ups in Singapore to apply online for the licenses needed to start their businesses. The award was given to recognise the government's efforts to streamline, simplify, and integrate the application of licences from various agencies to save time and costs for enterprises.

Overall, we have continued to do reasonably well for eGAP II and our achievements have ensured that Singapore continues to be ranked amongst the leading e-governments by international benchmarking studies conducted by the World Economic Forum, Accenture, and United Nations e-government survey.

TECHNICAL ARCHITECTURE— EARLY ENTERPRISE ARCHITECTURE

When the Singapore government embarked on eGAP, it became apparent that we needed a well-designed, reliable, and scalable infrastructure to support our e-government initiatives. In addition, the public sector needed a coherent collection of policies, standards, and guidelines to guide government agencies in the design, acquisition, implementation, and management of ICT. This was particularly so at a time when the rapid convergence of telecommunications, broadcasting, and information technology had opened up possibilities for a networked government. Until then, architecture development had only been done at intra-agency level at some agencies.

With the push toward the delivery of e-services for citizens and businesses and emergence of cross-agency integrated e-services, systems interoperability and the bridging of systems platforms across agencies became paramount. Moreover, cost benefits could be realised through the use of common systems and platforms for the deployment of e-services, and demand aggregation for the procurement of compatible technology products. Hence, a practical approach by way of a public sector service-wide technology standard for agencies was necessary.

This technology standard blueprint called the service-wide technical architecture (SWTA) was developed to provide a consistent framework for the effective management and protection of the public sector's IT assets that were implemented across the agencies.

According to META Group (1999b), the development of such a technical architecture still offered "the greatest opportunity for IT organisations to deliver prompt value to their business."

The SWTA, which was one of the key initiatives under the first eGAP, helped to create a better environment for interoperability and information sharing within the public service. The first five domain architectures in SWTA were published in October 2002. By April 2003, a total of nine domain architectures, as shown in Figure 2, were developed and published.

REVIEWS ON GOVERNMENT ENTERPRISE ARCHITECTURE

Achieving a networked government does not stop at just putting in place one of the technical enablers—viz technical architecture. The next step of development for ICT standards and

Figure 2. Architecture domains in service-wide technical architecture (SWTA)

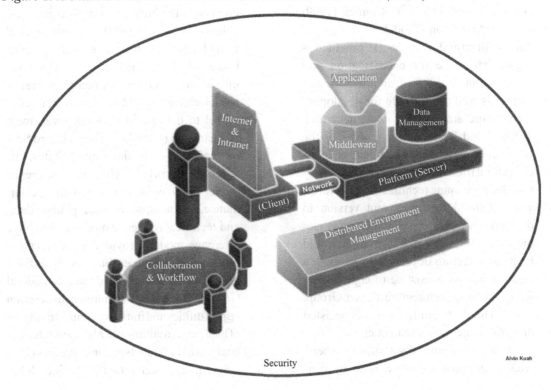

architectures was to explore the development of enterprise architecture.

This programme, identified in eGAP II, would increase cross-agency collaboration and systems integration, enable more innovative and business-transforming projects to be initiated and completed, and improve the public service's ability to anticipate and respond to rapid changes in the technology landscape when successfully executed.

Reviews were conducted to glean insights into enterprise architecture practices, their implementation at a government-wide level, and the approaches taken by other e-governments. Some of the key findings are summarised next starting from enterprise architecture components and concepts, and expanding into their implementations in other countries.

1. Enterprise architecture would comprise four elements, namely the business, information or data, solution or application, and technical architectures according to META Group (1999a, 1999b), U.S. CIO Council (1999) and the Open Group (2002).

2. An architectural framework provided a logical structure for classification and organisation of the four architecture elements, as well as guidance for developing architecture and systems implementation. TOGAF and Zachman were some of the frameworks reviewed. The open group architectural framework or TOGAF, originally used for developing technical architectures, was enhanced in the current version to develop other enterprise architectures elements as well. TOGAF's strength would be its architecture development method, a generic process consisting of eight phases for developing architecture (Open Group, 2002). The Zachman framework consisted of a two-dimensional matrix classification scheme in six columns (by what, how, where, who, when, and why) and five rows (by plan-

ner, owner, designer, builder, and contractor perspectives) for describing an enterprise appears comprehensive (Zachman, 1997). However, the Zachman framework did not have a process for developing an enterprise architecture, and the completion of such a matrix, either partially or full, for the whole-of-government seemed daunting.

3. In a government environment, enterprise architecture was deemed to be applicable at both government-wide and agency levels. Although both enterprise architecture implementations were conceptually similar, the construct was more complex in a government-wide context due to the scale and range of functions and diversity of the environment.

4. Government-wide enterprise architecture provides a service-wide perspective of business functions and their IT initiatives. In this context, the Canadian and U.S. Federal Governments have published reference models. The enterprise architecture effort in Canada comprises the business transformation enablement program and the governments of Canada strategic reference models, which had evolved over the last 15 years from the municipal level governments' reference model called the public service reference model to the provincial level government 10 years ago (Canada Treasury Board Secretariat, 2004). In the United States, the federal enterprise architecture reference model framework comprised the performance, business, service component, data, and technical reference models. These five reference models provided a classification scheme for government business operations and IT assets, and enabled the U.S. Federal Government's identification of collaboration opportunities and initiatives within five lines of business. In addition, it also facilitated the analysis of IT budgets and investments (U.S. Government Accountability Office, 2004;

U.S. Office of Management and Budget, 2005).

5.   It was also noted that the deliverables, documentation, and approaches for enterprise architecture were varied. Carbone (2004) had described that existing enterprise architecture approaches were too complex and theoretical and had proposed a simpler and improvised approach, such as the use of the Gane/Sarson methodology for diagramming. Whittle and Myrick (2005) asserted that formal models and architectures were "virtually nonexistent for business enterprises" and highlighted several models to describe a business architecture enterprise. Lastly, Perks and Beveridge (2002) had articulated the well-established process-centric TOGAF phases with clearer descriptions and details for practitioners use. These reviews from authors-practitioners showed that enterprise architecture deliverables and approaches needed to be "fit for purpose intended" and required customisation.

Hence, the Singapore government would adopt a federated architecture approach similar to the United States government. Reference models would need to be developed to serve as the whole-of-government enterprise architecture framework, with a suitable methodology and/or process as part of the framework to provide the guidance for architectural development. These reference models would enable new initiatives and projects

Figure 3. Elements of Singapore government enterprise architecture

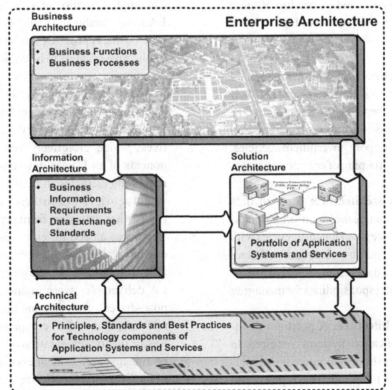

on common business functions and IT assets to be identified. The architectural documentation requirements would require continual research and localisation.

SINGAPORE GOVERNMENT ENTERPRISE ARCHITECTURE

Elements of Singapore Government Enterprise Architecture

The Singapore government enterprise architecture (SGEA) programme was established to support and enable the business strategies, objectives, and vision of a "networked government." Under this programme, a set of blueprints would be developed to provide a government-wide perspective of business functions, supporting data standards and ICT systems and services, regardless of the organisational structure and ownership of these functions and systems as shown in Figure 3 and descriptions next.

1. **Business architecture:** A holistic view of the organisation's key strategies and their impact on business. The contents define the lines of business and business functions performed by Singapore government agencies, as well as the grouping of common business processes.
2. **Information architecture:** A set of data models that examine the key information assets of Singapore government agencies with the aim of providing a shared, distributed, and consistent data resource. It also identifies individual responsibilities for managing information.
3. **Solution architecture:** A portfolio of integrated application systems required to satisfy business information needs and solutions, which facilitate rapid development and

delivery in a systematic and well-disciplined manner.
4. **Technical architecture:** This element details the organisation's technology strategies, its extended technology linkages, and their impact on business initiatives.

Our Approach

Out of the four elements in SGEA, only the business, information, and solution architectures would need to be developed as the technical architecture element was already addressed by the SWTA. The development of these EA elements would require substantial time and resource, and the same for its maintenance as well. Some of the key considerations underpinning the formulation of the strategy for the SGEA programme are as follows:

*   The implementation of a government-wide EA would enable the identification of common business processes to be streamlined, duplicative systems to be consolidated, and common systems to be implemented, leading to overall efficiency and effectiveness.
*   The Singapore government had previously implemented several service-wide initiatives, which effectively constitute components of an EA. In developing the three remaining elements in SGEA, the strategy would be to leverage on these existing initiatives rather than start from scratch.
*   There was a need for early results to demonstrate value and relevance of enterprise architecture to all stakeholders. Hence, the EA deliverables were intended to be purpose-driven, focusing on usefulness and relevance rather than comprehensiveness.
*   Lastly, the implementation of SGEA would be a means to effect business transformation in the Singapore public sector.

Government Business Architecture

The government business architecture (BA) was the first amongst three elements that we embarked on in the development of SGEA. The government BA was the key element in the SGEA, as it influenced the development of the other EA elements. The government BA, however, was also the most complex element.

First, unlike most organisations whose core businesses were clearer and more instinctive, there was voluminous information to be analysed due to the diversity of government business and absence of a singular set of overarching whole-of-government business objectives and performance measures. Second, there was no government-wide view of the lines of business and business functions. It was not practical to achieve a business architecture, which encompasses all business processes across the government either.

The government BA to be developed would be comprised of a high-level representation of government-wide lines of businesses and business functions. This would be sufficient to methodically identify agency collaboration opportunities or determine the need for common service-wide initiatives.

A top-down whole-of-government and business-driven approach was preferred for the development of government BA. Executive sponsorship and strong participation of business personnel was key to the success of the government BA effort. The stakeholders included chief information officers and corporate planning and strategic planning directors who were engaged for their directions throughout the BA development process. Their inputs and information on the business functions and agency level priorities were analysed and integrated into the government BA. This enabled government leaders to focus on priority areas instead of being overwhelmed by the voluminous information available.

The information for government BA was compiled into a structured format called the Singapore

Figure 4. Singapore government business reference model

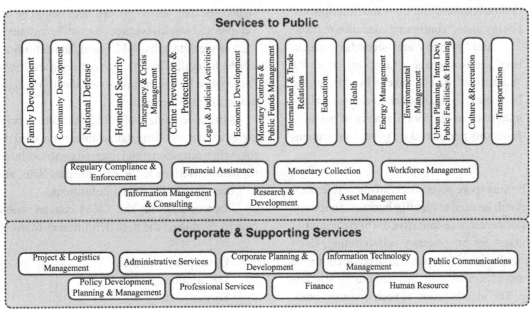

Alvin Kuah

government business reference model, which defined the business operations of the government using terminologies that were common across all government agencies as shown in Figure 4 diagram and described next.

1. The business reference model in Figure 4 has two broad categories of lines of businesses. Under the "services to public" category are 24 lines of businesses, which are external facing services that the Singapore government provides to citizens, businesses, and external stakeholders. Examples of these include the "family development," "public transportation," and "revenue collection" lines of businesses.

2. Under the "corporate & supporting services" category are nine lines of businesses representing all activities that support the delivery of services provided by the Singapore government to the public and all activities to operate the government effectively. Examples of these include "project & logistics management," "human resources," "finance" etc.

3. Within each line of business are a set of related business functions and descriptions. For instance, "continuing education & training" and "primary and secondary education" are two business functions under the "education" line of business. In addition, the business reference model would also include a set of cross-functional matrix of business functions performed by government agencies.

The Singapore government business reference model will be used to identify business functions that: (a) are resource-intensive or (b) are potential candidates for inter-agency collaboration. Each common business function within could comprise business processes with the potential for streamlining. The identification of such common business processes would facilitate optimisation and streamlining opportunities, resulting in generic business processes for use across the government or within a sector. The generic business processes and related information will then be incorporated as part of the desired future state (i.e., target architectures).

Government Information Architecture

The government information architecture (IA)—the second element to be developed in SGEA—focuses on the effective and efficient sharing of information among agencies and supports the business functions identified in the government BA.

Essentially, service-wide data standards would be developed to form a data reference model (Gartner, 2005). These efforts would be accompanied by the development of relevant data administration policy to establish proper accountability for the data as this would especially be crucial to address the privacy issue and protection of sensitive data.

To facilitate seamless sharing of data across the public sector, an information exchange framework to standardise data definitions of commonly used structured data across government would be developed and would leverage on existing initiatives such as the data hubs. Additional data definitions would be added into the information exchange framework from new initiatives identified in the government BA exercise.

In the development of DRM, the guiding principles used in defining data elements covered the following: (a) national and international standards, (b) data definitions in the existing data hubs, and (c) other standardised data definitions.

When completed, the DRM content would consist of at least the data definition as follows:

1. Data element name;
2. Description;
3. Format;
4. Allowed values or validation rules;

5. Special values;
6. Data element owner; and
7. Usage guidelines.

At the point of writing, the focus for the DRM was on the data elements in the existing three data hubs—people hub, business hub, and land hub. At present, the three data hubs have mechanisms established to facilitate the sharing of commonly used people, land, and businesses-related data. The people hub is a centralized database on common non-sensitive people data (e.g., contains unique identification number (UIN) for all Singapore citizens and residents). The land hub is a one-stop resource centre for comprehensive and accurate digitised land data in map and textual forms. The fundamental land base information includes buildings, roads, and cadastral data, which are the basic land information that are required in the development of most map-based systems. The business hub is a centralized database containing a comprehensive range of information pertaining

to businesses in Singapore. The types of business data captured include company/business identification number and particulars, company/business profile, name history, capital, and shareholder's share details.

The initial DRM is planned for release in 2006. The envisioned seamless information exchange between data owners, government agencies, and the public resulting from the use of the DRM and implementation of government IA is depicted in Figure 5.

Government Solution Architecture

The third element that needs to be developed is the government solution architecture (SA), which focuses on the ICT solutions and the systems and services required to address the needs of the government BA and IA.

The core deliverables for government SA would be a portfolio of service-wide and/or sector-wide systems and services. These will be shared

Figure 5. Implementation of government IA

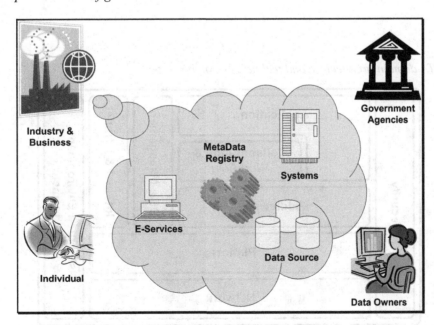

systems and services identified from collaboration opportunities and common business processes drawn from the government BA and existing ICT systems consolidated and implemented as shared components, which are reusable by agencies. Cost savings can then be better realised through such consolidation and standardization efforts.

At the point of writing, the government SA was at the stage of development. The government SA is targeted for implementation from 2007-2010 and would cover several public facing services as well as corporate and supporting services.

Government Technical Architecture

The service-wide technical architecture (SWTA) implemented in 2002 fulfils the role of a government technical architecture (TA). It has achieved inter-operability for systems in the government and was implemented for very practical reasons.

The SWTA is a logically consistent set of principles, standards, and guidelines that guide the public sector agencies in the design, acquisition, implementation, and management of ICT. This common set of principles and standards provides a semantic framework for information sharing and interoperability of systems amongst all agencies. A review process is carried out every half-yearly with agencies to ensure the currency of SWTA and its relevance to enterprise architecture development.

The SWTA architectural principles are high-level statements that describe preferred practices followed in the design and deployment of ICT in the public sector. The principles covered the following: (a) infrastructure reuse, (b) modular architecture, (c) open standards, (d) robustness, scalability, adaptiveness, and performance.

The SWTA framework consists of domain architectures, which are logical groups of related technologies. The content of each domain architecture includes:

1. **Technology components:** Description of relevant technology components.
2. **Technology standards:** International and industry standards that apply to the technology components selected and their status in terms of technology maturity.
3. **Products:** These are specific products in this domain.

Figure 6. SWTA domain architecture and technology components

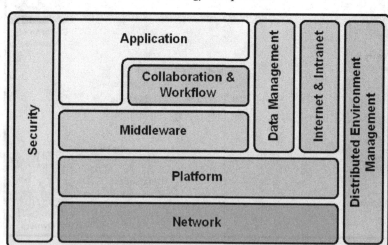

4. **Interoperability standards:** The standards and requirements that are mandatory for inter-agency interoperability.

5. **Central services:** Government-wide services that have been implemented and may be leveraged in this domain.

6. **Best practices:** Guidelines or practical advice based on the experience and research of project teams for implementing specific domain technology components or products.

7. **Technology watch:** Promising technologies that warrant further research and analysis for purpose of the domain.

There are nine domain architectures and these include: (a) application, (b) collaboration and workflow, (c) data management, (d) distributed environment management, (e) internet/intranet,

(f) middleware, (g) platform, (h) network, and (i) security. A diagram showing the nine SWTA domain architectures within is given in Figure 6.

Key Learning Points

Some of the key learning points over the last 12 months of our enterprise architecture journey are:

- EA development takes time and money. The first step is to get stakeholder buy-in, and senior leadership support is critical. There is a need to communicate to stakeholders the value of EA, particularly in relation to organisational goals and strategies.

- Effective communication means communication of outcome. For senior management and business owners, visual models should

Figure 7. ICT governance framework in the Singapore government

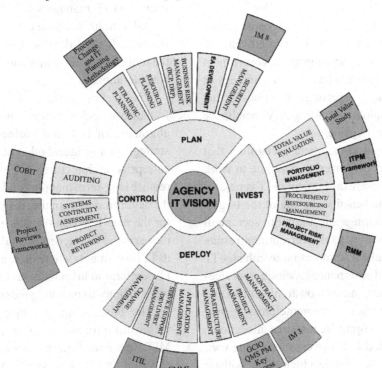

be used to help them understand EA better and focus on showing the outcome. It is necessary to leave the technical blueprints in the boiler room.

- Work on some "easier" areas that will meet less resistance from business owners to demonstrate quick wins and successes.
- EA is developed iteratively and evolves over time. Look at common areas and pick out three priority areas to focus on.
- Good governance is critical to the EA programme. The governance structure of an EA programme typically involves many stakeholder and working level committees. Leverage on existing committees and structures, where possible. Integrate EA into established forums for IT Governance within the organisation, if possible.

GOVERNANCE FOR ENTERPRISE ARCHITECTURE

Over the past few years, the Singapore public sector has been actively seeking improvements in IT governance. The Singapore government instruction manual on information technology or IM8, a comprehensive set of guiding policies that spells out the requirements for agency compliance on IT matters, is in place.

The Singapore government recognises that the public sector will need to continue to work collectively to ensure investment in IT generates the best possible benefits. As one of the largest spenders on IT in Singapore, the public sector will need to invest wisely to deliver optimal results from public funds. It is important to enhance IT management and governance capabilities servicewide and leverage on common architectures and shared infrastructures to promote cross-agency collaboration and optimise resource allocation.

The integrated ICT Governance framework in the pipeline is to provide a logical and holistic overview of the work involved in the public sector's

ICT deployment, and describes the positioning of the governance pieces as shown in Figure 7.

The framework adopts a lifecycle approach positioning IT governance needs and concerns around the agency's long term IT vision. The tools, policies, and methodologies are also positioned in the overview so that agencies can understand how these aids can help them.

It is structured as a three concentric-layered "onion" with the IT vision of the agency in the centre:

1. The first layer consists of the four-lifecycle stages of plan, invest, deploy, and control.
2. The second layer breaks this down into processes that an agency should consider for each stage.
3. The third layer identifies the policies, methodologies, and tools that best serve the agency in addressing the processes.

This framework helps chief information officers and IT managers to first understand the considerations necessary to achieve IT effectiveness. It then directs their attention toward the tools and policies that address the individual considerations.

The agency starts in the plan stage of the framework and examines and establishes the alignment of ICT and business goals through strategic planning and other processes including enterprise architecture. All of these processes require long-term mapping and need to be done at the beginning stage of the lifecycle. With the plan for the next few years in place, the agency then moves to the invest, deploy, and control stages for its IT investments where there are other tools like IT portfolio management and risk management methodology to provide guidance.

The positioning of enterprise architecture within this framework, which according to Sloan-MIT Research, form part of the IT governance equation (Weill & Ross, 2004). This will help agencies to better align IT assets and to "do more with less" by identifying and re-using components for shared systems and services, and will eventually articulate the real benefits of doing enterprise architecture.

CONCLUSION

Over the years, the ICT goals and priorities of the Singapore government had evolved. Starting from one focussing on productivity and operational efficiency in the eighties, to one emphasising "one-stop, non-stop" services in the nineties, and now on cross-agency, integrated public service online, we have come a long way. Architecting IT systems, whether at the agency or public service level, has always been seen as a means to the larger end of supporting the prevailing ICT goals and priorities. The establishment of data hubs to enable multilateral data sharing in 90s, and the implementation of the service-wide technical architecture in 2002 to facilitate systems interoperability were in practice early enterprise architecture efforts, though never labelled nor positioned as such. The formulation of the Singapore government business reference model, identification of common business functions and processes and their prioritisation to guide subsequent development of information exchange framework and data reference model, as well as the eventual deployment of solution architectures are all but examples of our pragmatic approach toward architecture development. The focus on meeting business needs and the principle of pragmatism will continue to guide us in the future work of developing and maintaining the Singapore government enterprise architecture.

REFERENCES

Canada Treasury Board Secretariat. (2004). *Business transformation enablement program.* Retrieved from http://www.tbs-sct.gc.ca/index_e.asp

Carbone, J. A. (2004). *IT architecture toolkit.* Upper Saddle River, NJ: Prentice Hall.

Gartner Inc. (2005, February). *Takes steps to improve government data sharing and reuse* (ID Number: G00125749). Stamford, CT.

META Group. (1999a). *Enterprise architecture strategies process model—Evolution 1999.* Stamford, CT.

META Group (1999b). *Holistic enterprise architecture: Beyond EWTA.* Stamford, CT.

Perks, C., & Beveridge, T. (2002). *Guide to enterprise IT architecture.* New York: Springer.

The Open Group (2002). *TOGAF, Version 8 Enterprise Edition.* Retrieved from http://www.theopengroup.org/

U.S. CIO Council. (1999). *Federal enterprise architecture framework version 1.1.* Retrieved from http://www.cio.gov

U.S. Government Accountability Office. (2004). *The federal enterprise architecture and agencies enterprise architecture are still maturing.* Retrieved from http://www.gao.gov

U.S. Office of Management and Budget. (2005). *Federal enterprise architecture.* Retrieved from http://www.whitehouse.gov/omb/egov/a-1-fea.html

Weill, P., & Ross, J. W. (2004). *IT governance on one page (CISR WP No. 349 and Sloan WP No. 4516-04).* Cambridge, MA: Massachusetts Institute of Technology.

Whittle, R., & Myrick, C. B. (2005). *Enterprise business architecture: The formal link between strategy and results.* Boca Raton, FL: Auerbach Publications.

Zachman J. (1997). *Zachman framework for enterprise architecture.* Retrieved from http://www.zifa.com

Section II
Governance and Management

Chapter VIII
Understanding and Communicating with Enterprise Architecture Users

Steven Thornton
National Institutes of Health, USA

ABSTRACT

The objective of this chapter is to educate chief information officers (CIO), information technology (IT) managers, and IT architects on the role of communications planning in implementing an enterprise architecture (EA) and its supporting programs and the applicability of user-centered analysis in effectively constructing the EA and communicating the organization's EA to the users of EA products and content.

INTRODUCTION

An effective communications strategy is a critical success factor for any organizational change or business reengineering effort. Implementing an EA program, which is a form of organizational change, is no exception. Poor communications is often in the top ten lists of why projects fail, including those that result in an organizational change rather than a software product. It is likely, therefore, that poor communications will be a major contributing factor to failed EA projects and programs within large organizations. To help mitigate the risk of failure, due to poor communications and communications planning, this chapter will provide a high-level view of effective EA communications planning, based on traditional marketing and communications practices. The primary focus of the chapter will be on how to develop an EA that is easy to use and apply from an EA user's perspective.

Many of the recommended approaches and practices are derived from current usability best practices (see *Additional Reading*). The National Institutes of Health (NIH), which is the custodian of biomedical research for the United States, is the case study. Recently NIH completed a yearlong project, which applied a user-centered development methodology to design, build, implement, and publish its EA Web site at enterprisearchitecture.nih.gov.

Because user research is a component of any user-centered development methodology, the NIH EA team has been able to apply lessons learned from this specific EA project to other communications channels and to other areas of the program to ensure that the NIH EA meets the needs of all of its stakeholders.

Included in the chapter are specific recommendations to create and communicate a more effective, usable, and targeted EA. The chapter will also introduce multi-channel communications concepts and their impact on EA communications planning. Communications channels include avenues for disseminating, collecting, or sharing information such as print, Web, executive communications, evangelism, training, and so forth. The chapter also provides some recommendations for communications resource management and for the production of EA products.

The objective of this chapter is to educate chief information officers (CIO), information technology (IT) managers, and IT architects on the role of communications planning in implementing an EA and its supporting programs and the applicability of user-centered analysis in effectively constructing the EA and communicating the organization's EA to the users of EA products and content.

BACKGROUND

A traditional architecture effort is a complex undertaking and an information technology architecture effort is no exception. In fact, IT

architecture efforts may be more complex, given the rapid evolution of technologies and the dynamic nature of large organizations that the systems are meant to support. The complexity is exacerbated in large, decentralize organizations like NIH. In traditional architecture, the laws of nature and physics do not change, although the materials and practices might. The same cannot be said for IT architecture. In fact, not only do the materials or technologies change, there is also a noticeable absence of laws or standards for IT. IT architecture is more akin to building on shifting, sandy soil within an earthquake fault zone, than building on solid bedrock. Nevertheless, an EA that does not simplify the complexities of an information systems design is a wasted effort. It is through the simplification of the organization's complex IT systems design and through a shared knowledge about those systems that the benefits of an EA can be realized.

There are some additional important differences between traditional architecture and EA that make EA more challenging, given today's IT environment. One of the most obvious differences is that enterprise architecture is a new field of knowledge compared to traditional architecture. Therefore, there are few worldwide or even national standards to apply to this knowledge area. In fact, there are probably as many different perspectives or approaches to enterprise architecture as there are organizations trying to apply it to their operations. This is not a new problem though. Other professions, including those in information technology, have shared this challenge.

Organizations have had either to ignore, create, customize, or buy EA frameworks and methodologies. Organizations must expend considerable resources to create a common understanding across stakeholders and to achieve buy-in about how to apply the methodology to solve business problems. Therefore, the EA team must plan for an effective communications strategy or plan for the effort to fail.

In this chapter, I will outline an approach for developing an effective communications plan and implementing your communications strategy. In some cases, I have arrived at a recommendation based on what we've learned at NIH, and in some cases, I have used my professional experience and expertise in the areas of marketing, communications, and user-centered design to arrive at a recommendation. Because every organization and every EA is unique, you may wish to focus on those areas that are most applicable or helpful to your organization today. My primary recommendation, however, is that in planning for an effective EA, keep the EA users at the center of the analysis, and engage them as much as possible and as early as possible. You will thereby ensure that what you are creating is useful and usable.

Throughout this chapter, the term "business" refers interchangeably to either a commercial, government, or other enterprise that works to accomplish some common objective. Though there are certainly differences in the way commercial and government organizations communicate and plan, the recommendations described in this chapter can be applied to either type of organization.

HOW TO COMMUNICATE ENTERPRISE ARCHITECTURE

EA as an Organizational Change

When an organization sets out to implement an EA program, it embarks on a major organizational change that impacts many parts of the business, not just the IT department. Because one purpose of an EA is to align information systems with the business needs or strategy, both the business and its constituent services are impacted.

Furthermore, because of the complexity of the information systems environment and the organizational politics that arise from limited resources, it takes considerable time and resources

to implement an effective EA and its supporting programs.

Because of changes in the business and IT environments, an organization must expend considerable resources to keep the EA current and accurate. Otherwise, the EA becomes a frustrating, academic exercise. Worse, an organization that attempts to apply an outdated EA will raise the cost of IT design and governance and will create disillusionment among its stakeholders.

So, the EA team must consider time and schedule when implementing and maintaining the EA and its supporting programs. There are three disciplines from which the EA team can borrow for its communications planning: *project, program*, and *product* planning.

First, the organization must successfully complete a project to implement an EA and its supporting programs. A critical success component for such a project will be the project communications plan, which includes the effective publication of milestones, schedules, risks, issues, and progress. The project team charged with implementing an EA and its supporting programs must plan for effective communications and must allocate the resources, including time, people, and money to create and execute an effective project communications plan.

Second, program communications planning includes those planning tasks and deliverables that support the ongoing communications about those activities that support the EA. Such activities might include governance, training, program budget, program planning, and risk management. As with project communications planning, the organization must plan for the ongoing communications planning required to support an EA program. The most significant difference between a project and a program is that a project has a definite end date, whereas a program may not. So, the activities that constitute program communications planning tend to be cyclical. For example, EA governance meetings will not end once an EA program has been established. Therefore, the

147

program communications plan must include the activities and resources required to support this set of recurring activities.

An EA program will likely include a portfolio of EA related projects even after the EA is implemented. Since each of the projects should have its own project communications plan and deliverables, the program communications plan and the projects' communications plans should be mutually supportive.

Finally, an EA is essentially a set of communications tools or products commonly referred to as blueprints or standards. The balance of this chapter will focus on this latter aspect of EA communications—communicating the EA products. Treating the EA as a product or set of products enables the organization to apply traditional marketing and communications concepts and practices to increase the usability and usefulness of the EA for its users.

Defining the Enterprise

An important step in creating an EA is to define the "enterprise." There may be multiple, faceted organizational layers—parent organizations, child organizations, peer organizations, matrix organizations, etc. So, in large, complex organizations the EA's scope must clearly define the organizational boundaries of the enterprise.

NIH (2005) defines the scope of the NIH enterprise architecture as such:

The NIH enterprise architecture policy directs that the scope of its enterprise architecture spans all [institutes and centers], including work completed or supported by outside agents. It specifically addresses the needs of NIH administrative and management functions, as well as interfaces to the external community with which it interacts.

Furthermore, especially in the case of hierarchical organizations or those with large operating divisions, if multiple EAs reside at different levels

in the organizational structure, the EA teams must be able to communicate how the EAs support or relate to one another. The key question for stakeholders throughout the large enterprise will be "What stakeholders at what layers of the organizations will need to use and understand which EA(s), and how do they apply the EA(s) to their work?"

From a design perspective, defining the enterprise and effectively communicating this definition will enable the EA team to have an identifiable, relatively fixed scope of work, and will thereby minimize scope creep, missed requirements, incorrect assumptions, redundant work, and poorly designed systems interfaces.

A related communications lesson can be learned from the military. In the military, areas of responsibility during a combat operation are as clearly defined as is reasonably possible, including responsibilities between different levels of the command structure and between geographically adjacent units. Clear definitions of the scope of the operation in terms of mission, time, and geography enable the units to minimize weak points and fratricide. Granted, failing to adequately define the enterprise may not lead to loss of life. However, failing to do so may lead to lost or corrupted data, security vulnerabilities, unusable user interfaces, and so on. More important to the area of EA communications, not defining the EA and the EA's position with respect to other EAs will lead to confusion and disillusionment about EA all across the entire enterprise.

Clearly defining the enterprise will also enable the users of EA information to distinguish which EA content is relevant to them within the organizational hierarchy without having to browse and search through endless pages of confusing, bureaucratic jargon. Also, defining the enterprises within various layers of a large organization will enable architects in the various enterprises to understand their organizational and system boundaries, which subsequently will highlight those areas about which they must sustain structured communications efforts, such as periodic architect forums.

Defining the Framework

The first level of decomposition for an EA is generally called the EA framework. From a communications perspective, the framework is a model or classification scheme for EA content. There are several standard frameworks that an organization can adopt or mirror. However, NIH, like many organizations, created its own customized framework because of local, unique business requirements and IT challenges.

The exact framework is less important than the requirement that the framework be easily understood for the target audience, consistently defined, and consistently communicated.

There are several reasons for consistency in communicating the EA framework. First, the framework is a component of the EA taxonomy and will be incorporated into many other EA deliverables and communications products. As the EA program matures and evolves, a minor change to the framework may incur significant hidden costs to update legacy EA content. Second, users become familiar with the EA framework as they navigate the EA content. The framework will begin to transform their mental model of EA. Therefore, changing the framework will generate hidden training costs and decreased productivity for these users.

If an organization is embarking on creating a new EA and does not have an existing EA framework, it is strongly advisable to engage EA users to understand how they would use and organize EA information. In this way, the organization can define a framework that is most useful to the broadest range of users, rather than a framework that fits only the architect or EA team's mental models.

The Approach to Effective EA Communications

Since NIH already had an existing EA when it began, its user-centered approach in developing an effective EA Web site, NIH performed the following tasks to better understand the EA users and how they use and interact with the EA content and products in an effort to make the EA more useful and usable:

- Assess the organization's current situation and understanding.
- Identify EA stakeholders.
- Identify EA users.
- Model EA users.
- Align user and organizational requirements.
- Identify the value proposition.
- Identify EA user tasks.
- Create the communications solutions.

Figure 1. Stair step model for effective EA communications planning

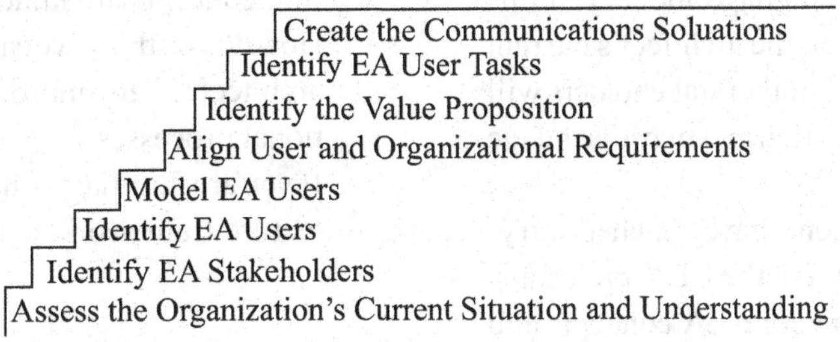

```
                                    Create the Communications Soluations
                              Identify EA User Tasks
                         Identify the Value Proposition
                    Align User and Organizational Requirements
                 Model EA Users
            Identify EA Users
         Identify EA Stakeholders
      Assess the Organization's Current Situation and Understanding
```

Figure 1 depicts these tasks in picture format.

It is important to note, however, that the EA team will never be entirely finished with communications. Not only will communications planning become an integral part of the overall EA program planning process, the EA team will have to revisit each of these steps as the environment in which the EA operates changes. Some examples of environmental changes that might necessitate revisiting these steps would include personnel changes, shift in corporate culture, change in executive management, organizational restructuring, buyouts and mergers, competitive pressures, technological advances, the organization's EA maturity level, and familiarity with EA concepts and the organization's EA specifically. The EA team must be aware of these various environmental forces and anticipate revisiting the communications plan every one to two years. This planning horizon will also enable the EA team to assess the effectiveness of their current communications plan and to reallocate scarce communications resources where they are most needed. It will also motivate the team to look at EA content and messages that may have become out of date.

Assess the Organization's Current Situation and Understanding

To communicate EA effectively within an organization, it is necessary to gauge and document the organization's current understanding of EA and the current organizational communications climate. One of the benefits of an EA is to create a common framework or language about IT. If this language is based only on the architect's current understanding, most of the other stakeholders will be left out of the conversation and may disengage from EA.

Different organizations have reached varying degrees of maturity for their EA programs. Whereas in some organization EA concepts and models may be very well understood, in other organizations EA concepts may be as foreign as a Martian alphabet. It is likely that even if a significant number of EA users understand EA concepts, the depth and breadth of understanding among users throughout the organization will vary significantly. Furthermore, because organizations are not stagnant and labor is highly mobile across organizations, and because EA concepts are highly localized and customized within different organizations, those users that have a good understanding of EA concepts will inevitably bring the mental model from their previous organization.

So, the next step is to understand a sampling of users' current understanding of EA in general and EA within the organization more specifically. This assessment can be accomplished in several ways, including meetings, individual interviews, and surveys. Examples of questions you might want your stakeholders to answer are:

- What does enterprise architecture mean to you?
- How would you define "enterprise"?
- Where do you currently go to get information about IT standards?
- What kinds of models do you use in your current design efforts?
- How do you think enterprise architecture can benefit this organization?
- Who do you think uses or will use enterprise architecture deliverables and how?
- Who do you think will contribute to enterprise architecture processes and how?
- How well do you think enterprise architecture concepts are understood?
- How do you think we can leverage enterprise architecture to improve IT and organizational processes?
- If you are familiar with the enterprise architecture framework, can you describe it?

- Have you ever used enterprise architecture concepts or deliverables either here or in another organization? How?
- What else would you like to tell us about enterprise architecture?

This list contains open-ended questions that require more than a "yes" or "no" answer. This approach will better gauge the users' understanding of EA than will leading questions. Furthermore, open-ended questions, especially in an interview situation, will help the user to open up and take the interview into a much more productive direction. It is likely that this type of research will provide some surprising insights and results that will inform your EA program. NIH, for example, learned that there was a significant knowledge gap about enterprise architecture for its EA users and other stakeholders and that additional communications and training resources were going to have to be budgeted for the EA stakeholders.

Include questions that will help identify the EA users and other stakeholders. NIH was able to use this information to select additional candidates for EA user research and for testing EA products, like the EA Web site. In the process, you will also expand the base of potential EA advocates.

Budget permitting, consider bringing a human factors or usability professional on board on a temporary and part time arrangement. These professionals are trained in identifying the correct users to interview, both the art and science of conducting user research, and interpreting and applying the research results. You may already have these resources in your IT or communications organizations.

Identify EA Stakeholders

The entire EA program depends on engaging the appropriate EA stakeholders. For communications planning specifically, identifying stakeholders will help the EA team to identify the audience for EA content and users of EA products. Furthermore,

EA stakeholders will influence EA communications frequency, format, and content, even if they don't directly consume EA products.

Some of the types of stakeholders NIH considered are:

- The EA team.
- Individuals or organizations impacted by the EA or EA program.
- Individuals or organizations that influence the EA or EA program.
- Individuals or organizations that help create or update EA products or content.
- Individuals or organizations that use EA products or content.
- Individuals or organizations that participate in IT governance.
- Individuals or organizations that are supported by the EA or the EA program.
- Individuals or organizations that support the EA or EA program.

Identify EA Users

The list of users can be derived by identifying those stakeholders that are also users of EA products or content. The list of users that NIH identified included the following:

- IT project managers
- IT program managers
- Software developers
- Systems designers
- Procurement specialists
- IT managers
- IT executives
- Business executives
- Business analysts
- Systems analysts

It may not be cost effective or useful to customize the presentation of EA content for every user. A typical user-centered approach, like the approach NIH used, is to categorize the list of users into a finite number of user segments or user groups. These segments are derived from a set of distinguishing, meaningful, and shared characteristics or needs.

For example, IT project managers, IT managers, and IT program managers may be lumped into a single user segment because these three groups of users are similar in most regards in relation to the EA. Specifically, they are mid-level managers who make decisions about IT projects and who acquire and manage project resources. Let's call this segment "planners."

Software developers may not fit in this segment because their needs with respect to the EA are significantly different. However, if they share common needs and characteristics with business analysts and systems analysts within your organization you may lump them into a second user segment. Let's call this segment "executers."

IT and business executives are sufficiently high up in the organization that their communications needs will be different than the other user groups. The mechanisms or channels for delivering content to them will be significantly different. Executives are a relatively small user segment, but they have enough influence over resources and other success factors that the EA team will do well to identify them and consider them in their communications planning. Let's call this segment simply "executives."

There is no single way to segment users. The goal is 3-5 significantly different user segments to make communications planning effective. The EA team, which is faced with limited resources and time, may not wish to devote as much time and effort into communications planning for some user segments.

As the EA program matures, different users may take on more or less importance. For example, executives and planners may be more important than executers early on and require more communications support. However, planners and executers may take on more importance than executives later on. It is also possible that a new user segment will enter into the picture that was of little import earlier in the program's history—external customers or business partners for example.

Understanding these segments will enable the EA team to focus and tailor the EA content. Different EA content will be important to different user segments and thus may be prioritized differently. The EA team can determine which channels work best for which users and focus on those user segments that are most important and deliver content to them in the most effective way.

Model Users

After the EA team has identified the user segments, the team can begin modeling the users. NIH used conventional usability methodologies to model its EA users, including the following:

- User profiles and demographics.
- Information needs.
- Task profiles.

User profiles include those user characteristics that describe the users in terms of their relationship to the EA or in terms of important demographic characteristics that impact communications planning. User profile characteristics might include:

- Health/age/gender
- Education
- Language
- Computer experience
- EA expertise
- Task knowledge
- Expectations of EA
- Business areas
- Preferred communications platforms
- Number of users

It isn't necessary to include every demographic characteristic when modeling EA users. Rather focus on those attributes that are important in understanding how the users might interact with the EA. For example, gender may have no relevance to EA communications within a given organization, whereas age might. Age might influence how users prefer to receive EA communications, including preferences for print vs. online. It may also influence language, level of detail, and information accessibility. Interviews, surveys, and direct observations are the best sources of information about EA users.

Add to this list or subtract from it to include those characteristics that will influence your decisions about EA communications planning. Consider statistical analysis to learn interesting and relevant trends, especially in large organizations. This kind of analysis can be summarized in a table similar to Figure 2.

Information needs may vary between user segments. It is probably the most important distinguishing attribute for the user segments. For example, executives may be more interested or concerned with EA governance and EA planning than they are with specific EA models. However, executers may be more concerned with specific IT standards and business models than they are with EA governance. Identify the EA information needs for each of the user segments. This step will allow you to identify the most important EA content that is used by more than one segment for

example and to focus EA communications efforts on this content.

At this stage, the EA team should also begin documenting what they believe the users will do with the EA content and products in terms of *task profiles*. Begin to answer questions like:

- How will they use the EA deliverables?
- What does the EA team need the users to do with the deliverables?
- What actions will be performed against or with the EA deliverables?
- What non-EA tasks or process will the EA deliverables support or be inputs into?

Understanding the tasks and what tasks are relevant to each user segment will enable the EA team to write and position EA content more effectively. It will also enable the EA team to publish specific instructions for using the EA. Grouping tasks by user segments enables the team to identify those tasks that are used by more than one user segment and therefore those that are most important and most frequently used. These tasks should be given priority in messaging and positioning within the various EA communications channels. A brief example of an EA task profile might look something like Figure 3.

Figure 2. Example user profile

Attribute	Executives	Planners	Executers
1. Age			
2. Education			
3. Language			
4. Computer experience			
5. EA expertise			
6. Task knowledge			
7. Expectations of EA			
8. Business areas			
9. Comm. platforms			
10. Number of users			

Figure 3. Example task profile

Task	Executives	Planners	Executers
Task 1: Learn about governance	X	X	
Task 2: Research models		X	X
Task 3: Apply standards		X	X
Task 4: Send e-mail about EA	X	X	X
Task 5: Certify project		X	
Task 6: Comment on standard		X	X
Task 7: Ask for help		X	X
Task 8: Request training		X	X
Task 9: Find meeting	X		
Task 10: Request waiver		X	

Other tools not addressed here that are available to the EA team for modeling and understanding EA users are:

- Personas
- User scenarios
- Use cases
- Storyboards

If you have a usability analyst on your team, the analyst can help leverage these analytical tools effectively in your communications planning.

Align User and Organizational Requirements

Any communications solutions that do not consider the needs of the EA team or supporting EA processes will be partial or perhaps misguided solutions. For example, users may want a collaboration tool to discuss to-be models. In this case, the EA team should be consulted to identify the requirements to moderate such a tool. Another example might include the processing of waiver requests. The EA team, not the EA users, will most likely identify the specific communica- tions requirements for the waiver process. The EA team will be impacted by virtually every EA communications decision and should therefore be consulted for their requirements, too.

Identify the Value Proposition

The EA value proposition is the intersection of the EA program's capabilities and the users' needs. Identifying it will help focus your scarce communications resources. Specifically, the EA value proposition identifies the set of EA products or services that EA users can use to benefit their work. The products are services are described in terms of how they benefit the users. Note that this is not the same as the benefits derived from having an EA in your organization. Rather, it describes the benefit of each EA product or service.

Figure 4a graphical representation of an EA value proposition shows this intersection of user needs and program capabilities. Because different organizations have different business requirements and are composed of different users with different individual needs, the value proposition may also be different for each organization.

Figure 4. Graphical representation of an EA value proposition

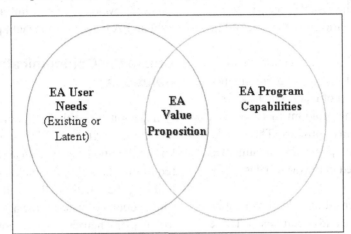

List what you have identified as the EA users' information needs or needs that can be met through EA-related tasks:

1. _____
2. _____
3. _____
4. _____
5. _____
6. _____
7. _____
8. _____
9. _____
10. _____

List what you have identified as the EA program's products or services that can be used to complete EA-related tasks:

1. _____
2. _____
3. _____
4. _____
5. _____
6. _____
7. _____
8. _____

9. _____
10. _____

Match the identified user needs with the existing EA program capabilities. The overlap is the current EA value proposition. Focusing on these capabilities and describing how they meet the EA users' needs will motivate users to use and apply these EA products and services. In effect, the value proposition becomes the "EA sell" and the call to action.

Identify User Tasks

The next step NIH took in planning for its redesigned EA Web site was to decompose the high-level user tasks into detailed user task flows. Rather than simply listing the tasks, as in a task profile, this analysis breaks these tasks down into process steps, decision points, and additional subtasks. Even if you don't plan to automate all of your program's EA processes, this detailed task analysis will help you to understand how the users will navigate and use the EA.

The detailed task flows are important inputs for the effective design of EA Web sites and other EA software products and tools. The team will use the task flows in conjunction with the EA taxonomy to develop the EA Web site's information architecture, navigation scheme, and online user scenarios.

As mentioned earlier in the section on aligning EA program and EA user requirements, there may be another set of tasks that arise from the requirements of the program that were not identified in the user task profiles. These tasks must be similarly decomposed and documented so that they are included in the overall design for the Web site or EA tool.

There is yet another set of tasks that must be identified, documented, and decomposed. These tasks create inputs to the EA processes and account for outputs from EA processes that feed other business processes. These process interfaces, which might include interfaces into such business areas as IT governance, IT project management, and procurement, will assist the team in identifying where users should encounter EA messages and content (link to the EA Web site) and how users should apply the EA to other business areas (link from the EA Web site).

The goal in identifying this set of tasks is to position the EA where it is most useful to the user and to use the EA as a springboard to other related business processes. The EA exists to support the business, not as a purely academic exercise. Some questions to ask in deriving these tasks are:

- Where is a need or requirement to use the EA likely to arise either online or in the real world?
- What other needs are likely to arise when using the EA that can be better met elsewhere, either online or in the real world?
- How will the user apply this part of the EA to their work?
- For what other business processes will the EA user use this specific EA content?

Answers to these kinds of questions will help the team develop a Web site linking strategy and to publish EA content at the right place and time.

Create the Communications Solutions

At this point during the communications planning process, the EA team will have a wealth of valuable knowledge about the EA user and the EA program requirements. All that remains is designing and building the solutions that will deliver the EA. This section describes some high-level guidance to consider when creating the content or building the EA communications solutions.

Deliver Effective EA Content

Communications is all about delivering the right message, to the right audience, at the right time, in the way that is most helpful to them. Effective internal communications has become increasingly important because more and more demands are being placed on employees' time. Furthermore, with the explosion of digital media there is an increasing number of competing, divergent communications sources in an organization. Finally, on the World Wide Web, other sources of information, whether good or bad, are a click away. Therefore, the current environment makes effective communications and communications planning more important than ever.

Users have neither the time nor motivation to decipher executive intent that underlies EA communications. The EA team must make it easy to understand EA content and apply it to their work. It is more likely that an EA team will be able to communicate effectively by understanding the users' needs and tasks. However, all of this analysis will be an exorbitant waste of time and money if the EA team doesn't write effectively and with the audience and intricacies of the various communications channels in mind.

If the EA team doesn't have effective writers, then consider investing in a good writer who is trained in technical writing and writing for the Web, or consider investing in your current team to develop these skills if you plan to use the Web as a primary communications channel. Some writers may also have experience with communications planning and can help in this area.

Another thought to consider when communicating about EA is to "keep it simple." One of the goals of an EA program is to simplify an inherently complex enterprise design for information systems. If the EA complicates the organization's understanding of the IT environment, either through an overly complex framework or taxonomy or through a poorly executed communications plan, then the EA adds little value and may increase the cost of IT significantly.

The 80-20 Rule for Content

Because users' time, attention span, and patience are all in short supply in today's fast paced business environment, communicators must effectively prioritize content. While working through the process of understanding and modeling EA users, identify the information that is most important to most users. A good rule of thumb is that 20% of your content will serve 80% of your users' information needs.

Therefore, this 20% of the content should be treated as the most important information asset for your EA program. Give it priority placement in your communications channels, especially on your Web site. Make this 20% of the content very easy to find and spend more of your time and resources on developing, improving, and communicating it. You'll get the biggest bang for your buck and most users will get the information they need from the 20%.

Keep in mind though that the specific content that falls into this 20% will change over time, as the EA program evolves.

EA Communications Channels

Consider all of the different communications channels available to reach EA stakeholders. Communicate with them where they prefer in the most cost effective way, given the organizational culture and available communications resources. Also, provide mechanisms for feedback since EA communications flow up, down, and laterally within an organization. Some of the available communications channels in a typical organization include:

- Web sites (Internet, intranet, and extranet, portals, etc.)
- Newsletters (within the organization or outside of the organization—online, print, e-mail)
- Online e-mail lists
- Discussion boards and other virtual collaboration environments
- Training
- Online training modules or computer based training
- Briefings to executives
- Briefings from executives and the architect executive road shows
- Meetings, discussion forums, and workshops
- Brochures
- White papers and case studies
- Online feedback forms
- Surveys
- Posters and table tents

NIH has leveraged all of these communications channels as part of its communications strategy for EA. However, because NIH is a decentralized, geographically dispersed organization, the Web plays the central role. The NIH currently maintains an intranet and Internet presence for its EA users to ensure the widest possible dissemination of EA content. The NIH has also leveraged collaboration technologies like discussion threads to foster asynchronous collaboration among EA stakeholders in the development of IT standards. NIH uses a subscription-based EA listserv for users who prefer to be notified of a change in the EA or to receive announcements about EA training opportunities. Executive communications, training opportunities, and the aforementioned communications channels are coordinated using a communications plan that considers the needs of both the EA user and the EA team.

The list available to you will probably be quite long. However, consider how you will best reach your most important user segments in the most effective way based on your understanding of your EA users. The communications plan should include a plan for each of your targeted communications channels so that the communications strategy is coordinated and synergistic. A communications plan should also help with creating and publishing consistent messages between the different channels so that you reinforce the message and prevent confusion resulting from possible inconsistencies. However, the messages may be tailored to realize the benefits of a given channel.

The focus on various communications channels may shift based on the maturity of the EA program. For example, NIH focused heavily on executive communications during its EA program's first two years in order to achieve executive buy-in, ownership, and direction. Thereafter, it shifted focus to the Web and other channels to disseminate information to a wider audience across the enterprise.

Communications Team and Resources

When building your EA team, include the resources required to develop, implement, and support your communications plan. Your team's skill set might include a combination of the following skills depending on your budget and the skills of your existing team members. Multiple skill sets may reside within a single individual. Some of these skill sets may reside with part time or temporary team members or may be task organized in a matrix organizational structure. The types of skills you will need will change over time. Some of the skills you will want to consider are:

- Communications manager
- Content manager
- Information architect
- Technical writer
- Web writer
- Training manager

Technical resources required to support your team will be based on your budget, your current technology environment, and on the requirements of the communications channels you decide to use as part of your communication plan. Such resources include commercial off-the-shelf (COTS) EA tools, content management systems, document management systems, collaboration systems, portals, modeling tools, etc. Try to leverage existing or low cost tools early in the process until you understand your program requirements and can make the most informed decision for your larger EA investments.

Consider the implementation of COTS EA tools carefully. These tools may be excellent for your EA team. However, they may not be the most effective communications channels for your user segments. They are feature rich and subsequently require a significant training investment. The problem you will eventually have to solve will be how to leverage the EA tool with your primary EA communications channels.

CONCLUSION

The bottom line is that to be successful you must plan for EA communications and not leave it to chance. Effective communications planning requires time, money, and persistence. To ignore this aspect of your EA planning is to set the conditions for failure. Plan and communicate well and you will increase buy-in and adoption of the EA.

When developing your communications plan, consider the EA users' needs as well as the EA program objectives. For EA to be an effective tool for IT design, the information contained within it must be thoughtfully constructed and effectively delivered. By taking into account the EA users' mental models, rather than solely the architect's mental model, you will deliver a more effective EA product.

REFERENCES

National Institutes of Health. (2005). *Approach at NIH*. Retrieved December 22, 2005, from http://enterprisearchitecture.nih.gov/About/Approach/

ADDITIONAL READING

A Guide to the Project Management Body of Knowledge Third Edition (PMBOK® Guide). Newton Square, Pennsylvania: Project Management Institute, Inc. 2004.

Department of U.S. Health and Human Services. Usability.gov.

European Union. *Usability.net*.

International Organization for Standardization (1998). *ISO 9241: Ergonomic Requirements for Office Work with Visual Display Terminals (VDTs) —Part 11: Guidance on Usability*.

International Organization for Standardization (1999). *ISO 13407: Human-centered design processes for interactive systems*.

Navalkar, A. (2006). *Usability Engineering –Quality Approach (ISO 13407)*. Retrieved March 27, 2006, from http://www.humanfactors.com/downloads/documents/UsabilityISO.pdf

The Schaffer-Weinschenk Method™ of User-Centered Design. Retrieved March 27, 2006, from http://www.humanfactors.com/about/sw-method.a

Chapter IX
Improving Stakeholder Communications and IT Engagement:
A Case Study Perspective[1]

Gail L. Verley

Federal Desposit Insurance Corporation, USA

ABSTRACT

Stakeholder engagement is critical to applying enterprise architecture (EA) principles and methodologies in order to achieve value from information technology (IT) investments. Stakeholders include the business owners, data owners, developers, and technical infrastructure operational staff. Obtaining stakeholder engagement is a continuous process and is necessary at all levels of the organization. It is also an integral aspect of the governance process for IT investments. This chapter addresses the following topics as they relate to stakeholder engagement:

- *Obtaining high-level stakeholder involvement in EA governing processes and addressing major challenges in building stakeholder engagement.*
- *Illustrating how stakeholder involvement can lead to consolidation and better management of IT investments.*
- *Identifying vehicles to communicate with EA stakeholders while ensuring the architecture accommodates the style and priorities of the stakeholder community.*

INTRODUCTION

Enterprise architecture is having a profound impact on the way organizations deal with IT. Responsibility for ensuring that IT delivers the required business results resides with the organization as a whole. EA can enable organizations to manage IT as a business that is, to drive IT decisions based upon business metrics, align IT to business objectives, and make financially sound decisions. Most organizations recognize that their business units must have an active, collaborative role with their IT departments in order to embrace new technologies, determine innovative approaches, and establish techniques to institutionalize best practices across the organization. This means that stakeholder engagement must be found at all levels in the organization—senior-level decision makers, operational management, and project sponsors. An engaged stakeholder community collaborates with the EA program staff to determine how to achieve the business objectives and maximize the technology investments life cycle. While standards, models, and protocols can be described and documented in the EA artifacts, a successful EA program results in cost savings and an agile IT environment that can easily respond to changing business needs.

BACKGROUND

Enterprise architecture is largely about change management and the behavior of people. In many organizations, it may be necessary to call the program something other than EA because the term is not well understood. In such cases, it would be better to label the program as "enterprise planning" or "IT rationalization" and to present the principles and methodologies using terminology familiar to the organization. Regardless of the term used to define your organization's EA program, the most important aspect for the program's success is stakeholder involvement. To involve stakeholders in their EA programs, organizations typically establish an approach that consists of the following five components:

1. **Identifying the stakeholders:** Who are they and why do they need to be engaged in determining the IT investment strategies and tactical implementations? EA stakehold-

ers include the business owners, the data owners, the developers, and the technical infrastructure operational staff. Each stakeholder has a very different perspective on the value of EA to his or her needs and how best to implement IT solutions considering the EA framework for the organization.

2. **Communicating the value of EA:** Unless stakeholders recognize that applying EA to the decision-making process is valuable to their needs, engaging stakeholders in applying EA principles and methodologies is useless. Establishing a communications or marketing plan is critical to the success as stated in a recent publication by Alex Cullen from Forrester Research, Inc. (Cullen, 2006). Although this chapter focuses on marketing the value of EA to the personnel of IT, the best practices described in this chapter still apply to the other stakeholders.

3. **Developing stakeholder roles:** Now that the stakeholders recognize that the value in applying EA to the decision-making process, they need to understand their roles within the process so they can actively participate. Gene Leganza noted in his article published by Forrester Research, Inc. in May 2001 that successful EA practices must consider the roles of the stakeholders in the organization, including the business leaders, IT management, and IT practitioners. Leganza also notes in a May 2005 article entitled *"Public and Private Sector Business Architecture"* that the business architecture unlocks the ultimate value of an EA program. Recognizing the value of the business stakeholder is an essential cornerstone in establishing an EA program. At the same time according to Leganza, EA artifacts must be created with a purpose and a target audience and be communicated to each stakeholder group.

4. **Marketing EA to developers:** Equally important to the implementation of an EA program is the support of the IT management

and IT practitioners. While many business owners see the value of strategically planning for implementing new IT solutions and are willing to take an enterprise approach to business solutions, IT practitioners may see EA as a hindrance or obstacle to achieving their IT solution. In some cases, these individuals disregard IT investment guidelines, ignore EA standards, and demonstrate an unwillingness to adopt EA practices. For example, while configuring a new solution for a particular business client, the developer may choose a solution familiar to the developer's expertise rather than implementing the solution using the standard platform prescribed by the EA standards and protocols. This set of stakeholders is equally important to the successful EA program. While the business or data owners may agree to implementing a common vision and shared set of standards, the IT practitioners may be the obstacles to implementing an enterprise solution or reusing code or solutions in the organization's IT portfolio.

5. **Establishing a governance framework:** An effective governance framework must be in place that includes the right leadership, focuses on the right issues, and asks the right questions. The governance structures have three characteristics according to Peter Weill and Jeanne W. Ross. They are (1) simple—mechanisms unambiguously define the responsibilities or objective for a specific person or group; (2) transparent—effective mechanisms rely on formal processes; and (3) suitable—mechanisms engage individuals in the best position to make given decisions. The mechanisms, however, do not act in isolation. The impact of governance mechanisms depends on interactions among the mechanisms (Weill & Ross, 2004).

To realize IT's potential to promote the organization's values and deliver on its mission,

senior leadership must craft a disciplined effort to identify and invest in IT strategies that will work best to those ends. This is a tough job. Widely divergent views on how best to use IT must be reconciled. Any organization with a single mission likely has components that contribute to it in very different ways. Varying in methods, procedures, objectives, and goals, they have different ways of measuring success that yield different ideas and priorities for IT. Differences can arise from knowing much about IT and having a vested interest, as well as from knowing little. Without IT governance to channel these forces productively, the main IT potential likely to be realized is that of absorbing large amounts of money with inconsistent results and uneven benefits.

The following ten strategies promote stakeholder engagement through simple, transparent, and suitable mechanisms:

1. Executive management "buy-in" provides the leadership and vision for ensuring that EA is considered when determining strategic and tactical IT investments.

2. Business accountability for IT projects provides a direct link for achieving the business value of the IT solution and ensures that the success of the implementation is dependent upon the business engagement in developing the solution.

3. Linking pay and performance to IT investment success places financial value on the outcome and, therefore, the commitment of resources to successfully implement the results.

4. Frequent communication of objectives, strategies, and activities is key to ensuring that all affected parties are up to date on the project status, as well as the short-term and long-term results anticipated by the EA initiative.

5. Clearly defined principles of EA are essential for the EA program to evolve.

6. Demonstrated tangible benefits to stakeholders with metrics such as cost savings, reduction in the duplication of IT technologies, and improved IT performance must be documented and tracked.
7. Governance bodies based upon the types of decisions that are required by the IT solution are established and actively engaged in IT management. According to Weill et al. (2004), well-designed IT governance arrangements distribute IT decision making to those responsible for outcomes.
8. Stakeholders are given responsibilities in leading and participating in IT strategic initiatives.
9. IT management has a seat at the business strategic table so that business strategies consider IT as a contributor, not simply the means to achieve the business result.
10. Successes are celebrated and all participants are recognized for their contribution.

Weill et al. observe that all enterprises have IT governance. Those with effective governance have actively designed a set of IT governance mechanisms (committees, budgeting processes, approvals, and so on) that encourage behavior consistent with the organization's mission, strategy, values, norms, and culture. Without strategic focus, organizations tend toward tactical IT decision-making of limited value that risks unintended conflict and inefficiency and fails to optimize the organization's success. By contrast, Weill et al. find that carefully designed IT governance provides a clear, transparent IT decision-making process that leads to consistent behavior linked back to the senior management vision while empowering everyone's creativity (Weill et al., 2004).

The following case study demonstrates how to engage stakeholders in the EA program. The case study addresses several components in establish-

ing a successful EA program, demonstrating that the stakeholder community demands an active role to ensure that the defined EA principles and methodologies are continuously applied. A recent research study by Gartner Research (Kreizman & Blanton, 2005) noted:

The Federal Deposit Insurance Corporation (FDIC) has capitalized on opportunities to make EA an alignment engine from strategic planning through development fueled by business attention to business issues. The FDIC first realized the value of EA in 1997, when two business executives had to reconcile data that had come from different systems for a high-profile report to the banking industry. This exercise demonstrated persuasively that their data was a corporate asset and they had to share a consistent view of that data. Essentially, they agreed that it made sense to plan the business processes and information across the enterprise first and then let technology follow. With high-level business sponsorship of the enterprise-wide approach from division directors who own each line of business, the EA program gained momentum.
The second driver for EA came in 2002 when the FDIC's Chairman emphasized stewardship, leadership and stability. In response, the Chief Financial Officer established a Capital Investment Review Committee to review and monitor investments. The EA provided discipline and targets for ensuring investments were aligned with the FDIC's strategic directions and were linked to real business needs. As a result, the agency sees EA as a planning tool for analyzing drivers, designing processes and then aligning IT. For the IT organization, this meant more detailed business cases that substantiated the business value for IT investments according to these characteristics.

Case Study: Federal Deposit Insurance Corporation

In response to the thousands of bank failures that occurred in the 1920s and early 1930s, Congress created the FDIC in 1933 to maintain stability and public confidence in the nation's banking system. An independent agency of the federal government, the FDIC, preserves and promotes public confidence in the U.S. financial system by insuring deposits in banks and thrift institutions for up to $100,000, by identifying, monitoring, and addressing risks to the deposit insurance funds, and by limiting the effect on the economy and the banking industry when a financial institution fails. Since the start of FDIC insurance on January 1, 1934, no depositor has lost a single cent of insured funds as a result of a bank failure.

The FDIC receives no Congressional appropriations. It is funded by premiums that financial institutions pay for deposit insurance coverage and from earnings on premiums invested in U.S. Treasury securities. The FDIC insures more than $3 trillion of deposits in U.S. financial institutions.

The FDIC examines and supervises approximately 5,300 banks and savings institutions--more than half of the institutions in the nation's banking system. To protect insured depositors, the FDIC responds immediately when a financial institution fails. Several options are available for resolving institution failures, but the one most frequently used is to sell deposits and loans of the failed institution to another institution. Customers of the failed institution automatically become customers of the assuming institution.

Historically, the FDIC's operations were decentralized with each division and office developing and implementing technology designed to support its business needs. The development efforts met business needs but were not directed by a centralized information resource management operation. Rather, they were managed by functional divisions that also managed the local area networks. The result was nonstandard, re-

dundant, and inefficient systems with accompanying data and quality problems. This was further complicated by the sunset of the Resolution Trust Corporation and its merger into the FDIC during 1995 and 1996, coupled with downsizing and organizational realignments.

In the years that followed, the FDIC focused considerable effort on centralizing management of its technology infrastructure and has developed a corporate perspective in its review and implementation of IT solutions. The development of a centralized IT investment model was initiated by the need to develop a secure local and wide area network, as well as a standard operating system and desktop platform across the country. The consolidation of the workforce and reduction in field locations supported moving the IT infrastructure responsibilities to a central IT organization. The FDIC made a strategic decision to realign the field structure and to provide for centralized IT and administrative support with limited IT and administrative functions in the field as staff of the central organizations. Former divisional IT and administrative staff were reassigned to the new central organizations, thus retaining the knowledge of the business functions while shifting reporting to the new organizations. This fundamental change provided the foundation for promoting a centralized approach for business systems and future enterprise solutions.

Obtain High-Level Stakeholder Involvement in EA Governing Processes

In order to effectively deliver IT services, the FDIC's IT division established the objective of becoming a strategic partner with its stakeholders. As a first step, with the support of the FDIC chairman, the chief information officer (CIO), the chief operating officer, and the chief financial officer (CFO), the FDIC established governing bodies to actively engage business line divisions in the FDIC's EA program.

The FDIC relies heavily on technology to support its analytical, communication, and operational business. The CIO reports directly to the Chairman, illustrating the importance of technology to the FDIC. Because business requirements change due to legislative initiatives, financial industry changes, and economic indicators, the FDIC must be able to respond and adjust to these changes. To ensure that IT decisions are aligned and responsive to all business needs, the FDIC established a collaborative governance structure. The FDIC's EA is considered a continuous, interactive, and integral part of the Corporation's strategic and capital planning processes. Because the Corporation recognizes the importance of the EA program, it is overseen by executive-level representation from across the Corporation's business lines. The FDIC's EA is developed in

a cooperative, managed, and coordinated effort facilitated by the CIO, with participation of the FDIC's divisions and subject matter technical experts.

The FDIC developed a capital investment policy, jointly issued by the CFO and the CIO, which conveys top-level recognition of the FDIC's reliance upon IT to deliver on its mission. The policy acknowledges that laws and executive orders regarding e-government represent industry best practices and states the FDIC's adoption, in whole or in part, to ensure sound IT capital investment planning and management. In addition to establishing the governance bodies illustrated in Figure 1, the policy defines the membership and roles in such a way as to promote broad and effective stakeholder participation. The governance committees work with one another and the EA

Figure 1. Illustrates the various committees and oversight groups that participate in the IT technology decisions and policies, noting that the stakeholders play a very active role in six of the seven governance bodies

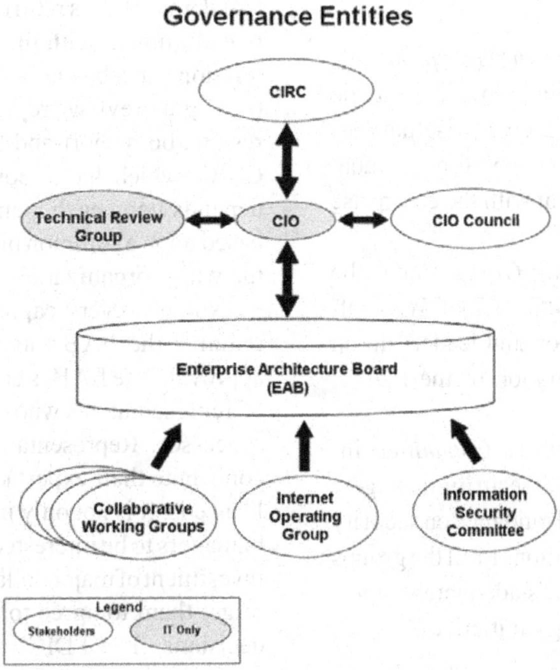

Governance Entities

program office to develop the architecture and a plan for migrating toward the target. Figure 1 illustrates the governance entities.

As described next, business leaders come together under this structure to represent all corporate interests:

- The *Capital Investment Review Committee (CIRC)*, comprised of senior-level division directors, evaluates the impact of IT investment decisions on the Corporation's capital investment portfolio by reviewing proposed major investments and making the final funding recommendations to the FDIC Board of Directors.

- The *CIO Council* is comprised of executive management in the FDIC's business line divisions and IT. This strategic group is key to obtaining stakeholder engagement in pursuing IT initiatives.

- The *Enterprise Architecture Board (EAB)* includes representatives from all divisions to ensure that all changes to the FDIC EA are aligned with other projects and corporate strategic goals including adherence to all IT security-related policies.

- The *Collaborative Working Groups* include key business staff who provide strategic direction for the FDIC enterprise data architecture and evaluate capital investment proposals for alignment with the enterprise data architecture.

- The *Internet Operating Group*, under the leadership of the FDIC's Chief Web Officer, provides direction and leadership on the content and navigation of the FDIC's external Web site.

- The *Information Security Committee* includes business line IT security managers who provide input and guidance on security architecture considerations to all the groups to ensure that security is adequately represented in all technology initiatives.

- The *Technical Review Group*, comprised of the senior management team for the IT division, reviews and evaluates technical solutions so that technology solutions meet the Corporation's enterprise technical needs and requirements.

In addition, the CFO established the Financial Analysis Committee (FAC) comprised of financial experts from all divisions to systematically review the financial profile of a project and work with the EAB to advise the CIRC on the FDIC's capital investments.

Each committee includes subject matter experts from every FDIC division appropriate to the committee's function. This structure gives stakeholders repeated opportunities to engage skilled subject matter experts, including IT and EA specialists, in determining IT solutions or opportunities that address their business needs. This structure also allows stakeholders to provide critical input that will influence the decision-making process. Projects are sponsored and implemented by individual FDIC divisions, but selection is based upon the development of a business case that demonstrates return on investment and positive alignment with the FDIC's strategic vision, mission, and business requirements. Selection, oversight, review, reporting, and judgment of results, both short-and long-term, belong to the CIRC, which has a corporate perspective and depends upon each member to make judgments based upon a common picture of what will benefit the whole organization.

Notably, every capital investment IT project requires the EAB's and the FAC's review and approval. The EAB is comprised of business and IT representatives who oversee EA products and processes. Representatives from each division contribute their expert knowledge of their area's IT needs. It is not only important to get top-level managers to be interested in making decisions on investment of major dollars in IT projects, but also to get them to agree to use EA to govern those decisions. The FDIC's challenges in reversing the proliferation of stovepipe IT solutions offered significant opportunities to demonstrate the value of involving IT subject matter experts on the front end in solving business problems. The challenge also generated appreciation among business leaders on the value of using guiding principles to rationalize IT development. Through this process, the FDIC ensures that changes to the architecture are cost-effective and make appropriate use of technological innovations.

The FDIC's capital investment policy demands the use of key performance indicators throughout the life of a project. Capital investment projects are measured quarterly in four areas: performance (meeting expectations), finance (adherence to budget), milestones or timeliness, and an overall assessment. The performance metrics are monitored through a balanced scorecard to document how well IT is aligning with the business. Specific metrics address:

- **Financial contribution perspective:** Is IT contributing to the FDIC's business success?

- **Customer perspective:** How well is IT aligning with the needs of the business?

- **Internal/innovation perspective:** How is IT performing operationally?

- **Growth and learning perspective:** How well is IT positioning itself to contribute to the FDIC business in the future?

The FDIC's CIO has focused intently on the fundamental principle that the business goals, objectives, and strategies of the corporation, and of each division, must drive IT development. The CIO Council provides a leadership forum and governance structure for discussing issues across organizational boundaries. Its members, representing the primary FDIC divisions and offices, advise the CIO on corporate IT strategies, policies, management issues, and practices and they work together on crosscutting issues such as EA management and IT investment management. The Council develops an IT strategic vision aligned with the FDIC's business strategies

to maximize the FDIC's ability to actualize its vision. The engaged stakeholders provide an essential ingredient for providing centralized IT resources. Stakeholders on the Council assure that the corporate strategic vision document covers each division's need for enhanced tools to better accomplish its work—offering to each stakeholder ready answers to the critical question, "What's in it for me?" The FDIC's Web site makes information available to stakeholders about this strategic alignment—where the FDIC's IT structure is now, where it is going, and how this direction is determined by specific corporate business interests. The information is available in multiple downloadable formats and presentations. In this way, the corporate focus of IT, as well as IT's role in achieving the FDIC's mission is continually provided to stakeholders. These communication strategies aid in preventing political barriers that could promote a return to the federated IT investment model that existed in 1996.

Stakeholder Involvement Encourages Consolidation and Better Management of IT Investments

Effective project execution is an important factor in determining IT's credibility with the business. In the past, the FDIC's IT investments were often exempt from rigorous business-case justification. Some investments were seen as mandatory, while others were seen as strategic and did not require an in-depth return-on-investment analysis. The FDIC designed a capital planning and investment management (CPIM) process to ensure that IT dollars are spent in the right place, with the FDIC getting the best value for its expenditures. The CPIM process requires that comprehensive business cases are produced and reviewed for each major investment. Proposals for new investments are considered against gaps in current capabilities in order to eliminate the possibility of redundancy.

The flow chart in Figure 2 illustrates the CPIM process.

This methodology provides the FDIC with a process for recognizing that while systems evolve, EA principles must be applied in adapting to these changes. It also demonstrates how people and systems work together to avoid "reinventing the wheel" and causing unnecessary delays and interruptions in the important business of the FDIC. As a part of this overall effort, the FDIC initiated an application rationalization project, focusing on a problem experienced by many other organizations that have, over time, accumulated a large and technically diverse portfolio of systems. Unmanaged, this type of portfolio is too expensive, inflexible, and unresponsive to change, and often not optimized to serve the mission of the organization. Furthermore, in a time of limited resources, it restricts the organization from taking on IT initiatives that are strategically important to its mission.

The application rationalization project addressed this problem in an enterprise-wide manner by engaging both the IT department and the business stakeholders in a joint, systematic effort to make targeted reductions in the FDIC's inventory of applications. This effort required close cooperation between the diverse stakeholder group and the IT staff. It also served to raise the awareness of staff and management throughout the FDIC of the life-cycle costs of applications and the increasing need for application integration and consolidation. Concurrently, the FDIC was able to implement several new enterprise-wide integrated applications that not only met the need to improve

Figure 2. FDIC's capital investment process is cyclical and continous throughout the lifecycle of an IT investment (EA principles are applied througout the lifecycle)

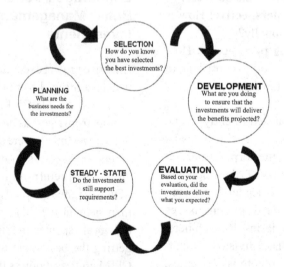

FDIC Capital Planning and Investment Management Process

SELECTION
How do you know you have selected the best investments?

DEVELOPMENT
What are you doing to ensure that the investments will deliver the benefits projected?

PLANNING
What are the business needs for the investments?

STEADY - STATE
Do the investments still support requirements?

EVALUATION
Based on your evaluation, did the investments deliver what you expected?

- Identify business needs
- Build a portfolio of investments
- Ensure that investments meet performance goals
- Compare actual vs. planned performance data
- Assess the effectiveness of mature systems in supporting mission requirements

business operations, but at the same time, replaced older, stove-piped legacy applications.

Concrete and measurable results were achieved within a two-year time frame. A 23% net reduction in the inventory of applications was fully realized by the end of 2005. Resources formerly devoted to managing the large legacy inventory were redeployed to more strategic uses. A few new enterprise-wide financial, legal, and human resource systems were implemented in 2005, while numerous marginal, stove-piped, and outdated applications were retired.

Since its inception in 2003, the CPIM process has provided oversight for strategic investments that have significantly changed each of the FDIC's major business areas: supervision, receivership, and operations. These systems, described next, have modernized business at the FDIC:

- *FDICconnect*, the FDIC's secure Web site for the exchange of information with financial institutions, has been expanded to offer additional business functionality in support of e-government. Financial institutions can now submit various applications and filings to the FDIC and retrieve quarterly deposit insurance statements online. Applications submitted by financial institutions using FDIC*connect* are shared with participating state banking departments via the FDIC's secure Extranet. In addition, certain filings submitted via FDIC*connect* are made available to the public via the FDIC's Web site, www.fdic.gov.

- The FDIC's *extranet* connects state and other federal regulators to the FDIC's corporate database allowing these business partners to share the corporation's structural, financial, and examination data. Using the secure sockets layer (SSL) protocol and certificates, the extranet addresses the challenge of securely transmitting confidential data across the Internet. This platform supports an expansion of applications—from basic data download tools to proactive applications that

alert subscribers to significant changes in an institution's financial condition by "pushing" notifications to them via e-mail.

- *The FDIC sales Web site* enables the FDIC to market and sell assets of failed or failing institutions by providing customers online 24/7 access to FDIC loan sales data. Customers have access to a full complement of sales-related information, and are notified when updates of sales information becomes available. This Web site was recognized by the 2003 President's Quality Award Program for excellence in expanding e-government. In addition, it was identified by the Federal Assets Sales Task Force as "a very strong candidate for adoption as a single online marketing portal for the purchase of financial instruments from federal agencies."

- The FDIC is in the midst of a multi-year effort to redesign and automate the *Deposit Insurance Claims System* used to process insurance claims and payments when an institution fails. This ongoing claims modernization project will provide an integrated solution that meets the corporation's current and future deposit insurance determination needs.

- *Virtual Supervisory Information on the Net* (*ViSION*) provides automated support for many aspects of bank supervision. ViSION provides one point of entry for supervisory examination personnel to complete all supervisory and insurance functions. Ongoing and future capabilities include implementation of support for large banks, case administration, off-site monitoring, supervisory tracking for safety and soundness, and supervisory tracking for IT examinations and comments.

- *Infrastructure modernization* of the FDIC's aging IT infrastructure included upgrading the mainframe, servers, and printers; installation of enterprise management software; replacement of computer monitors and projectors; modernization of voice and video infrastructure; and updates to the wide area network.

- The FDIC's *new financial environment* (*NFE*), a corporate initiative, focused on implementing an enterprise-wide integrated software solution for accounting and financial management.

Through a systematic method for reviewing and managing IT investments, the FDIC successfully integrated EA, portfolio management and strategic planning. The impact of these efforts is being realized in reduced IT operational expenses and successful IT project implementations.

Communicate with EA Stakeholders to Ensure the Architecture Accommodates the Style and Priorities of the Stakeholder Community

Enterprise architecture diagrams, a business-defined vocabulary, and numerous communication activities provide opportunities to explain IT's vision and value. By taking an enterprise point of view and creating a standard language used by the business and IT to communicate IT issues, EA leads to a better understanding of opportunities for business and IT innovation. Without communication, EA is not likely to deliver results. Communication channels range from one-on-one meetings with key stakeholders to Web sites, presentations, and online subscriptions. A multi-level communications program to market the need for, and benefits of, the EA work and compliance with EA provides an essential business understanding of the impact EA has on business results.

The FDIC uses high-level EA diagrams to show current applications mapped to business units, making it much easier to visualize how multiple applications support business activities. Other communication channels describe EA activities and accomplishments across the organization and are tailored to the audience. The FDIC is

implementing Troux, an EA repository product to provide an automated, comprehensive, and dynamic baseline of the enterprise architecture. This IT baseline provides the clear visibility needed to understand which IT investments support which lines of business, internal functions, and sub-functions.

Critical to effective communication is the role of the EA program staff in promoting an enterprise approach to systems development and technology innovation. These individuals think at both strategic and tactical levels, identifying and creating opportunities to apply an EA approach to problem resolution. The FDIC's enterprise architects have strong business domain understanding, are excellent communicators, have the capacity for abstract thought, and are technology generalists, patient, and persistent. One might characterize these individuals as "evangelizers" for EA or goodwill ambassadors.

While the EA program was beginning to make a difference in how IT investments were selected and managed, the CIO recognized that applying EA required a bolder approach. The CIO envisioned an overall IT program that would be more cost-efficient, customer-focused "best-in-class," as well as in complete partnership and collaboration with the business divisions. This transformation would clearly demonstrate alignment of the IT organization with the FDIC's overall business needs. In order to achieve this bold goal, it was necessary to concurrently make significant changes in sourcing, staffing, organization, and processes. After evaluating the risks, the CIO persuaded FDIC senior management to support this approach and become partners in the transformation. Specific improvements included consolidating 37 infrastructure contracts into a single contract and 40 development contracts into four long-term contracts, investing $33 million into modernizing the infrastructure; replacing the software development process with a more modern/flexible rational unified process; realigning the staff/contractor ratio; significantly flattening the organization by removing unnecessary management layers; providing new forums for customer input on IT projects and strategic direction; and adopting the Carnegie Mellon software engineering institute's capability maturity model integration standards.

To ensure that all stakeholders were included in the transformation process, the IT organization implemented an aggressive communications strategy to keep employees, union representatives, and the business lines informed as the transformation progressed. The CIO Council functioned as the executive-level advisory group and helped shape corporate IT strategy and activities and ensure IT-business alignment. The EA program was strengthened with additional resources and decision-making authority and a program management office (PMO) was established to implement standard repeatable project-management practices and improve the results of IT project-management activities. At the same time, the development of a methodology to derive and explain client costs contained in the IT budget was launched so the business lines could determine the impact that their IT-related decisions had on the corporate budget.

These communication efforts demonstrated a well-crafted approach to using multiple ways to get the message out to the EA stakeholders. Through ongoing communication, EA is understood from each stockholder's perspective with stakeholders collectively embracing an approach that ensures IT delivers required business results.

CONCLUSION

Successful EA requires clarity of vision, strong leadership, and effective communication. EA engagement is not about detailed standards, protocols, and technologies. Rather, it focuses on ensuring that the organization's business needs are clearly defined and on managing the delivery of IT initiatives aligned to these business needs. At the FDIC, these efforts are demonstrating the business value of EA and providing a critical step in identifying opportunities to consider common business processes or new business processes

from an enterprise perspective. An effective IT engagement model enables stakeholders to align business and IT, and to coordinate these interests and efforts at different organizational levels. Business units must have an active, collaborative role with IT departments in order to embrace new technologies, determine innovative approaches, and establish techniques to institutionalize best practices across the organization.

REFERENCES

Cullen, A. (2006). *IT must understand the value for EA groups to be successful.* Forrester Research, Inc.

Kreizman, G., & Blanton, C. (2005). *The research describes the federal deposit insurance corporation's effort to align IT to business through enterprise architecture.* Gartner Research ID Number: G00136042.

Leganza, G. (2005). *Public and private sector business architecture.* This article analyzes the differences between public and private sector business architecture and describes why EA documentation must be consciously designed for specific uses or it will be largely ignored. Forrester Research, Inc.

Weill, P., & Ross, J. W. (2004). *IT governance.* Boston, MA: Harvard Business School Publishing.

ENDNOTE

[1]   Special thanks to the following individuals for their contributions to the chapter and their participation in the application of EA at the FDIC: Susan Becker, Linda Collins, and Kenneth Weaver.

Chapter X
The Role of Change Management in IT Systems Implementation

Ron S. Kenett
KPA Limited, Israel and University of Torino, Italy

Sebastiano Lombardo
SINTEF, Norway

ABSTRACT

Implementation of IT enterprise systems triggers an inevitable organizational change. Managing an IT driven change requires a holistic approach to IT implementation. Such changes require an integration of best practices in project management, risk management, HR management, business process modelling, knowledge management, and software development. This chapter provides an introduction to the role of change management in IT systems implementation and describes the BEST methodology with three case studies from Norway and Israel.

INTRODUCTION

The chapter highlights the potential of an integrated holistic approach to IT systems implementation. It proposes tested approaches to harmonic enterprise architecture development. The chapter also provides a review of the theoretical background to holistic IT systems implementation.

Several case studies from the better enterprise system implementation (BEST) project funded by FP5 IST are presented to show how change management can facilitate IT driven enterprise architecture (EA) development. Some results on IT risk management from the FP6 IP project MUlti-industry, semantic-based next generation business INtelliGence (MUSING) are also mentioned.

IT IMPLEMENTATION AS AN EA DEVELOPMENT PROCESS

As often reported in the literature and practice, IT systems do not achieve expectations economically, organisationally, and in terms of anticipated gains in competitive advantage. Many IT system implementation projects suffer from budget and time overruns and sub-optimal or even detrimental results. A 2002 survey of 134 organisations in the U.S., Africa, Australia, and Europe, conducted by KPMG (2002), on the implementation of programme management, a new integrated management method, shows that about 60% of the companies studied have experienced failed projects within the previous year at an average cost of 12 million Euro each.

By IT or enterprise systems (ES), we refer to integrated software packages, which have been developed to support several aspects of a company's information management needs such as ERP, PDM, CRM, and KM. An IT system can be used to support tasks like product design and manufacturing, purchasing and logistics (material management, production planning), sales management and distribution, finance and controlling, and human resources management.

The implementation of a new IT system affects the enterprise architecture itself, touching key issues as business and organisational development. The IT implementation process triggers a complex set of change processes within the enterprises. We distinguish between issues related to IT implementation as a business development effort and organizational development implications.

IT Implementation as a Business Development Issue

An ES may integrate new tasks into the existing work processes and generate new management information. The outcome is dependent on the choice of ES and the configuration of the system. A key point is that an ES affects the work of many people in the organisation, influences work functions, but in general does not fully automate them. The overall perspective of this chapter is that enterprise architectures change as a consequence of implementation of an ES. We propose a change management methodology that is focused on key elements of an organisation and its key stakeholders throughout the implementation process. Effective change management requires an understanding of the impact on business of an IT system and its configuration. It is also necessary to understand which competencies are needed among the employees who participate in the change process, on the shop floor, as well as in administration, at management level, and others (Koch & Buhl, 2001).

From a business development perspective, a significant number of ERP projects are reported as failing to achieve anticipated benefits (Appleton, 1997), putting potentially a whole company at risk. Moreover, while new information technologies promise to significantly enhance organizations' performance, much of this potential is never realized (Kwon & Zmud, 1987; Nash, 2000). There is wide empirical evidence of unproductive use of IT systems. The "IT productivity paradox" is a well-known phenomenon, which, in this context, means that there is little correlation between a company's investment in IT and its productivity (Landauer, 1995, Willcocks & Lester, 1999). Problems have been identified not just to be technical issues, but also organisational and social ones—and this situation does not seem to have significantly improved over time.

IT Implementation as an Organisational Development Issue

In the literature, many IT implementation related problems are characterised as organisational and related to human resources. Technical problems are only a minor proportion of the reported problems. To confirm and refine this observation, the authors have analysed IT implementation processes with a reference framework that is based on a system model of organisations that centres on transformation processes in an organisation (Boer & Krabbendam, 1993).

The definition of an organisation underlying the system model is as follows:

An organization is seen as a purposeful system of people and means, which together perform certain activities or processes necessary to transform inputs into outputs that are useful for its environment, in order to achieve its objectives.

A system model views an organisation as an open system in constant development. An organisation interacts with its environment, which consists of suppliers, customers, competitors, government, and (labour) markets. The IT implementation normally affects these interactions. A set of activities is called a *process*. Processes are divided into primary, support, and management processes.

Primary processes are directly aimed at achieving the goals of the organisation. A primary process can be affected by internal and external changes with interrupts affecting its efficiency and effectiveness.

Support and management processes are needed to cope with these disturbances, both pro-actively and reactively. *Support processes* supply primary processes with resources, information, and tools needed to perform their tasks.

Management processes consist of strategic, adaptive, and operational processes each with a different scope and executed at different levels in the organisation.

People must have knowledge and skills to perform these processes. People perform processes to achieve various personal and organisational goals. Processes, people, and means are coordinated by means of organisational arrangements. Organisational arrangements can be subdivided into structural and cultural arrangements. Structural arrangements are the rules and procedures

that result from agreements made within an organisation, while cultural arrangements are the values, norms, and rituals in an organisation. Structural arrangements can be designed in contrast with cultural arrangements, which can only be developed by people in interaction (see e.g., Schein, 1985, 1996). These organisational dynamics significantly embrace the IT implementation process and influence its course.

An implementation process is usually organised as a project with a timeline, a budget, and an implementation plan. The IT implementation project lifecycle is therefore divided in phases such as "concept development," "initiation," "mobilisation," "ES deployment," "closing," and "ES operation." These project phases are the body of the implementation plan and include important tasks such as eliciting user requirements, adapting the software package, introducing the ES, training the users, communicating with the stakeholders, and measuring the improvements. Usually the real challenges come from unanticipated events.

RISK MANAGEMENT IN IT IMPLEMENTATIONS

All IT implementation projects carry important elements of risk, thus it is probable that progress will deviate from the plan at some point in the project life cycle. Risk in a project environment cannot be totally eliminated and must be managed. The objective of a risk management process is to minimise the impact of unplanned incidents in the project by identifying and addressing potential risks before significant negative consequences occur. Quoting the Project Management Institute (PMBOK, 2004): "Risk management is the systematic process of identifying, analyzing, and responding to project risk. It includes maximizing the probability and consequences of positive events and minimizing the probability and consequences of adverse events to project objectives."

The literature provides comprehensive insights and tools for risk management (Angling, 1985; Baccarini & Archer, 2001; Chapman & Ward, 2002, 2004; Gottfried, 1989; Grey, 1995; Lyons & Skitmore; 2004, Miller & Lessard, 2001; Raftery, 1994, Williams, 1996). The recent MUSING project (MUSING, 2006) combines semantic based information with quantitative data to derive operational risks estimates as required by BASEL II accord.

In general, IT risk management should be performed in such a way that the security of IT components such as data, hardware, software, and the involved personnel can be ensured. Risk management encompasses three processes:

- Risk assessment
- Risk mitigation
- Evaluation and assessment

Risk assessment is the first process in the risk management methodology. Organizations use risk assessment to determine the extent of the potential threat and the risk associated with an IT system implementation.

The output of this process helps to identify appropriate controls for reducing or eliminating risk during a mitigation process, which is the next step. *Risk* is a function of the *likelihood* of a given *threat-source's* exercising a particular potential *vulnerability*, and the resulting *impact* of hat adverse event on the organization.

Threat-sources must be identified and assessed. In assessing threat-sources, it is important to consider everything that could cause harm to the IT system and its processing environment. There are three main fields that affect the risk identification as well as the other processes of the risk management approach. They are: *Technology*, which concerns the implementation of the IT system (software and hardware); *Processes*, which are inevitably affected by the new IT system; and *Human Resources*, which implement the processes and use the new IT system.

Identifying risk for an IT system implementation requires comprehensive understanding of the system's processing environment. The outcome of the risk identification and analysis is a risk matrix indicating the position of each risk element in terms of probability of occurrence and impact level.

Risk mitigation involves prioritizing, evaluating, and implementing the appropriate risk-reducing controls recommended from the risk assessment process. Because the elimination of all risk is usually impractical or close to impossible, it is the responsibility of senior management and functional and business managers to use the *least-cost approach* and implement the most appropriate controls to decrease mission risk to an acceptable level, with minimal adverse impact on the organization's resources and mission. Risk mitigation options include:

- **Risk assumption:** To accept the potential risk and continue operating the IT system at a lower risk level.
- **Risk avoidance:** To avoid the risk by eliminating the risk cause and/or consequence.
- **Risk limitation:** To minimize the adverse impact of threats.
- **Risk planning:** To develop a risk mitigation plan that prioritizes, implements, and maintains controls.
- **Research and acknowledgment:** To lower the risk of loss by acknowledging the vulnerability or flaw and researching controls to correct the vulnerability.
- **Risk transference:** To transfer the risk by using other options to compensate for the loss, such as purchasing insurance.

Evaluation and assessment is the last phase of the risk management process. The purpose of carrying out this phase is to ensure that the assumption and estimates made by the risk management team are valid during the evolution of the project. This phase of the risk management process is also the trigger that initiates the next phase, providing material for the identification of new risks. For more results on IT risk management, see the MUSING Web site www.musing.eu.

MANAGING IT DRIVEN CHANGE

IT system implementation processes are usually complex and involve several different components, many people, and even different organisations. We describe the complexity of enterprise system implementation processes in more detail next, including a discussion of the dynamics of the process.

The Complexity of IT Implementation

Implementing an enterprise system in an organisation is a complex process. Besides the new technology, its impact on the organisation involves processes, tasks, knowledge and skills, and hierarchical levels and relationships with clients and suppliers.

An implementation process is typically performed as a project with an organisation that is different from the routine day to day permanent organisation. Such a project encounters many uncertainties, which cannot be all predicted or prevented from the beginning of the project. An enterprise system implementation project can therefore be considered as an organic structure (Burns & Stalker, 1961). IT system implementation processes are often treated as a technical endeavour while they should be considered as organisational change (Davenport, 2000; Leonard-Barton, 1988; Orlikowski, 1992). They are also often considered as an imperative for change while organisational change needs to be the starting point (Markus & Robey, 1988). Implementation of technology with an impact on several functions and levels of an organisation not only induces organisational change, but also requires organisational change.

Typically, the goals for change are often not very clear before implementation starts; moreover, implementation efforts are sometimes discontinuous creating more uncertainties. There may be a large time lag between successive implementation efforts and knowledge and skills built in one project are often lost before the next one starts.

Alignment between an enterprise system and the existing technology, or the enterprise system and the organisation is an important aspect. For example, traditional functional differentiation impedes IT implementation as the enterprise system requires a cross-functional process perspective, not just a narrow departmental or divisional perspective. Centralisation/decentralisation is another aspect an implementation project has to deal with. While a centralised IT architecture increases efficiency, local profit responsibility or decision autonomy is often not supported in the ERP system (Moch & Morse, 1977).

The project organisation may not be suitable for the complex task of implementing an enterprise system. Often, the number of people in the project is inadequate. Moreover, people may be insufficiently qualified. Finally, technical aspects are important and need to be understood by the people in the organisation affected by the system. The possibilities and benefits of the system are not always clear. Employees and middle management usually have very limited involvement in system definition and implementation, and thus lack ownership (Welti, 1999).

Enterprise system implementation is a journey requiring judgement and change of directions all the time. As a result, understanding of the complexity of implementing and operating/running enterprise systems needs to be developed while taking all the aspects touched upon previously into serious consideration. To this end, a combined understanding is necessary, going beyond the merely technical aspects of implementing and operating an enterprise system. In particular, an understanding is needed of the dynamics of an enterprise system implementation process.

The Dynamics of IT Implementation

All commercial enterprise systems have an inbuilt general and detailed "organisational model" together with predefined generic business processes for almost every work process in a company. The organisational model of the enterprise system has to be incorporated in, or has to be aligned with, the existing formal and informal work processes of the company. These include principles of design, production, workflow, management hierarchy, and internal and external coordination. Therefore, aligning organisation and enterprise system implies that the formal and informal organisation interact with the enterprise system and its implicit organisation model. Such alignment requires organisational change.

Organisational change cannot be fully predetermined. People involved in the process of change influence the process, while also changing circumstances may require a change in the direction to go. As such, an enterprise system implementation process is a dynamic process formed by the participating actors, their knowledge, interests, and social competence, but also constrained by the existing structure, norms, and rules.

Organisation and technology co-develop during enterprise system implementation requiring mutual adaptation and alignment during and even after the implementation process (Leonard-Barton 1988; Markus & Tanis, 2000; Orlikowski, 1992). As an enterprise system implementation process is social in nature, the social environments of participants in an enterprise system implementation process might largely differ. For example, the social context, organisational culture, and other social factors of enterprise system developers often differ largely from those of end users (Barley, 1986). As such, different social contexts add to the complexity of implementing technology. Barley (1986) for example, has observed that comparable starting situations for adopting and implementing new technology may lead to different outcomes due to organisational and people differences.

Dynamics are inherent in enterprise system implementation. An optimal set of initial conditions is neither complete nor sufficient. However, learning from dynamics, and identifying recurrent patterns might help to achieve a better start by enhancing awareness of what could happen and proposing a course of action when needed. Deviations from an implementation plan are not necessarily always negative. Situations may change because of various reasons, within or outside the control of the people involved in the implementation process. Some changes may create new options or challenges for the implementation process, while others might endanger a successful implementation process outcome. The term "disruption" is preferred to the word "problem" to indicate the complex character of the process--including both internal and external, favourable and unfavourable, intended and unintended, and expected and unexpected situations, which require immediate action.

Dynamics of an IT implementation process relate to the business in terms of the reasons for change, the goals to be achieved with the change, and the amount of change necessary to achieve the goals. They also relate to the implementation and change process itself in terms of determining the change coalition, configuration of the new technology and organisation, preparing the organisation for change, and handling post-implementation issues. Finally, they relate to the enterprise system technology in terms of learning about the technology and its potential, identifying the role of IT and the package selection, and developing a program to align the ES and the organisation. In any case, dynamics involve handling disruptions and their impacts, organising participation and communication, and facilitate organisational learning and knowledge gathering. All this has an impact on the development of a fit EA.

The BEST Holistic Change Management Approach

Given the growing significance and high risk of IT implementation projects, much research has been undertaken to develop better understanding of such processes in various disciplines. Yet, the literature on ESI, information technology, and organizational change management does not give substantial and reliable generalizations about the process dynamics and the relationships between information technology and organizational change. In order to fill this gap, a European FP5 project, Better Enterprise SysTem implementation (BEST), was launched in 2002 (BEST, 2002). The aim of the BEST project was to understand the dynamics of IT implementation processes and to help improve an organization's readiness to deal with such issues by acquiring knowledge of process dynamic from existing IT implementation projects. This general area is known in the literature as change management.

A holistic approach encompasses an effort to discover and take into consideration all the issues that the complexity and dynamics of IT implementation entails. The first part of this task will be an effort to structure the enormous volume of unstructured information about the IT implementation process that can be elicited. This demanding task has led the BEST project to the creation of a reference framework. This framework is used to capture knowledge and information from a number of sources. Based on this framework, the BEST assessment tool has been developed to produce a snapshot of the IT implementation process at a specific point in time. Based on this holistic, still punctual, understanding of the process the final effort is to highlight the change actions to be taken to secure a successful continuation.

The reference framework is aimed at recognising dynamic patterns, understanding the complex dynamics of IT implementation projects, and capturing their complexity, organising data collection, preparing for statistical analysis, and visualising the results for IT implementation professionals. The reference framework addresses the view of the overall enterprise characteristics and constitutive elements, which influence the implementation of an ES. The framework identifies important technical as well as organizational and human aspects that play a role in several processes. These processes are called dimensions and include the business process, the project management process, and the ES process. A more detailed definition of the three dimensions is listed below:

- The *permanent* **business** *process* for which the system is implemented. The focus process consists of all activities that will be supported or affected by the new enterprise system. The business processes are permanent processes, which may be subject to change continuously. The word permanent is used to distinguish the daily tasks from the temporary tasks of an implementation project.
- The *design and tuning of the new* **enterprise** *system*. The focus process consists of all activities that are needed to adapt or tune the system and align it with the business. Design and tuning of the enterprise system is a temporary process, but may extend beyond the implementation project.
- **Project management** of the implementation process. The focus process consists of all activities needed to plan and monitor the implementation process, select and perform the implementation strategy, select the system and implement it into the organization, compose a project team, manage project documents, etc. Project management is a temporary process.

In addition to these dimensions, the framework defines six organizational aspects.

The six aspects are defined as follows:

- **Strategy and goals:** Strategy and goals are the medium- and long-term goals to be achieved and the plans for realising these goals. The strategy and goals for the enterprise system and the implementation project should match the business goals and strategy.
- **Management:** The management aspect deals with setting priorities, assigning resources and planning, and monitoring processes.
- **Structure:** Structure involves the relationships between elements of the organisational system such as processes, people, and means. Structure includes tasks, authorities and responsibilities, team structures, process structure, and structure of the enterprise system.
- **Process:** Process involves the steps that are needed to perform the focus process of each dimension: the primary business process and relevant support and management processes, the project process and the enterprise system design and adaptation process.
- **Knowledge and skills:** This aspect refers to the knowledge and skills that are needed to perform the focus processes in each dimension.

- **Social dynamics:** The aspect social dynamics refers to the behaviours of people, their norms, and rituals. Social dynamics often become visible in informal procedures and (lack of) communication.

The 18 cells created by the intersection of dimensions and aspects are called focus cells (Buhl et al., 2004, Wognum, Krabbendam, Buhl, Ma, & Kenett, 2005). Combining aspects and dimensions generates the reference framework presented in Figure 1.

The framework has not only proven to be useful in analysing completed IT implementation cases, but also to structure ongoing workshop processes in companies. By using a graphical presentation of the reference framework (see Figure 1), people are enabled to assign their knowledge and experiences on enterprise system implementation to cells in the framework and discuss the results. Such an exercise leads to deeper insight and shared understanding of the implementation's complexity.

A Readiness Assessment Tool as a Change Management Tool

The goal of the BEST holistic approach is to provide a tool suitable for assessing a company's

Figure 1. The BEST framework

	Enterprise system	Project management	Permanent business
Strategy and goals			
Management			
Structure			
Process			
Knowledge and skills			
Social dynamics			

situation during each phase of the IT-implementation project.

The three dimensions and the six aspects are correlated. Following the columns of the reference framework, it is possible to explore each dimension in, and elicit detailed information. Following each row gives insight into how each aspect pervades the implementation process at different levels making it complex and dynamic.

The framework is used to elicit information through a predefined set of questions and multiple choice answers to be used in interviews and focus groups. The answer options reflect the degree of maturity and alignment of the situation identified by the question, ranging from an immature situation or insufficient alignment to an optimal situation or optimal alignment. For example, a high maturity level for the knowledge in the business of the enterprise system that is being implemented indicates that people in the business know and understand the enterprise system. Similarly, a low maturity level for the knowledge and skills in the permanent business to work with the system indicates that the people in the business are not fully ready to adopt the enterprise system.

Software is also available to gather this information and visualize it through a spider diagram. This software was developed by the BEST project consortium in 2004. It has been tested extensively by 10 experts related to the consortium in 11 companies and by 10 external experts (Ma,

Figure 2. Spider diagram resulting from the prototype tool

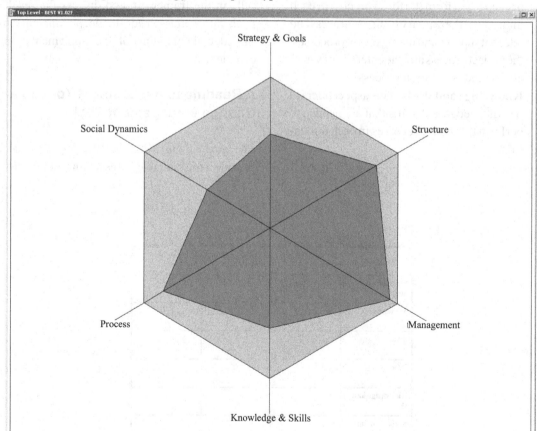

Loeh, Sedmak-Wells, Katzy, & Buhl, 2004) with promising results.

The red area in the spider diagram is the "maturity score" resulting from the connection of the overall score in each aspect-axis.

Although the problems captured are not different from those that can be found in the literature, the tool provides a means to develop a comprehensive overview of and insight into all dimensions and aspects that play a role in implementing a new IT system and puts problems into perspective.

THREE CASE STUDIES

This section reports on three case studies of change management initiatives taken in parallel to the enterprise system implementation (ESI). The first case involves the deployment of a product data management system in a large engineering firm. The second case involves the implementation of an ERP system in a research and development environment—quite a unique experience. The third case describes the blue print phase of an SAP implementation in a large health care organization serving over three million members. The context of each case is first described and complemented with the specifics of the change management effort. In addition, a section providing an assessment of the ESI is provided with lessons learned and gained insights. The final section of the chapter provides overall conclusions and direction for further research.

Case 1: Implementing a PDM System

Case Description

N1 is a global technology services group with a company founded in the beginning of 1900. N1 employs several thousand people worldwide. N1 is also a leading provider of exploration and production services, solutions, and technology to the international petroleum industry. In the late 1980s, N1 purchased a relatively new product data management system (PDM) from a small U.S.-based start-up company and installed it to assist in managing the engineering processes. This system became the source of the product design file information, which was subsequently loaded into the manufacturing system to plan and execute production. In 1993, it was decided that this same basic model would be standardized and implemented at other N1 sites throughout the world. A few years later, the PDM supplier was acquired by a competitor, who shortly after the acquisition, announced that the old PDM system would be discontinued in favor of their own PDM application. N1 had therefore to start the implementation of the new PDM system.

Case Assessment

At the initiation stage, the need for a new PDM system was stated by N1's top management. N1 launched a process to identify and evaluate other PDM suppliers and finally selected one as the N1's next generation PDM system. The first organization implementing the system was N1's site in Norway. Five to seven other "sites" would have then followed the Norwegian one. The implementation process in Norway represented an important pilot project that was to be used to gather experience, to chose solutions, and test implementation strategies. Vital questions were *"How to co-ordinate the user requirement task when you have thousands of users spread all over the five continents? How to emphasize the workflow analyses? How to adapt the standard system provided by the vendor to fit user requirements? How to communicate the vision of the top management? How to motivate department managers? How to encourage seniors to use the new system?"* These were some of the key questions to be answered by the global implementation team. All technical and organizational challenges had to be met and problems had to be solved before giving the baton to the next "site."

At the assignment stage, the contract with the vendor was negotiated intensively. After a few months, the contract was eventually signed and a total budget of approximately 10M€ was assigned to the implementation project. No major risk management activities were carried out at this stage though. The learning process at this stage was focused on gathering information about the vendor and its PDM system. At this stage, the BEST holistic approach was unknown to the company.

At the definition stage, a "global" implementation team was appointed to manage the task. An "introduction" plan was meant to give a detailed picture of all the tasks involved in the implementation project. The implementation team managed to edit a first draft of the plan.

At the beginning of the implementation process, many decisions were yet to be taken at the headquarters; it turned out to be impossible to plan in detail all the activities for the organization based in Norway. During the planning phase it was therefore enough to produce an overall description of the expected activities. Key personnel were appointed to manage crucial tasks such as user requirements elicitation, part classification structure, product life cycle design, etc. The challenges to be met were many: technical, cultural, organizational, and relational, among others. The BEST approach was then used to explore the situation and the results highlighted that the technical issues were attracting most of the management's attention. Nevertheless, through this approach the implementation team was discovering that human factors seemed to be a critical aspect of the implementation work. A line manager told us in that phase of the implementation project:

Planning with and for the users is the only way towards implementation success.

At the implementation stage, despite the dimension of the challenges mentioned above, any budget changes were refused by the top management. Extraordinary attention was therefore given to all critical tasks in the critical path, especially tasks related to change orders and software development. Besides this, as a consequence of the BEST diagnosis, a more general analysis was carried out to find out how the managers and future users of the PDM system would experience the change process resulting from its implementation in the organization. The analysis was more than registering IT architecture or assessing knowledge level among the users. It was an effort to understand the learning mechanisms to be addressed.

The organizational analysis was again based on the use of the BEST framework and encompassed:

1. Collecting information about the organizational starting point.
2. Trying to predict pitfalls and challenges.
3. Highlighting opportunities.
4. Tailoring information strategy to users' knowledge and awareness level.
5. Developing a communication plan.
6. Learning from future users.
7. Planning successful learning through training.

This kind of analysis helps managers understand the organizational mood prior to implementation. Line managers' thoughts about the coming change process were expressed in their own words. The implementation team used BEST framework as a tool to asses the changes and upgrade their general understanding of the process.

At the benefit realization stage, the management focus was directed on the project's overall achievements. The program was completed with a few months delay. The completion of the program did not univocally parallel the benefit realization. Many features of the system were still unutilized by most users. Some users creatively invented "smart workarounds" to avoid using features of the system they did not understand. Nevertheless, after having worked side by side with many end users during the whole project, the implementation team was known and accepted by their end user colleagues, so they used their stronger social position to trigger and accelerate the learning process. An information strategy document was created by the implementation team to support a major communication campaign throughout the Norwegian organizations.

Communication activities followed all the implementation processes from the very first day of the implementation project. According to the program manager who also was the main responsible for the information strategy during the IT system implementation:

Information and communication were based on openness and trust.

The information tasks included checklists and questionnaires to be used in order to follow up the user learning process. The benefits achieved by introducing the new PDM system were to be fully discovered only after a couple of years of intense training and of focusing on organizational learning.

Case 2: ERP in R&D

Case Description

N2 is a company in the R&D business, employing several hundred highly skilled people. The activities of the company are mainly in Europe. For several years, the company has had a badly integrated series of software packages used to manage human resources, finance, production, and some key logistics processes. That cluster of disconnected software had an ERP like function, but could hardly be considered an ERP system. The need for an ERP system that substitutes the exist-

ing software packages was therefore very clear, at least according to the head of the administration. The general attitude to change at N2 is negative as only the core business is really in focus. As a result, the administration's needs are not so visible or particularly prioritized. There was however, a group of enthusiasts, mainly internal consultants with business management background that strongly believed in the benefits that N2 could achieve implementing a new ERP system. Through lobbying and intense management buy-in activities, this group managed to get the ERP implementation process started.

Case Assessment

At the initiation stage, the CEO and the CFO considered the possibility of buying a new ERP system. The mission was not clear from the beginning and the top management had to specify it later on. The ERP was supposed to integrate new tasks into the existing work processes and generate new management information. The outcome was in any case dependent on the choice of ERP and the configuration of the system. A key point was that an ERP affects the work of many people in the organization, influences work functions, but in general does not dictate them. This introduced the need for some form of risk management planning. The overall perspective at this stage was more business change through implementation of an ERP, while considering key elements of an organization and its key stakeholders in the implementation process. This required a deeper understanding of the impact of an ERP and its configuration and necessary competencies of employees to participate in the change process, on the "shop floor," as well as in administration, production, at management level, and other levels. The BEST holistic approach was used to analyze the process up to that point and to plan the work to be done: The top manager explained during a focus group:

There is continuous pressure on our organization to improve its operational, tactical, and strategic processes. We can not avoid change.

Already at this point, the BEST framework clearly evidenced a lack of detailed knowledge of the different administrative routines throughout the company, and a distressing degree of incongruence between IT strategy and business strategy.

At the assignment stage, some additional analyses were carried out to figure out the budget need, as well as the expected return on investment. These analyses were performed by external consultants. The result was accepted by the CFO, who decided to allocate resources to perform the preparation work during the definition stage. According to the external consultants this stage should give:

A sound fundament for the rest of the implementation project, as far as risk management and project resources management are concerned.

It was interestingly noted how this external analysis failed to highlight the strategic incongruence discovered earlier by the internal implementation team using the BEST framework.

At the definition stage, the implementation process was organized as a program with a time-

line, a budget, and an implementation plan. The ERP program lifecycle was therefore divided in phases named "further concept development," "initiation," "mobilization," "ERP deployment," "closing," and "ERP operation." These program phases should be the body of the implementation plan and should include important tasks such as eliciting user requirements, adapting the software package, introducing the ES, training the users, communicating with the stakeholders, and measuring the improvements. The management acknowledged the need for organizing the ERP program with these phases. But further insight achieved through the BEST framework revealed that the real challenges come from unanticipated events described as disturbing events or disruptions, which called for reflection and action. Most of the potential disruptions were found along the strategy-aspect axes. This made further program planning difficult, but it did not remove the need for planning, it simply changed its scope as follows:

1. Plan in order to gain understanding.
2. Plan for unanticipated events—risk mitigation.
3. Consider the original plan as a guide to the future—it is not "the" future.

Figure 3. SAP implementation process

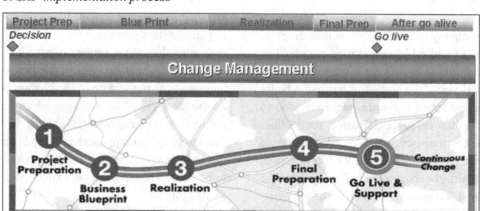

The implementation phase and the benefit realization phase were never carried out. The strategic incongruence had been so clearly highlighted that any further risk mitigation at lower detail levels was considered superfluous. During the definition stage, some key top managers resigned, the reasons being not related to the ERP implementation, and this resulted in a sudden stop of any activity. Altogether, the ERP project failed to achieve the anticipated benefits. The main reason was the sudden lack of program owners and decision makers. The lobbying work done by the group of enthusiasts that triggered the whole process turned out to be useless. A general feeling of a real need for a new ERP system in the company remained though. One of the line managers interviewed after this phase stressed that:

Things take time; this wasn't but the first act of a new long and exhausting ERP story!

A new initiation phase is expected to start when the new top management realizes the pressing need. Nevertheless, a significant amount of structured information regarding this ERP program "attempt" has been produced thanks to the BEST framework by internal and external consultants, and gathered by the head of the administration. Answers to old questions have been partly provided. This mainly concerned business process engineering issues. Almost all departments at this point are of the process informed that a new ERP is to be bought and implemented sometime in the near future. It can be argued that the organization has achieved a deeper understanding of their need for an ERP system and a deeper awareness of the challenges to meet during an implementation process. Much of the project planning is done and the lessons learned will turn useful as soon as the new CFO will start the new ERP implementation process.

Case 3: ERP in Health Care

Case Description

N3 is a large non-governmental and non-profit health care system in Israel with 14 hospitals and more than 1,200 primary and specialized clinics. Family doctors and hospital specialists cooperate to provide a broad medical-social perspective for the care of the individual, the family, and the com-

Figure 4. Change management work plan

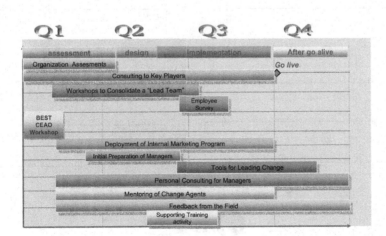

munity to 3,600,000 insured members from every ethnic group and every walk of life. N3 has made a strategic decision to implement an SAP ERP system in several implementation waves. The first wave is focused on logistics, human resources, and financial modules. Following a comprehensive preparation phase, 17 specialized blueprint teams were set up to specify blueprints of processes such as maintenance, supplier management, and training. The blueprints specify events (when should something be done), tasks or function (what should be done), organization (who should do it), and communication (what information is required to do the right task). From the blueprints business process, organization, authorization, and development master lists are prepared.

In addition to the 17 blueprint teams, three integration teams, one for each of the three modules were formed to handle vertical integration. An overall integration team was assigned the task of overall integration. Finally six horizontal teams were formed to handle issues of change management, quality assurance, interfaces, development, infrastructures and information

security. Overall 27 teams were set up to develop blueprint documents. A top management steering committee supervised the whole effort and provided strategic directions and tactical priorities. Change management was identified as an ongoing activity throughout the life of the project and, in that context, several activities were performed including a mapping of CEAO chains from the work of the blueprint teams. Change management activities were lead by the Human Resources Vice President in parallel to the SAP implementation (see Figure 3).

The detailed change management plan consisted of organization assessments, CEAO workshops, an internal marketing program to internally communicate the benefits of the ES, consulting and tools in change management and leadership, employee surveys and feedback mechanisms. The plan is presented in Figure 4.

Case Assessment

CEAO chains were identified by trained change management experts that participated as observ-

Figure 5. CEAO database

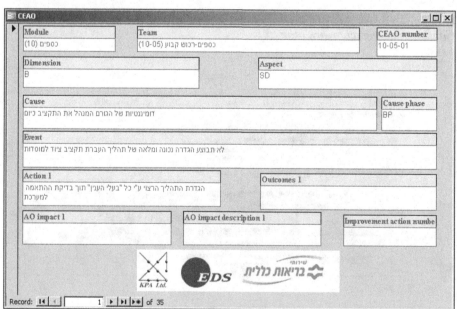

ers in the meetings of the blueprint teams. The reported CEAO chains were entered in a tailor made ACCESS application (see Figure 5).

An analysis of the CEAO database indicated that in change management events related to the financial module, 29% are attributed to process, 23% to structure, and 17% to knowledge and skills. The proactive corrective action was to refocus the effort to a wider horizon, re-emphasize the need for providing training to affected parties, and launch a focused effort to analyze structural implications from the point of view of job description and organizational charts.

CEAO chains related to ongoing business processes constituted 68% of all foreseeable events and only 6% to the SAP system. The implication of the finding was that special care had to be given to internal processes and not to the ES technology. This finding lead to a redefinition of work teams to enhance the presence of content experts as opposed to IT experts.

At the time of this writing, the project is still ongoing so overall conclusions are yet to be reached. The case study demonstrates how proactive actions can be taken at an early stage of the ES implementation using a structured databased approach. The challenge of mapping and analyzing change management information is addressed in Buhl et al. (2004) and Kenett and Raphaeli (2007).

CONCLUSION

The case studies were chosen based on the size of the companies, the complexity of the IT-driven EA-change process to be managed, and the fact that these companies accepted to use the holistic approach previously presented.

We described how traditional risk management approach to project management approach is used in the implementation of IT systems. However, there are a number of factors that this approach does not completely or sufficiently

cover. A comprehensive risk analysis together with professional project management does not seem to be any guaranty for a successful IT implementation. Organisational stress, clogged communication lines, business strategy consistency, social dynamics, and relationship to the suppliers are some of the many factors that must be taken into consideration.

This awareness opens new horizons for the management of IT driven enterprise architecture development.

The cases studied shed light on the feasibility of an approach designed to pay attention to the dynamic elements of IT-driven EA change and make visible their reciprocal relations. As a matter of fact, all companies had experience in risk management. N2 even sells risk management services. Risk management approach was therefore the most reasonable and immediate way to face the change process. However classic risk management and project management turned out to be insufficient to cope with the complexity and the dynamics of the change process.

Using a holistic approach like BEST was not an easy task either. The main reason for this is that the approach is new to most managers and consequently is often ignored, not appreciated, or even considered as a threat to more established methods.

Awareness of the resistance given by some executives to embracing a holistic approach was the key success factor in N1, N2, and N3.

The study shows how success can also mean creating the necessary insight to avoid starting an IT-implementation too prematurely. The success experienced by the BEST project should help researchers focus on these challenges, and motivate practitioners to embrace the holistic approach.

Future research involving the application of case based reasoning (CBR) expert system to change management problems has began (Raphaeli et al., 2004). A database of CEAO chains can be used to generate best practices that a CBR system can help retrieve, thereby improving the effectiveness of change management activities. This can lead to engineering the change management effort. Such research will have significant economical implications by positively affecting the success of IT implementations. In parallel, the new FP6 IP project on MUlti-industry, semantic-based next generation business INtelliGence (MUSING) is specifically handling IT operational risks and the integration of semantic based qualitative information with quantitative data. The combination of CBR and MUSING technology promises to offer innovation breakthroughs in managing change in IT systems implementation.

REFERENCES

Adam, F., & O'Doherty, P. (2000). Lessons from enterprise resource planning implementations in Ireland—Towards smaller and shorter ERP projects. *Journal of Information Technology, 15*(4), 305-316.

Angling, M. (1985). Assessing the relative priority of projects. *International Journal of Project Management, 3*(2), 114-120.

Argyris, C., & Schön, D. (1978). *Organisational learning. A theory of action perspective.* Reading, MA: Addison-Wesley Publishing Co.

Baccarini, D., & Archer, R. (2001). The risk ranking of projects: A methodology. *International Journal of Project Management, 19*(3), 139-145.

Bancroft, N. C., Seip, H., & Sprengel, A. (1997). *How to introduce a large system into a large organization.* Greenwich: Manning.

Barley, S. R. (1986). Technology as an occasion for structuring: Evidence from observations of CT scanners and the social order of radiology departments. *Administrative Science Quarterly, 28*, 245-273.

BEST. (2002). *FP5 IST project on better enterprise system implementation.* Received from www.best-project.com

Bikson, T., & Gutek, B. (1984). *Implementation of office automation.* Santa Monica, CA: Rand Corporation.

Blain, J., & Dodd, B. (1998). *Administering SAP R/3:The HR-human resources module.* Indianapolis.

Buhl, H., & Richter, A. (2004). Downplaying model power in IT project work. *Economic and Industrial Democracy, 25*(2), 239-267.

Buhl, H., Kenett, R. S., Lombardo, S., & Wognum, P. (2004). Methods to collect and analyze organizational change management data: The BEST approach. *European Network for Business and Industrial Statistics (ENBIS) 4th Annual Conference on Business and Industrial Statistics*, Copenhagen, Denmark.

Burns, T., & Stalker, G. M. (1961). *The management of innovation.* Oxford: Tavistock Publications.

Callaway, E. (1999). *Enterprise resource planning: Integrating applications and business processes across the enterprise.* Charleston: Computer Technology Research Corporation.

Chapman, C, & Ward, S. (2002). *Managing project risk and uncertainty.* Chichester: John Wiley & Sons.

Chapman, C., & Ward, S. (2004). Why risk efficiency is a key aspect of best practice projects. *International Journal of Project Management, 22*(8), 619-632.

Davenport, T. (2000). *Mission critical: Realizing the promise of enterprise systems.* Boston: Harvard Business School Press.

Eisenhardt, K. M. (1989). Building theories from case study research. *Academy of Management Review, 14*(4), 532-550.

Flanagan, J. C. (1954). The critical incidents technique. *Psychology Bulletin, 4,* 337-357.

Fleck, J. (1993). Configurations: Crystallizing contingency. *International Journal of Human Factors in Manufacturing, 3*(1), 15-36.

Giddens, A. (1984). *The constitution of society: Outline of the theory of structuration.* Berkely ; Los Angeles: University of California Press.

Gieskes, J. (2001). *Learning in product innovation processes. Managerial action on improving learning behaviour.* PhD Thesis, University of Twente, Enschede, The Netherlands.

Glaser, B., & Strauss, A. L. (1967). *The discovery of grounded theory.* Chicago: Aldine.

Goodman, S., & Griffith, L. (1991). A process approach to the implementation of new technology. *Journal of Engineering and Technology Management, 8,* 261-285.

Grey, S. (1995). *Practical risk assessment for project management.* Chichester: Wiley.

Griffith, L. T. (1996). Cognitive elements in the implementation of new technology: Can less information provide more benefits? *MIS Quarterly,* March, 99-110.

House, R. J. (2000). *Cultural influences on leadership and organizations.* Received from www.ucalgary.ca/mg/GLOBE/public/

Kenett, R., & Raphaeli, O. (2007). Multivariate methods in enterprise system implementation, risk management, and change management. *International Journal of Risk Assessment and Management,* to appear.

Kenett, R., & Zacks, S. (1998). *Modern industrial statistics.* San Francisco: Duxbury Press.

Kirchmer, M. (1999). *Business process oriented implementation of standard software: how to achieve competitive advantage quickly and efficiently.* Heidelberg: Springer.

Koch, C., & Buhl, H. (2001). ERP-supported teamworking in Danish manufacturing. *New Technology, Work, and Employment, 16*(3), 164-177.

KPMG. (2002) *Annual program management survey 2002.* Report 203-587. UK: KPMG-LLP.

Kwon, T. H., & Zmud, W. R. (1987). *Unifying the fragmented models of information system implementation. Critical issues in information system research.* New York: John Wiley.

Landauer, T. K. (1995). *The trouble with computers: Usefulness, usability, and productivity.* Cambridge, MA: MIT Press.

Lange-Ros, D. J. de (1999). *Continuous improvement in teams. The (mis)fit between improvement and operational activities of improvement teams.* Ph. D. Thesis, University of Twente, Enschede, The Netherlands.

Langenwalter, G. A. (1999). *Enterprise resources planning and beyond integrating your entire organization.* Washington, DC: CRC Press.

Lanzara, G. F., & Mathiassen, L. (1985). Mapping situations within a systems development project. *Information and Management, 8*(1).

Leonard-Barton, D. (1988). Implementation as mutual adaptation of technology and organization. *Research Policy, 17,* 251-267.

Lozinsky, S. (1998). *Enterprise-wide software solutions: Integration strategies and practices.* Boston: Addison-Wesley Pub Co.

Lyons, T., & Skitmore, M. (2004). Project risk management in the Queensland engineering construction industry: A survey. *International Journal of Project Management 2004, 22*(1), 51-61.

Ma, X., Loeh, H., Sedmak-Wells, M., Katzy, B., & Buhl, H. (2004). *BEST tool assessment and evaluation.* Deliverable 4.3 BEST_WP4_D4.3_20041010_V04, BEST project.

Markus, M. L., & Robey, D. (1988). Information technology and organisational change: Causal structure in theory and research. *Management science, 34*(5), 583-598.

Markus, M. L., & Tanis, C. (2000). The enterprise system experience: From adoption to success. In R. W. Zmud (Ed.), *Framing the domains of IT management: Projecting the future through the past* (pp. 173-207). Cincinatti: Pinnaflex Educational Resources, Inc.

Miles, M., & Huberman, A. M. (1984). *Qualitative data analysis.* Beverly Hills, CA: Sage Publications.

Miller, R., & Lessard, D. (2001). Understanding and managing risks in large engineering projects. *International Journal of Project Management, 19*(8), 437-443.

Moch, M. K., & Morse, E. V. (1977). Size, centralization, and organizational adoption of innovations. *American Sociological Review, 42,* 716-725.

MUSING. (2006). *FP6 IP project on MUlti-industry.* Semantic-based next generation business INtelliGence. Retrieved from www.musing.eu

Nash, K. S. (2000). Companies don't learn from previous IT snafus. *ComputerWorld,* October 30.

Orlikowski, W. J. (1992). The duality of technology: Rethinking the concept of technology in organizations. *Organization Science, 3*(3), 398-427.

Orlikowski, W. J., & Robey, D. (1991). Information technology and the structuring of organizations. *Information Systems Research, 2,* 143-169.

Pettigrew, A. (1987). Context and action in the transformation of the firm. *Journal of management studies, 24*(6), 649-671.

Project Management Institute. (2004). *A guide to the project management body of knowledge* (PMBOK® Guide) (3rd ed.). Newtown Square: Project Management Institute.

Raftery, J. (1994). *Risk analysis in project management.* London: E & FN Spon.

Raphaeli, O., Zahavi, J., & Kenett, R. (2004, July 4-7). Applying case based reasoning approach in analyzing organizational change management data. In P. Perner (Ed.), *Advances in data mining: applications in image mining, medicine and biotechnology, management and environmental control, and telecommunications, 4th Industrial Conference on Data Mining* (Vol. 3275, pp. 11-22), *Leipzig, Germany,* ICDM 2004. Lecture Notes in Computer Science, Springer Verlag.

Ruël, H. (2001). *The non-technical side of office technology.* PhD Thesis, Enschede, the Netherlands: University of Twente.

Schein, E. H. (1985). *Organisational culture and leadership, a dynamic view.* San Fransisco: Jossey-Bass Publishers.

Schein, E. H. (1996). Culture, the missing concept in organisation studies. *Administrative Science Quarterly, 41,* 229-240.

Welti, N. (1999). *Successful SAP R/3 implementation: Practical management of ERP projects.* Addison-Wesley Pub. Co.

Willcocks, L. P., & Lester, S. (1999). *Beyond the IT productivity paradox.* Chichester: Wiley.

Williams, T. M. (1996). The two-dimensionality of project risk. *International Journal of Project Management, 14*(3), 185-186.

Wognum, P., Krabbendam, J., Buhl, H., Ma, X., & Kenett, R. (2005). Improving enterprise system support—a case-based approach. *Advanced Engineering Informatics*, *18*(4), 241-253.

Yin, R. K. (1994). *Case study research: Design and methods*. Sage Publications, Inc.

Chapter XI
Managing Enterprise Architecture Change

Tim O'Neill
University of Technology Sydney, Australia

Mark Denford
University of Technology Sydney, Australia

John Leaney
University of Technology Sydney, Australia

Kyle Dunsire
Avolution Pty., Australia

ABSTRACT

Enterprise architecture (EA) is the recognised place where the engineering practice of systems architecture meets real-world enterprise needs. The enterprise computer-based systems employed by organisations today can be extremely complex. These systems are essential for undertaking business and general operations in the modern environment, and yet the ability of organisations to control their evolution is questionable. The emerging practice of enterprise architecture seeks to control that complexity through the use of a holistic and top-down perspective. However, the methodologies and toolsets already in use are very much bottom-up by nature. An architecture-based approach is herein proposed; one that has at its base a complete and formal architectural description (or model). This allows enterprise architects, strategists, and designers to confidently model, predict, and control the emergent properties of their respective systems from an architectural point of view. The authors conclude that by using an approach founded upon an architectural model to analyse software and enterprise systems, architects can guide the design and evolution of architectures based on quantifiable non-functional requirements. Furthermore, hierarchical 3D visualisation provides a meaningful and intuitive means for conceiving and communicating complex architectures.

ENTERPRISE ARCHITECTURE: NOUN OR VERB?

Enterprise architecture (EA) is the recognised place where the engineering practice of systems architecture meets real-world enterprise needs. The notion of EA is certainly still evolving, but can be defined broadly as:

The system of applications, infrastructure, and information that support the business functions of an organisation, as well as the processes and standards that dictate and guide their evolution.

Specifically, EA is not just a representation of an organisation's technical architecture, but also abstract business processes and the human organisation itself (Bernus, Nemes, & Schmidt, 2003; James, 2004; TOGAF, 2003). These three distinct elements form a "triad" of EA—focussed around the customer and governed by EA processes. Logically, any one element affects the others, and they cannot be properly understood without considering the relationships between them.

The open group specification for architectural frameworks (TOGAF) asserts the following:

The primary need for developing an enterprise architecture is to support the business by providing the fundamental technology and process structure for an IT strategy. (TOGAF, 2003)

The key word to focus on in that passage is "strategy." In the context of EA, we might define "IT strategy" as:

The practice of foreseeing the architectures most capable of satisfying the evolving business capabilities, and identifying and implementing procedures to ensure they are realised.

It follows then, that a core practice of an enterprise architect is to create architectures aligned to fit a pre-determined vision. The question is how does an architect guide that evolution? Architects are not, presumably, expected to stumble blindly toward a distant architectural target. To the contrary, they are expected to make incremental steps and each step should be fully justified not just in

Figure 1. The triad of enterprise architecture

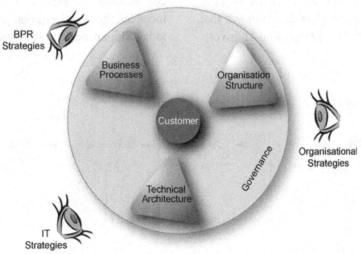

Managing Enterprise Architecture Change

terms of cost and function, but also in regard to technology choices.

NOT ART FOR ART'S SAKE[1]

The concept of EA is good in theory and most large companies now employ enterprise architects (expectantly). Sadly, the current practice of EA seems to be preoccupied with "box-ticking" implementations of "best practice" frameworks, processes, and toolsets. All too often enterprise architects are more concerned with creating endless documentation than any real architectural evolution.

A brief survey of the most popular EA tools on the market will readily confirm that view. For the most part, they are geared around creating documents and diagram sets, which are invariably out of date the minute they are produced. Hang them on the wall and post them on the company Intranet, but they are little more than art.

Five hundred years ago, Dante's famous quote "art for art's sake" warned that artists were becoming devoted to their craft rather than their social responsibility. Eventually art became so abstract that it had no useful purpose or meaning. History has a habit of repeating itself.

Clearly, EA should aspire to be more than pretty pictures. It should never be art for art's sake. Research (Hoffman, 2002) has shown that the companies with best-performing IT invest-

ments are often the most frugal IT spenders. The key lesson is that any IT spends must be leveraged and optimised against business benefits where "optimised" implies a deep level of analysis. EA should be about putting the gathered architectural information to work. It is about forward generation and planning—it is about strategy.

The premise of strategy is to choose the best path to an advantageous position. Logically, there should be some way of determining which path is the best. The following diagram shows the basic strategy steps and the implied feedback mechanism.

In practice, this mechanism is difficult and challenging to achieve. It is not possible to develop an architectural strategy without a suitable architectural understanding. To synthesise a strategy requires a comprehensive architectural model—across all elements of the enterprise.

It follows then, that the ability to synthesise solutions, analyse them, and extract guiding metrics is a highly desirable (even critical) ability of enterprise architecture practice. However, few organisations currently possess that capability. Organisations that obtain the capability clearly have a strategic advantage over organisations that don't.

The popularity of the balanced scorecard approach in management shows just how valuable combinations of various metrics can be. It is inconceivable that large companies could be run today without the highly evolved and standardised

Figure 2. Basic strategy

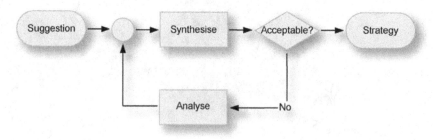

financial instruments that are currently employed. It should be similarly inconceivable that enterprise architectures can be evolved without the consideration of suitable top-level guiding metrics.

Another core function of enterprise architecture is that of IT governance, which we can take to mean the provision of an appropriate set of management principles and processes. Governance implies a certain degree of due diligence. An indication of what might constitute due diligence is currently given by examining the best practice EA frameworks.

Importantly, the common architecture frameworks such as TOGAF (2003), OGC (2000), CIOC (1999), OSD (1997), and Zachman (1987) encourage and promote the use of computerised tools to capture, control, and model architectures. Furthermore, TOGAF indicates that tools designed to model architectures should also be capable of simulating (or evaluating) the technical architecture.

Maturity models are used within the IT industry to assess the capability of organisations implementing EA. They are loosely based on the SEI capability maturity model (Paulk, Weber, Curtis, & Chrissis, 1995). The maturity is indicated by a rating from 0 to 5. Obtaining a level 4 maturity requires organisations to be able to not only model architectures but extract suitable architectural metrics (Rowe & Leaney, 1997).

To stress the point, the ability to synthesise solutions, analyse them, and extract guiding metrics should be a strategic capability within the IT function. Recent survey's and the experience of the authors suggest that few organisations currently posses that capability (EAS, 2003).

SEEK FIRST TO UNDERSTAND, THEN BE UNDERSTOOD[2]

Make no mistake, the enterprise systems employed by organisations today are extremely complex. Not only do they consist of countless hardware

and software products from many sources, but they often span continents, piggybacking on public networks (O'Neill, 2000). Considering the inherent risk of new technologies and the apparent immaturity of EA practices, the prevalence of IT mishap is not surprising.

Importantly, it is sheer complexity, not technology itself, that presents the biggest challenge to architects. A poorly understood system is a volatile one. But, how is it possible to reason about such complex systems?

Dealing with Non-Functional Requirements

It is only once a (complex) system has been built that certain intrinsic properties become apparent. Frustratingly, with gestalt systems[3], it is impossible to measure these things directly from the component pieces. A fundamental problem with complex systems, therefore, is that of predicting and controlling their emergent properties—"the principle that whole entities exhibit properties which are meaningful only when attributed to the whole, not to its parts" (Hitchins, 1992).

These emergent properties often reflect a system's overall "quality" in terms of the satisfaction its users and stakeholders experience when interacting with it. At an engineering level, such quality is expressed as non-functional requirements (for instance performance, reliability, openness, usability, and security).

If the non-functional requirements are not taken into proper consideration during system design, the consequences can be very expensive for the organisation. In the worst case, systems have to be completely re-designed because the non-functional requirements are not met (Bass, Clements, & Kazman, 2003). Furthermore, non-functional requirements directly influence the total cost of ownership, and are at least as significant as the functional properties of a system.

Therefore, if the mission of today's enterprise architects is to align their IT systems with their businesses needs, then it is fundamentally important to be able to control these emergent properties (Rechtin, 1991).

However, without the proper methodology and toolsets, trying to discern them is like gazing into a cloudy crystal ball.

The notion of "architecture" is so all-encompassing that research has shown it is fundamental to the evolvability, openness, performance, security, and reliability of a system, which are often spoken about but rarely catered for in design (Leaney, Rowe, & O'Neill, 2001; O'Neill, 2000; Payne, 1999). The architecture itself, not just the component pieces, directly affects the non-functional characteristics of a system. The ability to ascertain these emergent properties—or architectural metrics—provides access to invaluable information.

How to Tell a Good Architecture from a Bad One

A sound architecture might be considered a prerequisite of a sound system. But how is it possible to tell a good design from a poor one?

It is often said that the best designs are the simplest. This is also true in the realm of enterprise architecture. The aesthetic qualities of simplicity and elegance have long been the traditional design goals of system designers and architects. We suggest that good architectures should also exhibit the traditional qualities of symmetry, space, and balance, amongst others (Forty, 2000).

The quality of an architecture is reflected by the quality of its non-functional indicators. A good architecture should, at minimum, be evolvable, open, well performing, secure, and maintainable.

Figure 3. Emergent properties of complex systems

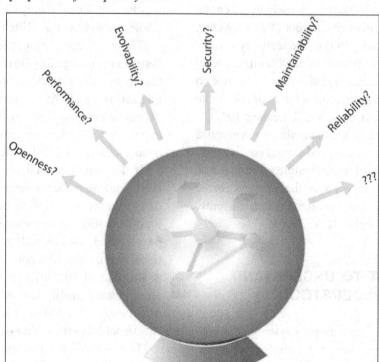

196

Some of these are self-evident, but openness and evolvability are particularly important:

Openness is the degree to which a complex system allows additions, replacements, or enhancements to be made without adversely affecting the operation of that system.

Evolvability is the degree to which a complex system may be changed to adapt to changing business needs before it degrades.

As a rule, any complex system, which is required to last any length of time, should have these two indicators as core requirements at least.

Current Methods of Dealing with Enterprise Architecture

The ANSI/IEEE definition of architecture is "the fundamental organization of a system, embodied in its components, their relationships to each other and the environment, and the principles governing its design and evolution" (IEEE, 2000).

When dealing with architectures it is important to think in the abstract; architecture is an abstract concept, not just a physical thing. It is a rich and comprehensive description or understanding of the structure of a system as a whole. It allows designers to capture a deeper understanding of all the system components, including how they implicitly and explicitly connect and interact.

Few methodologies allow architects to work from a truly architectural perspective.

Consequently, the common perception of architecture in the industry today is little more than that of various "box and line" diagrams. Architectures are commonly divided into four (sometimes up to 7) layer "EA stacks" consisting of layers such as business, information, application, and infrastructure (as shown in Figure 4). Typically, each layer has its own collection of diagram types.

To this day, most enterprise systems are poorly described and seldom understood. Often the architectural information exists—in one form or another—but is typically disseminated and in formats not easily digested. Design documents, Visio files, CAD drawings, UML diagrams, BPM diagrams, source code files, logbooks, sketches, and undocumented knowledge all form a part of the overall picture.

Figure 4. Traditional separate architectures approach (Adapted from Baschab & Piot, 2003)

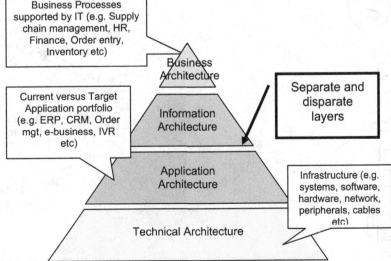

Consequently, organisations continue to address EA in a distinctly bottom-up fashion, arguing they have a "pragmatic" approach. The siloing of architectural information (in an effort to combat complexity) actually makes it impossible to reason about the entire architecture. This is compounded by the inherent inadequacy of current methods and toolsets. Despite the clear merits of working in a true unified architectural way, few organisations are capable of achieving it.

The Architectural Model

Re-collecting the diaspora of architectural information into a centralised repository, in a standardised format, is the starting place for managing architecture. Importantly, this information must be able to span the entire EA triad. Only with such a unified view does it become possible to visualise the complexity of enterprise systems. However, it would be of limited use if all you could do were use the repository to view the system.

The repository should be capable of completely representing all the important elements in an architecture—to any level of detail. It must also be capable of providing varied and customisable views of the architecture. Capturing this information in a digestible form gives the various IT services in an organisation, each with conflicting business requirements, the ability to evolve the enterprise architecture in the best possible way.

At the heart of the repository should be a formal architecture description language (ADL) comprising at least components, connections, and constraints. The scope of any model should cater for completely abstract entities (business goals and function flow) to concrete ones (servers, locations, and people).

Figure 5. Centralised architecture repository

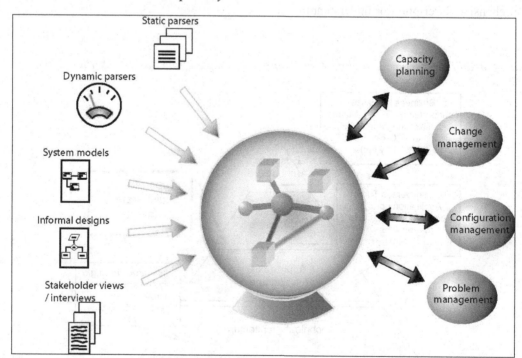

THE FIVE STEPS

Research by the University of Technology, Sydney, with some of Australia's leading technology organisations, has proven that the way to manage the risks associated with complex systems is through an architecture-based approach. An architecture-based approach is one that has at its base a complete and formal architectural description (or model). This allows enterprise architects, strategists and designers to confidently model, predict and control the emergent properties of their respective systems from an architectural point of view.

There are 5 integral steps:

1. Audit
2. Populate
3. Analyse
4. Visualise
5. Optimise.

1. **Audit:** Every journey needs a starting point. The starting point of an architecture-based methodology involves auditing the current architecture. The audit allows architects to present, familiarize, and discuss the existing architectural information with external experts. The goal is to objectively appraise the architectural information in regard to quality, quantity, and to some degree, completeness.

The input data can range in formality from source code through to designer/stakeholder knowledge, and in fidelity from informal designs in Visio/Powerpoint to dynamically parsed/monitored (runtime) results. An audit framework based on a vertical breakdown of (at least) people, processes, information, applications, and/or infrastructure, and a horizontal breakdown into (at least) domains, systems, regions, and/or geographies should be used. At the conclusion of the

Figure 6. The five steps

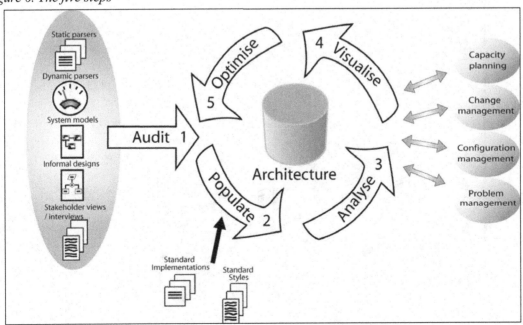

audit, the organisation will have an understanding of the relative maturity of its architecture information and processes.

2. **Populate:** The architectural model must next be populated. Initially, this requires discovery of the intrinsic architecture of a current system, or the proposed architecture of a system to be built. That is the set of components and structures necessary to satisfy the system's requirements. This process is not necessarily a one-off, as it is often necessary to discover the various essential and intermediate architectures of the system, before discovering the final implementation.

Discovery is performed by identifying the potential connections, components, properties, ports, implementations, and types required by the architectural model. The architect must find whatever sources of data are available and use these initially to define the architecture--ideally stored in an XML formatted repository. Discovery should be aided through the use of code parsers, export tools, SNMP sniffers, and import utilities wherever possible.

With the essential architecture in place, the entire model must be populated to the desired level of fidelity. This entails rationalising and consolidating the information within the architectural model, to enforce structure, and manage

Figure 7. Example 2D architecture diagram

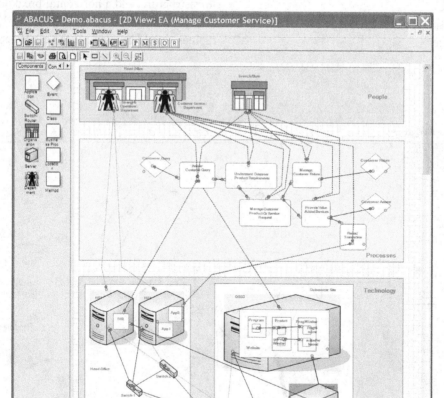

complexity. For example, there are often non-standard implementations and types that need to be refined. By the end of this stage, an architectural baseline will have been established.

To aid the construction or reconstruction of architectures, templates, styles, and patterns should be used. Templates should include the fundamental elements of components, connections, and properties, which can be extended and modified as required.

ADL's are not particularly user-friendly and population will often involve drawing of architectural elements. It is vitally important that any drawing tools map drawn elements directly to elements in the architecture itself.

3. **Analyse:** With a suitably capable and complete architecture model populated, evaluators should be run to extract useful metrics. The evaluators work by performing calculations, simulations, and tests on the architecture to appraise it in terms of the specified non-functional requirements.

Tailored application of the international standards (IEEE 1061 and ISO 9126) will yield practical and measurable metrics frameworks for non-functional requirements. However, the following metrics should form the basis:

*   **Performance:** The ability of the system to handle specified volumes of data/transactions in specified time, accuracy, and reliability constraints. Performance is suitably predicted using discrete event simulation.
*   **Openness:** The ability of the system to handle replacement of components with minimal impact.
*   **Evolvability:** The ability of the system to adapt to changes in business requirements.
*   **Modularity:** An indication of structure.
*   **Reliability:** And overall rating of mean time between failure.

*   **Total Cost of Ownership:** The total cost of a system over a given lifetime, taking into account hardware, software, and human resource costs.

Ideally, any toolset should provide a general purpose architecture calculator (GPAC) to allow evaluation of other metrics or key performance indicators (KPIs) that may be required.

4. **Visualise:** Now is the time for art. The results of the evaluations, along with the architecture itself, need to be presented in a range of meaningful visualizations, which are suitable for analysis. Comparative views and reports are developed to illustrate the relative meaning of the metrics gained from the architecture to the multitude of stakeholders at the relevant level of abstraction.

The visualisations need to convey complexity, structure, and metrics to the viewer. The visualisations should include hierarchical, three-dimensional views, which are ideal for visualising complexity. This should be supported by a range of other standard and customisable charts and reports, which highlight specific aspects of the system such as performance, layers of abstraction, evolutionary pathways, and real or potential problems.

Visualisation should allow:

*   Presentation of the entire enterprise architecture—across IT, business processes, and organization—in three-dimensions.
*   The ability to dynamically "zoom" up and down in the hierarchy viewing different levels of detail and abstraction.
*   Exploration of all assets in the architecture and how they connect to other elements.
*   Customisation of views—depending on architectural viewpoint or interest.
*   Identification of critical issues using customisable colours, shapes, and sizes.

Figure 8. Example 3D enterprise architecture view

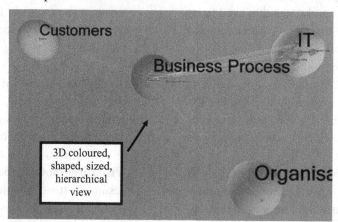

5. **Optimise:** Visualisations enable architects to reason about the qualities of their architecture through both structure and metrics. With an established baseline, an architect can effectively evolve the architecture to grow or rationalise in any way. Evolution is performed by repeating the populate-analyse-visualise process and comparing results against the baseline architecture.

While a system's implementation design is based on an architectural design with demonstrated capability, the actual system implementation will introduce further complexity (in the way of composition and structure) and constraints. The outcome may be that the desired capability is not achieved. Alternatively, the implementation of a system may bring unanticipated capability or undesirable properties. For this reason, it is necessary to consider a system capability space, which takes into account implementation factors and constraints. As we are most interested in establishing the implementation's ability to fulfill the required system capability, the final stage of the methodology is to develop a refined understanding of system capability via the architecture's capability space (Rowe et al., 1997).

Capability space is readily represented using Kiviat graphs where multiple properties from different versions of architectures can be easily compared. A typical multi-dimensional capability space is shown in Figure 9 with both a current and proposed architecture and only the behavioural or performance metrics. The point where the proposed architecture crosses the capability boundary indicates a requirement that is not satisfied.

The capability space is tailored to show any desired set of metrics. In this way, it becomes possible to compare and evolve the critical set of architectural metrics.

CONCLUSION

By using this approach and tools capable of the practices it describes, architects can predict and control the evolution of architectures. Research is already underway for ways to automate the optimisation and refinement process. In such a system, design rules, heuristics, and patterns would be used to automatically evolve and refine an architecture to meet predetermined sets of non-functional requirements.

Figure 9. Current and target implementation capability space (ICS)

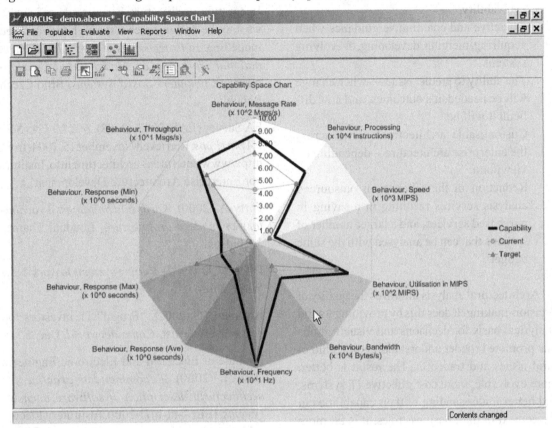

As the complexity of enterprise and computer systems continues to increase, so does the need for methodologies to handle them. The importance of emergent properties is recognised and it is clear that the only way to reason about them is through architecture. An architecture-based methodology and supporting toolset provides the following essential benefits:

- A tool to implement and execute the required strategic functions of enterprise architecture.
- The ability to collect and merge all enterprise architectural information of a system into a central, unified repository.
- The direct ability to evaluate system metrics, which cannot otherwise be evaluated—most importantly, performance, openness, and evolvability.
- Objective and quantitative guidance when acquiring, merging, developing, or evolving systems.
- The ability to predict issues—when change will be needed, it's outcomes, and how difficult it will be.
- Customisable architectural views across the enterprise architecture—depending on viewpoint.
- Reduction in the reliance on outsourced analysis services resulting in a saving in purchased services, and a larger number of systems that can be analysed with the same budget.

importantly, performance, openness, and evolvability.

- Objective and quantitative guidance when acquiring, merging, developing, or evolving systems.
- The ability to predict issues—when change will be needed, it's outcomes, and how difficult it will be.
- Customisable architectural views across the enterprise architecture—depending on viewpoint.
- Reduction in the reliance on outsourced analysis services resulting in a saving in purchased services, and a larger number of systems that can be analysed with the same budget.

Architectural analysis improves the quality of decision-making. It does this by providing a solid analytical basis for decisions and visualisations that promote broader understanding of architectural issues and tradeoffs. The result is better, more evolvable, more cost effective IT systems, and better understanding of their capabilities in the context of their business roles. It is far more than art for art's sake.

REFERENCES

Baschab, J., & Piot, J. (2003). *The executive's guide to information technology*. Hoboken, NJ: Wiley & Sons.

Bass, L., Clements, P., & Kazman, R. (2003). *Software architecture in practice* (2nd ed.). Reading, MA: Addison-Wesley.

Bernus, P., Nemes, L., & Schmidt, G. (2003). *Handbook of enterprise architecture*. Berlin; New York: Springer.

CIO Council (CIOC). (1999). *FEAF—Federal EA framework, version 1.1*. The CIO Council, USA.

Colquitt, D., Leaney, J., & O'Neill, T. (2004). Integrating architecture-based trade-off analysis into the design process through tool-assisted modelling. In *Proceedings of the 2nd IEEE International Workshop on Model-Based Development of Computer- Based Systems*, Brno Czech Republic.

EA Survey (EAS) 2003. (2003). *IFEAD Pres SG-EA part1.pps*. Retrieved November 15, 2004, from http://www.enterprise-architecture.info, Institute For Enterprise Architecture Development.

Forty, A. (2000). *Words and buildings: A vocabulary or modern architecture*. London: Thames & Hudson.

Hitchins, D. (1992). *Putting systems to work*. New York: Wiley.

Hoffman, T. (2002). "Frugal" IT investors top best-performer list. *Computerworld*, Dec. 6.

Institute of Electrical and Electronic Engineers (IEEE). (2000). *Recommended practice for architectural description of software intensive systems*. IEEE-std-1471-2000, Institute of Electrical and Electronic Engineers Publications, New York, USA.

James, G. (2004). *MarketScope: Enterprise architecture tool market document M-21-6251*, Gartner Corp., USA.

Leaney, J., Rowe, D., & O'Neill, T. (2001). Measuring the effectiveness of computer based systems: An open system measurement example. In *Proceedings of the IEEE Conference and Workshop on Engineering of Computer- Based Systems 2001* (pp. 179-189). New York: Institute of Electrical and Electronic Engineers Publications.

O'Neill, T. (2000). *Architecture-based performance analysis of open computer based systems*. Doctoral Thesis, University of Technology, Sydney. Sydney, Australia.

O'Neill, T., Simpson, H., Leaney, J., et al. (2000). IEEE engineering of computer based systems 1999 technical committee architecture working group (AWG) report. In *Proceedings of the IEEE Conference and Workshop on Engineering of Computer- Based Systems 2000* (pp. 383-389). New York: Institute of Electrical and Electronic Engineers Publications.

Office of Government Commerce (OGC). (2000). *ITIL—The IT infrastructure library*, version 1.2, Office of Government Commerce, UK.

Office of the Secretary of Defense (OSD). (1997). *C4ISR—Command, control, communications, computers, intelligence, surveillance, and reconnaissance architecture framework*, version 2.0, Office of the Secretary of Defense, USA.

O'Neill, T., Rowe, D., & Leaney, J. (1998). An open computer based system quality metrics framework. In *Proceedings of the IEEE Conference and Workshop on Engineering of Computer-Based Systems 1998*. New York: Institute of Electrical and Electronic Engineers Publications.

Paulk, M., Weber, C., Curtis, B., & Chrissis, M. (1995). *Capability maturity model, the guidelines for improving the software process*. Addison-Wesley.

Payne, C. N. (1999). Using composition and refinement to support security trade-off analysis. In *Proceedings of the 22nd National Information Systems Security Conference*, Arlington, Virginia.

Rechtin, E. (1991). *Systems architecting: Creating and building complex systems*. Prentice Hall.

Rowe, D., & Leaney, J. (1997). Evaluating evolvability of computer-based systems architectures—an ontological approach. In *Proceedings of the IEEE Conference and Workshop on Engineering of Computer- Based Systems 1997*. New York: Institute of Electrical and Electronic Engineers Publications.

Shekkerman, J. (2003). *E2AMM*. Retrieved November 10, 2004, from http://www.enterprise-architecture.info, Institute For Enterprise Architecture Development.

TOGAF. (2003). *TOGAF—The open group architectural framework*, version 8.1, The Open Group.

Zachman, J. (1987). A framework for information systems architecture. *IBM Systems Journal, 26*(3), 276-295.

ENDNOTES

1 Habit 5 from Stephen Covey's "7 Habits of Highly Effective People"

2 Habit 5 from Stephen Covey's "7 Habits of Highly Effective People"

3 The gestalt movement, or gestalt psychology, was concerned with the principle that the whole is greater than the sum of the parts. What might be exhibited by a system is not directly attributable to the characteristics of individual entities (Hitchins, 1992).

Section III
Transformation and Value Realization

Chapter XII
Architecture–Driven Business Transformation

Chris Lawrence
Old Mutual South Africa, South Africa

ABSTRACT

Enterprise architecture (EA) has primarily a business focus, but it involves the kind of systems thinking typically associated with information technology (IT). Any one of its component architectures could theoretically drive a business transformation. The example of process architecture is chosen because of its implications for other architectural domains; because of the link between customer-centricity and process-centricity; and because inherited attitudes to process desperately need overhaul. An imagined diagnostic in a financial services company provides context. The diagnostic recommends a holistic alternative to current approaches to process. It articulates an explicit logical meta-model from which it draws out a number of key concepts implementable as generic physical constructs. The resulting process architecture can drive radical business transformation given the right program management, governance, and, above all, sponsorship.

INTRODUCTION

An enterprise can choose to see enterprise architecture (EA) primarily in business terms or primarily in technology terms. The choice is itself an enterprise-architectural choice. An enterprise which sees EA as primarily a business thing, is likely to be very different from one seeing EA as primarily a technology thing. It may be that people with IT backgrounds are more likely to think architecturally than people with other backgrounds, but this doesn't mean architecture is only about IT.

This chapter assumes that EA is primarily a business concern, but that the A in EA involves applying to business the sort of conceptual and "systems thinking" more associated with "IT" than "pure business" (whatever these terms actually mean in the 21st Century). We start with a general discussion of EA and what it incorporates. We then position the relationship between EA and business transformation by looking at an organization's bill of health. This leads to a discussion of diagnostics.

Because the diagnostic will differ widely from one organization to another, what counts as architecture-driven business transformation will also differ widely. Further progress means choosing a representative direction. For the purposes of this chapter, the choice is of a transformation based on process architecture. The approach is first established at a purely logical level by way of a meta-model. This then generates an implementable process architecture, which can form the basis of a business transformation.

BACKGROUND

The process-architectural meta-model is articulated in greater detail in Lawrence (2005), part of which is also reproduced in Fischer (2005). In 2004, Old Mutual South Africa adopted substantially the same approach as the "Old Mutual Business Process Methodology" (OMBPM).

An important source of the meta-model is experience in designing and implementing the sort of process-architected systems described in Jackson and Twaddle (1997). It is in implementation in particular where the full business-transformational potential of integrated process architecture starts to show.

TRANSFORMATION THROUGH ARCHITECTURE

Enterprise Architecture

Strategy and architecture are not the same, but they are intimately related. Business transformation is either intentionally directed or it just happens to an organization as a result of external influences. When intentionally directed it is essentially strategic. So on the face of it there seems to be a link worth exploring between architecture and intentionally directed business transformation.

Enterprise architecture typically refers to the highest or most generic level at which architecture applies in an organization. It incorporates and links together other architectures: business architecture, people and organization architecture, process architecture, information architecture, application architecture, infrastructure architecture, and so on. EA is not just the arithmetic sum of these architectures. It also considers for example how process architecture influences (or is contained within) business architecture; how application architecture implements or subverts process architecture; and how information architecture supports or frustrates business architecture.

These are all clues to how architecture can transform a business. They also point to the immense variety of ways in which that transformation can happen.

A lot will depend on current reality. At the most basic level, an organization may either have an architecture or not have one—or at least not one worth speaking of. Simply moving from having no architecture to having one (or perhaps from not knowing it has one and therefore not knowing what it is, to having the one it has chosen to have) can be a business transformation in itself.

Then at an ostensibly more sophisticated level, a business wanting to transform itself can choose to effect that transformation—wholly or partly—by moving from one known current architecture to a new, intended, planned (and therefore known) architecture. (*Choose* is deliberate. Transformation does not have to be architecture-led, and it is illuminating to consider alternatives.)

The field seems wide open. Does every business need an architecture? Must it know what its architecture is? Must every business transform itself? A corner shop employing an enterprise architect to document its current state and then recommend an architected transformation could well be driven out of business by the diversion of resources and management focus. So is it to do with size, or complexity?

In Sickness and in Health

I would like to suggest two apparently opposite directions across the field. One is from the perspective of sickness, the other from that of health. But they seem to arrive at the same place.

Businesses fail or decline for many reasons. To restore a business to health, it first needs a correct diagnosis. If we take "low staff morale" as a possible ailment which could be (but doesn't have to be) at the opposite extreme from "architecture," then investing in architecture could well make morale even worse. But if the illness itself has an architectural component, the cure will probably need one too.

In the case of a healthy business on the other hand, investment in architecture *appears* to be more a question of choice or management style. (Do you want an architecture? Do you want to know what your architecture is?) But then businesses succeed because of sequences of good, mutually coherent decisions. There are good and bad choices. Other things being equal, good choices are ones that promote health and avoid illness. It could be just as wrong to overstress architecture (perhaps by diverting resources or focus better spent elsewhere) than to ignore it. Ultimately, the question is about avoiding

architectural problems. Hence, the architecture question comes to the same thing in sickness and in health. Architectural investment is related to architectural problems—curing them in a sick business, avoiding them in a healthy business.

If this argument is accepted, we should bank it as a principle: the importance of *diagnostics* in any architecture-related definition or implementation of strategy. It is also a good place to start the discussion.

Diagnostics

The diagnostics step should, in theory at least, have a brief broader than architecture. Its objective is to identify actual or potential illnesses and to recommend remedial or preventative treatment. It should not prejudge the result and only look for architectural complaints.

But it must be both analytic and holistic. There is little point in documenting a thousand cases of poor data integrity in an outfit heading for cash-flow disaster or in chronicling how a conglomerate's fragmented applications have resulted from years of growth by acquisition--when the real problem is that no one wants to work there. But maybe the outfit's cash-flow crisis comes from the escalating cost of manual workarounds to shield customers from data which doesn't add up? And the reason people are leaving the conglomerate in droves is their heads cannot take any more system and process knowledge?

Hence the qualification "in theory at least." To respond to an earlier question, Yes it is partly to do with size and complexity. For a sole trader, the organizing principle is the individual. A bigger organization relies less on the individual or individuals *per se*, and more on roles interconnecting, selection of individuals to fill roles, and management of performance within roles. *People and organization architecture* means this if it means anything.

We can therefore suggest a second guiding principle. Although the diagnostic should not presuppose that all its findings and recommendations would be architectural, it should nevertheless be alive to all possible architectural implications. It should construe *architecture* as broadly as possible.

Next Steps

We have reached a point where it is difficult to progress further across a broad front. The nature of any strategic intervention, and in particular any with a significant architectural component will depend on the results of the diagnostic and the nature and scope of its recommendations.

Even if we restrict ourselves to the domains of enterprise architecture already suggested, it is easy to see that a strategic transformation initiative addressing (say) people and organization architecture could be very different from one addressing (say) infrastructure architecture.

To make headway, we need to narrow our scope and consider an example of a transformation which a diagnostic might have recommended. It will be more generic than a case study, but its features will not apply to all architectural transformations and other architectural transformations will have features the example excludes.

Example: Process-Based Transformation in a Financial Services Company

A process-based transformation is chosen because of its potential implications for a number of other architectural domains. Business process is also currently high on corporate agendas. But while process has almost universal applicability in organizational contexts, it is only an example. Not every architecture-driven business transformation will necessarily have a significant process component or any process component at all.

Financial services is chosen because it is a paradigm case of the kind of knowledge-intensive and rule-based service and administration activity

which the modern world sees absorbing increasing amounts of time and energy. (The category also includes central and local government administration, large areas of education, tourism, law etc, and both internal and business-to-business transactions like accounting, ordering, invoicing, settlement, reconciliation, governance, and so on.) The "knowledge-intensive and rule-based service and administration" sector also lends itself particularly well to architecture-driven business transformation.

Choosing a sector like this narrows the scope of "process" and exposes sector-specific features, which provide important process-architectural guidelines. These will be drawn out under *Findings and Recommendations*.

Findings and Recommendations

We shall assume the diagnostic found the organization was losing competitive advantage because of unacceptable unit costs and poor service delivery. It traced both problems to inadequate definition, support, and implementation of key business processes, and recommended a strategic transformation based on a conception of "process" radically different from its current understanding.

In fact part of the problem was that no one concept of "process" was shared across the organization. A cross-section of staff was asked to define "process." Responses ranged from "computer functionality" via "sequence of computer functions" to "sequence of activities with a defined outcome." Although some interviewees were familiar with the concept of process rules, most assumed that process came first and rules came second. A few IT people on the other hand insisted on the priority of rules, even to the extent of denying that "process" was anything other than business rules.

It is important to identify why the recommendation is specifically architectural. It has a lot to do with rigor and governance. Before unpacking the recommendation and its implications in more detail, it would be useful to consider two analogies. (Both will eventually emerge as more than analogies.)

Analogy 1: Double-Entry Accounting

Imagine the diagnostic had discovered that the organization was heading for ruin and the root cause was no understanding or implementation of basic accounting principles. There were records of cash in and cash out, and lists of unpaid invoices and income not yet received. But no understanding of how double-entry principles can define and structure accounting records so they always reconcile against themselves--and how this reconciliation helps ensure the records correspond with reality.

The gap would be profound at the level of logical architecture. It would have implications for data and information, skills, and application systems. With no understanding of double entry, there would be no true accounting skills. Accounting systems would not exist or they would only support simple categorized lists of monetary items, as these would be all the accounting data model would need to support. Understanding, skills, systems, and data would all reinforce each other. Understanding would determine choices about systems and system usage. Nothing about the chosen systems and implemented data models would challenge prevailing perceptions and skill sets.

Now step back. Why is the example so bizarre? It is hard to imagine how an organization like this could survive alongside peers and trading partners using "proper" accounting practices. Where would it find its idiosyncratic accounting system? How could it not have stumbled across standard packages?

The double-entry paradigm has been in existence since the beginning of modern mercantile activity several hundred years ago. It is no longer an architectural choice. In the business world, it would be like choosing to breathe. So let's look at something more recent.

Analogy 2: Relational Data Model

Imagine the diagnostic had instead uncovered a range of quality issues resulting in a low productivity level and traced the problem to a generally poor understanding and implementation of data. Not only were principal application systems based around flattened file structures, much control data was still in program code if it was anywhere, and even recently installed management information systems displayed suboptimal data design. MIS data was only extracts from administration systems, with no restructuring or normalization. Masses of data were replicated even at the transaction level so production metrics were systematically inaccurate. Key data relationships were missing, hampering the use of information to manage the business.

This scenario also seems far-fetched. But 30 or 40 years ago, very few organizations had anything like a "management information system" and extracting data from administration systems was a challenge even if there was somewhere to put it. Administration systems were often built around a single sequential or indexed-sequential file with one record type containing many different entities compressed as attributes or repeating groups. Tape-based storage technology cast a long shadow.

Over the years since then the relational model and normalized data structures have become more and more universal. Forty years ago, organizations could survive without them because none had them. Imagine an equivalent diagnostic carried out 20 years ago. It might have discovered that the client organization was losing competitive advantage because of unacceptable unit costs and poor service delivery and traced both problems to inadequate definition, analysis, and implementation of key business data entities and their relationships. It might have recommended a strategic transformation based on a conception of *data* radically different from how the organization currently understood it.

Manner and Degree of Permeation

Isn't there a difference though between the *accounting* and *data* diagnostics and the *process* diagnostic? Process is surely what people (business users) do. Data on the other hand is malleable and can be translated into different structures and formats. Business users may be unaware of the implications of different approaches to data. A new approach to data may not have to permeate through the organization. Although it would no doubt be good if the principles of normalization, primary, foreign keys, and so on were commonly understood, this is only likely in something like a software company. In general, people go about their work fairly oblivious to the principles an organization has adopted as to how it treats its data.

There would be some implications largely implemented through governance. Business users would not be able to dictate how data is organized in different systems (e.g., whether it needs to be physically present in a system or just available to it) and in the latter case, business users might feel the impact of integration overheads.

A more direct implication could be explicit ownership. The more normalized the logical data model, the more of a distinction will emerge between primary and secondary repositories. The customer data "bible" is likely to be the customer file or table. Customer data may be replicated elsewhere but the customer file would be the source- -the single point of truth. Once the sovereignty of the customer file has been established (in respect of all other customer data stores), a business owner can be found for it. A different business owner could be found for the chart of accounts, another recognizable data entity.

We find a similar variable distribution in the double-entry accounting analogy. Not everyone will understand every implication of double entry- -how control accounts work and why cash book debits and credits seem the wrong way round. But there will be general knowledge of debits and credits and of assets and liabilities. And the governance principle of account ownership will usually be rigorously applied. A manager owning a cost centre owns a section of the general ledger and is literally accountable for every transaction across a defined set of accounts.

Both analogies illuminate the process diagnostic. Both are significant at the level of logical architecture—what concepts and definitions are used and what relationships are identified. Decisions at the logical level translate into design and acquisition choices at physical solution architecture level and into organizational and operational changes. In both cases, both translations may call for pragmatic governance.

The process diagnostic is similar. There will be implications at the logical architectural level: concepts, definitions, and relationships. Some implications will translate into choices around physical solution architecture and operational organization; some translations will require explicit governance. But because process is also what people do (not just what it is done on), and because we are assuming the recommended architecture-driven business transformation will be carried out, the translation will also require holistically managed change.

Implicit to Explicit

We shall now unpack the diagnostic summary *inadequate definition, support, and implementation of key business processes* in a bit more detail. The problem is that the current process architecture is implicit, not explicit. It is what people do either within or outside the various systems the organization has built, bought, and integrated over the years. An implicit process architecture is where processes happen around systems (and often in spite of them) and where processes are the way they are because systems are the way they are. In an explicit architecture, processes are the way they need to be to meet business needs, and the rest of the architecture is optimized to implement those processes.

On Not Taking Process Seriously

An explicit process architecture is one where process is taken seriously as an architectural domain in its own right. There are many ways of not doing this, for example:

1. Process could be reduced to data and rules about data, typically rules about what counts as a well-formed master record (bank account, insurance policy, purchase order, customer or client record, etc.).
2. Process could be reduced to document flow: paper, scanned images, digitized documents of any kind, or links to digitized documents. This can happen when a generic "workflow" package is implemented, particularly one originally designed to support the "paperless office."
3. Process could be seen in terms of what people do, either within or outside the systems established in the organization. This is the classic business process re-engineering (BPR) perspective, with its roots in manufacturing and distribution.

All three are supplier-centric. The data approach (1) is concerned with the supplier's data, its integrity, and its conformance with rules. The document-flow approach (2) concentrates on the paperwork, which accounts for a large part of the supplier organization's activity and cost. And the BPR approach (3) focuses on what the supplier resources do and how they can be deployed more effectively and efficiently.

The three are frequently seen together in the same organization. They are also not necessarily wrong. But they are incomplete, which is why they

often coexist as each tries to fill the gaps the others leave. Coexistence comes at a price however, as different development and implementation paradigms vie with each other and create duplication and confusion. An organization may not see this duplication and confusion (and may not want to see it) if it doesn't take the process seriously.

The financial services diagnostic will have identified examples of this. The company has a number of administration systems supporting its product range. In one of these, process is implemented as in the data-centric approach (1) because this was where the increasing sophistication of its designers and architects had reached at the time. The company has also implemented a generic workflow package, and over the years has extended it across a number of business areas including those using the data-centric administration system. So processes were also implemented as "workflows" defining the paths which links to digitized documents were allowed to take from one person to another (2). Then a BPR exercise (3) mapped processes across a number of areas, including ones supported by the data-centric administration system, by the generic workflow system, and by both. Diagrams showed activities involving both systems, but depicted the processes themselves as independent of the systems—interacting with them, but not physically implemented in them. No wonder "process" meant different things to different people.

Now translate this into the two analogies. Imagine an organization where different people had different views of where the principal accounting records were, how they were constructed, how many accounts (or lists) there were, what account types were represented, and so on. Or where different people disagree over what is and is not customer data, where it is stored, what the source or master is or should be, what the unique identifier(s) should be, what foreign keys in other entities or data groupings reference the customer data, and so on. We would say the first organization did not take accounting seriously and the second did not take data seriously. By extension, the financial services company in the diagnostic does not take process seriously. When something can mean anything, it means nothing.

Process Meta-Model

Simplicity is the ultimate sophistication said Leonardo da Vinci. This can work both ways. Sometimes it is worth being a bit more sophisticated to achieve a bit more simplicity.

The diagnostic argued that a particular meta-model underlay the financial services company's overall approach to process (see Figure 1).

This model is familiar, ostensibly simple, and again neither false nor wrong. It holds generically across all processes—not only "business processes"—and can inform quality improvement initiatives. But it also does not challenge the coexistence of the three incomplete approaches (1)-(3).

Particularly when dealing with the kind of business processes featuring in a rule-based environment like financial services, it is worth being a bit more stringent (see Figure 2).

In the input-process-output model, the only logical connection between input and output is that inputs are needed to generate outputs.

In the request-process-outcome model, on the other hand the request and the outcome are described in the same terms. The request is for the outcome; the outcome fulfils the request. An entity can therefore be identified—the request itself—which travels through the process.

The request-process-outcome model is from Lawrence (2005), which explores its implications in a lot more detail. For now we shall just indicate a few practical benefits this more "sophisticated" simplicity bestows.

The request entity and its related data set can be identified and analyzed for any particular process, which means defining precisely what level the process operates at. In financial services, this is crucial but often glossed over. Is the process operating at customer level, at account level, at portfolio level, at policy level, at claim level etc?

The diagnostic found a glaring flaw of this kind in the way the workflow package had been implemented.

Because the data design of the workflow package was largely unchanged from its paper-less office days, its *process instance* entity was effectively an extension of a *document* entity. A *document* was something that had to be digitized (e.g., scanned) and then indexed so that the image could be retrieved by business keys. Indexing attached a maximum of six business keys to each image. Because the solution was generic, the same six applied across all document types.

Figure 1. Input-process-output model

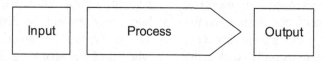

Figure 2. Request-process-outcome model

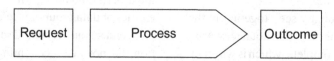

The request-process-outcome meta-model exposes the inadequacy of this approach. The data set in terms of which the request is worded (which therefore identifies the level the process operates at) may not be uniquely referenced by one of the six (or a concatenation of more than one). And if it is, it only needs that one business key. To apply other keys is to risk de-normalization and data conflict.

For example, assume the business keys include the customer account number, customer reference, and intermediary code. If the process is at customer account level, then it would be right to use the customer account number as the business key index. Adding customer reference would be redundant, and adding intermediary code would be wrong. This is assuming a customer account is necessarily tied to a customer but only contingently (and perhaps temporarily) linked to an intermediary. If a customer account could belong to more than one customer, then it would also be wrong and not only redundant to add (just one) customer reference.

Or the process could be at the level of a unit holding on an investment contract holding units in several funds. The required business key might be the concatenation of contract reference and fund reference. But this might not be available within the six available keys so only contract reference can be used. The example may look small, at an almost trivial level of detail. But it is important to appreciate its significance in both architectural and service quality terms. The business user closes the gap by making sure the process (unit surrender or switch) takes place on the right unit holding. This may be acceptable when the workflow system and administration system are unconnected (artificially held at a low technological level), but it will bedevil future integration attempts. The workflow system has been allowed to dictate how processes are viewed with negative implications for process architecture, data architecture, application architecture, and skills requirements. What would happen if the business user didn't close the gap properly and the wrong unit holding was surrendered? Someone would have to pay.

These examples are not academic. They are real and familiar muddles with implications for data, processing, work, and service quality. They are evidence of not taking process seriously--the unfortunate assumption that normal data analysis and design principles don't apply around "process," when in fact observing those principles in a process context is crucial in today's increasingly competitive, increasingly customer-oriented, and therefore increasingly process-centric world.

Process and Well-Formed Data

The meta-model also demonstrates both the truth and the incompleteness of the view (1) that process can be reduced to rules about well-formed data (except, it must be added, from the most holistic perspective). Many business processes in administration contexts create master records: opening a bank account, issuing an insurance policy, placing an order, etc. Rules about what counts as a well-formed account, policy, or order record (and a well-formed related customer record) will be intimately linked, if not identical, to rules governing the process itself. So much so that it would be otiose to insist on a distinction between "data rules" (including perhaps product rules) and "process rules."

Many subsequent business processes, particularly in the paradigm case of financial services, will also be controlled by data rules. A transaction across a bank account must have a date, amount, account number, debit or credit—if a debit it must be from a recognized and authorized source etc. But to focus on the data set to the exclusion of the request, the data set is linked to is to risk ignoring the thread of intentionality, which makes a business process what it is, with all its contingencies and logistics and loops.

A well-formed input data set is a necessary but not sufficient condition for a successful process outcome. An insurance claim must specify x, y,

215

and z. But what if it doesn't? What are the rules about asking for missing information? What documentation needs to be attached? What if it is incomplete? How should it be followed up? What if it never turns up? When must the claim be settled by? How is this affected by missing information or missing documentation? Who must do what, and when, and in what sequence? What if the customer requests a change of address at the same time? How much is the administration of the claim allowed to cost the insurance company? How are queues of work managed? Do some claims have priority over others?

Questions like these are all part of the "process" and they go beyond the quality and integrity of administration system data. Hence, the incompleteness of the view that process can be reduced to rules about well-formed data. Ultimately, however, every what-if, performance target, case priority rule, follow-up rule, and process integration rule can be expressed as control data. And the passage of the request entity plus related data set along the process in accordance with every control data rule can be seen as the validation of a transaction to ensure it is well formed. So hence the caveat: the incompleteness of the data-centric approach starts to disappear when viewed from the most holistic perspective.

The challenge is to achieve that perspective, and the request-process-outcome meta-model can move us toward it.

Process, Subprocess, and Task

Defining the request entity as the subject of the process is the first step in developing the meta-model into a full logical process architecture. Again, the discussion here summarizes a more detailed exposition in Lawrence (2005).

As the request entity (e.g., customer order or claim) passes through the process (order process or insurance claim process respectively), it undergoes changes in business status relating to the things that need to happen for it to be fulfilled.

These things may be either sequential or parallel, and depend on pure logic or contingent business rules. For example, an order may be first captured, then validated, then credit-checked, then matched against stock, then authorized, then dispatched. Or the rules may allow or require credit checking and matching against stock to happen in parallel.

These business statuses can be defined in terms of what has just happened, or—more usefully—what needs to happen next: awaiting validation, awaiting credit check, etc. As they reflect the workflow of the request, we can call them the possible *workflow statuses* the request entity can have.

We can now use the concept of workflow status to analyze *process* itself into two more lower levels. The first is *subprocess*:

- Each process consists of one or more subprocesses.
- Each subprocess represents the work required to take the request entity from one workflow status to the next, disregarding any differences in the possible attribute values of the request entity or its related data set.

The next is *task*:

- Each subprocess consists of one or more tasks.
- All the work of a subprocess, and therefore of a process, is contained in its tasks.
- A task may be manual or automatic.
- The tasks within a subprocess, and the routing between them, are determined by what needs to happen to achieve the workflow status transition of the subprocess, taking account of all possible attribute values of the request entity and its related data set.

The result is an explicit logical architecture, which takes process seriously and is customer-centric by design. It unifies the three incomplete approaches (1)-(3), incorporates their strengths, and closes their gaps.

Connections with Other Architecture Domains

Process architecture is particularly powerful in the way it informs other architectures. These connections in themselves indicate how broad and deep an architecture-driven business transformation can be. Conversely, a business transformation is all the more effective and profound when propelled by the centripetal force of architectural unification.

Process architecture is both explicit and sovereign when processes are the way they need to be in order to deliver against customer needs, and where the rest of the architecture is optimized to implement those processes.

The meta-model generates a logical process architecture, which can translate into logical and physical data models. Hence the implication for data and/or information architecture. Organizations that are not process-based tend not to see process entities (process type and instance, task type, and instance etc) as parts of their logical data model. The revelation that process entities can be modeled with attributes and relationships just like other business entities can profoundly influence for example the use of integrated data analysis to support financial control and continuous process improvement.

This is just a start. How thorough and physical the connections would be will depend on the organization's appetite for architectural transformation and its perception of how urgent it is. To pursue the envisaged diagnostic, process architecture in a financial services operation could completely determine application architecture in the sense that applications could be incrementally designed and built and/or re-engineered around the kind of design patterns and constructs the meta-model generates. (Because the meta-model translates into logical and physical data models,

the process architecture can be implemented in physical application architecture.) This would be a 180° shift from the current state in which application architecture determines process architecture; the intended state has it the other way round.

Implemented process architecture can then determine (or at least profoundly influence) people and organization architecture: by defining roles in terms of patterns of access rights to manual tasks in implemented processes; by instituting and requiring "process owner" roles; by redefining managerial and supervisory roles by reducing or eliminating their process-management component; and so on.

Transformation Pathway

So far, we have only sketched the possible transformation target—the intended outcome enabled and implemented by the intended architecture. How to get there is a subject all by itself.

The transformation must succeed on many levels, and governance and sponsorship structures are needed to ensure the intent is not eroded.

Since the transformation is architecture-driven, whoever is responsible for program sponsorship must understand this, and understand the nature and importance of architectural governance. This does not mean the sponsor must be an architect—indeed an architect would be unlikely to have the degree and extent of organizational authority the sponsorship role needs. Ideally, a sponsor of any business change initiative should be that person who has the most to gain from the success of the initiative and the most to lose from its failure.

This is possibly the most significant logistical challenge of architecture-driven transformation. With the right sponsorship, almost anything is possible. The difficulty is to get the right sponsorship, because the wrong sponsorship can be disastrous.

The link between strategy and architecture was mentioned early on. To state the obvious, transformation is where the two overlap. In business, not all strategies are architectural—leader's strategy could be 100% political or 100% financial. But architecture is by nature strategic because it projects intention into the future. Architecture is about making something that lasts into the future, or about ensuring that something that already exists lasts into the future. So the sponsor must not only be a strategic thinker, he or she must also be in no doubt about why the transformation target depends on its architectural preconditions.

The sponsor will maintain this certainty all the more easily if every opportunity is taken to make the architecture physical, and as early as possible. The kind of process architecture summarized here and detailed elsewhere (Lawrence, 2005) can be built as generic constructs to enable demonstration prototypes to be crafted, and phased implementations to be scoped and planned. What eats up time and blocks physical implementation is not the architectural complexity of the target (remember Leonardo da Vinci), but the labyrinthine legacy of past incomplete solutions; and even more the legacy mindsets which have crafted them and been crafted by them. All the more reason to build demonstration prototypes as early as possible.

It is only when business stakeholders come to grips with what true, unified, process architecture means in practice that they can begin to understand and support the radical and extensive changes it requires and facilitates. No more "tracking" systems to deduce where processes are from data extracted from administration and workflow applications; "tracking" is just a customized window on implemented process architecture. No more "customer contact" systems in some specialized "CRM" domain; "customer contact" is just a customized configuration of generic constructs, incorporating "tracking" deep within the process architecture, which articulates the business, which in an increasingly real sense *is* the business. And what about the skills which need developing and preserving? In a process-architected environment, they too are

architected into categories. There are front-line skills represented by the residual manual tasks defined within the model of each implemented process type. There are supervisory and operational management skills related to the throughput, productivity, quality, and performance against service-level agreements; supported by metrics for the most part automatically falling out of the process architecture. (This is no empty promise. Process architecture models the work required to deliver against recognized customer requests. Its implemented data model cannot but be what production metrics require). And there are the IT-related skills needed to keep the process-based architecture in place, to improve its quality and productivity, to extend it, and change it when changes in product, distribution or regulatory environment demand.

Holistic architecture calls for holistic thinking, transcending legacy categories like *product administration, customer information management, workflow, work management, document management, MIS*, and *business rules*. Of course product administration, customer information management, workflow, etc., will continue being done, but there cannot be "product administration systems" developed and supported by "product administration system teams" and "workflow systems" developed and supported by "workflow teams." A process-architectural transformation, which doesn't address this, is no transformation. Such is the sponsorship challenge.

This is just to sketch a few examples of the possible dimensions of a true and truly successful transformation driven by process architecture. A more specific and detailed case study is available in Lawrence (2005). But even this only scratches the surface a little deeper.

Other Transformations

Not all architecture-driven business transformations will involve process architecture. Process was picked as an example but it was not arbitrary.

Process is one of the more relevant and central architectural domains in the current business world, possibly the most relevant and central. It is certainly one with extensive implications on multiple dimensions. But whether process or otherwise, if architecture-driven business transformation is so involved and so perilous, why risk it? No law ordains it but the law of survival. For some organizations, the change might be just too wholesale to contemplate. Not every organization will transform or have to. An increasing number of start-up organizations will be process-architected from day 1 as there were many with relational data structures from day 1. Other things being equal they were the ones that survived and prospered.

Transformation does not have to be architecture-led. The diagnostic might not identify significant actual or potential architectural problems, but still recommend a productivity and/or quality transformation based for example on a re-engineering paradigm like Lean or Six Sigma. The difficulty comes when architecture is to be addressed as well. Re-engineering and re-architecting can struggle to stay compatible so an organization must be very clear about its strategic intent.

Lean (and/or Six Sigma) and process architecture inhabit a similar problem space—both having to do with "process." Lean engineering and work management principles can be entirely compatible with process architecture. If a strategic decision has been made to take a process-architectural route, then Lean can be the icing on the cake. Process architecture will define and implement residual manual tasks, and Lean will inform how they are tackled, managed, prioritized, and measured, how the results will be visually displayed, and how teams will be built and maintained to optimize accountability, productivity, and quality.

But if instead the strategic decision is to go the Lean route, and as a result the Lean initiative is given sovereignty, then there is a risk that Lean will declare a monopoly over radical thinking. Because it is typically associated with the re-engineering process paradigm (3), this can reinforce legacy thinking wherever Lean itself doesn't challenge it. Lean initiatives often involve external consultancies whose engagement models require networking among the status quo to minimize risk. The result can constrain radical architectural re-thinking.

CONCLUSION

Can architecture drive business transformation? Yes, because process architecture can, which is the example explored here.

Much current business process thinking is constrained by the belief that it must be generic across all types of process, including those in manufacturing and distribution, which necessarily deal with material objects. Popular process improvement approaches like Lean and Six Sigma have their roots in these environments. But a significant and growing proportion of work in the modern world is only contingently related to material objects. This work is both rule-based and digitizable. It is more than just supported by IT. IT defines the work itself and the world the work is done within.

A customer-oriented, process-architectural approach is available, which can transform the business operations where this kind of work takes place. The architecture itself is disarmingly simple. The only challenge is the labyrinthine legacy of incompleteness in both technology and thinking so all it needs is time.

REFERENCES

Fischer, L. (2005). *Workflow handbook 2005*. Lighthouse Point, FL: Future Strategies Inc.

Jackson, M., & Twaddle, G. (1997). *Business process implementation: Building workflow systems*. Harlow, UK: Addison Wesley Longman Limited.

Lawrence, C. P. (2005). *Make work make sense: An introduction to business process architecture*. Cape Town, South Africa: Future Managers (Pty) Ltd. Retrieved from http://www.makeworkmake-sense.com

Chapter XIII
Maturity of IT–Business Alignment:
An Assessment Tool

Nel Wognum
University of Twente, The Netherlands

Fan Ip-Shing
Cranfield University, UK

ABSTRACT

Enterprise systems hold a large promise for organisations to enhance their strategic position. However, adoption and implementation of enterprise systems is not without problems. Many problems have been reported in the literature with implementation of new technology, many of which seem to reoccur over and over again. It seems difficult for organisations to learn from previous experience and successfully organise and manage complex dynamic projects like an enterprise system implementation project. Although current project and change management methods offer support in organising and managing complex projects, more is needed to increase insight into the specific situation at hand. In this chapter, research is presented aimed at collecting knowledge on the dynamics of enterprise system implementation projects. The knowledge can serve to increase awareness of potential risks and pitfalls in specific new enterprise system implementation situations. To make the knowledge accessible, a tool has been developed for assessing a start-up situation of an enterprise system implementation project in an organisation. The key concept in this assessment is the level of mutual alignment between various organisational aspects of the business in which the system is implemented, the enterprise system, and the implementation project.

INTRODUCTION

More and more enterprise systems are implemented and used in organisations to support enterprise-wide processes. Such processes involve several departments in an organisation or even may cross organisations' borders (see e.g., Davenport, 2000). Examples of enterprise-wide processes are the order-throughput process from customer order to finished product, including purchasing and distribution and the design and engineering process from idea to product specification, including possibly early transfer of information to downstream processes. A well-known enterprise system is an enterprise resource planning (ERP) system, which supports all processes involved in processing customer orders. Another example is a product data management (PDM) system, which supports management of lifecycle aspects of product information. Knowledge management (KM) is yet another solution to managing enterprise-wide information.

Despite the many potential advantages, implementation of an enterprise system is not without problems. About half of all implementation projects only partly meet the envisioned goals or fail completely (see e.g., KPMG, 2002; Kwon & Zmud, 1987; Nash, 2000). Many other projects may meet the goals, but only by consuming considerably more resources than budgeted. In the literature, many dos and donts have been described as well as success and failure factures (see e.g., Adam & O'Doherty, 2000). In addition, many best-practice project management approaches and change management methods are offered that can support people in successfully implementing an enterprise system (Bancroft, Seip, & Sprengel, 1997; Callaway, 1999; Lozinsky, 1998; Welti, 1999). However, the dos and donts and best practices do not sufficiently guide people in organisations in managing a complex process like implementing an enterprise system. Available guidelines and methods apparently are abstracted from real contexts and are difficult to specify for specific situations.

Moreover, in practice, most of the identified problems seem to reoccur over and over again as can be concluded from a vast amount of literature on real-life experiences with implementing new technologies (see e.g., Davenport, 2000; Ruël, 2001). The problems reported are multi-faceted. They are both technical and organisational in nature, with less than 10% of a technical nature. The majority of problem is related to organisational and human issues (Bikson & Gutek, 1984). It seems that in real practice, insight into the specific situation at hand is insufficient for engaging in and managing an enterprise system implementation project.

Enterprise system implementation projects are inherently complex and dynamic, which means that the process and its outcomes cannot be fully predicted. Technology and organisation need to co-develop during an implementation project (Leonard-Barton, 1988; Orlikowski & Robey, 1991), which means that the envisioned outcomes for technology and organisation may change during the project. Moreover, the course of the project may change due to internal and external disturbances or unexpected new opportunities. Although current project and change management methods offer support for managing such projects, they need to be complemented with methods to increase insight into the specific situation in which an enterprise system is to be implemented.

There is a large need for people with extensive experience of managing complex projects. Such people could be consultants who have been guiding and managing many projects in various companies. In-depth experience is, however, scarce. Similarly, people in organisations may have gained experience in earlier implementation projects. Knowledge in organisations may, however, fade away due to possibly large time lag between implementation projects or because people may leave the organisation. The question is how people and organisations can learn from previous experience gained in other similar situations. The challenge is to collect such experiences and transfer them into a tool for increasing awareness of the areas that need attention in a specific implementation situation. With such a tool, the start of an implementation project would be improved by the ability to anticipate situation-specific risks and problems.

In this chapter, a tool is presented for assessing the readiness of an organisation to start an enterprise system implementation project. The tool is the result of research performed in the BEST project[1] (Wognum, Krabbendam, Buhl, Ma, & Kenett, 2004). The research was aimed at capturing experiences of enterprise system implementation projects and making these available to other projects through the tool. The resulting tool is based on the view that implementation of an enterprise system occurs in a socio-technical system in which several systems co-exist (see Section 3). The degree of alignment between these systems is a measure of the readiness of an organisation.

We will address two questions in this chapter:

1. What needs to be considered in anticipating problems in an implementation project? To answer this question, a model is needed incorporating relevant aspects of a socio-technical system, as well as a model of the systems that co-exist during an implementation project. Such a model will be suited to capture and structure knowledge of real-life implementation projects.

2. What potential problems can be expected in the start-up phase of a particular implementation project? To answer this question, a tool will be presented that visualises the weak areas that need attention in a specific situation. The potential risk areas are rated on a maturity scale that indicates the degree of alignment between the different co-existing socio-economic systems.

The previous questions will be addressed in the following sections. Section 2 will present the background of enterprise systems and their use for current organisations. The need for an architectural view will be explained. In Section 3 the architectural view adopted for the presented research will be presented. Section 4 briefly presents the research performed and the results gained. Section 5 introduces the tool for assessing the readiness and maturity of an organisation to start an enterprise system implementation project. This chapter ends with a summary and ideas for further research.

BACKGROUND

Business functions, business units, and companies become more and more connected all around the globe to meet the challenges of current market needs. Interconnectivity requires that information needs to flow seamlessly across the various boundaries (Davenport, 2000). Enterprise-wide information systems are implemented to generate, store, retrieve, share, and transfer information across the company and beyond. Enterprise resource planning systems (ERP), for example, manage information throughout the whole order-throughput process, from order intake to product delivery, from supplier to distribution, involving many different business functions or even supply chain partners. Product data management (PDM) systems manage data throughout the whole design and engineering process involving downstream processes where needed and possibly, suppliers and design partners. Web technology is increasingly being integrated with enterprise information systems to enable the transfer of information between companies (Laudon & Laudon, 2004).

The most important characteristic of enterprise systems is that data is centrally managed and can be accessed by all business functions inside and outside the company that are involved in the supported business process. Central data management

223

requires shared agreement on data definitions and formats across the various business functions. Other agreements involve the streamlining of processes and workflow to achieve integration between the various business functions (Laudon et al., 2004).

Enterprise systems have several characteristics that need to be taken into account when implementing such systems in an organisation (Markus & Tanis, 2000):

- They integrate information flows through a company—involving (e.g., financial and accounting information, human resources information, supply chain information.

- They are commercial packages bought from or leased by software vendors. This means that traditional IT skills are not sufficient for implementing a software package like an enterprise system, while organisational requirements and processes need to be mapped to the processes and terminology embedded in the enterprise system. Organisations need to manage their dependency on vendors.

- They are based on best practices, which force organisations to adapt to a less proprietary way of working. Often considerable redesign of a company's processes is needed, also influencing organisational structure, tasks, workflow, etc.

- Assembly is needed of the enterprise system with the company's existing infrastructure, legacy systems, or modules or programs from other vendors. Markus et al. (2000) state that today's enterprise systems do not yet meet all the information-processing needs of the majority of organisations.

- Evolution of enterprise systems is continuously happening to meet the changing demands of current business involving continuous updates of a company's enterprise system and accompanying organisational changes.

The impact of enterprise systems on the organisation is, however, often underestimated (Davenport, 2000). Many enterprise system implementation projects are still considered to be a responsibility of the IT people in the organisation. This fact is often mentioned as an important reason for failure. In selecting and adopting an enterprise system, a thorough analysis is needed of many aspects of the organisation such as business strategy, business processes and tasks, organisational culture, existing infrastructure and systems, and people knowledge and skills. Top management cannot sit aside in this process.

Many problems are reported in the literature in the past decades with implementing new technology in an organisation. Many problems seem to reoccur and are not restricted to one type of technology (see e.g., Boer, 1990; Markus et al., 2000; Ruël, 2001). Despite of the many different situations, some regularities can be found, which may help people in managing an implementation project. Project and change management methods have been developed to manage complex projects and offer methods to manage or prevent many of the common problems. However, despite the availability of advanced project and change management methods, problems still keep appearing.

The process of implementing an enterprise system is extremely complex and different for each different situation. Moreover, technology implementation projects are not deterministic. Even with similar starting situations, outcomes may be different (see e.g., Barley, 1986). An implementation project is dynamic because at any phase different things can go wrong, problems may stay unnoticed for a while, many actors are involved with their own perspectives and goals, business situations may change, a wide range of decision options exist, etc. Moreover, system and organisation co-develop (Leonard-Barton, 1988). People influence the way a system is used (Orlikowski, 1992) possibly leading to adaptations to the system, while better understanding of the system might lead to identification of new opportunities for the organisation, which requires additional organisational changes.

Implementing an enterprise system requires a team approach involving many different disciplines, technical as well as organisational, and several organisational levels, from top-level management to the worker level. Experience of implementation projects is indispensable. However, in-depth experience is scarce. Similarly, implementation knowledge in organisations may fade away due to possibly large time lags between implementation projects or because people may leave the organisation. The question is how people and organisations can gather knowledge and learn from previous experience gained in other similar situations. The challenge is to collect such experiences and make them available for increasing awareness of the areas that need attention in a specific implementation situation. In this way, the start of an implementation project would be improved by the ability to anticipate situation-specific risks and problems.

In the EC project BEST (Better Enterprise SysTem implementation), case studies have been performed to capture dynamics of enterprise system implementation projects. Process fragments have been gathered that represent an unexpected or undesired course of action. As such, the process fragments serve as mini-cases of real-life experiences of enterprise system implementation projects. By reading such mini-cases, people may better understand their own situation and improve their own implementation project. The mini-cases have been used to build a tool for identifying possibly weak or problematic situations at the start of a new enterprise system implementation project (Wognum et al., 2004). The tool also offers an index to the set of mini-cases that are relevant to a specific start-up situation.

The tool offers a snapshot of a company at the start of adopting an enterprise system. The snapshot shows weak areas of the implementation project to start. By increasing awareness of the potential risks involved, the tool may support establishing conditions that may be necessary for achieving a successful outcome. However, these conditions may be necessary, but are not sufficient. Because of the dynamic and emergent nature (Soh & Markus, 1995) of enterprise system implementation projects as previously argued, adequate project and change management methods are indispensable. Repeated snap-shots may be needed to redirect and change the course of the project.

ENTERPRISE ARCHITECTURE AND SOCIAL DYNAMICS

The main challenge of implementing an enterprise system in an organisation is to achieve alignment between the system and the organisation. Achieving alignment requires an integrated approach to all aspects of an organisation, technical as well as organisational. Enterprise architecture may offer an important support for achieving such integration (Lankhorts, 2004). In this chapter, we will not discuss modelling languages or tools for enterprise architectures, but we will discuss the elements and relationships of an enterprise architecture that offers an integrated analytic view on the processes involved in implementing an enterprise system.

The research performed in the BEST project is based on a system view of organisations (see e.g., Daft, 2004; Flood & Jackson, 1991). An organisation is viewed as a socio-technical system in which technology and organisation need to be aligned with each other to achieve the organisational goals. In a socio-technical systems approach, many different disciplines, technical as well as social, need to collaborate (Laudon et al., 2004). Next, we introduce the socio-technical system approach adopted in the BEST project, which serves as the basis for the resulting enterprise architecture.

Enterprise Architecture

In the systems view, an organisation is viewed as a purposeful whole in which people perform processes with the help of means, like methods and tools to satisfy certain needs in the environment of the organisation (Boer & Krabbendam, 1993). Processes transform inputs of material and/or information into outputs, which are products and/or services needed in the environment. The processes directly aimed at achieving the goals of the organisation are called primary processes. The primary processes are controlled and buffered against disturbances from the environment by management processes, which consist of strategic, adaptive, and operational management processes. Strategic processes determine the long-term goals and strategy of the organisation including the performance goals (see e.g., Slack, Chambers, Harland, Harrison, & Johnston, 1998). Adaptive management implements these goals into suitable organisational configurations. Operational processes manage the daily processes within the goals and strategy set by strategic management. To perform the primary, management, and sup-

port processes, sufficient and sufficiently qualified people and means are necessary for which support processes are responsible. Finally, organisational arrangements consist of all formal and informal structural and cultural relationships between people, between means, and between people and means in an organisation. An architectural view on an organisational system for a manufacturing organisation is depicted in Figure 1, which can be considered an enterprise architecture. The model has been used as a component in an architecture of a virtual organisation to identify essential capabilities needed for mature performance (Wognum & Faber, 2002).

In the enterprise architecture presented in Figure 1, the processes have not been explicitly subdivided into management, primary, and support processes. Processes consist of activities, each of which also may consist of lower-level activities until basic activities are reached. The architecture shows the information on the process and product that flows between activities. Two types of process activities have been distinguished, transformation and communication activities. Transformation activities transform input information into out-

Figure 1. Architectural model of a manufacturing organisation

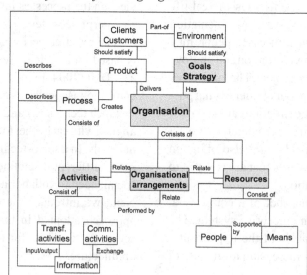

226

put information. Examples of such activities are the transformation of product requirements into a conceptual design in a product development process. Similarly, information on the product status in order processing is transformed when the order is processed (the architecture does not show the material flow). Communication activities transfer information from one activity to another and, as such, between the people that perform the activities. The document flow between activities represents the formal communication in a company, for example. Information on the product and process is important to consider when implementing an enterprise system (e.g., a PDM system for supporting a product development process).

A system is more than the sum of its elements (Flood et al., 1991). The behaviour of a system as a whole cannot be found in any of its elements. A system view, therefore, is a holistic view. It is possible to analyse parts or aspects of a system, but without taking into account their relationships with other parts or aspects, conclusions may not be very reliable. A system view is, moreover, an analytic way to focus analysis on a coherent part of the world.

Determining system borders is an important part of organisational analysis and design. Examples of systems to be analysed are the manufacturing process (Boer, 1990), the R&D process (Weerd-Nederhof, 1998), or the collaborative design process between organisations (Faber, 2001). Determining system borders and the relevant system elements starts with selection of a focus process. The enterprise architecture presented in Figure 1 may represent various primary processes in a manufacturing environment.

In case of an enterprise system implementation project, selecting a focus process is not very simple. Focusing only on the project process is not sufficient. Focusing only on the business process that is impacted by the enterprise system on the other hand might lead to ignorance of the project and change process. Moreover, the enterprise system itself is also a system with a business process embedded in it with a related workflow and dataflow and task definition, which need to be tuned to the business process and vice versa. An enterprise architecture for an enterprise system implementation project should incorporate these three processes (see Section 3.3).

In an enterprise implementation project, an enterprise architecture must be supplemented by a detailed process model in which the different activities and the transformation and flow of information can be recognised. Such a model can be compared with best practice models as, for example, are offered by enterprise system package vendors (see e.g., www.sap.com). Comparison of the process models will help in determining the changes needed in the business process. More is needed, however, to estimate the amount of effort needed to implement an enterprise system as we will describe next. An enterprise architecture helps in determining the areas of attention. This also means that enterprise architectures should differ for different application areas. In Section 3.3, an enterprise architecture for enterprise system implementation will be presented.

Modelling important elements and relationships is not sufficient. To analyse if and how an organisation achieves its goal, the behaviour of an organisation needs to be studied. Next, organisational behaviour is discussed in more detail.

Social Dynamics

The processes performed in an organisational system determine its behaviour. Processes are expected to proceed as designed (i.e., as laid down in process schemes and process handbooks in ISO certified companies). However, this is often not the case, not only because of unexpected disturbances like broken machines or insufficient supplies, but also because of the culture, politics, power, and other aspects involved in collaboration between people (Schein, 1996).

Organisational arrangements as previously introduced provide the glue between the other elements of the organisation. They consist of the formal and informal arrangements, the structure and culture of an organisation, which allow material and information to flow from one process step to another, and support communication between people.

The structure and culture of an organisation consist of various normative relationships between the elements in an organisation. Normative relationships are not only the organisational hierarchy, reporting relationships, process structure, infrastructure, team structures, normative procedures, and routines, but also the values, rules, and norms that constitute a relatively coherent and consistent set of beliefs and prescriptions that govern the behaviour of people (Scott, 1992). The normative relationships can be considered to constrain and channel human behaviour in the organisation.

On the other hand, actual behaviour often differs from behaviour intended in the normative part of the organisational arrangements. This actual behaviour depends not only on individual human characteristics, but also on relationships and interactions between people. Commitment, attitude, sentiments, conflicts, autonomous activities are examples of characteristics that influence organisational behaviour.

There is a duality (Giddens, 1984) between normative and actual behaviour in an organisation. Actual behaviour may shape the normative relationships, while normative relationships shape behaviour. In this chapter, we will use the term social-dynamics to indicate actual behaviour.

An Enterprise Architecture for Enterprise System Implementation

The architectural model previously presented has been used in the BEST project to frame thinking and structure knowledge on the process of enterprise system implementation. As previously indicated above, in an enterprise system implementation project several organisational systems co-exist (see e.g., Lange-Ros, 1999). These systems may need separate configurations and may behave differently. In the socio-technical view, these systems need to be internally as well as mutually aligned for achieving successful implementation. While organisational theories may support internal alignment (see e.g., Daft, 2004), mutual alignment requires understanding the different needs and characteristics of the different organisational systems.

Figure 2. Enterprise architecture for enterprise system implementation

	Enterprise system	Project management	Permanent business
Strategy and goals			
Management			
Structure			
Process			
Knowledge and skills			
Social dynamics			

The first system that can be recognised is the permanent business, which needs to proceed as usual during an implementation of a new enterprise system, while at the same time gradually adapting to the new situation. The second system is the implementation project, which requires specific resources, processes, and structure. The third system is the process to configure and tune the enterprise system with its embedded processes and structure. Each of the three systems can be studied apart from the others, although the distinction is purely analytic. In practice, the three systems interact and are mutually dependent. They need to be aligned to achieve success. For example, people involved in the implementation project need to have sufficient knowledge and skills to enable them to understand differences between their daily situation and the project, with respect to respective tasks and ways of working.

The model has been applied to each of the three organisational systems with their own focus processes. These organisational systems are called dimensions. Initially the full model was used in an initial step to gather knowledge from experts in enterprise system implementation. Experts, like enterprise system implementation consultants, have been asked to write down their experiences of past implementation projects. They had to remember events that have influenced the course of the implementation project, the perceived causes of these events, the actions that were taken to react to the events, and the eventual outcomes of these actions (see also Section 4). The causes of the events have been put into one of the dimensions and one of the organisational elements, which are called aspects. Based on the outcomes of this step, the initial model was reduced to the model depicted in Figure 2.

The external part of the architectural model has been left out, while the number of remaining elements, called aspects, has been reduced. We will explain the aspects that have remained part of the model:

- **Strategy and goals:** Strategy and goals are the medium- and long-term goals to be achieved and the plans for realising these goals. The strategy and goals for the enterprise system and the implementation project should be explicit and should match the business goals and strategy.
- **Management:** The management aspect deals with setting priorities, assigning resources and planning, and monitoring the process. Business management in this respect differs from project management.
- **Structure:** Structure involves the normative relationships between elements of the organisational system. Examples are process structure, hierarchy, team structure, or technical architecture. The process structure of the enterprise and the enterprise system belong also to this aspect. Process structure reflects the (formal) flow of information and material.
- **Process:** Process involves the steps that are needed to perform the focus process of each dimension: the primary business process and relevant support processes, the project process, and the enterprise system design and adaptation process. This aspect reflects the different activities.
- **Knowledge and skills:** This aspect refers to the knowledge and skills that are needed to perform the focus processes in each dimension. As previously indicated, the knowledge and skills needed for each of the focus processes are different.
- **Social dynamics:** This aspect concerns the actual behaviour of people individually or in groups. Social dynamics often become visible in informal interaction and (lack of) communication.

The dimensions and aspects together form an enterprise architecture for enterprise system implementation. In Figure 2, the full socio-technical architecture used in the BEST project is depicted. This architecture covers part of the enterprise architecture of Figure 1. The purpose of this chapter is not to specify a formal enterprise architectures. Instead, this chapter aims at presenting an approach to use the content and structure of an enterprise architecture to understand real-life problems in implementing enterprise systems.

The enterprise architecture of enterprise system implementation is used for structuring thought and knowledge. The experiences collected in the BEST project are classified into the cells of the architecture, thus populating the architecture with specific knowledge. In this way, more in-depth knowledge of each of the cells is achieved. The architecture may serve as such as a reference model for enterprise system implementation.

CAPTURING KNOWLEDGE

Research methods like surveys and questionnaires are not very suited to gather knowledge on process dynamics and understand context influences. Instead, in-depth case studies are needed. A case study is a research methodology suitable to understand process dynamics within specific contexts (Miles & Hubermann, 1984). Yin (1994) and Eisenhardt (2000) have developed systematic and rigorous approaches for developing theory through comparative case studies. In particular, Eisenhardt has developed a roadmap for building theory from case study research, which synthesizes Miles et al.'s (1984) work on qualitative methods, design of case study research by Yin (1994), and grounded theory building by Glaser and Strauss (1967). It extends this work in areas such as a priori specification of constructs, triangulation of multiple investigators, within-case and cross-case analysis, and the role of existing literature (Eisenhardt, 2000).

The initial constructs used in the BEST project are the cells of the enterprise architecture of Figure 2, which have been specified for capturing experience of enterprise system implementation projects.

The architecture incorporates a socio-technical view because mutual alignment between the organizational aspects and between dimensions is assumed. Each dimension incorporates both technical and organizational aspects. Triangulation has been realized, because multiple investigators have been involved in several parts of Europe, while several sources of knowledge have been used (see below). The knowledge gathered allows for within-case and cross-case analysis. Within-case analysis has been performed in performing the case study and feeding the results back to the respective company. The research in BEST has focused on cross-case analysis. For this purpose context characteristics have been identified for distinguishing different interesting subclasses of the knowledge gathered. The results will be described in Section 5.

Because of the time frame available in the BEST project, retrospective case studies have been performed. Different actors who have been involved in an enterprise system implementation project have been interviewed according to a particular protocol. Actors with different roles have been selected such as a senior manager, an end user, a key user, an IT person, a functional manager, and a project manager. Each interview has focused on identification of events that have had a major influence on the course of the implementation project. After putting the events in order of decreasing importance and impact, the top three events were selected for further analysis. For each event, causes as perceived by the interviewees have been identified, as well as actions taken to repair or manage the impact of the events and outcomes for each of the actions. The causes, events, actions, and outcomes are process fragments. Together these process fragments give an impression of the dynamics of the enterprise system implementation project studied.

The construct used to capture the process fragments is the CEAO (cause-event-action-outcome) chain. In total, 264 chains have been gathered from 24 cases all over Europe. Typically, for each

Table 1. Distribution of causes in enterprise architecture

Aspect	Dimension			
	Business	**Enterprise system**	**Project management**	**Total**
Strategy and goals	20	2	3	25
Management	40	4	12	56
Process		22	19	41
Structure	16	27	4	47
Knowledge and skills	24	4	11	39
Social dynamics	32	7	17	56
Total	132	66	66	264

in-depth case study, 10-15 CEAO chains have been gathered. In addition, for each case, context information has been gathered through a demographic questionnaire. This context information allows for cross-case analysis. Different context factors have been defined, such as organizational size, cultural region, type of primary process, type of enterprise system implemented, type of company, etc.

The process fragments can be considered as mini-cases or what-if patterns that can be used to increase learning on what might happen if a problematic situation is not taken care of or has not been recognised. The presentation of such mini-cases to people responsible for an enterprise system implementation project can take the form of:

IF <sitiation> THEN <possible event> REQUIRING <action> WITH <possible outcome>

The total set of CEAO chains is, however, too large to present in specific situations. An index is needed to reduce the set to contain only those chains that are useful in a specific situation. The chains have been analysed by means of the enterprise architecture of Figure 2, which gave them an internal structure and application area. Each cell in the architecture, filled with the knowledge from the chains, has then served to formulate questions

and answers on the level of alignment between dimensions. With the questions and answers a tool has been built for assessing the maturity of the start-up phase of an enterprise system implementation project in terms of level of alignment between dimensions. The analysis of the chains and the resulting tool are presented below.

KNOWLEDGE ANALYSIS

Causes are an important part of CEAO chains. These causes represent situations that have led to situations called events, which have required people to act and may have changed the course of the project. By identifying situations like the ones mentioned in the causes, weak spots in the start-up phase might be determined allowing proper actions to be taken to prevent potential problems to occur.

Each of the causes of the 264 chains has been assigned to a cell of the enterprise architecture. The resulting distribution of causes is presented in Table 1. For the cross-case analysis, we refer to another article published on the BEST results (Wognum et al., 2004).

The main problems seem to exist in business management (lack of management support, lack of vision, insufficient assignment of resources), in social dynamics in the business (consisting of user resistance especially in large enterprises), and in enterprise system structure (alignment with business process structure, clarity of embedded process, user interface). The business process as such does not present problems with respect to the implementation project.

To illustrate the analysis process, we will give an example of assigning a cause of a CEAO chain to a cell in the enterprise architecture. In Table 2, a specific CEAO chain is presented as well as the specific cell to which the chain's cause has been assigned. Thorough knowledge on the fundamentals of the enterprise architecture is needed to perform the cause analysis. Nevertheless, the analysis process has been performed by the research team of the BEST project consisting of seven people. After an initial learning process, most causes have been assigned to one cell unanimously.

The resulting contents of the cells of the enterprise architecture have been translated into questions and related answers options. An example of one question-answer pair is given in Table 3.

Each of the answer options are rated on a scale of 0-4, where 0 means no alignment between dimensions and 4 means optimal alignment between dimensions. The score of optimal alignment is considered as the benchmark for the final score. With the questions and answer options a tool has been built for assessing an organisation's readiness for enterprise system implementation.

ASSESSMENT TOOL

The tool built in the BEST project is a prototype that will be subject to further adaptation and development based on additional knowledge

Table 2. An example of a CEAO chain and assignment of cause to enterprise architecture

CEAO chain		
	Text	**Assignment**
Cause	People have limited time for internal projects. It is hard to find only the most capable people in the organisation that are available for internal projects.	Business/management
Event	No priority on internal projects. Resources are limited for internal projects.	
Action	1. Project plan adjusted by mutual agreement with consultant. 2. People in project team have been carefully chosen. Only people with empathy for the ESI project are selected.	
Outcome	1. Postponement of deadlines. 2. Expectation of a positive influence of the chosen persons. Not all departments have carefully chosen the right people, thus limiting the marketing of the enterprise system in their department.	

Table 3. Example of question-answer pair

Question (Business/management)	What is the priority of the enterprise system implementation project?
Answers	1. The project is very important for us. 2. Day-to-day business has priority over the internal project. 3. Enterprise System priority is only high during project life. 4. Project priority is highly dependent on other internal projects. 5. Project priority is low.

gathered through in-depth case studies. A session with the user of the tool consists of filling in the user details and filling out all answers in the tool. For each cell in the enterprise architecture, two or more questions with accompanying answers have been formulated. In Figure 3, the output of a specific session with the tool is depicted.

After a session, CEAO chains relevant for the specific company are shown from which the most applicable ones can be selected. From a repository of improvement actions, relevant ones are shown. This option is especially useful for a consultant supporting a company in selecting and adopting an enterprise system. With his or her knowledge, the relevant chains and improvement actions can be selected. The option is also useful to people in a company who want to learn about potential problems that may occur.

The tool has been validated with 10 experts related to the BEST consortium, with 11 compa-

nies and with 10 external experts. The overall performance, reliability, easiness to be understood, easiness to be learned have all been rated as good, while the capability to be maintained and adapted has been rated as average. The coverage of common risk elements, the logic of the tool structure, the consistency between constructs and cases and literature, characterisation of aspects and dimensions have been rated as good. The feeling about questions and answers, the presentation of questions and answers, the scoring mechanism of question, and answers and the integration of tool components have been rated good. Finally, attractiveness to practitioners, business value, and innovativeness have all been rated as good.

Although the tool still requires adaptation and improvement before commercial use will be possible, the results are promising. The tool helps a company to understand its own situation, anticipate potential problems, and decide on taking

Figure 3. Spider diagram resulting from the prtotype tool

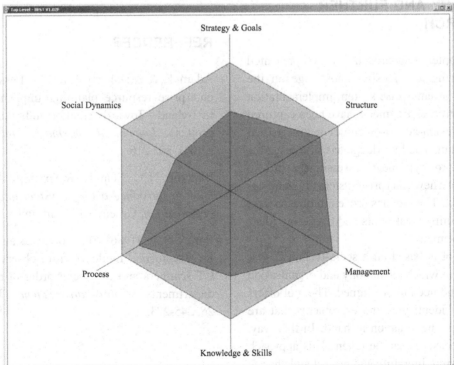

actions to prevent these problems to occur. The knowledge captured shows real process fragments, which trigger thoughts in other, similar, situations. Although the problems captured can also be found in the literature, the tool provides a means to develop a comprehensive overview of and insight into all dimensions and aspects that play a role in implementing a new enterprise system and puts problems into perspective. Moreover, the tool supports a company in focusing on those areas that may need specific attention.

The tool is considered particularly useful for a project manager of an enterprise system implementation project preferably assisted by a consultant with extensive experience of such implementation projects. The tool is meant to be used at the start of an implementation project to discover areas that require attention. The tool can also be used during an implementation project, especially when the project has changed its course of action or its goals.

SUMMARY AND FURTHER RESEARCH

In this chapter, an approach has been presented for capturing and reusing knowledge on the dynamics of enterprise system implementation projects. Process fragments have been captured in a cause-event-action-outcome construct called CEAO chain. The knowledge has been used for building a prototype tool for assessing the start-up situation of a new enterprise system implementation project. The tool has proven to be powerful in determining weak spots and triggering ideas for improvement.

The tool is based on a socio-technical system view in which technology and organisation co-exist and need to be aligned. The tool offers support in identifying those problems that are relevant for the situation at hand. In this way, suitable measures can be taken. This approach refines current literature and project and change

management methods in reducing efforts to those areas that need attention.

Of course, during the course of a complex project like an enterprise system implementation project, other problems may occur which were not obvious or anticipated from the start. Additional tool sessions may be needed along the project path to identify those problems.

The tool currently supports people with experience of implementing enterprise systems in judging a particular situation. On the other hand, the tool can be used as a learning tool for consultants. In academic and industrial education, the tool can be used to visualise different scenarios. The tool is also considered useful in further research for setting up comparative case studies.

ACKNOWLEDGMENT

We thank all people involved in the Best project and all people from the companies who have been involved in the case studies.

REFERENCES

Adam, F., & O'Doherty, P. (2000). Lessons from enterprise resource planning implementations in Ireland—Towards smaller and shorter ERP projects. *Journal of information technology, 15*(04), 305-316.

Bancroft, N. C., Seip, H., & Sprengel, A. (1997). *How to introduce a large system into a large organization.* Greenwich: Manning.

Barley, S. R. (1986). Technology as an occasion for structuring: Evidence from observations of CT scanners and the social order of radiology departments. *Administrative Science Quarterly, 28*, 245-273.

Bikson, T., & Gutek, B. (1984). *Implementation of office automation.* Santa Monica, CA: Rand Corporation.

Boer, H. (1990). *Organising for manufacturing innovation: The case of flexible manufacturing systems* (Ph. D. Thesis). Enschede, The Netherlands: University of Twente.

Boer, H., & Krabbendam, J. J. (1993). *Introduction in organisational science.* Enschede, The Netherlands: University of Twente (in Dutch).

Callaway, E. (1999). *Enterprise resource planning: Integrating applications and business processes across the enterprise.* Charleston: Computer Technology Research Corporation.

Daft, R. L. (2004). *Organisation theory and design* (8th ed.). USA: Thomson.

Davenport, T. (2000). *Mission critical: Realizing the promise of enterprise systems.* Boston: Harvard Business School Press.

Eisenhardt, K. M. (2000). Building theories from case study research. *Academy of Management Review, 14*(4), 532-550.

Faber, E. C. C. (2001). *Managing collaborative new product development* (Ph. Thesis). Enschede, The Netherlands: University of Twente.

Flood, R. L., & Jackson, M. C. (1991). *Creative problem solving: Total systems intervention.* Chichester, UK: John Wiley & Sons.

Giddens, A. (1984). *The constitution of society: Outline of the theory of structuration.* Berkeley; Los Angeles: University of California Press.

Glaser, B., & Strauss A. L. (1967). *The discovery of grounded theory.* Chicago: Aldine.

KPMG. (2002). *Annual program management survey 2002* (Report 203-587). UK: KPMG-LLP.

Kwon, T. H., & Zmud, W. R. (1987). *Unifying the fragmented models of information system implementation. Critical issues in information system research.* New York: John Wiley.

Lange-Ros, de D. J. (1999). *Continuous improvement in teams. The (mis)fit between improvement and operational activities of improvement teams* (PhD Thesis). Enschede, The Netherlands: University of Twente.

Lankhorts, M. M. (2004). Enterprise architecture modelling—The issue of integration. *Advanced Engineering Informatics, 16,* 205-216.

Laudon, K. C., & Laudon J. P. (2004). *Management information systems. Managing the digital firm* (8th ed.). NJ: Pearson Education, Inc.

Leonard-Barton, D. (1988). Implementation as mutual adaptation of technology and organization. *Research Policy, 17,* 251-267.

Lozinsky, S. (1998). *Enterprise-wide software solutions: Integration strategies and practices.* Boston: Addison-Wesley Publishing Co.

Markus, M. L., & Tanis, C. (2000). The enterprise system experience—From adoption to success. In R.W. Zmud (Ed.), *Framing the domain of IT management. Projecting the future...through the past* (pp. 173-207). Cincinnati, OH: Pinnaflex educational resources, Inc.

Miles, M., & Hubermann, A. M. (1984). *Qualitative data analysis.* Beverley Hills: Sage.

Nash, K. S. (2000). Companies don't learn from previous IT snafus. *ComputerWorld,* October 30.

Orlikowski, W. J. (1992). The duality of technology: Rethinking the concept of technology in organisations. *Organisation Science, 3*(3), 398-427.

Orlikowski, W. J., & Robey, D. (1991). Information technology and the structuring of organizations. *Information Systems Research, 2,* 143-169.

Ruël, H. (2001). *The non-technical side of office technology* (PhD Thesis). Enschede, The Netherlands: University of Twente.

Schein, E. H. (1996). Culture, the missing concept in organisation studies. *Administrative Science Quarterly, 41*, 229-240.

Scott, W. R. (1992). *Organisations. Rational, natural, and open systems.* Englewood Cliffs, NJ: Prentice-Hall, Inc.

Slack, N., Chambers, N., Harland, C., Harrison, A., & Johnston, R. (1998). *Operations management* (2nd ed.). London: Financial Times Management.

Soh, C., & Markus M. L. (1995). How IT creates business value: A process theory synthesis. In *Proceedings of the 16th International Conference on Information Systems* (pp. 29-41). Amsterdam, The Netherlands.

Weerd-Nederhof, de P. C. (1998). *New product development systems, operational effectiveness, and strategic flexibility* (PhD thesis). Enschede, The Netherlands: University of Twente.

Welti, N. (1999). *Successful SAP R/3 implementation: Practical management of ERP projects.* Boston: Addison-Wesley Publishing Co.

Wognum, P. M., & Faber E. C. C. (2002). Infrastructures for collaboration in virtual organisations. *International Journal of Networking and Virtual Organisations, 1*(1), 32-54.

Wognum, P. M., Krabbendam, J. J., Buhl, H., Ma, X., & Kenett, R. (2004). Improving enterprise system support—A case-based approach. *Advanced Engineering Informatics, 18*, 241-253.

Yin, R. K. (1994). *Case study research: Design and methods.* Sage.

ENDNOTE

[1]   BEST (Better Enterprise SysTem implementation) is a project within the Information Systems (IST) domain of the fifth Framework Programme of the European Union. It started in June 2002 and finished in November 2004 (www.best-project.com).

Chapter XIV
The Integrated Enterprise Life Cycle:
Enterprise Architecture, Investment Management, and System Development

Frank J. Armour
Armour IT LLC, USA

Chris Emery
U.S. Architect of Capitol USA

Jonathan Houk
U.S. Architect of Capitol USA

Stephen H. Kaisler
SET Associates, USA

John S. Kirk
U.S. National Science Foundation, USA

ABSTRACT

The enterprise architecture provides benefits to the organization that embraces it. However, in many organizations, the enterprise architecture effort is not tightly coupled and integrated with other enterprise level programs such as investment management and system development processes. This chapter will identify the process integration and enterprise architecture touchpoints from the perspective of the investment management process and it outlines an overall integrated enterprise life cycle process flow. Specifically, this chapter explores Why it is important for an organization to follow an architecture-driven integrated enterprise life cycle? What are the processes of an enterprise life cycle and how do they fit together, specifically the enterprise architecture, investment management, and system development processes? What is an organizational structure for managing and executing the integrated enterprise life cycle? What is an approach for implementing an integrated enterprise life cycle?

INTRODUCTION TO ENTERPRISE ARCHITECTURE AND THE INTEGRATED ENTERPRISE LIFE CYCLE

An enterprise architecture provides significant benefits to an organization that embraces it. However, in many organizations the enterprise architecture effort is not tightly coupled and integrated with other enterprise level programs such as investment management and system development processes. (Bernard, 2005; Rechtin, 1991)

The target enterprise architecture and the IT initiatives needed to achieve the target should be managed in an IT portfolio within an overall investment management process. Additionally, as these IT initiatives are being implemented and deployed, there is a need for oversight and good project management. To ensure comprehensive IT governance and business/IT alignment, the enterprise architecture must be integrated into an overall "integrated enterprise life cycle" that includes not only the enterprise architecture, but also an investment management process as well as the individual system development life cycles. The challenge for most organizations is that the guidance, responsibility, and skill sets for these various processes can be spread out across the organization and are often implemented in a silo, nonintegrated fashion. Only by viewing these processes as a whole can an organization achieve the maximum benefits that an enterprise architecture can provide. This chapter will identify the process integration and enterprise architecture touchpoints from the perspective of the investment management process and it outlines an overall integrated enterprise life cycle process flow. Specifically, we will discuss:

- Why it is important for an organization to follow an architecture-driven integrated enterprise life cycle?
- What are the processes of an enterprise life cycle and how do they fit together, specifi-

cally the enterprise architecture, investment management, and system development processes?
- What is an organizational structure for managing and executing the integrated enterprise life cycle?
- What is an approach for implementing an integrated enterprise life cycle?

BACKGROUND AND MAJOR PROCESSES OF THE ENTERPRISE LIFE CYCLE

We start by defining the major processes of the integrated enterprise life cycle (IELC) which include the following:

- **Enterprise architecture:** The enterprise architecture establishes a comprehensive understanding of an organization's core business processes and defines the technology that supports and optimizes them. (Armour, Kaisler, & Liu, 1999a)
- **Investment management planning and oversight:** The investment management process (IMP) is a fluid, dynamic process by which an organization selects and monitors both proposed and ongoing IT investments (initiatives) throughout their life cycle. An organization evaluates IT investments to assess the impact on future initiatives and to benefit from any lessons learned. The IMP can contain three phases (GAO, 2004):
  - The *select phase* discovers and selects the IT investments that best support the organization's mission needs and identifies and analyzes each project's risks and returns before committing significant funds to a project.
  - The *control phase* ensures that, as the investment is implemented, the project continues to meet mission needs at the expected levels of cost and risk.

- The *evaluate phase* compares actual vs. expected results for the implemented project.
- **System development life cycle:** A system development life cycle (SDLC) program provides guidelines and procedures for system acquisition, development, implementation and deployment, and project management. The SDLC guidelines address such areas as configuration management, risk management, requirements management, design, acquisition management, test management, and quality assurance throughout the life cycle of a project from its inception to its completion. The SDLC supports the organization's enterprise architecture and investment review processes by providing guidance for selecting appropriate methods, techniques, and tools based on specific organizational and project factors.

Figure 1 expresses an IELC that encompasses investment management, enterprise architecture and systems development (SDLC). Key components of the enterprise life cycle are discussed in the next sections.

Integrated enterprise architecture, investment management, and systems development processes are similar to a set of gears whose output is greater then the sum of the parts. The enterprise architecture provides the structure and vision as to where the organization is and where it needs to go. The investment provides the IT governance, discovery, selection, and control for the portfolio of initiatives that are needed to acknowledge the enterprise architecture target vision. For each of the individual initiatives, a system development life cycle methodology provides standard detailed guidelines for project managers. The investment management process, enterprise architecture, and systems development life cycle (SDLC) should be highly integrated to ensure projects have the needed process support.

To be most effective, these enterprise processes need to be highly integrated with multiple touchpoints. For example, to maintain alignment

Figure 1. Integrated enterprise architecture, investment management, and system development

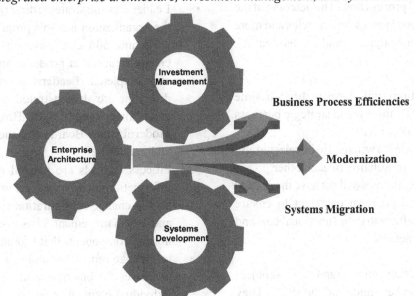

with the organization's goals and objectives, the investment management processes should perform portfolio management to select, prioritize, and control its key IT initiatives, as this highly influences and is in turn influenced by the target enterprise architecture including its business, application, data, and technical dimensions. As new initiatives are proposed, they need to be mapped against and comply with the enterprise architecture. (Armour et al., 1999a; Armour, Kaisler, & Liu, 1999b). New initiatives are guided by the organization's defined architectural principles. (Lindstrom, 2006; Open Group, 1999) As these initiatives are developed and implemented, they need to follow an organizationally defined system development life cycle (SDLC) that specifies the project management and technical activities. The SDLC has touchpoints with the enterprise architecture to ensure that an initiative's evolving requirements, designs, and technology continue to adhere to the target enterprise architecture. In addition, the SDLC specifics integration points to the investment management process in such areas as project status reports to a project review board and risk management. This chapter identifies the process integration and touchpoints from the perspective of the enterprise architecture and outlines an overall IELC process flow. The outcome of the IELC is improved business efficiencies and more efficient system mitigation and modernization. Without an IELC:

- Organizations will have a difficult time aligning IT initiatives to strategic business goals and objectives.
- These initiatives will tend to be selected and developed in isolation of each other.
- Ongoing initiatives will not have the needed project and program oversight to ensure that they adhere to their functional cost and resource metrics.

The organization's mission and business objectives provide the key input into the IELC. They can include the organization's mission, vision, business drivers, strategic goals, strategic business objectives, information needs, IT vision, IT objectives, and guiding architectural principles. This business direction is used as a guidance tool and remains relatively stable over time. It is critical that alignment among IT applications and technology and the organization's mission and objectives be defined and maintained throughout the entire IELC. In this chapter, we use the investment management process as the framework to demonstrate the integrated of the investment, enterprise architecture, and SDLC activities.

Throughout this chapter, we will use an example to combine the concepts in this chapter with an example of a technology implementation. The example we will use is the implementation of an asset inventory system that will support the business on managing their assets.

INTEGRATED ENTERPRISE LIFE CYCLE ORGANIZATION

For an organization to fully implement and institutionalize the IELC there needs to be:

- Leadership and strategic direction, whether the organization is a sole proprietorship or a Fortune 500 company, are required to ensure the services, products, and processes are completed. Leadership and strategic direction are demonstrated by having a viable Investment Review Board (IRB), a Modernization Board, and the enterprise architecture.
- Process controls are needed that include information security, project management, SDLC, change/configuration management, and data management. These are among the normal components that should be in place to manage repeatable and ever improving processes for business efficiencies. Many individual companies use the CMMi as a

way of providing a guide to creating and maintaining those processes.

- The final key element is financial control through investment management and quality assurance processes. These two elements ensure appropriate use of funding and ensure that the processes being used by the organization are followed and efficient.

With these three elements, your organization starts to have the components needed to establish an IELC. From financial management to strategic direction to controlling the quality and security of the product, the IELC ensures that the support mechanisms are in place.

To implement the IELC, an integrated organization needs to be created. The components of the organization that will be discussed in this chapter include the following in Table 1.

Table 1 lists the organizational components of the IELC. The Investment Review Board is made up of key leadership positions representing the head of the organization, the business units,

the chief financial officer (CFO), and the chief information officer (CIO). This board ensures that the strategic direction, transition plan (sequencing), and the prioritization of scarce resources are allocated to the correct portfolio.

For example a proposed asset control system that is presented to the IRB will have an executive sponsor, a project management team, and an implementation team that combines technical staff from the CIO and business subject matter experts from the business unit(s).

IELC INVESTMENT MANAGEMENT PROCESS

The Investment Management Process (IMP) is a fluid, dynamic process by which an organization monitors proposed and ongoing IT investments throughout their life cycle. The process evaluates IT investments to assess the impact on future initiatives and to benefit from any lessons learned. The IMP contains three phases—select, control,

Table 1. IELC organizational components

Organization component	Role/Responsibility
Investment Review Board (IRB)	Directs the strategic direction of the transition plan; approves the portfolio; assigns executive sponsorship; and sets priorities for the organization.
Office of Information Technology (OIT) (or similar organization)	Responsible for leading the planning, acquisition, implementation, operation, and management of the automated information systems.
Modernization board	Responsible for establishing and maintaining the organization's enterprise architecture reviews project proposals to ensure alignment with the enterprise architecture as part of the funding process researches new technology.
EA program office	Provides architectural oversight of all EA and SDLC projects.
Enterprise Architecture (EA) executive steering committee	Provides IT technical and managerial oversight of the EA.
Project Review Board (PRB)	Project oversight; oversees all projects assigned to OIT; monitors schedules, costs, and risks.
Information technology outreach	Coordinates with stakeholders; receives feedback on issues and progress.
Change Control Board	Addresses SDLC change issues/requests.
System Development Life Cycle methodology	Quality assurance and system development guidance

and evaluate as defined earlier in this chapter.

The IMP has been designed to scale to the unique characteristics of the information technology projects. The steps are grouped into the three phases—select, control, and evaluate to align with the investment management framework. The process described in this section is intended as a starting framework for an organization. An organization, based on such factors as size, culture, and the external environment that it operates in, should be prepared to adjust and modify this process to meet its specific needs.

THE SELECT PHASE

The first phase of the IMP includes procedures for ranking and selecting new investments and related projects based on several factors including costs, value, risk, alignment with the enterprise architecture, and the portfolio.

The activities in the select phase help to ensure that there is a solid alignment with mission and business needs and that the investments will fit within current portfolio of IT investments. This phase also provides an initial determination of the oversight level and validates whether an IT investment meets all technical and project requirements. Figures 2 and 3 highlight the key activities within the select phase; the activities are discussed in more detail next.

Yearly/Annual Budget Formulation-Select Phase Process

Before the start of every fiscal year, a budget formulation process determines the approved, baselined IT portfolio for the coming year. The yearly/annual budget call begins with a call for new projects or a renewal of projects for the next fiscal year. The OIT, working closely with the business stakeholders, compiles the projects into a proposed IT portfolio. The proposed IT portfolio is then submitted to the investment review board (IRB). The IRB reviews and analyzes the IT portfolio, making any needed adjustments to the portfolio (based on such factors as cost, benefit, risk, and priority) and approves the IT portfolio for the upcoming year. The portfolio is then baselined to include costs, alignment, as well as conformance with the enterprise architecture transition plan to that demonstrates the transition from the current state of business to the to-be state of the business.

For example, if an asset management system had been proposed, it could be selected as an item for development during this process and be weighed against other processes. If the IRB approves the development of a new asset management system, then a formal project would be started. In order for the IRB to make that determination, a concept of operations, a costing proposal, and a cost benefit analysis would be included in a business case for the initiative. The

Figure 2. Annual investment review select phase

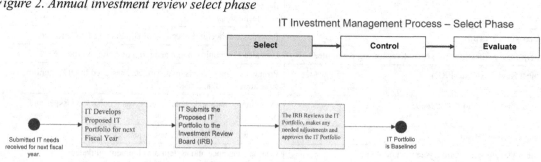

Figure 3. Ongoing investment review select phase

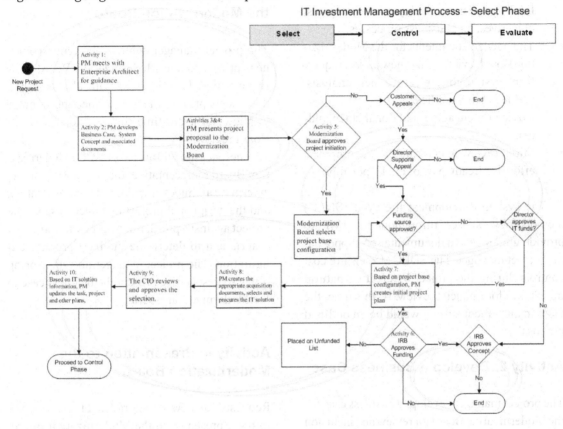

business case would also address how the initiative is aligned with the enterprise architecture's target vision, architectural principles, and the appropriate EA technical standards. Ranking of the project should be from the IRB only after the CIO has had an opportunity to review and pre-rank the projects.

Ongoing Select Review Process

During the fiscal year, when a new IT project request is received, the following ongoing select review process occurs as depicted in Figure 3. This includes reviewing the EA transition plan (Armour & Kaisler 2001) to ensure that integration points are not out of sequence as timetables, costs, and

deliverables change. We will assume that an asset management system has been proposed as a new IT project in the following discussion.

Activity 1: Initial Project Setup Meeting

The project manager meets with the Enterprise Architect and Modernization Board representatives for guidance on the project approval process[1]. The EA and Modernization Board representatives, based on the initial understanding of the project's scope and characteristics, provide the project manager with guidance and advice that includes, but is not limited to:

- Initial advice on ensuring conformance with EA target vision and alignment with goals, objectives, and business processes.
- The needed documents for the Modernization Board review such as new project request form, system concept, cost benefit analysis, and feasibility studies.
- Advice on engaging additional stakeholders.
- Initial review to determine if the proposed effort is already part of the IT portfolio.

The system development life cycle (SDLC) methodology is used throughout the IMP to provide guidance and documentation support to the project manager. The SDLC also ensure cost controls during the project by creating natural milestones for financial review. At this time, the asset management system would be an outlined proposal.

Activity 2: Develop a Business Case

The project manager develops a business case for the Modernization Board for review and inclusion into the proposed IT portfolio. Other documents that may be submitted but are not necessary include a detailed costing proposal, concept of operations, detailed cost/benefit analysis, and resource plan. The business case is a means for the business community to engage and ensure that the asset management system they are proposing has the buy in of its stakeholders and the IT community. Some key questions that should be answered by the business case include:

- Will the asset management system supporting the goals and objectives of the organization?
- Does it make fiscal sense to build an automated system?

Activity 3: Submit Business Case to the Modernization Board

The project manager submits the request for a new project to the Modernization Board. The request must be submitted with all associated documents prior to the review meeting in order to allow sufficient time for the Modernization Board review.

The requestor will also work with a Modernization Board representative, the sponsoring office, enterprise architect, a senior CIO representative, and the designated project manager to score the project against a pre-defined set of value and risk criteria and to determine the base project configuration. The project manager and sponsoring office representative present the business case to the Modernization Board.

Activity 4: Presentation to the Modernization Board

Requests for new or upgraded IT projects are initially presented to the Modernization Board, which either approves the item as being in alignment with the enterprise architecture (EA), agrees to grant a waiver for the item or denies the request, possibly with a request for modifications before resubmittal. The Modernization Board will bring in stakeholder subject matter experts as appropriate to provide input on proposals.

When the Modernization Board reviews the business case, it is specifically reviewing it with the following in mind:

- Determines if the project adheres to all elements of the enterprise architecture such as architectural principles, business roles, technology standards, application data, and security principles.

- Determines key risks on the project and recommends how to address them.
- Determines if the project fits within the IT portfolio (for cost, risk, benefit, and priority).
- Determines if the project aligns with the organization's goals, objectives, and business processes.
- Recommends a base SDLC project configuration template to use. Example templates include small project, medium project, and infrastructure project.
- Determines a project's mission criticality.
- Determines if IRB approval is needed.
- Provides other guidance as needed.

Activity 5: Modernization Board Approval

The Modernization Board approves/disapproves the project. If the project is approved, it is added to the IT portfolio. The Modernization Board can also ask that it be resubmitted with modifications or additional information.

If the project is denied, the project requestor has the right to appeal to the IRB or executive agent of the organization along with the signature of the CFO and the CIO, for a final and binding decision. A waiver will be granted only by consensus (consensus in the context of this document means the majority opinion of the Modernization Board). Generally, waivers are decided on a case-by-case basis, but a few possible reasons are:

- Replacement of existing proprietary technology where it would be too expensive to convert to an entirely new set of platforms (hardware, software, telecom).
- Only one vendor provides the necessary functionality (with a proprietary system) and this can be justified based on cost, schedule, or satisfying certain unique requirements. Or if it would be too costly to customize a commercially available package to meet the

requirements.
- The system is required to interface with an externally provided system that uses proprietary technology which is mission critical to the.

If the project under consideration has an impact on the EA technical reference model (TRM), the Modernization Board will determine, based on project characteristics such as risk, cost, and benefit, whether to accept or reject the proposal and what updates, if needed, will be made to the TRM. The Modernization Board will then make the final determination of proposal acceptance or rejection.

In our example, the asset management system will need to develop a proposal for purchase or development of the system. During that time, the approval of the Modernization Board would help mold that proposal based on the current technology investment, standards, and costing for the project. The asset management system may have constraints because it has to integrate with the financial system. If so, during the impact analysis with respect to the EA, the asset management system may have additional requirements added to the scope of the project including business functions as well as technical integration requirements.

Activity 6: Investment Review Board Approval

Once a project has been approved by the Modernization Board, and if it is a project that requires funding beyond what the organization can accommodate in its current budget, it will go to the IRB. The project manager will present the business case along with a concept of operations, cost benefit analysis, and feasibility study to the IRB. Projects that need funding are addressed under two scenarios: During the annual budget cycle (new project requests) and previously unplanned projects that come up during the year (e.g., new legislation, technology no longer supported by vendor, etc.) for which funding is not available.

The IRB will vote to approve or deny funding. If denied, the business unit may appeal to the CEO or head of organization based on the merits of the project. However, the CIO and the CFO as official stewards of information technology and financial management must be included. It is important that these appeals be reflected in the EA transition plan as well as the target enterprise architecture to reflect the decisions by senior management. The CEO or head of the agency that approves this may ask for an impact analysis by the enterprise architect to have an independent view of the impact to the organization as a whole.

For example, the EA transition plan may show that a delay of the acquisition of an asset management system is required if the business functions are not completely defined or the development of other systems have not been done that have more strategic importance. The enterprise architect would discuss with the CIO with IRB the relationship between systems and develop a transition plan that would help ensure the successful completion of the portfolio. The asset management system may be delayed if a major shift in the financial system was going to be done the same year because of risk or cost.

Activity 7: Initial Project Plan Development

Based on project characteristics (size, risk, etc.), the project manager develops the initial project plan, initial task plan (WBS), and other associated documentation. The focus on initial project plan is detailed planning for the upfront procurement and analysis activities. The project task plan is entered into a project management tool. (*Note: Regular PRB status reporting starts at this point*). The asset management system project plan would be input here.

Activity 8: Acquisition and Source Selection

Working with procurement, the project manager creates the appropriate acquisition documents and selects and procures the IT solution. This a strong touchpoint to enterprise architecture. Part of the acquisition and source selection of a tool or product to automate a process should be reviewed by the enterprise architect to ensure coherence with the future alignment of the business and the technology.

This is an iterative process because the business subject matter experts should ensure the system works for them. The OIT should ensure that the systems are interoperable and the CFO before the signature of the selection should ensure that it is fiscally responsible. The asset management system acquisition cycle should include those reviews to ensure business function, financial feasibility, and system integration are included.

Activity 9: CIO Approval

The CIO (senior IT manager) and executive sponsor (business unit representative) review and approve the selection to ensure that the IT solution continues to align with the goals, objectives, and business objectives.

Activity 10: Updated Project Plan

Based on IT solution information, the project manager updates the task, project, and other plans and updates them in the project management tool. As the project plan changes, deviations greater than 5% require that the enterprise architect check to see if the EA transition plan is being impacted.

THE CONTROL PHASE

The control phase of the IT investment management process provides the consistent monitoring of ongoing IT projects, reprioritizing them as conditions change, and re-selecting them for continued funding. This phase ensures that the project remains aligned and compliant with the EA.

The control phase focuses on oversight and review of a project from requirements validation through implementation. The purpose of this phase is to ensure that the project manager manages and implements the approved project in a structured manner, using sound management practices and ensuring involvement of all key parties. Each approved investment must ensure:

- Continued compliance of the proposed solution with the enterprise architecture.
- Ensure that the project adheres to the SDLC.
- Ensures scope is maintained during the project design and implementation.
- Continued alignment with goals, objectives, and business processes.
- Compliance with the systems development life cycle processes (project planning and management, requirement management, configuration management, quality assurance, testing, contractor management, etc.).
- Compliance with systems security standards and requirements.
- Continued viability assessed by compliance with project costs, schedule, and performance measures.

The project review board (PRB) has primary responsibility for ensuring that the project manager properly manages investments on an ongoing basis. Projects will continue to draw on and utilize the SDLC for direction in these areas. The IRB ensures that the investment continues to meet business and mission objectives and address any critical issues related to these. Figure 4 highlights the key activities within the control phase; the activities are discussed in more detail next.

For example, the asset management system that was purchased may have financial functions for deprecation and for investment cycles. This is where the IELC is of great value. The enterprise architect, the business subject matter experts, executive sponsor, and the project manager would work with the vender and the business units involved to resolve where the functions of the financial management of assets belongs. If the original concept of operations didn't include this business function, then the Modernization Board would review the scope change and recommend to the IRB a change. If the business function is automated in another system then it is hoped that the concept of operations included an integration point, if not then a change of scope would happen again. The enterprise life cycle should be flexible enough to include these changes.

Activity 11: Initial Project Review Board Review

The project plan and any associated information is submitted to the PRB. The project manager meets with the PRB to review project approach and setup project oversight including project review schedules, as well as SDLC artifacts and activities. The PRB provides input, guidance, addresses risks, determines review gates, and approves the project. In the case of the asset management system, the PRB may identify a scoping issue that would be sent to the modernization office.

Activity 12: Baseline Project Plan

The updated initial project plan is baselined. At this point again, any changes to the associated milestones or resource allocation changes should be reported to the enterprise architect to ensure that the sequencing plan is updated and dependencies are reviewed. If there are financial impacts those should be submitted to the financial management office to ensure funding is available.

Figure 4. Investment review control phase

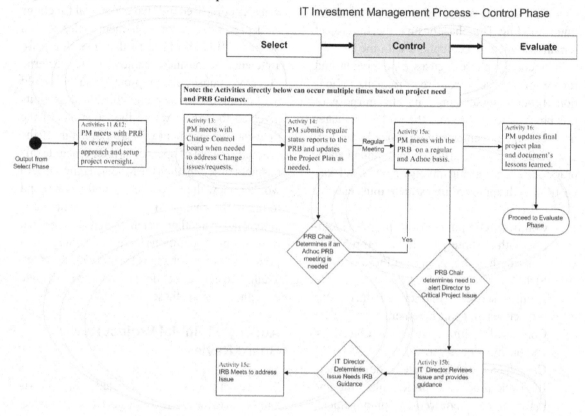

Activity 13: Change Control Review

The project manager meets with Change Control Board (CCB) when needed to address change issues/requests. (*Repeated throughout the project as needed*). The role of the change control board are to maintain the integrity of the system life cycle during the life of the project. This includes the documentation, code, and requirements during the design and implementation of the system.

Activity 14: Project Status Reporting

The project manager submits regular project status to the PRB chair. The PRB chair may, based on the status reports, initiate a meeting with the project manager and/or call a PRB review. Project

status reports and any actions taken are captured for program management reporting. (*Repeated throughout the project*). A copy of the project status report should be given to the enterprise architect and a full project status review should be conducted if the deviation from the baseline is greater than 5%.

Activity 15: Project Status Review

The project manager meets/informs with the PRB based on a regular and adhoc review schedule. The PRB will review the project deliverables and provide guidance. The enterprise architect will continue to monitor the project during these reviews to ensure continuing EA alignment. During this activity, the appropriate SDLC artifacts are reviewed (e.g., project plan, requirements documents, design documents, test plan, etc.) to determine their quality and provide feedback and guidance to the project team. (*This activity is repeated throughout the project as needed*).

If the PRB chair determines that the project has incurred such risks or issues that a higher-level review is required, the CIO is alerted. The CIO will review the project status and provide direction and guidance. If however, there are critical risks and issues that will significantly affect the project's outcome and alignment with business objectives and performance measures the IRB will be alerted.

The IRB may review the project, its progress, and issues and make a determination as to corrective action, including cancellation of the project. This review can be requested at any time.

Project statuses and any actions taken are captured for program management reporting.

Activity 16: Update Final Project Plan

At the conclusion of the project, the project manager will update the final project plan and document the lessons learned.

THE EVALUATE PHASE

The final phase of the investment management process is the evaluate phase. A "lessons learned" (post implementation review (PIR)) meeting will be held to evaluate completed projects, a set of user satisfaction interviews/surveys will be performed, and any needed process improvements will be recorded.

Information captured will:

- Include best practices used in completing tasks in an effective and efficient manner, as well as suggestions on activities to be modified.
- Feedback on the application of the SDLC, its artifacts, and activities.
- A final assessment of a project's impact on commission the completed project.
- Capturing measurements of actual vs. projected performance.
- An updated EA based on the deployed project's impact to the organization's business, technical, and information characteristics.

The lessons learned will be feedback into the selection and control phases. The main goals of

Figure 5. Investment review evaluate phase

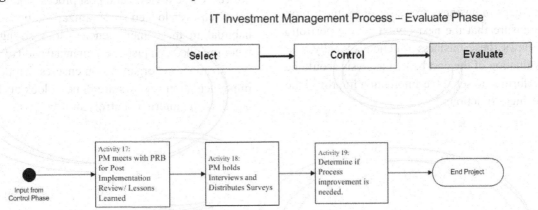

the evaluate phase will be to answer the questions "Were the business objectives accomplished by completing this project?" and "Were the means the most effective and efficient way to get to the end result?" Adjustments to the investment review and project monitoring process will be made. In addition, baseline project plans and costs will be compared to the actual project timeline and cost in order to improve future estimation efforts. Figure 5 highlights the key activities within the evaluate phase; the activities are discussed in more detail next.

This step is not just a review of the project but also the associated processes to ensure that they are efficient. The evaluation process should include answering the question of whether the IELC was cost effective and reduced business risk. This question is both objective as well as subjective so the evaluation should be a quantitative as possible.

In our example, the asset management system was have been deployed at this point. Like most projects, the implementation of the system had surprises along the way at this point the IELC processes could be improved. For an example, a change in scope may demonstrate that a more detailed concept of operations should have been done before the start of the project. The requirements may not have been fully vetted and that caused a change in scope or missed requirements, which had an impact on costs.

At this point, it is important to also review any gaps in business processes or in integration to ensure that the next review of the portfolio reviews these business functions. Finally, an evaluation of the cost benefit analysis should be performed to see if the automation improved the business function.

Activity 17: Post Implementation Review/ Lessons Learned (PIR)

The project manager will meet/submit with the OIT Deputy Director/PRB for the project closeout meeting. The project manager will submit the final project plan, lessons learned, and completed system user and technical documents for review and closeout approval.

Activity 18: Surveys and Interviews

Perspectives and insights of project participants, executive sponsor, and sponsoring business and end users, is also collected through:

- Surveys and interviews of end users, customers, project management, project staff, contractors, and developers.
- Project management and staff interviews.
- Interviews with senior decision makers involved in investment oversight.

Activity 19: Process Improvement

Information from the quantitative data, the post implementation review, and the surveys are used to make adjustments to the investment management process. In addition, baseline project plans and costs will be compared to the actual project timeline and cost in order to improve future estimation efforts. These reviews and post process analysis are often over looked so organizations become habitual in these inefficiencies. It is strongly recommended that just like a financial audit of an organization, the organization ensures that post implementation reviews are done to look at the health of the internal controls and systems.

CONCLUSION

Throughout this chapter, we have discussed the integration of the enterprise architecture, investment management process, and the system development life cycle. While we did this via an investment management framework of select, control, and evaluate, the critical aspect is the actual integration itself. Whatever approach an organization takes, it should be aware of the importance of the overall IELC and the multiple integration and touchpoints between the activities that make it up.

Going forward, the U.S. Office of Budget and Management (OMB) has issued and continues to evolve a set of enterprise architecture reference models (FEA) (OMB, 2005) that address the business, application, data, service component reference model, and performance dimensions of an organization. Organizations are expected to develop and specify these views (both baseline and target) and formally document how a proposed application will adhere to them in its business case. An organization is then expected to track the performance of initiative as it progresses to ensure that it remains in alignment with the views. At the same time, the U.S Government's General Accountability Office continues to evolve its investment management maturity framework (GAO, 2004) that addresses how IT projects are determined, tracked, and controlled.

REFERENCES

Armour, F., & Kaisler, S. (2001, Nov-Dec). Enterprise architecture: Agile transition and implementation. *IEEE IT Pro.*

Armour, F., Kaisler, S., & S. Liu. (1999a). A big picture look at enterprise architectures. *IEEE IT Pro, 1*(1), 35-42.

Armour, F., Kaisler, S., & S. Liu. (1999b). Building an enterprise architecture step-by-step. *IEEE IT Pro, 1*(3), 49-57.

Bernard, S. (2005). *An introduction to enterprise architecture* (2nd ed.). Bloomington, IN: Authorhouse. Boar, B. (1998). Constructing blueprints for enterprise IT architectures. New York: Wiley & Sons.

GAO. (2004). *GAO information technology investment management: A framework for assessing and improving process maturity, Version 1.1.* Washington, DC: U.S. Government Accountability Office.

Lindstrom, A. (2006 January 4-7). On the syntax and semantics of architectural principles. In *Proceedings of the 39th Hawaii International Conference on System Sciences*, Kauai, HI.

OMB. (2005). *FEA consolidated reference model document.* May 2005. Washington, DC: U.S. Office of Budget and Management.

Open Group. (1999). *Enterprise architecture.* Retrieved from http://www.opengroup.org/architecture

Rechtin, E. (1991). *Systems architecting: Creating and building complex systems.* Englewood Cliffs, NJ: Prentice Hall.

Rechtin, E., & Maier, M. W. (1997). *The art of systems architecting.* Boca Raton, FL: CRC Press.

ENDNOTE

[1] The Modernization Board representative and other personnel will be available to consult with the project manager throughout the investment management process.

Chapter XV
Promoting Netcentricity through the Use of Enterprise Architecture

Supriya Ghosh
Arcadia-Concepts LLC, USA

ABSTRACT

This chapter describes the DoD (Department of Defense) policy goal toward Net centric transformation as an example of enterprise architecture in practice. An integrated architecture across the enterprise provided by the DoD Global Information Grid (GIG) is a key ingredient toward meeting Net centricity. The chapter provides background information on key concepts and details the steps necessary to meeting the Net-ready key performance parameter (NR-KPP). The DoD architecture framework provides the Supporting System View, Operational View, and Technical Standards View architecture products that each DoD program must create to meet the Net-centric model. The Net-centric transformation is detailed based on the Net-centric data strategy, Net-centric IA strategy, use of service-oriented architecture, and use of a communications transport strategy. The path toward Net centricity is a significant and long-term effort and the chapter focuses on specific areas that affect DoD programs on their path toward Net-centric compliance. The implementation of enterprise services and the use of key technical standards are also discussed as emerging efforts.

INTRODUCTION

This chapter provides a specific example of enterprise architecture (EA) in practice by describing how EA acts as the principal enabler in promoting Net-centric warfare. The United States Department of Defense (DoD) has been successful in its efforts in promoting Net centricity as a concept to address modern warfare. Modern warfare is enabled by a Net-centric environment, which promotes a seamless sharing of data among users, applications, and platforms. Today's military is a global operation that includes land, air, sea, and space-based communications that all need to work together effectively to achieve greater levels of interoperability. Interoperability has been a big buzzword that needs to level set expectations for information systems in use by the military user community, government officials, and public citizens at large.

To address interoperability across the entire government, U.S. federal agencies are adopting EA guidelines as has been prescribed by the office of management and budget (OMB). The U.S. federal government has recognized that EA is critical in tying information technology investments to current and future business goals. The OMB has mandated each federal agency to develop an enterprise-wide architecture that provides a rational basis for each agency's information systems. The OMB has developed a set of Federal EA reference models that provides an organized structure to provide services to citizens—this includes a business reference model (BRM), performance reference model (PRM), services reference model (SRM), technical reference model (TRM), and data reference model (DRM). These reference models provide a basis for all federal agencies to comply with OMB policy and architecture mandates.

Within the DoD, EA is a key construct in transforming the military to the Net-centric vision. DoD EA is designed to manage complexity, allow interoperability, and provide the blueprint for the realization of mission-critical goals within the organization. DoD EA is implemented based on the DoD architecture framework (DoDAF), which has been in wide use and provides the central enterprise architecture framework that is abided by all DoD component organizations. This includes the Armed Forces, Air Force, Army, Navy, Marines, and DoD financial, business, and health organizations.

The path toward Net centricity requires DoD component organizations and information systems to achieve greater levels of interoperability.

Defining a stable enterprise architecture helps to resolve complexities that arise in connecting information systems together. Current challenges stem from the fact that many of the systems are isolated and "stove-piped" and do not effectively communicate with other systems within DoD or other Federal agencies. There are differing levels of heterogeneity of hardware and software, differing levels of information assurance and security controls, use of a variety of common and proprietary standards, and differing abilities for sharing and collaboration of data. Users also have a hard time being knowledgeable of current information. The Net-centric initiative intends to address these issues head-on and provides a path for greater interoperability within DoD component systems.

This chapter provides background as to the definition of Net centricity as has been intended based on DoD policies and guidelines, delineates the requirements necessary to meet the Net-ready key performance parameter, and provides an overview of the DoDAF architecture views. The chapter then discusses the goals set forth for the DoD Net-centric data strategy and DoD Net-centric IA strategy and describes how the creation of integrated architecture views accomplishes Net-centric goals. The chapter then discusses how DoD programs must abide by the Net-centric checklist and describes the use of service-oriented architecture and a communications transport strategy. Within the upcoming and future trends, it identifies the implementation of enterprise services and a set of emerging technical standards.

BACKGROUND

This section provides a description of the concept of Net centricity and defines key terms that help the audience understand the subject matter. The section covers the following topics and provides a background for each concept.

1. Net centricity.
2. GIG and interoperability.
3. Net-ready key performance parameter (NR-KPP).
4. DoDAF EA views.
5. DoD IT standards registry.

Netcentricity

According to the DoD Net-centric data strategy published as a DoD CIO memorandum, the Net-centric initiative is defined as follows:

Net centricity is the realization of a networked environment, including infrastructure, systems, processes, and people that enables a completely different approach to war fighting and business operations. The foundation for Net-centricity is the Defense Department's Global Information Grid (GIG). The GIG is the globally interconnected, end-to-end set of information capabilities, associated processes, and personnel for collecting, processing, storing, disseminat-ing, and managing information on demand to warfighters, defense policymakers, and support personnel."..."The approach to implementing the GIG uses communications, computing, and applications technologies, but also recognizes that the cultural barriers against trust and data sharing must be addressed. To this end, DoD is using a comprehensive, integrated approach to deliver the foundation for Net-centricity.

The DoD has developed a two-pronged approach that creates an overall Net-centric data strategy and a DoD Net-centric information assurance strategy that effectively coordinates with the layered implementation of the GIG. This concept is depicted within the DoD CIO memorandum as an integrated approach illustrated in Figure 1.

Net centricity is a complex term that works as depicted in a layered manner and intends to accomplish the following threads:

*   Securely interconnects people and systems independent of time or location.
*   Supports a substantially improved military situational awareness.
*   Allows better access to business information and dramatically shortened decision cycles.

The model starts with a foundation layer of an integrated EA that includes technical standards, architecture governance, engineering and policy, DoD guidance doctrines, and a communications spectrum. The model then addresses the communications layer consisting of different communications types including use of broadband and fiber. The computing layer includes key information system functions such as messaging, collaboration, mediation, and storage. The application layer addresses all of the current and future DoD information applications that serve the business and user community. The top layer consists of the capabilities layer that defines all of the information management/information technology capabilities

Figure 1. Integrated approach to a Net-centric environment

that are addressed within the DoD submission to the U.S. federal budget.

Within this new paradigm, Net centricity plans to better serve its user community that consists of military warfighters and support personnel, government officials, and public citizens at large. Users are empowered to be able:

- To better protect assets to effectively exploit information.
- To more efficiently use resources.
- To create extended, collaborative communities to focus on the mission at hand.

GIG and Interoperability

The Defense Acquisition Guidebook as detailed within DoDD 5000.1 and DoDI 5000.2 has defined the GIG as follows: "The Global Information Grid (GIG) is the organizing and transforming construct for managing information technology (IT) throughout the Department. GIG policy, governance procedures, and supporting architectures are the basis for developing and evolving IT capabilities, IT capital planning and funding strategies, and management of legacy (existing) IT services and systems in the DoD. In discussing the GIG and how a particular program interacts with, supports, or relies upon the GIG, it is useful to think of the GIG from three perspectives—*its vision, its implementation, and its architecture.*"

The GIG vision as stated by the Defense Acquisition Handbook, is "to empower users through easy access to information anytime and anyplace, under any conditions, with attendant security." "This vision requires a comprehensive information capability that is global, robust, survivable, maintainable, interoperable, secure, reliable, and user-driven."

The GIG implementation depends on the model set up by Net centricity and depends upon the ability of systems, units, or forces to provide and accept to and from, data, information, materiel, and services to operate effectively together. The

DoD intent is to implement the GIG throughout the organization and this will provide the central construct that will coordinate attachment to all DoD component systems.

The GIG architecture consists of the composite DoD EA that provides the overall framework for all DoD component system architecture. The GIG architecture uses the DODAF architecture framework and creates a complete set of EA views to depict the overall DoD enterprise. Each DoD component system architecture then is traced back to the GIG enterprise as the parent architecture. This level of interoperability is the goal of DoD guidance documents written within the Defense Acquisition Handbook.

Interoperability is defined by DoDI 4630.8 within this GIG construct as "both a technical exchange of information and an end-to-end operational effectiveness of that exchange of information as required for mission accomplishment." Interoperability is defined as more than just information exchange. Interoperability characteristics include systems, processes, procedures, organizations, and missions over the life cycle and must be balanced with information assurance. The GIG model includes interoperability and supportability needs and asks that interoperability and supportability deficiencies have been identified, and are based on an approved or established rule set.

Net-Ready Key Performance Parameter (NR-KPP)

To fully realize the Net-centric vision, the Assistant Secretary of Defense for Network and Information Integration (NII) otherwise known as the DoD CIO, has set up a set of performance parameters known as the NR-KPP (Net-ready key performance parameter). The NR-KPP defines a set of tenets that enforce compliance actions from all DoD component systems. Once it is ascertained that a system is compliant with each of these tenets then the DoD CIO continues with the system acquisition life cycle for the program. The

NR-KPP tenets consist of verifiable performance measures and associated metrics required to assess information needs, information timeliness, information assurance, and Net-ready attributes. The NR-KPP is comprised of each of the four elements listed as categories next.

1. **Support of integrated architecture products:** DoD component program compliance to the Net-centric vision is measured through the adherence to a full set of supporting integrated EA products. This is demonstrated through inspection and analysis of developed architecture products to determine conformance with DODAF specifications and that all required EA products have been produced. The DODAF EA products include the All View (AV), Operational View (OV), System View (SV), and Technical Standards View (TV). The detailed procedure to create the appropriate architecture products are detailed within the DoD guidance documents: Chairman of Joint Chiefs Instruction (CJCSI) 3170.01 and CJCSI 6212.01. The DODAF EA views are described in more detail later in this chapter.

2. **Compliance with the NCOW RM:** The Net-centric attributes have been incorporated within the GIG architecture and implementation to establish the Net-centric operational warfare reference model (NCOW RM). This reference model describes activities required to establish, use, operate, and manage the Net-centric enterprise information environment. Figure 2 provides the GIG architecture high-level Operational View (OV-1) diagram published within the DoD NII public Web site that ties in all facets of the reference model.

DoD component program compliance with the NCOW RM is demonstrated through inspection and analysis of the system capabilities:

Figure 2. Net-centric operations and warfare reference model (NCOW RM)

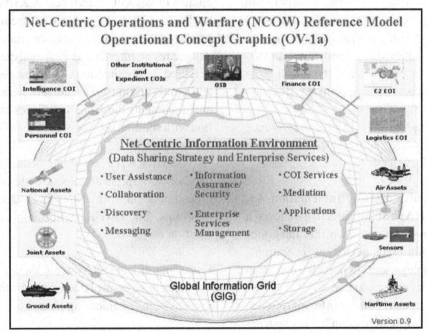

- Use of NCOW RM definitions and vocabulary.
- Incorporation of NCOW RM Operational View (OV) capabilities and services in the materiel solution.
- Incorporation of NCOW RM Technical Standards View (TV) information technology standards developed for the materiel solution.

Compliance with DoD Information Assurance Requirements

The Defense Acquisition Handbook defines information assurance as "measures that protect and defend information and information systems by ensuring their availability, integrity, authentication, confidentiality, and non-repudiation. This includes providing for the restoration of information systems by incorporating protection, detection, and reaction capabilities."

To meet the NR-KPP mandate, DoD component system program managers have to comply with regulatory requirements governing information assurance (IA). This includes the following steps: defining IA requirements, incorporating IA in the program's architecture, developing an acquisition IA strategy, conducting appropriate IA testing, and achieving IA certification and accreditation for the program. Satisfaction of these requirements results in IA compliance verification of the program capabilities.

Requirements for DoD information assurance certification and accreditation are specified within the following documents:

- DoD directive 8500.1, **"Information Assurance (IA)"**: This directive follows a defense-in-depth approach that integrates the capabilities of personnel, operations, and technology, and supports the evolution to network centric warfare.
- DoD instruction 8500.2, **"Information Assurance Implementation"**: This instruc-

tion implements policy and procedures for applying the integrated, layered protection mentioned in under DoDD 8500.1.

- DoD instruction 8580.1, **"Information Assurance (IA) in the Defense Acquisition System"**: This instruction implements policy and procedures to integrate information assurance (IA) into the defense acquisition system.
- DoD instruction 5200.40, **"DoD Information Technology Security Certification and Accreditation Process (DITSCAP)"**: This instruction is the current method for receiving certification and accreditation for a DoD component program. However, it will be superceded by DoD 8500 series of guidance documents when the new guidance is adopted.

Compliance with Applicable GIG Key Interface Profiles

GIG key interface profiles (KIPs) provide a Net-centric-oriented approach for managing interoperability across the GIG based on the configuration control of key GIG interfaces. A KIP is defined by DoDI 4630.8 as "the set of documentation produced as a result of interface analysis which designates an interface as key; analyzes it to understand its architectural, interoperability, test, and configuration management characteristics; and documents those characteristics in conjunction with solution sets for issues identified during the analysis."

The GIG KIPs are implemented based on the DoD enterprise architecture views, and key milestone documents written for DoD component programs. The GIG KIPs are enforced via the creation of:

- Operational and Systems View products.
- Interface control document/specifications.
- Systems engineering plan.

- Configuration management plan.
- Technical Standards View (TV-1) with an SV-TV bridge.
- Procedures for standards conformance and interoperability testing.

DoD component system program manager compliance with applicable GIG KIPs is demonstrated through inspection of acquisition milestone documentation and test plans, and compliance with DoD and CJCS instructions.

DoDAF Integrated EA Views

The DoD architecture framework (DoDAF) specifies a common approach for describing, comparing, and presenting enterprise-wide DoD component architecture. It describes a set of 26 architecture product views to ensure uniformity and standardization in documenting defense-wide architectural concepts.

DoDAF artifacts are delivered as work products and are organised into four views: Operational View (OV), Systems View (SV), Technical standards View (TV), and an overarching All View (AV). Figure 3 is excerpted from the DoD joint technical architecture (JTA) Version 6.0, Volume II, and illustrates the architectural relationships between each view.

All View (AV)

All View (AV) products provide the overarching description of the entire architecture and define the scope and context of the architecture. The AV products are defined as:

- AV-1 overview and summary information.
- AV-2 integrated dictionary.

Operational View (OV)

The OV products provide descriptions of the tasks and activities, operational elements, and information exchanges required to accomplish

Figure 3. Architecture views relationships

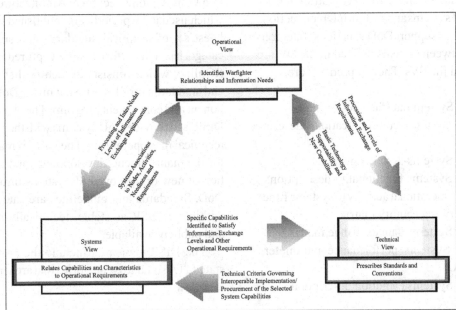

DoD missions. The OV provides textual and graphical representations of operational nodes and elements, assigned tasks and activities, and information flows between nodes. It defines the type of information exchanged, the frequency of exchanges, the tasks and activities supported by these exchanges, and the nature of the exchanges. The OV products are defined as:

- **OV-1:** High level operational concept graphic.
- **OV-2:** Operational node connectivity description.
- **OV-3:** Operational information exchange matrix.
- **OV-4:** Organizational relationships chart.
- **OV-5:** Operational activity model.
- **OV-6a:** Operational rules model.
- **OV-6b:** Operational state transition description.
- **OV-6c:** Operational event-trace description.
- **OV-7:** Logical data model.

Systems View (SV)

The SV products provide graphical and textual descriptions of systems and system interconnections that provide or support DoD functions. Interconnections between systems defined in the OV are described in the SVs. The SV products are:

- **SV-1:** System interface description.
- **SV-2:** Systems communications description.
- **SV-3:** Systems-systems matrix.
- **SV-4:** Systems functionality description.
- **SV-5:** Operational activity to systems functionality traceability matrix.
- **SV-6:** Systems data exchange matrix.
- **SV-7:** Systems performance parameters matrix.
- **SV-8:** Systems evolution description.

- **SV-9:** Systems technology forecast.
- **SV-10a:** Systems rules model.
- **SV-10b:** Systems state transition description.
- **SV-10c:** Systems event-trace description.
- **SV-11:** Physical schema.

Technical Standards View (TV)

The TV products define technical standards, implementation conventions, business rules, and criteria that govern the architecture. The TV products are as follows:

- **TV-1:** Technical standards profile.
- **TV-2:** Technical standards forecast.
- **SV-TV Bridge:** This is a new product that allows direct correlation of technical standards to a DoD component system view.

DoD IT Standards Registry (DISR)

The DoD has currently implemented an online repository to store all of the technical standards that are relevant for the DoD enterprise. The DoD IT Standards Registry (DISR) was previously known as the Joint Technical Architecture (JTA), which used to be periodically published with the latest set of technical standards and standards categories. This effort is now captured as DISROnline, which consists of technical standards and standards profiles for each major DoD component and component program. The objective of DISR is to provide DoD systems with the basis for technical interoperability. The DISR is mandated for the management, development, and acquisition of new or improved IT systems throughout DoD. Standards and guidelines are categorized within the DISR as stable, technically mature, and publicly available.

The DISR standards include the previously stated JTA standards categories that are separated as follows:

- **Information processing standards:** This describes Government and commercial information processing standards DoD uses to develop integrated, interoperable systems that meet the information processing requirements.
- **Information transfer standards:** This describes the information transfer standards and profiles that are essential for information transfer interoperability and seamless communications.
- **Information modeling, metadata, and information exchange standards:** This describes the use of integrated information modeling and applicable standards. Information modeling consists of activity, data, and object modeling. This section also mandates information standards, including message formats.
- **Human-computer interface standards:** This provides a common framework for human-computer interface (HCI) design and implementation in DoD systems.

- **Information security standards:** This prescribes the standards and protocols to be used to satisfy security requirements.

NET-CENTRIC COMPLIANCE TO AN INTEGRATED EA

This section provides specifics as to how Net-centric parameters use the integrated DoD EA products to capture enterprise architecture compliance for Net centricity. Each of the mandated architecture products is discussed along with traceability as to why the depiction of these architecture product views is important. The section then provides specifics on the Net-centric data strategy and Net-centric IA strategy. An introduction is then given to service-oriented architecture, communications transport strategy, and use of upcoming technical standards.

Table 1. Mandatory architecture products required for Net-centric compliance

DoDAF Product	Product Name	Description
AV-1	Overview and summary information	Scope, purpose, intended users, environment depicted, analytical findings
OV-2	Operational node connectivity description	Operational nodes, operational activities performed at each node, connectivity, and information exchange needlines between nodes
OV-4	Organizational relationship chart	Organizational role or other relationships among organizations
OV-5	Operational activity model	Operational activities, relationships among activities, inputs and outputs, overlays can show cost, performing nodes, or other pertinent information
OV-6c	Operational event-trace description	One of three products used to describe operational activity sequence and timing--trace actions in a scenario or sequence of events and specifies timing of events
SV-4	Systems functionality description	Functions performed by systems and the information flow among system functions
SV-5	Operational activity to systems function traceability matrix	Mapping of systems back to operational capabilities or of system functions back to operational activities
SV-6	Systems data exchange matrix	Provides details of system data or information exchange requirements between systems
TV-1	Technical standards profile	Extraction of standards that apply to the given architecture

Integrated Architecture Products

The establishment and implementation of Net-centric principles leads to building an integrated architecture that aligns with the GIG EA for the DoD. The GIG architecture principles include:

- A secure, dependable, and reliable network with seamless connectivity and collaboration capabilities, at all times, across geographical, organizational, and mission boundaries.
- Information that must be available to the people who want it, the way they want it, when they want it.
- No technical limitations on the capabilities to access, retrieve, share, disseminate, or fuse information resilient against information warfare, and terrorist and criminal activities.

- Information that is protected, secure, and resilient against information warfare, and terrorist and criminal activities.

These set of principles are achieved by presenting mandated supporting architecture views that depict Net-centric compliance for a DoD component system or program. The mandated DoDAF architecture views are stated within DoDI 4630.8 and CJCSI 6212.01 guidance documents and are described in Table 1.

Each of these views was chosen to be mandatory from the perspective of interoperability and traceability to the overall GIG architecture. In coordinating with the full set of DoDAF architecture views, the other named architecture views are deemed to be optional from the perspective of program compliance.

For a specific DoD program, the AV-1 provides the overall scope of the program and acquisition

Figure 4. Flowchart of supporting integrated architecture products

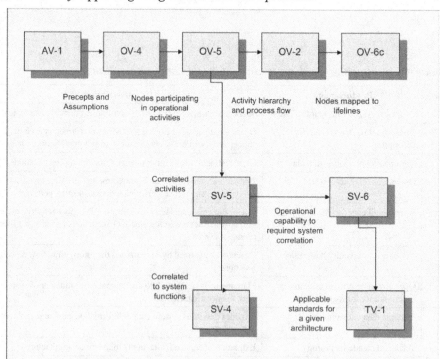

milestones. The OV-2 delineates the high-level operational nodes that provide the overall program interfaces. The OV-4 provides a listing of the relationships between the operational facilities of the system and its interface to different external organizations. The OV-5 provides an activity model that traces high-level program capabilities to information technology activities. OV-6c is an operational trace diagram that provides timing and data sequences for information to flow through the system. The SV-4 is a listing of all the high and low-level functions that the system performs. The SV-5 provides a mapping traceability between system functions in SV-4 and the operational activity listed within the OV-5. The SV-6 lists all of the Information Exchange Requirements that are exchanged between the DoD system and other internal and external components. The TV-1 provides a technical standards profile of the system and lists each of the standards that are in use within each system component.

Figure 4 illustrates a flowchart of the integrated architecture products and how they work together to ensure interoperability.

To ensure that each of the DoD component programs are current on their information technology posture and are abiding by integrated architecture views, DoD NII has developed a Net-centric checklist that assists program managers to move toward a Net-centric environment. The Net-centric checklist focuses on a number of key areas that this section will now go into further detail.

- Net-centric data strategy.
- Net-centric IA strategy.
- Service-oriented architecture (SOA).
- Communications transport strategy.

Each of these areas describes the facets of the Net-centric strategy and how it advances the goal of an integrated EA. Since Net centricity is a complex term that is implemented in layers, it is very important to ensure that all pieces of the activity are coherently put in place.

B. Net-Centric Data Strategy

The DoD Net-centric data strategy is a key enabler of the department's transformation since it establishes the foundation for managing the department's data in a Net-centric environment. Key attributes of the data strategy includes the following:

- Ensuring data is visible, accessible, understandable, and trustable when needed and where needed to accelerate decision-making.
- "Tagging" of data, whether it is intelligence, non-intelligence, raw, and processed with metadata to enable discovery by known and unanticipated users.
- Posting of data to shared spaces for users to access except when limited by security, policy, or regulations.
- Protection of sensitive data to ensure that authorized users obtain reliable secure information, even in the presence of adversarial disruption.

Table 2 is excerpted from the DoD Net-centric data strategy and provides a description of the seven major Net-centric data goals.

This data strategy also tries to involve the various DoD communities of interest (COIs) that support the different DoD component domains such as the warfighter, business, and intelligence domains. The intent is to make sure that internal and external stakeholders are all included within the "system of systems" and "network of networks." The DoD CIO calls this ability "power to the edge," in which people throughout the network are empowered by their ability to access information and take action on the knowledge provided by that information.

Table 2. Net-centric data strategy goals

Goal	Description
Goals to increase enterprise and community data over private user and system data	
Visible	Users and applications can discover the existence of data assets through catalogs, registries, and other search services. All data assets (intelligence, non-intelligence, raw, and processed) are advertised or "made visible" by providing metadata, which describes the asset.
Accessible	Users and applications post data to a "shared space." Posting data implies that (1) descriptive information about the asset (metadata) has been provided to a catalog that is visible to the Enterprise and (2) the data is stored such that users and applications in the enterprise can access it. Data assets are made available to any user or application except when limited by policy, regulation, or security.
Institutionalize	Data approaches are incorporated into department processes and practices. The benefits of enterprise and community data are recognized throughout the department.
Goals to increase use of enterprise and community data	
Understandable	Users and applications can comprehend the data, both structurally and semantically, and readily determine how the data may be used for their specific needs.
Trusted	Users and applications can determine and assess the authority of the source because the pedigree, security level, and access control level of each data asset is known and available.
Interoperable	Many-to-many exchanges of data occur between systems, through interfaces that are sometimes predefined or sometimes unanticipated. Metadata is available to allow mediation or translation of data between interfaces, as needed.
Responsive to user needs	Perspectives of users, whether data consumers or data producers, are incorporated into data approaches via continual feedback to ensure satisfaction.

Figure 5. Net-centric data strategy scope

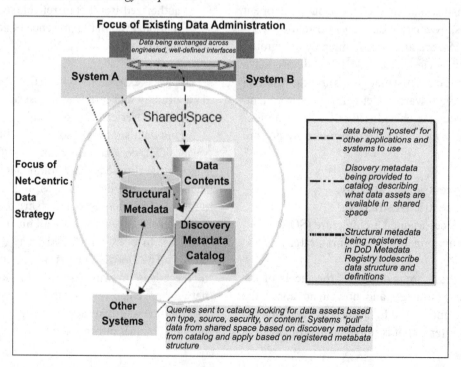

In an environment where information technology systems are continually being implemented, migrated, or replaced, there is a necessity for making allowances for unanticipated interfaces. The data strategy addresses this need by shifting the focus from tightly engineered, predefined systems to enterprise-level data standardization within the DoD. Figure 5 illustrates the expanded scope of the Net-centric data strategy.

To make data visible throughout the organization, the system would have to provide discovery metadata for data posted into shared spaces. Users and applications maintaining private data will have to provide mechanisms for making data available to the COI community. The focus is to develop an enterprise-level DoD metadata registry that would record all of the different structural metadata that is in use throughout the component programs.

Use of common languages such as XML would be the communications mechanism for data transfer between automated systems. Systems need to adhere to common standards for implementing Web services such as SOAP (simple object access protocol), WSDL (Web services description language), and UDDI (universal description, discovery and integration).

To make data accessible, the system needs to ensure that data can be sent to external entities and potential consumers of the data. The data can be accessed via an application client, Web portal, as a Web service, or as a shared XML data construct. To make data understandable, all system documentation needs to be clearly written and explained. Enterprise-level data naming and tagging schemes should be used that abides by the DoD metadata registry and is compliant with the DoD discovery metadata specification. Automated mechanisms for data mediation or translation should be made available via standards such as XSL (extensible stylesheet language) or XSD (XML schema definition).

Net-Centric Information Assurance Strategy

The Net-centric IA strategy stems from DoD component programs complying with the latest DoD directives and instructions regarding information assurance. This refers to the DoD 8500 series of documents that includes DoDD 8500.1, DoDI 8500.2, and DoDI 8580.1 policy documents. The information assurance strategy is defined as measures taken to protect and defend our information and information systems to ensure confidentiality, integrity, availability, identification and authentication, and non-repudiation. This also includes the accountability to achieve protect, detect, monitor, and react, capabilities. Based on these directives, when a program transitions to a Net-centric environment, the following objectives are coordinated within the system or program:

- An integrated identity management, permissions management, and digital rights management solution for the system.
- Ensuring that adequate confidentiality, availability, and integrity are provided as part of the NCOW RM to the GIG.
- Providing information assurance capabilities to users for DoD military operations, DoD business operations, and department-wide enterprise management operations.

This viewpoint is possible within a service-oriented, inter-networked, information infrastructure where users request and receive services that enable operational capabilities across the DoD enterprise. The Net-centric IA strategy provides a set of IA and security measures (IAS) core enterprise services (CES), which serve as a framework and family of services that provide a foundation to implement uniform, consistent, and effective IA.

The Net-centric IA posture ensures that a mission assurance category (MAC) level is assigned to each DoD component program. This MAC level and confidentiality level needs to be appropriate for the system in context with the system architecture and IA architecture views, and should be traced through the NCOW RM to the DoD GIG.

In relation to identity management, the system needs to identify the mechanisms for authentication that includes biometrics, common access card, or username and password. DoD has also adopted a public- private key infrastructure (PKI) that is now being implemented in a coordinated manner throughout the enterprise. To better able security information to be shared with external systems, the DoD program should mediate security assertions such that the system allows security information to be passed between processes, domains, and interfaces.

If the program needs to exchange information across security domains, the mechanism or capability should be fully documented. This data could be e-mail, structured data sets, unstructured documents, imagery, or multimedia objects. Data encryption is a key technique in securing data at rest, and data during transit. The National Institute of Standards and Technology (NIST) has established a number of federal information processing standard (FIPS) publications to address data encryption. FIPS 140-2 and FIPS 197 are recent standards that are being adopted across the federal and DoD enterprise that define data encryption standards for programs to use.

Service-Oriented Architecture

The Net centric data and IA strategy demands a service-oriented architecture (SOA) paradigm to be followed across the DoD. SOA is a design style for building flexible, adaptable distributed-computing environments, and is fundamentally about sharing and reuse of functionality across diverse applications. Within the DoD, SOA design focuses on the following best practices:

- Develop application and system functionality through accessible and reusable services.
- Expose Web-based services through programmatic interfaces.
- Insert an abstraction layer between service interfaces and service implementations.
- Define service interfaces using DoD standardized metadata.
- Publish and subscribe services using standard service registries.
- Communicate with external services using standard protocols.

As a key enabler to Net centricity, SOA provides an environment that enables the rapid development and deployment of services. SOA provides well-defined, realizable capabilities that can be used with other external services to provide a wide range of simple and complex functions. In the Net-centric checklist, the focus is to move to the Net-centric environment as part of a SOA-based architecture within the GIG construct. The Net-centric checklist ensures that DoD programs address specific issues with regard to SOA-based implementation:

- Is the system architecture based on loosely coupled interactions, enabling the internal components to map to well-defined external interfaces?
- Is the program implementing Web services and are a core set of technical standards such as WSDL, UDDI, and SOAP being used?
- Are open architecture standards as for example, published by the W3C consortium, being adopted?
- Are XML foundational and metadata standards being used?
- Is object-oriented modeling and programming techniques used?

Communications Transport Strategy

The Net-centric transformation is dependent upon a communications transport strategy as an infrastructure foundation for the DoD and the intelligence community. The GIG demands a dependable, reliable, and all-consuming network that eliminates stovepipes and responds to the GIG enterprise architecture. The Net-centric model asks the DoD to construct a transport infrastructure that will:

- Follow the Internet model.
- Create the GIG from smaller component building blocks.
- Design with interoperability, scalability, and simplicity in mind.

The next generation of the Internet is dictated based on the Internet protocol version 6 (IPv6) specification, and the DoD presently has a transition plan in place for moving toward a IPv6-based network. Each DoD component program is asked to take advantage of the new IPv6 technical standards and capabilities. This includes the expanded addressing capability, the ability of Internet messages to demand a better quality-of-service, and the ability to have better mobile and broadband IP-based networking and communications.

DoD programs that are connected to the GIG can take advantage of a packet switched infrastructure that ensures that all information flow within a system and external to a system is in the form of IP packets and datagrams. For a DoD program, it is best to adopt layering and modularity techniques within the communications infrastructure, so that system failures are minimized. Based on the Internet model, the systems connected to the GIG must also be designed to accommodate change. These changes may occur at different rates in different elements of the network. As the IPv6 and broadband network evolve, the GIG transport goal is to have full convergence of traffic (voice, video, and data) on a single IP inter-network. Network connectivity can be provided to all end points based on wide area networks or mobile and satellite transmissions.

UPCOMING AND FUTURE TRENDS

There are a large number of upcoming trends on the path toward Net centricity. This section picks two trends that are deemed to be key in moving forward on the Net-centric goal:

- Implementation of enterprise services.
- Use and adoption of key emerging technical standards.

Implementation of Enterprise Services

One emerging trend on the path to Net centricity is for DoD programs to implement and reuse enterprise services (ES). These services stem from the use of SOA-based systems that exchange services between all DoD component systems. Net-centric enterprise services (NCES) has been identified by DoD NII as a key component of DoD's strategy for meeting its transformation goals. NCES will eliminate duplicative services within DoD by providing a common set of interoperable ES supporting users in the war fighter and business domains.

NCES and GIG ES is the DoD strategy to provide a suite of value-added information, Web, and computing capabilities to support Net-centric warfare and operations. The strategy is to provide access anytime, anywhere to reliable decision-quality information through the use of cutting-edge, Web-based, networked services.

The core set of ES for implementing SOA-based DoD programs involve the following activities:

- **Discovery:** The enabling of all users no matter where they are to find the necessary information required no matter where it is located or stored
- **Collaboration:** This service will enable real-time situational updates to time critical planning activities among all DoD partners
- **Mediation:** This service enables users to post and use previously posted data no matter what format in order to support rapid decision-making.
- **Messaging:** This service provides a Web browser-based e-mail system, secure messaging, notifications and alerts, message boards and newsgroups, mailing and distribution, wireless support, messaging policies, and procedures.
- **Enterprise services management (ESM):** This service will provide assured end-to-end service availability, assured information protection, and assured information delivery.
- **Application:** Provides a protected hosting environment consisting of common services for hardware platforms, operating systems, and applications that is developed and delivered.
- **Storage:** Provides the warfighter and business user with storage hardware and software services to store all necessary information.
- **Information assurance services:** Provides authentication, access management, and domain security services.

The DoD plans to implement these ES across the enterprise in the upcoming future to enable the path to SOA and Net centricity. Defense Information Systems Agency (DISA) is currently working with different DoD component systems to develop and integrate the ES throughout the DoD infrastructure and attachments.

Use of Key Emerging Technical Standards

The path toward Net centricity requires a clear knowledge of emerging technology and technical standards. DoD NII has been working on a technical standards forecast (TV-2) that presents emerging technical standards that are to be adopted enterprise-wide throughout the department. A large number of new technology arenas have come into focus in relation to the Net-centric vision. This includes object-oriented development, Web services, XML-based transactions, standardized metadata, common criteria security standards, next generation Internet standards, and broadband networking. DoD NII expects all DoD programs to monitor the technical standards that are in use within their program and create a program-level technical standards profile (TV-1) that can then be inserted into DISROnline. DISR standards are coordinated by DoD NII and DISA to ensure that there is interoperability within the department. To ensure that programs are committed to the Net-centric vision, a key set of technical standard categories and standards are being encouraged for further research and adoption. The following provides an abbreviated list:

- **XML-based standards:** Use of XML schema, XPath, XQuery, XHTML, ebXML, XML-based workflow (XPDL), XSL, XSL transformations.
- **Web services standards:** SOAP, UDDI, WSDL, WS-security, WS-addressing, WS-messaging, WS-reliable messaging, WS-ReliableExchange, WS-management, WS-federation.
- **Metadata standards:** WS-MetadataExchange, metadata encoding and transmission standard (METS), Dublin core, directory interchange format (DIF), geospatial metadata standards.

- **IPv6 standards:** IPv6 addresses, IPv6 hosts and routers, unicast address allocation, TCP and UDP for IPv6, advanced sockets API, Internet control message protocol, transmission of IPv6 packets, global unicast address format, mobile IPv6, router renumbering, quality of service.

CONCLUSION

The chapter uses the transformation of the United States Department of Defense to a Net-centric environment as a specific example of EA in practice. The road to Net centricity is a difficult one. The DoD is a very large and complex organization, and to initiate fundamental change requires long-term vision and steadfastness. The EA principles are known and well defined within the DoD architecture framework, and it is a matter of discipline as to how this enabler helps in defining the DoD GIG enterprise. The Net-centric approach requires active participation from all of the DoD component organizations and communities of Interest. A significant amount of effort is necessary in defining future enterprise services that standardize data, information, knowledge, and intelligence across the DoD enterprise and other Federal agencies. In executing the Net-centric strategy, it is also important to sequence how legacy systems can be migrated to the Net-centric model, and how to effectively insert the latest technology within large information systems. The ultimate goal is to move up to a higher level of interoperability—one where all information capabilities are effectively intertwined to provide seamless communication with the user.

REFERENCES

Bass, T. (2005). Information management challenges on the path to Net-centric operations. *IEEE Milcom 2005*, Atlantic, City, NJ.

Chairman of the Joint Chiefs of Staff (CJCS) Instruction 3170.01E. (2005). *Joint Capabilities Integration and Development System (JCIDS)*.

Chairman of the Joint Chiefs of Staff (CJCS) Instruction 6212.01C. (2003, Nov 20). *Interoperability and Supportability of Information Technology and National Security Systems*.

Computer Associates White Paper. (2004). *Leveraging technology to enable Net-centric warfare*.

Department of Defense. (2003). *Joint Technical Architecture* Volume II.

Office of the Assistant Secretary of Defense for Networks and Information Integration, Department of Defense, Chief Information Officer. (2003). *DoD Net-Centric Data Strategy*.

Office of the Assistant Secretary of Defense for Networks and Information Integration, Department of Defense, Chief Information Officer. (2004). *DoD Architecture Framework* (Version 1.0).

Office of the Assistant Secretary of Defense for Networks and Information Integration, Department of Defense, Chief Information Officer. (2004). *Net-Centric Checklist* (Version 2.1.4).

Office of the Assistant Secretary of Defense for Networks and Information Integration, Department of Defense, Chief Information Officer, Directive 5000.1. (2003). *The Defense Acquisition System*.

Office of the Assistant Secretary of Defense for Networks and Information Integration, Department of Defense, Chief Information Officer, Directive 5000.2. (2003). *Operation of the Defense Acquisition System*.

Office of the Assistant Secretary of Defense for Networks and Information Integration, Department of Defense, Chief Information Officer, Directive 8500.1 (2002), *Information Assurance*.

Office of the Assistant Secretary of Defense for Networks and Information Integration, Department of Defense, Chief Information Officer, Directive 8500.2. (2003). *Information Assurance Implementation.*

Office of the Assistant Secretary of Defense for Networks and Information Integration, Department of Defense, Chief Information Officer, Instruction 4630.8. (2004, June 30). *Procedures for Interoperability and Supportability of Infor-*

mation Technology (IT) and National Security Systems (NSS).

Office of the Assistant Secretary of Defense for Networks and Information Integration, Department of Defense, Chief Information Officer, Instruction 8580.1. (2004). *Information Assurance (IA) in the Defense Acquisition System.*

Zenishek, S. G., Usechak, D. (2005). Net-centric warfare and its impact on system-of-systems. *Defense Acquisition Review Journal, 39.*

Section IV
Implementation and Deployment

Chapter XVI
Enterprise Architecture as an Enabler for E–Governance:
An Indian Perspective

Raghunath Mahapatra
Ernst & Young India, India

Sinnakkrishnan Perumal[1]
Indian Institute of Management Calcutta, India

ABSTRACT

E-governance in India is different from those in developed countries due to the peculiarities in administrative structure, geo-political and organizational culture, and process management. U.S., UK, and Denmark have effectively used enterprise architecture frameworks for e-governance implementation. In this chapter, we analyze how enterprise architecture concepts and methodology can be used to implement an efficient and effective e-governance system for citizen services administration by the Government of India. There are several enterprise architecture frameworks like Zachman framework, FEA CRM, TOGAF, DODAF, etc. We have based our analysis on the Zachman framework due to its simplicity and since most of the other frameworks have either been guided by or derived from it. We develop a framework to be applicable to the Indian initiatives and identify how it can guide the e-governance implementation in India and facilitate solving the traditional problems associated with the governance system in India through better processes.

INTRODUCTION

Following the global tradition, India has undertaken pioneering initiatives in governance domain. As a consequence, there have been several e-governance initiatives in India. An analysis of the different projects of e-governance undertaken in India indicates that they are more of islands of attempts rather than an integrating one. There have been two levels of attempts, first at the central government level and second at the state government level. There have been no initiatives taken by the local authorities—the municipalities on their own. While the efforts of the central government projects have attempted some amount of integration, all the efforts at the state government level have been more of e-government rather than e-governance (i.e., the attempts have been to automate the existing government services using ICT especially the Internet and Web-related technologies and not focused on process reengineering). Vincent and Mahesh (2005) state that "Though administrative improvements brought about through the use of technology are welcome, the real goal should be enhanced governance."

The other aspects of these initiatives have been the following:

- There were no national level directives for e-government or e-governance.
- There has been no overall goal for achievement of deliverables.
- All the processes in any department, where the initiatives are undertaken, have not been automated.
- The efforts have taken more of a low hanging fruit approach keeping in view funds available, acceptance within the department, protection of turf, and preserving the status quo in mind.

Overall, no comprehensive framework has been used for e-governance in India.

While the success of the implementations will need effective legislation (e.g., citizen charters and the right to information act and other enablers), there is a strong need for an integrative framework for the isolated attempts to be holistic.

This chapter attempts at the following:

- Analyzing the present situation in India in terms of e-governance initiatives.
- Identifying the needs felt for the progress of the initiatives.
- Role of enterprise architecture in fulfilling the needs.
- Various enterprise architecture frameworks existing at present.
- A suggested approach for using enterprise architecture for e-governance in Indian context.

Figure 1. Some of the e-governance initiatives in India

- National E-Governance Action Plan (NeGAP)
- Centre for E-Governance (CEG)
- Bhoomi
- Stamps Registration and Archiving (SARITA)
- VOICE
- e-Seva
- Gyandoot
- e-Choupal
- VidyaVahini
- Aarakshi
- Web based Citizen-IT Interface (WebCITI)
- Drishtee
- New Agent of Information – District level Integrated Services of Haryana for All (NAIDISHA)
- Saukaryam
- Akshaya
- GramSampark
- Dairy Information Services Kiosk (DISK)
- Community Information Center

BACKGROUND

E-governance initiatives in India have taken major strides following the increased emphasis on improving the traditional governance mechanisms through information technology systems. India's Information Technology Act, 2000, provides a legal framework for information and transactions carried out through Internet, thus facilitating the e-governance initiatives. Manufacturers association of information technology (MAIT, 2005) details various e-governance initiatives in India (see Figure 1).

Of the previously mentioned e-governance initiatives, e-Choupal is a private sector initiative undertaken by the company ITC Limited to procure farm products directly from the farmers by providing them with the price and other information about the market. e-Seva is a citizen-centric service delivery implemented in selected cities of Andhra Pradesh state to provide a one-stop service for citizen-interactions with the government. Bhoomi is a self-sustainable project for rural land records delivery and management. Bhoomi has successfully curbed the issue of corruption and red tape (manufacturers association of information technology (MAIT), 2005). E-Seva, Bhoomi, and e-Choupal are proving to be very successful projects and are getting scaled up to extend the benefits to other regions (Department of Information Technology (DIT) & National Council of Applied Economic Research (NCAER), 2004, p. 83).

The national e-governance action plan (NeGAP) formed by the Government of India envisages a set of core policies and infrastructure facilities to facilitate central level, state level, and integrated level e-governance initiatives to provide citizen-centric and business-centric service delivery.

The CEO of NISG said in a summit that the following are the challenges for e-governance in India (quoted from Shirur, 2006, p. 18):

- Last mile connectivity, availability of power, line of sight, etc.
- Sustainability and maintenance of infrastructure created (SWAN, CSC, etc.).
- Lack of standards and architecture especially in information management.
- Lack of content.
- Backend computerization of departments.
- Lack of local language content.
- Lack of awareness of what content is available.
- Quality of content.
- Needs assessment and community participation.
- Issues in sharing infrastructure and information between departments.
- Projects designed in silos.
- Lack of suitable legal frameworks.
- Complexity of dealing with multiple government departments for private partner.

Shetty (2002) states the risks associated with any e-government initiative can be of two types, citizen-side risks, and government-side risks. He further states that citizen-side risks can be classified into digital divide, low expectations, lack of familiarity, not easy to use, lack of trust, and misconceptions, and government-side risks can be classified into complexity, department/agency-centric paradigm, lack of capacity, human resource constraints, and financial resource constraints.

Heeks (2006) refers to Barret and Greene (2001) and Doherty and Horne (2002) and states that "Many public organizations also find themselves in situations of constant and largely uncontrollable flux from factors such as changeover in ruling political parties, constant circulation of senior politicians and officials, emergence of new political initiatives and legislation that alter organizational activities, priorities and even structures, sudden imposition of cost-cutting measures, sudden external crises that demand a reaction, changes within the client groups the organizations serve, and changes in IT, IT standards, and IT suppliers"

(p. 62). All this leads to a consistent chaos in the governance systems, leading in turn to a need for an architecture that is constantly updated and used for the purpose of designing an efficient and effective e-governance system.

The NASSCOM (2003) report identifies operational hurdles, economic hurdles, planning and implementation hurdles, and personnel hurdles in implementing e-governance in India. Various planning and implementation hurdles identified in this report are (quoted from NASSCOM, 2003):

- No clear roadmap with measurable milestones.
- Focus on computerization and hardware spend.
- Low emphasis on process re-engineering.

This shows a lack of holistic view in implementing e-governance in India. Need for a holistic view is also emphasized by the Joint Secretary for e-governance in Ministry of IT, India as: "When you look at e-governance from a citizen's point-of-view, you sense a need for a common framework and approach. It may not be a grand holistic blueprint for the entire country, but it should be a foundation on which governments and departments can provide citizen services," (as stated in "India's e-governance plan," 2006). In this chapter, he further talks about the evolution of such a blueprint in India.

Previously mentioned risks associated with e-governance initiatives along with the consistent changes in the government structure and need for a holistic view call for a comprehensive blueprint for the e-governance system across the entire nation. E-governance implementation without this blueprint will be akin to an organization without any management plan. Such a blueprint is provided by the enterprise architecture by providing the mapping between management plans and their reality for various organizational perspectives. In addition, enterprise architecture provides the necessary baseline for any change management

initiative by clearly depicting the AS-IS situation and hence making it easier to achieve the TO-BE situation.

The Department of Information Technology (DIT) and National Council of Applied Economic Research (NCAER) (2004) studied e-governance readiness of various states in the year 2004 and identified strategies for improving e-governance mechanisms in the respective states. They analyzed various e-governance initiatives based on Sen and Brown's evaluation frameworks and sustainability and scalability of the initiatives. They have come up with the recommendations based on the following premises (quoted from Department of Information Technology (DIT) and National Council of Applied Economic Research (NCAER), 2004, pp. 83-84):

- Second generation reforms.
  - ° Modernize public services.
  - ° Improve transparency and efficiency in delivery.
  - ° Economize on delivery.
- Empowering and including marginalized sections through evolution of networked states/provinces.
- Sustainable/scalable/profitable rural development initiatives.
- Adopt proactive policies to consciously move the states up the pyramid to the status of "average achievers" and above.
- Match potential of Indian states for IT application with actual level of applications in the state with assistance from the Central government.
- Developing a domestic market for IT applications to reduce vulnerability from the external environment.
- Improving readiness of verticals.
- Increasing awareness of potential benefits of ICT in rural development.

The first five of the previously mentioned premises can be facilitated by having an enterprise architecture for the complete and pan-Indian e-governance system. The other three can also be addressed through extended versions of the enterprise architecture framework.

E-GOVERNANCE IN INDIA

E-governance initiatives in India are more of the nature of administration of citizen services. Peristeras and Tarabanis (2004) have proposed three primary administrative government functions—declaration, direction, and interrogation and four generic types of public services—certification, control, authorization, and production. The previous classifications focus more on the types of services that are delivered to the citizens. These can be termed as the front-end of the government functioning.

They further classified the overall function of a government into three categories—provide service, formulate public policy, and support operations. We classify the overall function of a government into policy, regulations, and service delivery. While the policy can be seen as the equivalent of the declarative and directive functions of the government, and policy along with service delivery can fulfill interrogation function, regulations, both outside and inside, are important for efficient functioning and transparency.

The present e-government initiatives in India are focusing on the front-end parameters of the service delivery only. Analysis of various such initiatives and projects shows that most of the projects have one or more of the following in different stages:

- Preparing a Web site for various departments of the government.
- Converting government forms and documents into electronic forms.
- Enabling citizens to download the forms, but submission to be made offline.

- Displaying applications' status on Web sites for online tracking of progress.

In addition to the previous, some of the departments and ministries of the government at the central level have done the following:

- **Submission of the forms electronically:** This is not expected to be 100% in the near future since the submissions need supporting documents that are in physical format held by the citizens. Hence, a physical submission across the counter is the accepted method and is expected to continue for a long time until all old documents are dematerialized and the necessary frameworks incorporating indexed citizen database, repository for the documents, security, etc., are in place.
- **Transactions on the Internet:** This is primarily done by ministries like railways and has been very successful.

Mahapatra and Perumal (2006) have compared some of the e-governance initiatives in India—Gyandoot, E-seva, SETU, Warana project, and FRIENDS taking various parameters considered appropriate for e-governance initiatives in India. The parameters chosen were the following (quoted from Mahapatra et al., 2006, p. 9):

- Existence of strong and committed leadership.
- Detailed project management.
- Involvement of stakeholders.
- Internal process efficiency.
- Inter-departmental coordination/integration.
- Easy access for citizens.
- Established standards.
- Scaling up.
- Financial viability ensured.
- Privacy aspects taken care of.
- Data security taken care of.

The comparison concluded that except a few, most of the projects are weak when judged according to the previous parameters. Hence, it can be inferred that there is a long way to go before e-governance initiatives in India can be termed as successful and useful.

While the initiatives are similar across the world, the Indian exercise will be more complex than those in the developed countries due to the following reasons:

- **Data related issues—storage, indexing, and ageing:** In developed countries, data has been maintained in a structured manner even before the information technology and the advantages thereof were available. Hence, building up the repository entailed digitalization and automation. The focus in these countries, hence, was on optimal and efficient database design and implementation. However, in India, data storage is a known and acknowledged problem. Data is fragmented, incomplete, and geographically dispersed.

- The federal structure of governance in India has led to segregation of responsibility into three levels—that of center, state, and concurrent. The concurrent areas of responsibilities have a constitutional supremacy of center over the states in terms of decision-making and initiatives, but it requires active cooperation. Sometimes, this also leads to conflict of political and economical interest since the focus of the states is local while that of the center is more global.

- India has more than 20 recognized languages with their own scripts, in addition to the two national languages—Hindi and English. The states store the data and formats in the vernacular languages. However, citizens are mobile across India. Ideally, once the citizen moves out of one place, the data should be able to follow him. This will require data to be seamlessly portable while the storage of the data can be either decentralized with porting protocols or centralized with access protocols in place. However, since the data is in vernacular format, it becomes difficult to access, collect, and use the data by users not familiar or proficient in the native language. Also, it is not possible for a single person to be familiar with so many languages or employ multiple persons for the purpose. Hence, a cross-country integration framework is necessary to address these issues.

- India has a multi-tier governance structure (see Figure 2). Since India is a predominantly rural and agriculture focused country, it is important to focus the initiatives that will fulfill the need of rural population for the benefits to reach most of the citizens. Hence, a framework should be adopted that will enable the sub-state—districts, municipalities, and gram panchayats to implement the initiatives. Since it will be impossible to cater to all the requirements at one go, the framework should have scalability built into it.

Figure 2. Administrative structure of India

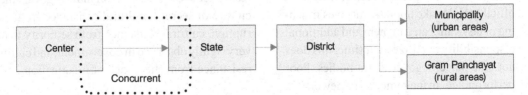

Further, except the center, all other entities have similar functions and offer similar services to the citizens with some differences as justified by the local issues and conditions. In case of the areas coming under the purview of central government, the state and sub-state governance units are responsible for implementing most of the regulations especially related to enforcement, certification, taxation, and welfare.

- For citizen services, multiple government departments are involved. Recent e-governance initiatives at the central level are focusing on integrating the function of different departments involved in the process. This has involved automating various departments related to the deliverable and streamlining and integrating the processes involved. An example of this is the issuance of passport to the citizens of India. Issuing a passport involves more than three departments that come under the purview of different ministries--passport office under Ministry of External Affairs, police department under Home Ministry, and Department of Public Grievances under Home Ministry. The e-government initiative attempts to integrate the information availability by combining the information from passport, police, and grievance departments on one Web site.

- Government departments are governed by established rules and working procedures. It has been observed that the workload of all the officials in the government is not the same or proportionate. Some of the officials are overloaded while some others are under-utilized. Inappropriate work allocation is a dominant cause of this. While in other kinds of organization—private sector, interested official might take upon themselves finishing of tasks allocated to them and additional responsibility to utilize their time; this does not take place in government bodies. Poor performance management framework in government organization is the primary influencing factor for such condition. Due to the previous conditions, compliance, and conformity, rather than initiative is the driving force for the performance of the government officials.

Previous issues are in addition to the usual ones e.g., an old nation steeped in unique cultural milieu, sociological dogmas, feudal mindset and the residual effect of outdated legal, and official framework of the colonial rule, etc. The results have been a deliberate and redundant use of the Official Secrets Act to withhold information from citizens, patronizing attitude of government officials toward the citizens, insecurity in the minds of officials, and use of information as a controlling rather than facilitating tool. Garg and Khataokar (2003) state that "Due to corruption deep routed in the political and administrative system, majority of the people at the authoritative positions in the respective functional departments may dislike the transparent and smooth working after e-governance initiative." Some of these are being tackled now through the Right to Information Act in combination with e-governance initiatives. Further, Garg et al. (2003) say, "Poor requirement-gathering (particularly in the case of frequent policy changes) and non-involvement of end-users during this process, poor or negligible awareness about information technology among decision-makers, poor management of knowledge and human resources, non-compatibility between IT projects and business processes, poor risk management, choice of technology and over-ambitious projects are among the root causes of problems in achieving significant e-governance benefits." Vittal (2001) identifies four sources of cultural resistance to e-governance in India—government culture of secrecy, cultural resistance from corruption, cultural resistance from seniority that is very rigidly observed in government, and cultural resistance from sheer lack of imagination.

THE IMPERATIVES

Judging from the previous description, it can be inferred that to provide seamless and effective citizen services the following will be necessary:

- Integration of the processes and approaches at national level along with identification of the localized requirements.
- Standardization of the processes, parameters, and data.
- Ease of replicability and avoiding duplication of effort among the functions in states and sub-state level will need normalization of the tasks along with the standardization of processes. This will require identification and definition of common tasks and creation of common task language across the governments both at center and especially amongst the states through the use of uniform semantics and taxonomy. While the foundation in the form of tools to fulfill these necessities have been created by different governments across the world, it is necessary to adopt and adapt the appropriate ones and create new ones as necessary.
- Interoperability of parameters among the processes. This can be achieved through modularization of the standardized process thereby developing reusable components. Modularization of process can be achieved by adopting object orientation approach.
- Since e-governance is a long-term exercise and has to be achieved in a gradual and phased manner, it is important to have scalability parameters built into the design of the processes during standardization and modularization. It will be easier to create modules for new processes as and when they are necessary and also to modify the existing modules without affecting the complete service value chain, if any of the existing processes gets modified due to improve-

ment or due to external impact (e.g., new processes).
- Judicious use of ICT and related parameters like hardware and software to achieve better return on investment (IT for Change, 2003).

In this context, an integrating framework with the technological enablers will facilitate the execution by providing the implementer a structured platform for reference and action.

ENTERPRISE ARCHITECTURE

Enterprise architecture provides such an integrating framework. The concept of enterprise architecture was introduced by John Zachman in 1987 in Zachman (1987). Zachman defines the framework (Zachman framework)[2] as a "Logical structure for classifying and organizing the description representations of an enterprise that are significant to the management of the enterprise as well as to the enterprise's system."

The institute for enterprise architecture developments (n.d.) defines enterprise architecture as "about understanding all of the different elements that go to make up the enterprise and how those elements interrelate." It further defines elements as "all the elements that enclose the areas of people, processes, business, and technology. In that sense, examples of elements are strategies, business drivers, principles, stakeholders, units, locations, budgets, domains, functions, activities, processes, services, products, information, communications, applications, systems, infrastructure, etc."

IEEE (2000) (as cited in Tang, Han, & Chen, 2004, p. 640) defines architecture as "the fundamental organization of a system, embodied in its components, their relationships to each other and the environment, and the principles governing its design and evolution." Analysis of this definition provides several insights into the way architecture for any organization can be viewed. The architecture has to deal with the following:

- Fundamental aspects of the way a system is (as-is) or can be (to-be) organized.
- The manner in which these aspects are related to each other and the environment, which can be either internal or external to the organization (i.e., the intra-play among the aspects and the inter-play between the aspects and the environment).
- The policies and principles on which they are based. These define the intangible foundation of the system and are indicators of its robustness and flexibility. The flexibility that the policies permit along with the checks and balances therein influence the evolution of the same in tune with the changing dynamics.

Enterprise architecture can be complex for comprehension and implementation. Zwahr and Finger (2004) have analyzed various definitions and bodies of work and have shown that enterprise architecture can be seen as a tool dealing with methodologies and styles for designing purposeful activities obtaining a comprehensive view of the organization for efficient functioning.

ENTERPRISE ARCHITECTURE FOR E-GOVERNANCE

While enterprise architecture was designed for information systems in the corporate organizations, it has evolved over a period of time to address the issues and cater to the needs of different kinds of information systems. At the same time, governments and governance have also evolved to assume, and progressively internalize, the characteristics of the corporate sector. This independent evolution has made it possible now to analyze the governance in the context of the applicability of enterprise architecture to it.

Enterprise architecture approach to e-governance would provide the following benefits:

- Efficiency and effectiveness through an integrated approach: As the enterprise architecture functions as the overall guiding framework, integration of the activities will lead to streamlining and removal of slack and redundancy.
- Improved citizen service in terms of accuracy, reduction in duplication of data and effort and time spent by the officials in processing the data, and time spent by citizens by approaching multiple avenues.
- Collaboration across departments, enabling the integration, will improve system efficiency.
- Process-oriented rather than department-oriented approach will reduce redundancy in effort of the officials, and improve the transparency of the system and smooth ensuring of workflow.
- Re-use of design, technology, processes will assist in replicability and scalability.
- Standardization of data, technology, and processes will ensure transparency and improve efficiency.
- Easy access to data will be possible because of the improved data management policies and systems being in place.
- Rigorous monitoring of process execution will be possible thus improving the performance management system.

Several architectures have been developed for e-governance. Few examples of them will be the federal enterprise architecture framework (FEAF) of the U.S. government, The open group architecture framework (TOGAF), e-services development framework of UK, and DoDAF that is developed specifically for application in the department of defense of the U.S. government. All of these have either referred to or used Zachman framework. There have been attempts to analyze these frameworks for their applicability toward e-governance effectiveness. Zwahr et al. (2004) analyze how various enterprise architecture frameworks such as the open group architecture framework (TOGAF), Zachman framework, and DoD architecture framework (DoDAF) can be used for e-governance. In addition, they provide a two level e-governance framework in which the top-level layer has e-governance matrix plotting *technology* against *state transformation*. The second level layer has four dimensions of e-governance framework such as *level, actor, function,* and *technology.*

ENTERPRISE ARCHITECTURE FOR E-GOVERNANCE IN INDIA

Taking into account the context and imperatives mentioned in previous sections, enterprise architecture can be used to address the imperatives.

The Zachman framework, being the foundation of most other frameworks, has been used by the authors. The Zachman framework analyzes the organization from two dimensions in a matrix form that are considered to be both comprehensive and primitive. The rows of the matrix consist of perspectives and the columns consist of the six interrogative dimensions—who, what, where, when, why, and how. The perspectives are effectively points of view (i.e., analysis through the eyes of the stakeholders). These interrogative dimensions reduce the results of analysis to the primitive form thus constituting the foundation.

The cells in the matrix of Zachman framework provide dedicated focus in identifying the need and hence each approach can be separate while being part of a whole. While implementing the framework, this will assist in dedicating teams to take care of the content of individual cells and an oversight team can be responsible for ensuring inter-relationships amongst them. Any e-gover-

nance initiative with wide scope will need the involvement of multiple departments. In a federal structure, that is in India, any e-governance initiative will involve the entities subsequent to the initiating entity as depicted in Figure 2. While the nodal coordinating body will belong to the initiating agency, the executing agency will belong thereafter. For example, for a project initiated by center, coordination will be made by central bodies while the execution will involve agencies and departments belonging to the state government and sub-state entities. Hence, the existence of a framework will enable seamless implementation.

Keeping the expected outcomes previously outlined as targets, the authors have developed a usable framework. While the framework can be for any e-governance initiative, it is focused on Indian context and contains relevant dominant factors. The same is presented in Table 1 and explained subsequently. The alphanumeric representation for unique identification of cells has been adopted to make reference easier.

Objective/Scope (Contextual)

A1 (Contextual: Planner—What: Data): Details Pertaining to Citizen Services

The major objective of any e-governance initiative is providing efficient delivery of citizen services. To fulfill this objective, it is important to have the details pertaining to citizen services. The data will include those pertaining to the citizens and those related to the rules for processing these data. At the contextual level, it is important to make a roster of all the data necessary and develop an appropriate structure for collecting such data in a periodic manner at different geographical locations.

Table 1. Enterprise architecture framework for e-governance in Indian context

		1 DATA *What*	2 FUNCTION *How*	3 NETWORK *Where*	4 PEOPLE *Who*	5 TIME *When*	6 MOTIVATION *Why*
A	**Objective/scope** *Contextual* *Role: Planner*	Details pertaining to citizen services	Citizen service delivery processes (internal and external)	Citizen interaction points	Government bodies/ departments, NGOs, private sectors etc.	Offline, physical and online interactions, internal processes	Governance vision and objectives -transparency, efficiency, etc.
B	**Enterprise model** *Conceptual* *Role: Owner*	Citizen service components	Optimized and integrated citizen service delivery processes	Pan-Indian network	Operating procedures, delegation of authority, performance metrics	Recurring service delivery plan	Rollout plan, phasing, robust project monitoring plan
C	**System model** *Logical* *Role: Designer*	Data management plan	Integrative architecture including service and service components	Pan-Indian system architecture for service and service components	Single window, online and distributed facilities plan	Integrative, seamless model	International benchmarks, best practices and OVIs, efficiency targets
D	**Technology model** *Physical* *Role: Builder*	Modular structure, cluster maps	Replicable, scalable model	Location—service specification map	Easy citizen access offices, online kiosks and bulletin boards, User-friendly multi-lingual Web sites	Project execution monitoring plan, robust workflow and built-in feedback system	Government rules and regulations

A2 (Contextual: Planner—How: Function): Citizen Service Delivery Processes (Internal and External)

Viewing government as an extended corporate service that involves the citizens of the country makes it a complex environment that will need multitude of processes for efficient execution. Given the layered administrative structure of India, processes will be many and vary in their complexity, objective, and span of influence. At present, there are several processes running at different places and levels depending on the necessities, rules, and regulations. It is necessary to prepare a list of all the processes, and identify the fundamental processes that will form the nucleus of the integrative approach and other processes will be treated as complementary and/or supplementary.

A3 (Contextual: Planner—Where: Network): Citizen Interaction Points

Citizen interaction points are important variables for efficient delivery of citizen services. Currently, most of the transactions take place across the physical counters and there have been several successful initiatives to shift the interaction points to online system like Web pages. Additional facilities like information dissemination and transaction kiosks through public private partnership initiatives are being explored and some have been tested successfully.

A4 (Contextual: Planner—Who: People): Government Bodies/ Departments, NGOs, Private Sectors, etc.

The parties involved in the citizen service delivery processes are government bodies and officials. Long term focused frameworks should have facilities to include other parties like NGOs and private sector players. This will lessen the burden on the government infrastructure and create a self-sustaining model while ensuring transparency since involvement of local level bodies will reduce the opacity in the system and will harness the efficiencies of other agencies.

A5 (Contextual: Planner—When: Time): Offline, Physical, and Online Interactions, Internal Processes

The transactions related to citizen services delivery take place, currently, during the regular office hours. There are several factors that prevent a higher level of efficiency in the process. One of the dominant factors is the official time being the same as that for effective economic activity for the citizens. Thus, citizens have to interrupt their normal daily routine activities for availing the services. It will be a benefit to reduce this and related inconvenience. These kinds of initiatives have been undertaken by private sector service providers—banks through ATMs and Internet enabled banking for round-the-clock service delivery possible with reduced cost and increased efficiency. To achieve similar operational levels, it is important to document the present and possible future interactions and develop a suitable framework.

A6 (Contextual: Planner—Why: Vision): Governance Vision and Objectives— Transparency, Efficiency, etc.

The contextual reasons for the framework will be the governance vision espoused by government and the evolving governance context in India. The Government of India has formulated a plan called the National e-Governance Action Plan (NeGAP) to achieve this. In addition, the National Institute of Smart Governance has been entrusted with drawing up the e-governance road map for Indian states.

Enterprise Model (Conceptual)

B1 (Conceptual: Owner—What: Data): Citizen Service Components

Services rendered to citizens across India are dispersed, but similar in nature. Hence, one of the imperatives is to modularize the service offerings by creating replicable service components. For this, it is necessary to identify the components and conduct a cross-state nation-wide comparison to categorize the components and their inter-linkages.

B2 (Conceptual: Owner—How: Function: Optimized and Integrated Citizen Services Delivery Processes

Integration of citizen services delivery processes as described will result in efficiency gains in the short term. However, to provide seamless service delivery processes, it will be necessary to continuously review them and strive for optimizing them periodically to maintain it in the long term. Hence, a model/framework should be put in place for integration and optimization aspects of the delivery processes with the phasing plan for setting milestones. Developing a set of metrics will help in setting up a list of objectively verifiable indicators (OVIs). Standardization of processes should form part of the plan.

B3 (Conceptual: Owner—Where: Network): Pan-Indian Network

For the previous step to be possible, it is important that the logistics system should be of cross-country in nature since all the administrative units of the country will be integrated in the long term. In addition to the communication network, it should include data, human resource in terms of skill sets, and service rendering formats.

B4 (Conceptual: Owner—Who: People): Operating Procedures, Delegation of Authority, Performance Metrics

For the systems to work effectively, it is important that the officials of the government and its partners, the NGOs, private sector players, etc., follow a systematic working procedure. Hence, a robust operating procedure should be in place with the delegation of authority and responsibilities delineated for the officials and other stakeholders. Central government in India has "Central Secretariat—Manual of Office Procedures," which is in line with the previous. Efforts are being made to establish a robust set of operating procedures in line with the above in the states. Key responsibility areas (KRAs), key performance indicators (KPIs), and similar metrics should be incorporated to make the system accountable and self-governing.

B5 (Conceptual: Owner—When: Time): Recurring Service Delivery Plan

In case of citizen services delivery, most of the services are recurring in nature. A plan should be in place to recognize the recurring nature of the services and provide smoother delivery of the same.

B6 (Conceptual: Owner—Why: Vision): Rollout Plan, Phasing, Robust Project Monitoring Plan

E-governance in India will require phased implementation, considering factors like geographical diversity and existing delivery systems. Hence, a plan has to be in place for prototyping, phasing of the activities and rolling out the initiatives in different places with the integration aspects in mind. To ensure success of such exercises, robust project monitoring plan will be necessary. Efforts should be made to incorporate the lessons from the existing projects in future projects.

System Model (Logical)

C1 (Logical: Designer—What: Data): Data Management Plan

Citizen-related data that can be used for providing services are not available in an organized manner in India due to sub-optimal archiving facility. This is also due to the fact that data collation did not receive priority earlier. Hence, many a time data is found missing thus, generating discontinuity. In recent years, the situation has improved substantially.

Due to the linguistic diversity of India, different states use different scripts. Different measurement systems are used in different states based on the legacy. These pose challenges to integration. Technology solutions can help in addressing the language issues. An international measurement system (e.g., metric system can be used for conversion among the different units).

C2 (Logical: Designer—How: Function): Integrative Architecture Including Service And Service Components

The system architecture should be integrative and should be focused on providing citizen services keeping in mind the replicability and scalability aspects. There are several established architectures—service-oriented architecture and component-based object-oriented architecture that can cater to these needs. Depending on the justification, the architectures can be used as available or might be modified to fulfill the desired objectives.

C3 (Logical: Designer—Where: Network): Pan-Indian System Architecture for Service and Service Components

It will be necessary to make the system architecture keeping the administrative structure of India in mind so that all the segments are catered to.

C4 (Logical: Designer—Who: People): Single Window, Online, and Distributed Facilities Plan

Currently, the citizen is required to spend time and effort by approaching several government departments to avail the services. Government of India and state governments have a vision of providing single window delivery mechanism where the citizen will have one point of contact and the internal processes will be integrated. Online and distributed facilities like information kiosks that might involve private entrepreneurs will be supplementing and complementing these efforts.

C5 (Logical: Designer—When: Time): Integrative, Seamless Model

The internal processes to be used by the system implementers and stakeholders should provide for seamless and modular integration taking into account the information, human resource, processes, and the information technology.

C6 (Logical: Designer—Why: Vision): International Benchmarks, Best Practices and OVIs, Efficiency Targets

There have been many successful e-governance implementations in the world. Some of the examples can be Singapore and Dubai. While these countries do not have the geographical diversity and procedural complexity present in India, they can be used as learning points and efficiency benchmarks. Best practices from international implementations can be used to set the targets and objectively verifiable indicators (OVIs) should be decided to track the variances and take corrective measures, if needed.

Technology Model (Physical)

D1 (Physical: Builder—What: Data): Modular Structure, Cluster Maps

Technology, being the enabler for successful implementation of e-governance initiatives, should be used optimally. E-governance initiatives in a country like India are going to be hardware intensive needing large investments. Hence, the structure should be modular that provides better scalability. At the same time, software should be capable of handling diverse technologies involving operating systems, databases, and user interfaces. Data should also be structured in a modular manner.

D2 (Physical: Builder—How: Function): Replicable, Scalable Model

Designing for the technology should take into account factors like replicability and scalability. It should be adaptive so that changes can be made with minimum investment in hardware and software.

D3 (Physical: Builder—Where: Network): Location—Service Specification Map

Since there will be multiple locations with varied facilities in terms of infrastructure, a detailed map of locations with the service delivery scope should be developed. This will enable resource allocation optimization.

D4 (Physical: Builder—Who: People): Easy Citizen Access Offices, Online Kiosks and Bulletin Boards, User-Friendly Multi-Lingual Web sites

Web sites that are integral to the success of efficient citizen service delivery standards should be user friendly and multi-lingual with provision for local vernacular language display (IT for Change, 2003).

To supplement the Web sites, information kiosks, electronic bulletin boards, and similar tools can be used for disseminating the information and convenience of user. This will ensure that the initial resistance to change is minimized, thus increasing the chances of adoption.

It is anticipated that the physical interaction points for the citizen services will co-exist with the online facilities. Hence, it is important that these are factored into the initiatives, and the facilities are designed to extend the convenience and transparency that the e-governance will ensure.

D5 (Physical: Builder—When: Time): Project Execution Monitoring Plan, Robust Workflow, and Built-In Feedback System

Technology enabled controls for checks and balances should be put in place.

D6 (Physical: Builder—Why: Vision): Government Rules and Regulations (Continued Compliance)

Because e-governance will entail a paradigm shift in the way government operates in India, the regulations need focus. The rules and regulations should be formulated in a manner to ensure fairness and equity especially those involving private sector players.

Since the data will be available through Internet/Web sites, security of the data will need

Figure 3. Mapping between imperatives and the framework

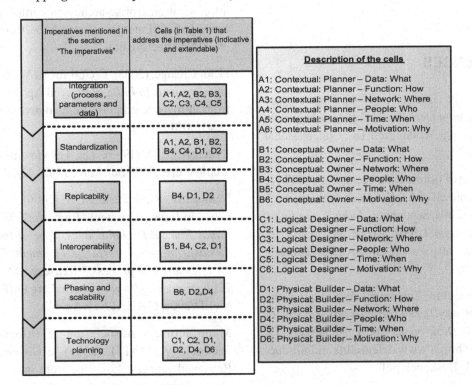

attention and will need robust cyber laws. India has enacted various laws including the Right to Information Act with some exceptions in accessing information. However, various states have implemented it in varying degrees.

Investment in technology should also consider the optimal usage due to issues arising out of rapid obsolescence of hardware and software systems, opportunity costs in not catering to high priority areas, etc.

Mapping the imperatives previously mentioned to the framework suggested, the following summary is achieved (see Figure 3).

CONCLUSION

E-governance is slowly emerging as a strategic tool for governance and international relations.

India has undertaken several initiatives in this domain with varying degrees of success. The authors have proposed that to learn from these initiatives and for the initiatives to be successful, the use of enterprise architecture will be beneficial. This chapter refers to existing body of work in the domain of enterprise architecture as applicable to e-governance. Using the Zachman framework for enterprise architecture, the authors have developed a framework for e-governance in India. The architecture is aimed at catering to the imperatives that have been found from existing works and the experience of authors. The frameworks are dependent on perspectives that come from the stakeholders. It is important that pertinent stakeholders are identified to obtain the correct perspectives.

While the framework is based on established references and experience, it is necessary to put it to use for its validation and further improvement.

REFERENCES

Barrett, K., & Greene, R. (2001). *Powering up: How public managers can take control of information technology*. Washington, DC: Congressional Quarterly.

Department of Information Technology (DIT) & National Council of Applied Economic Research (NCAER). (2004, September). *India: E-readiness assessment report 2004*. Retrieved January 15, 2005, from http://www.mit.gov.in/ereadiness/CHAP8.PDF

DoD Architecture Framework Working Group. (2004, February 9). *DoD architecture framework version 1.0 Desk book*. Retrieved January 15, 2006, from http:// www.defenselink.mil/nii/doc/DoDAF_v1_Deskbook.pdf

Doherty, T. L., & Horne, T. (2002). *Managing public services-implementing changes: A thoughtful approach to the practice of management*. London: Routledge.

Garg, V. N., & Khataokar, A. (2003, December). *E-governance in India: Implementation issues*. Retrieved April 9, 2006, from http://www.i4donline.net/issue/nov03/implementation_full.htm

Heeks, R. (2006). *Implementing and managing eGovernment: An international text*. London: Sage.

IEEE. (2000). IEEE recommended practice for architectural description of software-intensive systems. *IEEE Std. 1471-2000.*

India's e-governance plan. (2006, February 28). Retrieved April 9, 2006, from http://www.computerpartner.nl/article.php?news=int&id=2627

Institute for Enterprise Architecture Developments. (n.d.). *Enterprise architecture definition*. Retrieved October 6, 2005, from http://www.enterprise-architecture.info/Images/Extended%20Enterprise/Extended%20Enterprise%20Architecture.htm

IT for Change. (2003). *E-GOVERNANCE: 20 hot eGov projects in India*. Retrieved April 9, 2006, from http://www.dqindia.com/content/top_stories/103101501.asp

Kruchten, P. B. (1995). The 4+1 view model of architecture. *IEEE Software, 12*(6), 42-50.

Mahapatra, R., & Perumal, S. (2006). E-governance in India: A strategic framework. *International Journal for Infonomics, Special Issue on "Measuring e-Business for development: Toward an international process."* Retrieved March 6, 2006, from http://www.i-journal.org.uk/Papers/MeBD/2006/MAHAPATRA.pdf

Manufacturers Association of Information Technology (MAIT). (2005). *e-Governance*. Retrieved January 15, 2005, from http://www.elcot.com/mait-reports/e-Gov.pdf

NASSCOM. (2003). *e-Governance in India accelerating, but roadblocks exist, says NASSCOM*. Retrieved April 9, 2006, from http://nasscom.org/artdisplay.asp?Art_id=1572

Office of Management and Budget. (2005). *FY07 budget formulation FEA consolidated reference model document*. Retrieved December 1, 2005, from http://www.whitehouse.gov/omb/egov/documents/CRM.PDF

Peristeras, V., & Tarabanis, K. (2004). Governance enterprise architecture (GEA): Domain models for e-governance. In M. Janssen, H. G. Sol, & R. W. Wagenaar (Eds.), *Proceedings of the 6th International Conference on Electronic Commerce* (Vol. 60, pp. 471-479). New York: ACM Press.

Shetty, K. A. V. (2002, September). *E-government: Blueprint for the State of Tamil Nadu, India*. Retrieved April 16, 2006, from http://www.idd.

bham.ac.uk/research/dissertations/2001-2002/shetty.pdf

Shirur, P. (2006, April). Public sector summit 2006: Connecting government, empowering citizens. *egov, 2*(4), 17-18. Retrieved April 9, 2006, from http://www.egovonline.net/pdf/april06.pdf

Sowa, J. F., & Zachman, J. A. (1992). Extending and formalizing the framework for information systems architecture. *IBM Systems Journal, 31,* 590-616.

Tang, A., Han, J., & Chen, P. (2004). A comparative analysis of architecture frameworks. In IEEE (Ed.), *Proceedings of the 11th Asia-Pacific Software Engineering Conference (Apsec'04)* (pp. 640-647). Washington, DC: IEEE Computer Society.

The Chief Information Officers Council. (1999). *Federal enterprise architecture framework: version 1.1.* Retrieved October 6, 2005, from http://www.cio.gov/archive/fedarch1.pdf

The Open Group. (2003). *TOGAF (the open group architecture framework) Version 8.1: Enterprise Edition.* Retrieved October 6, 2005, from http://www.opengroup.org/architecture/togaf/#download

Vincent, S., & Mahesh, A. (2005). *E isn't everything.* Retrieved April 9, 2006, from http://www.indiatogether.org/2005/apr/edt-egovern.htm

Vittal, N. (2001, October 20). *Cultural dimensions of e-governance.* Retrieved April 9, 2006, from http://cvc.nic.in/vscvc/cvcspeeches/sp4oct01.pdf

Zachman, J. A. (n.d.). *Concepts of the framework for enterprise architecture: Background, description, and utility.* Retrieved December 1, 2005, from http://members.ozemail.com.au/~visible/papers/zachman3.htm

Zachman, J. A. (1987). A framework for information systems architecture. *IBM Systems Journal, 26,* 276-292.

Zwahr, T., & Finger, M. (2004). *Enhancing the e-governance model: Enterprise architecture as a potential methodology to build a holistic framework.* Retrieved September 10, 2005, from http://au.itpapers.zdnet.com/whitepaper.aspx?kw=it%20governance%20model&docid=135159

ENDNOTES

[1] This research was partially supported by Infosys Technologies Limited, Bangalore under the Infosys Fellowship Award.
[2] "Zachman Framework" is the copyright of The Zachman Institute for Framework Advancement.

Chapter XVII
Federated Enterprise Resource Planning Systems

Nico Brehm
Carl-von-Ossietzky-Universität Oldenburg, Germany

Daniel Lübke
University Hannover, Germany

Jorge Marx Gómez
Carl-von-Ossietzky-Universität Oldenburg, Germany

ABSTRACT

Enterprise resource planning (ERP) systems consist of many software components, which provide specific functionality. As ERP systems become more complex, the financial expenditures that are associated with the application of such systems dramatically increase. Furthermore, ERP system development of nowadays is product-oriented and coordinated by only one instance at any one time. Consequently, each product has a separate data model, which is the basis for the integration of various types of business applications. Based on this fact, the selection of the covered functional enterprise sectors as well as the implemented functions is controlled by the respective vendor, too. Thus, enhancements and modifications of the standard software product are incumbent upon the software vendors. A cross-vendor standardization of data models for ERP systems and the establishment of unified architectural model, however, would change this situation. The new idea is to develop a novel ERP system architecture, which facilitates an overall reusability of individual business components (BC) through a shared and non-monolithic architecture based on Web services. The presented approach uses Web services to wrap up ERP components that are provided within a distributed system, which appears as an ERP community and serves as a vendor-independent platform.

INTRODUCTION

Since the advent of Web services during the last years, software components can be easily distributed and remotely accessed. These components become small services, which provide clients with specific functions. These can be invoked using standardized protocols like simple object access protocol (SOAP) (Gudgin, Hadley, Mendelsohn, Moreau, & Nielsen, 2003). The goal is to create an infrastructure allowing business applications to seamlessly discover and use Web services. This will hopefully make the integration of different applications and the development of distributed applications easier. This kind of architecture, called service oriented architecture (SOA), provides a transparent environment in which applications can be composed out of services.

Some hopes and visions are associated with SOA, for example, enterprise application integration (EAI) strives to seamlessly connect different systems in an enterprise mainly by utilizing Web service standards. While EAI has become an objective for larger enterprises due to the huge number of deployed systems, small- and medium-sized enterprises (SME) still struggle to support business processes using integrated IT systems. SMEs compete against larger corporations utilizing their flexibility and their ability to innovate. In order to compete better, these SMEs need to deploy ERP systems to support their business processes. But to stay as flexible and competitive as today, SMEs have to customize their ERP system each time the business processes change. However, ERP systems are complex and their customization as well as maintenance is costly. Therefore, investments into large and powerful ERP systems often do not pay off financially for SMEs who do not have the necessary financial resources to deploy and maintain such systems at all.

Two approaches try to fill this gap: Cheaper ERP systems with less functionality have been offered and the concept of application service providing (ASP) has emerged. However, both solutions have their drawbacks. ERP systems offering less functionality do not realize all possible opportunities and do not address maintenance costs. Even worse, ASP (i.e., the operation of systems by a third party in an external data-center) has been rejected by the market because enterprises are not willing to store their valuable data externally and the distribution of responsibilities creates management problems (Walsh, 2003). Our aim is therefore a solution, which combines local data management with reduced costs and flexible support for changing and optimizing business processes.

The result is an ERP system whose logic is completely composed of Web services called federated ERP (FERP). The Web services are dynamically arranged to support the company's business processes (Krüger, Marx Gómez, Rautenstrauch, & Lübke, 2004). Such an ERP system has the advantage of storing all relevant data in-house as well as being extensible by integrating as many Web services as required for realizing the desired functionality. For implementing these ideas, some challenges have to be overcome. In course of this chapter, we will focus on the following problems:

- Management of user interfaces in highly dynamic, model-driven environments.
- Server-side data-management.
- Organization and standardization of Web services for the envisioned FERP system.
- Security considerations.

This chapter is structured as follows: Within the next section, we present background information and definitions of the most important terms. In the third section, we discuss the four main points as previously presented. The open research questions and future problems are presented in the fourth section. Finally, a conclusion is given.

BACKGROUND

An ERP system is a highly integrated software system representing different types of business application systems. In the majority of cases, there is a smooth transition between these system parts whereby it is almost impossible to locate isolated components. In fact, ERP vendors provide packages of business functions, which can be associated to different enterprise sectors. These functions are interwoven, which means that a function can invoke another function without a central control instance. This characteristic causes the problem that it is difficult to isolate a group of functions as a discrete component. With the intention of a sustainable reusability of discrete software components, ERP vendors started redesigning their products step by step.

The main objective is to achieve a component-oriented software design. One example for this phenomenon is the company SAP®AG with their ERP system SAP®/R3™. Earlier versions of this product appeared as a monolithic solution. With the BAPI technology (business application programming interface) (see SAP Library, 2005), it is now possible to encapsulate single business functions in business objects. Furthermore, there is the possibility to remotely access these business objects or to recombine them within business workflows.

This chapter introduces the conceptual foundation of FERP systems and shows how a component-oriented ERP solution is transferred to a Web service-based FERP system. The visionary development process of such a system is supposed to be pushed by a community of ERP software

Figure 1. Conventional ERP system architecture

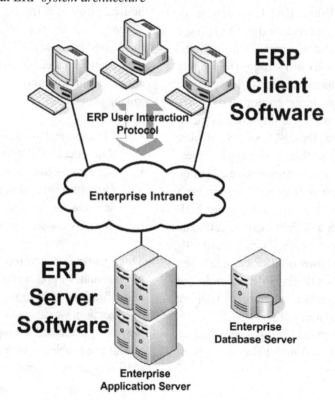

vendors whereby the degree of implementation varies according to the different entrepreneurial motives of different developers.

Definition 1

An *ERP system* is a standard software system, which provides functionality to integrate and automate the business practices associated with the operations or production aspects of a company. The integration is based on a common data model for all system components and extents to more than one enterprise sectors (see Rautenstrauch & Schulze, 2003; Robey, Ross, & Boudreau, 2002).

Conventional ERP architectures are based on n-tier models including presentation tier, potentially different application tiers, and a database tier. The functional software components of ERP systems are administered on a central application server, which is responsible for the coordination of interactions with end users, for the execution of business logic, and for the communication with the enterprise database server. The communication between the application server and GUI clients can be either based on standard protocols like HTTP or proprietary protocols like the DIAG protocol, which was developed by SAP® in order to exchange requests and responses between SAP®GUI and SAP®R3 servers or in later versions SAP® enterprise central component servers, which act as applications servers in this context. In cases where different application servers have to be interconnected (e.g., in order to invoke remote functions calls), protocols like RFC or also HTTP are used. Figure 1 shows the architecture of today's ERP systems.

ERP system development of nowadays is product-oriented and coordinated by only one instance at any one time. Consequently, each product has a separate data model, which is the basis for the integration of various types of business applications. Based on this fact, the selection of the covered functional enterprise sectors as well as the implemented functions is controlled by the

respective vendor, too. Thus, enhancements and modifications of the standard software product are incumbent upon the software vendors. Various managerial motives (e.g., actual situation of the company, missing know-how, strategic objectives, or inadequate empathy for cooperation) are the deciding factors for the mostly compromise-driven orchestration of ERP system components. A cross-vendor standardization of a data model for ERP systems and the establishment of unified architectural model, however, would change this situation. Thus in theory a cross-vendor composition of ERP functions becomes possible whereas the coordination of this process is individual and vendor-independent.

Definition 2

A *federated ERP system* (FERP system) is an ERP system that consists of system components that are distributed within a computer network. The overall functionality is provided by an ensemble of allied network nodes that all together appear as a single ERP system to the user. Different ERP system components can be developed by different vendors.

Definition 3

An *ERP system component* in this case is a reusable, closed, and marketable software module, which provides services over a well-defined interface. These components can be combined with other components in a not foreseeable manner (see Turowski, 2003, p. 19).

Figure 2 shows the two approaches in comparison to each other. The left hand side represents the architecture of a conventional ERP system where a closed amount of ERP components (C1, C2, ..., C6) are installed on the same application server and were developed by the same software vendor. The right hand side shows an open ERP network where each node is assigned to one ERP component, which is provided as service (S1, S2, ..., Sn). This network consists of allied network nodes that all together represent a feder-

Figure 2. Conventional ERP system with ERP components (C1-C6) vs. a federated ERP system that provides its ERP components as services (S1-Sn)

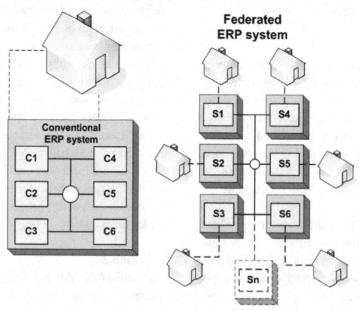

Figure 3. Vision of a federated ERP system landscape where ERP software components can be developed and provided by different software vendors

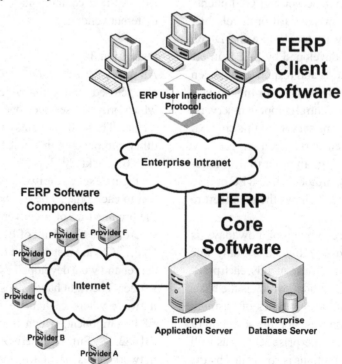

ated ERP system. New components are added as new network nodes that provide corresponding services.

The main disadvantages of conventional ERP systems are that in most cases, not all of the installed components are needed, high-end computer hardware is required, and that the customizing of such systems is very expensive because product specific know-how of experts is necessary. Due to the expensive proceedings of installation and maintenance, only large enterprises can afford complex ERP systems, which provide business logic of all sectors of the functional enterprise organisation. Contrary to these aspects, FERP systems allow the separation of local and remote functions whereby no local resources are wasted for unnecessary components. Furthermore, single components are executable on small computers and due to decreasing complexity of the local system also installation and maintenance costs subside. Figure 3 shows how the ERP system is supplied by a network of FERP business logic components, which provide all potentially needed business functions.

ARCHITECTURE OF FEDERATED ERP SYSTEMS

Overview

The federated ERP-system as presented in the second section is a distributed system composed of Web services. Therefore, the underlying architecture needs to fulfill the following requirements:

- Integrate the Web services to provide the needed functionality.
- Execute and control the workflow.
- Manage data access and storage.
- Authenticate and authorize users.
- Provide usable interfaces to the users.

For minimizing customization effort and reduction costs for changing business processes, the following non-functional requirements hold:

- Changes in business processes should be easy to introduce into the system.
- Changes in the federated ERP-system should be easy to incorporate.
- Changes in the federated ERP-system should require minimal software distribution effort for changes.

Requirements were grouped and assigned to layers resulting in a three-tier system design (see Figure 4):

1. Web services are the standard logic components of the system and the set of all Web services forms the first layer.
2. The Web service orchestration and business process layer is in charge of managing the data and control flow of the application through the business processes.
3. The presentation layer generates user interface descriptions for interactive steps in the business processes.

We decided to use an application server infrastructure in order to be able to centralize many tasks. Thus, many updates need only be done on the application server and do not affect clients. For our prototype implementation, we used the J2EE platform represented by a Tomcat Web container

Figure 4. Layers of a federated-ERP system

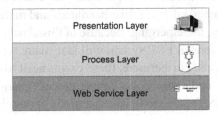

and the AXIS Web services framework. The clients were implemented in Java Swing.

For better explanation of the concepts, we will use the same example process throughout the next sections (the process is taken from Lübke, Lüecke, Schneider, & Marx Gómez, 2006). The example is a simple process of an order acceptance. The profit margin of an incoming order is checked. If the profit margin has been breached, a manager must decide if the order is accepted or not. For example, some orders of important clients can be seen as advertising and therefore, need to make not as much profit as orders normally would do. If the order is accepted, it is forwarded to production. The whole process is illustrated as an event-driven process chain (EPC) in Figure 5. EPCs consist of so-called events symbolizing the state of an organization and functions representing actions taken within the process. A function is triggered by a certain state and results in a new state. A whole process is triggered by events as well and results in a changed overall system. Therefore, an EPC is roughly an alternating event-function sequence starting and finishing with an event. To control the execution of process connectors can be added for splitting and joining the control flow as illustrated in the example process. EPCs are used for modeling all business processes in the Federated-ERP project and are stored at the application server in EPML (Mendling & Nütt-gens, 2005).

User Interface Generation

Every ERP system needs to be operated by users. In the end, they need to make decisions, retrieve data, or enter new records. While classical ERP systems offer clients for personal computers only, now mobile devices, like handhelds and mobile phones, are emerging. Because of this situation, the federated ERP system will face many types of clients. Furthermore, these clients need to be easily updatable. For a simple process change, it is not feasible to update hundreds of possibly

mobile or distributed computers. Thus, the user interface must be managed on the server-side and must be platform-neutral.

Our approach for minimizing the effort needed to develop and customize the user interface is to automatically generate the interfaces from the business process descriptions. Much research has been done in the field of model-based user interface (MB-UI), which aims to model user interfaces in the way program logic is modeled in UML. Research in these fields has been going on for more than a decade. For example, Paterno (1999) gives an overview over of the field of MB-UI. Numerous design environments have been proposed as result of MB-UI. Each differs in the number and type of models used (for a thorough overview the reader is referred to da Silva (2002). However, most approaches share a common element: the task model. Fortunately, this task model is easily related to our approach. The business process model is in fact a task model on a very high abstraction level

Figure 5. Example order process

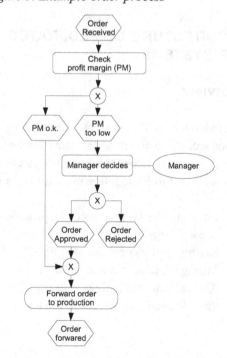

(see Trætteberg, 1999). Furthermore, the field of MB-UI has matured; especially insight into reasons for failure of some approaches has been beneficial for our research. Common mistakes and problems concerning practical adoption of MB-UI techniques are listed by Trætteberg, Molina, & Nunes, 2004): The biggest problem has been the complexity of the introduced models. While complex and detailed models give the designer the best level of control, such models are difficult to learn, time-consuming to design, and hard to maintain. Therefore, our approach particularly strives to reduce the inherent complexity. This is especially important for being useful for the targeted, non-expert audience.

Because we assume the business process to be already modeled, the user interface is expressed by stereotyping business functions. Four stereotypes have been introduced:

- **Selection:** The user shall select data from a collection of possible choices. For example, select product from a catalogue.
- **Edit:** The user shall edit some information object from the data model. For example, edit order.
- **Control:** The user wants to explicitly invoke some action. This is used to model navigational decisions. For example, "Accept order."

- **User:** The user has to do something by himself (e.g., planning, comparing, etc.).

These four actions can be attached to a business function and are visualized by small icons on the left-hand side of the function. The annotated business processes are downloaded by the client software, which generates user interfaces from these models and sends the data and user decisions back to the server. This way, the user interface can simply be edited by installing new business process models on the server. For generating the user interfaces, the data types are used to create matching editors: Because Web services are based on XML, the data types are represented by XML Schema definitions. XML schema recursively defines data types: Primitive types can be grouped to complex types. Complex and primitive types can be grouped to new complex types and so on. Editors are created by traversing this tree-structure and look for matching editors registered in the system. At least for each primitive type, like integers and strings, an editor is provided by the system. Therefore, a (possibly primitive) editor can be generated for each XML Schema. Figure 6 shows a simple generated editor for a customer record.

Figure 7 shows the hierarchical refinement of the example process with user interface stereotypes and the resulting user interface using a

Figure 6. Generation of a simple user interface for a customer record

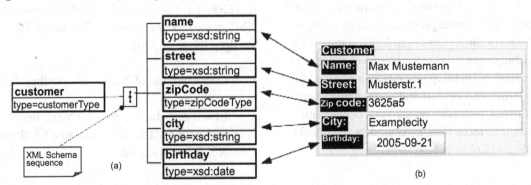

Figure 7. Refinement of the business process and user interface generation

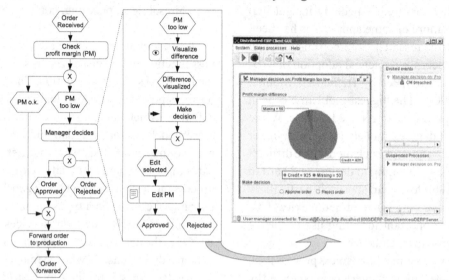

custom editor. The client application shows the processes needing further action by the user and the processes, which are currently executed by someone else. This information is given on the right hand side.

Since the user interface generation is based on the business process description, context information can be given to the user. For example, descriptions of the currently active business function can be displayed. In our prototype, these are realized by giving tool-tip information. At this point, it is even possible to integrate experience bases to facilitate the communication between developers, process designers, and end users.

Since this approach is based on the process description only, it is possible to generate user interfaces for different target platforms. For example, a connector for XForms—an XML standard for describing input forms—is under development and generation of HTML pages is possible as well for integration into intranet and portal applications. For further discussion on the topic of generation of user interfaces from EPC models see Lüecke (2005) and Lübke et al. (2006).

Server-Side Data Management

When executing a process model, which can not only include user interfaces but also Web service calls, corresponding data in terms of business objects needs to be managed. If a process shall be started, the application server creates a new process instance. The instance represents a running process including its whole state. The state is comprised of the data objects currently in use and the statistics which business functions have already been executed in order to evaluate the joins in the control flow. The data management currently follows the blackboard approach as presented by Alonso, Casati, Kuno, and Machiraju (2004). All process instance data is stored as XML at the process' instance. The advantages of the deep usage of XML are:

- Consistent use of XML between the whole platform.
- Efficiency during development because powerful XML technologies like XPath and XSLT are available.

- Easy user interface generation through XML schema.

Using XML throughout the application has the advantage that Web services' parameters can be simply extracted from the blackboard by use of XSLT. The Web services' output can be stored after XSLT transformations to the native XML Schema, too. The application server needs to offer local services for data management. The business processes need to be able to store and retrieve persistent data. The corresponding functionality is offered by the means of services. Data objects referenced by XPath expressions can be used from the business processes. The application server must retrieve the matching business objects from the database and save any changes made.

However, some disadvantages are also connected to this approach:

- XML processing is not efficient. Using plain objects would increase performance.
- If non-XML technologies are to be used like relational database systems or CORBA services instead of Web services, the XML data need to be transformed, which is an expensive operation.
- The XML data format is very space-consuming hindering replication within cluster environments.

These weaknesses can be addressed by building scalable applications, which can be distributed to many servers in order to improve performance. To overcome the third disadvantage, "sticky sessions" can be used in which a process instance is always run on the same server. Thus, replication is minimized.

Organization and Standardization of Web Services

Starting from the syntactical standardization approach of FERP systems as proposed in Brehm

& Marx Gómez, 2005), it is possible to define dependencies between the different operations of FERP Web services. This structure is based on the preliminary idea that FERP Web services are classified according to the enterprise sector which their offered operations belong to. The basis of the FERP Web service specification model is the summarization of all functions (Web service operations) that belong to the same sector of the functional business organization. Functions of the same sector are assigned to the same FERP Web service. In this first proposal, we classify the following Web service types in the context of FERP systems whereas we have to mention that this classification is incomplete and only serves as an example:

- Production planning and controlling.
- Accounting.
- Logistics.
- Sales and distribution.
- Materials management.
- Quality management.
- Project management.
- Human resource management.

According to a literature review in the area of component standardization models as Turowski (2003) described, the standardization of FERP Web services must include the following levels:

- Syntactic level
- Behavioral level
- Synchronization level
- Quality-of-service level

Figure 8 shows an uncompleted example syntactic specification of a production planning and controlling (PP) Web service as presented in Brehm et al. (2005). Based on the specification of data types (e.g., BOM, work plan, operation, etc.), message types are specified. These message types are used to describe the functions of the PP Web service. Out of this functionality specification, different Web services can be derived, which implement the overall component functionality in a different completeness. The Web service descriptions are expressed in the Web service description language (WSDL).

Semantic Web services are Web services whose properties, capabilities, interfaces, and effects are encoded in an unambiguous, machine-understandable form (see McIlraith, Son, & Zeng, 2001). Research works that deal with semantic Web services aim at the provision of a comprehensive Web service description, discovery, and mediation framework. Because UDDI, WSDL, and SOAP are not sufficient, other specification languages like Web ontology language (OWL) (see W3C, 2004) and the resource description framework (RDF) (see W3C, 2004a) are used. This approach is more abstract then the presented proposal because the efforts within the scope of

semantic Web services do not concentrate on a specific type of Web service. The shown proposal is based on XML schema to define a fixed language for ERP systems as basis for the communication between software components of a distributed application.

Security Considerations

Security Model and Requirements

In connection with the common use of distributed applications, several *security problems* exist. The most important security objectives in the case of distributed ERP systems are:

- *Confidentiality* of transmitted data.
- *Integrity* of transmitted data.
- *Authenticity* of communication partners.

Figure 8. Uncompleted example FERP Web service specification and three possible Web service descriptions (see Brehm et al., 2005)

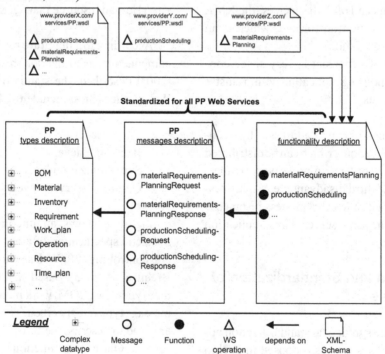

- *Availability* of data and functionality.
- *Anonymity* of communication partners against unauthorized parties.
- *Non-repudiation* of transactions.
- *Reliability* (trustability) of communication partners.

Constructing a security layer and involving it into the already existing architecture, attention should be paid to the different specifications of individual security requirements of different companies. Within the shown context of a shared ERP system, those requirements commonly correspond to message integrity, authenticity, and data confidentiality of all interface calls and responses and thus, of the whole network traffic. As these strategic security objectives differ from each utilizing enterprise to another, it is essential that the security model is open for virtually all security mechanisms and standards, which allows the processing of generic definitions of security policies. Referring to the existing security mechanisms, security policies describe the concrete security requirements of the appropriate network node including the respective configuration parameters. Based on this approach, a suitable policy processor is able to audit all incoming messages for security conformance on the enterprises security policy and to extend all outgoing messages according to the security policy of the remote network node, which is commonly the service provider as proposed by Brehm, Marx Gómez, and Rautenstrauch, 2005b). Attributes of such security policies can partly be modeled directly in the EPCs. Functions in EPCs can be assigned to security mechanisms like encryption or decryption algorithms or user roles (e.g., the manager role in Figure 5).

Local and Remote Security

Within the context of FERP systems, local and remote security considerations have to be differentiated. Concerning this matter, the primary tasks of the FERP system core component, which is installed on the application server of an enterprise, can be split into responsibilities regarding access control and the assurance of confidentiality. Local access control mechanisms use role-based authentication and authorization models (e.g., passwords or public key infrastructure (PKI) elements like certificates) as to authenticate local users and to permit or deny their requests accordingly. Therefore, the system is equipped with a user management module, which maps possible activities to user permissions. A typical requirement in this case is that only users in the corresponding role can invoke a function or may access the corresponding user interface. However, in some situations the roles must be fine-grained. For example, it may be necessary to have a special manager who has to approve the order. In our example, it may be necessary that the manager of the customer's consultant must approve the order. For realizing this functionality, conditions can be appended to the roles: These conditions can access the process' instance data. In this case, the order is assigned to a customer who is assigned to his consultant. Therefore, the manager role can have the restriction of being accessible only to the consultant's manager. This security information can be used during run-time to control the access to ERP functionality.

Contrary to conventional ERP systems, FERP systems have to access functions of potentially not well-known component providers whereas the authentication of these providers and the establishment of a secure communication channel are not sufficient. Following the vision of a flexible and open FERP network where FERP component vendors can provide their functionality to all participating network nodes as straight forward as possible, it is not practicable to establish trust relationships, which are exclusively based on directly applied human intelligence (e.g., by persons who are talking to each other). This aspect is still unsolved and shows a frequently discussed research question. A number of trust models as for instance centralized rating systems as applied in *Ebay* and *Amazon* auctions or social network analysis techniques (e.g., Friend of a Friend (FOAF) networks) have been developed in e-commerce, e-business, security, and multi-agent systems, which have to be investigated according to their practicability in future research work.

FUTURE TRENDS AND RESEARCH

Many options concerning process modeling and service composition have to be researched. While SOA promises to better integrate software with its underlying processes, the models are still not integrated well nor even are unified. Our approach so far has been to simply use and extend EPCs, which are a business process modeling language. However, they are not as powerful as some workflow languages. If in practice, these additional abilities of workflow languages like Petri nets are needed, much research has to be done how to synchronize between different models. Business models are an important part of the software requirements and therefore often need to be traced forward and backward during the development. If EPCs cannot be used everywhere, a mapping between EPCs and the workflow language used needs to be established. However, tracing problems still arise if only using EPCs; Software requirements are more than business processes. For example, use cases are a very beneficial way of documenting software requirements. These need to be linked to the processes. The same holds true for test cases, which are based on requirements and the executable processes.

On the technical side, the internal modeling and mapping between business objects and their external representation in XML can be improved. While the deep use of XML and the blackboard approach is sufficient for use within our prototype, this approach is not well suited for productive use. XML processing is very slow in contrast to the use of native objects like Java Beans. Further-

more, other types of services like those offered by Enterprise Java Beans via RMI and CORBA cannot be called with XML data. However, the migration to an object-oriented approach for data management results in the need for converting huge amounts of data from and to XML. Furthermore, the use of practical techniques like XPath has to be emulated. The system's user interface part can be extended with modules for generating interfaces for mobile devices and Web applications. The necessary infrastructure is already existent making these tasks easy to solve.

Chances, Problems, and Risks

The difficulties of the application of conventional ERP systems are based on the complexity of the currently available products. The ERP market offers small, medium, and large ERP systems, which can be classified by the amount of covered enterprise sectors and the amount of included functions. Starting from the general statement that small- and medium-sized enterprises (SME) have almost the same functional ERP system requirements like large enterprises have, a dilemma opens up. Because SME cannot afford large ERP systems such as SAP®R3, Oracle®E-Business Suite, or SSA®Baan ERP 5, choices are based on compromise-driven decisions. Contrary to conventional ERP systems, FERP systems feature the following advantages, which aim at the solution of these problems:

- Due to the provision of isolated components, it is possible to charge the utilizing enterprises according to their needs and by this to decrease the overall ERP system application costs.
- Enterprises do not have to run high-end hardware in order to meet the requirements related to the application of complex ERP systems. Hardware can be made available by service providers.

- ERP service providers only have to make a part of the total system available, which reduces their time to market and their financial investment.
- A distributed system architecture is more scalable then a monolithic system.
- Distributed systems may be more reliable then monolithic systems. If one service goes down, then other services might continue to work. Moreover, it might be possible to replace the service with another one.

Beside this advantages various disadvantages, problems, and risks exist:

- Security considerations play an important role when a public network is used as communication basis. Particularly confidentiality of enterprise data is a critical aspect, which has to be considered in this context. Furthermore, a distributed access control model has to be developed in order to ensure the protection of local and remote resources, which means that only authorized users are permitted to access these resources. A federated identity management provides a solution of this problem (see Siddharth et al., 2003).
- The relationships between the different participating parties are based on different trust levels. Trust not only refers to misuse aspects but also the professional correctness of the provided functionality has to be secured. This was already discussed in Brehm and Marx Gómez (2005a), but trust measurement techniques deserve closer attention in this case.
- Performance problems will arise because the volume of data to be submitted is going to be immense in many cases (e.g., a large number of input and output data has to be exchanged between accounting-service consumer and service provider in order to calculate an actual target report).

Data models, interfaces, and architectural components have to be standardized in order to make FERP services interoperable. A solution for this problem was already previously shown and proposed in Brehm et al. (2005).

CONCLUSION

Comparing distributed ERP systems and ERP systems running on only one computer, distributed systems offer a lot of advantages. However, the design and development of such architectures are subject to a number of problems. The chapter presents a basis for the introduction of FERP Web services and discusses the pros and cons of an ERP solution as part of a service landscape where different vendors are appealed for the implementation and provision of ERP Web services in a federated manner. The proposed approach tunes in to the vision of a development process, which abstracts from concrete implementations. Nevertheless, there are a lot of open questions left which hinder machines to interact as providers of ERP software based on a process model even if ERP Web services act on standardized requirements. Because ERP systems process confidential enterprise data, security considerations play an important role when an open network like the internet is used. The future work must pick up these problems to realize the vision of a loosely coupled ERP system, which allows the combination of software components of different providers.

REFERENCES

Alonso, G., Casati, F., Kuno, H., & Machiraju, V. (2004). *Web services—Concepts, architectures, and applications. Data-centric systems and applications.* London: Springer.

Brehm, N., & Marx Gómez, J. (2005). Standardization approach for federated ERP systems based on

Web services. *Proceedings of the 1st International Workshop on Engineering Service Compositions*, Amsterdam.

Brehm, N., & Marx Gómez, J. (2005a). Resource sharing in ERP networks based on secure Web services. *International Journal on Information Privacy and Security (JIPS), 1*(2), 29-48.

Brehm, N., Marx Gómez, J., & Rautenstrauch, C. (2006). Security architecture of federated ERP-systems for small and medium enterprises. *International Journal of Information Systems and Change Management (IJISCM), 1*(1), 99-111.

Brehm, N., Marx Gómez, J., & Rautenstrauch C. (2005b). Web service-based ERP systems and an open security model. In *Proceedings of 16th IRMA International Conference—Managing Modern Organizations with Information Technology, (IRMA'2005)*, San Diego, (USA)

da Silva, P. P. (2002). User interface declarative models and development environments: A survey. In Palanque, & Paterno (Eds.), *DSV-IS, volume 1946 of Lecture Notes in Computer Science* (pp. 207–226) London: Springer.

Gudgin, M., Hadley, M., Mendelsohn, N., Moreau, J. J., & Nielsen, H. F. (2003) *SOAP Version 1.2 Part 1: Messaging Framework*. Technical report, World Wide Web Consortium, Retrieved January 5, 2005, from http://www.w3.org/TR/2003/REC-soap12-part1-20030624/

Krüger, O., Marx Gómez, J., Rautenstrauch, C., & Lübke, D. (2004). Developing a distributed ERP system based on peer-to-peer-networks and Web services. In J. Marx Gómez (Ed.), *Proceedings of the Workshop for Intelligent Mobile Agents in Peer-to-Peer Networks, EIS 2004.*

Lübke, D., Lüecke, T., Schneider, K., & Marx Gómez, J. (2006). Using event-driven process chains for model-driven development of business applications, In M. Nüttgens & J. Mendling (Eds.), *Proceedings of the XML4BPM 2006.*

Lüecke, T. (2005). *Development of a concept for creating and managing user interfaces bound to business processes*. Unpublished Master Thesis, University Hannover, Germany.

McIlraith, S., Son, T., & Zeng, H. (2001). Semantic Web services. In *IEEE Intelligent Systems* (Special Issue on the Semantic Web)

Mendling, J., & Nüttgens, M. (2005). EPC markup language (EPML)—*An XML-based interchange format for event-driven process chains (EPC)*. Technical report, Vienna. University of Economics and Business Administration.

Paterno, F. (1999). *Model-based design and evaluation of interactive applications*. London: Springer-Verlag.

Rautenstrauch, C., & Schulze, T. (2003). Informatik für Wirtschaftswissenschaftler und Wirtschaftsinformatiker, Berlin et al.

Robey, D., Ross, J., & Boudreau, M. (2002). Learning to implement enterprise systems: An exploratory study of the dialectics of change. *Journal of Management Information Systems, 19*(1), 17-46.

SAP Library. (2005). *Business application programming interface (BAPI)*. Retrieved from http://help.sap.com/saphelp_erp2004/helpdata/en/7e/5e11ee4a1611d1894c0000e829fbbd/frameset.htm

Siddharth, B. et al. (2003). *Web services federation language (WS-Federation)*. Retrieved from http://www-128.ibm.com/developerworks/library/specification/ws-fed/

Trætteberg, H., Molina, P. J., & Nunes, N. J. (2004). Making model-based UI design practical: Usable and open methods and tools. In Vanderonckt, Nunes, & Rich (Eds.), *Intelligent user interfaces* (pp. 376-377). ACM.

Trætteberg, H. (1999). Modelling work. Workflow and task modelling. In Vanderdonckt, & Puerta (Eds.), *CADUI* (pp 275-280). Kluwer.

Turowski, K. (2003). *Fachkomponenten: Komponentenbasierte betriebliche Anwendungssysteme*, Aachen.

W3C. (2004). *OWL Web ontology language*. Retrieved from http://www.w3.org/TR/owl-features/

W3C. (2004a). *RDF vocabulary description language 1.0: RDF Schema*. Retrieved from http://www.w3.org/TR/owl-features/

Walsh, K. R. (2003). Analyzing the application ASP concept: Technologies, economies, and strategies. *Communications of the ACM, 46*(8), 103-107.

Chapter XVIII
A Network–Based View of Enterprise Architecture

Bala Iyer
Babson College, USA

David Dreyfus
Boston University, USA

Per Gyllstrom
PFPC Worldwide Inc., USA

ABSTRACT

Traditional notions of architecture have focused on the components and (or domains of interest—process, data, and infrastructure) aspects of architecture. Their goal is to separate concerns into modules and provide interfaces between modules. This view helps designers understand the ideal or espoused view of architecture. In our work, we view architecture from a dependency perspective. These dependencies evolve over time, creating an emergent architecture. The emergence is influenced by both technical and social factors. Dependencies occur during the design, production, and use of enterprise components. This leads us to use network-based analysis techniques in order to understand the emerging dependency networks.In order to provide architects with support tools to communicate and make decisions about architecture, we describe the data requirements and algorithms that can be used to build a decision support system that enable enterprises to incorporate a network perspective in their decision-making process. We present our approach and methods in the context of a case study

INTRODUCTION

A fundamental assumption behind this work is that reasoning with architecture is a key determinant of successful information systems design, maintenance, and evolution. Stakeholders need architectural representations in order to make resource allocation decisions and perform risk assessment. In addition, we believe that current techniques fall short in providing stakeholders with a vehicle that help them make informed decisions about information system design. Part of the problem is that IS architecture has no universally accepted definition in either the research arena or in the practitioner world (Ross, 2003). Architecture has been viewed strategically (Henderson & Venkatraman, 1993; McKay & Brockway, 1989; Morris & Ferguson, 1993; Ross, 2003; Sauer & Willcocks, 2002), organizationally (Byrd & Turner, 2000; Dreyfus & Iyer, 2006; Duncan, 1995; Iyer & Gottlieb, 2004; Richardson, Jackson, & Dickson, 1990; Weill & Broadbent, 1998), and technologically (Malone & Crowston, 1994; Messerschmitt & Szyperski, 2003; Nezlek, Jain, & Nazareth, 1999; Parnas, 1972). These perspectives, while individually interesting, do not provide the integrated view of architecture that is required to analyze risk and make resource allocation decisions. Another part of the problem is that these perspectives often focus on the idealized system and not the system in use.

Previous studies have summarized that an IS architecture includes a group of shared, tangible IT resources (i.e., hardware, software, data, training, management, etc.) that provide a platform to launch present and future business applications (Duncan, 1995; Kayworth, Chatterjee, & Sambamurthy, 2001; McKay et al., 1989; Weill et al., 1998). Architecture, as implemented through its IT infrastructure, should be flexible, reliable, robust, scalable, and adaptable (Byrd et al., 2000; Duncan, 1995; Kayworth et al., 2001). It should support the reuse of business components within a firm while supporting firm responsiveness, innovativeness, and economies of scope (Kayworth et al., 2001). A review of these and other articles clearly illustrate that when the given definition for architecture is translated into action, the concept becomes very complicated.

Architecture implementation also involves learning effects. As researchers have explored organizations making changes to architecture, they have identified two strategies: localized exploitation or enterprise-wide integration (Allen,

1977). Most techniques seem to support the former and there are many tools that support the latter. These techniques and tools, however, focus on the system at a point in time. Changes to the system, on the other hand, do not occur in one step, they occur in stages (Ross, 2003). Although seemingly obvious, these insights don't seem to have been translated into tools or techniques.

Architecture is more than technology. It reflects and supports business strategy. Architecture is not just concerned with the allocation of resources at the physical level, but also with the support of strategic business goals. The architectural challenge is not just cost minimization in the allocation of task to computational device, but the alignment of the task structure (Gasser, 1986) supported by the information system with the business objectives of the organization. Thus, the approach we take to architecture must enable communication and decision making between and by business and technology stakeholders.

Zachman provides a useful framework that identifies the components of an IT architecture as well as the various perspectives taken during the design and implementation of an architecture by the different stakeholders (Zachman, 1987). According to Zachman, there is no such thing as a single information architecture; there are many. Separate architectures exist for scope/objectives, business model, information system description, technology model, detailed description, and machine language description. For these six categories, there are also the descriptions for *who, what, how, where, when,* and *why.* Altogether, there are 36 possible architectures. This insight liberates us from the constraint of a single architectural perspective.

D'Souza and Wills (1999) describe the architecture of a system as the set of design decisions that constrain its implementation and maintenance. They discuss the need for many different architectural views of a system, each using a different set of elements (abstractions) and each conveying significant design decisions. Some common architectural views focus on technology deployment (hardware, networks), processes, software packages and their structure, object types, and relationships.

Iyer et al. (2004) identified three views through which we can examine architecture. The first view is the espoused (architecture-in-design). It is the outcome of the process of defining and modeling the architecture and describes the planned dependencies between system modules. They argue that although there may be multiple participants in the design process, the espoused view is the province of the IS architect. This is the view we most commonly associate with architecture. In reality, most if not all enterprise architectures are the result of individual "silo" application implementations or applications brought into the enterprise though mergers and acquisitions, resulting in an enterprise architecture that likely will differ from the espoused view. This emergent architecture is the second view. It is a descriptive view of the actual dependencies that exist among system modules. It is the system as it exists at a point in time. Finally, Iyer et al. (2004) define the third view, architecture-in-use (architecture-in-operation). The in-use view highlights the dependencies between and among system components and organizational groups that arise from the business of doing the work of the enterprise—selling products, buying supplies, managing employees, etc.—as employees, suppliers, and other stakeholders interact with the system.

The emergent architecture, the focus of this chapter, can be a result of conscious or unconscious action (Alexander, 1964). That is, organizations with information systems can evaluate projects with the intent to understand how the project will impact the emergent architecture, or they can evaluate projects without this architectural perspective. An organization can develop an architecture, implement it according to plan, and then have a series of subsequent IT projects that, in response to specific or general business requirements, modify it. Iyer et al. (2004) argue

that the way architecture emerges may subsequently impact how well the firm can achieve IT/business strategy alignment as well as the goals of flexibility, reliability, robustness, scalability, adaptability, and reusability.

In the quest to align IT and business strategy, many approaches are relevant. Take, for example, the technical perspective taken by architecture modeling (Zhao & Siau, 2002). UML modelers develop use cases from which models are developed, structured analysis highlights the relationships between data elements and processes (Yourdon & Constantine, 1986), and Petri-Nets have been used to analyze coordination constraints (Gunter, 2000).

Most of the approaches described so far have focused on the components. In some cases, they focus on data and process independently, or, as in the case of objects, they encapsulate data and process, but deal with them as a combined independent entity. These approaches are useful to understand espoused or intended architecture when we are interested in static systems. However, most systems deal with dynamic environments and the accompanying changes in requirements. These changes affect both individual components and their dependencies with other components. As a result, we have to focus on the direct and indirect (cascading) dependencies as well. Network analysis techniques are a natural fit for this task.

A network approach enables us to conceptualize large-scale information systems and their emergence over time. Through the techniques and concepts we will present in subsequent sections, architects can better communicate across stakeholder groups, better cope with emergent complexity, and better manage risk.

Network Approach

Central to our approach to architecture, is representing information systems as a network. All renderings of actual information systems are abstractions; in our case, information systems are drawn as networks comprised of nodes and links. In particular, a node is a component with a well-defined interface. As such, it may be used by other components without the user of the component being aware of its implementation details. Ideally, the component is separately buildable, installable, and manageable. In practice, it is hard to substitute one component—even if part of the same product class—for another.

The links between nodes represent conduits through which information, ideas, and knowledge flow. In the case of information systems, the most obvious links between systems are those in which two systems exchange data. That is, two nodes are linked if they share data. As a dependency, we would say that system A depends on system B for data. However, by drawing on the coordination literature (Malone et al., 1994) and organizational research on interdependence (Thompson, 1967), we understand that there are multiple types of dependencies by which we could characterize the tasks represented by systems: resource sharing, producer/consumer, and simultaneity. Links between nodes are limited to data flows in this chapter, but they can be expanded to include a great variety of dependencies that are found in practice.

A resource dependency exists when system A depends on data managed by system B. For example, applications that share a common Oracle database have a dependency on the shared data resource managed by Oracle. The database management system (DBMS) has many facilities to manage the dependency on this shared resource. A producer/consumer dependency exists when system A depends upon the results of system B. For example, a general ledger application depends upon the data processed in a sales order application. A simultaneity dependency exists when two or more tasks must be completed before a third task can begin. For example, a reporting application may need data from multiple systems before compiling the report.

Network analysis has been utilized in a great many areas to describe many complex phenomena (Barabasi, 2002). Software researchers have proposed metrics (Chidamber & Kemerer, 1998) to assess the structural properties of software and measure complexity using techniques such as DSM (MacCormack, Rusnak, & Baldwin, 2005). In our approach, we are introducing the concepts of social network analysis into the examination of architecture because information systems are both the product of social construction (Pinch & Bijker, 1987) and are first-class actors in the network that includes the stakeholders of the information system (Akrich, 1992). It is imperative that the architect understand how the information system fits within the larger network that is the organization. The computer-based information system is the manifestation of an ongoing dialog between the different stakeholders of the system. It is both shaped by the organization and will shape the organization in a cyclic, recursive process (Glaeser, Kallal, Scheinkman, & Shleifer, 1992; Orlikowski, 2000). Therefore, the information system architect plays a role in shaping both the information system and the subsequent organization. Changes made by business managers shape both the organization and the subsequent information system.

Enterprise architects are interested in such variables as IT project complexity, cost and success, as well as system flexibility, robustness, adaptability, and performance. They are also responsible for the ongoing evolution of the enterprise architecture. These outcomes are the result of an interaction between system and organization that system architecture influences (Glaeser et al., 1992). Project cost and maintenance is directly related to complexity (Banker, Datar, Kemerer, & Zweig, 1993), which is a description of interdependency. If the goal of architecture is to provide flexibility, robustness, and adaptability, then any change to the architecture will affect those characteristics.

Managers looking to address IT project performance and overall system performance must balance the needs of various internal and external organizations, and even engage in the negotiations that decide whether a system is a success or failure (Wilson & Howcroft, 2002). Dependencies between components of the IS architecture reflect dependencies between the organizations that utilize the components. The architect's ability to modify the network is constrained by the interdependencies of the groups utilizing the existing components. Moreover, the interdependencies evolve as the information system is adapted by the organization, and as the organization adapts to the information system. Through frequent intervention, the architect can influence the evolution of the information system, but may not be able to control it.

If we assume that the architects cannot control all the components of the information system, then the question the architect wants answered is which components should be controlled or more actively managed. That is, what are the architectural control points? Similarly, how does the espoused architecture influence subsequent emergence and control points? Are there architectures and simple rules that minimize the change in control points? The control points may be identified according to a specific set of criteria (i.e., their autarky value),

or they may be identified due to their network position within the espoused architecture (i.e., their positional value). In a system of emergent interdependencies, however, the systems identified as core by one set of managers, at one point in time, may not be identified as the most important by either the original set of managers or other groups of stakeholders at another point in time. That is, the loci of interdependence may shift over time. In our approach, we identify and emphasize importance by network position, as described later, in order to complement traditional approaches. The network approach in no way minimizes the need to actively manage systems with high intrinsic value.

New Measures and Visualizations

Networks provide two benefits to understanding architecture. First, they provide a good metaphor to communicate architectural issues. One of the challenges architects face is that architectural models and specifications are often useful only to other architects. Enterprise architects, chartered with a long-term, global architecture strategy, are often challenged to convey how they contribute to the day-to-day business. This includes conveying what the key issues are and why projects get out of control (fail, run over budget, ship late, fail service level agreements, etc.) to their business colleagues. Networks are both simple in their symbols and rich in describing complexity. Second, networks are amenable to certain analytics that can help the architect compute relevant metrics.

Network approaches have been used in other settings such as inter-organizational networks and social networks. In those setting, researchers have used several network metrics and provided interesting interpretations. One particular metric that is important in analyzing architectures is centrality.

Degree centrality of a node refers to the number of direct connections that a node has at a given point in time. A node with more direct

Figure 1. A sample network

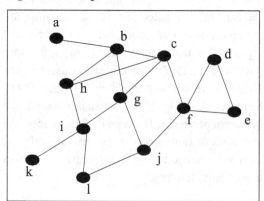

connections to other nodes is considered to be more central than other nodes. For example in Figure 1, node g has a degree of 4 and node h as a degree of 3.

Other centrality measures include the effect of indirect ties between nodes. (Node h may be directly connected to node b, but node h is also indirectly connected to node a (by going through node b)). For example, closeness centrality (one of the simpler measures incorporating indirect ties) measures the distance using shortest paths from each node to all other nodes. The node that can reach all other nodes in the fewest steps is considered most central.

Researchers and practitioners alike have been interested in the pattern of connections between nodes. Historically, researchers have assumed that the nodes are connected to one another randomly. As a result, if we were to plot the probability distribution of the number of links in the network, we expect to see a bell shaped curve that is centered on a mean number of links. However, in reality, when researchers observed connections between nodes in real networks they found that the distributions did not match the random expectation. In fact, they encountered several networks with a probability distribution that resembled what they called power-law distributions. This meant that these networks had a great majority of nodes with very few connections and few nodes with a great many connections. This result does not occur by accident. In fact, Barabasi listed two conditions for making any network scale-free (Barabasi, 2002). First, the network should be growing with new nodes appearing at random times. Second, a new node should preferentially attach to an existing node based on the number of connections that the existing node already has.

Centrality and the way links are formed over time has implications for control and risk. When nodes occupy a central position, they have the ability to influence the entire network. As a result of this, they gain importance. Within the architectural context, such nodes have to be

managed closely or they could adversely impact the network as a whole. If nodes connect to other nodes randomly, complexity is not managed and the network represents a random network. If nodes connect to other nodes under the preferential attachment logic, a few nodes become very central-critical—to the network as a whole. These nodes may be very hard to modify and could expose the firm to undo risk if they are not controlled or are uncontrollable. If nodes most often connect to nodes within their local domain, but have some links to other clusters of nodes, then a small world network may emerge. These networks are more robust to perturbations than random networks. Researchers have created a metric called small world quotient, or Q, to measure this (Uzzi & Spiro, 2005). The measure of design preservation is captured through the network's small world quotient. A high value represents a high ratio of clustering to short path lengths, relative to a random network with the same node count and arc density.

Within the architecture domain, a few requirements stand out. Most enterprise architects are interested in identifying what they call the shared core. These are the set of components (systems, services, applications) that are used by most other components. Visualization packages such as Pajek, a freeware program (Batagelj & Mrvar, 2004), can be used to draw network diagrams and generate meaningful and replicable visualizations of very large networks (networks having hundreds of thousands of vertices). From within the many network drawing algorithms within Pajek, two algorithms—Fruchterman-Reingold (FR) (Fruchterman & Reingold, 1991) and Kamada-Kawai (KK) (Kamada & Kawai, 1989)—can be used to help the analyst identify the shared core. These algorithms use "spring-embedded" techniques to derive minimum energy states of the underlying networks.

A second requirement is identifying components that, if not working, will cause the most significant negative impact on the enterprise's ability to provide its services. Using an appropriate network model, the single most important node can be identified through an appropriate centrality measure. However, architects interested in risk management may be interested in the group of systems that represent those systems that must provide 24×7 availability or be maintained collectively to minimize disruption to the network. Identifying the critical set of systems is a greater challenge than identifying a single node. In order to do this, we utilize KeyPlayer (Borgatti & Dreyfus, 2005). It implements the KPP-NEG test (Borgatti, 2003) in which we identify the N nodes that have the potential to maximally disrupt the network.

The third requirement is similar to the second. Impact analysis helps us identify the set of systems that have the greatest impact on the rest of the network. Where traditional approaches would identify the direct and indirect systems affected by a proposed change to a specific set of systems, the impact analysis we suggest in this chapter is identifying the set of nodes that would have the largest impact on the network. In effect, this impact analysis finds the points of greatest leverage on the rest of the system. In order to do this, we again utilize Key Player but utilize the KPP-POS metric in which we identify the N nodes that collectively have the greatest reach in the network (Borgatti, 2003; Borgatti et al., 2005). Although none of these nodes may be the most central, they may be the most important when we consider only their collective positional value in the network.

The final requirement (at least in this chapter), is to identify the best decomposition of a set of components that minimizes dependencies across clusters while maximizing dependency within a cluster. Enterprise architects are familiar with the notion of tight and lose coupling. Our challenge is to use network analysis techniques to create and analyze useful clusters. In our case study with FinServ (see next section), we have not yet done this analysis. Since FinServ has decided to adopt

a service-oriented architecture (SOA) to rearchitect its applications and components as a set of services, this will be an important requirement. The problem of finding a grouping of vertices, such that for all vertices in each group they are powerfully connected within (homogeneity) and weakly connected to others (separation), remains an NP-complete problem since Karp (Karp, 1972) identified it as such. Social network analysis methods have provided polynomial-like algorithms, mostly applicable to boolean graphs (e.g., LS sets: Lawler (1973), Lambda sets: (Freeman, Borgatti, & White, 1991)), that have been implemented in various software packages (e.g., Ucinet)[1].

A Case Study

In order to highlight the suggestions we have previously made, we present the following case study to explore data collection requirements and interesting questions that network models of the enterprise architecture can help provide answers to.

Our research setting was within a financial services company (FinServ) that provides processing services to the investment management industry. In addition to our own primary data collection, we used details listed in Westerman & Walpole (2005) to inform our case study. FinServ has over a trillion dollars in assets under management. They provide full service transfer agency and accounting services globally.

Over the last couple of decades, FinServ has grown rapidly primarily through mergers and acquisitions and also by launching new services and entering new regions. As companies were acquired, each line-of-business (LOB) has maintained much of the decision rights to control most aspects of their (line-of) business, including design, sales, back-end processing, and IT services. The resulting implied enterprise architecture is one with duplication of functionality, limited integration, and applications with different look and feel. This was sustainable during the economic growth phase in the 90s. Each LOB was empowered to focus on and independently respond to specific opportunities and needs.

A combination of the dot-com crash and the associated stock marked decline coupled with increased competition caused FinServ to find that the market conditions quickly changed. This new market is very competitive. A commoditization of services has increasingly squeezed the company's profit margins. New demands on flexibility, agility, and improved time-to-market have become differentiators. Furthermore, as a result of 9-11, oversight bodies have stepped up the requirements on the financial industry with governance and compliance mandates (such as Sarbanes Oxley). These factors together have moved FinServ from being in a high growth profitable market to one where cost cutting, activity-streamlining efficiency improvements are a necessity to stay competitive. While the strategic, long-term direction was clear, FinServ's existing architecture was not compatible with these changes. The attributes of the FinServ architecture had several challenges, such as tight coupling between systems and monolithic solutions, often not well documented, that duplicated functionality in multiple systems. This prevented FinServ from quickly responding to changing market conditions.

In response to this predicament, FinServ hired a new CIO and created a new corporate initiative to address the problems. The IT organization was changed, creating an enterprise architecture team, a management oversight committee, and an organization to provide company-wide shared application services. A FinServ enterprise architecture strategy was created and a Global Platform SOA-based enterprise architecture was defined. Their core mandate was to reduce IT spending though the elimination of redundant systems, componentization, and exposure of core functionality through accessible services, redesign of strategic shared applications and components and the provision of mutually consistent customer access channels (Web, voice,

wireless, etc.). This organization invests in a strong enterprise architecture organization and actively practices architecture-driven application development with accompanying architecture governance via an Architecture Review Board. This involves investing in technology, processes, people, and organizational structures that can help them deliver on their mandate.

This multi-year effort required significant changes to FinServ's IT applications. To support the CIO's call for action, corporate IT organized an all-day planning session that resulted in the identification of the following goals:

1. Rationalize the application portfolio and eliminate redundant systems and applications.
2. Restructure the legacy applications to create core components and re-architect highly reusable capabilities into shared services.
3. Componentize and service-enable the components (create open interfaces to legacy code).
4. Create an enterprise architecture—a single platform across all LOBs.
5. Enable significantly improved ability to design new customer-facing applications (agility).
6. Enable efficient integration of existing and new components.

We began our project by taking inventory of the applications within FinServ. The chief enterprise architect at FinServ had already collected information on applications and their dependencies. As a start, he collected dependencies that included data sharing, function calls and message passing. This information was stored in an Access™ database and updated constantly as new information trickled in from business units. Besides tracking systems and dependencies, the Access application generated Pajek and Key Player input files to support the visualizations and analysis.

Based on the inventory of all applications from FinServ, we drew the network diagram of the deployment architecture shown in Figure 2. Each node in the figure is a system within FinServ and each link represents a dependency previously described.

Node colors denote if the system is internal to FinServ or an external system that is used by FinServ. A blue color (darker shade) denotes an external system and a red color (lighter shade) denotes an internal one. Almost immediately, one can see that several blue nodes occupy key positions within FinServ. This presents a challenge since they are both vital to the performance of other core systems and outside FinServ's control.

When we presented this picture to the architects, it stimulated a lot of discussion. They observed that some aspects of the figure were obvious to them. For example, some red notes occupying the middle of the picture were their key transaction processing systems. What surprised them was the presence of blue nodes in the middle. This got them discussing these systems in great depth, not from a cost or performance perspective

but from the ownership perspective. Are all the blue colored nodes truly outside FinServ's control? In other words, this was a data quality question. If they are indeed outside FinServ's control, why are these systems outsourced? What kinds of service level agreements do they have with those vendors? What are some of the risks? What platforms are these applications running on (UNIX, Linux, Windows, etc.)? What is the number of developers or users associated with each application? How far along (in terms of completion) are the projects associated with each application?

Another byproduct of the network analysis was the identification of the key players—the architectural control points. The top set of core nodes that were identified by our key player algorithm contained most of the core systems that the stakeholders had already identified. Given that they had close to 200 systems in their inventory, they were a little surprised about a few systems that showed up very high on our key player set. Upon further analysis, they were able to justify why these systems were important. A similar concern was raised about nodes containing either

Figure 2. Enterprise architecture

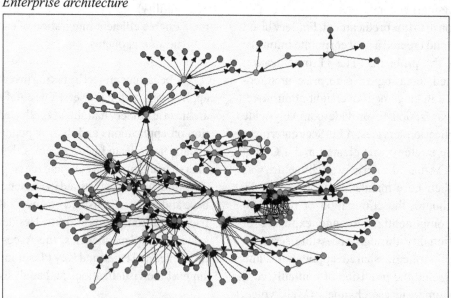

only incoming links or outgoing links. Once again, the question about data quality came up. An architect in the meeting raised an interesting point that he could use these pictures to determine the degree of difficulty in making changes to a system. He opined that systems with a large number of links, if these links were of different types, would be very expensive to modify. While there were many other smaller questions that came up, the chief architect summed up the session to us by saying that these figures had changed the nature of discussion from raw counts to business related issues and complexity/change management concerns.

Another issue that came up during the discussions was the presence of small clusters that were disconnected from the larger group. While on the surface these islands were disconcerting, some of the architects raised the possibility that there was missing information about the links. In fact, this session led them to look closely at the dependencies.

The visualizations were also valuable as a basis for communication among the architects, development managers, business managers, and senior management. The challenge for any technical group is explaining what they do and why things are as difficult as they are. For a perceived overhead function such as the enterprise architecture group, the challenge is greater because they also have to continuously justify their existence. It appears that the visualizations accomplish both tasks.

The graphics are simple enough in their nomenclature that people not familiar with the terminology can still understand them. To both senior management and line-of-business management, the visualizations provide an abstract view of the organization and its information flows. Managers can see how and where their systems fit into the larger picture. Managers can visualize the complexity and understand why certain changes are being recommended. The nodes represent the systems the managers' people use every day. The links highlight the managers' interdependencies with everyone else.

Initially we have limited the architectural view to a deployment view. The graphics represent the state of the enterprise systems and their dependencies as of today. By creating renderings of the information system at different points in time, people can see how the system evolves. In our prototype project, we maintained an Access database with an inventory of systems and dependencies. In time, this can be replaced by an asset management application dedicated to this task. Central to this type of architectural decision-making is a running inventory of the organization's information system assets. Unfortunately, the missing piece in many asset management systems is the management of the dependencies. These aren't assets or liabilities in the traditional sense, yet are as important, if not more important, than the assets and liabilities usually tracked.

Creation of network models representing other architectural and/or organizational views can provide further significant insight of the current state of the architecture.

Data Collection Requirements and Limitations

Based on our initial analysis, we presented our findings to the enterprise architecture group at FinServ. During our presentation, members of the architecture group had several clarification questions and also identified many new questions. Since they did not have enough time to discuss these new questions during that session, they decided to meet separately and have a separate brainstorming session. Coming out of the session were a set of broader questions and accompanying data collection requirements. Although our analysis was limited to an initial set of data gathered, we have had several rounds of follow-on discussions with stakeholders and as a result identified broader needs.

Enterprise architects planning to use our approach need to decide which architectural views are important to them. The architectural view is dependent on the question that the architect chooses to address. After the creation of the specific network model representation (the semantic meaning of arcs, nodes, colors, directional arcs, etc.) the necessary data has to be collected, such as, for example, information on systems, projects, the project team, and business users. Our technique hinges on finding the proper level of information. The best place to start is to consider a deployment architectural view of the set of existing components and their inter-relationships. On this project, we were able to begin discussions and interpretations based on a sample of the total data on systems. This was helpful because follow-on discussions resulted in the identification of new and relevant data elements.

Components can be anything from hardware, operating system, and communication network components (e.g., Intel/Linux), application software components (e.g., customer service applications), business service components (e.g., shareholder services), and their respective interfaces, to software technology services (e.g., BPM, Security). For an architectural view of application software components, the modules of Oracle Financials, for example, constitute a single component. For each component, we need to know the components it calls, the components that call it, and information about the type of system it is (database, workflow, analytics, decision support, etc.).

For each component (piece of major software, hardware) in the network, other useful information to collect includes the date it went into service, the project name associated with its introduction, prerequisite hardware and software platform information, and the names of the other systems it integrates with. For each integration point, we suggest collecting the information regarding the type of data exchanged and the method of exchange (e.g., CORBA, RMI, WebServices, RPC,

synchronous or asynchronous messaging, batch file exchange, file system access, database access). The format of the data exchange should also be tracked. In addition to the static information we have just described, we recommend maintaining information regarding the frequency and volume of data exchange. This information can help the analyst better understand the nature of the dependency between the components within the production architecture.

Because the information system grows through projects, and projects are frequently the item that is budgeted, it is important to have each project name, description, components touched, project justification, and budget. In addition, data on the estimated time (elapsed and person-hours) and actual time (elapsed and person-hours), plus any extenuating circumstances, is also important. This data can be used to understand how interdependency between systems can affect project outcomes.

We also recommend collecting data regarding the people who work on the projects. Collect data on who worked on each project, who the project lead was, the role each person played on the project, and the components each person managed. This data can be used to develop insight into the social network of project teams, and aid in understanding how this network influences project outcomes.

On the user side, we recommend collecting data on which business users (groups) use which components of the system and which groups coordinate with which other groups independent of their use of the system. That is, it is useful to understand which groups work together, how they work together, and why they do so. With information on projects and business unit success, the analyst can start connecting the information system to project and business value. Based on our discussions with stakeholders, they consider the following to be successful outcomes: project estimation accuracy, degree of reuse, quality of the system, and changeability or flexibility, and ROI.

CONCLUSION

Viewing architecture from a network perspective provides two clear benefits. Networks provide a useful metaphor to communicate and interpret architecture and, based on their graph-theoretic underpinnings, provide a basis for analytics to compute metrics that may help explain variation in the performance of architectural and organizational flexibility, robustness, and risk management.

Our case study at FinServ helped create a decision support system and a set of metrics that are useful for making architectural decisions. In building the decision support system, we were able to identify the methodology and data required to successfully manage architecture based decisions. While the current version of the system requires users to input the information, in future versions FinServ is planning on automating the data collection and looking at live architectures.

REFERENCES

Akrich, M. (1992). *The description of technical artifacts*. In W. E. Bijker & J. Law (Eds.), (pp. 205-224). Cambridge, MA: MIT Press.

Alexander, C. (1964). *Notes on the synthesis of form*. Cambridge: Harvard University Press.

Allen, T. J. (1977). *Managing the flow of technology*. Cambridge, MA: MIT Press.

Banker, R. D., Datar, S. M., Kemerer, C. F., & Zweig, D. (1993). Software complexity and maintenance costs. Association for Computing Machinery. *Communications of the ACM, 36*(11), 81.

Barabasi, A. L. (2002). *Linked: The new science of networks*. Cambridge, MA: Perseus Publishing.

Batagelj, V., & Mrvar, A. (2004). *Pajek program for large network analysis*. Retrieved from http://vlado.fmf.uni-lj.si/pub/networks/pajek/

Borgatti, S. P. (2003). The key player problem. In R. L. Breiger, K. M. Carley, P. Pattison, & N. R. C. U. S. C. o. H. Factors (Eds.), *Dynamic social network modeling and analysis: Workshop summary and papers*. Washington, DC: National Academy of Sciences Press.

Borgatti, S. P., & Dreyfus, D. (2005). *Key player* (Version 2.0). Harvard, MA.

Byrd, T., & Turner, D. (2000). Measuring the flexibility of information technology infrastructure: Exploratory analysis of a construct. *Journal of Management Information Systems, 17*(1), 167-208.

Chidamber, S., & Kemerer, C. (1998). A metrics suite for object oriented design. *IEEE Transactions on Software Engineering, 20*(6), 476-493.

D'Souza, D., & Willis, A. (1999). *Objects, components, and frameworks with UML: The catalysis approach*. Addison-Wesley.

Dreyfus, D., & Iyer, B. (2006). *Enterprise architecture:* A social network perspective. Paper presented at the *Proceedings of the 39th Annual Hawaii International Conference on System Sciences (HICSS-39)*, Koloa, Kauai HI.

Duncan, N. (1995). Capturing flexibility of information technology infrastructure: A study of resource characteristics and their measure. *Journal of Management Information Systems, 12*(2), 37-57.

Everitt, B. S., Landau, S., & Leese, M. (2001). *Cluster analysis*. Arnold Publishers.

Freeman, L., Borgatti, S., & White, D. (1991). Centrality in valued graphs: A measure of between-ness based on network flow. *Social Networks, 13*(2), 141-154.

Fruchterman, T., & Reingold, E. (1991). Graph drawing by force-directed relacement. *Software Practice and Experience, 21*, 1129-1164.

Gasser, L. (1986). The integration of computing and routine work. *ACM Transactions on Office Information Systems, 4*(3), 205-225.

Glaeser, E., Kallal, H., Scheinkman, J. A., & Shleifer, A. A. (1992). Growth in cities. *Journal of Political Economy, 100*(61), 1126-1152.

Gunter, C. A. (2000). Abstracting dependencies between software configuration items. *ACM Transaction Software Engineering Methodologies, 9*(1), 94-131.

Henderson, J. C., & Venkatraman, N. (1993). Strategic alignment: Leveraging information technology for transforming organizations. *IBM Systems Journal, 32*(1), 4.

Iyer, B., & Gottlieb, R. M. (2004). The four-domain architecture: An approach to support enterprise architecture design. *IBM Systems Journal, 43*, 587-597, IBM Corporation/IBM Journals.

Kamada, T., & Kawai, S. (1989). An algorithm for drawing general undirected graphs. *Information Processing Letters, 31*, 7-15.

Karp, R. M. (1972). Reducibility among combinatorial problems. In M. A. Thatcher (Ed.), *Complexity of computer computations* (pp. 85-103). Plenum Press.

Kayworth, T., Chatterjee, D., & Sambamurthy, V. (2001). Theoretical justifcation for IT infrastructure investments. *Information Resources Management Journal, 14*(3), 5-14.

MacCormack, A., Rusnak, J., & Baldwin, C. (2005). *Exploring the structure of complex software designs: An empirical study of open source and proprietary code.* Unpublished manuscript.

Malone, T. W., & Crowston, K. (1994). The interdisciplinary study of coordination. *ACM Computing Surveys, 26*(1), 87-119.

McKay, D., & Brockway, D. (1989). Building IT Infrastructure for the 1990s. *Stage by Stage, 9*(3), 1-11.

Messerschmitt, D., & Szyperski, C. (2003). *Software ecosystems: Understanding an indispensable technology and industry.* Cambridge, MA: The MIT Press.

Morris, C., & Ferguson, C. (1993). How architecture wins technology wars. *Harvard Business Review, 71*(2), 86-97.

Nezlek, G. S., Jain, H. K., & Nazareth, D. L. (1999). An integrated approach to enterprise computing architectures. *Communications of the ACM, 42*(11), 82-90.

Orlikowski, W. J. (2000). Using technology and constituting structures: A practice lens for studying technology in organizations. *Organization Science, 11*(4), 404-428.

Parnas, D. L. (1972). On the criteria to be used in decomposing systems into modules. *Communications of the ACM, 15*(12), 1053-1058.

Pinch, T. J., & Bijker, W. E. (1987). The social construction of facts and artifacts. In T. Pinch (Ed.), *The social construction of technological systems* (pp. 17-50). Cambridge, MA: The MIT Press.

Richardson, G., Jackson, B., & Dickson, G. (1990). A principle-based enterprise architecture: Lessons from Texaco and Star Enterprise. *MIS Quarterly, 14*(4), 385-403.

Ross, J. (2003). Creating a strategic IT architecture competency: Learning in stages. *MIS Quarterly Executive, 2*(1), 31-43.

Sauer, C., & Willcocks, L. P. (2002). The evolution of the organizational architect. *Sloan Management Review* (Spring), 41-49.

Thompson, J. (1967). *Organizations in action.* New York: McGraw-Hill.

Uzzi, B., & Spiro, J. (2005). Collaboration and creativity: The small world problem. *American Journal of Sociology, 111*(2), 447-504.

Venkatraman, V. N., Lee, C. H., & Iyer, B. (2005). Is ambidexterity a valuable organizational capability? An empirical test in software product introductions, 1991-2002. Boston: Boston University.

Weill, P., & Broadbent, M. (1998). *Leveraging the new infrastructure: How market leaders capitalize on information technology.* Boston: Harvard Business School Press.

Westerman, G., & Walpole, R. (2005). PFPC: *Building an IT risk management competency.* CISR Working Paper.

Wilson, M., & Howcroft, D. (2002). Re-conceptualising failure: Social shaping meets IS research. *European Journal of Information Systems, 11*(4), 236.

Yourdon, E., & Constantine, L. (1986). *Structured design: Fundamentals of a discipline of computer program and systems design.* Englewood Cliffs, NJ: Yourdon Press.

Zachman, J. A. (1987). A framework for information systems architecture. *IBM Systems Journal, 26*(3), 276-292.

Zhao, L., & Siau, K. (2002). Component-based development using UML. *Communications of the Association for Information Systems, 9*(12), 207-222.

ENDNOTE

[1]   An introduction to clustering methods can be found in Everitt, Landau, and Leese (2001).

Chapter XIX
Enterprise Architecture by a Small Unit in a Federated Organization

Roger Sliva
State of Nevada, USA

ABSTRACT

This chapter provides specific guidance for enterprise architects who are part of a small team in a federated organization. Architects in that situation may be compelled to drastically limit the scope of their program. This chapter offers architects several actions they can take to perform current architecture, target architecture, and architecture governance as part of a wider-scoped program. Emphasis is placed on using an architecture repository tool, focusing on open standards, planning for shared business services, supporting a governance process, and building trust relationships within and between the organization's departments.

INTRODUCTION

This chapter assumes the reader is part of a small enterprise architecture (EA) team, or possibly solely responsible for performing enterprise architecture in a federated organization. A federated organization (as described later) presents challenges for performing enterprise architecture for any size team and a small team may feel the need to drastically limit the scope of their architecture efforts. This chapter will suggest actions for a small architecture team that can help them perform a wider-scoped architecture program that includes capturing the current view of your organization, planning for a business-aligned target environment, and supporting an enterprise architecture governance process.

Those three main tasks—developing current architecture (or as-is environment), planning for target architecture (or to-be environment), and promoting architecture governance—are the three legs of a substantive program that even a small team can perform. For these three legs of an architecture program, I will provide an overview of resources to leverage, deliverables to produce, and actions that the small team can perform to ease their difficult task. The goal of this chapter is to provide the small enterprise architecture team with a few key tools and resources to help them be as effective and relevant as possible under difficult circumstances.

BACKGROUND

Small Architecture Team

A "small" enterprise architecture team is defined as an architecture team that lacks any resources, facilities, manpower, funding, and sponsorship such that the team can not possibly fully implement an architecture program as defined by one of the EA frameworks (Table 1).

Architecture Frameworks

The standard resource for a fully scoped architecture program is the enterprise architecture framework. There are numerous EA frameworks with several of the most common listed in Table 1.

These frameworks provide key definitions and objectives for the elements of an architecture program. They are in effect how-to manuals. Each architecture framework has its strengths and when followed will provide templates for effectively performing the three legs of an EA program. A small architecture team should survey these frameworks to determine their potential for use. Due to the complexities of a federated organization and their own limited resources, the small architecture team can't guarantee success by diligently following a standard framework, and can't guarantee that they can diligently follow the framework in the first place.

The Federated Organization

A federated organization is an organization consisting of autonomous or semi-autonomous departments (or units, agencies, and so on). Note that the terms federated or federal, and organization or enterprise can be used interchangeably. The independence of the departments in a federated organization presents special challenges for enterprise architects. Even if the departments share an executive authority, mandates are unlikely. These departments will have their own agenda and priorities, and they may be more self-concerned than concerned about the organization as a whole. Collaboration and compromise are required to get anything done across departmental boundaries. Departments in a federated organization may have political and funding autonomy as well as organizational autonomy. They may have different funding sources, political structures, security requirements, customer bases, and customer ser-

Table 1. EA frameworks

Zachman	http://www.zifa.com
The open group architecture framework	http://www.opengroup.org/togaf/
The federal enterprise architecture reference models	http://www.whitehouse.gov/omb/egov/a-1-fea.html
National Association of State Chief Information Officers (NASCIO) enterprise architecture tool-kit	http://www.nascio.org

vice responsibilities. More importantly, they may have their own IT shops, policies, and standards. A federated organization is a *set of enterprises*.

THE SCOPE OF THE ENTERPRISE ARCHITECTURE EFFORT

Considering individual departments of a federated organization as their own enterprise implies that the scope of an architecture effort is increased by a magnitude above the single enterprise effort. Let's assume that it is impractical for the small EA team to fully apply an EA framework to the whole set of enterprises. With limited resources, a small architecture team must cut back the scope of their program somewhere and will only be able to implement a portion of one the EA frameworks. It is also possible for the EA team to take the more feasible portions from multiple frameworks and weave them into a new framework suitable for a small EA program. Either way I summarize the scope of enterprise architecture effort for a small team in a federated organization as:

- Develop a repository to store information about the current state of the organization across the major departments. Identify elements of your organization such as business strategies and business goals, business services provided and used, and related technical systems. Populate the repository with these elements based upon a common architecture framework such as Zachman. This becomes your current architecture.

- Analyze the repository data and identify the common strategic goals, business needs, and service requirements of the departments in your organization. Identify and document current common industry IT service solutions, best practices, open standards and specifications, and near term trends that satisfy the aforementioned analysis. Then develop recommendations for business re-

lationships, business services, policies, and standards that promote enterprise strategic goals. These deliverables become your target architecture.

- Establish and support a multi-departmental enterprise architecture governance structure and process. Allow the governance process to guide the development and application of the target architecture deliverables to support IT and business decision-making.

THE CURRENT ARCHITECTURE

The current architecture is sometimes called the as-is or baseline architecture. Simply put it is the current answer to what, how, where, who, when, and why for every aspect of the organization. It can include data that describes every software package used, each department's location, a department's strategic principles, the lines of business, models of routers and networks, lists of databases, the data relationships in the HR database, and so on. Frameworks such as Zachman and the federal enterprise architecture provide models for organizing and classifying the all this data to provide strategic, business, or service perspectives of the enterprise. An architecture repository tool is most useful to capture and classify this data and build those perspectives.

Architecture Repository and Repository Tools

An architecture repository tool is a software program that manages the data in a database called an architecture repository. An architecture repository is useful to store discrete elements of information about the organization. These discrete elements are also called artifacts. An architecture artifact can be anything that in any way describes your organization. Or an artifact can be a composite of other artifacts. A user role, a business strategy, a technical specification, a data relationship, an operating system, an office location, an enterprise project, and a business relationship are all artifacts. The type of artifacts identified and how they are categorized and organized in the repository for later reporting or analysis should be based on your framework. Using an enterprise architecture repository tool will simplify the capture, categorization, organization, and reporting of EA artifacts. Although there are many architecture repository tools that are specific to enterprise architecture programs, there are also generic UML modeling and CASE tools that can be used effectively as well. The following list shows several tools that can be used by a resource-constrained EA team that are either low or no cost.

Besides these, there are many appropriate products at various cost levels. The following links provide more information on various free or low cost architecture modeling/repository tools:

- http://dmoz.org/Computers/Programming/ Methodologies/Modeling_Languages/Unified_Modeling_Language/Tools/
- http://www.enterprise-architecture.info/ EA_Tools.htm

These types of architecture repository tools allow architecture artifacts to be managed as objects. An object can be re-used, associated or linked with other objects, and manipulated through a graphical object browser. This makes it easy to use tools such as UML modelers to organize architecture artifacts using frameworks such as the Zachman framework. Figure 1 shows a

Table 2. Repository tools

Altova UModel™	UML Modeler	http://www.altova.com
MagicDraw™ (community edition)	UML Modeler	http://www.magicdraw.com
Protégé (plus plug-ins)	Ontology Editor	http://protege.stanford.edu
Sparx Systems Enterprise Architect™	UML Modeler	http://www.sparxsystems.com.au
StarUML™	UML Modeler	http://www.staruml.com
Visual Paradigm™ (community edition)	UML Modeler	http://www.visual-paradigm.com

Figure 1. Modeling a framework

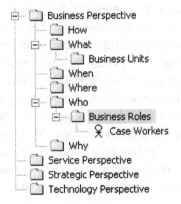

Figure 2. Modeling a taxonomy

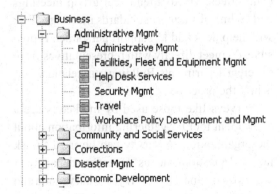

portion of a Zachman-like framework represented in a UML modeler's object browser.

Another use of the object browser is to categorize. The federal enterprise architecture framework has taxonomy for lines of business in the U.S federal government. This taxonomy may be represented in the object browser. Figure 2 shows how a portion of a similar taxonomy might look like in a UML modeler's object browser.

Getting the Artifacts

The information in the architecture repository has to come from somewhere. In a federated organization, the autonomous departments may be unwilling to share information about what they do, how they do it, and so forth. For a small architecture team it may be difficult to meet with every department and determine what they know about themselves. Even if you could, don't be surprised if the people you talk with aren't aware of everything their department is doing. A broad and multi-leveled approach is needed. Of course, if there are privacy and sensitivity restrictions that constrain your team from acquiring architecture artifacts from certain departments, then there is not much you can do. I recommend meeting with as many people as possible and also do surveys.

Every meeting you attend and every discussion you have with staff members or partners can contain intelligence that describes the organization. Make notes and add the information into the repository. Work with the members of IT governance committees. Try to attend user group meetings and technical status or standards meetings. Talk with help desk and IT support personnel. If possible, do meet directly with representatives from different departments. Building trust relationships is half the process.

Surveys like those used by marketers are a convenient tool for gathering information about the organization. A survey can be used to ask targeted questions such as "Does your department use it's own e-mail server? If yes, what version and how many users are served?" A targeted survey is especially useful when the team is trying to fill in gaps in the current view. Surveys can be e-mailed out with little front-end effort by your team. Although some people won't participate, others find this mode convenient because it allows them to respond at their pace.

Modeling and Reporting

The artifacts in the repository are useful when analyzed to identify patterns, relationships and trends, and to use those to form opinions about where the organization is now and where it should head with respect to IT and business solutions. Using the modeling capabilities of the architecture repository tool, the artifacts can be associated graphically to visually impact decision-making. Repository queries and other reports can be used to mine for the patterns, relationships, and trends. Note that architecture repository tool vary in their ability to produce reports and models. However, even simple models can provide insight into the patterns, relationships, and trends that feed into the preparation of target architecture deliverables.

THE TARGET ARCHITECTURE

The target architecture or to-be architecture is the set of deliverables that describes the future state of the organization in line with strategic principles and business objectives. The nature of those EA deliverables may be determined from the EA framework being used. There are a large number of potential deliverables including models (diagrams of all types), strategic plans, project plans, project recommendations, policies, standards, best practices, specifications, principles, investment requests, transition recommendations, and others. The deliverables should have an impact somewhere in the organization. Specifically they should have some impact on an IT decision-making process. In a federated organization, deliverables should advance IT interoperability, sharing, automation, simplification, cooperation and trust between departments depending on the principles most important to your organization.

The small EA team should allow the nature and scope of EA deliverables to be within the purview of the architecture governance process (discussed later) to ensure cross-department buy-in and to have the authoritative weight of a governance committee behind the deliverables. In a federated organization, expect that many different departments or other entities will want to be included in the EA deliverable development and approval process.

How to Eat an Elephant

The target architecture has to be broken into pieces to be manageable. Some frameworks recommend dividing up the effort into IT domains addressed by domain teams. Domains are a convenient way to group similar aspects of IT business and infrastructure services. Example IT domains might include:

- Security and privacy.
- Computing platforms.
- Networks and telecommunications.
- Application.
- Information.
- Integration and middleware.

The IT domains in turn can be sub-divided further to provide greater granularity when developing target architecture deliverables. These sub-divisions are often business service specific. A small architecture team should focus on a prioritized subset of potential services that are most important to the organization's business. In addition, the team should consider how such services could be expanded across the organization. Without going into all possible options, here's a sample list of shared enterprise services:

- Enterprise content management/work flow management.
- Federated identity management.
- Enterprise storage.
- Enterprise application server.
- Computing virtualization.
- Enterprise database management.
- Data standardization and integration.
- Digital signing.

The EA team and the EA governance process can tackle each shared enterprise service one at a time as a target architecture initiative. The types of services and their priority can be aligned with the strategic and business goals of the organization as a whole.

Service Federation

Service federation is an alternative to consolidating services that may be unattainable in a federated organization. Service federation allows service control and provisioning to occur close to the business needing those services. Federating shared enterprise services requires architecture mechanisms to support mediation between distributed systems. There are added complexities in a federated service model over a consolidated service model, but the departments may accept the federated model more willingly. If proposing a federated model for an architecture initiative, then develop deliverables that promote open standards for the service interfaces and protocols to limit the complexity of the mediating infrastructure.

Domain Experts

As previously noted, some frameworks suggest using domain teams to handle certain target architecture initiatives. For a small architecture team, establishing and managing formal domain teams may be unreasonable. However, it is most likely that domain experts exist across the various departments. Leverage these experts if possible.

User and interest groups may already exist in an organization that can take on the role of a domain team and provide input into deliverable development.

When addressing specific domains and disciplines, the architecture team may discover other groups already supporting shared enterprise services, they may be way ahead of any EA program planning and deliverable development. In that case, collaborate with them. Learn what they are doing (see Current Architecture) and help them fill in the holes and span the gaps.

Enterprise-Wide Strategy Alignment

Although one or more business units or agencies in your organization may have outlined strategic goals, it is useful for organization-wide (enterprise) strategic goals to be developed and prioritized to support effective target architecture efforts. A small team needs all the support it can get, especially executive support. Promote an enterprise strategic process and align architecture deliverables with executive direction.

Affecting Decision-Making

The EA team and the EA governance process need to identify the specific functions in the organization where target architecture deliverables will affect a decision-making process. For any EA initiative, the deliverables should be specifically targeted for that audience. Typical functions include strategic and technical planning, budgeting and investment requests, requests for information and proposals, contracts, and project oversight. The earlier the deliverables are applied in an IT project's lifecycle the better.

Open Standards and Specifications

Support an organization's decision-making process by helping departments standardize on the interfaces and protocols used by IT systems. Open standards and specifications are key to planning a target architecture where departments benefit from data sharing and system interoperability. Table 3 lists common standards bodies with their relevance to enterprise architecture. Table 4 lists a few of the relevant open standards that can be addressed as part of a target architecture initiative.

Enterprise Architecture Governance Process

An enterprise architecture governance process can set the agenda for EA initiatives and their deliverables, advise on EA deliverables, review and approve EA deliverables, and have deliverable compliance and exception authority. These governance functions may be distributed across several groups, teams, and committees including the EA team, an EA review committee, an executive or advisory committee, sub-committees, and domain teams. A fully implemented governance process can consume a small EA team's time and energy. A small EA program may need to limit the governance structure to a formal enterprise architecture committee and a formal advisory committee. Then informally collaborate and engage with the various technical groups and domain experts to support deliverable development.

The Enterprise Architecture Committee

Establish an enterprise architecture committee that consists of representatives from major IT stakeholders, representatives from other governance committees, and knowledgeable third parties. Most importantly, the committee must represent a cross-section of the organization. Use this committee for review and approval of deliverables.

The Advisory or Executive Sub-Committee

Establish an advisory or executive sub-committee of the enterprise architecture committee to set the target architecture initiative and to advise on potential deliverables and their audience. Populate this group with enterprise-minded and committed enterprise architecture committee members to ensure the program moves forward.

RESOURCES

In addition to the frameworks as a resource, an architecture program may subscribe to a consulting service such as Gartner, The Burton Group, or the Cutter Consortium to name a few. These consultants provide subscription services to research papers and reports that give advise on best practices and scoping for an EA program. Cutter Consortium as an example has many relevant reports such as *What It Takes to Be a Great Enterprise Architect* (Bredemeyer & Malan, 2004). These types of reports provide theory, practical steps, trends, and case studies for architecture program management and architect development. Reports such as Cutter Consortium's *Applying EA Roadmapping: An SOA Roadmap* (Kiepuszewski, Paluskiewicz, Stokalski, Konkol, & Ruszynski, 2004) are useful for a small team's efforts in formulating target architecture plans.

In addition, there are books on IT governance and strategic planning that provide best practices for architecture governance development. The book *IT Governance* (Weill & Ross, 2004) weaves enterprise architecture current and target planning, and architecture governance in its discussion of overall IT governance that includes strategic, business, and investment planning in federated organizations.

Service-oriented architecture (SOA) is an application development and implementation model that incorporates several key principles for planning for target architecture in a federated organization. Distributing services and having loosely coupled services are consistent themes in SOA literature. Issues with SOA implementation can be mapped to target architecture issues. SOA literature such as *Web Services and Service-Oriented Architectures* (Barry, 2003) and *Enterprise SOA* (Krafzig, Banke, & Slama, 2005) provide that mapping.

CAVEATS FOR A SMALL TEAM

Enterprise Architecture Shelfware

Shelfware is a term for an EA deliverable that once developed is relegated to sitting on a shelf unused or unreferenced. Every deliverable developed by your architecture team or the governance process should be applicable—either directly or as an intermediate step—to a decision-making process in the organization's business life cycle. This includes presentations or other marketing materials developed for educating others on your architecture program. There are many models that can be produced from the current architecture repository data, and many models that can be developed to describe the ideal target architecture scenario, but if those models can not be used to affect an IT decision then they won't have very much value.

Independent Enterprise Architect Efforts

In a federated organization where there are multiple IT shops and where there's some duplicity of roles, be aware of other people or groups working toward enterprise goals independent of your architecture efforts. Engage with these individuals or groups and try to avoid opposing efforts. Let the EA governance committee know what's happening and see if those independent efforts can be correlated with your own.

Relevancy

Some enterprise architecture initiatives may require a long time to produce deliverables. Others may interpret this as a lack of relevancy of an enterprise architecture program. One way to maintain relevancy is to engage the EA team and governance committees in a more tactical initiative. This initiative must align with the strategic architecture initiatives in place or intended. Again, rely on the advisory sub-committee to establish the agenda for a tactical initiative. For the deliverable produce a relevant, formal position paper, policy recommendation, or project recommendation that can be used by other governance committee's such as technical standards, or by IT planners or contract management, etc. Examples of tactical initiatives include:

- Open source software including Linux.
- Unified e-mail address book/directory.
- Biometric authentication.
- Wireless networking.
- IPv4 to IPv6 migration.
- Database modernization.

Be warned that your team's involvement in a tactical initiative may create disharmony above and beyond what already exists in the federated organization. A tactical initiative's immediacy can make individuals and departments more reactionary. Include subject matter experts from various departments of the organization into the tactical initiative process to avoid negative reaction at the technical level of the organization. Tactical initiatives are usually more visible and get more attention from stakeholders than strategic initiatives and a successful short term, energetic process can boost the relevancy of EA planning within an organization. The long term IT strategic planning work still needs to be done though.

TRUST: THE FINAL RECOMMENDATION

This chapter has provided a number of resources and actions aimed at making a big job easier for a small team. Regardless of how thoroughly your repository is maintained, or how well your target is planned, or how finely you have tuned your governance process, it is people working together that results in an effective, efficient, organization—an organization where IT serves the business needs and keeps costs down. The final recommendation for a small enterprise architecture team is to build trust relationships between the departments of the federated organization. Especially in a federated organization, the architect(s) should engage with the largest scope of inter-departmental and intra-departmental groups as possible. The enterprise architect team can centrally position itself and act as a conduit, an enabler, an advocate, and a coordinator of all the separate agents of change within an organization. Working from that center the EA team helps build trust relationships that are the basis for the success of all other enterprise efforts. From that trust comes cooperation, and cooperating departments offer up their current artifacts more readily, work towards a consensus target vision, and willingly participate in the EA governance process. With cooperation, the small enterprise architecture team can accomplish big tasks.

REFERENCES

Barry, D. K. (2003). *Web services and service-oriented architectures.* San Francisco: Morgan Kaufmann Publishers.

Bredemeyer, D., & Malan, R. (2004). *What it takes to be a great enterprise architect.* (Enterprise Architecture Advisory Service Executive Report Vol. 7, No 8). Arlington, MA: Cutter Consortium.

Kiepuszewski, B., Paluskiewicz, M., Stokalski, B., Konkol, S., & Ruszynski, M. (2004). *Applying EA roadmapping: An SOA roadmap*. (Enterprise Architecture Advisory Service Executive Report Vol. 7, No 9). Arlington: Cutter Consortium.

Krafzig, D., Banke, K., & Slama, D. (2005). *Enterprise SOA*. Upper Saddle River, NJ: Prentice Hall Professional Technical Resource.

Weill, P., & Ross, J. W. (2004). *IT governance*. Boston: Harvard Business School Publishing.

APPENDIX

Table 3. Standards bodies

NAME	DESCRIPTION	WEB
Ecma International	Provides Internet standards	http://www.ecma-international.org
FSG (Free Standards Group)	Provides Linux standards	http://www.freestandards.com
Globus Alliance	Provides standards for distributed computing	http://www.globus.org
IEEE (Institute of Electrical and Electronics Engineers)	Provides IT and communications standards	http://www.ieee.org
IETF (Internet Engineering Task Force)	Provides Internet standards	http://www.ietf.org
Internet2	Promotes Interoperability Standards	http://www.internet2.edu/
IOSN (International Open Source Network)	Promotes use of open standards	http://www.iosn.net
ISO (International Organization for Standards)	Leading provider of IT standards	http://www.iso.org
ITU (International Telecommunications Union)	Provides telecommunications standards	http://www.itu.int
OASIS (Organization for the Advancement of Structured Information Standards)	A leading provider of open standards for business, Internet, etc.	http://www.oasis-open.org
ObjectWeb	Provides middleware standards	http://www.objectweb.org
OFBiz.org (Open For Business)	Promotes open source office productivity	http://www.ofbiz.org
OGC (Open GIS Consortium)	Promotes open GIS standards	http://www.opengis.org
OMG (Object Management Group)	Promotes UML and Model Driven Architecture (MDA) development standards	http://www.omg.org
OSDL (Open Source Development Labs)	Develops Linux Kernel	http://www.osdlab.org
OSI (Open Source Initiative)	Ensures open source licensing compliance	http://www.opensource.org
W3C (World Wide Web Consortium)	Provides Internet standards	http://www.w3.org

Table 4. Common standards for enterprise architecture

BPEL, BPEL4WS (Business Process Execution Language)	OASIS	XML-based language for describing and executing business process rules. BPEL4WS is specific to Web services.
CSS (Cascading Style Sheets)	W3C	Web page formatting.
H.23x, H.26x	ITU	Videoconferencing communications (H.23x) and encoding (H.26x) standards.
HTML, XHTML	W3C	Web Display language.
HTTP, HTTPS	IETF / W3C	Web protocol.
IPv6 (Internet Protocol v. 6)	IETF	Network layer protocol.
Java (J2SE, J2EE, J2ME)	Sun Microsystems	Application development and server environment.
JavaScript	ECMA	Application development for browsers.
JSP (Java Server Pages)	Sun Microsystems	Web application development and server environment.
LDAP (Light Directory Access Protocol)	IETF	Standard for directory services.
LSB (Linux Standards Base)	ISO	Standard for Linux operating environment and application compatibility.
ODF (OpenDocument Format)	OASIS	XML-based file format standard.
WMS, WFS, GML (Web Map Service, Web Feature Service, Geography Markup Language)	OGC	File format and data storage protocols for GIS (graphic information systems).
PDF (Portable Document Format)	ISO	Document format and display.
PGP (Pretty Good Privacy)	IETF	Privacy key--see RFC 1991, 2015, 2440, and 3156.
PKI (Public Key Infrastructure)	ISO /ITU X.509	Privacy key and digital signature standards.
RTF (Rich Text Format)	Microsoft	Document formatting.
SAML (Security Assertion Markup Language)	OASIS	Markup language for exchange of authentication and authorization assertions.
SMTP (Simple Mail Transfer Protocol)	IETF	E-mail transport protocol.
SNMP (Simple Network Management Protocol)	IETF	Network management protocol.
SOAP	IETF / W3C	XM-based protocol supporting inter-platform communication including those for Web services.
SQL (Structured Query Language)	ANSI	Database query language for relational databases.
TCP, UDP	IETF	Network communications protocols.
UML (and MDA)	OMG	Systems modeling--model driven architecture.
WSDL (Web Services Description Language)	W3C	XML format for describing the interface and communication protocol for a Web service.
XML (eXtensible Markup Language)	W3C	Ubiquitous markup standard for data description and interchange.
XSL / XSLT (eXtensible Style Sheets)	W3C	Formatting transformation for XML documents.

Chapter XX
The Syngenta Architecture Story

Peter Hungerford
Syngenta AG., Switzerland

ABSTRACT

We share the experiences of an enterprise architecture (EA) practice within a young global company, Syngenta. We will see how EA within the company has evolved and matured. We will reveal our general architecture experiences, plus insights gleaned from case studies in widely differing business areas. EA nowadays aspires to cover all aspects of the enterprise—particularly business process and information. A theme that we emphasize is that architects can no longer dictate to the organization by reason of analytical/technical superiority, but need the skills to affect strategic decisions and directions by influencing. This leads to the conclusion that effective EA is as much a social activity as a technical one, where personal skills are clearly as important as analytical. In addition, we have found that considering architecture challenges through the lens of business efficiency, growth, and innovation provides a framework for a deeper understanding of the issues, constraints, inevitable trade-offs, and potential architecture solutions to particular business problems.

INTRODUCTION

We will tell the Syngenta architecture story, starting with a general introduction to Syngenta as a company, its business, and its aspirations. We will briefly review the IS organization. With this as context, we report on the evolution of our EA practice and its development to its current relatively mature state. We will highlight people, process, and technology aspects. We give particular emphasis to the softer issues such as skills, culture, and communication.

We will then consider a number of our key architecture initiatives in the form of case studies, analyzing the business problem, the architectural challenges, and the decisions taken. Through the course of this discussion, we will provide a summary of key do's and don'ts.

In addition, we consider a simple architecture framework that allows us to classify our activities and provides guidelines for further understanding.

In conclusion, we look at where we, as enterprise architects within Syngenta, would like to be heading, identifying the key EA challenges that we are facing, and pinpointing where we need academia and industry to help others and us.

The specific objectives of this chapter are:

- Share EA experiences, learning, and insights from a global company.
- Highlight the social aspects needed for successfully implementing EA in a multi-national business environment.
- Discuss actual architectural experiences within a simple framework.
- Provide suggestions for areas of EA research via our experience and needs.

We hope that our wide experiences and findings will provide assistance for other companies on a similar journey.

BACKGROUND

In order to provide an overall context for the subsequent architecture discussions, we will provide a brief background to Syngenta as a company. In addition we will present an overview of the IS department, including the position of the global strategy and architecture group (the custodians of EA), the reporting line, and the information technology used within the company.

The Company

Syngenta (www.syngenta.com) is a world-leading agribusiness committed to sustainable agriculture through innovative research and technology. The company is a leader in crop protection, and ranks third in the high-value commercial seeds market. Syngenta employs some 20,000 people in more than 90 countries.

The company was founded in the year 2000 by a merger of Novartis Agribusiness and Zeneca Agrochemicals; it has its headquarters in Basel, Switzerland.

Syngenta has a substantial research and development function with some 5,000 employees working in research, technology, and development.

The company business strategy is summarized inFigure 1, which focuses on three broad major market areas—Agri, consumer-led, and new.

Another way of labeling these areas would be *efficiency, growth,* and *innovation*, terms, which we will be using later in the discussion.

The IS Organization

In order to support our 20000 end users, situated at about 420 sites world wide, Syngenta IS is organized as shown in Figure 2.

The global strategy and architecture group is part of global IS and is responsible for the development, maintenance, governance, and communication of the EA. Of the approximately 450 IS people, there are 11 full time enterprise/IS architects. It should be highlighted that the Global IS Shared Solutions is our services organization. The IS organization mirrors the Syngenta business structure.

IS change management follows a well-established lifecycle methodology that is based on a strong portfolio review process, which in turn is closely linked to the Syngenta business strategy and financial review processes.

Figure 1. Business strategy

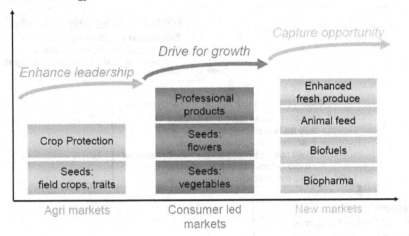

Figure 2. IS Organisation

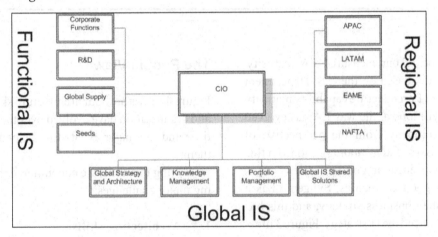

The IT strategy is to consolidate on and exploit the toolsets from leading platform vendors. Software infrastructure is based primarily on Microsoft technology and business applications are based on SAP. A notable exception to this is within research and development, where a greater diversity of systems exists to support the unique business requirements.

OUR ENTERPRISE ARCHITECTURE EVOLUTION

Since the company's formation (and with the committed support of our CIO), the IS organization has been actively pursuing EA and considers itself a leader in the field. This statement is based on discussions with many other companies and

Figure 3. IS Strategy

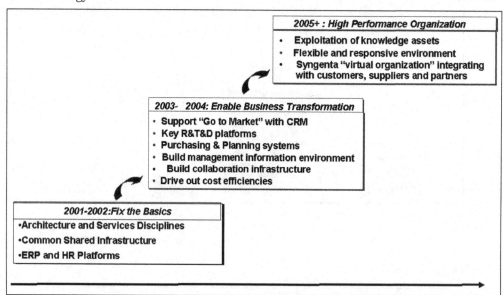

by comparison of our measured EA maturity. We use a model based on the U.S. Department of Commerce IT architecture capability maturity model. We will look at the way EA has evolved within the company from the perspective of *people*, *processes*, and *technology* and from this share our experiences and best practices.

As in all good companies, Syngenta has a well-established business strategy, and this has strongly influenced the IS strategy. Figure 3 illustrates the IS strategy that we have been following consistently since the original merger.

One could say that we spent the first years of our existence like a young child, learning how to walk, followed by a growth spurt, and ending up in young adulthood. Again, we could label the three phases with *efficiency, growth, and innovation* since we can align them with the business strategy areas we saw earlier.

This strategy puts into context the growth of EA within the company, which we will now explore from the viewpoints of people, processes, and technology.

The People View

Figure 4 shows how our architecture skills, roles, and organization have evolved over the course of time and the major events that helped to shape them.

During this time, we encountered the following major challenges:

1. **Architecture skills:**
   - What makes a good architect? There are differing views on this, depending on whether, for example, you are sitting in an architecture function or within a services organization.
   - How do architects deal with the ever-increasing pace of change? Architects not only have to learn new soft skills but also still need to deal with technology. How do we keep the necessary technical skills fresh?
   - How can architects bridge between business and IS? The focus is changing from technology to one of dealing with information and business issues. Moving from local to global

Figure 4. Evolution of skills, roles and organization

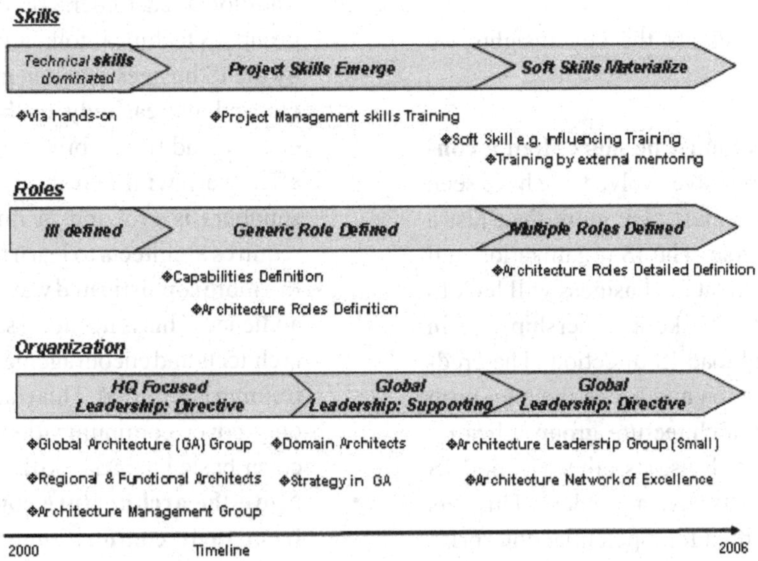

scope we found that, in order to achieve the desired ends, we need to be able to *influence* an organization rather than dictate through technical knowledge.

2. **Roles:**

We needed a learning period to understand, identify, and agree the architecture roles. Different parts of the organization initially had differing expectations as to what degree of detail architecture should cover (*One man's architecture is another man's design*) and hence the role and corresponding skill set that the architects should have. These became clearer after going through a formal definition of the architecture role and the corresponding capabilities, although since the role of the architect is continuously evolving within the company this needs to be revisited at intervals.

3. **Architecture organization:**

Finding the optimal constitution of the architecture board, or organizing so as to gain informed commitment from all stake-

holders is not easy. Assigning membership of the architecture board was a challenge and involved a trade-off between ensuring representation for all key stakeholders and having a functional, manageable size. We initially tried with an inclusive model and found great difficulty in making a quorum; this led to impasse and no decisions being made. Over the course of time we elected to switch to a much smaller group of key enthusiastic members from various parts of the IS organization which, of course, places a greater emphasis on effective communication and consultation. Supporting this group is an extended architecture community. This model has been more successful, primarily owing to an increased trust by the organization in the smaller group and the feeling that, via the extended architecture community, interested individuals can still influence decisions.

The Key Insights

The following highlights the key insights we have identified:

- **The architect must be more than a consultant:** As we have evolved, we have seen that architects must play more than just a consultancy role. The IS organization and to a certain extent the business will look to the architects to take a leadership role in determining broad IS direction. The credibility (reputation and hence the long term value) of the architecture group relies on making correct decisions, otherwise both IS and the business have a problem. This sets the bar very high for a potential enterprise architect—he or she must have personal credibility.

- **Make the architecture group a desirable career step:** Building on the previous point, in order to obtain the high-caliber people that an architecture group requires, it must be seen as a desirable career step. In the past it was the natural progression for the IS technical community, now this is no longer so clear. The traditional supply of new architects via the services organization is drying up with no clear natural successor. Equally, the architecture group must not be seen as a career graveyard—it must be a career step. The open question is; What is the next position for an architect?

- **Understand who the architecture group's customers are and be able to speak their language:** As architecture has evolved, the traditional customers of the architecture group, IS technical folk, are being replaced by the IS business-facing group, IS managers, and, increasingly, the business managers. In addition, ability to communicate effectively with and influence third party suppliers is growing in importance. This requires architects to learn to communicate in a more sophisticated way, tailored to their audience. This is not necessarily easy for all architects and encouragement and/or formal training is required. This training should not only cover communication skills but also cover basic business skills.

- **Move the architecture community away from their comfort zone around infrastructure to the higher value of applications, information, and business process:** We, the current architects, tend to be of a certain age and come with an IT background strongly influenced by technical issues (let's face it—we are a bunch of old techies at heart!). Even now as architects, we are more comfortable in having a technical discussion (how do we get that data from A to B?) rather than looking at the bigger picture (is that the correct information flow to support the business process?). It requires a mindset shift of the architecture organization to get this new view, and constant challenging of one another to begin with. However, once this has set in it appears to be self-sustaining.

- **The Rule of Three:** Architects need to work on three levels of abstraction: The level of

Table 1. The architect must be a leader, must be good, and must be right

Do	Don't
• Formally agree the role description of architects. • Have a training program, which includes presentation, influencing, and negotiation skills.	• Think that architects will only have an infrastructure background; a business process analyst make also may a great architect. • Consider that architecture is the end point of an IS career.

Figure 5. Evolution of governance, communication and architecture development

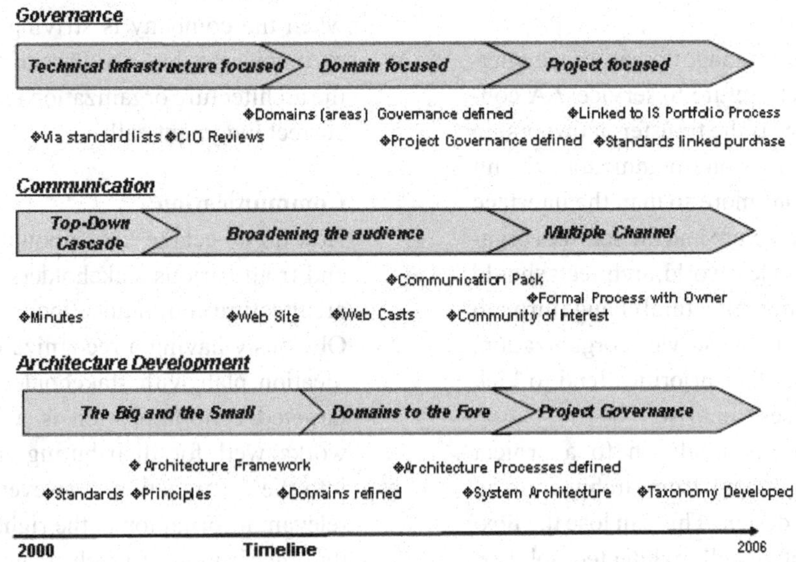

the current problem, the level above in order to put work in context, and the level below in order to be sure that the proposed solution is likely to work. They also work to three time scales: Mostly medium term but in context of the long-term (where the strategy drives) and the short-term (what needs to be done now—can we realistically get there from here). Finally, it can be argued that they need to have been involved with three major projects before they can call themselves qualified.

The Process View

Figure 5 shows our progression in terms of architecture governance, communication and architecture framework, and process development.

During this five-year development period, we encountered the following major challenges:

1. **Governance:**
   How to get visibility of projects and get involved at the right time? In a large organization, it is essential but often difficult to obtain visibility of those projects that are likely to have significant effect on the EA at a time when they can be easily challenged and, if necessary, their direction altered. Having a portfolio process where all IS projects are recorded is a start. However, in a global organization, a set of clear criteria as to what makes a significant project from an architecture perspective is also required.

Not all expensive projects will cause significant architecture impact, but it's a fair bet.

If architecture gets involved too late, the project will already have acquired too much momentum and it may not be possible to change its approach, if it is required.

If it comes to a fight, projects generally win over architecture.

- How do we best manage transition of ownership from architecture to services? A constant challenge is the transfer of ownership of a project from one organizational unit to another, none more so than the interface between architecture and the services organization. In an ideal world, architects should accompany an architectural change through the transition to the services organization, but in reality, other priorities tend to kick in. So two cases can arise:
  - Architecture holds on to a project too long, going from architecture to solution design. This can lose the flexibility of a well-architected solution by being too detailed, and, when it is finally transferred, causes ownership problems.
  - The opposite case is when architecture lets go too early and the original concept is lost during the design stage.
- How do we get middle level business management to buy into EA? In Syngenta, where the CIO forcefully advocates EA and evangelizes it well to the board, the value of EA is well accepted at the higher business management levels. However, the architecture message often gets diluted at the middle management layers where local projects, budgets, and priorities are naturally seen as paramount, overriding the enterprise view.
- What are the correct things for us to govern? Resources are limited and an organization must carefully consider the activities that it pays detailed attention too. As we will see later, this can vary depending on the strategy an enterprise or business area is following (efficiency, growth, or innovation). For example, in times when efficiency is paramount, detailed examination by

architecture into the number and variety of desktop packages would make sense, but when the company is striving for growth or innovation less so. Part of the skill of the architecture organization is making the correct judgment call.

2. **Communication:**
   How do we get the right amount of detail to and from various stakeholders? The art of architecture communication is very subtle. Obviously having a recognizable communication plan with stakeholders receiving targeted communication is a basis. This works well for distributing information into the organization. However, obtaining relevant information at the right time from the organization is a much greater challenge. This is probably the issue that Syngenta architecture has struggled with, and may not yet have optimized.

3. **Architecture development**
   - How do we avoid losing architecture benefits in design? Good architecture can, to a large extent, be negated by failings at design stages. It is critical for major new projects to have direct attention from the architecture group or to have established processes and organization structures that are fully conversant with the architectural intent. We use design authorities: A person or organization responsible for reviewing individual project design plans against the underlying architecture within a specific area (e.g., Enterprise Data Warehouse) and accepting, revising, or escalating if necessary.
   - What is relevant for non-architects? Architecture is not performed in a vacuum; a large amount of the output should be aimed at the external world (business or IS) and as such must be seen to be relevant and accessible. The appearance of too much

intellectual rigor can in fact be counter-productive with architects seen as living in an Ivory Tower.

The Key Insights

- **CIO support is imperative:** You absolutely need a CIO who actively supports the EA endeavor generally and the chief architect specifically in cases of conflict. At times, our CIO uses the word architecture in every second sentence! This, of course, in turn makes it all the more essential that the architect be right. If an organization is into a TCO discussion about the value of EA then the outlook is bleak.

- **Get the timing right:** This is especially true for getting an organization to accept major architectural changes. The seeds of an idea have to be planted within the organization and allowed to mature before pushing for formal acceptance. Timing is of paramount importance. Attempting too early you will often encounter roadblocks (e.g., in the case of IS managers holding infrastructure budgets. Signs that the organization has accepted the idea are:
  - The CIO espouses the idea and is asking when it will happen.
  - Key IS managers are wondering where the money is going to come from rather than asking why the change is needed.
  - Business managers are asking for pilot implementations.

Too late in applying for ratification and the momentum is lost, the organization has turned its attention elsewhere and is no longer interested in pursuing the change. In fact, there may be a feeling that it has done without and therefore does not need the proposal.

- **Actively monitor processes and have owners for them:** Architecture processes, for example governance or communication, once established seldom run by themselves. They need constant nurturing and monitoring and for this, it is critical that a single individual be given the accountability.

- **Recognize the battle that must be won:** Not every architecture confrontation can be actively fought, let alone won. The energy required to do so is too great and the overall value to the enterprise not proportionate. It requires individuals or the architecture organization to assess the situation coolly with as little emotion as possible and rationally decide whether this is the conflict that must be won. An important aspect to consider is whether the timing is right. Quite often if a particular architecture initiative is being blocked by the organization, it is more effective to back off, analyze the stakeholders and their issues, and take a more strategic view rather than force the issue.

- **Making architecture reviews a win-win situation:** Successful reviews are win-wins for both the architecture group and the proj-

Table 2. Timing is everything; Not only must you do the right thing, it must be at the right time

Do	Don't
• Have a formal communication plan. • Get the CIO to *believe* in EA. • Recognize the correct point for architects to let go of a project.	• Pursue the right activities at the wrong time. • Be perceived as the command and control group. • Tightly govern projects that only have minor impact on the EA.

ect that is being reviewed. A key point is the tone that the interviewing architects set. It is important to make the review a learning experience for both sides, with the architects being willing to learn from the project, while discussing the bigger picture issues that may not be apparent at the project level in a positive manner. Interrogation and acting superior will clearly lead to entrenchment of the project's position, and most likely no willing change to the architecture proposals. Strategic influencing is a key skill that needs to be part of the architects' repertoire. A key point is making sure that reviews are held at a time where changes can still be instigated relatively easily.

The Technology View

Figure 6 diagram shows the evolution of our architecture documentation and collaboration and communication.

We encountered the following major challenges:

1. **Documentation technologies:** Regardless of the underlying approach to documenting the architecture it is difficult to:

   - Get the correct level of detail.
   - Keep documentation up to date.
   - Provide the correct views for differing stakeholders.

   In order to get the organization to start documenting at all, we deliberately took a light touch approach to the use of formal architecture tools. This proved successful; now however, as anticipated, we have to deal with the issue of consistency.

2. **Communication and collaboration technologies:** Initially as an organization we only had rudimentary collaboration technologies with no common means for collaborating and sharing information. This problem has been alleviated as we roll out a standardized collaboration service. The architecture group was instrumental in proposing and championing this extension to our infra-

Figure 6. Evolution of documentation approaches and collaboration/communication technologies

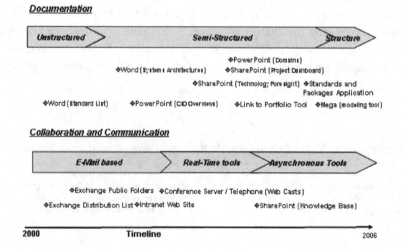

structure and was heavily involved via pilots in refining the service.

The Key Insights

- **Technologies and tools are less important than people and processes:** It certainly has been our experience that the technology support for EA plays a secondary role to the *people* and *process* aspects. Of course, it is highly desirable to have EA artifacts recorded as far as possible in a structured format, but for a developing EA function this certainly comes after defining the basic architecture processes or agreeing the architecture roles.

- **Visio is a great tool for the "hobby" architect:** Visio is much maligned as a tool for recording EA information for the obvious reason that there is very little support from the tool itself for ensuring consistency or validating the information recorded. However, in terms of ease of use it is hard to beat. We found that with well-thought-out stencils it was the ideal tool for broad use in recording information in a developing EA function. At a later phase, more structured tools can be introduced; we are currently at this phase.

- **Documentation doesn't have to be perfect to be useful—initially:** In an organization where architecture information is mostly in people's heads (perhaps including some who have left the company), having any documentation at all is better than nothing. Clearly as the level of detail required increases then the accuracy, comprehensiveness and completeness will have to improve. This relates to the previous point.

- **Artifacts for communication are long term:** The organization takes time to assimilate key architecture artifacts (e.g., architecture domains). There are some diagrams that are always referred to within the organization and give structure to many discussions. It is important that once the organization has taken to these (in fact assumed ownership) that they are not lightly changed, e.g., in order to introduce more refinements. This leads to uncertainty.

CASE STUDIES

In this section, we will look at several major architecture initiatives that we have been through within the company. We will describe the business challenge and the architectural approach taken, and use this to provide detailed lessons learned and insights gained specifically through this work.

Table 3.

Do	Don't
• Recognize that certain diagrams/documents become key to describing the EA. Changes to these artifacts should be handled with care. • Realize that creating an EA is a collaboration exercise and needs correct tools for support. • Recognize the broad industry trend to provide standard EA frameworks and processes supported by tools.	• Put the technology view before people and process. • Over-document—there is a point where it becomes a diminishing return.

Server Rationalization and Building Global Infrastructure Services

The Business Challenge

A benchmark exercise indicated that although our cost of management per server was best in class, we needed to reduce by 40% the number of servers. This spurred us to launch a project aimed at consolidating and rationalizing the servers that Syngenta owned. At the same time, we made the decision to create standardized infrastructure services.

The Architectural Approach

We undertook the architecture work in partnership with a third party who would subsequently be responsible for running these services. This third party was responsible for creating the architecture and designs, while Syngenta architects provided direction, challenged, and validated the architecture proposals. Together we created an initial architecture framework that recognized the major global services we had to deliver: database, Web server, thin client, directory, messaging, and application. Architectural principles included location of data centers. Based on these, detailed architectural proposals for the services were produced. To validate these proposals we held extensive review and approval workshops, including all major stakeholders (e.g., delivery and production managers).

Challenges

The major challenge was financial and technical modeling of the key services to understand how best to perform consolidation. This involved balancing the trade-off between network bandwidth usage (costs and performance) and server consolidation. We had extensive discussions before we came to a common view of the different classes of data centers. A final point was the harmonization of individual service designs into an overall, consistent design.

Key Insights

- As we work with more external suppliers, we need to recognize that although we (Syngenta) have ownership of our architecture, there will be others who can assist with our architecture work.
- There is the potential over the course of time that in-house architects, while still owning the architecture, may not actually produce any of it, but more often manage partners and others who are better able to produce the artifacts (This may even change the nature of the artifacts we need e.g. in the case of a utility service). This will be especially true

Table 4. Ownership of architecture remains in the company but there may be many partners supplying architecture contect

Do	Don't
• Realize that architecture ownership remains within the enterprise, but that others can and should contribute. • Get broad agreement that the architecture is correct by allowing enough time and opportunity for the organization to understand, comment on, and buy into the proposals. • Arrange for a smooth transition out of the architecture group, monitor and if necessarily update in the light of design or implementation. Ensure that the ownership is recognized at every stage of the project.	• Think that architecture is the same as design.

for the base infrastructure components of the architecture.

- Although primarily concerned with the front end of any major change, architects need to be concerned with its full life cycle, being prepared to revaluate the architecture proposals based on design or implementation findings and ensuring that the architecture intent is adhered to.

Provide an Integrated "Go-to-Market" Platform

The Business Challenge

We had to provide a global integrated platform for supporting the company's *Go-to-Market* strategy. This platform was to be used by major sales countries within Syngenta, recognizing that individual countries had different business requirements. This platform covered the following functional areas: B2B, CRM, sales team support, marketing, and contact center support.

The Architectural Approach

It was agreed for CRM that there would be a common technology platform with an approved template for country implementation. We identified standard common business functions that

allowed the reuse of common technology components relating to these functions. Individual countries then implemented the design. For B2B we also identified a common technology platform (centrally hosted). Standard middleware was used overall for connecting different systems. A CRM/B2B network of excellence (network of excellence is a Syngenta term for a community sharing a common long-term project goal), with both IS and business membership was used for establishing business requirements, building consensus and first architectural approval. A central dedicated IS and business team drove the program and provided full time resources.

Challenges

It is perhaps not surprising given the nature of the project that reuse, at the process, information and technology levels, was the biggest major architectural issue. There was a constant need for us to balance between country and global requirements.

Key Insights

- Agreeing the overall global architecture is one thing, keeping to the spirit at a local design level is another.

Table 5. Agreeing the overall global architecture is one thing, keeping to the spirit at a local design level is another

Do	Don't
• Look in detail at data flows and data processes before architecting the technology solutions. • Beware of moving from architecture into design: (a) As an architect you are probably too removed from the details to be able to do this successfully; (b) you restrict the possibility of others to provide innovative designs within the architecture. • For large/long programs of work have an empowered, stable mixed IS/Business team which has regular face-to-face meetings.	• Underestimate the amount of effort needed for agreeing data standards especially when legacy systems are involved. • Think that reuse is simple and always cost effective. • Architect a system from the IT perspective--think rather from the point of view of the customer.

- Reuse seems better at the system level (e.g., complete B2B systems), rather than at the level of individual components. This involved making a copy and then adapting.
- With end customers facing solutions, recognize that local requirements will lead to a limited amount of reuse and that the architecture proposals should allow for a large degree of local specializations.

Providing a Unified Research Platform

The Business Challenge

As part of our research organization strategy, we had to replace the legacy companies' research support systems by a new global platform. This platform was to support the research organization and its major processes, and was to cover structured and semi-structured data.

The Architectural Approach

We agreed research-specific architectural principles, e.g., location and organization-independent systems and major architectural building blocks. These included:

- A common document storage system to store all Research documents and with this platform provide a means for document-centric collaboration.
- A system for recording chemical and test information to be built in-house, based on a relational database as repository, including some third party software with interfaces to laboratory and logistic equipment. The system was built from scratch, by distributed development teams. The software modules were built in parallel with the aim of going live in one major push.
- A common, single instance dictionary/reference data system for use across all systems.

For most of these systems, we took a service-oriented architecture (SOA) approach.

Challenges

Some of the problems we encountered were intrinsic to the technology used. These included the use of SOA, where the chosen technology did not perform as anticipated, especially in the areas of authentication, transactions, and performance. Other issues we encountered were organizational, where design teams were embedded in historical legacy organizations.

Table 6. The company memory plays an important role in specific architecture solutions

Do	Don't
• For important systems using new technology make sure that the architecture is validated by proofs of concept that test all major functionality. • Try to avoid a Big Bang approach to going live. Incremental implementations allow better validation of the architecture and/or the design and allow changes to be made if necessary. • Ensure that the architecture group shepherd the design work to ensure that it keeps to the essence and if necessary can feed back into the architecture. • Promote and foster the architecture principle of simplicity.	• Make IS the means to force common business processes. • Architect a solution before enough time is taken to obtain an agreed business process. • Think that current SOA technologies are mature enough for easy implementation, especially across technology platforms. • Assume compensation logic is the same as two-phase commit. • Underestimate the coordination effort for dispersed teams.

Key Insights

- An architecture that has been developed by people who have had previous experience and use an approach of evolution from previous systems is likely to be less risky but produce a less flexible/innovative solution.
- A company has a *memory* and if this *memory* goes (people moving on) then projects and architects start afresh. This has *pros* (new ideas) and *cons* (making the same mistakes). Often updating a system provides feedback to the architects. There is probably an optimal time for introducing major changes into a systems landscape; one of the factors in this is the experience (memory) of the architects.
- How can we communicate architecture to the business owners? Physical architects can construct a model from which the business owner can visualize the final result. This is not true for IT architecture. We can mock up screens for users, but this is like showing individual rooms to a buyer without showing him what the building looks like.
- For modular systems consider carefully how these modules are to be created: (a) all at once; (b) serially; (c) each a bit at a time. There are significant trade-offs between the different approaches (e.g., in how to perform systems integration tests).

Providing Enterprise-Wide Business Intelligence

The Business Challenge

Our existing business intelligence solutions were no longer fit for purpose. The issues were many but the main drivers were information inconsistency, lack of trust in the data, lack of transparency regarding the origin, and treatment of the data. In addition, new data warehousing requirements were emerging that required new solutions.

The Architectural Approach

We took the decision to build a new foundation for our future BI landscape, the enterprise data warehouse (EDWH). This EDWH is the single source for all information reporting. The heart of the EDWH is the DWH layer, also called the single point of truth (SPOT). This layer is all about reusability. Data is extracted exactly once into the SPOT layer, where it is kept on a granular level. Using the master data information, the data is integrated, but neither flavored nor interpreted. This way we ensure that the data can still be reused across different business areas. The data marts take the data from the SPOT layer. Here the data is processed to serve a set of scope-specific

Table 7. The architecture solution needs to recognize and be congruent with the maturity of the organization as a whole

Do	Don't
• Ensure that (EDWH) concept is underpinned with a strong vision to ensure buy-in. • For major projects ensure strong sponsorship by business stakeholders, and make sure that the CIO shows leadership. • Realize that you need a master data management initiative alongside the EDWH initiative. • Ensure local flexibility, but global compliance.	• Wait for business to lead, but do make sure business is taken along the journey. • Try to solve the master data management issues within the EDWH • Think that data quality improvement is a one-off action. • Think that moving from silo to enterprise thinking is a short-term activity.

Table 8. A simple framework for architecture: Business drivers

Business Driver	Innovation	Growth	Efficiency
Relative investment (Cost)	Medium	Willing to invest most	Must be Low
Expected financial benefit	Unclear but hope is high	High	Low/medium
Risk business is willing to take	High	Medium	Low
Time scale to deliver solutions	Medium	Short since the markets are changing rapidly	Long
Business approach	Managed portfolio	Targeted investment (including M&A)	Rationalization and offshore/ outsourcing for low cost supply

Table 9. A simple framework for architecture: Architecture toles and skills

Architecture Roles & Skills	Innovation	Growth	Efficiency
In relation to the IS Organization	• Providing technology foresight. • Providing rich collaboration and information finding architectures. • Provide sandbox environment. • Disconnected standalone approach.	• Establish base architecture but rapid handover to implementation groups who can better provide business relevant designs.	• Identifying the common components (technology & information) • Decommission. • Micro-managing standards. • Detailed architecture reviews. • Emphasis on infrastructure services.
In relation to the Business	• Providing a standard platform that can be reused in multiple Business PoC/ Venture approaches. • Broker to connect different parts of the organization.	• External focus. • Connect external/market signals into standard business processes (Market sense and respond).	• Strategic sourcing. • Optimizing the business process. • Providing standard, centralized services. • Internal company focus.
Skills	• Out of the box. • Entrepreneurial. • Understand emerging technologies within the business context. • Ability to link to and influence IS expertise embedded within the business unit.	• Able to talk to business. • Deep understanding of what the business wants. • Ability to recognize major change and interpret for the business.	• Project management. • Thoroughness. • Technical credibility in IS.

solutions. The data gets interpreted and organized in a performance-optimized way to be accessed by BI tools. We have a very strong focus on maximizing reuse across projects and business areas for the benefit of the entire company. With the EDWH, we changed the focus from silos to enterprise solutions, supporting the business in obtaining *one set of numbers*. We also built in the concept of reusing data from the EDWH as feeds into other systems.

Challenges

The most important challenges revolved around data quality and alongside this master data management. We also found a degree of resistance in changing the mindset of the organization to support the enterprise solution focus.

Key Insights

- The architecture solution needs to recognize and be congruent with the maturity of the organization. You can't expect skyscrapers to be built with mud and sticks.
- Many parts of the business need the same basic information, which turns the focus from silo to enterprise solutions. This needs to be reflected in the supporting organization and processes.
- Timing needs to be right. It's almost as through the business needs to feel the pain of an outdated solution in order to be ready for the journey.

EFFICIENCY, GROWTH, AND INNOVATION: A SIMPLE FRAMEWORK FOR ARCHITECTURE?

Introduction

Our EA approach is evolving from homegrown frameworks and processes to a framework based on Zachman (see Zachman Institute for Framework Advancement Web site http://www.zifa.com/) and a process guided by the TOGAF (See the open group architecture forum Web site) approach. However, in addition to this formal basis we have noted another means of architecture classification that has the potential to provide insights into architecture development. We will now explore this.

As part of our business strategy, the terms *efficiency, growth, and innovation are* often used to describe our approach to different market areas:

- **Efficiency:** Markets where there is no expectation of growth and our business advantage comes from efficient execution.
- **Growth:** Markets that Syngenta expects to expand.
- **Innovation**: Markets are new (to Syngenta).

Moreover we can also see in terms of business processes a similar categorization:

- **Efficiency:** Operational (finance and administration, order fulfillment).
- **Growth:** Leadership (market sense and respond).
- **Innovation:** Management (new product introductions and management information).

Table 10. A Simple Framework for Architecture: Qualities and Dimensions

Architecture qualities & dimensions	Innovation	Growth	Efficiency
Qualities			
Scalability	Local	Market focused	Enterprise wide
Usability	Visualization	Query and drill down	Optimized for repetitive use
Extensibility	Often thrown away if not fit for purpose	Design for scale up	A *given* for a shared service
Flexibility	Capable of targeted, specific usage	Optimized, must be capable of rapid adapting for emerging business needs	Generic
Reliability	Less important	Important	Essential
Simplicity	Not necessary	Desirable	Essential
Security	"Good enough"	Important and outward focused	Essential and historically inward focused (but changing)
Dimension Infrastructure	Thin: small number of common components	Medium number of common components operated as individual services	Maximize common components operated as common services
Applications	Home grown, problem specific functionality, human-centric	*Best of Breed*, collaborative, competitive advantage functionality	Packages, transactional, industry standard functionality, machine-centric
Information	Structured, non-transactional, standardization less important	Semi-structured	Predominately structured, transactional based standardization important
Business Process	Loose, changing organization		Well-defined, fixed stable organization

Intrigued by the usage within a business context, we have tried to take these terms and use them as a simple framework for architecture classification (these are shown in Tables 8 & 10). With this framework, we will attempt to provide a deeper insight into the characteristics of the architecture activities. We note that this framework has similarities with those found in IT portfolio management. For example, see Cranfield grid (Ward & Peppard, 2002), Ross/Beath framework (Ross & Beath, 2002), or Geoffrey Moore core/ context analysis framework (Moore, 2002).

Discussion of the Case Studies in the Light of the Framework

We believe that this framework can provide broad, although not detailed, guidance for architects and we try to explore this next.

We see *efficiency, growth,* and *innovation* structures within a particular business area. For example, research as a whole would be labeled *innovation* but there are clearly areas of efficiency (e.g., high-throughput screening of chemicals) and growth (data mining).

Possible consequences of the framework are:

- For architecting in a given area (*efficiency, growth, innovation*), keep to the style as given by the table. Only mix if you have made an explicit, considered decision.
- Business change and new technology both tend to follow a natural progression *innovation* to *growth* to *efficiency* and followed by outsourcing/retirement. For each step there is an opportunity to consider re-architecting.
- An end-to-end business process will often transcend business areas, which fall into different categories. For example, bringing a new product to market involves research, development/registration, manufacture, and commercial departments. Of course there will be interactions between differing domains, e.g., registration (*efficiency*) and research (*innovation and efficiency*). These will have technical and informational implications (e.g., interfaces, form of system coupling), but we believe that the biggest potential difficulty is at the people/organization level where there may well be a clash of mindsets. The architect in producing solutions should be well aware of this.
- Also possible are substructures, for example *efficiency* within *innovation* (e.g., chemical logistic support systems within a research system). These, however, seem less problematical, perhaps because the superstructure sets the context for the substructure.

Looking at our case studies, we can in the first instance categorize them as:

- **Innovation:** Providing a unified research platform for structured and semi-structure data.
- **Growth:** Providing an integrated "go-to-market" platform. Providing an enterprise-wide business intelligence.
- **Efficiency:** Server rationalization and building global infrastructure services.

We do not have space to go into an in-depth analysis here but would like feedback from readers as to whether they agree with our analysis and whether they feel there is value in pursuing this approach.

FUTURE TRENDS AND RESEARCH

As we move forward in Syngenta, we find that we are being challenged in the following areas.

- As the pace of delivery increases, how can we best architect at speed? Must quality be sacrificed?
- How do we recognize the key architectural building blocks within an enterprise? How can we provide industry standard building blocks?
- What are the characteristics of a good architecture—how do we all recognize one?
- As the focus changes from just the enterprise to the extended enterprise—having to deal with many partners, suppliers, and customers—architecture and architects will have to take an even broader view. Will this, perforce, lead to greater architecture standardization?
- What is the career path for an architect? Where is the next generation going to come from?

We believe that we are not alone and most of these are industry issues. We believe there is an urgent need for research to provide a solid foundation and/or the establishing of best practices to address some of these concerns. Moreover, for the next generation of architects we need universities to recognize and embrace EA in their curricula.

CONCLUSION

In conclusion, we would like to say that through our experiences we are coming to recognize that, for architecture to be effective within an enterprise, architects need more than analytical skills. The ability to influence and lead the IS and even business organizations is vital, especially for significant changes to the EA. This leads us to say that effective EA within a large company is as much a social activity as a technical or an analytical one.

We have seen that a simple framework based on recognizing areas of activity classified as *efficiency, growth,* or *innovation* can provide a framework by which we can view our architecture activities and judge them for consistency of approach.

Finally as we move forward, it is important to build upon our successes and adopt a mindset of seeing opportunities rather than problems. If we cannot convince our business partners that we can enthusiastically keep adding value to their endeavors then we will move from the mainstream to the backwaters of commodity computing alongside such activities as data entry, tape changers, Cobol coders .... would we really want that?

We hope that by sharing our experiences and insights that we can help to contribute to the practice of enterprise architecture.

ACKNOWLEDGMENTS

I would like to thank the following colleagues for detailed discussions and invaluable feedback to this chapter: Jeff Brown, Frank Dugrillon, Alec Fitton, Steve Holt, Allen Lo, Mike Meysner, Pierre Pfister, and Armin Weltin. Without them and many other colleagues, this would not be the Syngenta architecture story. Val, as always, gets my heartfelt thanks for putting up with all of this.

REFERENCES

Moore, G. A. (2002). *Living on the fault line: Managing for shareholder value in any economy.* Collins.

Ross, J. W., & Beath, C. M. (2002). Beyond the business case: New approaches to IT investment. *MIT Sloan Management Review*, Winter

TOGAF see the Open Group Architecture Forum web site, http://www.opengroup.org/togaf/

U.S. Department of Commerce IT Architecture Capability Maturity Model see http://www.osec.doc.gov/cio/arch_cmm.htm

Ward, J., & Peppard, J. (2002). *Strategic planning for information systems.* John Wiley & Sons.

Zachman Framework, see Zachman Institute for Framework Advancement web site http://www.zifa.com/

Chapter XXI
The Use of GERAM for Design of a Virtual Enterprise for a Ship Maintenance Consortium

John Mo
Commonwealth Scientific and Industrial Research Orgainsation, Australia

ABSTRACT

This chapter describes the key elements in the application of GERAM to the analysis of the virtual enterprise of a ship maintenance consortium, the ANZAC ship alliance. The ANZAC ship project built 10 ANZAC class guided missile frigates for the Royal Australian Navy and the Royal New Zealand Navy. The ships have a service life of 25 to 30 years in which changes are required to keep up-to-date with latest warfare. In this study, VERA was adopted as the generic enterprise reference architecture to guide the systematic study of the anatomy of the virtual enterprise. The issues of creating and managing the logistics and information infrastructure that are necessary to support successful operation of the virtual enterprise are examined. Particular models were created according to GERAM for the timely support of the projects as the virtual enterprise grew.

INTRODUCTION

The generalised enterprise reference architecture and methodology (GERAM) describes a set of principles that can be used for the design, management, continuous improvement, and operation of enterprises (ISO, 2000). It was developed by the IFIP-IFAC Task Force (Williams et al., 1994)

and adopted as an Appendix of ISO 15704:2000. GERAM defines a complete methodology that captures the engineering and integration requirements for any organisation to develop a fit-for-purpose enterprise model supporting its business (Bernus & Nemes, 1996). GERAM encompasses essential enterprise concepts of life cycles, life history, partial models, and generated views (Noran,

2005). It distinguishes the functions of modelling framework, modelling languages, and modelling tools in the process of design, implementation, and operation of enterprise architectures.

Business enterprise is inherently a complex entity. The application of GERAM is not a straightforward task. The generality of GERAM helps the enterprise engineers to encapsulate the wide range of functions and processes that may exist within the business enterprise when it interacts with its clients. However, continuous innovation and changing business conditions drive enterprises into a dynamic ever-evolving environment. Many enterprises have gone through a number of organisational changes, not only within its own authoritative boundaries, but also involving external entities. Typical changes are growth through the absorption of outside business entities and the consolidation of key projects leading to loss of corporate knowledge and expertise (Nousala, Miles, Kilpatrick, & Hall, 2005). The matter gets messier as the business entities that are involved in the merger processes bring along their heritage resulting in disparate process assets, a varied understanding of process value and disjoint actions and reactions to industrial requirements within the enlarged enterprise (Hall, Dalmaris, & Nousala, 2005). Furthermore, customers are seeking solutions that are reliable and flexible (Syntera, 1998). The sophistication of the products and services demanded by customers requires a wide variety of expertise and integrated specialisation that almost no one enterprise can handle the business alone. Companies increasingly need to seek collaboration opportunities with other organisations. A new concept known as virtual enterprise has added another level of difficulty in the application of GERAM to the new paradigm (Bernus, Baltrusch, Tolle, & Vesterager, 2002).

The virtual enterprise concept captures the fact that many manufacturing, industrial, service, and commercial activities are organised into collaborative teams in networked organisations (Beckett, 2003). The operating conditions of the business environment are characterised by frequent changes in products, services, processes, organisations, markets, supply, and distribution networks (Tharumarajah, 2003). They form a temporary alliance to deliver a project or product and they dissolve when the job is completed. The teams work together as an entity for a goal but the relationships among themselves and the individual companies they come from often rely on trust and industry practices. Success for achieving the goal therefore demands well-coordinated agility in all internal and external aspects of the virtual enterprise. This level of agility can only be achieved if the partners share common views and models, which represent the relevant parts of their operations within the virtual enterprise. Furthermore, these models have to be linked to represent the dynamic relations allowing key performance indicators to be established on compatible platforms. To provide the required inter-operability, the models have to adhere to a common representation for both model enactment and human understandability (Kosanke & Nell, 1999). GERAM has been developed by the IFIP-IFAC Task Force after investigating a number of enterprise architectures including PERA (Williams, 1994), GRAI-GIM (Chen, Vallespir, & Doumeingts, 1997), and CIMOSA (Kosanke, 1995). The outcomes are recommendations for achieving a "complete" architecture by selecting and combining the best features of the available architectures. Hence, GERAM is adopted as the basis for modelling the virtual enterprise.

This chapter describes the key elements in the application of GERAM to the analysis of the virtual enterprise of a ship maintenance consortium. The adoption of an appropriate generic enterprise reference architecture (GERA) to the investigation is critical to the success in the systematic study of the anatomy of the virtual enterprise. The issues of creating and managing the logistics and information infrastructure that are necessary to support successful operation of the virtual enterprise are examined. Particular models were created according to GERAM for the timely support of the projects as the virtual enterprise grew.

VIRTUAL ENTERPRISE REFERENCE ARCHITECTURE

The GERAM metamodel (Figure 1) outlines the elements of an enterprise engineering process that will lead to suitable executable reference architecture for an organisation. The starting point of the methodology requires the availability of a GERA. For the study of virtual enterprise, a reference architecture describing the life cycles of business entities interacting in a dynamic, loosely coupled environment is essential.

The concept of virtual enterprise has been studied in many research projects (Aerts, Szirbik, & Goossenaerts, 2000; Cheng & Popov, 2004; Mills, Brand, & Elmarsi, 1998). The most well known project is the intelligent manufacturing systems (IMS) project GLOBEMEN, which defines the virtual enterprise reference architecture (VERA) (Zwegers, Tolle, & Vesterager, 2003).

The important characteristic of VERA is the change of architecture requirements in different phases of the enterprise entities. This concept originates from the Purdue enterprise reference architecture (PERA) (Williams, 1994). Conceptually, PERA is a time-based modelling framework describing the functions, activities, processes, systems, and other aspects of an enterprise through its life cycle. It starts with the identification of the enterprise with a mission and elaborating from there the concepts, policies and requirements to fulfil the mission. When it comes to the actual establishment of the enterprise, PERA defines three architectures: information systems, manufacturing equipment, and human and organisational architectures. Information systems and manufacturing equipment architectures represent automation of information and materials flow. Human and organisational architecture sits between the two architectures and serves as the operating centre of the virtual enterprise.

VERA, which originates from GERAM, illustrates the logical, recursive relationships between the "network," the "virtual enterprise," and the "product" entities (Figure 2). These entities are themselves representing an enterprise model (EM) in the evolution history of virtual enterprise. Each EM contains a life cycle with phases that the enterprise will go through in its life span from

Figure 1. GERAM metamodel

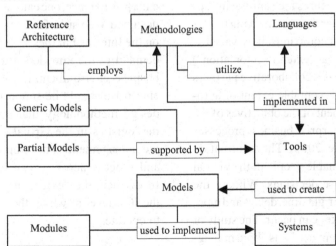

Figure 2. Enterprise models relationships in VERA

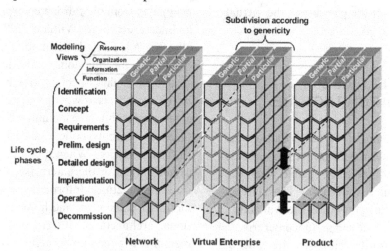

identification to decommission. VERA illustrates that an instance of a "network" can create VEs in its operation phase and, correspondingly, a VE can create "products" (in a general sense, and/or services) in its operation phase. It is noted that the generic and partial models are not real entities and hence they do not have operation phase. Hence, VERA inherits the PERA concepts with the definition of three architectures in each of the VERA entities.

It is essential that a balance is required to ensure all three architectures are running in supporting each other rather than one moving too far (or behind). Individual companies may vary the balancing point (known as "extent of automation") but in a virtual enterprise, collaborative partners must find a common acceptable extent of automation, that is, alignment of the objectives of the amalgamated inter-enterprise business processes (Van den Berg & Tolle, 2000). The information system is the link to enable people in the virtual enterprise making wise decisions. Without the right information at the right time, delays and more seriously costly mistakes can occur. The study of the logistics of virtual enterprise is about manag-

ing the information flow and data architecture across company boundaries to support the work in the virtual enterprise.

Most virtual enterprise developments have been concentrated on the "content" of the information infrastructure rather than its "functions" (Hussein, Nor, Karim, Mamat, & Anom, 2005). While internet technology has substantially improved the communication ability between different organisations, there are other factors affecting the information architecture in a virtual enterprise. Hence, one can easily find a lot of nicely designed Web sites for companies and alliances on the Internet but they fail to meet the stringent demand of the knowledge users in competitive business environment. It is crucial that a virtual enterprise should be supported by a systematic design methodology that adequately describes the logistics in the virtual enterprise and helps the management to develop well-defined policy and process across organisational boundaries. In essence, the "extent of automation" defines the ICT level at which the virtual enterprise is to operate.

THE SHIP CONSORTIUM AS A VIRTUAL ENTERPRISE

The ANZAC ship project is to build 10 ANZAC class guided missile frigates for the Royal Australian Navy and the Royal New Zealand Navy. The first ship was delivered in 1996 with the last two to be delivered by 2006. The ships are planned to have a service life of 25 to 30 years. In this time period, there will be changes in the operational requirements for these vessels. These will lead to major changes in the mission systems, platform systems, and how the ship is operated and used. The long product life cycle means that people, skills, experience, companies, society, and government will change. Documentation is an important starting point to support the product but it can only cater for existing information and has limitation when changes occur (Hall, 2000). In this context, it is important that a well-defined policy and process should be put in place to ensure that knowledge and decision references are applicable over such a long period.

The ANZAC ship alliance (ASA) is an organization formed by an agreement between Tenix Defence, Saab Systems, and the Australian Commonwealth with the aim to provide design and implementation of changes to the in-service ANZAC class frigates over the lifetime of the "product." It is an attempt of all parties involved in the creation of the ANZAC fleet to provide a stable support environment ensuring that the ships are combat ready, "fit for the purpose" at any given time with the best value outcome. The Alliance is not a legal company entity. It draws its resources such as staff and assets from the member organizations as required. To establish a framework for coordinating the supply chain and service team members from different companies across company boundaries, a virtual enterprise study was conducted.

Tenix had built up a long standing relationship with the CSIRO via the GLOBEMEN project. GLOBEMEN is an international project involving 22 companies and research institutions around the world. The project enables partners to work together in a VE environment to develop the theoretical background for global integration of enterprises and to carry out experiments involving real enterprises collaborating on real projects. The new ASA was recognised as having a business structure and objectives that could potentially benefit from the expertise developed via GLOBEMEN. Likewise, GLOBEMEN was able to research the practical aspect of its findings such as VERA.

The approach adopted in this study was the combination of the theoretical understanding of the system nature together with the top down process of segmenting the complex enterprise system into a stepwise phase-oriented architecture for more detailed analysis. GERAM is a general framework, which adopts the best available architecture for specific enterprise integration task. In the case of virtual enterprise integration, VERA in essence adopts PERA in its life cycle analysis. The particular model of ASA is therefore created using the enterprise engineering methodology (EEM) and enterprise modelling language (EML) stipulated by PERA. The PERA methodology (Li & Williams, 2000) helps the virtual enterprises to capture their logistics from objectives to individual tasks. All virtual enterprise operating elements including role functions, project execution guides, document repository, documentation, workflow control, and entry portal can then be specified.

ENTERPRISE ENGINEERING METHODOLOGY FOR ASA

Three steps are involved in establishing the three architectural requirements of the virtual enterprise (Mo, Nemes, Zhou, & Anticev, 2003). First, we developed the ASA particular EM through a one-day initial briefing session with the key executives of the ASA (Figure 3). The foundation model served as an important guiding tool

Figure 3. The particular EM of the ANZAC ship alliance

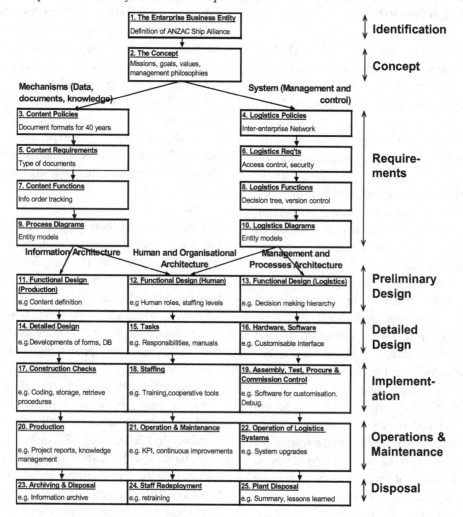

for formulating questions and focusing the effort of investigation during subsequent meetings and process examination.

The second step was to solicit information to populate the particular EM through a comprehensive questionnaire. Each part of the particular EM examined different aspects of the virtual enterprise including the specific objectives of the virtual enterprise in a particular area, the actions that were taken to achieve the objectives and the performance indicators that the enterprise

adopted. The questionnaire was distributed to all levels of personnel in the ASA.

The third step was to conduct a series of in-depth interviews with selected personnel. The objectives of the interviews were to clarify answers and analyse the coherence between replies. Interviews were conducted for individual and in small group discussions over 5 days at several locations of the ASA offices in Melbourne, Adelaide, and Perth.

The ASA has gone through a series of consortium creation activities over a long period. There are a number of steps identified through the study leading to the formation of the ASA:

- Identification.
- Definition.
- Alliance agreement.
- Development of the management plan.
- Formation of the ASA management office (ASAMO).
- Dissolve.

In this period, the companies participated in many forums in which the potential of collaboration and the format of the joint venture were explored. There was no fixed agenda in many of the meetings and the outcomes were not always aligned with a specific goal. According to VERA, this period is best modelled by the "network" EM. The steps of creating the ship maintenance consortium can then be mapped to VERA (Figure 4).

It is interesting to note the steps align well with the generalised model except the practical difficulty of distinguishing the "concept," "requirements," "preliminary design," and "detailed design" phases from "definition" and "alliance agreement" phases respectively. When the ASAMO is formed, the ASA ("network") is said to be in operation.

The outcome of this study was a re-definition of the enterprise business entity (Mo et al, in press). Conflicting views from different parties (individuals as well as organisations) indicated that there were at least three possible types of the virtual enterprise:

- A design VE has the focus is to develop change solutions. The ASA has the responsibility to provide design of the changes. Hence, the design of the virtual enterprise architecture will be focussed on enabling designs to be developed within the VE.

Figure 4. Mapping of ASA formation phases to the generalised network EM of VERA

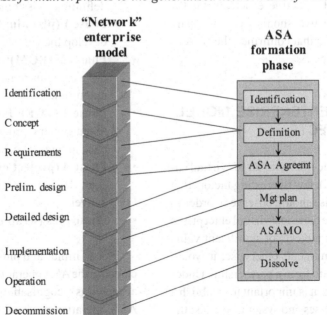

- A manufacturing VE has the focus is to ensure that the industry partners (i.e., "shareholders") undertake change for the ANZAC ships. The ASA has the responsibility of not only designing capabilities that will catalyst the change, but also requires certain degree of control over the capabilities of its "shareholders" to implement the change.

- A consultant VE has the focus to facilitate the change programme. The VE has no obligation to effect change to occur if the "shareholders" refuse to make changes. It is an arm's length situation that the ASA only coordinates specialists to support the changes but the prime responsibility of implementation rests with the "shareholders." The implementation actions in this sense include creating design, project management, cost control, scheduling, manufacturing, and so on to the completion of the change.

It is important that the members of the VE understand the primary goal of the organisation. Immediately after this part of the study, the Alliance held a series of workshops involving all levels of personnel to define exactly what the organisational objective should be. The result was a clear statement that confirmed the ASA as a "consultant VE."

PARTICULAR ENTERPRISE MODEL OF ASA PROJECTS

The experience of the ASA as a "large" virtual enterprise highlighted a few interesting factors that any virtual enterprise should observe in order to succeed. We assume that most virtual enterprises will be working on projects of significant value and resource commitment; otherwise, it would not be cost effective to form a partnership. Under these circumstances, it is important to establish a framework of processes and systems to assist the operation of the virtual enterprise for attaining

highest possible efficiency, even at a small percentage of savings. To achieve this goal, we need to develop particular enterprise models for ASA projects. This development signified that the ASA had moved into the operation phase and certain parts of the ASA EM needed to be analysed for system design and constraint identification.

Adopting a pragmatic approach, the ASA agreed to use one of its major projects known as Harpoon to be the pilot project level study. The Harpoon project is a major modification on the ships and will extend over a period of 5 years until all ships are upgraded. A series of investigative activities took place at one of the working sites of the project. Most of the meetings were held using teleconference facilities linking members from different states of Australia.

As a starting point of investigation, the ASA operation protocol was consulted. The ASA operation protocol describes the process that all partners in the consortium should follow when forming ship change programs. There were six phases:

- **Phase minus (project creation):** Project definition, mission, objective statements.
- **Phase 1 (planning):** The estimated cost to develop the concept.
- **Phase 2 (ROM):** Concept development, policies, requirements, and rough order of magnitude.
- **Phase 3 (TCE):** Preliminary design plans (management, procurement, configuration, etc.), and target cost estimate.
- **Phase 4 (project execution):** Detailed design, develop, procure, integrate, support, deliver.
- **Phase plus (wrap up):** Audit, archive.

Phases minus and plus were not originally included in the ASA operation protocol but were later accepted as recognisable phases in this study. The ASA operation protocol describes the life cycle of a typical project under ASA. The inclusion of the two pre and post project phases highlights the completeness of the project management process and maps well onto the "virtual enterprise" EM of VERA.

Phase minus defines the mission and objective of the change program and is equivalent to the VERA phases "identification" of the business entity. Phase 1 estimates the cost of the change concept and is equivalent to the VERA phases of "policies" and "requirements." Phase 2 develops the ROM, which is the "preliminary design" of the change. Phase 3 produces the TCE, which requires substantial details of the design including work breakdown structures, design modeling and expanded drawings, quotations, and pre-procurement activities. This phase can be mapped to the "detailed design" phase of VERA. Phase 4 includes activities such as detailed design, procurement, delivery, and system integration. Phase 4 is therefore mapped to the VERA "implementation" and "operation" phases. Finally, phase plus maps to "disposal" phase.

As the mission of the ASA entity has been clarified as the "consulting VE," the execution of the project is the responsibility of the "shareholders." For management consideration, the change program is led by an ASA partner in collaboration with the other partners. It was agreed as part of the ASA operation protocol that the same project life cycle process will be adopted by the partners to implement the change. The implementation life cycle operated by the ASA partner is mapped to the "product" EM of VERA.

Together with the ASA particular EM discussed earlier, the specific processes at different stages of the ASA operation are mapped to VERA in Figure 5. It is noted that the identification and concept and phases in the "product" EM are not executed from the "execution" phase of "virtual enterprise" EM because the information has already been defined in the early phases of the "virtual enterprise" EM. The ASA operation protocol confirms this characteristic by the fact that "project creation" is a carry over knowledge from the "virtual enterprise" entity.

GERAM allows for EMs to be partially developed for coping with emerging enterprising issues. Partial EMs are not complete models, but rather enable enterprise engineers to concentrate efforts to areas with accessible information that enables models to be effectively created to support the immediate work at hand. In this case of

Figure 5. Mapping of ASA operation protocol to particular EMs in VERA

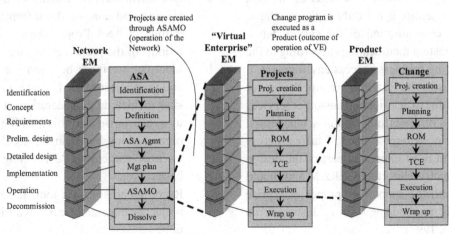

the ASA, it was at the early history of the virtual enterprise and so not all the information required is available. For example, resources and functional constructs were only speculative and hence were not complete for the purpose of this study. However, the use of GERAM in this process ensures the completeness of the methodology and future connectivity to other parts of the enterprise when new information are solicited or new areas are investigated.

INFORMATION ARCHITECTURE DEVELOPMENT

As the technology for setting up information systems becomes more complex and capable, many companies tried to apply its own ICT model to collaborate with their business partners. In the late 1990s, companies believed that video conferencing was the key to success of distance collaboration (Mo, Kovacek, & Cirocoo, 1998). They spent millions of dollars to set up their communication networks for video conferences. The result was a mix of success and failures. There are other aspects of virtual enterprise like project coordination, resources management, team building, document management, and information control, all of which require careful planning and management (Redman & Mo, 1999). The impact to the enterprise can be enormous as the cost of such an exercise is not only in the purchase, setup, and customisation of the system but it requires constant modifications according to the ever-changing business process environment. It is also necessary to take into account the loss of businesses due to deteriorated customer services and the loss of opportunity on new businesses. Companies need to recognise ICT infrastructure development is an important part of the design of information architecture GERAM and should be dealt with the support of proper enterprise engineering methodology (Lim, Juster, & de Pennington, 1997).

At the initial stage of the ASA formation, there was a question about what ICT infrastructure should be implemented to support the work of the ASA. There were barriers within the partner companies to achieve satisfactory coordination. Due to the nature of the virtual enterprise, ASA partners have their own practices and standard procedures when dealing with one another in various business matters. For example, different companies use different file formats and rules for scheduling and costing. Sometimes it was impossible to have a direct conversion from the data set of one company to another due to the treatment of the information when the data was accumulated. It was also an issue where some data was just missing from one company's management process. Information about where to find certain documents in the virtual enterprise was scarce. In addition, ASA was considering deploying a Web-based project collaboration tool to support the ASA operation. The commercial Web-based system was recommended by a consultant company commissioned by ASA as candidate software meeting ASA's project management requirements. Hence, the first task of information architecture study was to evaluate a number of commercial products against some unknown system criteria that this study eventually identified.

The objectives of this task were:

a. Document the requirements for information sharing and analyse the information flow within an ASA Project during the first 2 months of the project execution.

b. Identify interfaces between the ASAMO and the project office (at the lead partner's site) to include consideration of the need to synchronise activities within the two organisations, based on the ASAMO "need to know" rather than "everything possible" basis.

c. Recommend software tools to support the project management activities during execution.

To fulfil this task, the ASA particular EM was reviewed. The primary concern in the design of the information architecture is the requirements at each level of the organisation. The ASA consultant's documentation of recommending the commercial system across the whole virtual enterprise is the starting point of understanding the rationale behind the proposed design. However, more importantly, the specification supporting related architectural investigations was solicited from the project staff. Examples of the information acquired were:

- All ASA partners use a range of Microsoft Office tools extensively. It is necessary that information flow should comply with these common office tools.
- The ASA partners agreed to deploy Web enabled DRMS (a requirement specification tool) on the network. This tool will provide document and record management within the ASAMO. It is expected also to fulfil similar functions for projects during execution.
- Workflow support is necessary to enable online work submission, review, approval, and execution processes.
- Inter-operability with costing and scheduling data from some of the software systems used by ASA partners including Cobra, OpenPlan, MS Project, and others.
- To support the work of individuals, the system should have the ability to view data in various forms of Gantt charts, graphs, and diagrams. Online document authoring, red-lining, and reviewing are necessary as an integral part of proper document version control mechanism.
- A single reference data repository is required to support the distributed engineering teams across the country, and possibly with overseas contractors.
- Responsibility for system administration support should be identified when the commercial software is installed

Based on the requirements previous determined, a series of evaluation criteria was developed to assess the suitability of the commercial software recommended by the ASA consultant.

- The information architecture should provide support to activities both within the ASAMO and project activities within the projects during development and execution. This architecture will include Web access from all ASA work sites and remote access to all users via dial up connections.
- Simple facilities for project collaboration and information sharing such as file upload and download, discussion forum, and process improvement are essential.
- Many ASA projects require massive data transfer up to tens and hundreds of MB.
- The access speed and system responses to slow network access must be managed within the context of the application.
- Security on the internet is a non-tolerable aspect that must be addressed before any confidential information can be put on the system.
- Reliability of the user interface, in particular, when the user is accessing the system while on transit or through unreliable network links, must be assured.
- Due to the dynamic VE environment, the system should be capable of supporting customisation in the future.

To understand the workflow, the human and organisational architecture must be modelled. The organisational chart of the ASA was collected as shown in Figure 6.

The document flow paths for different types of documents and processes were described in a series of review and approval procedures (Figure 7). The diagram shows the roles and responsibilities of ASA key personnel. For example, a proposal review process is initiated by the project engineer. The proposal is sent to the section manager for

Figure 6. Organisational chart of ASA

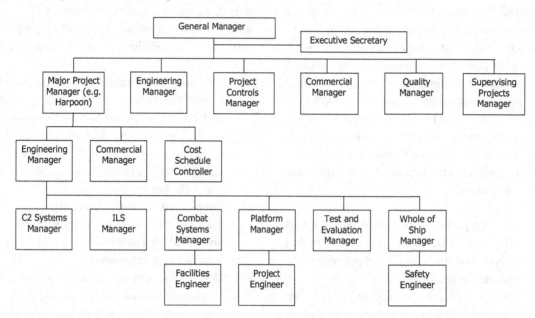

Figure 7. Document work flow and access control analysis

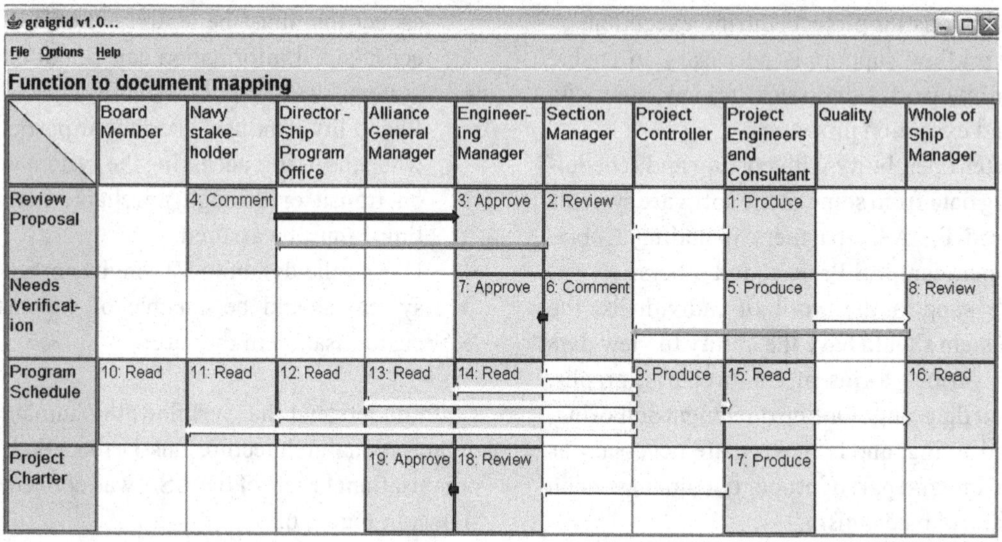

graigrid v1.0...

File Options Help

Function to document mapping

	Board Member	Navy stake-holder	Director - Ship Program Office	Alliance General Manager	Engineer-ing Manager	Section Manager	Project Controller	Project Engineers and Consultant	Quality	Whole of Ship Manager
Review Proposal		4: Comment			3: Approve	2: Review		1: Produce		
Needs Verificat-ion					7: Approve	6: Comment		5: Produce		8: Review
Program Schedule	10: Read	11: Read	12: Read	13: Read	14: Read		9: Produce	15: Read		16: Read
Project Charter				19: Approve	18: Review			17: Produce		

review. After the review, the proposal is sent to Navy stakeholder for comments and finally approved by the engineering manager. Figure 7 is an adaptation of the GRAI-GIM (Chen et al., 1997) at the short-term time horizon.

Based on the evaluation criteria and process modelling, several commercial-off-the-shelf ICT products, including the consultant recommended system, were evaluated. Unfortunately, the outcome of this evaluation was not favourable. For the recommended product, a number of problems were reported. For example, the access speed to the test server was good on a broadband network, but the performance degraded rapidly when the network was slow or congested. This caused some frames not loading properly. Clicking on the "refresh" button on the Internet Explorer logged the user out. The document management facility is very limited. It failed to upload a large file (about 50M) without giving any error message. It also refused to upload two files with the same file name but belonging to different folders/categories in the same project. The facility of the software to view data in different format was impressive, but it occasionally failed to load the data files, especially for the large data sets and Gantt charts. The diagrams and charts generated by other software such as Cobra were of poor quality, and couldn't be easily adjusted. The support for workflows was very simple. Online document authoring, redlining, and reviewing were missing, and there was no proper document version control mechanism. Documentation for system administration was poor. Customisation or extension to the system was difficult without the help of system developer. The most devastating feature was the breach of security. The system allowed entry to the system without username or password through a normal user access procedure. The administration security could also be bypassed easily.

It was therefore recommended that the recommended software was not suitable to ASA and other systems should be evaluated more thoroughly. Subsequently, a customised Web-based system was developed by the project as a pilot to support the work of Harpoon project.

CONCLUSION

The design of the ANZAC ship alliance virtual enterprise has been studied using GERAM. The key outcome of this study was to assist the ASA to define the mission of the virtual enterprise as the "consulting VE," which has the responsibility of facilitating the changes on the ANZAC ships but the primary responsibility of implementation rests with one of the partners in the virtual enterprise as the prime "shareholder." In this study, the VERA was used as the underlying GERA of the EEM. The enterprise models for the reference architectures in VERA, namely, network, virtual enterprise, and product were developed. The use of GERAM ensures that connectivity and compatibility of the current models can be maintained for supporting any future developments.

This chapter illustrates how the generalised methodologies can assist the evaluation of commercial ICT systems that are recommended for consideration without thorough analysis of its suitability to the virtual enterprise. The information architecture of ASA has been developed as part of the life cycle analysis in GERAM and was assessed against the functionality, capability, and implementation of the proposed Web-based system. Subsequently, a recommendation to ASA to consider other more capable systems was made.

The study showed significant changes have to be made on the operations within the virtual enterprise in order to adapt the system to differences stemmed from the practices in individual companies. The application of GERAM has been particularly useful to enable a comprehensive assessment of the enterprise architectures adopted in ASA.

REFERENCES

Aerts, A. T. M., Szirbik, N. B., & Goossenaerts, J. B. M. (2000). Flexible infrastructure for virtual enterprises. In J. P. T. Mo, & L. Nemes (Eds.), *Global engineering, manufacturing, and enterprise networks* (pp. 26-37). PA: Kluwer Academic Publishers.

Beckett, R. C. (2003). Determining the anatomy of business systems for a virtual enterprise. *Computers in Industry, 51*, 127-138.

Bernus, P., & Nemes, L. (1996). A framework to define a generic enterprise reference architecture and methodology. *Computer Integrated Manufacturing Systems, 9*(3), 179-191.

Bernus, P., Baltrusch, R., Tolle, M., & Vesterager, J. (2002). Better models for agile enterprise—The enterprise and its constituents as hybrid agents. In I. Karvonen, R. van den Berg, P. Bernus, Y. Fukuda, M. Hannus, I. Hartel, & J. Vesterager (Eds.), *Global engineering and manufacturing in enterprise networks,* (pp. 91-110). PA: VTT Technical Research Centre of Finland.

Chen, D., Vallespir, B., & Doumeingts, G. (1997). GRAI integrated methodology and its mapping onto generic enterprise reference architecture and methodology. *Computers in Industry, 33*, 387-394.

Cheng, K., & Popov, Y. (2004). Internet-enabled modelling of extended manufacturing enterprises using process-based techniques. *International Journal of Advanced Manufacturing Technology, 23*, 148-153

Hall, W. P. (2000). Managing technical documentation for large defence projects: Engineering corporate knowledge. In J. P. T. Mo & L. Nemes (Eds.), *Global engineering, manufacturing and enterprise networks* (pp. 370-378). PA: Kluwer Academic Publishers.

Hall, W. P., Dalmaris, P., & Nousala, S. (2005, November 28-29). A biological theory of knowledge and applications to real world. In D. J. Pauleen (Ed.), *Conference proceedings, knowledge management in Asia Pacific*, Willington, New Zealand.

Hussein, R., Nor, M. H. S., Karim, S. A., Mamat, A., & Anom, R. B. (2005, November 28-29). The impact of organizational factors on IS success.

An empirical investigation on the Malaysian electronic government agencies. In D. J. Pauleen (Ed.), *Conference Proceedings, Knowledge Management in Asia Pacific*. Willington, New Zealand.

ISO. (2000). Annex A: GERAM. In *ISO 15704:2000 industrial automation systems – requirements for enterprise reference architectures and methodologies*. ISO/TC184 (Ed.). PA: ISO.

Kosanke, K. (1995). CIMOSA—Overview and status. *Computers in Industry, 27*, 101-109.

Kosanke, K., & Nell, J. G. (1999). Standardisation in ISO for enterprise engineering and integration. *Computers in Industry, 40*, 311-319.

Li, H., & Williams, T. J. (2000). The interconnected chain of enterprises as presented by the Purdue enterprise reference architecture. *Computers in Industry, 42*, 265-274.

Lim, S. H., Juster, N., & de Pennington, A. (1997). Enterprise modelling and integration: A taxonomy of seven key aspects. *Computers in Industry, 34*, 339-359.

Mills, J., Brand, M., & Elmarsi, R. (1998, May 18-20). AeroWEB: An information infrastructure for the supply chain. In J. J. Mills, & F. Kimura (Eds.), *IFIP TC5 WG5.3/5.7 3rd International Conference on the Design of Information Infrastructure Systems for Manufacturing (DIISM'98)*, (pp. 323-336). Fort Worth, Texas, USA.

Mo, J. P. T., Kovacek, M., & Cirocoo, L. (1998, September 9-12). A framework for round the clock design and support. In G. Jacucci, G. J. Olling, K. Preiss, & M. J. Wozny (Ed.), *Proceedings of the 10th International IFIP WG5.2/5.3 International Conference PROLAMAT 98, Globalisation of Manufacturing in the Digital Communications Era of the 21st Century: Innovation, Agility, and the Virtual Enterprise*, (pp. 439-450). Trento, Italy.

Mo, J. P. T., Nemes, L., Zhou, M., & Anticev, J. (2003, April 6-8). Content management system and its alignment to business processes. *The 7th IFAC Workshop on Intelligent Manufacturing Systems—IMS 2003*, Paper 24, Budapest, Hungary. PA: Elsevier Science

Mo, J. P. T., Zhou, M., Anticev, J., Nemes, L., Jones, M., & Hall, W. P. (in press). A study on the logistics and performance of a real virtual enterprise. *International Journal of Business Performance Management.*

Noran, O. (2005). A systematic evaluation of the C4ISR AF using ISO 15704 Annex A (GERAM). *Computer in Industry, 56*, 407-427.

Nousala, S., Miles, A., Kilpatrick, W., & Hall, W. P. (2005, November 28-29). Building knowledge sharing communities using team expertise access maps (TEAM). In D. J. Pauleen (Ed.), *Conference proceedings, knowledge management in Asia Pacific*, November 28-29, Willington, New Zealand.

Redman, J., & Mo, J. P. T. (1999, November 18-20). Process modelling for global work team creation and management. The 2nd *International Conference, Managing Enterprises '99* (pp. 275-280), Newcastle, Australia.

Syntera, H. (1998, October 6-8). Challenges in global manufacturing (as seen in Globeman21). In N. Martensson (Ed.), *Proceedings, The European Conference on Integration in Manufacturing (IiM) 1998, IMS Workshop*, Gothenburg, Sweden.

Tharumarajah, A. (2003). A self-organising view of manufacturing enterprise. *Computers in Industry, 51*, 185-196.

Van den Berg, R. J., & Tolle, M. (2000). Assessing ability to execute in virtual enterprises. In J. P. T. Mo, & L. Nemes (Ed.), *Global engineering, manufacturing and enterprise networks* (pp. 38-45). PA: Kluwer Academic Publishers.

Williams, T. J. (1994). The Purdue enterprise reference architecture. *Computers in Industry, 24*(2-3), 141-158.

Williams, T. J., Bernus, P., Brosvic, J., Chen, D., Doumeingts, G., Nemes, L., Nevins, J. L., Vallespir, B., Vlietstra, J., & Zoetekouw, D. (1994). Architectures for integration manufacturing activities and enterprises. *Computers in Industry, 24*, 111-139.

Zwegers, A., Tolle, M., & Vesterager, J. (2003). VERAM: Virtual enterprise reference architecture and methodology. In I. Karvonen, R. van den Berg, P. Bernus, Y. Fukuda, M. Hannus, I. Hartel, & J. Vesterager (Eds.), *Global engineering and manufacturing in enterprise networks* (pp. 17-38). PA: VTT Technical Research Centre of Finland.

Chapter XXII
Information Systems Architecture for Business Process Modeling

Michel Spadoni
Ecole Nationale d'Ingénieurs de Metz &
Laboratory for Industrial and Mechanical Engineering, France

Anis Abdmouleh
Metz University & Laboratory for Industrial and Mechanical Engineering, France

ABSTRACT

The purpose of this chapter is to present our contribution in business process modeling within the CAS (CIMOSA Application Server) project. In this project, a referential, which helps enterprises to model their internal or collaborative activities within an enterprise chain (i.e., extended enterprise) is proposed. The referential is supported by a meta-model, which consists of a process modeling concept and a methodology as a user modeling guide. Enterprise activities modeling is based on a business process approach CIMOSA-based and that we define into an enterprise system. In this manuscript, the implementation of the referential is detailed within an information system by a component approach and a framework, which integrates the modeling methodology. The referential components are developed with .NET Microsoft technology.

INTRODUCTION

The enterprise concept refers to a set of activities implemented by some resources to reach a purpose through one or more objectives. Manufacture, contractor, training, or research enterprises can be mentioned.

Nowadays, many enterprises realize that it is not enough to be efficient to stay in business. Indeed, due to fierce competition, customer demands are so diverse and the actors involved in the production supply chains are so numerous that any enterprise is facing a highly interdependent situation with its partners. This is the reason why the challenge is no more productivity of the enterprise itself but productivity of the entire supply chain. Consequently, enterprise modeling, a key step in enterprise engineering, should no more be limited to the scope of a single enterprise but must encompass the entire enterprise network (be it a supply chain, an extended enterprise or a virtual enterprise) to cope with the entire system implications.

A major outcome of enterprise modeling is to provide some form of knowledge capitalization about a single or networked enterprise as a result of producing descriptive and behavioral models. Indeed, these models can represent essential aspects of an enterprise (especially concerning its objectives, structure, functionality, and behavior) in a form that can be understood by many business users and can be shared and exploited by various tools (as numeric models).

The enterprise knowledge core is materialized by the representation of business processes, which have a direct impact on enterprise results, long-term sustainability, and customer satisfaction. It is therefore essential to precisely model business processes and related entities, which have an impact in their design (engineering phase) and their execution (operational phase).

Following an analysis of the major enterprise modeling approaches such as IDEF, GRAI, CIMOSA, PERA, GERAM, ARIS, Olympios, or ACNOS (Bernus, Nems, & Williams, 1996; Vernadat, 1996), prime attention was given to business process centric methods. Among these, CIMOSA (Esprit, 1993) was the very first to propose the concept of system modeling and control based on business processes and not only on activities as it was previously the case in, for instance, GRAI (Doumeingts, Vallespir, & Chen, 1993) and IDEF (Menzel & Mayer, 1999).

The chapter focuses on CAS (CIMOSA Applications Server) project (Abdmouleh, 2004b). In fact, the CIMOSA aspects, which interest the project are presented. In addition, the referential meta-model and components are detailed.

PROBLEM

To be more competitive, enterprises improve their productivity by integrating different technologies in their information system, such as ERP (enterprise resource planning).

However, large enterprises suffer from their important existing applicative park, which is costly to evolve. On the other hand, small enterprises could not provide the required resources to implement an information system.

In this context, it is necessary to move the database application toward client/server architectures or Web services (Tomas, 1999). This approach is particularly based on information, reuse (Ezran, Moriso, & Tully, 1999), integration, and interoperability (Dogac, Kalinichenko, Ozsu, & Sheth, 1998; Vckouski, 1998), which are crucial to externalize processes. Many projects are released, especially, on interoperability. Among them, ATHENA (http://www.athena-ip.org), UEML (http://www.ueml.org), and INTEROP-NoE project (interoperability research for networked enterprises applications and software).

Consequently, two essential issues are studied:

- Managing enterprise information, which is related to processes. So, implementing an opportunist information system is necessary.
- Externalizing the process modeling into extended enterprises and defining activities within individual enterprise.

Before going further, let us define the process concept. Indeed, several definitions (Afnor, 1992; Bernus et al., 1996; Esprit, 1993; Mathieu, 2000) exist, but they remain general. The definition used in CAS project is as follows: "a process is a sequence of correlated activities. A process transforms input objects into ones output by means of required resources to achieve objectives."

THE CAS PROJECT

The principal motivation of the CAS project is to implement an information system useful for enterprise system modeling and designing (Abdmouleh, 2004b).

An enterprise system is the set of methods and techniques, which provide a definite function to produce a result. Thus, it is important to specify its objectives and concepts.

The core concepts of an enterprise system are entities, processes, and actor roles (Eriksson & Penker, 2000). In fact, the control flow of a system is described by processes. The latter transform inputs into outputs by using resources and are called business processes (Vernadat, 1996). They have a direct impact on the enterprise results and they represent the enterprise behavior while achieving strategic objectives.

To model an enterprise system, the information system must be able to describe it faithfully through its entities, processes, and actor roles.

In deed, a referential is proposed to support the information system. This referential regroups different components (Bachman, 2000), which are distributed and exploited by:

- Application designers via a framework. The latter gives documents, which can be shared by Windows or Linux users.
- Enterprise systems via a framework to obtain XML documents, which can be shared and handled by application designers and internet users.

The proposed information system can be represented by four layers architecture (Figure 1):

- **Layer 0—CIMOSA referential:** Based on CIMOSA approach, this layer is useful to model processes. It is shared by all extended enterprise nodes.
- **Layer 1—enterprise systems:** This layer is represented by an enterprise systems reposi-

Figure 1. Information system layers in an enterprise net (from Spadoni, 2004)

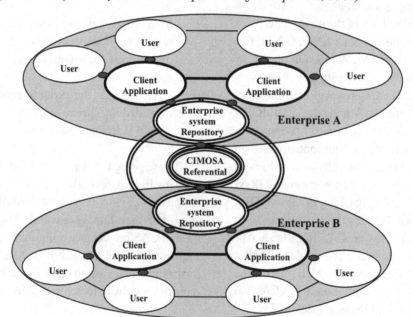

tory assigned for each individual enterprise. One repository can be used by another enterprise according to partnership.

- **Layer 2—applications:** Here, all enterprise applications are regrouped to be reused and shared by authorized internal users.
- **Layer 3—users:** Users can be internal or external to one individual enterprise. Consulting enterprise applications can be this one is represented by the whole of the users of the same enterprise. Those can be of type Windows, Linux, or Internet.

The architecture, which implements the information system of the project, integrates an interoperable framework. The latter is used to help developing models by instantiating the meta-model through referential components.

THE CIMOSA APPROACH

Principle

CIMOSA (which stands for open system architecture for CIM) is a full-fledged framework proposed to analyze, design, and make operational large-scale integrated manufacturing systems (Dogac et al., 1998; Esprit, 1993; Ezran et al., 1999; Vernadat, 1996). It has been developed by the ESPRIT Consortium AMICE as a series of ESPRIT Projects (EP 688, 5288, and 7110) over the period 1985-1995. More than 21 enterprises and research units from seven European countries have directly contributed to CIMOSA, plus additional partners in validation or sister projects (e.g., VOICE, CODE, CIMPRESS). The major outcomes of CIMOSA have been: (1) to be the pivotal foundation of GERAM (generalized enterprise reference architecture and methodology) together with GRAI and PERA (Bernus et al., 1996), (2) to be the baseline for standards development on enterprise modeling and integration at the European and international levels (CEN

ENV 40003, CEN ENV 12204, ISO/IS 15704, ISO/DIS 14258 among others), and (3) to inspire enterprise modeling and workflow tool developers (e.g., ARIS Toolset, FirstSTEP, PrimeObjects, CimTool, to name a few).

One of the major strengths of CIMOSA relies on its enterprise modeling approach based on systems theory, process algebra, and object orientation. Indeed, CIMOSA views any enterprise (single enterprise or networked enterprise) as a large set of concurrent processes executed by communicating resources and exchanging objects and messages, all these being organized in business domains (or functional areas) to be coordinated (Afnor, 1992; Vckouski, 1998).

The following concepts form the core of the modeling approach defined as modeling constructs in CIMOSA, for which a syntax and semantics are provided: event, process, activity, operation, resource, and object view (Ezran et al., 1999; Vckouski, 1998). It is worthwhile to point out that the activity concept is the structuring concept in the sense that it federates all other constructs by means of well-defined relations with them.

It is fundamental to clearly distinguish the concept of activity from the concept of process. An activity defines a piece of functionality of the enterprise while a process defines a piece of behavior of the enterprise. The following definitions are therefore used:

- An *activity* is the locus of action, which utilizes time and resources to perform a task in order to transform an input state into an output state. Each task requires capabilities or skills.
- A *process* is a partially ordered set of activities, the execution of which will result in the achievement of some objective of the enterprise. This execution needs to be enabled by some trigger called event.

In other words, a process can be the subject of planning (like a project) but only in seldom cases of scheduling. Activities are subject to scheduling and need allocation of resources according to roles to be played (i.e., required capabilities or skills).

CIMOSA MODELING FRAMEWORK AND CONCEPTUAL MODEL

The CIMOSA modeling framework is based on four abstraction views (function, information, resource, and organization views) and three modeling levels (requirements definition, design specification, and implementation description). Particular models (i.e., the actual model of a business entity, whole or part of a single or networked enterprise) are obtained by directly instantiating CIMOSA constructs provided in the generic layer and/or by customizing some partial models retrieved from model repositories of the partial layer to particular needs. The generic and partial layers of the CIMOSA cube define the reference architecture. Only the CIMOSA association or standardization bodies are allowed to update, expand, or populate the reference architecture. The particular layer defines the particular architecture of the enterprise.

The four modeling views are provided to manage the integrated enterprise model (design, manipulation, access). The role of each view is to filter or screen components of the model according to given perspective, allowing it to focus on some aspects and leaving out other aspects. This is an essential mechanism to deal with complexity of the model. For the sake of completeness, a brief description of each modeling view follows.

Function View: It is used to organize the enterprise as a set of interacting functional domains and to describe the concurrent processes, their triggering conditions, and their execution. Indeed, from a functional standpoint, a large-scale business entity is a collection of disjoint parts called *enterprise domains* (DM). Each domain is made

of end-to-end processes called *domain processes* (DP) interacting with one another (e.g., customer order processing, production planning, bills-of-materials processing…). The domain processes are triggered under certain circumstances or conditions, denoted *events* (e.g., machine breakdowns, customer order arrivals, management orders…). Events correspond to state changes in the system. Events can be generated internally by elements of the enterprise (resources or enterprise activities), by clock times, or by the system environment (external actions). They can be solicited (deterministic or scheduled actions) or unsolicited (happenings, perturbations). Each domain process may comprise *business processes* (i.e., sub-processes) and at the lowest level of functional decomposition *enterprise activities* (EA). Enterprise activities represent elementary steps in a process. The process logic (i.e., the process behavior defined as a partially ordered sequence of steps) is described in the form of an activity network defined by means of a so-called *behavioral rule set* (BRS). A BRS can be formally defined as a stochastic automaton or a stochastic Petri net. In CIMOSA, it is defined by means of operators (called rules) to connect activities (namely, triggering rules, forced sequential rules, conditional sequential rules, synchronous and asynchronous spawning rules, rendezvous rules, loops, ending rules) (Afnor, 1992; Vckouski, 1998). Enterprise activities can be further decomposed into elementary actions called *functional operations* (FO). An FO must be executed by exactly one actor (or active resource) of the enterprise. An EA transforms an input state into an output state by activating the FO's. When it is completed, it generates an *ending status* (ES) (i.e., a value identifying the termination status among all possible statuses foreseeable for this activity). Finally, each activity is defined by a set of capabilities or skills required for its execution (capability set).

Information View: It is used to describe entities used by activities and processes, information and object flows, as well as constraints applicable to informational entities, all described as a conceptual data model supporting integration. From the information standpoint, input and output states of activities in processes are defined in terms of *Object Views* (OV). An object view represents a particular state and manifestation of one or more *enterprise objects* (EO). An enterprise object denotes any class of useful objects of the enterprise (e.g., products, parts, bills-of-materials, orders...). In the model, an EO is defined by its list of properties called *information elements* (IE) and abstraction mechanisms (specialization, aggregation). An object view is defined over an enterprise object is made of a subset or a combination of these information elements. Furthermore, object views can be of two types: physical view (the materialized object itself) and information view (set of information elements). This allows it to model the information flows and the material flows separately. Finally, information elements as data properties are subject to *integrity constraints* (IC) to express and check data validity, plausibility, and consistency in the information model.

Resource View: It is used to declare and define those objects that play the role of resources in the execution of activities. CIMOSA defines a generic construct called *resource* that must be specialized in two major classes: components, that describe passive resources (e.g., a tool, a cart, a truck...), as opposed to *functional entities* (FE), that describe active resources (i.e., those able to provide and execute functional operations (e.g., a CNC machine, a robot, a truck driver...). Functional entities can be divided into three main types: humans (for human beings), machines (for any device instrumented with a controller) and applications (for computer or IT systems). All kinds of resources can be characterized by their *capability set* (CS) (i.e., the set of capabilities that can provide, in the case of humans, the term competency set or skills must be used).

Organization View: It is used to describe the organizational and decisional structures of the business entity and to assign responsibilities and authorities to components of the particular architecture. CIMOSA provides two essential constructs for this: *organization unit* (OU), to define a position (a job) or an elementary decision center, and *organization cell* (OC), to organize organization units into cells and cells into higher level cells, and so on. For instance, jobs are grouped into sections, sections into departments, departments into divisions, and divisions into plants.

In this manuscript, we have represented only the CIMOSA core constructs used to model complex systems and organizations. For a detailed description of these constructs, the reader is referred to references (Esprit, 1993; Ezran et al., 1999; Vernadat, 1996).

DESCRIPTION OF AN ENTERPRISE SYSTEM (*FUNCTIONAL POINT-OF-VIEW*)

Modeling Approach

An enterprise system is modeled from strategic objectives and their deployment (Berrah, Clivillé, Harzallah, Haurat, & Vernadat, 2001). CIMOSA modeling framework proposes four levels to deploy these objectives: domains, domain processes, business processes, and activities.

However, the definition of a domain process concept is limited to the main process of a domain. In this project, this concept is especially exploited to organize business processes, detail objective decomposition, and expand the assigned responsibilities layer. Consequently, the process reengineering is focused, in this project, on domain processes. Therefore, a domain process and objective-oriented organization is proposed.

In fact, a global approach concerning particularly functional decomposition is represented in this manuscript. The approach is detailed in four steps (Figure 2):

- **Step 1:** After defining the system objectives (SO), these ones are decomposed into sub-objectives called domain objectives to define the system domains (DM). Relationships are defined between communicant domains, which exchange information and objects.
- **Step 2:** For each domain, a list of existent business processes is established (BP). These processes must contribute to achieve domain objectives.

- **Step 3:** Business processes are grouped into parent processes, which correspond to domain objectives decomposition. Each domain process is triggered by one or more events, which are defined in this step.

The set of possible grouping solutions are represented by OR graph. Only one grouping solution is retained according to the different constraints (e.g., financial, economical, marketing, technical, etc.) of the enterprise.

Figure 2. Enterprise system approach (from Abdmouleh, 2004b)

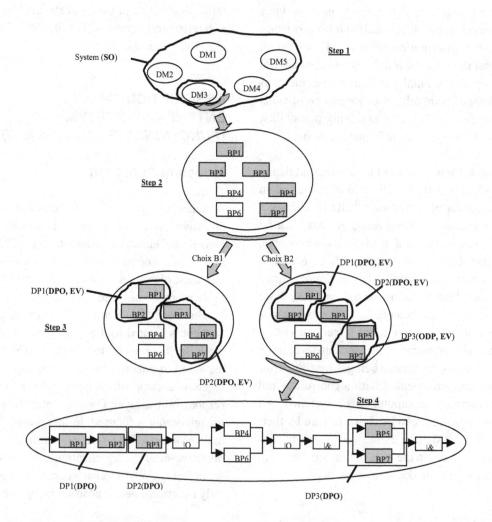

• **Step 4:** When a solution is selected, a functional decomposition of business processes is released to define, also, activities and functional operations. This helps to model control flow, define inputs/outputs, and associate required resources.

Structure solutions of an enterprise system are capitalized in the enterprise system repository. The capitalization and the management of a model structure is supported by a research engine based on actions plan called SIRS (Système Interactif de Recherche de Séquence) (Spadoni, 2001).

The proposed approach to model an enterprise system is integrated into a framework, which refers to the referential components and applies required concepts such as domain, business process, object view, functional entity, etc.

Example

Given a manufacturing enterprise defined by domains set, these domains treat the market situation, define the resulting product, study costs, deal with customers, study planning and manufacturing, deal with suppliers, analyze and validate design of the product, buy needed products, store design documents, etc.

Each domain regroups some of business processes, which can achieve sub-objectives of the domain one.

In fact, this enterprise can be modeled as a system by defining its objectives (i.e., reduce production costs, improve product quality, reduce development costs, and reduce time-to-market). Then, by identifying the different domains and specifying those that will be modeled (see Figure 3). CIMOSA domains (i.e., product design, produc-

Figure 3. System objectives

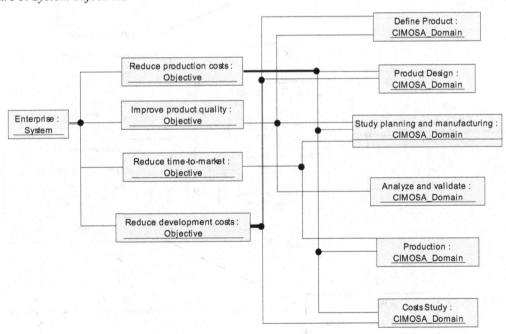

tion, study planning and manufacturing, analyze and validate, costs study, and define product).

For each domain, business processes are defined to achieve business objectives (e.g., sub-objectives of the domain objective). These business processes are managed and regrouped into domain processes (Figure 4). After defining the different events that can trigger domain processes and the corresponding process objectives, the quality regrouping must be evaluated and validated by technical experts and business responsibles. If the result is not satisfactory, regrouping must be reviewed and rectified according to business and domain objectives.

THE REFERENTIAL

The Components

Definition

There are many different definitions of a component, especially in software technology. But, the common points to all definitions are: independent, deliverable, and reusable services (Brown & Short, 1997). Independence does not necessarily mean that a component has no dependency on other components. It means that the component can be handled as one entity (Brereton & Budgen, 2000). Deliverable service means that the component

Figure 4. Business and domain processes (from Abdmouleh, Spadoni, & Vernadat, 2004a)

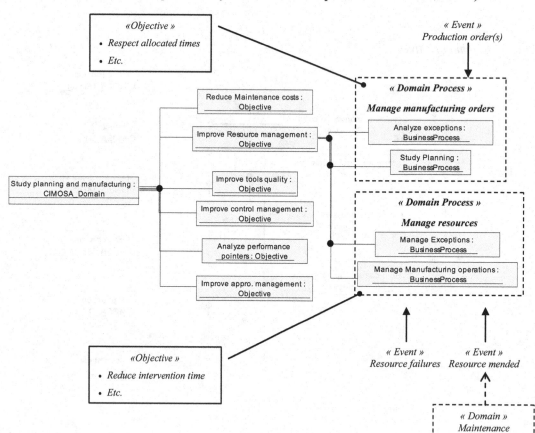

will produce identified and expected end-result. Reusable means that the same component can be used in several places in the system model.

A component can either be a class, a specification, a document, a source code, an interface (e.g., CORBA, DCOM, ActiveX, EJB, etc.) or have a framework form (Kobryn, 2000). Thus, a generic application can itself be viewed as a software component.

Another definition given in UML 1.3 assumes that a component is a physical, replaceable part of a system that packages implementation and provides realization of a set of interfaces (OMG, 1999).

A business component (or enterprise component) is defined in this chapter as an operational component whose function is to perform services for one or many enterprise business objects.

In our work, a component type consists of a set of classes. Each component of this type will be an instantiation of this type.

Determination of component types is an important step in systems engineering to integrate reusability of business modeling know-how (Hopkins, 2000). This makes the creation of software components that can be used in different applications in the same domain possible. Therefore, it is important to make a careful analysis of business functionality and actor requirements for the enterprise domain being investigated.

Identification

To model an enterprise system with the last approach, some modules are essential to deal with aspects according to CIMOSA views.

In deed, by starting with the generic tasks called use cases (Booch, 1999), the problems of enterprise systems are appreciably detailed.

A first aspect corresponds to the functional view of CIMOSA. This is encapsulated into two modules, which allow developing a process map of a system and behavior rules to define the control flow into each process. The latter operation also consists of defining activities and functional operations.

To design activities or processes, resources and treated objects should be attributed by different enterprise actors into different organization entities. One can point out three distinct modules to analyze resources, information (objects) and organization structure. These modules must be reusable in different contexts of an enterprise system and interoperable with information systems and applications that are supposed to exist in enterprises.

All the modules, also called packages, together represent the meta-model of the referential, which are implemented by five computing components (Hopkins, 2000). This referential regroups these components to respond to a users community to develop enterprise system models.

We have called these components *enterprise modeling components (EMC)* (Abdmouleh et al., 2004a). These components are as follows:

- **Process management and design:** It is used by business actors to design processes (domain and business processes) and group them into domains in one system.
- To describe the behavior processes and specify functionalities, another component is define. It is called "dehavior component"
- **Resources management:** It is used by process designers and managers to define and determine the required resources, to specify the capability sets, as well as to control functionality execution and achieve process objectives.
- **Information management:** It is used by process designers and managers to define and determine activity inputs and outputs (object views) and describe information flows.
- **Organization structure:** It is used by process designers and managers to associate responsibilities, authorities, and roles to the different processes, resources, and object

views and to allocate them to organization units and cells.

The Meta-Model

On the basis of the CIMOSA conceptual model, the referential meta-model is proposed. The aim of this meta-model is to provide assistance in managing and designing business processes during the enterprise engineering stage of the system life cycle methodology (Zelm, Vernadat, & Kosanke, 1995).

The meta-model covers functional (i.e., domains, processes, and activities), informational

Figure 5. The referential meta-model (from Abdmouleh et al., 2004a)

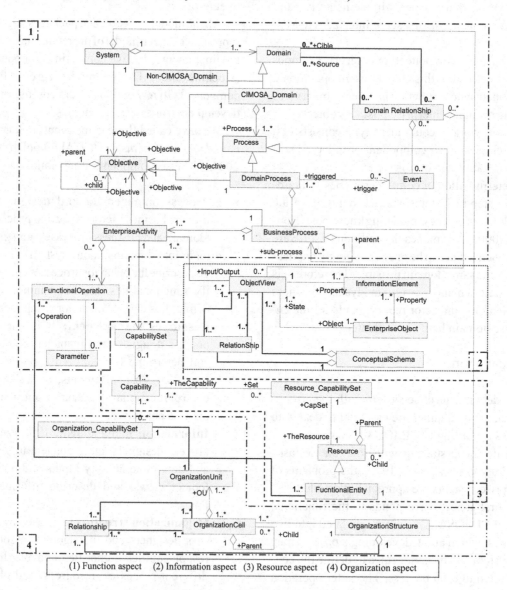

(1) Function aspect   (2) Information aspect   (3) Resource aspect   (4) Organization aspect

Figure 6. Interaction of the framework with the referential and resultant models (from Abdmouleh, 2004b)

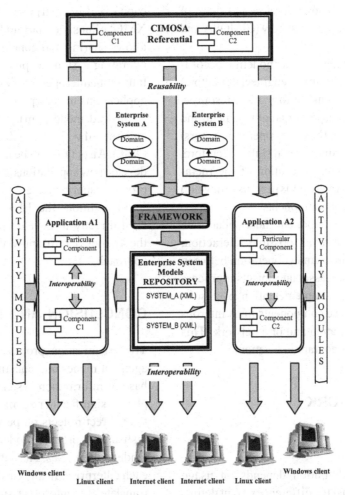

(i.e., enterprise objects and their object views), resource (i.e., functional entities and capability sets), and organizational (i.e., organization units and roles) aspects of manufacturing business entities (see Figure 5).

The static structure of the meta-model is depicted by a class diagram expressed in UML (unified modeling language) (Booch, 1999; OMG, 1999). It is used by enterprise modelers and designers to develop a business system design according to the CIMOSA approach. The system under scrutiny is defined by its business objectives, functional domains, and overall organizational structure.

The static aspect of the concepts suggested in the meta-model allows a static development of models per instantiation. So the dynamic description of the meta-model is necessary to allow modeling of a part or a whole system behavior. Consequently, the behavior of the various meta-model concepts is defined at the time of the implementation definition. This is carried out by an approach allowing reuse and share of the business modeling know-how (CIMOSA and business patterns).

This approach must allow modeling according to a modeler (business engineering actors) point of view (functional, information, resource, and/or organization aspect), his environment, and the model end-users (business operation actors) requirements, according to their skills. Therefore, one can propose implementation of the meta-model aspects separately. This permits to develop the five independent components.

However, each component must collaborate with each other to make possible interaction, information exchange, and cooperation between aspects concepts (i.e., associate objects as process inputs). Therefore, at implementation level (software modules), these components must interoperate at one workstation and/or a network. This depends on users geographic location.

THE FRAMEWORK

Definition

The framework definition depends on usage constraints. Against the different existent definitions, one can quote the one of Johnson (1997): "a framework can be defined as micro-architecture which provides an incomplete definition of systems in a given domain. This architecture can be a reusable design or an application skeleton which can be personalized by developer."

Framework CIMOSA-Based

In the present project, a framework is defined as a set of components, which describe a model. The latter corresponds to the meta-model.

Consequently, the framework refers to the EMC components (Figure 6). It permits model-

ers to develop enterprise system models while following the modeling approach. Models are capitalized in enterprise system repository with XML "eXensible Markup Language" form. This allows sharing and consulting models with any operating system or plate-form. Here, one can talk about interoperability with the other existing applications in enterprise.

In deed, models can be displayed via a network and filtered with eXtensible style sheet language (XSL). Also, they can be handled by designers to develop new applications (e.g., design, simulation, process supervision, etc.)

In addition, the EMC components can be used directly to develop models without using the framework to apply the enterprise system approach.

CONCLUSION AND PROSPECTS

The organization process structures the management modes and constitutes the architecture base of information systems. Indeed, processes play a significant role in enterprise thanks to their direct reflects on performance. Therefore, distributing process models is privileged in extended enterprises. Activities remain private to each enterprise. In any case, modeling processes translate the enterprise specifications to fulfill requirements.

To contribute in modeling processes, the proposed meta-model integrates different know-how of business process modeling, particularly with CIMOSA approach, which is an international standard in this domain.

The meta-model benefit is to allow enterprises to develop their particular (own) models by instantiating the standard concepts of the first.

However, to manage business processes efficiently, enterprises need flexible and extensible technologies proportional with the globalization. Consequently, one can propose the Web service approach (Freemantle, Weerawarana, & Khalaf,

2002) to make contracting services easier without caring about enterprise geographic location or plate-form operation system. Therefore, integration is centered on the services interoperability.

In this context, the proposed meta-model is developed by using component approach to implement services and by the way the Web services.

In CAS project, developing Web services based on enterprise system modeling is the current step. The obtained results will allow users to model enterprise systems directly on an Internet navigator and capitalize them into the corresponding repository. In other words, the framework proposed is migrating to Web services by using DOTNET technology of Microsoft (http://msdn.microsoft.com/asp.net).

REFERENCES

Abdmouleh, A. (2004b). *Composants pour la modéliation des processus metiers en productique, bases sur CIMOSA*. Phd thesis, University of Metz, France.

Abdmouleh, A., Spadoni, M., & Vernadat, F. (2004a). *Distributed client/server architecture for CIMOSA-based enterprise components. Computers in Industry*.

AFNOR. (1992). *Gérer la qualité: Concepts et terminologie*. Paris, tome 1, Afnor (Ed.).

Bachman, F., Bass, L., Buhman, S., Comella-Dorda, S., Long, F., Seacord, R., & Wallnau, K.C. (2000). *Technical concepts of component-based software engineering*. Tech. Rep. CMU/SEI-2000-TR-008, Software Engineering Institute, Canegie Mellon University.

Bernus, P., Nems, L., & Williams T. J. (1996) *Architectures for enterprise integration*. The Findings of the IFAC/IFIP Task Force. London; Chapman & Hall (Ed.).

Berrah, L., Clivillé, V., Harzallah, M., Haurat, A., & Vernadat, F. (2001*). PETRA: Un guide méthodologique pour une démarche de réorganisation industrielle*. (Tech. Rep.). France: LGIPM & LLP.

Booch, G. (1999). UML in action. *Communications of the ACM, 42*, 26-70.

Brereton, P., & Budgen, D. (2000*). Component-based systems: A classification of issues. Computer, 33*, 54-62.

Brown, A. W., & Short, K. (1997). On components and objects: The foundations of components based development. In *Proceedings of the 5th IEEE International Symposium on Assessment of Software Tools and Technologies* (pp. 112-121). Los Alamitos.

Dogac, A., Kalinichenko, L., Ozsu, T., & Sheth, A. (1998). *Workflow management systems and interoperability*. Berlin: Springer Verlag.

Doumeingts, G., Vallespir B., & Chen, D (1993). GRAI grid decisional modelling. In *Handbook on Architectures for Information Systems* (pp. 313-337). Berlin: Springer-Verlag.

Eriksson, A. E., & Penker, M. (2000). *Business modeling with UML-business patterns at work*. New York: John Wiley & Sons.

ESPRIT Consortium AMICE. (1993). *CIMOSA: Open system architecture for CIM* (2nd and extended ed.). Berlin; Springer Verlag.

Ezran, M., Moriso, M., & Tully, C. (1999). *Réutilisation logicielle*. Paris: Eyrolles.

Freemantle, P., Weerawarana, S., & Khalaf, R. (2002). Enterprise services, enterprise components and services. *Communication of the ACM, 45*(10).

Hopkins, J. (2000). Component primer. *Communications of the ACM, 43*, 27-30.

Johnson, R. E. (1997). Frameworks = (Components + patterns). *Communications of the ACM, 40*(10), 39-42.

Kobryn, C. (2000). Modeling components and frameworks with UML. *Communications of the ACM, 43*, 31-38.

Mathieu, S. (2000). *Comprendre les normes ISO 9000 version 2000*. Paris: Afnor.

Menzel, C., & Mayer, R. J. (1999). The IDEF family of languages. In *handbook on architectures for information systems* (pp. 209-242). Berlin: Springer Verlag.

OMG. (1999). *Unified modeling language specification Version 1.3.* Document ad/99-06-08. Object Management Group. Retrieved from http://www.omg.org

Spadoni, M. (2004). Project CAS: Proposition d'une méthodologie de conception de modèles de processus distribués d'entreprise, basée sur la méthode CIMOSA. *Journal Européen des Systèmes Automatisés, 38*(5), 497-527.

Spadoni, M., Gardoni, M., Abdmouleh, A., & Nsingi-Menamo, T. (2001). Un formalisme générique pour la représentation d'informations structurées et de savoir-faire en ingénierie de fabrication et gestion de production. *Journal Européen des Systèmes Automatisés, 35*(6), 747-781.

Tomas, J. L. (1999). *ERP et progiciels intégrés.* InterEdition.

Vckouski, A. (1998). *Interoperable and distributed processing in GIS.* London: Taylor & Francis.

Vernadat, F. B. (1996). *Enterprise modeling and integration: Principles and applications.* London: Chapman & Hall.

Zelm, M., Vernadat, F. B., & Kosanke, K. (1995). The CIMOSA business modelling process. *Computers in Industry, 27,* 123-142.

Chapter XVIII
Enterprise Architecture within
the Service-Oriented Enterprise

Section V
Technology and
Service-Oriented Architecture

Chapter XXIII
Enterprise Architecture within the Service-Oriented Enterprise

Scott J. Dowell
Shirnia & Dowell LLC, USA

ABSTRACT

In his best selling book The World is Flat, *Thomas Friedman proclaims "We are entering a phase where we are going to see the digitization, virtualization, and automation of almost everything ... the real information revolution is about to begin" (Friedman, 2005). Certainly, the prevalence of high-speed connectivity has eliminated the barriers of doing business around the world. Lower cost and talented workforce in India and China are now easily if not transparently accessible and online. To thrive in the global economy, CEOs are using outsource, in-source, and offshore models to create strong partner-networks throughout the value chain. Technology leader Intel Corporation states in a recent whitepaper, "businesses are enjoying increased agility that allows them to rapidly respond to changing market needs and opportunities" (Intel Corporation, 2005). Enter a new paradigm called the "service-oriented enterprise" (SOE). In the SOE model, an organization views itself as a set of "business services" supported by adaptable, scalable, and reliable technology. Early-adopters of this model are benefiting through global collaboration, real-time business responsiveness, and productive mobile work forces. By grasping this paradigm shift, enterprise architects can guide organizations in building agility model and compete in the global economy.*

INTRODUCTION

Something has changed in our world. In an interesting twist to "who moved my cheese," the era of a single, integrated "enterprise architecture" is disappearing. The demand to increase efficiency, decrease costs, reduce time to market, and expand revenue streams are causing business leaders to evaluate and re-think their execution models. Collaboration is becoming increasingly important. Martin Brodbeck, Director, Global Application Architecture at Pfizer, Inc. states "... it's about connecting business processes in a much more horizontal fashion ... having a federated infrastructure that provides an architecture and security foundation to be able to run these components consistently across your enterprise." Both public and private sector organizations are moving to a model where the "enterprise" crosses partner boundaries to deliver services within the value chain. In financial markets, investors refer to this business model as a "platform company," that is, one where knowledge capital is the differentiator and execution is through a set of service providers—each specializing in a particular segment of the value chain. Those that refine their role in the value chain and establish the right complimentary partner-networks deliver faster, cheaper, and better—trumping those who use standalone models. To better understand this paradigm shift, let us review the trends occurring in public and private sector organizations as well as how technology vendors are addressing the emerging model.

In the public sector, organizations within U.S. Federal Government are creating internal partner networks by embracing "line of business" (LOB) with supporting centers of excellence (COE). This shift began in 2001 when the Hon. Mark Forman, former administrator of information technology and e-government at the Office of Management and Budget instituted the shared services model to support the Presidents Management Agenda and the eGovernment act. This model allows the Federal Government, a traditionally bureaucratic institution, to act as a private sector organization. Enterprise architecture is the key enabler as agencies strive to eliminate redundant, disparate solutions and create COEs that provide common, commodity services within an LOB. To become a COE, an agency establishes a best practice that can be selected, controlled, and evaluated for efficiency, cost effectiveness, and quality. When an agency is selected to become a COE, it can then "supply" services for a fee to fellow "demanding" organizations. Much like private sector organizations, control and trust are addressed using Service

Level Agreements (SLAs) as a form of binding contract. Today, LOBs include case management, human resources, financial management, grants management, geospatial, and IT infrastructure. Using this model, agencies can focus on delivering core competencies of the Federal Government value chain such as land management, housing, tax collection, or border security while relegating common, commodity services to the appropriate COE partner. Savings from this approach in terms of eliminating redundancy, increasing efficiency, and improving quality are estimated to be in the billions of dollars.

Private sector organizations such as Toshiba, UPS, Pfizer, and FedEx are using in-source, outsource, and offshore models to address costs, efficiency, and quality in what they deliver to customers. Thirty percent of the world's largest 1000 firms are sending work offshore. This percentage is expected to increase in accordance with the expected growth rate (20-30%) for offshore industries in India and China. Outsource and offshore models are prevalent, but let's look at how organizations use in-sourcing to exploit the partner-network model within a value chain. An example cited by Friedman (2005) in the *World is Flat* is a good one. Consider the Toshiba/UPS partnership where UPS has established a computer and printer repair hub in Louisville, Kentucky. Toshiba customers are told that if their laptop needs repair to send it in via UPS. When picked up, the laptop travels to the UPS hub, where UPS employees fix it, and ship it back to the customer. No longer does the laptop need to take the extra trips to a Toshiba center, nor does Toshiba need to dedicate resources to a lower value-add service. By understanding laptop repair can be a commodity service, it can be relegated to a partner and the resulting Toshiba value chain streamlined. According to Friedman (2005), UPS has invested $1 billion dollars in creating supply chain management expertise and is an integrated service provider for such companies as HP, Nike, Jockey, and even Papa Johns Pizza. It is doing more than delivering packages, it is moving into the value-chain of its complementing network of partners. In the private sector, agility is the new mantra and using a partner-network creates a flexible value chain that can be tweaked to address changing market needs, competitive threats, and new opportunities.

Technology thought-leaders quickly began acting on the service-oriented paradigm shift. In 2003, Bill Coleman recognized the convergence of applications, computer resources, and widespread communications leading to a dynamic infrastructure fabric and formed Cassatt Corporation. In 2005, Intel Corporation published a whitepaper on its Web site stating, "This is a fundamental shift to a set of innovative business processes supported by a very modular, manageable IT infrastructure" (Intel Corporation, 2005). Leading vendors such as BEA, Cassatt, EMC, IBM, and Intel are delivering tools to create a modular, manageable IT infrastructure fabric supporting what is termed as the service-oriented enterprise (SOE). These solutions virtualize hardware, network, and storage resources to reduce complexity, lower costs, and increase flexibility of the IT infrastructure. Tools, such as Collage from Cassatt Corporation, extend infrastructure virtualization to support service level automation. Through service level automation, organizations use policy-based optimization to dynamically adjust computing capacity (adding, allocating, and removing infrastructure components) to meet defined service levels. Service levels can be managed in real-time in accordance to the needs of the organization. IT is experiencing a greater role in business transformation. With the maturity of virtualization and service level automation, organizations are adopting IT services management (ITSM) framework to form an "IT as a service" model. This model allows organizations to correctly position IT services within the value chain.

Enterprise architects need to be aware of these changes in business and the technology that has

sped the SOE adoption in both public and private sector organizations. Moving to SOE introduces new concepts and changes to the organization to include business services, service-oriented solutions, infrastructure services, and IT organization. Each area is briefly described below:

- **Business services:** Are meaningful functions provided in response to a business need within the value chain. They are managed using service level agreements that stipulate performance metrics and measured using financial and quality benchmarks. In SOE, they are classified as core (differentiators) and commodity (non-differentiator).

- **Service-oriented solutions:** Enable the business services of the organization through automation. Two popular trends are "software as a service" and service-oriented architecture. They are characterized as component-based architecture that can be orchestrated to solve a business service. Acting as plug-n-play components, the solutions can be constructed and re-constructed based on service level to enable the agility aspects of the SOE.

- **Infrastructure services:** Are the underlying hardware, software, storage, and network resources of an organization. This infrastructure creates a "fabric" containing pools of compute resource capability. This fabric will span the enterprise providing the ability to dynamically scale (up or down) to satisfy the business needs using service level automation.

- **IT organization changes:** The people aspects and business model of IT operations are changing focus to act as a business within the organization. IT organizations will be adopting the information technology services management to increase efficiency and contribution to the organization.

In this chapter, we discuss key areas of which enterprise architects should be mindful as they address the SOE business model. Beginning with an overview of the SOE, the chapter addresses changes in IT strategy, solutions, infrastructure, and the IT organization.

THE SERVICE-ORIENTED ENTERPRISE

The SOE differs from the traditional enterprise in several ways. A recent article in the IBM Systems Journal highlighted the differences in the two models in terms of business ecosystem, business process, and organizational issues. The comparison is shown in Figure 1.

As we see, IT plays a strategic role in transforming the organization to the service-oriented model. Enterprise architecture and its understanding of people, process, and technology is central to its success. Let's review what else is different in the two models.

SOE emphasizes forming and managing a strong partner-network to create and sustain value. Today, the scope of the value chain typically remains within a single enterprise under strict control of the business executives. In the

Figure 1. Comparison of a traditional enterprise with a service-oriented enterprise (Cherbakov, Galambos, Harishankar, Kalyana, & Rackham, 2005)

	Traditional Enterprise	Service-Oriented Enterprise
Business Ecosystem		
IT role in business (business/IT alignment)	IT has supporting role ("enabler" of business activity). Business organization has the challenge to ensure that IT understands and supports business requirements.	IT plays a strategic role in business transformation, including creation of new sources of business revenue. IT systems mirror the attributes of the business they enable.
Business value creation	Value is created in each phase in the value chain (e.g., from raw goods to finished products). Business value is created mostly within the enterprise.	Real-time information moves across the value net among cooperating businesses, facilitating dynamic relationships among partners. The business value is created through services provided by participants.
Business requirements/ fulfillment coupling	Business requirements are often generated and fulfilled by the same business unit/ enterprise.	Logical separation of business need (service consumption) from fulfillment (service provision). The same business need can be fulfilled by multiple providers.
Business Process		
Process flow and composite services	Process flow is often sequential; value creation is cumulative and based on the value chain. Composition of services is limited.	Process flow is net-like, through composition and enhancement (and often parallel execution) of existing services provided by participants in the business ecosystem.
Process design	Static, sequential flow with decision points in predefined sequence. Modeling is focused on decomposition.	Dynamic, based on execution results of subprocesses. Nearly real-time dynamic orchestration.
Organizational Issues		
Organizational structure	Hierarchical	Horizontal, network-like structure based on service consumer-service provider relationship.
Intermediaries	Limited applicability	Service intermediaries are needed to accelerate negotiations and facilitate switching providers.
Common interpretation of service definitions	Limited applicability	Essential in the service-oriented environment.

SOE, real-time information will move among cooperating organizations to facilitate relationships among partners. The logical separation of business need (service consumption) from fulfillment (service provision) will use multiple providers to create value. Partners are continually measured and monitored using service level agreements (SLAs). In this model, the enterprise will expand in scope across partner boundaries, extending its traditional organizational boundary scope.

Business process flow and design is different in the SOE as well. In the SOE, process flow is less sequential and uses "net-like" patterns. Processes become somewhat autonomous services that are dynamic in nature, orchestrated to execute, and execute based on real-time results. Enterprise architects will be responsible for expressing the organization as a set of business services that are responsible for delivering goods and services in alignment with business goals and objectives. The efficacy of a business service will be measured using financial data such as capital and operational expenses as well as performance and quality metrics found in comparative industry benchmarks. Enterprise architects will be responsible for determining the best method to satisfy the business service. They will advise executives in selecting from a variety of techniques including internal provider, partner collaboration, outsource, or moving offshore using a lower cost workforce. Managing services using SLAs, executives can readily evaluate costs, quality, and performance within each segment of the value chain.

The traditional enterprise structure is typically hierarchical, whereas the SOE structure is more horizontal or network-like to enable the service consumer-service provider relationships. In this regard, we may see changes in reward and recognition systems. Enterprise architects addressing organization change may need to structure programs based on service level achievement where internal and external service providers alike meet service level commitments in order to be rewarded.

As such, they will likely become increasingly focused on how they best deliver value.

In the SOE, the role of IT becomes more prominent in achieving business transformation. As the SOE technical architecture comprises infrastructure and applications as a set of malleable components that can be dynamically constructed and re-constructed to support the value chain. Organizations are becoming dependent upon IT to support the partner-network and monitor service delivery. The resulting infrastructure must be flexible, scalable, and reliable where capacity is dynamically adjusted based upon service level requirements. IT has greater responsibility in managing delivery throughout the value chain.

As we can see, the SOE and traditional organization differ in structure, flow, and execution. In this new model, IT plays a significant role in business transformation. Enterprise architects shape the SOE of the future. They must correctly apply this paradigm in defining a successful strategy and the services, solution, and infrastructure that serve its execution.

FORMING THE SOE STRATEGY

Transforming an organization begins with strategy. The elements of the strategy should address where the organization can maximize value. Its contents include vision, goals, objectives, critical success factors (CSFs), and business drivers that link to strategic outcomes through value chains. In this section, we address the linkage from strategy to measurable outcomes using a strategy map. Strategy maps, developed by Kaplan and Norton (2004), are closely aligned with the balanced scorecard—successful in many public and private sector organizations. The model emphasizes the cause-and-effect relationship of goals, objectives, and outcomes that comprise a value chain. It provides a uniform and consistent way to describe the strategy so that objectives and measures can be established and managed through execution.

A strategy map is a four-perspective model provides a common language that executives can use to discuss the direction and priorities of their organization. It is used to link vision and strategy to strategic outcomes

While the definition of the perspectives slightly differs between public and private sector organizations, the concepts and application are the same. The model uses linkages between financial, customer, internal, and learning and growth perspectives to align strategy to measurable outcomes. Through this linking, enterprise architects identify core and commodity services lie within the value chain.

As an overview in applying the model, the first two perspectives, financial and customer, are closely aligned in defining value outcomes. The second two perspectives, internal and learning

and growth, are linked to the execution processes. All four perspectives work together to form a living strategy. Let us take a look at a map using an example of "laptop repair."

In the financial perspective, an organization describes what they hope to achieve in traditional financial terms such as ROI, shareholder value, profitability, and revenue. Here we align objectives with a balance of short-term results such as cost reduction with long-term profitable gains in revenue growth. Financial outcomes show how well the strategy is succeeding or failing. They typically address increasing sales or reducing costs. An example financial value statement for a personal computer manufacturer may be focused on improving laptop repair services. Creating a statement to "reduce laptop computer repair and maintenance costs by 50%" indicates value in addressing efficiency and quality services. The outcome will attack cost structure and possibly promote revenue growth by addressing a customer

Figure 2. Strategy map

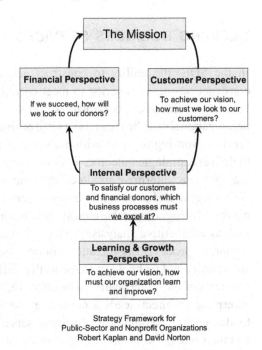

Strategy Framework for
Public-Sector and Nonprofit Organizations
Robert Kaplan and David Norton

Strategy Framework for
Private Sector Organizations
Robert Kaplan and David Norton

requirement for quick turn-around when using the laptop repair service. With this statement in place, the next step is to align it with the remaining perspectives.

Satisfying customers is the way organizations sustain value. The customer perspective identifies targeted consumer segments and the value proposition to satisfy them. If the targeted base value is reliable, quality products, then skills, systems, and processes that result in quality products and services are of obvious importance to the organization. An example customer value statement is "If my laptop breaks, promptly repair it for me in 3 days or less". If during the course of using a quality product the customer has an issue, it should be a seamless, painless process to have it back in working order. A continual alignment of goals to the customer perspective and internal efficiencies will reveal core business services of the organization.

While financial and customer perspectives describe outcomes, effective and aligned internal processes determine how value gets created and sustained. The internal perspective identifies the efficiencies that are critical in achieving the outcomes listed in financial and customer perspectives. This perspective is where value chain elements and business services are identified. Outcomes may link to partner-network solutions. For example, if the organization wishes to increase the value of its fix and repair service by reducing costs and turn-around time, it may decide a relationship with UPS is the best method to perform the repair service, as Toshiba did. The internal perspective is linked with learning and growth as organizations must determine how solutions impact valuable intangible assets of intellectual and human capital.

The learning and growth perspective identifies which positions, systems, and working environment are needed to create the value creating internal processes. These elements represent the most critical elements of an organization, its

human and intellectual capital. In responding to the internal process of using an in-source solution with UPS, the learning and growth perspective determines the impact to the intangible assets of the organization. How much intellectual capital is lost in repairing laptops? How much must be retained if the business service is performed by the partner? To be successful, the organization must sustain the knowledge, culture, and leadership while balancing financial, customer value. In this perspective, the organization will confirm core business services.

The strategy map is an easy way to meaningfully link strategy formulation and strategy execution. It helps organizations consider how partnerships can satisfy objectives financial terms, customer value, internal efficiency, and learning and growth. The model works well in the SOE as organization can define the business services within the value chain and the events that govern them. For further understanding of this model, the text *Strategy Maps* by Kaplan and Norton is an excellent study.

DEFINING BUSINESS SERVICES

In the SOE, the ability to construct and re-construct business scenarios to meet changing business environment is critical. To do so, the organization should be viewed as a set of business services working together within a value chain to deliver a strategic outcome. With the strategy map in place, enterprise architects shift focus to defining core and commodity business services measured using comparable industry benchmarks such as competitive analysis. Business services comprise process, organization, information, application, and technology elements that fulfill segments of the value chain. To be effective, the enterprise architect needs a consistent method to define and communicate business services and their role in fulfilling strategic outcomes. In this section, we discuss using a supply/demand framework to define and communicate business services.

In the SOE, business services act as providers or consumers working together in fulfilling a strategic outcome. For those familiar with object-oriented methodology, the model is relatively straightforward in that a provider contributes a service whereas a consumer uses it in its processing to produce a desired result. However, the SOE model extrapolates this theory several notches to that of partnerships within the value chain.

While we understand the business service concept, teams may struggle with communicating and modeling it in a consistent manner. A framework developed by Gordon Babcock of Computer Sciences Corporation (CSC) for the Department of Education (Computer Sciences Corporation, 2005) is a very good way to model business services. The model uses a business perspective to ensure the organization gets the results it needs absent of technology bias. It uses a consistent language to describe concepts from strategic to implementation level. In this model, a customer consumes a service that leads to results. A service is a meaningful function provided by a component for a customer. A component is a tangible provider of services. Results desired by the customer create a demand for a service in the form of requirements for functionality delivered at satisfactory performance and quality levels. A component, which is ultimately constructed with tangible resources (especially technology and people) and which is capable of delivering a service that meets the customer's service requirements, provides the service for the customer. In so doing, the component is the supplier of the service that meets the customer demand. The framework provides a set of patterns that reflect typical transaction types within an organization. These patterns use the same modeling constructs in greater and greater levels of detail.

In the process of defining business services, enterprise architects should identify those that are considered "core" and key differentiators from the competition. Most organizations find that 25% of their services are "core" and allow them to differentiate themselves from competi-

Figure 3. Supply demand framework

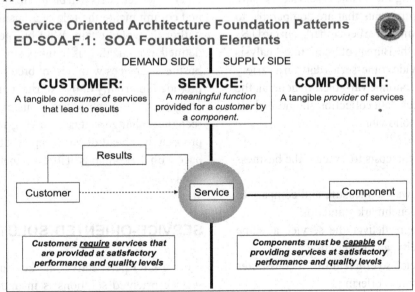

tion. Typically, organizations will find commodity services in the following areas:

- **Supply chain:** Companies like FedEx and UPS have embedded themselves within partner-networks to support product delivery to consumers. China has significant manufacturing resources and processes working today.
- **Human resources:** Firms have moved recruiting, benefits management, and payroll to business process outsource firms who specialize in these areas. Delivering these services better, faster, and cheaper than internal functions.
- **Information technology:** Application development has been moved offshore to India or to popular system integration companies like Accenture, EDS, CSC, and IBM.
- **Customer service:** Call centers and help desk functions are sent offshore from the U.S. to be supported by companies primarily located in Europe and India. Because of widespread, high-speed connectivity, this service can be provided without regard to location.

When defining the business service, be sure to collect measurements that are comparable to industry and competitive benchmarks. In the U.S., a good source is the Bureau of Economic Analysis (BEA) as it provides time-series data on a variety of U.S. macroeconomic variables. In general, the business services data collection should include answers to the following:

- What are the costs to execute the business service?
- Is there a way to measure and compare to industry benchmark standards?
- Can partners deliver the service at same level, quality, and lower cost?
- Is the service so efficient that it constitutes a new business offering?

By answering these questions, the organization will understand what areas provide greatest value to the business.

The goal of any SOE solution is the ability to change and adapt based on business need. From a strategic perspective, business services are implemented using internal processing or by a partner using in-source, outsource, offshore model. Most organizations have expertise in core aspects and have other areas that are non-differentiating or commodity operations. The reason a business wants a partner to perform a particular business service is because the partner is considered an expert in that particular area. Consuming a service is usually cheaper and more effective than doing the work internally. Organizations must be able to easily employ a partner to perform non-core, commodity services in a more cost effective manner with the same or better service levels.

Using the strategy map framework, enterprise architects can link strategy to strategic outcomes and identify which business services are critical to the organization. They will identify where the business services fit into the value chain and define sets of strategic and tactical initiatives that will have significant return on investment and deliver the business vision. Using the framework enterprise architects will be able to quickly define and communicate the role of a business service within the value chain. With business services defined, organization is in the position to link its business services with best of breed capabilities provided internally or by external partners. This component-based structure, a business is able to recognize change as it is occurring and react appropriately, ahead of the competition, and keep pace with the demands of its customers, partners, and employees.

SERVICE-ORIENTED SOLUTIONS

From a CIO perspective, the key managing to service-oriented solutions is in understanding, defining, and measuring service level achievement to meet strategic outcomes. The enterprise architect understands that in the service-oriented world business services are susceptible to change and as such they are good candidates to be implemented using a plug-and-play, component-based model. In this manner, they too can be ostensibly constructed and re-constructed based on the needs of the organization in a close to real-time manner. As creating and managing SLAs are much discussed in other texts, the contents of this section briefly address considerations in selecting an approach service-oriented software solutions.

Today, industry is touting two options satisfying service-oriented needs. The first option is employing the software as a service (SaaS) model where an organization subscribes to software offerings from a partner provider. Popular offerings include SalesForce.com delivering CRM; employees delivering HR; and NetSuite delivering financials. The second option is service-oriented architecture (SOA). While SOA is not a new concept, its popularity has recently increased with the advent of Web services, orchestration, and infrastructure virtualization. Enterprise architects should understand that it is the service-oriented concepts, not just technology, that instills the component-based framework and orchestration necessary to drive the SOE. It is the ability to freely subscribe, use, and release a service for a specific business purpose that makes the architecture so valuable.

With the prevalence of communication bandwidth, companies can offer software applications as a service to those organizations who do not want the infrastructure. The key architectural principle for selecting a SaaS solution is ensuring a single instance of the software runs on the provider environment—and all users log into that instance. Releasing organizations from managing servers, version control, and disaster recovery, Providers have made SaaS a feasible model for the SOE. These products, once considered only viable for small-to-midsize businesses, are now used by the large corporations as well. They enable organizations to be up and running faster, better, and cheaper. The enterprise architect can find these offerings for most back office functions—those that are typically considered commodity services. The SaaS selection should be based upon standard evaluation criteria as well as the ability to extend the information model and possibly personalize the application to meet unique operational needs. With SaaS, the organization can define service levels for application performance execution while continuing to perform the service in-house. In some cases, organizations are fearful to fully move service to a partner. However, the next logical step is to find the provider that can perform the same business service with better quality at a lower cost. For commodity services, the move is inevitable.

SOA represents many things to many people today. In this discussion, it is considered a loosely coupled architectural strategy that is technology and vendor agnostic. The SOA concept naturally fits the SOE paradigm with its separation of presentation, business logic, and data tiers, orchestration, and asynchronous messaging. Using a range of technologies, architects designate applications services at an elementary-level. Because they are at the elementary level, the application services can be orchestrated, into a series of steps, to reflect how a particular business service will execute based upon a given event or result. Abstraction is a key mechanism to de-constructing and re-constructing components and integrating partner solutions without interruption to business. In this approach, the application and data are abstracted from its implementation, so its provider is transparent to the customer. Like SaaS, the consumer does not need to know if the application service is housed internally or subscribed from a provider.

In December 2005, Michelson of the Patricia Seybold Group attended the SOA InfoWorld Conference and stated in her review that:

Enterprises are using SOA to provide both agility and productivity for business and IT. The secret is to approach SOA as an architectural strategy. In such, make decisions based on your business, technology portfolios, and people. Don't be misled by vendors who claim SOA can be bought in a box. Don't be misled by technology snobs who claim SOA is Web Services. Remember loose-coupling, well-defined interfaces, and standards based messages. (Michelson, 2005).

This is sage advice for all enterprise architects to follow.

While service-oriented solutions are viable today, some gaps still exist in reliability, legacy support, and data semantics. These gaps will be remedied soon, but the architect must be mindful of them while defining solutions. In terms of reliability, the best service will only be as strong as its weakest link or slowest performing component. This means, we need the correct infrastructure, one that can ensure adequate performance and compute resources that are continually available to the service. In terms of legacy support, there will be tightly-coupled, domain-specific applications supporting business services like finance, payroll, or marketing. Oftentimes, these applications and infrastructures are stovepipes of hardware, software, connectivity, and license fees. This implementation is expensive, encourages hardware/OS/SW disparity, and prohibits easy growth in accordance with the demand of the business. In the SOA model, the first step is to define how these applications can offer services for consumption by other applications or providers. They need standard interface points or consumption mechanisms to integrate with external services and support partner collaborations that require access. In terms of data semantics, the architect should create a data model that can be considered the single source of key naming terms, definitions, and relationships. To implement the SOA correctly, the data model is used as a refer-

ence point where services only message each other rather than exchange specific logic.

As application services support business services, they too are measured through SLAs directly tied to business requirements. The SLAs define performance, financial, and qualitative metrics and are regularly measured to industry benchmarks or competitive analysis data. If the SLA is not being met, it should go under review and a new solution selected.

Case Study: Pfizer Global Pharmaceuticals (Manasco, 2005)

Pfizer Global Pharmaceuticals (PGP) is one of the world's largest drug companies. In the competitive pharmaceutical marketplace, leveraging technology to its fullest value is mandatory. In 2005, Pfizer examined how the services oriented approach could be leveraged to improve business capability. The following case study was found on Information week (www.informationweek. com).

PGP needed an enterprise-wide services-oriented architecture to make application integration operational. Key business data from line of business applications reside in differing business units, on differing computing platforms, located in differing geographies, must be shared. Shared services comprise both technical and business services, and must be leveraged by multiple lines of business (LOB) across the world, regardless of disparate technologies. The key functional objectives of the shared services strategy included leveraging existing data across a wide number of processes, supporting flexibility in business processes, establishing consistent standards for IT systems, and preserving the value of their existing IT assets. PGP wanted to maintain and enforce consistent policies across their computing infrastructure—deemed critical to making shared services usable enterprise-wide.

The PGP technical architecture includes Web services that are security aware with business process management, content management, and XML firewalls as important elements of their new integration infrastructure. Brodbeck, Application Architecture Director of PGP, states, "Most technology investments made in the past five years have driven efficiencies in vertical processes (e.g., order process). Pfizer's opportunity with SOA is to drive efficiency in processes that match Pfizer's strategic needs across multiple groups within the company—either line of business, geographic, or technical group—and have an impact on unique elements of the business (e.g., clinical trials). The products must be standards-based and actually service-oriented themselves. Just putting a Web services interface on a monolithic product only gets you so far." The goal for PGP is to alter the competitive dynamics within the pharmaceutical industry. At PGP, the Enterprise SOA Fabric™ provides the potential to accelerate the core processes around Pfizer's drug discovery and clinical trials while greatly reducing the cost of this enabling infrastructure.

As Pfizer is successful at driving efficiencies in areas like drug discovery, clinical trials, and drug marketing, they will garner a substantial and defensible competitive advantage. PGP is altering the operating dynamics of IT by redefining their infrastructure capabilities. Working with Blue Titan's Network Director and Cassatt Collage, the company leveraged existing technologies and platforms across operating units and lines of business. PGP developed a shared services strategy that now enables it to draw on existing data from a wide array of processes, establish consistent standards for IT systems, and enforce IT policies across infrastructure. Shared services have made it possible for developers to roll out and deploy applications much more quickly. The PGP approvals portal, the first productivity driving application of its SOA efforts, is a single place for executives to gain approvals for project expenses and invoices by providing access to 20 systems on the back-end. The solution condensed employee training from one week down to one day and

help desk costs related to project management were cut by 50%.

INFRASTRUCTURE SERVICES

In SOE, the key principle is easily changing all components of the enterprise. This principle applies to the supporting infrastructure layer as well. Infrastructure comprises the hardware servers, network, storage, and software configuration items managed by IT in support of application services. In the SOE, the infrastructure must be reactive, flexible, and scalable to continually meet the demands stipulated in the business service levels. Today, technology vendors are creating tools that apply virtualization, compute resource pooling, and service level automation to make infrastructure compatible to the service-oriented concept.

Infrastructure costs a lot. A 2004 IDC study found nearly $95 billion dollars was applied to managing infrastructure in North America. The report estimated that 57% of the IT budget is attributed to rote maintenance and administration tasks such as patch management. Most data centers are over provisioned with servers running at 15%-20% of peak utilization levels. Applications are stove piped into segregated hardware, software license, data resources, and network elements. This architecture is in-flexible and costly and does not support the SOE concept. Instead, it stymies the organization as it cannot quickly shift computing resources to where they are needed. It requires the business to purchase licenses for each CPU where the specific software will run—not per utilization or transaction load associated with a particular service level. This view of infrastructure must change to implement the SOE.

Enterprise architects will solve this dilemma by establishing a principle stating infrastructure must be "on-demand" and applying infrastructure virtualization. While virtualization has become a broad term that refers to the abstraction of resources, in the infrastructure context we are referring to network, servers, and storage resources. Combining virtualization and service level automation creates an infrastructure that can continually change and self-manage. Self-management tasks include server failover, server image provisioning, hardware provision, operating system provision, and software provision, supporting application services. In service level automation solutions, the infrastructure components are dynamically managed using business rules that are defined based upon the SLAs of the business service.

Software license fee structures will change. With infrastructure virtualization, organizations can shift license fee models from "pay per CPU" structure to that of a "usage based" structure. Because the infrastructure will constantly and dynamically react to service level demands, servers can no longer be tracked as static entities with assigned software components. Instead, software components (such as Web server, application server, operating system, etc.) are "in-use" when dynamically added into the infrastructure or "not used" when dynamically removed from the infrastructure. For license management, the infrastructure will track usage (number of CPUs, time, transactions) during a specified usage period. The IT department, enterprise architect, and vendor will negotiate the period—monthly, quarterly, yearly—to apply the cost of licenses and the maintenance fee. This approach is more in-tune with the service-oriented model.

Several technology vendors offer infrastructure virtualization solutions. While companies such as IBM, EMC, and Sun have interesting tools, Cassatt Corporation appears to have the best approach. Cassatt Collage is technology agnostic and uses network, data, and compute resource virtualization to make the infrastructure flexible and dynamic to the needs of the business. It automates many of the daily system administration tasks such as patch management and hardware provision-

ing. Its application of service level automation ensures the infrastructure meets commitment levels specified in the business service.

Case Study: Cassatt Corporation

Cassatt Collage combines goal-driven automation and virtualization control to respond to change and drive higher service levels. In Collage, business priorities and service-level agreements are used to create simple policies for balancing resources across applications. Drawing from a common resource pool, Collage assigns resources to meet service level requirements and automatically reassigns them as conditions change. Sharing peaks and valleys in capacity drives higher utilization rates and thus reduces hardware and associated maintenance costs. Where traditional management software focuses on physical resources such as servers and networks, Collage manages both physical and virtual entities. Collage enables this transformation of IT functions using existing, off-the-shelf hardware, operating systems, network switches, and applications. The tools comprise three areas: Goal driven automation, virtualization control, and infrastructure management. Each area is briefly described next.

Goal-driven automation is used to optimize resource allocation by taking existing policies, priorities, and service level agreements and mapping them to goals. Based on these goals, an optimization engine automatically responds to critical events. If the optimization engine analysis determines that an application does not meet its service levels, it applies best-fit algorithms to determine the optimal course of action to bring the application into compliance.

Virtualization control is used to deliver unified control of all the application components required to deliver the appropriate service levels. Collage leverages a variety of virtualization technologies, including virtual machine managers (VMM),

Java virtual machines (JVM), virtual local area networks (VLAN), and its own virtualized image deployment, the image delivery service.

Managing the environment includes defining policies and detailing application resource requirements. An activity reporting facility tracks which servers are running, which software, and when changes were applied for billing, auditing, and compliance. In addition, Collage provides management tool integration APIs to interface with various enterprise management systems.

The features of Cassatt Collage represent the infrastructure toolset of the SOE. Through these tools, enterprise architects can establish a lower cost, efficient environment that is managed dynamically using SLAs specified in the business service.

Cassatt at Pfizer

To explain how virtualization is making headway in the private sector, *Information Week* reported the progress made at Pfizer Pharmaceuticals in the March 2006 issue. The article shows how Cassatt Collage is supporting the Pfizer PGP architecture and its range of technology platforms. The article includes a brief comparison to other companies supporting the infrastructure virtualization space. Pfizer's core business unit, Pfizer Global Pharmaceuticals, plans to virtualize more of the company's middleware, particularly its BEA Systems' WebLogic application servers, and use them as a flexible, dynamically allocateable resource.

In this initial foray into infrastructure virtualization, Pfizer planned to make 14 WebLogic application servers (running on 14 hardware servers in the data center) into a single virtualized resource using Cassatt Collage software and its Web Automation Module (WAM). Using WAM, the Pfizer business applications are no longer constrained by a specific physical application server, but will be virtualized to acquire compute resources and application server services from underutilized servers within the infrastructure. With Cassatt Collage and Web automation, Module Pfizer can "manage our WebLogic environment as if it were one machine," even though it's spread across multiple servers, says Richard Lynn, VP of global applications and architecture. As the first phase is completed, Pfizer plans to add another 86 servers into the Cassatt management environment by the end of 2006.

Pfizer plans to have 500 servers under virtualization by 2007 using a combination of Cassatt and VMware technology. Plans include extending virtualization to include portal servers and portal applications as well as Oracle DBMS, IBM DataStage for ETL, and Microsoft Windows Server applications. The benefit of managing servers using virtualization is obvious now. "We would need at least double the 500 servers if we weren't running Collage and VMware," reported Lynn.

The Collage software management is based upon SLA or other built-in performance rules to provision servers based on utilization levels. With WAM, the WLS software is separated from the hardware servers on which they run, and as such, are treated as a pool of resources. This is different than "load-balancing" on clusters as it understands the middleware component and its relationship to the overall goal of the SLA. Treating middleware independent of hardware and applications offers greater operational flexibility and efficient use of hardware resources.

In contrast, the WebSphere Extended Deployment can also virtualize application server resources. It creates many small virtual machines in logical partitions on IBM servers and allocates JVMs and application server units as demand increases. This solution is software platform dependent, unlike the hardware resource approach of Cassatt.

Using the Cassatt software over a three-year period, Pfizer plans to save "several million dollars" by reducing operations and software costs. The savings stem in part from higher server usage levels as Lynn estimated the WebLogic servers will go from about 40% utilization to more than 75% utilization. This is important as most data center servers run at approximately 15%-30% utilization—tying up unnecessary costs within the infrastructure (Babcock, 2006).

IT ORGANIZATION CHANGES

The SOE means changes to people, processes, and technology. We discussed the changes from a strategy perspective with creating business services; application perspective with SaaS and SOA; and an infrastructure perspective with virtualization and service level automation. This section discusses how the IT organization will change to execute "as a business" in the role of service provider for such things as service level management, application management, capacity management, security management, infrastructure management, and problem resolution. To make this change, private and public sector organizations are adopting the de-facto standard of information technology services management (ITSM) to run their operations in a common, structured manner.

ITSM and the IT infrastructure library (ITIL) combine to provide a framework of common IT processes and services. Emphasizing alignment of IT and business objectives, ITIL comprises a library of best practices and processes to support management and delivery of IT services to the organization. By implementing the ITSM/ITIL processes, organizations have a standard means to measure efficiency and cost effectiveness of their IT services as compared to industry benchmark. The ITSM Forum is a standards body that has categorized the ITIL processes into several modules matching the activities and duties of a common IT Organization. Each module is briefly described below:

- **Service delivery:** This module includes the processes associated with planning and delivery of quality IT services. It focuses on strategic processes required with improving the quality of the IT services delivered. Activities under service deliver include service level management, capacity management, financial management, availability management, and continuity management.

- **Service support:** This module describes the processes used in day-to day support and maintenance activities associated with provisioning IT services. Service support activities include configuration management,

Figure 4. ITSM framework

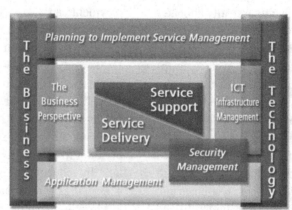

change management, release management, incident management, and problem management.

- **ICT infrastructure management (ICT IM):** This module describes all aspects of infrastructure management to include identification of business requirements through the tendering process, to the testing, installation, deployment, and ongoing operation and optimization of the components and IT services.

- **Planning to implement service management:** This module examines the issues and tasks involved in planning, implementing, and improving service management processes within an IT organization. The module addresses cultural and organizational change, developing vision and strategy, and the method of approach.

- **Application management:** This module describes processes to manage applications from the initial business need, through all stages in the application lifecycle including application retirement. It focuses on the alignment of IT projects and strategies to the business.

- **Security management:** This module describes the process of planning and managing levels of security for information and IT services. The scope includes all aspects associated with reaction to security Incidents. The module also addresses the assessment and management of risks, vulnerabilities, and countermeasures.

IT departments in both the public and private sector are adopting ITSM but are struggling with creating the best procedures to manage its services. Because data centers often vary in structure from plan and attack to chaos and react, the adjustment to standard processes is difficult. To operate as a business, IT organizations must change the way they execute to reflect a set of

services with measurable service levels. ITSM and ITIL are becoming the de-facto standard for IT processes within private and public sector alike. By developing a set of standard services based upon the ITSM/ITL framework, corporations have a measurable way to gauge how effective their organization is operating. Industry experts report that IT organizations can reduce their annual IT operating costs by as much as 30% by adopting these best practices.

Case Study: Wipro Technologies

The following article found in the January 2006 itSMF Research paper at www.itsmf.org describes the benefits of applying ITSM in one of the largest offshore development companies located in India—Wipro Technologies. The study attributes a dramatic improvement in service delivery and service management from applying the ITSM framework to its operations.

Wipro Technologies doesn't just adhere to the principles of ITIL, it shares them with customers worldwide. One of India's largest IT services vendors, Wipro, began implementing ITIL best practices in 2001 as part of an enterprise-wide quality initiative aimed at lowering costs and improving efficiencies in the company's technology infrastructure services (TIS) unit. TIS operates Wipro's Global Command Center (GCC), which manages IT services for nearly 300 global customers. In the highly competitive services industry, "We need to remain at the top as a quality service provider," says Viswanathan Sankara, manager of mission quality in Wipro TIS. "ITIL is the world's de facto standard for best practices around managing IT infrastructure." Wipro's challenge: How could it create a flexible, reliable management system to support the scores of incidents the GCC handles daily? Ultimately, Wipro improved internal operations through better workflow automation, better response time, and ITIL best practices. As a result, most of Wipro's clients have seen direct benefits. One has seen an estimated 35% cost savings, mainly from automating tasks, which have helped reduce the support team's headcount from 46 to 35, an effort savings of 24%, response time, which has improved from an average of two hours to 30 minutes, and global sourcing, co-locating the support team onsite in the UK and offshore in India, where labor costs are significantly lower. Sankara also cites several soft benefits as well. "ITIL, as a framework helps marry IT and business needs. It reminds us, for example, that our users view e-mail not as a technology, but as a critical business tool." To achieve such success requires a top-down management commitment to excellence. That commitment is held with Chairman Azim Premji, whose mantra is: "Quality, like integrity, is nonnegotiable" (itSMF, 2006).

CONCLUSION

In conclusion, the move to the service-oriented enterprise model is inevitable. With the acceptance of capitalism in India and China and availability of high-speed connectivity, the scope of the "enterprise" is dramatically extended. Using strategy maps to link strategy to strategic outcomes, organizations can identify key business services that impact the value chain. Private and public sector organizations are stronger and more efficient through adoption of the partner-network model and the ability to adjust to a changing global market. Private sector organizations find competitive advantage based by understanding how they best contribute to the value chain and relegating commodity services to partners. Public organizations too find value by embracing SOE and promoting shared services in the context of centers of excellence. From a technology perspective, application services now support the service-oriented paradigm as well. Organizations can choose to enable current software into loosely coupled, message-based environment or make agreements with SaaS partners. Technology vendors like IBM, Cassatt, EMC, and others are

providing infrastructure virtualization tools that enable storage, servers, and network to be reactive, scalable, and manageable through service level automation. IT organizations are adopting the service-oriented paradigm using ITSM and running IT as a business.

Enterprise architects are the primary resource in implementing the SOE within the public and private sector organizations of the future. In this role, they must understand direction, strategy, and differentiator segments of the value chain of the organization. They will help executives determine which business services are differentiators and which are considered a commodity. For each business service, enterprise architects will select the correct model—internal, in-source, outsource, or offshore—to deliver the best solution in alignment with business direction.

Success in execution will be measured using SLAs and industry benchmarks. The enterprise architecture team will monitor the ability of each business service in meeting the service level commitment. They will institute change as necessary.

While SOE does not equal SOA, the emergence of service-oriented applications allows teams to create component-based solutions that are adaptable to changing business needs. Using such technologies as Web services and orchestration tools, a plug-and-play environment can be established to facilitate reuse and exploiting partner relationships. In terms of infrastructure, virtualization and service level automation tools from thought-leading companies like Cassatt Corporation allow IT departments to manage capacity and compute power based on SLAs. These tools remove the costly stove-pipe and over provisioned server hardware found in many data centers around the world. The ability to ratchet-up or ratchet-down compute resources based on service level demands reflects the service-oriented of the global business.

From a people perspective, organizations are embracing a service-oriented culture where focus is in delivering quality service to the enterprise. Roles will somewhat change in both business and IT organizations when moving to the service-oriented enterprise. Personnel must understand how the action they take affects the overall ability to deliver on agreed upon service levels. Changes to reward and recognition systems will include how well teams meet service levels and quality of service requirements. Communication strategies must include messaging that reflects the importance of services and service level achievement of the organization.

In this world of interchanging parts, the IT organization and their business operations brethren must adopt the service-oriented perspective. Adopting ITSM, the IT department is able to act as a service within the organization. ITSM helps IT teams define common services executed by the department. Using SLAs, organizations will measure the effectiveness of the IT department and make changes to increase value. When the business is viewed as a set of services that can be coupled or de-coupled at will—then all must understand their value to the corporation. People must understand how their work affects the business and its components or they risk being replaced by a vendor that can do it better, faster, and cheaper.

Today, the service-oriented concept impacts the business, organization, application, and technology domains of the enterprise architecture model. This important trend should be embraced by any enterprise architect who wishes to remain viable in the next decade. Prepare for enterprise architecture within the service-oriented world of the future.

REFERENCES

Babcock, C. (2006). *Virtualization's next stage.* Retrieved March 20, 2006 from http://www. informationweek.com/showArticle.jhtml;jsessio nid=1YDF1RNVNUYZCQSNDBECKH0CJU MEKJVN?articleID=183700351

Cherbakov, L., Galambos, G., Harishankar, R., Kalyana, S., & Rackham, G. (2005). Impact of service orientation at the business level. *IBM Systems Journal of Service-Oriented Architecture, 44*(4).

Computer Sciences Corporation. (2005). *Service-oriented architecture (SOA) patterns and practices, Draft 1.0.*

Friedman, T. L. (2005). *The World is flat.* New York: Farrar, Straus, and Giroux.

Intel Corporation. (2005). *Service-oriented enterprise—The technology path to business transformation.* Retrieved April 3, 2006, from http://www.intel.com

itSMF. (2006, January). *itSMF USA research letter Volume 2 Issue 1: Wipro ITIL gains.* Retrieved May 16, 2006, from http://data.memberclicks. com/site/itsmf/Research_Newsletter_-_January_2006_Issue.pdf

Kaplan, R. S., & Norton, D. P. (2004). *Strategy maps.* Boston: Harvard Business School Press.

Manasco, B. (2005). *Pfizer's SOA strategy.* Retrieved February 21, 2006, from http://blogs.zdnet. com/service-oriented/?p=215

Michelson, B. M. (2005). Best practices, lessons learned, and takeaways from enterprise SOA practitioners. *A Report from InfoWorld's SOA Executive Forum.* Retrieved March 26, 2006.

Chapter XXIV
A Fundamental SOA Approach to Rebuilding Enterprise Architecture for a Local Government after a Disaster

Zachary B. Wheeler
SDDM Technology, USA

ABSTRACT

As a result of Hurricane Katrina, the destruction of property, assets, documentation, and human life in the Gulf Port has introduced a myriad of challenging issues. These issues involve human, social, government, and technological concerns. This chapter does not address the many immediate human and social concerns brought forth from a natural disaster or major terrorist attack (NDMTA); this chapter addresses a small but significant problem of re-establishing or laying the groundwork for an enterprise architecture for local government during the response phase of the disaster. Specifically, it addresses constructing a high-level data model and fundamental SOA, utilizing the remaining local assets, XML (extensible markup language), and Web services.

INTRODUCTION

Disaster preparedness, response, and recovery received a lot of attention immediately after the terrorist attacks of 9/11 and eventually faded from the forefront of attention after the invasion of Iraq and the global war on terrorism. However, recent natural disasters such as the Indonesian Tsunami in 2004 and the devastating Hurricane Katrina in Louisiana have refocused attention on these three prominent areas. Specifically, the lack of preparedness, inadequate response, and slow recovery has burdened local, state, and federal governments as well as citizens.

The presented enterprise approach and implementation process covers an area that is void in the disaster preparedness and response phase; however, it is applicable in each phase: preparedness, response, and recovery. It is recommended that the presented approach be included as part of the disaster preparedness phase, implemented in the response phase, and eventually expanded in the recovery phase. The approach is unique because the enterprise implementation takes place during the actual response phase of the disaster and utilization of the fundamental SOA leads to further expansion during and after the recovery phase.

The approach introduced in this chapter takes advantage of the Zachman framework system model perspective by utilizing Web services on a local level and introducing a practical but efficient method for populating the initial data model. A series of basic assumptions are introduced based on information regarding the recent Gulf Port, Hurricane Andrew, Indonesian Tsunami, and 9/11 disaster events. These assumptions are based on the physical, environmental, and technological conditions immediately after disaster strikes. The assumptions are there will be limited or nonexistent landline and wireless communication, a lack of ability to use generators for power source, limited or nonexistent Internet and intranet, major IT system destruction, and the incapacitation of local government services.

This chapter addresses the problem of reestablishing or laying the groundwork for an enterprise architecture for local government during the response phase of the disaster. Specifically, it addresses constructing a high-level data model and fundamental SOA by utilizing the remaining local assets, XML, and Web services.

BACKGROUND

The fundamental role of local government is to protect the people, provide basic human services, and assist in strengthening communities. This is typically accomplished by establishing various local agencies and departments. These departments are structured to provide essential services for the community. For instance, the fire department role is to help citizens in immediate danger due to fire, gas, or chemical hazard. The role of the health department is to establish policy, programs, and standards regarding health and health related issues. An additional role of the health department is to assist citizens in obtaining basic health care services. Each established department or agency has a role in assisting the community and its residents by providing relevant services. In a typical municipality, each agency has a database of information relating to the citizens and the services provided to the citizen by the agency. For instance, the police department maintains a database of criminals, criminal activity, and citizen complaints. The Department of Human Services maintains a database of child immunization records. In short, each agency maintains a database and application system to enter data, process data, and execute business rules. However, in the wake of an ND-MTA, these systems along with other IT assets are destroyed or rendered useless. For instance, Hurricane Katrina destroyed most of New Orleans including property, buildings, human life, landline and mobile communications, Internet services, intranet services, and essentially incapacitated local government. In the terror attacks of 9/11, the same asset destruction was prevalent within a specified geographic area. Hurricane Andrew wreaked havoc among Florida communities and followed the same line of asset destruction and local government incapacitation as Hurricane Katrina. In each of these cases, major response and rebuilding were needed to help reestablish public safety, government, and services to the remaining citizens. This approach suggests that reestablishing a basic framework for IT services can be facilitated during the response phase of a disaster. In that regard, the proposed approach is unique in that the role of rebuilding typically takes place during the recovery phase (University of Florida, 1998).

The extended Zachman Framework system model perspective will be utilized to establish high-level data elements for the model. The utilization of Web services will be used to lay down a basic framework for a fundamental service oriented architecture that can be extended to an enterprise level once essential government services have been restored. In addition, a data collection process is provided for initial population of the primary data elements from the remaining survivors.

The System Model and Zachman

In the initial framework provided by Zachman (1987), he identifies five different perspectives of an enterprise architecture, three views of the enterprise, and introduces the six questions pertaining to an enterprise. The six questions are what, how, where, who, when, and why.

Zachman provides a clear and concise identification of the various views of an enterprise and shows how each view is proper and correct. In 1992, the Zachman framework was extended by Zachman and Sowa (1992). In addition to answering the final three questions, they introduce the conceptual graph to represent the ISA and replace the "model of the information system" with the more generic system model reference

for row 3 or the designer perspective. Hence, the various perspectives identified by Zachman are scope, enterprise model, system model, technology model, and components. Our perspective will cover the system model or designer perspective. In the conclusion, the what, how, and where questions of the ISA will be answered.

MAIN THRUST OF THE CHAPTER

Basis for a Conceptual Data Model

The ISA system model perspective represents the system analyst role in information technology. The system analyst is responsible for determining the data elements and functions that represent the business entities and processes. Zachman suggests introducing all of the entities; however, the construction of all data elements, processes, and functions for a local government would be beyond the scope of this chapter, therefore, a high-level perspective for core data elements utilized during the response phase will be presented.

Primary Data Elements

One of the main priorities of local government is to provide services to the citizens of the community. Regardless of the service provided, most government agencies interact with its residents

Table 1. Zachman's enterprise questions

Zachman's Six Enterprise Questions	
What?	What entities are involved?
How?	How they are processed?
Where?	Where they are located?
Who?	Who works with the system?
When?	When events occur?
Why?	Why these activities are taking place?

and maintain some form of database of citizen information. In a disaster area, the citizens of the community are the disaster survivors. From a data acquisition perspective, we can obtain valuable information from the survivors and with this information begin to develop a conceptual data model for the emerging enterprise. Typically, the conceptual data model does not show actual data details of the entities. Instead, the conceptual data model provides a high-level entity view using the entity relationship diagram (ERD) (Rob & Coronel, 2002). Entity details will be provided in tabular format for clarity; however, the ERD will only show the entities and the defined relationships. Utilizing the following assumptions, we can define each remaining citizen as unique:

- Every entity has a name (names are not unique).
- Every entity has or had an associated address (address is not unique).
- Every entity has a sex (unique).
- Every entity will have an identifying unique number (ID card, green card, federal em-

Table 2. Person entity details

PERSON	
Unique_Id	Not Null
Unique_ID_Type	Not Null
First_Name	Not Null
Middle_Name	
Last_Name	Not Null
Name_Suffix (i.e. Jr, Sr, etc....)	
Date_of_Birth	Not Null
Sex	Not Null
Status(Living,Deceased)	Not Null
Phone(Optional)	
Address_Id	

Table 3. Address entity details

ADDRESS	
Address_Id	Not Null
Street_Number	Not Null
Prefix	
Street_Name	Not Null
Street_Type	Not Null
PostDir	
City	Not Null
State	Not Null
Zip	
Current_Address (Y,N)	Not Null

ployee identification number, social security card, or driver's license).

Note: Newborns or infants will be given a temporary generic unique id if they do not have a SSN.

If we further assume that each remaining survivor (citizen) has an associated address then we can define the following address entity.

We are working under the assumption that local assets and asset information have been destroyed, which includes the destruction of roads, streets, bridges, highways, and previously existing addresses. Thus, when the data collection process begins, during the response phase, local officials, or management can glean a geographic representation of survivors and establish a basic address information repository. During the recovery phase, old and new street, road, bridge, highway and address information will be added to the system thus creating a complete address reference or

even an address database. For instance, an entity that contains parcel information (square, suffix, and lot) and an instance that contains ownership information (owner name, owner address, etc...) will be needed, however, during the response phase, only the address entity defined above is necessary. The person and address entities are termed primary data elements.

Secondary Data Elements: Extending the Core Elements

In the event of NMDATA, there must be a continuation of basic essential services for the remaining citizens. These essential services required during a disaster, according to Davis (1998), are public safety, public works, and health services. This position is further bolstered by our knowledge of the recent events in the Gulf Port and the establishment of the following five essential services for that particular region.

Table 4. Essential local government agencies

Essential Department/Agencies	
Police Department	for maintaining order and protecting the people from physical harm
Department of Health	for maintaining control and administering of basic health services including disease and disease outbreak
Emergency Medical Services	for assisting in medical data collection and medical services
Department of Pubic Works	for cleaning and clearing of debris, corpses and other related health hazards
Fire Department	for maintaining fire, gas, and chemical controls and basic rescue operations

Table 5. Police entity object relating to person

POLICE	
Unique_Id	Not Null
Unique_Id_Type	Not Null
Arrested(Y,N)	Not Null
Officer_Id	Not Null
Comments	
Crime_Id	Not Null

Table 6. Health services entity object relating to person

HEALTH	
Unique_Id	Not Null
Unique_Id_Type	Not Null
Temperature	Not Null
Eyes(Normal,Dialated)	Not Null
Blood_Pressure_Systollic	Not Null
Blood_Pressure_Diastollic	Not Null
Heart_Rate	Not Null
Recommendations	
Comments	
Treatment	
Medicine_Prescribed	
Disease_Id	

Table 7. EMS entity object relating to person

EMS	
Unique_Id	Not Null
Unique_Id_Type	Not Null
Service_Provided_Id	Not Null
EMS_ID	Not Null
Comments	
Service_Provided_Id	Not Null

Table 8. Public works entity object relating to person and address

PUBLIC WORKS	
Work_Order_Id	Not Null
Unique_Id	
Unique_Id_Type	
Address_Id	
Comments	

Table 9. Fire department entity object relating to person and address

FIRE	
Call_Id	Not Null
Response_Unit_Id	Not Null
Address_Id	Not Null
Unique_Id	
Unique_Id_Type	
Comments	

Based on the five essential departments, five basic data elements can be identified. These essential data elements are termed secondary data elements. Although there are more possible data elements than presented here, an expanded view of potential secondary elements is provided for clarity.

Now that the primary and secondary elements have been identified, we have enough high-level data elements to begin the construction of our conceptual data model. In the overall enterprise, entities can be identified and added as service agencies are added or new requirements are determined.

WEB SERVICES

The construction of our enterprise architecture, from a technology perspective, relies on the utilization of the data model, Web services, and SOA. In our approach, we take advantage of three different definitions of a Web service while saliently maintaining that a Web service, based on the Web services architecture, is considered a software system (Guruge 2004).

- **Definition 1:** Web services are modular, self-contained "applications" or application logic developed per a set of open standards (Guruge, 2004).
- **Definition 2:** Web services are extensible markup language (XML) application mapped to programs, objects, or databases or to comprehensive business functions (Newcomer, 2002)
- **Definition 3:** A Web service is a particular implementation of a protocol (SOAP), Web services description language (WSDL), and universal description discovery and integration (UDDI) (Fermantle, 2002) where
  - SOAP
  - Uses a RPC or a request-response mechanism based on HTTP.

- Utilizes an XML message format that contains an address, possible header, and body.
- Contains one or more elements.
  - The elements are defined using common interoperable data formats (integers, strings, and doubles).
  - The parameters are maybe encoded as child elements of a common parent whose name indicates the operation and whose namespace indicates the service.
- Can be sent over a common transport typically-HTTP.

WSDL
- Offers the ability to describe the inputs and outputs of a Web service.
- Allows a Web service to publish the interface of a service, thus if a client sends a SOAP message in format A to the service, it will receive a reply in format B. The WSDL has two basic strengths:
  - It enforces the separation between the interface and implementation.
  - WSDL is inherently extensible.

UDDI
- A discovery mechanism used to discover available services.

Although a Web service is a particular implementation of a protocol (SOAP), Web services description language (WSDL) and UDDI, the Web service is composed of one or more independent services. A service represents a particular function of the system and has a well-defined, formal interface called its service contract that:

- Defines what the service does and
- Separates the services externally acces-

sible interface from the services technical implementation (Newcomer 2002).

For instance, a Web service can contain a service that performs the function of adding data, another service that performs the function of retrieving data, and another service that performs the function of generating reports for management. A service can be either an atomic (simple) or a composite (complex) service. An atomic service does not rely on other services and are usually associated with straightforward business transactions or with executing data queries and data updates (Newcomer, 2002). A composite service uses other services, has a well-defined service contract, is registered in the service registry, can be looked up via the service registry, and can be invoked like any other service provider (Newcomer, 2002). Regardless of the service type (atomic or composite), the services are required to satisfy the following basic requirements (Fermantle, 2002):

- **Technology neutral:** Each service is non-technology dependent and can be invoked through the standardized lowest common denominator technologies.
- **Loosely coupled:** Each service has a life of its own, each service remains independent of all other services, and each service does not have knowledge about other services.
- **Support location transparency:** Services should have their definition and location information stored in a repository such as UDDI and is accessible by a variety of clients that can locate and invoke the services irrespective of their location.

The Basic Services

During the response phase and part of the recovery phase, several assumptions are made, such as limited landlines, limited mobile communications, and limited Internet and intranet services. The main objective, however, is to form a basic framework using Zachman's framework (system model perspective), Web services, and service-oriented architecture. By maintaining our focus on basic services for the Web service, a foundation is created for extending our Web services to a service oriented architecture later in the recovery phase.

If we utilize the best practice approach of Krafzig, Banke, and Slama (2004), we can identify two crucial basic service types: simple data-centric services and logic-centric services. A data-centric service is used to handle data manipulation, data storage, and data retrieval (Krafizig, Banke, & Slama 2004). We can easily incorporate logic-centric services at a later date to handle business processing and application logic. In a data centric service, an entity can be encapsulated into a service (Krafizig et al., 2004). This encapsulation acts as data layer and all services developed in the future will have to access these services to access and manipulate the data. In this chapter, the primary data elements are wrapped into services and then a composite service is created that utilizes the simple services of person and address. An example is presented in the following screen shot for clarity.

The PersonAddress Composite service will be used in the initial data collection process for the disaster survivors. The SOAP XML message format representation for the PersonAddress_Composite service is provided for clarity.

```
POST /Primary_Core_Service/Service1.asmx
HTTP/1.1
  Host: localhost
  Content-Type: text/xml; charset=utf-8
  Content-Length: length
  SOAPAction: "http://tempuri.org/Primary_Core_Ser-
vice/Service1/PersonAddress_Composite"

  <?xml version="1.0" encoding="utf-8"?>
  <soap:Envelope xmlns:xsi="http://www.w3.org/2001/
XMLSchema-instance" xmlns:xsd="http://www.
```

```
w3.org/2001/XMLSchema" xmlns:soap="http://schemas.
xmlsoap.org/soap/envelope/">
  <soap:Body>
  <PersonAddress_Composite xmlns="http://tempuri.
org/Primary_Core_Service/Service1">
   <Person>
   <Person>
    <Person_ID>string</Person_ID>
    <Person_Id_Type>string</Person_Id_Type>
    <First_Name>string</First_Name>
    <Middle_Name>string</Middle_Name>
    <Last_Name>string</Last_Name>
    <Name_Suffix>string</Name_Suffix>
    <Date_Of_Birth>string</Date_Of_Birth>
    <Persons_Sex>string</Persons_Sex>
    <Living_Status>string</Living_Status>
    <Phone>string</Phone>
   </Person>
   <Address>
   <Address_Id>int</Address_Id>
   <Street_Number>string</Street_Number>
   <Predir>string</Predir>
   <Street_Name>string</Street_Name>
   <Postdir>string</Postdir>
   <Suite_Apt>string</Suite_Apt>
   <City>string</City>
   <State>string</State>
   <Zip>string</Zip>
   <Current_Address>string</Current_Address>
   </Address>
   </Person>
  </PersonAddress_Composite>
  </soap:Body>
</soap:Envelope>
HTTP/1.1 200 OK
Content-Type: text/xml; charset=utf-8
Content-Length: length

<?xml version="1.0" encoding="utf-8"?>
<soap:Envelope xmlns:xsi="http://www.w3.org/2001/
XMLSchema-instance" xmlns:xsd="http://www.
w3.org/2001/XMLSchema" xmlns:soap="http://schemas.
xmlsoap.org/soap/envelope/">
  <soap:Body>
```

```
<PersonAddress_CompositeResponse xmlns="http://
tempuri.org/Primary_Core_Service/Service1">
   <PersonAddress_CompositeResult>string</Per-
sonAddress_CompositeResult>
  </PersonAddress_CompositeResponse>
  </soap:Body>
</soap:Envelope>
```

Individual person and address services were necessary for the initial data population and to make data available to entities and agencies as they are developed. For instance, the police may spot a crime taking place at a particular address thus they must be able to retrieve or add that address to the database thereby identifying the crime location. In another instance, the DMV will require basic person and address data for license issuance, fines, and motor vehicle infractions. The creation of individual and composites services, using data centric services, for each of the essential agencies can be generated for immediate data collection and tracking purposes. Later in the recovery phase, logic centric services can be integrated to provide business rule processing. In the example, below the services are extended to include the Department of Health.

The SOAP message format for the Health Service and PersonHealth_Service is provided below for clarity

```
POST /Primary_Core_Service/Service1.asmx
HTTP/1.1
Host: localhost
Content-Type: text/xml; charset=utf-8
Content-Length: length
SOAPAction: "http://tempuri.org/Primary_Core_Ser-
vice/Service1/Health_Service"

<?xml version="1.0" encoding="utf-8"?>
<soap:Envelope xmlns:xsi="http://www.w3.org/2001/
XMLSchema-instance" xmlns:xsd="http://www.
w3.org/2001/XMLSchema" xmlns:soap="http://schemas.
xmlsoap.org/soap/envelope/">
  <soap:Body>
   <Health_Service xmlns="http://tempuri.org/Pri-
```

```
mary_Core_Service/Service1">
    <Health>
    <Health_Id>int</Health_Id>
    <Person_Id>string</Person_Id>
    <Person_Id_Type>string</Person_Id_Type>
    <Persons_Temperature>double</Persons_Tem-
perature>
        <Persons_BP_Systollic>double</Persons_BP_
Systollic>
        <Persons_BP_Disstollic>double</Persons_BP_
Disstollic>
    <Eyes>string</Eyes>
        <Persons_Heart_Rate>int</Persons_Heart_
Rate>
        <Recommendations>string</Recommenda-
tions>
    <Treatment>string</Treatment>
    <Comments>string</Comments>
        <MedicinePrescribed>string</MedicinePre-
scribed>
    <Disease_Id>int</Disease_Id>
    </Health>
    </Health_Service>
 </soap:Body>
</soap:Envelope>
HTTP/1.1 200 OK
Content-Type: text/xml; charset=utf-8
Content-Length: length

    <?xml version="1.0" encoding="utf-8"?>
    <soap:Envelope xmlns:xsi="http://www.w3.org/2001/
XMLSchema-instance"  xmlns:xsd="http://www.
w3.org/2001/XMLSchema" xmlns:soap="http://schemas.
xmlsoap.org/soap/envelope/">
    <soap:Body>
    <Health_ServiceResponse xmlns="http://tempuri.
org/Primary_Core_Service/Service1">
    <Health_ServiceResult>
    <Health_Id>int</Health_Id>
    <Person_Id>string</Person_Id>
    <Person_Id_Type>string</Person_Id_Type>
        <Persons_Temperature>double</Persons_Tem-
perature>
        <Persons_BP_Systollic>double</Persons_BP_
```

```
Systollic>
        <Persons_BP_Disstollic>double</Persons_BP_
Disstollic>
    <Eyes>string</Eyes>
        <Persons_Heart_Rate>int</Persons_Heart_
Rate>
        <Recommendations>string</Recommenda-
tions>
    <Treatment>string</Treatment>
    <Comments>string</Comments>
        <MedicinePrescribed>string</MedicinePre-
scribed>
    <Disease_Id>int</Disease_Id>
    </Health_ServiceResult>
    </Health_ServiceResponse>
 </soap:Body>
</soap:Envelope>

Composite Person_Health Service
POST  /Primary_Core_Service/Service1.asmx
HTTP/1.1
    Host: localhost
    Content-Type: text/xml; charset=utf-8
    Content-Length: length
    SOAPAction: "http://tempuri.org/Primary_Core_Ser-
vice/Service1/PersonHealth_Service"

    <?xml version="1.0" encoding="utf-8"?>
    <soap:Envelope xmlns:xsi="http://www.w3.org/2001/
XMLSchema-instance"  xmlns:xsd="http://www.
w3.org/2001/XMLSchema" xmlns:soap="http://schemas.
xmlsoap.org/soap/envelope/">
    <soap:Body>
    <PersonHealth_Service xmlns="http://tempuri.
org/Primary_Core_Service/Service1">
    <PersonHealth>
    <Person>
    <Person_ID>string</Person_ID>
    <Person_Id_Type>string</Person_Id_Type>
    <First_Name>string</First_Name>
    <Middle_Name>string</Middle_Name>
    <Last_Name>string</Last_Name>
    <Name_Suffix>string</Name_Suffix>
    <Date_Of_Birth>string</Date_Of_Birth>
```

```
<Persons_Sex>string</Persons_Sex>
<Living_Status>string</Living_Status>
<Phone>string</Phone>
</Person>
<Health>
<Health_Id>int</Health_Id>
<Person_Id>string</Person_Id>
<Person_Id_Type>string</Person_Id_Type>
<Persons_Temperature>double</Persons_Tem-
perature>
    <Persons_BP_Systollic>double</Persons_BP_
Systollic>
    <Persons_BP_Disstollic>double</Persons_BP_
Disstollic>
    <Eyes>string</Eyes>
      <Persons_Heart_Rate>int</Persons_Heart_
Rate>
        <Recommendations>string</Recommenda-
tions>
    <Treatment>string</Treatment>
    <Comments>string</Comments>
        <MedicinePrescribed>string</MedicinePre-
scribed>
    <Disease_Id>int</Disease_Id>
    </Health>
   </PersonHealth>
  </PersonHealth_Service>
 </soap:Body>
</soap:Envelope>
HTTP/1.1 200 OK
Content-Type: text/xml; charset=utf-8
Content-Length: length

<?xml version="1.0" encoding="utf-8"?>
<soap:Envelope xmlns:xsi="http://www.w3.org/2001/
XMLSchema-instance" xmlns:xsd="http://www.
w3.org/2001/XMLSchema" xmlns:soap="http://schemas.
xmlsoap.org/soap/envelope/">
  <soap:Body>
    <PersonHealth_ServiceResponse xmlns="http://
tempuri.org/Primary_Core_Service/Service1">
        <PersonHealth_ServiceResult>string</Person-
Health_ServiceResult>
    </PersonHealth_ServiceResponse>
```

```
  </soap:Body>
 </soap:Envelope>
```

DEFINITION OF SOA WITH WEB SERVICES

SOA is a design model with a deeply rooted concept of encapsulation application logic with services that interact via a common communications protocol. When Web services are used to establish this communications framework, they basically represent a Web based implementation of an SOA (Krafizig et al., 2004).

We can begin to visualize the development and basis of a service-oriented architecture for our enterprise. Our services can be put into action during the response phase of the disaster. This may appear implausible based on our assumptions; however, in the next section we discuss the implementation and data collection process.

IMPLEMENTATION AND DATA COLLECTION

Implementation

In our approach, a single Web service is created, the primary data entities (persons, address, personaddress), one essential agency health services (health, personhealth), and the basic data centric services are created.

The Web service is implemented on a single or multiple servers capable of operating as a Web server for IIS or Linux. We define this as a local or single instance installation. Based on assumptions with regards to limited Internet and intranet capabilities, local instance installation is necessary. If mobile units are used as mechanisms for data collection or multiple servers are setup at different data collection points then data reconciliation can take place at the end of the day.

The Web services approach is crucial because of the ability to easily implement and extend the Web services across the Internet or intranet once landline and wireless services become readily available and reliable.

Data Collection

In our approach, data collection is crucial. Based on our assumptions, local assets have been lost or destroyed and city residents have been dispersed or congregated into localized specified areas (i.e., convention center, stadium, etc.). On the surface, data collection from disaster survivors can appear to be a daunting task as survivors may initially feel hysteria, shock, and confusion. However, SDDM technology has observed and identified three stages during which primary data collection can and should be accomplished.

The three stages identified for data collection are food relief, medical relief, and post evacuation. A structured and orderly method of dispensing food and medical supplies to survivors will allow designated staff to capture primary data about disaster survivors using a local installation. For brevity and clarity, we outline a data collection process based on two of the three stages.

Proposed Structured Data Collection Process

In order to maximize data collection and minimize staff efforts SDDM technology proposes the following structured approach.

Food and Medical Relief
- Survivor enters food dispensing station.
- Survivor provides primary data (see primary data) to staff.
- Staff enters primary data into data collection device.
- Staff saves data.

- (Optional) staff issues identification card with photo (data is barcode scanned).
- Staff instructs survivor to food dispensing station.
- Survivor obtains care package.
- Staff walks survivor to medical treatment station.
- Medical staff retrieves primary data from server.
- (Optional) medical swipes id thus retrieving data.
- Medical staff collects and records basic vital signs.
- Medical staff provides basic medical care (if needed).
- Survivor exits process.

SERVICE-ORIENTED ARCHITECTURE

In our approach, we have not explicitly defined the application front-end because the application front-end can be a Web application utilizing the local installation of the Web server or it can be a windows application and still utilize the Web services on the local server. The only requirement with regards for the application front-end is that it must be user interactive for data collection purposes.

For local installation, we do not need a services repository (Krafizig et al., 2004), however, for the extension of the services to the enterprise a services repository will be needed for identifying the location of services and identifying their functions. The service bus for this approach may rely on the technology implementation, for instance enterprise Java Bean, .NET, or IBM MQseries. We make these statements to show that our approach adheres to the definition of a services-oriented architecture given by Krafiz (2004).

Definition of Service-Oriented Architecture

A service-oriented architecture (SOA) is a software architecture that is based on the key concepts of an application front-end, service, service repository, and service bus.

In fact, Krafzig et al. identifies three expansion stages of SOA: fundamental SOA, network SOA, and process-enabled SOA. Based on our assumptions, we take full advantage of the characteristics of a Fundamental SOA (Krafizig et al., 2004) identified by Krafzig, and imply the extension to a full SOA at later stages during the disasters recovery period and beyond.

CHARACTERISTICS OF A FUNDAMENTAL SOA

- A fundamental SOA consists of two layers: the basic layer and the enterprise layer.
- Enables two or more applications to share business logic and live data.
- Provides a strong platform for large enterprise application landscapes.

Enables the enterprise to start small on the technical side and focus on other critical success factors.

WEB SERVICE TRANSACTIONS (LOCALLY)

The ability to apply all or nothing data commit process is paramount in our SOA both on a local and wide area network (WAN) scenario. This all or nothing data commit process is called a transaction. The ability to model and implement transactions is a frustrating and difficult task with regards to services. According to Newcomer, the difficulty lies in the loosely coupled interfaces of services (Newcomer & Lomow, 2004).

On a local level, the two-phase commit transaction process is ideal as the services are relatively close to each other (Newcomer et al., 2004) (they exist on the same server) and a single uniform data repository is used for the initial data collection. Data collection can take place on local servers during the response and certain parts of the recovery phases and data reconciliation, replication or integration accomplished at specified time frames throughout theses two phases. However, with the expansion of our SOA during the recovery and rebuilding phase service transactions will play an important role.

SOA Expansion and Web Service Transactions (Distributed)

As resources and services expand, the fundamental SOA will expand to include other services,

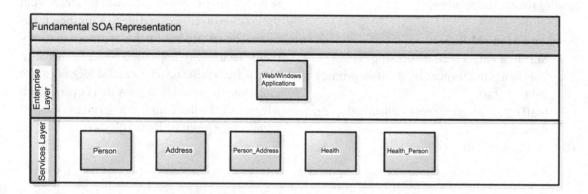

business process and data repositories and the reliance on local data stores and Web servers will decrease significantly. A more dispersed and hopefully more robust enterprise will develop while continuing to build on our basic services for the primary agencies. In short, a distributed government and information technology environment will evolve that will require distributed transactions process and distributed transaction systems (DTS). Although there are several distributed transactions system specifications and models to choose from:

- WS-composite application framework.
- WS-transactions

The WS—transaction specification developed by BEA, IBM, and Microsoft are recommended for our approach. The WS-transaction specification, based on a WS-coordination (WS-C), has the ability to utilize the two-phase commit process defined for our local data collection process. In fact, the WS-transaction is composed of a family of specifications (Newcomer et al., 2004)

- **WS-AtomicTransactions (WS-AT):** A two-phase commit protocol for Web services interoperability.
- **WS-BusinessActivity (WS-BA):** An open nested protocol for long running business processes.
- **WS-Coordination (WS-C):** A pluggable coordination framework supporting WS-AT and WS-BA.

For a more detailed explanation of the implementation of the WS-transaction, we defer to Newcomers et al.'s Understanding SOA with Web services (2004).

SOA Expansion and Other Information Systems

The fundamental SOA by design is expandable to be inclusive of other services, business processes, and data repositories while utilizing the services developed for the response and recovery phase. Over the course of the recovery and rebuilding phases, independent information systems will be developed by vendors. These independent systems will be integrated into the enterprise (SOA) using Web service integration tools, XML, and XML translation.

The creation of our enterprise using the service-oriented architecture will allow a smoother integration transition due to the inherent nature of Web services and XML. Various services, interfaces, data wrappers, application wrappers, and application programming interfaces (API's) can be developed to extract and utilize data and business processes within the framework.

FUTURE TRENDS AND RESEARCH

SDDM technology is in the process of researching Web service security, citizen privacy issues, and the implementation of smart card technology. The maturity of the Web and Web services over the past three years have produced several security specifications worth researching and implementing to provide for tighter and stronger security protocols. In addition, citizen privacy issues will play a major role with the introduction and implementation of smart card technology. Smart card technology will facilitate data collection and data integrity across the municipality. A brief description of this technology is presented for clarity.

Integrating Smart Card and Smart Card Technology

Once the primary data has been collected, the survivor data can be recorded onto a smart card (SC). Smart card technology has been around since 1968 when German inventors Jurgen Dethloff and Helmut Grotrupp applied for the first ICC related patents with similar applications in Japan in 1970 and France 1974 (Litronic, 2003) In 1984, the French Postal and Telecommunications began using the smart card for telephones and by 1996, 150 million smart cards were in use for this purpose. Over the past 20 years, smart cards have been used throughout Europe successfully for a variety of purposes. They range from storing bank account information, to storing health care and health related information, as well as transportation information (Jacquot, 2003). In the United States, smart cards are beginning to garner interest since the events of 9/11 and the increase in identity theft. Current U.S. applications for the smart card are identity security authentication, personal identification, and transportation services. For thoroughness, a brief description of smart cards and smart card technology is provided. The majority of the background information was taken directly from the U.S. Government Smart Card Handbook (GSA Card Handbook, 2004).

What is a Smart Card?

A smart card is a simple plastic card that resembles a credit card in size. It is considered a smart card because a small microprocessor and memory is embedded inside the card. A smart is card is used for storing. In addition to storing data a smart card can also store applications and perform mostly basic and a few complex calculations. The U.S. Government Smart Card Handbook provides an excellent description of a smart card and we will use that description as our basis for the definition of a smart card.

Definition: Smart Card: A smart card is a credit card-sized device that contains one or more integrated circuits (ICs) and also may employ one or more of the following machine-readable technologies: magnetic stripe, bar code (linear or two-dimensional), contactless radio frequency transmitters, biometric information, encryption and authentication, or photo identification. The integrated circuit chip (ICC) embedded in the smart card can act as a microcontroller or computer. Data are stored in the chip's memory and can be accessed to complete various processing applications. The memory also contains the microcontroller chip operating system (COS), communications software, and can also contain encryption algorithms to make the application software and data unreadable.

Although smart cards remain relatively the same, they do not perform the same functions. In fact, the function of the smart card is based on two factors: the chip type and the interface used to communicate with the card reader. In short, there are three chip types: memory only, wired logic, and microcontroller.

- **Memory-only integrated circuit chip cards (including serial protected memory chip cards):** Memory-only cards are "electronic magnetic stripes" and provide little more security than a magnetic stripe card. Two advantages they have over magnetic stripe cards are: (a) they have a higher data capacity (up to 16 kilobits (Kbits) compared with 80 bytes per track), and (b) the read/write device is much less expensive. The memory-only chip cards do not contain logic or perform calculations; they simply store data. Serial-protected memory chip cards have a security feature not found in the memory-only chip card; they can contain a hardwired memory that cannot be overwritten.

- **Wired logic integrated circuit chip cards:** A wired logic chip card contains a logic-based state machine that provides encryption and authenticated access to the memory and its contents. Wired logic cards provide a static file system supporting multiple applications, with optional encrypted access to memory contents. Their file systems and command set can only be changed by redesigning the logic of the IC (integrated circuit).

- **Secure microcontroller integrated circuit chip cards:** Microcontroller cards contain a microcontroller, an operating system, and read/write memory that can be updated many times. The secure microcontroller chip card contains and executes logic and calculations and stores data in accordance with its operating system. The microcontroller card is like a miniature PC one can carry in a wallet. All it needs to operate is power and a communication terminal.

Smart Card Interfaces

There are two primary types of chip card interfaces—contact and contactless. The terms "contact" and "contactless" describe the means by which electrical power is supplied to the integrated circuit chip (ICC) and by which data is transferred from the ICC to an interface (or card acceptance) device (reader). Cards may offer both contact and contactless interfaces by using two separate chips (sometimes called hybrid cards) or by using a dual-interface chip (sometimes called "combi" cards).

Contact Smart Card

- **Contact smart cards:** A contact smart card requires insertion into a smart card reader with a direct connection to a conductive micromodule on the surface of the card.
- **Contactless smart card.**

If the smart card does not have a contact pad then the connection between the reader and the card is done via radio frequency (RF). Contactless smart cards can exchange data without having to make contact with the reader using radio frequency (RF). Hence, contactless smart card communication can take within a perimeter of 10 centimeters or 3.94 inches.

Combo Smart Card

A combo or hybrid card can have both contact and contactless communication with the card reader.

The memory only card could be used for both human and non-human asset data capture during the response phase; however, since we have developed a framework for the future enterprise and we view the survivor data as dynamic and consistently changing due to the addition of agencies and services. Thus, we recommend the contact multi-application cards for issuance to the survivors. A multi-application card has the advantage of having multiple applications on a single card and each application can be managed by a different agency. Thus, when the department of motor vehicles comes online with services the citizen can simply show the card to motor vehicle staff (MVS), MVS will read the primary data off of the card (name, dob, address, etc….), initiate the immediate process, update the DMV entity(s) utilizing data centric and logic centric services and finally update the smart card with DMV data. Thus we have shown how two separate and distinct agencies (DOH, DMV) with different functions and data requirements are linked by a survivors primary data and how information can be added, updated, retrieved and shared using a smart card. A high-level overview is provided in the following diagram.

With regard to public safety assets, although the maintenance of data will change over time, it will remain static for most of the lifetime of the asset. Integrating smart cards during the response phase will produce immediate returns for emergency workers and government. For instance, the ability to determine and track food rationing (based on food dispensation), the ability to immediately view a survivors vital signs, and possible treatments and the ability to identify public and public safety assets (i.e., street lights, catch basins, down power lines, roadways, alleys, etc).

Smart Card Authentication/ Authorization

A natural question that arises with the utilization or implementation of smart card technology with our approach is the issue of authentication and authorization. To be fair, authentication has received the most interest. We define authentication and authorization utilizing Wikipedia dictionary (Wikipedia Dictionary):

Initial high-level Web services infrastructure

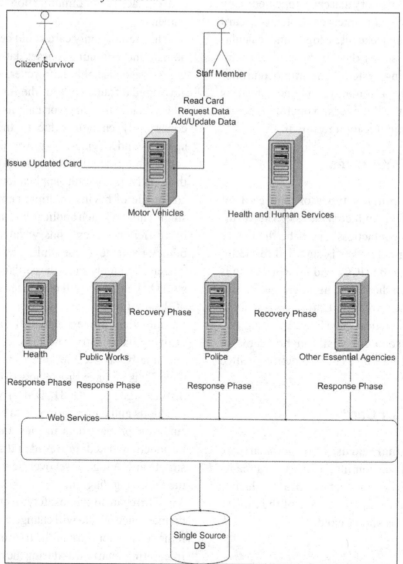

- **Authenticaion** is the act of establishing or confirming something (or someone) as authentic, that is, that claims made by or about the thing is true. Authenticaion of an object may mean confirming it provenance. Authentication of a person often consists of verifying their identity.
- **Authorization** is the process of verifying that a known person has the authority to perform a certain operation.

With regards to authentication, there exists three basic types or categories which are:

- Something the user **is** (e.g., fingerprint or retinal pattern, DNA sequence (there are assorted definitions of what is sufficient), voice pattern (again several definitions), signature recognition, or other biometric identifier.
- Something the user **has** (e.g., ID card, security token, software token, or cell phone).
- Something the user **knows** (e.g., a password, a pass phrase, or a personal identification number (PIN)).

The three authentication categories provide a basis for single factor or multiple factor authentication. In single factor authentication only one of the categories is used for authentication purposes. If more than one category used for authentication then the authentication process is called: multiple-factored authentication. In our approach we suggest a two factor authentication process using:

- Something the user has (smart card).
- Something the user knows (PIN).

It is recommended that the Unique ID (SSN, drivers license number, green card number, etc.) defined in our high level data model be used as the PIN. Thus, the authentication level provides a uniform consistency of the citizen and the de-

fined levels of authorization would apply to the particular (application) service provided (DMV, emergency medical services, etc.).

CONCLUSION

This chapter strongly emphasizes an implementation approach that rests on the Zachman system model perspective. This approach was formulated after the visual confusion of the aftermath of Hurricane Katrina and the lack of preparedness thereof. It is important to note in the conclusion that this approach be considered in the preparedness phase as to circumvent or assist in answering organizational and logistical challenges at the local, state, and federal government level. Natural questions will arise, for instance:

- Where will the back bone of the enterprise be located?
- Which agencies and business processes are next to come online?
- Who will be in control of the fundamental enterprise (SOA)?

The author hopes that viewing this approach as part of the disaster preparedness phase will answer many of the organizational and logistical challenges that face government during and after the disaster.

We have attempted to establish a basic framework for the development of an enterprise architecture for local government immediately after a natural disaster or major terrorist attack. As a basis for our development, we have applied Zachman's system model perspective and defined two basic types of data elements: primary data elements and secondary data elements. These elements were then wrapped into simple services and utilized by composite services to establish a Web services environment on a local server level. The ability to extend the local server level to a broader audience among local government through the Internet or intranet is obvious. In the future SDDM technology will continue to refine the concepts and explore the areas of process and functionality in more detail. The expectation is that this approach will be deemed practical and useful as a model for assisting local government to gain valuable information from survivors, assist survivors in medical need, and eventually provide the basis for a an enterprise utilizing a service-oriented architecture in the rebuilding of local government.

REFERENCES

Davis, T. (1998). *The role of government in a disaster.* The Disaster Handbook 1998 National Edition Institute of Food and Agricultural Sciences. Chapter 3, Section 3.7: University of Florida.

Erl, T. (2004). *Service-oriented architecture: a field guide to integrating XML and Web services.* Upper Saddle River, NJ: Prentice Hall.

Fermantle, P. (2002). Enterprise services: Examining the emerging field of Web services and how it is integrated into existing enterprise infrastructures. *Communications of the ACM, 45*(10), October.

GSA., U.G.S.A., (2004). *Government Smart Card Handbook.*

Guruge. A. (2004). *Web services theory and practice.* Burlington, MA: Elsevier Digital Press.

Jacquot, J. N. (2003). Application Note 104: Smart Cards. Exfo Photonic White Paper.

Krafzig, D., Banke, K., & Slama, D. (2004). *Enterprise SOA: Service-oriented architecture best practices* (The Coad Series). Upper Saddle River, NJ: Prentice Hall.

Litronic, S. (2003). *Introduction to smart cards: A White Paper.* Retrieved September 2005, from www.litronic.com

Newcomer, E. (2002). *Understanding Web services XML, WSDL, SOAP, and UDDI.* Indianapolis, IN: Addison Wesley.

Newcomer, E., & Lomow, G. (2004). *Understanding SOA with Web services.* Indianapolis, IN: Addison Wesley.

Rob, P., & Coronel, C. (2002). *Database systems: Design, implementation, & management.* Boston: Course Technology.

Wikipedia, Defining Authentication and Authorization, from http://en.wikipedia.org/wiki/authentication

Zachman, J. A. (1987). A framework for information systems architecture. *IBM Systems Journal, 26*(3).

Zachman, J. A., & Sowa, J. F. (1992). Extending and formalizing the framework for information systems architecture. *IBM Systems Journal, 31*(3).

Chapter XXV
Business Networking with Web Services:
Supporting the Full Life Cycle of Business Collaborations

Diogo R. Ferreira
IST-Technical University of Lisbon, Portugal

ABSTRACT

This chapter describes how the latest advances in Web services technology are paving the way toward dynamic B2B integration. It begins by distinguishing between three kinds of life cycles: the operational life cycle, the B2B trading life cycle, and the business networking life cycle. In the past, most B2B integration solutions have been designed to support the operational life cycle by specifying a set of pre-defined B2B conversations. We will show that Web services can be used to settle those conversations at run-time, and that they can support the B2B trading life cycle all the way from partner search to contracting, operation, and evaluation. In general, though, the B2B trading life cycle may change across different markets, which requires mechanisms for a company to retrieve information about how it should proceed once it enters a new market. These mechanisms belong to the business networking life cycle, and they can be supported by Web services as well. The conclusion is that Web services provide the required features to support the full life cycle of business collaborations.

INTRODUCTION

The Web has an unparalleled potential to reshape the way companies conduct their businesses. As a globally connected and widely accessible network infrastructure, the Web allows an enterprise to find and establish business relationships with new business partners. At the same time, it allows an enterprise to integrate its systems and processes with those of its business partners. Provided with a common, global network infrastructure, enterprises can associate with each other in order to become more competitive or to offer improved products or services. The result is the development of business networks, which combine the competencies of several business partners.

Solutions such as EDI, sophisticated Web sites, e-marketplaces, e-procurement systems (Albrecht, Dean, & Hansen, 2005), and B2B frameworks (Shim, Pendyala, Sundaram, & Gao, 2000) have been at least partly successful in achieving B2B integration by providing either the infrastructure or the data formats for message exchange. The challenge today is to come up with a technological solution by means of which an enterprise could search for, evaluate, select potential business partners and interact with them in a mostly automated way. We will refer to this kind of dynamic B2B integration as *business networking* (Österle, Fleisch, & Alt, 2001). We will show in this chapter that Web services, more than any previous technology, display an unprecedented potential to support business networking.

WEB SERVICES AS AN INTEGRATION TECHNOLOGY

Before the arrival of Web services technology, integration was about defining interfaces and making sure that systems correctly implemented or invoked those special-purpose interfaces. There was RPC, there was message-oriented middleware, there were transaction-processing monitors, and there was CORBA. Then Web services came along and with it came the capability of discovering and binding to interfaces either at build-time or at run-time. Not that the concept is entirely new—CORBA, for example, included a mechanism called dynamic invocation interface (Vinoski, 1997)—but the ability to describe and deploy components that can be easily discovered and invoked, possibly in an automated way, came only with the adoption of WSDL (Chinnici, Moreau, Ryman, & Weerawarana, 2005) and UDDI (Clement, Hately, von Riegen, & Rogers, 2004) standards.

As the foundation of Web services technology matures, it becomes clearer how they will be able to achieve the ultimate goal of dynamic B2B in-

tegration. From enterprise application integration to enterprise-wide service-oriented architectures, and then to supporting B2B interactions between different organizations, Web services technology is a cross-level integration paradigm that allows an application to invoke another component, as well as a company to interact with another organization. At first, the single key enabling feature to these scenarios seemed to be the possibility of publishing, searching for, and discovering Web services. Today, the problem of integration is known to require other features such as service composition, orchestration, and coordination, besides addressing, routing, security, and policy capabilities.

Most of these features are being addressed by separate standardization efforts, such as WS-coordination (Cabrera, 2002), WS-transaction management (Bunting, 2003), WS-BPEL (Arkin, 2005), WS-Addressing (Box, 2004), WS-security (Atkinson, 2002), and WS-policy (Bajaj, 2004). As the technological landscape becomes cluttered with acronyms and different standards, it might seem that the original goal of dynamic B2B integration may take long to achieve. Truth is however that most, if not all, challenges have been already identified, and several authors have introduced advances to Web service technology in features such as negotiation, contracting, security, matchmaking, monitoring, composition, and coordination as we will show in this chapter.

There is not much more to wait on the way toward supporting dynamic B2B integration—what we call business networking—if only one is able to sort out and combine the available contributions in Web service technology. This is precisely what we aim at in this chapter by describing the contributions that are most relevant to supporting the full life cycle of business collaborations. Rather than reiterating how Web services can support B2B exchanges—solutions for that have been available for a long time—our purpose is to introduce a full life cycle approach, showing how Web services can support every phase of business collaborations, from the time business partners search for each other to the time they perform and evaluate their interactions.

THE CONCEPT OF LIFE CYCLE IN INTEGRATION

Many solutions for B2B integration focus on defining the protocols and specifying the message format between business partners. It is clear that these frameworks concern the operation phase when two or more organizations, that have previously met, interact with each other. But business networking concerns more than just the operation phase: there must be mechanisms to search and find business partners, to establish contracts with them, to monitor exchanges, and to evaluate each other's performance. Operation is therefore just a single phase within a broader life cycle that includes search, selection, contracting, operation, and evaluation (Ferreira & Ferreira, 2004).

The concept of having a life cycle, which requires different integration mechanisms across different life cycle phases is known since the beginning of enterprise integration as a discipline. The reference architecture CIMOSA (AMICE, 1993), one of the first major enterprise integration architectures, established the distinction between a "system life cycle" and a "product life cycle," the latter unfolding within the operation phase of the former. Then GERAM (IFIP-IFAC, 1999), the generalized reference architecture, generalized the concept of nesting the life cycle of different entities within the operation phase of one another.

The same approach can be applied to develop a framework for business networking. B2B exchanges take place within the operation phase of a larger life cycle comprising also search, selection, contracting, and evaluation. We will call this the "B2B trading life cycle" (Ferreira & Ferreira, 2004). In this larger life cycle, B2B exchanges are no longer fixed by any particular

Figure 1. The business networking life cycle hierarchy

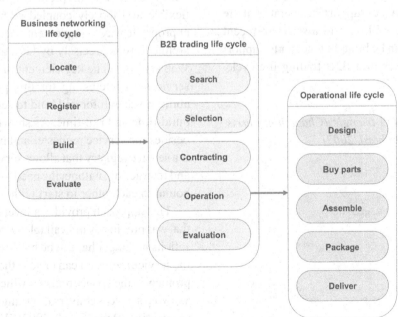

B2B standard. Rather, the conversations that take place during the operation phase and between different organizations depend upon the interactions that those organizations have agreed to perform. Defining these interactions is part of the B2B trading life cycle, and it happens during the contracting phase.

But then, depending on the markets that organizations find themselves in, the B2B trading life cycle may include these or other phases. And because a company may outsource some of its activities or associate itself with other partners according to an arbitrary structure, the selection and contracting phases for this company may be more elaborate than for other participants. So how can an organization learn about the B2B trading life cycle that takes place in a particular market? It becomes apparent that the B2B trading life cycle, on its turn, is just a single phase within an even broader life cycle—the business networking life cycle, which describes how organizations can enter a market and obtain information about how business networks are developed within that market. Figure 1 illustrates the relationships between these different life cycles.

In the following sections, we begin by describing how Web services support the operational life cycle. Then, we will refer to a series of recent advances that can be brought together to support the typical phases of a B2B trading life cycle.

Figure 2. The SOA triangle (Champion, Ferris, Newcomer, & Orchard, 2002)

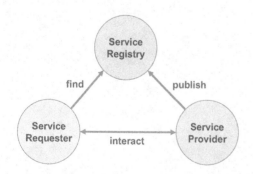

Finally, we explain how Web services can be used to support the business networking life cycle as well. We will conclude that all these life cycles can be supported by recursively applying the basic principles of Web services technology.

SUPPORTING THE OPERATIONAL LIFE CYCLE

Supporting B2B operational exchanges has always required companies to incur in costly system integrations. Even the adoption of XML and B2B frameworks (such as RosettaNet) has not dramatically reduced the amount of effort required to attain B2B exchanges, since it is still necessary to integrate the B2B side with internal back office systems. This is often done by interfacing B2B systems with the enterprise messaging bus, which requires customized interfaces between different systems and produces tightly coupled solutions. These solutions will have to be reworked as soon as the partners, the conversation protocols, or the supporting systems change.

Service-oriented architectures (SOAs) are known to alleviate this problem by allowing more flexible and loosely coupled architectures. An appropriate way to implement a service-oriented architecture is precisely by taking advantage of Web services. The key element that makes Web services so interesting for this purpose is the ability to search for and bind to services both at build-time and run-time. As shown in Figure 2, besides the service requester and provider, there is a service registry that allows service discovery and interaction, without the need to have services bound to each other to start with.

This approach provides a level of indirection that was previously unavailable since B2B conversations no longer have to be hard-wired. Instead, the service requestor can look up the conversation protocol in the service registry, which can be given as a Web services conversation language (WSCL) description (Banerji et al., 2002). WSCL is able to specify a set of interactions (one-way or two-way), how these interactions follow one another, and what are the document formats (XML schemas) used in each interaction. Configuring a B2B conversation is therefore no longer a programmer's task; rather, it can be readily supported by the underlying service infrastructure.

Once the conversation is taking place, an open issue is how to correlate requests and responses without mixing them with messages from other simultaneous conversations. Brambilla, Ceri, Passamani, and Riccio (2002) discuss five different correlation mechanisms and present the advantages and disadvantages of each of them. These mechanisms include transport-level correlation, which requires asynchronous transport protocols not widely supported, and application semantics correlation, which requires shared data structures. They also include correlation mechanisms are based on metadata, to be included in every message regardless of its particular format. The metadata relates each message to a particular operation type and instance, and possibly also to a particular conversation type and instance.

An alternative approach to specifying conversations as a set of one-way or two-way operations is, as in Hanson, Nandi, and Levine (2002), to describe them as a complete state machine together with the operations that trigger changes in state. This state machine is referred to as the *conversation policy*. The main advantage of this approach is to be able to nest an entire conversation policy into a single state of another one, allowing conversations to be described by a composition of sub-conversations. This may be useful in order to be able to reuse sub-conversations or change them without impacting the overall behavior.

SUPPORTING THE B2B TRADING LIFE CYCLE

In addition to the operation phase, in the B2B trading life cycle we are interested in support-

ing partner search and selection, contracting, configuration, and evaluation. Supporting these phases requires different kinds of mechanisms, but the underlying infrastructure can be the same as before:

- Partner search and selection involves querying service registries and applying search criteria in order to match goals, processes, or even QoS (Quality of service) parameters.
- Contracting requires facilities to support negotiation, which can be regarded as a kind of B2B conversation, and languages to describe service-level agreements (SLAs).
- Configuration deals with making resources properly accessible (e.g., via Web services) in order to carry out the agreed B2B conversations during the operation phase.
- Evaluation may involve active monitoring during the operation phase and its ultimate purpose is to assess the performance of the operation phase.

There have been recent advances in Web services technology that are relevant to all of these phases. We will organize the discussion by dividing these contributions according to the B2B trading phase where they seem to be most useful.

Supporting Partner Search and Selection

One of the first tasks in the B2B trading life cycle is to look for potential business partners that will satisfy given criteria. Since Web services technology inherently provides publishing and discovery capabilities, it is convenient to use those capabilities (notably UDDI) to search for business partners. However, UDDI registries are centralized repositories. Unless there is a global agreement on which repository to use, there will always be multiple UDDI registries that could be potentially relevant to the partner search being performed.

Zhang, Chao, Chang, and Chung (2003) address the problem of searching in multiple UDDI registries and aggregating the search results. They do this by expressing search queries in a UDDI search markup language (USML), which can be used to specify different registries, the queries to be performed in each registry, and the aggregation operator that determines how the search results are to be consolidated (this can be as simple as an AND or OR operator). The USML is passed on to a search engine which parses the query, builds search commands, dispatches them to UDDI registries, and finally combines the responses and sends the end result back to the requester.

Whereas USML makes use of UDDI data elements to specify queries, other authors have proposed the use of more sophisticated criteria. Dumas, Benatallah, Russell, and Spork (2004) propose a framework to describe trading intentions as constraints on attributes of a given schema (ontology). The example given is that of a car buyer who wants to find a car of a certain model, not older than a number of years and within a certain price range, where model, year, and price are attributes defined by the given schema. The matchmaking with the trading intention of a car seller (or anyone else, for that matter) is done by satisfying the conjunction of the constraints in the two intentions.

Besides satisfying goals, a company may actually want a business partner that carries out their activities in a particular way. In this case, the challenge is to be able to find business partners that comply not only with a given trading intention but also with a given message exchange sequence. Wombacher, Fankhauser, Mahleko, and Neuhold (2003) introduced such an approach, where finite state automata (FSA) are used to describe message-exchange sequences. Basically, the proposed algorithm computes the intersection of two FSA, which describe both the desired sequence and the provided one. It is shown that if the intersection contains an empty automaton, then the two sequences do not match, otherwise they are compatible. The use of FSA is motivated by the fact that they can be mapped to WSCL in a straightforward way.

Other search criteria may require potential business partners to comply with given QoS preferences. As with trading intentions, matching QoS preferences can be done with constraint satisfaction algorithms. For example, Lin, Xie, Guo, and Wang (2005) employ fuzzy logic to express QoS preferences and a branch-and-bound algorithm to support service composition. This composition is achieved by selecting candidate Web services with different QoS criteria values. Zeng et al. (2004) propose a set of concrete QoS criteria to be used in service composition: execution price, execution duration, reputation, successful execution rate, and availability. They also discuss how to implement QoS-driven service selection either by local optimization (selecting the one from a set of similar services) or by global planning (selecting the services that optimize the overall composition).

In any case, it is necessary to make sure that the selected services are actually provided the required input in order to carry out their job, and that they are actually able to produce the desired outputs. In addition, there may be a set of preconditions that must be satisfied so that the service can be performed. Tomaz, Labidi, and Wanghon (2003) propose a system that can deal with inputs, outputs, and preconditions at the semantic level using the DAML-S (now OWL-S) ontology language to express buyer requests and supplier advertisements. The matchmaking is done by a semantic engine which, based on the given ontology, will determine the best fit by computing the distance between different concepts in the taxonomy tree.

Supporting Negotiation and Contracting

Despite the fact that business contracts must be objective, unambiguous and complete, the negotiation that precedes a contract is to a large extent an unstructured process, in the sense that it may require an unspecified number of interactions until all parties are satisfied with the result. This poses a challenge to the automation of negotiation and contracting. It is apparent, however, that most negotiation processes end up following similar patterns (Robinson & Volkov, 1998) and that these patterns can be supported by Web services technology in different ways.

Chiu, Cheung, Hung, Chiu, and Chung (2005) propose a methodology to manage negotiation processes, which has been implemented with Web services. The methodology relies on contract templates, which can either refer to the negotiation process of a previously established contract or to a new negotiation process to be supported. Once the contract template has been created, its execution is supported by a negotiation support system (NSS), which provides the Web services required for each activity in the negotiation process. For example, in some negotiations dealing with requests for proposals there is a Web service for placing the request and another Web service for suppliers to submit the proposals. Negotiation processes based on bargaining and auctions are supported as well.

The same degree of automation may be achieved as suggested by Kim, Segev, Patankar, and Cho (2003) who explore the possibility (and problems) of describing negotiation processes with BPEL (business process execution language for Web services). Even though the authors focus only the abstract process and not on creating an executable process model, it is evident that BPEL can be used to support the automation of a negotiation process by the orderly invocation of Web services residing at different organizations. The approach is illustrated in an RFQ (request for quote) scenario.

Some authors (Lamparter, Mutschler, Luckner, Stockmar, & Laborde, 2005) actually argue that full automation of contracting is not possible, where full automation is understood as contracting without any human intervention. It should be noted, however, that it is possible to automate with human intervention. For example, the invocation of a Web service may result in placing a new task in the to-do list of an employee. When the task is done the same or another Web service may send a reply back to the requester. The point of Lamparter et al. (2005) is that contracting may involve negotiable as well as non-negotiable clauses, which can only be evaluated by humans. Therefore, they propose an ontology-based modeling framework that is directed at negotiable clauses only.

As in partner search and selection, contracting may also involve the specification of QoS parameters. In this context, the contracts are usually referred to as service-level agreements (SLAs). Sahai, Machiraju, Sayal, Jin, and Casati (2002) discuss how to describe an SLA as a set of service-level objectives (SLOs). An SLO is a specification of what parameter is to be measured, when it should be measured, how it is to be measured and evaluated, and what action should be done after measuring. One of the most common parameters is the client-side response time (Debusmann & Geihs, 2004). This is usually measured by "instrumenting" the Web service or the Web service platform, as we will see ahead when discussing support for monitoring.

The negotiation of QoS parameters can be automated if QoS information about service providers is readily available. This information may be published in the UDDI registry in the form of WSOL documents (Tosic, Pagurek, Patel, Esfandiari, & Ma, 2003), an extension to WSDL that is able to express QoS constraints and combine them into boolean expressions. Besides constraints on QoS attributes, it will be useful to include the parameters of utility functions (Comuzzi & Pernici, 2005) that specify how much a value of a QoS parameter is worth to the service requester or provider. If both the QoS information from the requester and from the provider are available, the negotiation can be fully automated by a third-party broker. If only the QoS information from the provider is available, it is still possible to make use of semi-automated negotiation (Comuzzi et al., 2005), which requires interacting with the service requester.

Supporting Configuration and Pre-Operation

From a technological point of view, a contract can be especially useful if it specifies the B2B conversation to take place between business partners during the operation phase. If such information can be gathered during the contracting phase, then it is straightforward to express it using WSCL, BPEL, or another orchestration language. In order to carry out that B2B conversation, however, partners must have their service platforms properly configured. This particular task can also be automated, even if partners have different infrastructures: the task of generating Web service wrappers from the specification of a B2B conversation is similar to that of generating Web service proxies/stubs from a WSDL description. In scenarios where the Web service infrastructure is already in place, configuration may turn into a problem of service composition. Several authors have explored these different possibilities.

Baghdadi (2004) addresses the problem of generating Web services from coordination requirements. The approach is holistic in the sense that it starts by creating an overall business model of the main systems in an enterprise information infrastructure. This business model is expressed in terms of business objects, events, processes, and states—the so-called "elements of discourse." Then the concept of "factual dependency" is introduced: what elements must be created/updated/removed/retrieved when a given event occurs. The proposed approach is based on

generating a Web service that implements each factual dependency. The same approach could be used to generate the Web services that implement a B2B conversation, described as a set of factual dependencies between different business partners.

Shan, Chiu, and Qing (2005) get closer to achieving this goal using workflow views rather than factual dependencies. A workflow view is a flow graph of activities with input and output messages, and it is a publicly available subset of the actual process taking place within an enterprise. A B2B conversation is the result of connecting workflow views of different partners via message exchange, and it is described with BPEL. These conversations are then orchestrated by a workflow-based B2B process engine. It is interesting to note that the proposed system supports the generation of Web service definitions (in WSDL) from workflow views, where each activity is mapped onto a WSDL port. This effectively provides a jump start to the configuration of B2B interactions.

Other authors address precisely the inverse problem; if the Web service infrastructure is already in place, and there are multiple service offerings to choose from, then what B2B interaction should be used to achieve a given business goal? This problem falls within the scope of dynamic service composition (Tosic et al., 2001) and an effective way to solve it is to rely on planning techniques (Madhusudan & Uttamsingh, 2004). According to this approach, each Web service is modeled as a collection of elementary operations as specified in the corresponding WSDL description. The point is that some service requests may be satisfied by invoking an elementary operation, while others require the invocation of several operations from the same or different Web services. In the latter case, the sequence of required operations and Web services is computed via hierarchical task network (HTN) planning. The same technique could possibly be used to determine the B2B conversation that must be carried out in order to satisfy the business goals expressed in a contract.

Supporting Monitoring and Evaluation

The last phase of the B2B trading life cycle is the evaluation phase when business partners assess the performance of each other and gather information that may be useful in future partner selections. Evaluation is related to decision-making so the opportunity for technological support is in focusing on gathering information to facilitate evaluation. This explains why monitoring is so relevant for the purpose of evaluation. Thus, even though monitoring takes place during the operation phase, its purpose is to support the evaluation phase. Among other issues, recent advances in monitoring have addressed performance evaluation, compliance with SLAs, data quality management, and trustworthiness of the service infrastructure.

Monitoring can be done at the lowest level of the Web services stack by intercepting and logging every SOAP message (Cruz, Campos, Pires, & Campos, 2004), which may be useful to extract information about service use and performance. A more convenient way to obtain such information is by "instrumenting" the Web services platform. Debusmann et al. (2004) illustrate how to instrument the Axis platform using aspect-oriented programming. Since there are two separate request and response handlers, it is possible to measure the client-side response time by means of the interval between their invocation, for a given pair of correlated request and response. McGregor and Scheifer (2003) make use of instrumentation in order to maintain an audit-trail of all status changes during B2B conversations, described as WSFL flows (Leymann, 2001). Sahai et al. (2002) make use of instrumentation in order to monitor SLAs and to record any violation of SLOs.

Monitoring and evaluation become an even more pressing need when the end product of a B2B collaboration must comply with quality management standards. Whereas the scope of these standards is traditionally confined to the environment of a single organization, B2B collaborations require quality management techniques to be extended to inter-organizational settings. This has already been approached for the case of information products (Shankaranarayanan & Cai, 2005) by means of a data quality metadata specification. The metadata associated with an information product describe how data flows and is processed across business partners to create that information product. The metadata is shared among business partners by means of a Web service architecture, which collects and provides metadata upon request. This architecture makes use of a central metadata exchange (MX) service which retrieves and consolidates metadata provided by the MX services running at each organization.

Another important role of the evaluation phase is to contribute to the development of trust among business partners. Since this subject goes far beyond the scope of Web services technology, we will refer only to the problem of improving the trustworthiness of the underlying service infrastructure. Zhang, Zhang, and Chung (2004) propose a framework to control the trustworthiness of computing in Web services. Basically, the framework requires certain pieces of information to be included in the WSDL description of a Web service. This information concerns resources (roles and how to invoke them), policies (e.g., security policies), validation (ensuring predictability and handling exceptions), and management (tracking and monitoring). Resource, policy, and validation info are expressed using WS-resource, WS-policy and BPEL, respectively, while trustworthy management depends on the monitoring capabilities of the run-time platform.

SUPPORTING THE BUSINESS NETWORKING LIFE CYCLE

Much like the eCo framework once proposed by Tenenbaum, Chowdhry, and Hughes (1997), which comprised several layers ranging from services up to markets and networks (eCo Working Group, 1999), the business networking life cycle can be regarded as the top layer above the B2B trading life cycle. In the B2B trading life cycle discussed previously, organizations search for and select business partners, and settle, configure and evaluate the interactions that take place with those partners. These tasks are just a single phase within the business networking life cycle, as shown in Figure 1, where companies locate and enter markets in order to build trading relationships with other players in that market.

In the previous section, we discussed the latest developments toward providing Web service infrastructures with search, contracting, and monitoring capabilities, among others. Now,

regarding the business networking life cycle, the required capabilities are those that provide companies with the ability to organize themselves into markets and to join and develop collaborations within those markets. A market may be either vertically oriented, being industry- or product-specific, or horizontally oriented, dealing with goods and services that are common to multiple industries (Sahai & Machiraju, 2001). In addition, each market may have its own set of rules, such as how to advertise purchase needs, how to select partners, how perform negotiations, etc.

The way a company enters a market and starts interacting with other players in that market resembles the way a peer enters a P2P network, joins a peer group, and starts interacting with the peers within that group. In the JXTA platform (Traversat et al., 2002), for example, peers join peer groups where special-purpose services are available. Peer groups are described by XML advertisements published in the network, and services are described by advertisements published

Figure 3. The role of Web services technology in B2B collaborations

	Networking life cycle	Trading life cycle	Operational life cycle
Service Registry	Maintain information about markets, participants, regulations and available services.	Maintain partner information such as profile, processes, QoS preferences, semantics.	Maintain information about service definitions and run-time conversation protocols.
Service Provider	Create and manage markets. Register, configure and advertise service offers.	Publish information about service provision. Negotiate, configure and operate trading exchanges.	Provide information about service interfaces. Carry out requested run-time activities.
Service Requester	Locate, enter markets and register. Submit purchase needs and select service offers.	Search for, negotiate with, coordinate and evaluate the performance of business partners.	Retrieve service info and bind to service interfaces. Issue requests and receive responses.
Technologies	Discovery, advertisements, grouping, description, coordination, choreography, ...	Discovery, matchmaking, composition, coordination, QoS, semantics, resource, policy, ...	Discovery, description, transaction, conversation, addressing, security, ...

within a peer group. Both kinds of advertisements can be found by means of a discovery service, and they contain the necessary information to bind and interact with other resources (peers and peer groups).

The analogy between peer groups and electronic markets is striking, as well as between JXTA service advertisements and WSDL definitions, and the JXTA discovery service can be seen as a decentralized version of the service registry concept. Therefore, Web services technology does provide the required features for a business networking infrastructure, although not as decentralized as in a P2P platform, since Web services rely on a centralized service registry. In the business networking life cycle, the role of the service registry is to allow companies to find markets and, once they have entered a market, to retrieve information about the trading life cycle that applies within a market—whether it is the five-phase life cycle described earlier or any other kind of service choreography. This choreography can be described by means of a WSCL or WSFL, for example, and it can be retrieved from the service registry within the market.

Albrecht et al. (2005) make a comparison of five different approaches toward supporting electronic marketplaces, and Web services stand out as an appropriate infrastructure to support loosely connected marketplaces, being hampered only by the lack of standards. As standardization is evolving in several fronts, a more severe handicap may be the fact that Web services technology relies on centralized services, so it is still not entirely clear how to make use of it in highly distributed environments (Huang & Chung, 2003). Nevertheless, the developments described in the previous sections span across all the different phases of business collaborations, from the business networking life cycle down to the operational life cycle. Figure 3 illustrates the role that features of Web services technology can play each of these phases.

As suggested in Figure 3, a large amount of information stored in the service registries concerns the description of B2B conversations to take place between business partners. This means that Web services technology, besides providing dynamic binding via a service registry, should also include process management capabilities in order to support the design, execution, and monitoring of those conversations. In fact, a survey of Web service architectures (Myerson, 2002) shows that key technology vendors intend to provide workflow capabilities on top of their Web services stack. This may be eased by the fact that Web services seem to be a suitable foundation for business process management both within and across enterprise boundaries (Leymann et al., 2002).

As an example of how such capabilities can be implemented on top of Web services, Gomez, Hernandez, Olmedo, and Bussler (2005) propose a B2B conversational architecture organized in four layers. The Web services layer encompasses basic features such as publishing and searching for service information in a UDDI registry. The composite Web service layer makes use of a second repository, which keeps information about available composite services, with compositions being described by means of BPEL documents. The enterprise intra-workflow layer deals business processes that are described as orchestrations of composite services, and stored in a third repository as WS-CDL documents (Kavantzas, Burdett, & Ritzinger, 2004). The top-most layer is the enterprise inter-workflow layer, which makes use of a fourth repository in order to store rules, policies and regulations that govern B2B interactions. Except for the bottom Web service layer, each layer is associated with an engine that provides execution and monitoring capabilities.

CONCLUSION

In the operational life cycle, Web services support B2B exchanges as they encapsulate the business activities within a B2B collaboration. In the B2B trading life cycle, Web services also encapsulate business activities, but now the purpose of these activities is to search for and select business partners, and to settle, configure, and evaluate the interactions that take place with those partners. In the business networking life cycle, Web services will again encapsulate a set of business activities. These business networking activities deal with locating and entering markets, where a company will build relationships and undertake collaborations with other players in that market.

Web services technology is pervasive in the way that it is able to provide a common infrastructure that supports B2B conversations at each of these different levels. The key enabling features are the same across these levels: the ability to publish, search for, and interact with remote services. This chapter has drawn attention to the latest developments in Web services technology that are paving the way toward supporting the full life cycle of business collaborations. Clearly, there is a wide range of research challenges that still lack a definite answer. Yet, Web services have already succeeded in gathering a community that is developing the capabilities required to turn Web services into a business networking platform.

REFERENCES

Albrecht, C., Dean, D., & Hansen, J. (2005). Marketplace and technology standards for B2B e-commerce: Progress, challenges, and the state of the art. *Information & Management, 42*(6).

AMICE ESPRIT Consortium. (1993). *CIMOSA: Open system architecture for CIM*. Springer-Verlag.

Arkin, A., Askary, S., Bloch, B., Curbera, F., Goland, Y., Kartha, N., Liu, C., Thatte, S., Yendluri, P., & Yiu, A. (2005). *Web services business process execution language*, OASIS Committee Draft.

Atkinson, B., Della-Libera, G., Hada, S., Hondo, M., Hallam-Baker, P., Kaler, C., Klein, J., LaMac-chia, B., Leach, P., Manferdelli, J., Maruyama, H., Nadalin, A., Nagaratnam, N., Prafullchandra, H., Shewchuk, J., & Simon, D. (2002). *Web services security (WS-security)*. IBM, Microsoft, and Verisign.

Baghdadi, Y. (2004). A business model for B2B integration through Web services. In *Proceedings of the IEEE International Conference on e-Commerce Technology* (pp. 187-194).

Bajaj, S., Box, D., Chappell, D., Curbera, F., Daniels, G., Hallam-Baker, P., Hondo, M., Kaler, C., Langworthy, D., Malhotra, A., Nadalin, A., Nagaratnam, N., Nottingham, M., Prafullchandra, H., von Riegen, C., Schlimmer, J., Sharp, C., & Shewchuk, J. (2004). *Web services policy framework (WSPolicy)*. BEA, IBM, Microsoft, SAP, Sonic, Verisign.

Banerji, A., Bartolini, C., Beringer, D., Chopella, V., Govindarajan, K., Karp, A., Kuno, H., Lemon, M., Pogossiants, G., Sharma, S., & Williams, S. (2002). *Web services conversation language (WSCL) 1.0*. W3C Note.

Box, D., Christensen, E., Curbera, F., Ferguson, D., Frey, J., Hadley, M., Kaler, C., Langworthy, D., Leymann, F., Lovering, B., Lucco, S., Millet, S., Mukhi, N., Nottingham, M., Orchard, D., Shewchuk, J., Sindambiwe, E., Storey, T., Weerawarana, S., & Winkler, S. (2004). *Web services addressing (WS-addressing)*. BEA, IBM, Microsoft, SAP, Sun.

Brambilla, M., Ceri, S., Passamani, M., & Riccio, A. (2004). Managing asynchronous Web services interactions. In *Proceedings of the IEEE International Conference on Web services* (pp. 80-87).

Bunting, D., Chapman, M., Hurley, O., Little, M., Mischkinsky, J., Newcomer, E., Webber, J., & Swenson, K. (2003). *Web services transaction management (WS-TXM)*. Arjuna, Fujitsu, IONA, Oracle, Sun.

Cabrera, L. F., Copeland, G., Feingold, M., Freund, R., Freund, T., Johnson, J., Joyce, S., Kaler, C., Klein, J., Langworthy, D., Little, M., Nadalin, A., Newcomer, E., Orchard, D., Robinson, I., Shewchuk, J., & Storey, T. (2005). *Web services coordination (WS-coordination)*. Arjuna, BEA, Hitachi, IBM, IONA, Microsoft.

Champion, M., Ferris, C., Newcomer, E., & Orchard, D. (2002). *Web services architecture*. W3C Working Draft.

Chinnici, R., Moreau, J. J., Ryman, C., & Weerawarana, S. (2005). *Web services description language (WSDL) Version 2.0 Part 1: Core Language*. W3C Working Draft.

Chiu, D., Cheung, S., Hung, P., Chiu, S., & Chung, A. (2005). Developing e-negotiation support with a meta-modeling approach in a Web services environment. *Decision Support Systems, 40*(1), 51-69.

Clement, L., Hately, A., von Riegen, C., & Rogers, T. (2004). *UDDI Version 3.0.2*, OASIS UDDI Spec Technical Committee Draft.

Comuzzi, M., & Pernici, B. (2005). An architecture for flexible Web service QoS negotiation. In *Proceedings of the 9th IEEE International EDOC Conference*.

Cruz, S., da, Campos, M., Pires, P., & Campos, L. (2004). Monitoring e-business Web services usage through a log based architecture. In *Proceedings of the IEEE International Conference on Web services* (pp. 61-69).

Debusmann, M., & Geihs, K. (2004). Towards dependable Web services. In *Proceedings of the 10th IEEE Pacific Rim International Symposium on Dependable Computing* (pp. 5-14).

Dumas, M., Benatallah, B., Russell, N., & Spork, M. (2004). A configurable matchmaking framework for electronic marketplaces. *Electronic Commerce Research and Applications, 3*(1), 95-106.

eCo Working Group. (1999). *eCo architecture for electronic commerce interoperability*. CommerceNet.

Ferreira, D., & Ferreira, J. J. (2004). Building an e-marketplace on a peer-to-peer infrastructure. *International Journal of Computer Integrated Manufacturing, 17*(3).

Gomez, J., Hernandez, G., Olmedo, J., & Bussler, C. (2005). A B2B conversational architecture for semantic Web services based on BPIMS-WS. In *Proceedings of the 10th IEEE International Conference on Engineering of Complex Computer Systems* (pp. 252-259).

Hanson, J., Nandi, P., & Levine, D. (2002). Conversation-enabled Web services for agents and e-business. In *Proceedings of the International Conference on Internet Computing*.

Huang, Y., & Chung, J. Y. (2003), A Web services-based framework for business integration solutions. *Electronic Commerce Research and Applications, 2*(1), 15-26.

IFIP-IFAC Task Force. (1999). *GERAM: Generalised enterprise reference architecture and methodology*. Version 1.6.3.

Kavantzas, N., Burdett, D., & Ritzinger, G. (2004). *Web services choreography description language Version 1.0*. W3C Working Draft.

Kim, J., Segev, A., Patankar, A., & Cho, M. (2003). Web services and BPEL4WS for dynamic ebusiness negotiation processes. In *Proceedings of the International Conference on Web Services*.

Lamparter, S., Mutschler, S., Luckner, S., Stockmar, K., & Laborde, C. (2005). A modeling perspective on Web service contracting. In *Proceedings of the Workshop on Contract Architectures and Languages, The 9th IEEE International EDOC Conference*.

Leymann, F. (2001). *Web services flow language (WSFL) Version 1.0*. IBM Software Group.

Leymann, F., Roller, D., & Schmidt, M. T. (2002). Web services and business process management. *IBM Systems Journal, 41*(2).

Lin, M., Xie, J., Guo, H., & Wang, H. (2005). Solving QoS-driven Web service dynamic composition as fuzzy constraint satisfaction. In *Proceedings of the 2005 IEEE International Conference on e-Technology, e-Commerce, and e-service* (pp. 9-14).

Madhusudan, T., & Uttamsingh, N. (2004). A declarative approach to composing Web services in dynamic environments. *Decision Support Systems* (to appear).

McGregor, C., & Scheifer, J. (2003). A framework for analyzing and measuring business performance with Web services. In *Proceedings of the IEEE International Conference on E-Commerce* (pp. 405-412).

Myerson, J. (2002). *Web service architectures.* Tect.

Österle, H., Fleisch, E., & Alt, R. (2001). *Business networking: Shaping collaboration between enterprises.* Springer.

Robinson, W., & Volkov V. (1998). Supporting the negotiation life cycle. *Communications of the ACM, 41*(5), 95-102.

Sahai, A., & Machiraju, V. (2001). Enabling of the ubiquitous e-service vision on the Internet. *E-Service Journal, 1*(1).

Sahai, A., Machiraju, V., Sayal, M., Jin, L., & Casati, F. (2002). *Automated SLA monitoring for Web services.* HP Technical Report HPL-2002-191.

Sakata, Y., Yokoyama, K., & Matsuda, S. (2004). A method for composing process of nondeterministic Web services. In *Proceedings of the IEEE International Conference on Web services* (pp. 436-443).

Shan, Z., Chiu, D., & Qing, L. (2005). Systematic interaction management in a workflow view based business-to-business process engine. In *Proceedings of the 38th Annual Hawaii International Conference on System Sciences.*

Shankaranarayanan, G., & Cai, Y. (2005). A Web services application for the data quality management in the B2B networked environment. In *Proceedings of the 38th Annual Hawaii International Conference on System Sciences.*

Shim, S., Pendyala, V., Sundaram, M., & Gao, J. (2000). Business-to-business e-commerce frameworks. *IEEE Computer, 33*(10).

Tenenbaum, J., Chowdhry, T., & Hughes, K. (1997). Eco system: An Internet commerce architecture. *IEEE Computer, 30*(5), 48-55.

Tomaz, R., Labidi, S., & Wanghon, B. (2003). A semantic matching method for clustering traders in B2B systems. In *Proceedings of the 1st Latin American Web Congress* (pp. 144-153).

Tosic, V., Pagurek, B., Esfandiari, B., & Patel, K. (2001). On the management of compositions of Web services. In *Proceedings of the Object-Oriented Web services Workshop*, ACM Conference on Object-Oriented Programming, Systems, Languages, and Applications.

Tosic, V., Pagurek, B., Patel, K., Esfandiari, B. & Ma, W. (2003). Management applications of the Web service offerings language (WSOL). *Lecture Notes in Computer Science* (Vol. 2681, pp. 468-484).

Traversat, B., Abdelaziz, M., Duigou, M., Hugly, J. C., Pouyoul, E., & Yeager, B. (2002). *Project JXTA virtual network.* Sun Microsystems.

Vinoski, S. (1997). CORBA: Integrating diverse applications within distributed heterogeneous environments. *IEEE Communications Magazine, 14*(2).

Wombacher, A., Fankhauser, P., Mahleko, B., & Neuhold, E. (2003). Matchmaking for business processes. In *Proceedings of the IEEE International Conference on E-Commerce* (pp. 7-11).

Zeng, L., Benatallah, B., Ngu, A., Dumas, M., Kalagnanam, J., & Chang, H. (2004). QoS-aware middleware for Web services composition. *IEEE Transactions on Software Engineering, 30*(5), 311-327.

Zhang, L., Chao, T., Chang, H., & Chung, J. Y. (2003). XML-based advanced UDDI search mechanism for B2B integration. *Electronic Commerce Research, 3*(1-2), 25-42.

Zhang, J., Zhang, L. J., & Chung, J. Y. (2004). WS-trustworthy: A framework for Web services centered trustworthy computing. In *Proceedings of the IEEE International Conference on services Computing* (pp. 186-193).

Chapter XXVI
Enterprise Integration Architecture for Harmonized Messaging

Dat C. Ma
The University of Queensland, Australia

Belinda M. Carter
The University of Queensland, Australia

Shazia W. Sadiq
The University of Queensland, Australia

Maria E. Orlowska
The University of Queensland, Australia

ABSTRACT

Integrating business processes across disparate systems of partner organizations is known to be one of the biggest challenges facing enterprise systems development. Recent developments in service technologies and advanced middleware solutions, together with efforts toward standard interfaces, have helped overcome some of the difficulties. However, managing the rules that govern the interactions between cross-organizational business processes is still under developed. In this chapter, we present an approach for enterprise integration facilitated through a rule based messaging technology. In particular, we will present insights into rule specification, verification, and execution for such an enterprise integration architecture.

INTRODUCTION

With the current business trends toward outsourcing and virtual alliances, the importance of business process integration has emerged very strongly. Business process integration (BPI), understood as the controlled sharing of data and applications within and across an enterprise boundary, is considered to be one of the main strategies of many organizations. BPI offers new business opportunities, benefits of maximizing operational productivity, and business resource usefulness, and also supports businesses in gaining competitive advantages through customer and supplier satisfaction.

However, the research efforts and development paths pursued by many research groups and system developers to target heterogenous system integration have not been easy and have not always delivered effective and practical results. From a technical perspective, the challenges that BPI systems or large-scale collaboration systems deal with are:

- **Scalability:** The great number of instances that come as and are delivered by the systems per a unit of time, in the number of geographical locations, the number of systems/applications/functions involved, the number of organizations participating, the number of products/services offered, the amount of data needed to retrieve and update.
- **Volatility:** A characteristic of the business environment, which refers to a dynamically changing environment where data and services can appear, be removed, or be updated in a timely manner, where the changes can be predictable or not.
- **Autonomy:** The flexibility to change one's own processes with controlled reduction of impact on other partners. The limited trust in trading partner relationships, however, will be present, thus requiring the traceability

and controlled monitoring of the automated processes that are established between the trading participants.
- **Heterogeneity:** Customers do not want to rip and replace legacy applications and so diverse systems exist across a trading community. There are countless business applications, data formats, and points of integration that increase the process integration complexity exponentially.

Historically speaking, process enablement has been a driver for enterprise systems for a significant period of time. The pitfalls of functional over-specialization and lack of overall process control has been well documented. Technology response to this business demand was met with a suite of technologies, ranging from groupware and office automation, to workflow systems, and more currently business process management (BPM) technologies. Recently, BPM has been used as a broader term to reflect the fact that a business process may or may not involve human participants and may also cross organizational boundaries.

It is this integration aspect of business process management that has attracted significant interest in academia and industry. We can find in literature a range of technologies, standards and formal approaches that have been put forth to address this complex problem.

Our study also indicates that it is well known that messaging technologies play a key role in BPI. This role is primarily that of facilitating interactions between partner organizations running potentially heterogeneous systems. Message-oriented middleware is known to tackle some key issues of cross enterprise data exchange without violating individual system autonomy.

Process enactment systems traditionally rely on the control flow defined within the process model, which triggers the invocation of the underlying application component(s). Even though the interaction between the application components and the process engine may take place through a messaging protocol instead of a method call, the order of application execution is driven by the process.

This approach has been highly successful in coordinative processes. The ability to abstract the process logic and then utilize it to drive the business activities is a key feature of workflow systems. However, this approach becomes arguable for collaborative processes that are characterized by asynchronous and highly dynamic business activity between heterogeneous and autonomous systems of business partners.

In collaborative processes, it is expected that independent specialized application components both within and across organizational boundaries will be capable of detecting the events that dictate subsequent process flow. These events can be many and can arise at any time during the overall process and cannot be anticipated by related or dependent components. Thus, in a message driven process, the component detecting an event would need to communicate relevant data pertaining to the event to the process enforcement system. It is natural to contemplate that this would take the form of message passing.

Modelling a collaborative process through the exchange of messages rather than through a rigid control flow between its activities is significantly different albeit more natural way of capturing the logic behind collaborative processes. Thus, business activity takes place within application components, the manner in which the context for the business activity is provided by message harmonization. How the business activity deals with the message is not the question, instead capturing which business activity may need to be informed about a particular event, and when, is the question at hand.

The critical factor is that the process enforcement system is empowered with sufficient intelligence so that the appropriate action can be taken when a particular message arrives. This action basically constitutes communicating the relevant data to the right process participant, for example, an application component, a business activity performer, or a workflow management system at the right time. This onward communication can also be assumed to take place through a messaging protocol. Thus, an incoming message representing a process event is interpreted and evaluated against given conditions, and an appropriate outgoing message is created. We refer to such handling of messages as message harmonization. In this chapter, we will present an enterprise integration architecture based on message harmonization.

The chapter is structured as follows: In the next section, we present the overall vision for the proposed enterprise integration architecture based on harmonized messaging. Then we provide an overview of related technologies, specifically ongoing research in the area of event-based and rule-based systems. Foundations for expressing rules that govern harmonized messaging are also considered, which include a discussion on correctness criteria and verification of the rules. We then show the overall execution environment and the issues and challenges in rule execution due to the particular characteristics of message harmonization rules. The chapter concludes with an outlook on trends and future developments in this area.

In summary, the chapter will present an emerging architecture for enterprise integration based on messaging technology. The core of the architecture is in the specification and execution of complex rules that govern the integration logic between multiple partners collaborating in long duration business processes. The chapter will provide value to practitioners as it is well positioned within the current trend of BPI solutions, as well as to the research community owing to the presented formal foundations, which help in understanding requirements and limitations in this area.

ENTERPRISE INTEGRATION ARCHITECTURE BASED ON HARMONIZED MESSAGING

During the past several years as enterprise software has evolved, there has been extensive research on enterprise architectures in pursuit of the evasive business-IT alignment.

From the technology perspective, the most significant development in the recent past impacting on enterprise architectures has been through service-oriented architectures (SOA) (Erl, 2004). Although SOA has generated unrealistic hype at times, there is clear evidence of advances in configurable solutions due to standardization of service interfaces. Although Web services standards are an essential stepping stone for *service enablement* of enterprise applications, they do not provide the complete solution for BPI.

Achieving communication between disparate enterprise applications through messaging is well established in message-oriented middleware (Middleware.org, 2005). An essential component in enterprise architectures is an intelligent middleware solution that can scale beyond the traditional hub-and-spoke message broker, thus providing the ability to provide *service communication* through messaging. The extended functionality of the enterprise service bus (ESB) (Chappell, 2004) is currently a dominant approach in this respect, providing the ability to store messages. Figure 1 illustrates the use of ESB in establishing streamlined service communication.

Recent developments from business software vendors have identified the need for solutions that go beyond service enablement and communication capability. These provide a development environment that allows multiple services both within and across enterprise systems to be collated into value added composite applications (see enterprise services architecture (SAP AG, 2005a) and associated composite application framework (SAP AG, 2005b).

Figure 1. Role of ESB in streamlining scattered communication (Angeli & Grice, 2005)

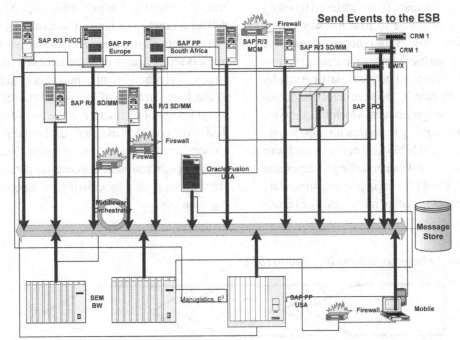

We observe that a critical aspect of current enterprise architectures based on the previous approaches is the management of the rules for *service interaction*. This functionality would naturally reside in middleware components and is the main driver for our vision behind harmonized messaging technology (HMT). Figure 2 presents the path to BPI and a consequently high level of business agility. While there have been significant developments within the first two phases of service enablement and communication, the last phase of managing service interaction still holds many challenges.

In HMT, each process participant contributes to the collaboration by offering one or several services (such as issuing invoices, approving purchase requests, etc.). In practice, services interact with each other through message exchange, which is the typical mechanism for sharing data among services (or participants).

To achieve a collaborative process, a HMT system (called harmonised messaging management system—HMMS) is used (Figure 3). The HMMS uses rules to facilitate service interactions. Interactions between a service of participant A and that of a participant B are achieved by using the HMMS as a bridge to pass messages (thus data) between A and B. In other words, service interactions are achieved by manipulating the flow of messages exchanged between participants by the HMMS. Rules in HMMS can detect the occurrences of incoming messages (which are events) to generate new outgoing messages for appropriate participants. The HMMS also acts as a mediator that passes relevant data pertaining to the events between participants by incorporating these data in the contents of outgoing messages. The result-

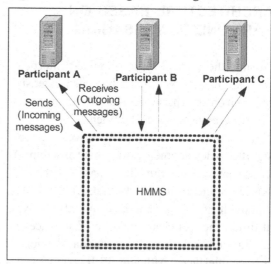

Figure 3. Service integration using the HMMS

ing collaborated process can later be reused as a service for other collaborative processes.

In the subsequent sections, we will focus on the specification and execution challenges for rules of service interaction. However, we first present an overview of the architecture for HMT. While the driving factors behind known messaging middleware solutions have been primarily based around scalability and performance, HMT must deliver on this front but is also distinguished in two respects. First, the *persistence* and *traceability* of message exchange must be achieved since it is an essential requirement in business systems due to the long duration of business activities. The second point of distinction is the *use of rules* to deal with complex message exchange patterns for service interactions that subsume the typical point-to-point and publish-subscribe patterns that are well supported by existing message brokering solutions.

Figure 2. Path to business process integration (BPI)

The main functional components of a HMT system (or the HMMS) are illustrated in Figure 4.

The components of the generic HMT model are briefly described next. Various concepts (e.g., collaboration space, message types, etc.) are further elaborated in subsequent sections.

Collaboration Modeller

The collaboration modeller provides a toolset for the designers to establish collaboration spaces (CSs). Collaboration designers are in charge of identifying and designing the set of message types needed for collaboration where the messages that are exchanged between a participant and the HMMS must conform to message types in that set.

In addition, the designers also provide the rules needed by the CSs to support message exchange. To be effective, the collaboration modeller must be equipped with a language to express the rules that govern the harmonization requirements.

Harmonization Engine

The harmonization engine is the core driving force for the system supporting essential functionality. This engine is primarily responsible for managing the collaboration spaces defined within the system, which use rules, message type definitions, and participant information for run-time rule execution based on the data received from external participants. The harmonization engine is also responsible for the management of message instances and maintenance of the system log.

Figure 4. System architecture for harmonized messaging technology (HMT)

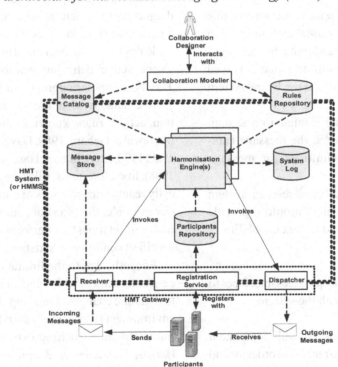

HMT Data Sources

The HMT framework will be supported by a number of underlying databases essential for the persistent storage and management of data driving various aspects of the system. These consist of:

- **Message store:** The message store allows reliable and persistent of messages. A relational DBMS can serve this purpose. The messages need to be stored in the message store while in transition from one participant to another and/or during the execution of complex rules defined on those messages.
- **Participant's repository:** Data about the collaboration participants (parties, processes, and other objects) that need to exchange messages must be maintained. At a minimum, participant profiles would include registration information, privileges, and requirements.
- **Rule repository:** The harmonization engine needs rules within a collaboration space to effectively manage and route the messages. At design-time, this information is placed in the rules repository for use by the system at run-time.
- **Message catalogue:** Similar to a system catalogue in a DBMS, the message catalog stores type definitions for message objects.
- **System log:** Data about all relevant system events must be maintained in order to provide system reliability and transactionability.

HMT Gateway

The messaging gateway provides interfaces to participants to interact with the system.

- **Registration service:** This sub-component allows participants to register in order to send messages to and receive messages from the system.

- **Receiver:** This sub-component evaluates the validity of incoming messages based on definition of message types, processes the information of the sending participants, and invokes the harmonization engine for processing.
- **Dispatcher:** This sub-component routes the messages to respective receiver participants.

RELATED WORK

Business processes are driven by domain-specific knowledge and one way to represent such knowledge is through rules that express what must or should happen when certain conditions are met. Rule-based systems (RBS) automate problem-solving know-how, providing a means for capturing and refining human expertise (Hayes-Roth, 1985) using rules to provide recommendations or diagnoses, or to determine a course of action in a particular situation (Coppin, 2004).

Rules have long been used to implement reactive or "active" behaviour in information systems. The most popular approach to facilitating these "active databases" is the use of "event, condition, action" rules, known as the ECA paradigm (Agrawal & Gehani, 1989; Dayal et al., 1988; Haas et al., 1990; Stonebraker, Hanson, & Potamianos, 1988). In such systems, rules are used to automatically react to occurrences of database operations (for example, the insertion, deletion or update of tuples in relations) by performing an action if a specified condition is satisfied.

Recently, due to the limitations of some process enforcement technologies in the adaptation to dynamic changes stemming from the business environment (Rahm et al., 2005), combined with limitations in modelling expressiveness (Aalst, Barros, Hofstede, & Kiepuszewski, 2000), as well as the requirement to extend its functions to accommodate advanced process requirements such as the grouping or ungrouping of activity instances (Sadiq, Orlowska, Sadiq, & Schulz, 2005), there is a movement toward the application of rule-based technology to the process enforcement domain. The appearances of many vendor products (such as Biztalk Server, 2006, Microsoft, 2006, ILOG's Business Rule Management System (ILOG), PegaRULES (PEGA), Corticon's Business Rule Management System (CORTICON)) as well as research prototypes (such as CEP (Luckham, 2002), EDEE (Abrahams, Eyers, & Bacon, 2002), and TriGSflow (Kappel, Rausch-Schott, & Retschitzegger, 2000) reflect this trend.

Such active system behaviour is centered around the notion of an event and so events receive significant attention in academic society. In advanced active database systems and BPM systems, events can be considered either primitive or composite, where primitive events are considered to be atomic incidences of database operations or business activities, and there is a mechanism to create composite events from the primitive ones by using event operators such as sequencing, disjunction, and conjunction. Such composition is achieved through the use of event algebras, which differ based on the richness of predefined primitive event types as well as the availability of event operators, such as HiPAC (Dayal et al., 1988), Compose (Gehani, Jagadish, & Shmueli, 1992), Snoop (Chakravarthy, Krishnaprasad, Anwar, & Kim, 1994), RAPIDE (Luckham, 2002), and TriGS (Retschitzegger, 1998).

For the process enforcement service in BPM systems, complex composite events can be expressed to represent advanced business patterns. However, the employment of event algebras in BPM systems requires techniques to detect errors in rule specifications to verify that they reflect the intended business logic at system design time as well as techniques to efficiently execute such rules at run time. The verification of large rule sets is known to be a hard problem, because although individual rules can be easy to understand on their own, interactions that can occur between rules are

not obvious (Grossner, Chander, Radhakrishnan, & Preece, 1996). These tasks become especially challenging when the composed events involve a temporal dimension.

FOUNDATIONS FOR RULE EXPRESSION

Expressing the rules that govern the interaction logic between multiple partners of collaborative business processes is a highly challenging issue that requires both an understanding of practical requirements, as well as insight into formal rule specification and limitations. In this section, we will provide a detailed discussion on HMT rules, including issues relating to verification of rule sets.

Basic Concepts

We now introduce the foundation concepts within HMT through a simple business scenario where multiple business partners are engaged in a common process. A merchant company places orders to two separate manufacturers. Order delivery to shipment partner needs to be synchronised within and between the two orders (for example, to save delivery fee, or to facilitate some management purpose). That means shipment is to take place not when the entire quantity of one order has arrived, but it is to wait for the arrival of the second order items as well.

In this case, orders and shipments can be seen as communication messages (termed *message instances*), which conform to predefined conventional schemas (termed *message types*). The merchant, shipment, and all partners engaged in the collaboration are termed *participants*. The system capable of facilitating the message-based communication is called *harmonized messaging management system (HMMS)*. In a nutshell, the main concepts that facilitate message harmonization in HMT are:

- **Participants:** A participant is a primitive concept used to represent a component process, an organization, or a program participating in collaboration. Participants can send and/or receive instances to/from the system (HMMS).
- **Rules:** Rules constitute the most critical aspect of collaboration. The ability of the system to receive and generate instances of certain message types represents the system behaviour, and rules provide the means of enforcing this behaviour. For example, there are simple rules enforcing the system to generate a purchase order upon receiving a purchase request, or to dispatch a receipt after receiving an acknowledgment for shipment. However, there is evidence that these rules can involve complex expressions surpassing data, time and ordering dependencies.
- **Message types:** All the communication message instances must conform to predefined schemas, which are defined through message types. Each message type contains various *fields*. Each field can only accept values from a set called its *field domain*. A *field definition expression* refers to values of fields within or outside the message instance to calculate value of a field. Fields also carry *field constraints*, which include restrictions on fields such as mandatory/optional, subtype, or subset constraints, etc.

Considering that XML is currently the most popular standard for document exchange on the Web, each message type can be represented as an XML schema. Fields are implemented as XML elements or attributes. Therefore, domains of fields correspond to element/attribute domains, and the field constraints can be defined as constraints within XML schemas. In this manner, each instance is represented as an XML document.

Based on the HMMS's receipt and dispatch functions, message types are classified into two classes:

- Incoming message types (or IMTs), which are the schemas of instances coming to the HMMS. Denoted as, $\overline{T}_i$ (where i is the ID of the IMT).
- Outgoing message types (or OMTs), which are the schemas of instances dispatched from the HMMS. Denoted as, $\underline{T}_i$ (where i is the ID of the OMT).

Generally, based on the receiver and sender of its instances, a message type is classified to be an IMT or an OMT. If the receiver of its instances is the HMMS, it is an IMT, and if the HMMS is the sender of its instances, it is an OMT. Note that the status of a message (incoming or outgoing) will always depend on the context of the system that receives/sends it. For example, a purchase request will have outgoing status in the context of a CRM (customer relationship management) system, but will have an incoming status in the context of a SCM (supply chain management) system. When the class of a message type is not a concern, we use T_i to denote the message type for the sake of simplicity of specification.

Lastly, we denote a field of a message type as $\overline{T}_i.F$, $\underline{T}_i.F$, or $T_i.F$, where F is the ID or the name of the field.

- **Collaboration space:** In order to perform a collaboration of processes by harmonizing messages, participants need to communicate with each other by exchanging instances of different message types following a collection of rules. Thus it is required to form a collaboration space (or CS), which is a 3-tuple of: <set of participants, set of rules, set of message types >

The concept of collaboration space takes inspiration from the concept of database space in relational database systems. A HMMS can have several collaboration spaces, each with its own rules, message types, and participants, similar to a DBMS having multiple database spaces.

Rules for Message Harmonization

A system is envisaged that processes and responds to incoming messages as they occur according to the set of defined rules. The rules of HMT take inspiration from the well-established paradigm of ECA (event condition action) (Widom & Ceri, 1996) and are given to be of the form:

Event, Condition → Action.

In the context of message-based business process enforcement, the event part typically refers the receipt of one or more messages, the condition part is defined as a logical expression involving the content of such messages, and the action part involves the composition and dispatch of one or more outgoing messages. Accordingly, we present the types of events, conditions, and action for rules in HMT next.

Event Types

Although event based systems have been studied widely (Luckham, 2002) and span a large variety of possible types of events, particular events of interest from the perspective of facilitating the execution of message-driven business processes are the following:

- Arrival (or dispatch) of a message instance.
- Occurrence of a specific time value (or clock event).
- Detection of the completed state (i.e., all the fields constraints are satisfied) of an outgoing message instance.

Conditions

The condition of a rule is a first order formula, which is built on constants, fields, events, and NOW (variable refers to the current time point) using Boolean operators ($\neg, \wedge, \vee$).

Example: $(\overline{T_{PO}}.Total > 10000)$ is a condition, which will evaluate to TRUE if the total value of a purchase order is more than 10,000. One important use of HMT conditions is for correlating events. For example, the composite event receiving a purchase order and a receipt is meaningful only when they are correlated to each other, for example by the customer number, here the customer number is called the correlated field. A specific value of the correlated field is used to group events that trigger the same rule. Besides, the correlated field is also be used to correlate events that generate instances of different OMTs belonging to the same execution of a process (instance), where the value of the correlated field represents the flow of information across multiple outgoing message instances. The selection of correlated field is varied from case to case; however the correlated field must be a mandatory field for all the message types of the correlated events, and also a mandatory field for the OMT.

Action Types

When the condition part of a rule is evaluated to be TRUE (that is, the rule is triggered) the system will react by performing an action. In the context of harmonizing messages, there are three different types of actions that need to be considered when generating a new outgoing message instance:

- **Associate:** Associates an event with the suitable OMT to create a "blank" OMT's instance (rule type 1).
- **Assign (or Populate):** Assigns field definition expressions which assign values to

corresponding fields of the OMT's instance (rule type 2).
- **Send:** Sends the completed OMT instance (rule type 3)

Consequently, there are three *rule types*, each dealing with one action type.

In practice, before collaboration, an agreement on message types must be achieved between the HMMS and all participants. Contents for individual instances of an IMT are decided by participant(s) and contents for instances of an OMT are populated by the HMMS using rules.

The interactions between any two services are explicitly captured by rules of type 1 and 3, while the real data to be passed between them is encapsulated by the field definition expressions and/or rules type 2. Rules with various building components can express a wide range of message exhange patterns, which put event, data, and temporal contraints on messages (a detail formalisation of rule types and their expressive power is documented in Ma, Orlowska, & Sadiq (2005). As a result, complex service interactions can be implied.

Example

We use a simple purchasing process in an organisation to illustrate the deployment of rules.

Typically, a customer will initiate the purchase process by submitting a purchase request; a purchase order will be created after a quote is supplied by the vendor and the approval is obtained from the customer's manager; the invoice and the shipment notice will then be delivered to the customer; and then a payment from the customer will finalise the process.

The following steps are involved to perform the above process in HMT:

- A customer sends a purchase request (PR) (an instance of $\overline{T_{PR}}$) to the purchasing system.

- The system will generate a request approval (RA) (an instance of T_{RA}) to the purchasing manager to ask for the approval.
- After approving, an approval (AP) (an instance of $\overline{T_{AP}}$) is sent back to the system from the purchasing manager.
- Based on the approval, a quote request (QR) (an instance of T_{QR}) is sent to the vendor to ask for the product quotes.
- The vendor replies with a quote (QO) (an instance of $\overline{T_{QO}}$).
- Then the system will automatically generate a purchase order (PO) (an instance of T_{PO}) on the behalf of the customer.
- When a PO is received, the vendor will place a shipment order (SO) to the shipping company and send back the system an invoice (IV) (an instance of $\overline{T_{IV}}$).
- After receiving the IV and the shipment notice (SN) (an instance of $\overline{T_{SN}}$), the system will issue the payment (PM) (an instance of T_{PM}).

In this example, the participants that participate in the process are: the purchasing system, the customer, the purchasing manager, the vendor, and the shipping company. They communicate with each other by utilizing the following message types: $\overline{T_{PR}}$, T_{RA}, $\overline{T_{AP}}$, T_{QR}, $\overline{T_{QO}}$, T_{PO}, $\overline{T_{IV}}$, $\overline{T_{SN}}$, T_{PM}.

The HMT system takes its role in the process by generating instances of T_{RA}, T_{QR}, T_{PO}, and T_{PM} based on the following rules of three types:

- **Rule type 1:** Rules to associate OMTs:
  (R11) Associate T_{RA}
  IF a PR arrived THEN create a blank RA
  (R12) Associate T_{QR}
  IF a RA is sent AND the correlated AP arrived THEN create a blank QR.

In this example, the RA and the AP are correlated with each other when they have the same reference no. The reference no. is unique and is created by the system each time a PR arrives, and propagated to all the instances (i.e., the reference no. is copied to RA, AP, QR, QO, PO, SN, IV, PM) that belong to the same process instance.

- **(R13) Associate T_{PO}**
  IF a QR is sent $\overline{\text{AND}}$ the correlated QO arrived AND the correlated AP arrived THEN create a blank PO.

- **(R14) Associate T_{PM}**
  IF a PO is sent $\overline{\text{AND}}$ the correlated IV arrived AND the correlated SN arrived THEN create a blank PM.

- **Rule type 2:** In this example due to the space limitation, we consider only the assign rules to populate the content of $\underline{T_{RA}}$.

For purposes of illustration, consider a typical PR received by the system as given in Figure 5. Each field of the PR has a value followed by the field id. For example: From: ITEE-UQ (F3), then the From field has id 'F3' and in this PR it gets the value "ITEE-UQ."

The content of a correlated request approval (RA) will be populated by the system in accordance with the assign rule, the field definition expression, and field constraint (i.e., mandatory). This is illustrated in Figure 6. For example, To: Mr Lee (F5:= "Mr Lee"). The "To" field has id "F5," and in this RA gets value "Mr Lee" from the field definition expression, which is shown to be a constant here, but more often will by dynamically generated from data contained in the previous corresponding received messages.

Figure 5. A purchase request (PR)

	Message Type: T_{PR} *(F0)*
PURCHASE REQUEST	Message ID: PR-001 *(F1:=SYSTEM)* Reference No.: Ref-001 *(F2:=SYSTEM)*

From: ITEE – UQ   *(F3)*
Email: itee@uq.edu.au   *(F4)*

To: Purchasing System *(F5)*
Email: ps@uq.edu.au *(F6)*

Time, date received: 08:10:20 - 06/09/04 *(F7:= SYSTEM)*

Vendor: Dell Australia Company *(F8)*
    Vendor ID: V001 *(F9)*
    Email: sales@dell.com.au *(F10)*

Requested by: Mr. Alex *(F11)*
    Staff ID: S0012 *(F12)*
    Depart: ITEE *(F13)*
    Email: alex@itee.uq.edu.au *(F14)*

Requested date: 06/09/04 *(F15)*
    Need by: 10/09/04 *(F16)*

Ship to: ITEE *(F17)*
    Add: GP Building, St Lucia Campus. *(F18)*

Account with vendor: ACC-0001 *(F19)*

(Tab1)

Item *(Tab1.F1)*	Description *(Tab1.F2)*	Quantity *(Tab1.F3)*
1	PC DELL – Dimension 8400	10
2	Server DELL-Precision 470DT	3

Note: *(F20)*
Signature: ALEX *(F21)*

Figure 6. A request approval (RA) and the rules to populate it

---

REQUEST FOR APPROVAL

Message Type: T_{RA} *(F0)*

Message ID: RA-002 *(F1:=SYSTEM)*
Reference No.: Ref-001 *(F2:= T_{PR} .F2)*

From: Purchasing System *(F3:= "Purchasing System")*
Email: ps@uq.edu.au *(F4:= "ps@uq.edu.au")*

To: Mr Lee *(F5:= "Mr Lee")*
Email: lee@uq.edu.au *(F6:= lee@uq.edu.au)*

Time, date sent: 08:10:22 - 06/09/04 *(F7:= SYSTEM)*

Vendor: Dell Australia Company *(F8:= T_{PR} .F8)*
   Vendor ID: V001 *(F9:= T_{PR} .F9)*
   Email: sales@dell.com.au *(F10:= T_{PR} .F10)*
Requested by: Mr. Alex *(F11:= T_{PR} .F11)*
   Staff ID: S0012 *(F12:= T_{PR} .F12)*
   Depart: ITEE *(F13:= T_{PR} .F13)*
   Email: alex@itee.uq.edu.au *(F14:= T_{PR} .F14)*

Requested date: 06/09/04 *(F15:= T_{PR} .F15)*
   Need by: 10/09/04 *(F16:= T_{PR} .F16)*
Ship to: ITEE *(F17:= T_{PR} .F17)*
Add: GP Building, St Lucia Campus. *(F18:= T_{PR} .F18)*

Account with vendor: ACC-0001 *(F19:= T_{PR} .F19)*

(Tab1)

Item (Tab1.F1)	Description (Tab1.F2:= T_{PR} .Tab1.F2)	Quantity (Tab1.F3:= T_{PR} .Tab1.F3)
1	PC DELL – Dimension 8400	10
2	Server DELL-Precision 470DT	3

Note: .... *(F20:= T_{PR} .F20)*
Signature: ALEX *(F21:= T_{PR} .F21)*

- **Rule type 3:** Rules to send OMT's instances are:
  - (R31) When RA (T_{RA}) is in completed state send it.
  - (R32) When QR (T_{QR}) is in completed state send it.
  - (R33) At 8 o'clock everyday, any ready POs (T_{PO}) will be sent.
  - (R34) When PM (T_{PM}) is in completed state send it.

It is important to note that there is often a requirement to extend the functionality of the system to adapt better to changes or exceptions in the real business environment. For example, the aforementioned process could be required to handle business cases such as customer cancellations or insufficient customer credit. These cases are exceptions in the business sense (i.e., they do not follow the "typical" process previously described) and if the process enforcement is performed by traditional process management systems then it is difficult to accommodate these policies, due to the complex problem of dynamic instance management (Reichert & Dadam, 1998). This requires the creation of new system functionality to deal with the changes or exceptions or they can be handled as errors (Adams M. et al., 2005; Sadiq, 2000).

However, in the HMT approach, the insertion or modification of further rule can provide support for these new or changed policies without requiring new system functionality. For example, the above cancellation policy can be accommodated in the system by introducing a new message type for order cancelling (CA) and modify rule R13 as:

- (R13a) IF a QR is sent AND the correlated QO arrived AND the correlated AP arrived AND NOT a correlated CA arrived THEN create a blank PO.

CORRECTNESS CRITERIA AND VERIFICATION ISSUES

While rule-based systems provide immense power in specification, it is with regards to analysis and verification that rule-based approaches have often taken a back seat in business process modelling. In this section, we propose the essential correctness criteria (that is, constraints to avoid errors) for rules in HMT and discuss some critical issues related to the task of verifying such rule sets.

There are two phases of verification—first verifying individual rules and subsequently verifying rule sets (that have generally been defined within the context of a collaboration space).

Individual Rules

We present rules in a semi-formal language for the purpose of this chapter. However, these rules are expected to be specified using high-level modelling tools (as depicted in Figure 4), and subsequently transformed into machine readable format for execution purposes. Thus, the discussion next relates to rule verification at a conceptual level, and is independent of any particular implementation.

Syntactic Correctness: Syntax checks are generally simple and can be provided through language parsers. Examples of syntax checks for HMT rules include:

- An Assign rule must ensure that it always assigns a field definition expression to field.
- Events that are referred to by the condition part must appear in the event part of the rule.

- An optional field cannot be referenced by a field definition expression of a mandatory field.
- There is no loop reference in field definition expressions where, for example, the field definition expression of field T1.F1 refers to T1.F1, or the field definition expression of T1.F1 refers to T1.F2 and the field definition of T1.F2 refers to T1.F1.

Safety of Rules: A rule may be syntactically correct, but the condition in a rule may be formulated in such a way that it leads to unsafe behaviour. Unsafe behaviour is typically found in rules that refer to the absence of events and are unbounded by time. This may result in infinite triggering of the rule.

The concept of safety of a rule is formally defined as follows. We call a substitution of values for terms in the condition part (a first order logic formula), for which the condition evaluates to TRUE—an evaluation of the rule's condition. A rule's condition is safe if and only if the set of all its evaluations is a finite set.

For example, the rule "when a purchase order has not been received, send an acknowledgement" is not a safe rule because at every tick of the system clock or the occurrence of any event other than the arrival of a purchase order would trigger the sending of an acknowledgement message.

In Ma, Orlowska, and Sadiq (2005), a mechanism to check rule safety is provided, which addresses the problem of determining rule safety without reverting to finding the set of all the evaluations of the formula (the satisfiability problem) known to be an NP complete problem.

Rule Sets

Individual rules may be syntactically correct and safe, however, rule sets may still introduce conflicts and inconsistencies that leads to erroneous execution. We define two criteria of correctness for rule sets, namely atomicity and conformity.

We first introduce the concept of an interaction. An interaction is the execution of rules of three rule types, in order to associate, assign values to all the fields (or populate), and send an OMT's instance. This forms a logical unit for system processing, which results in a completed OMT's instance being sent to a participant. An interaction that generates (i.e., associates, populates, and sends) an instance of OMT is denoted as:

Atomicity: An interaction is atomic if and only if whenever an OMT's instance is initiated, it must be populated, and then dispatched, or the OMT's instance is not initiated at all. The atomicity is a desirable property of interactions, since imitating OMT instances that will never be populated and sent would lead to an immense build up of dead instances, eventually compromising system performance. This requires that:

- Each OMT must have a rule (type 1) to associate it,
- Every field must have a field definition expression or an assign rule,
- Each OMT must have a rule (type 3) to send its instances.

Conformity: In practice, the collaboration space of a system often contains a large number of OMTs, and consequently a large number of rules controlling these OMTs. The execution of these rules will generate a great number of interactions. Since these interactions are actually steps within larger business processes, it is essential to control the order of execution of these interactions thereby reflecting the logic of the intended business process. We term this requirement as process conformity. For example the generating of a purchase order must take place in advance of the generating of the corresponding receipt, where the purchase order and the correlated receipt are the results of distinct interactions.

In this chapter, we restrict the relationship between any two interactions to precedency. In particular, in order to represent the fact that precedes, we introduce the sequence operator (denoted as .). The sequence operator is a Boolean binary operator, which takes two interactions as arguments, and will be evaluated to be TRUE when the following properties hold:

Let T1 and T2 be the OMTs such that their instances are generated by I1 and I2; T1.F and T2.F are fields in T1 and T2, the event of detection of the completed state of an instance of T1 is denoted as:

- (P1) Rules in I2 can refer to T1.F (i.e., used as terms in conditions or in field definition expressions). If we assume that only field values in a completed OMT's instance can be referred by a different OMT's instance, then is an event to associate T2.
- (P2) Rules in I1 can not refer to T2.F. These two properties guarantee that the correlated instance of T1 is initiated, completely populated before an instance of T2 is initiated, and populated. However, this does not guarantee that correlated instance of T1 is sent before an instance of T2. The intention here is to separate the process of initiating, and populating an instance, from the sending of this instance, which will suit well in the case of long running business process where the rule executions in each interaction can be performed in an interleaving manner.
- (P3) A stricter way to guarantee the sequence of interactions is by including the event of dispatching a correlated instance of T1 as an event to associate T2. This property guarantees that T2 can not be associated, populated, and sent before an instance of T1 is sent.

A sequence of interactions is valid if every pair of consecutive interactions satisfies properties (P1) and (P2). It is called strict if it is valid and every pair of consecutive interactions satisfies property (P3).

Example

We will now demonstrate through the example introduced in the verification of individual and collections of rules according to the previous correctness criteria.

INDIVIDUAL RULE VERIFICATION

Syntactic Correctness

- Every field has a field definition expression.
- As indicated in Figure 5 and Figure 6, the field definition expressions of fields and violate the syntactic correctness criteria since they refer to values of the optional fields in a PR (and) to calculate mandatory field values.
- There is no loop reference in field definition expressions.

Safety of Rules

- The only rule that refers to the absence of event is R13a, the absent event here is "CA NOT arrived." The absent event is bounded with other correlated events (i.e., QR sent, QO arrived, AP arrived) and by the Reference No, therefore, the rule is considered safe (Ma et al., 2005).

Rule Set Verification

Atomicity

- Each of the OMTs— , , , —has a rule to associate it (i.e., R11, R12, R13, R14).
- Each field in an OMT must have a rule type 2 or a field definition expression to assign its value. In this example, for the RA, every field of it has a field definition expression.

- Each of the OMTs— , , , —has a rule to send it instances (i.e., R31, R32, R33, R34).

Conformity

In this example, to reflect the logic of the intended business process, the order of interactions to generate correlated instances of OMTs must be as follows: . . . . Consider the rules to associate , , and   (rules type 1):

- The sending of a I_{RA} is an event to associate.
- The sending of a I_{QR} is an event to associate.
- The sending of a I_{PO} is an event to associate.

These rules guarantee that the interactions will occur following the expected order, thus conforming to the business logic. Furthermore, the interaction sequence is strict (satisfies property P3).

For a simple example like the previous where the number of participants, message types, and rules are small, the verification task can be handled manually. However, we understand that meaningful applications in BPI may require the number of message types and rules in the order of hundreds if not more to effectively capture interaction patterns (typical and exceptional) among a large number of participants. Thus, the previous discussion provides groundwork for verification requirements, acknowledging that an implementation of the previous into a verification tool will clearly greatly assist in managing the rules.

EXECUTION ENVIRONMENT

In previous sections, we have discussed aspects related to the design-time phase of collaborative business process enforcement—in particular, the definition of rules to describe the interactions between collaborating partners that comprise such processes. In this section, we discuss some of the run-time issues associated with the underlying system to enable such rules to be executed. First, we outline the requirements for the execution of such a system in order to evaluate the conditions of the rules described above, and then we briefly outline execution approaches for such systems to support this evaluation.

Rule Evaluation

In order to facilitate business processes, the supporting system must process and respond to incoming messages as they occur, according to the set of defined rules. This may be as simple as routing a single message immediately upon receipt to a recipient based on its content. However, due to the complex nature of business, responses to events will often depend on the context in which they are received, leading to the more complex condition expressions. Reacting to events in this "stateful" manner allows business policy to be enforced. The state of the system is updated with each new event produced or received by the system. Therefore, each condition expression may be dependent on the receipt of multiple messages and each such message may contribute toward the evaluation of multiple expressions in different ways.

The evaluation of such expressions can be considered in two ways. First, each expression can be considered to be associated with a truth value of either FALSE or TRUE, where it is FALSE until it is TRUE (if ever), and where the action associated with the condition in the rule is performed at the time the expression turns to TRUE (if ever). The alternative approach is that each expression is associated with one of three (3) truth values—TRUE, FALSE, and UNKNOWN, where the expression is UNKNOWN until requisite messages are received to evaluate the expression to TRUE, or to deem that the expression may never evaluate to TRUE (no matter which

messages are subsequently received), at which point the expression is considered FALSE. Note that both approaches yield the same externally visible system behaviour, that is, that the action is performed if and only if the expression is TRUE, otherwise, nothing happens.

The receipt of each message may allow one or more expressions to be evaluated to TRUE where the associated action should be performed, as previously noted. A truth value of FALSE may also be associated with expressions that may never be evaluated to TRUE (due to the sequence of messages that have already been received by the system), depending on whether such data is beneficial in system execution (for example, to improve performance).

In any case, the "many-to-many" relationship between events and conditions means that many expressions will be in a state of "partial evaluation" until the expression is found to be TRUE (or possibly FALSE, depending on the approach adopted). Due to the unpredictable order of the events (arrival of messages) contributing toward the evaluation of these complex expressions, thousands of such expressions may be in a state of "partial evaluation" at any given time. Processes to enforce business policies may span months or even years, further contributing to the massive build up of "partially evaluated" expressions. While the effective management of this state information is an interesting question in itself, the real challenge arises when the system must operate in an intensive environment in which a very high throughput of messages is expected. In such an environment, efficiency, and scalability become critical factors for the success of the technology.

Execution Approaches

In this section, we briefly discuss two alternative approaches for the execution of such systems. Since each expression may require that multiple messages be received before it is satisfied, and message data is consequently used in the composition of outgoing messages, it is clear that messages must be stored persistently, at least for some time. The obvious method for evaluation of expressions is therefore to execute the query associated with each expression on the persistent message store each time a message is received that may impact on the evaluation of the expression (that is, may cause a truth value of True or False to be assigned to the expression). We refer to this execution model as a "brute force" approach because it (generally) requires multiple passes over each message in the persistent message store during expression evaluation. Depending on the set of rules to be executed and the incoming message stream driving such execution, such brute force models may have limited performance due to I/O cost and would not scale well.

Caching data by maintaining materialised views is a well-known technique to address such issues (e.g., Goldstein & Larson, 2001; Pal et al., 2004; Sawires, Tatemura, Po, Agrawal, & Candan, 2005). An alternative to the brute force approach is to extract "relevant" data on receipt of each message and cache some representations of it. Since the intermediate data being maintained in the cache can be derived from the stored messages, it can be considered a materialised view defined on this data. Although the volume of data in the repository is large, only a subset of it is used during expression evaluation. Only a subset of the data being exchanged between collaborating parties in business processes is used for routing purposes (i.e., referenced in the expressions)—most of the data is either intended for the receiving application or is present due to standardisation requirements.

Summarising the data from each message that is relevant to expression evaluation prevents multiple passes over messages in the persistent message store. We refer to execution models that make only one pass over the messages during expression evaluation as streaming models since they can be used in data streaming applications where

storage of the data is not possible. Data structures that store the cached data in a compressed format will reduce the volume of data on which subsequent processing (expression evaluation) is performed, increasing the probability that it is maintained in memory, and therefore reducing I/O costs incurred during system execution. In particular cases (that is, when the expressions are complex), materialisation strategies are required in order to attain reasonable and scalable performance in such systems.

In summary, evaluation of rules to drive collaborative business processes is a challenging issue due to the complex relationships between the data (messages) and expressions defined on this data. In the previous discussion, we have presented an overview of the issues and challenges involved in providing a suitable execution model for the proposed technology. Further investigation is required to derive conclusions regarding the appropriateness of the proposed alternative approaches.

SUMMARY AND OUTLOOK

A complete BPM solution must cover multiple aspects ranging from business process design and governance, to managing the deployment of BPM solutions in Web centric environments. The presented concepts specifically target business process management in a collaborative setting, where multiple participant services work towards common collaborative process goals. In particular the focus is on handling the interactions between participant services.

There exists a significant body of knowledge relating to reference models for enterprise systems architectures. In this chapter, we have presented an approach that is well positioned within current enterprise systems development trends that advocate configurable solutions for large scale integration through service enablement and communication. Specifically, the work targets the underlying foundations for facilitating interactions between participants of collaborative business processes. The presented approach is based on harmonized messaging, a rule based approach for managing interactions in business process integration. The essential requirements for specification, verficication and execution have been presented.

From a practical perspective, two aspects in particular require further consideration—first, the usability of the system and the ability to provide intuitive design tools to mask the underlying complexity of the rule specification; and second, an analysis of the scalability and performance of the rule evaluation engine in the presence of high volume message streams. These two considerations form the core of our current and future work.

REFERENCES

Aalst, W. M. P., Barros, A. P., Hofstede, A. H. M., & Kiepuszewski, B. (2000). Advanced workflow patterns. Paper presented at the *Proceedings of the 7th International Conference on Cooperative Information Systems (CoopIS 2000)*, Berlin, Germany.

Abrahams, A., Eyers, D., & Bacon, J. (2002). An asynchronous rule-based approach for business process automation using obligations. Paper presented at the *Proceedings of the 2002 ACM SIGPLAN Workshop on Rule-based Programming*, Pittsburgh, Pennsylvania, United States.

Adams, M., Arthur, H. M., ter Hofstede, E. D., & Wil, M. P. v. d. (2005) Facilitating flexibility and dynamic exception handling in workflows through worklets. Paper presented at the *17th Conference on Advanced Information Systems Engineering Forum (CAiSE05 Forum)*, Porto, Portugal.

Agrawal, R., & Gehani, G. (1989). ODE: The language and the data model. *Paper presented at the ACM-SIGMOD Conference on Management of Data*, Portland, Oregon, United States.

Angeli, A., & Grice, L. (2005). *Can ESA really work*? A practical guide to risk-free ESA introduction. Klee Associates, Inc. SAPtips.com. Retrieved October 1, 2006, from http://searchsap. techtarget.com/whitepaperPage/0,293857,sid21_gci1148549,00.html

Chakravarthy, S., Krishnaprasad, V., Anwar, E., & Kim, S. K. (1994). Composite events for active databases: Semantics, contexts, and detection. *Paper presented at the Proceedings of 20th International Conference on Very Large Data Bases (VLDB' 94)*, Santiago, Chile.

Chappell, D. A. (2004). *Enterprise service bus* (1st ed.). Sebastopol, CA: O'Reilly Media, Inc.

Coppin, B. (2004). *Artificial intelligence illuminated* (1st ed.). Boston: Jones and Bartlett Publishers.

CORTICON. *Corticon's Business Rules Management System*. Retrieved March 10, 2006, from http://www.corticon.com/html/products.html

Dayal, U., Blaustein, B. T., Buchmann, A. P., Chakravarthy, U. S., Hsu, M., Ledin, R., et al. (1988). The HiPAC project: Combining active databases and timing constraints. *ACM's Special Interest Group on Management Of Data (SIGMOD), 17*(1), 51-70.

Erl, T. (2004). *Service-oriented architecture: A field guide to integrating XML and Web services*. NJ: Prentice Hall PTR.

Gehani, N. H., Jagadish, H. V., & Shmueli, O. (1992). Event specification in an active object-oriented database. *Paper presented at the Proceedings of the 1992 ACM Special Interest Group on Management of Data International Conference on Management of Data (SIGMOD'92)*, San Diego, California, United States.

Goldstein, J., & Larson, P. A. (2001). Optimizing queries using materialized views: A practical, scalable solution. *Paper presented at the Proceedings of the 2001 ACM SIGMOD International Conference on Management of Data*, Santa Barbara, California, United States.

Grossner, C., Chander, P. G., Radhakrishnan, T., & Preece, A. D. (1996). Revealing the structure of rule-based systems. *International Journal of Expert Systems: Research and Applications, 9*(2), 255-278.

Haas, L. M., Chang, W., Lohman, G. M., McPherson, J., Wilms, P. F., Lapis, G., et al. (1990). Starburst mid-flight: As the dust clears. *Knowledge and Data Engineering, IEEE Transactions, 2*(1), 143-160.

Hayes-Roth, F. (1985). Rule-based systems. Communications of *ACM, 28*(9), 921-932.

ILOG. *ILOG's Business Rule Management System*. Retrieved March 10, 2006, from http://www.ilog.com/products/businessrules/

Kappel, G., Rausch-Schott, S., & Retschitzegger, W. (2000). *A framework for workflow management systems based on objects, rules, and roles*. ACM Computing Surveys, 32(1es), Article No. 27.

Luckham, D. C. (2002). *The power of events: An introduction to complex event processing in distributed enterprise systems*. Boston: Addison-Wesley.

Ma, D. C., Orlowska, M. E., & Sadiq, S. W. (2005). Formal considerations of rule-based messaged for business process integration. *Cybernetics and Systems: An International Journal, 37*(2-3), 171-196.

Microsoft. (2006). *Biztalk Server 2006*. Retrieved March 10, 2006, from http://www.microsoft.com/biztalk/default.mspx

Middleware.org. Retrieved March 10, 2006, from http://www.middleware.org/

Pal, S., Cseri, I., Schaller, G., Seeliger, O., Giakoumakis, L., & Zolotov, V. V. (2004). Indexing XML data stored in a relational database. *Paper presented at the Proceedings of the 13th International Conference on Very Large Data Bases (VLDB 04')*, Toronto, Canada.

PEGA. PegaRULES. Retrieved March 10, 2006, from http://www.pega.com/Products/RulesTechnology.asp

Rahm, E., Greiner, U., Robert, M., Ramsch, J., Heller, B., & Löffler, M. (2005). *Adaptive workflow management*. Retrieved February 08, 2005, from http://dbs.uni-leipzig.de/en/Research/workflow.html

Reichert, M., & Dadam, P. (1998). ADEPTflex—Supporting dynamic changes of workflows without losing control. *Journal of Intelligent Information Systems, Special Issue on Workflow and Process Management, 10*(2), 93-129.

Retschitzegger, W. (1998). Composite event management in TriGS—Concepts and implementation. *Paper presented at the Proceedings of the 9th International Conference on Database and Expert Systems Applications (DEXA 98')*, Vienna, Austria.

Sadiq, S. (2000, April 12-13). On capturing exceptions in workflow process models. *Paper presented at the Proceedings of the 4th International Conference on Business Information Systems (BIS, 2000)*. Poznan, Poland.

Sadiq, S., Orlowska, M., Sadiq, W., & Schulz, K. (2005). When workflows will not deliver—The case of contradicting work practice. *Paper presented at the 8th International Conference on Business Information Systems (BIS, 2005)*, Poznan, Poland.

SAP AG. (2005a). *Enterprise services architecture*. Retrieved January 10, 2006, from http://www.sap.com/solutions/esa/index.epx

SAP AG. (2005b). *SAP composite application framework*. Retrieved January 10, 2006, from http://www.sap.com/solutions/netweaver/cafindex.epx

Sawires, A., Tatemura, J., Po, O., Agrawal, D., & Candan, K. S. (2005). Incremental maintenance of path-expression views. *Paper presented at the Proceedings of the 2005 ACM Special Interest Group on Management of Data (SIGMOD) International Conference on Management of Data*, Baltimore.

Stonebraker, M., Hanson, E. N., & Potamianos, S. (1988). The POSTGRES rule manager. *IEEE Transactions on Software Engineering, 14*(7), 897-907.

Widom, J., & Ceri, S. (1996). *Active database systems: Triggers and rules for advanced database processing*. San Francisco: Morgan Kaufmann Publishers.

About the Authors

Pallab Saha is currently a member of the faculty with the National University of Singapore (NUS). His current research and consulting interests include IT governance, enterprise architecture, and business process management. He has published several research papers in these areas. Dr. Saha teaches courses in enterprise architecture, IT governance, and business process management at the post-graduate and senior executive levels (including CIOs). His current consulting engagements are in enterprise architecture for Singapore government agencies. Dr. Saha is also a faculty member of the newly formed Center for E-Government Leadership (CeGL) in NUS and delivers executive programmes to senior government officials from several countries. He is a frequently invited speaker at international and local conferences on enterprise architecture and IT governance and is currently engaged in the development of an enterprise architecture methodology and toolkit for the Government of Singapore. Prior to academics, he was instrumental in managing Baxter's Environmental Health and Safety Offshore Development Centre in Bangalore as head of projects and development. He has worked on engagements in several Fortune 100 organizations in various capacities. Dr. Saha received his PhD in information systems (1999) from the Indian Institute of Science, Bangalore. His PhD dissertation was awarded the best thesis in the department and also received a special research grant for the same. Earlier he completed an MBA in information systems and prior to that gained a BSc in electronic sciences.

***

Anis Abdmouleh received his PhD degree in industrial engineering and automatic control at LGIPM (Mechanical Production and industrial engineering Laboratory) and Metz University/France. He is working on projects about process modelling in enterprise by using component approach in purpose to develop manufacturing Web services CIMOSA-based. He teaches enterprise modelling, integration, and office automation in Metz University. He has contributed and is the author of a number of papers in international conferences and journals. He is also a technical freelance consultant about total quality management, lean management, and process re-engineering.

Frank J. Armour is a senior IT consultant and a faculty member at the School of Information Technology and Engineering, George Mason University. He has extensive experience in both the practical and academic aspects of applying advanced information technology. His work and research includes enterprise information, technology architectures, requirements analysis, system development cycle development (SDLC), and object-oriented development. He is currently consulting to both government and private organizations on the effective application of enterprise architecture and object-oriented system requirements and design approaches. He is the coauthor of *Advanced Use Case Modeling*.

Isaac Barjis is an assistant professor in New York City College of Technology of the City University of New York. His research interest is focused on business process management, information system design, and bioinformatics (modeling biological systems). He received his PhD in bioinformatics (2002), an MS in molecular biology (with second major in information systems) (2000) from the World Distributed University, and BSc in biomedical sciences and nutrition from the Metropolitan University of London (formerly known as University of North London) (1996). Dr. Barjis is professional member of numerous biology and bioinformatics organizations such as The International Organization of Bioinformatics, The Society for Modeling and Simulation International (SCS), and the Metropolitan Association of College and University (MACUB). He is also member of the organizing or program committee of numerous fully refereed international conferences (SCSC, IRMA). Dr. Barjis's research offspring resulted in numerous refereed publications in international conference proceedings, book chapters, and journal articles.

Joseph Barjis is a faculty in the Department of Information Technology of Georgia Southern University. Prior to that, he worked in The Netherlands and United Kingdom where he had teaching and research appointments. Dr. Barjis has both MSc (with highest honors) and PhD in computer science and a post-doctorate in information systems. His research interest is focused on areas such as business process analysis, design, modeling and simulation, IS design, systems analysis and design, enterprise architecture, and petri nets. Offspring of his research activities in these areas are published in over 80 works: three edited books, two college handbooks, six book chapters, five journal articles, and over 70 papers in fully peer-refereed international conference proceedings. Dr. Barjis is a member of several professional organizations (ACM, AIS).

Gan Wei Boon is the project manager of the Singapore Government Enterprise Architecture and the Service-wide Technical Architecture programmes. He works with business leaders, users, and "techies" across the government, with the mission to connect them to streamlined business processes, shared systems, and data. Prior to assuming his current appointment in 2005, he was head (IT Projects) at the Ministry of Home Affairs where he was the programme manager for Homeland Security IT projects. He is a certified IT project manager.

Nico Brehm studied computer science at the University of Applied Sciences in Wernigerode (Germany) and is currently a research assistant at the working group of business information systems at the University of Oldenburg. He is working on his PhD thesis at the Department of Computer Science in Oldenburg. His research work focuses on enterprise resource planning (ERP) systems, IT security, and service-oriented architectures (SOA).

Belinda M. Carter received a Bachelor of Information Technology (Honours I) from the University of Queensland, Australia, in 2002. She is currently working towards a Ph.D within the School of Information Technology and Electrical Engineering at the same institution. Her research interests include workflow, rule-based systems, data integration in heterogeneous environments, and the facilitation of inter-organizational business processes.

Mark Denford holds a bachelor of engineering degree in computer systems and a PhD from the University of Technology, Sydney (UTS). In the last 5 years, Dr. Denford has published over 10 internationally refereed papers and consulted on large systems engineering projects in all sectors in Australia and overseas. Currently he is the chief technical officer of Avolution Pty Ltd.

Scott J. Dowell is the executive consultant of Shirnia & Dowell, LLC. With over 20 years in the information technology industry, he assists Fortune 500 and Agency CxOs develop IT vision, strategy, and architecture that transform the enterprise. Mr. Dowell has led IT organizations as they implement enterprise architecture, portfolio governance, shared business services, data center consolidation, business process outsourcing, and offshore development. Mr. Dowell applies his hands-on experience as an enterprise architect, applications director, and IT executive to guide teams in defining and delivering large-scale, and global strategic programs. His solutions include such emerging trends as service-oriented architecture, service-oriented infrastructure, multi-platform Web services, on-demand/autonomic computing, and applying information technology services management (ITSM).

David Dreyfus is a doctoral student in the Information Systems Department at the School of Management, Boston University. He holds a bachelor of arts in computer science and a masters in business administration from the University of California at Berkeley. He also worked in the software industry for over 20 years before resuming his graduate studies. His current focus is on studying emergence in software systems with a particular emphasis on their social contexts. He has presented papers at the International Conference on Information Systems, the Hawaiian International Conferences on System Science, the Design Science Research in Information Systems and Technology conference, and the Decision Science Institute conference.

Kyle Dunsire holds a bachelor's degree in electrical engineering gained from the University of Technology, Sydney (UTS). He has 15 years experience in the engineering of computer-based systems, particularly real-time automation systems and in technical writing.

Chris Emery is the chief enterprise architect for the Architect of the Capitol (AOC). AOC is a federal agency responsible for the facilities maintenance and historic preservation of the U.S. Capitol, Senate, and House Office Buildings, Library of Congress, and Supreme Court. Dr. Emery has 28 years of information technology experience, including eight years at the White House. Dr. Emery earned his bachelors degree in information systems management from the University of Maryland, where he has also conducted graduate work in technology management.

Diogo R. Ferreira is assistant professor of information systems at IST—Technical University of Lisbon. A graduate of electrical and computer engineering at the University of Porto (1999), he received his PhD (2004) from the same institution following a comprehensive work on workflow management and business networking. From 1999 to 2003, he has been a researcher at INESC Porto where he developed workflow-based solutions for a wide range of applications including teleworking, total quality management, enterprise application integration, and supply chain management. Between 2003 and 2006, he has been assistant professor at the Faculty of Engineering, University of Porto, before joining IST at the campus in Taguspark.

Supriya Ghosh is currently principal architect for Lockheed Martin and is responsible for providing strategic and technical direction for federal government programs. In his role, he provides leadership and expertise in architecture, systems integration. and large-scale software implementation. Mr. Ghosh has been a thought leader in enterprise architecture and is currently a member of the American Council for Technology Enterprise Architecture SIG. He worked for a number of years for the DOD as a contractor and has developed knowledge and expertise in net centricity, interoperability, and service-oriented architecture. Mr. Ghosh is active in various working groups that prepare technical papers in new and upcoming technologies. He has received an MBA from Johns Hopkins University, an MS in aeronautics and astronautics from the University of Washington, and a BS from the California Institute of Technology.

Jorge Marx Gómez studied computer engineering and industrial engineering at the University of Applied Science of Berlin (Germany). He was a lecturer and researcher at the Otto-von-Guericke-Universität Magdeburg where he also obtained a PhD degree in business information systems with the work Computer-Based Approaches to Forecast Returns of Scrapped Products to Recycling. In 2004, he received his habilitation for the work Automated Environmental Reporting through Material Flow Networks at the Otto-von-Guericke-Universität Magdeburg. From 2002-2003, he was a visiting professor for business informatics at the Technical University of Clausthal (Germany). In October 2005, he became a full professor of business information systems at the Oldenburg University (Germany). Professor Gomez's research interests include business information systems, business intelligence, e-commerce, Web intelligence, material flow management systems, life cycle assessment, eco-balancing, environmental reporting, recycling program planning, disassembly planning and control, simulation, and neuro-fuzzy-systems.

Floris Gout was a late starter in information technology. After eight years as a dancer in the performing arts, he worked in engineering (for which he had prior training) on large iron ore, petroleum, and gas projects in Western Australia and Malaysia until 1987. Following those two exciting careers, Dr. Gout studied for his bachelor of applied science majoring in information science and graduated in 1990. Dr. Gout has worked across industry sectors in a range of roles. From his beginnings as a maintenance programmer, he has built research databases for epidemiological studies, developed application requirements, managed a data warehouse project, managed technology and infrastructure conversion projects, written numerous business cases for business applications, and facilitated information plans. Dr. Gout's major interests lie in modelling and project management. He has modelled systems at the enterprise and software application levels. Dr. Gout has developed a skill to reverse engineer a database and assess its alignment to business objectives and IT governance. His project management interest focuses on risk and rewards, and demonstrating the alignment of an architectural model to the business case.

Per Gyllstrom is the chief architect at PFPC Inc. where he runs the Enterprise Architecture group. He has created a company wide architecture, Global Enterprise Architecture (GEA), which his team has been rolling out across PFPC. Over the past 25 years, Dr. Gyllstrom has been a methodologist, development manager, architect, standards leader, and a program manager at Bell Laboratories, Digital Equipment Corporation, Xerox, Platinum Technology, and Computer Associates. During this time, he has made a contribution in several areas including distributed scheduling algorithms, high-performance transaction systems, and to integration methodologies. Dr. Gyllstrom has a PhD in computer science from the University of Iowa in the area of fault-tolerant algorithms.

Jonathan Houk has 11 years of experience managing technology at all levels of Federal organizations and has been involved in the standing up key organizations and delivery of information technology projects. He has held a number of leadership and technical roles for such organizations as the Transportation Security Administration where he served as chief architect, information analysis and infrastructure protection, where he served as deputy chief information officer, Department of Homeland Security as deputy director of information and application delivery, Federal Aviation Administration as a program manager, and currently at the Architect of the Capitol as deputy director of ITD.

Peter Hungerford is an enterprise architect within the IS Strategy and Architecture Group of Syngenta. His current work areas are collaboration technologies, future IT technologies, and architecture processes within Syngenta. He is also a Senior Syngenta Fellow. His previous work has taken him from being a physicist (D Phil from the University of Sussex, England) to IT developer to IT architect. This involved the development of real-time control systems, database systems and a variety of infrastructure designs, working in diverse locations in Europe (France, Germany, UK, and Switzerland). Outside of work, sailing, surfing (wind), skiing, sport climbing, squash, stargazing, and family are important.

Fan Ip-Shing is the course director of the MSc in enterprise system implementation in Cranfield University, UK. Taking a socio-technical approach, he works to develop understanding of and methods in more effective introduction and use of enterprise systems. He has been the coordinator of the European Commission supported research project BEST, Better Enterprise Systems Implementation. In this 4 million euro project, with 12 partners in 10 countries, tools have been developed to provide organisation and human factor readiness assessment for enterprise systems and assist in formulating change management plans to improve the readiness. Dr. Fan has gained his doctorate in computer integrated manufacturing in Cranfield Institute of Technology and has completed his bachelor degree in industrial engineering in the University of Hong Kong.

Bala Iyer is an associate professor of information systems at Babson College. Iyer received his PhD from New York University with a minor in computer science. His research interests include exploring the role of IT architectures in delivering business capabilities, designing knowledge management systems, querying complex dynamic systems, and model management systems. He has published papers in the California Management Review, Communications of the ACM, Communications of AIS, Decision Support Systems, Annals of Operations Research, Journal of the Operational Research Society, and in several proceeding of the Hawaii International Conference of Systems Sciences.

Stephen H. Kaisler is currently with SET Associates, a firm specializing in science, engineering, and technology research, development, and integration. Prior to joining SET, he was technical advisor to the chief information officer of the U.S. Senate, where he was responsible for systems architecture, modernization, and strategic planning for the U.S. Senate. Dr. Kaisler has been an adjunct professor of engineering in the Department of Computer Science at George Washington University. He earned a DSc (computer science) from George Washington University, an MS (computer science), and BS (physics) from the University of Maryland. He has written four books and published over 25 technical papers.

Ron S. Kenett is CEO and senior partner of KPA Ltd., an international management consulting firm with headquarters in Raanana, Israel, and professor at the University of Torino, Torino, Italy. Dr. Kenett has over 25 years of experience in restructuring and improving the competitive position of organizations by integrating statistical methods, process analysis, supporting technologies, and modern human resource management systems. His 130 publications are on topics in industrial statistics and quality management. He is co-author of four books including *Modern Industrial Statistics: Design and Control of Quality and Reliability* (with S. Zacks), *Multivariate Quality Control: Theory and Applications* (with C. Fuchs), *Software Process Quality: Management and Control* (with E. Baker), Professor Kenett's PhD is in mathematics from the Weizmann Institute of Science (1978); he earned a BSc in mathematics with first class honors from Imperial College, London University (1974). Professor Kenett is president of ENBIS, the European Network for Business and Industrial Statistics (www.enbis.org).

Cheol-Han Kim is an associate professor in the Department of Information System Engineering at Daejeon University. Before joining Daejeon, he had many years of experience working for LG software Ltd. and Samsung SDS. He obtained his BS and MS degrees from Hanyang University, and PhD degree from Pohang University of Science and Technology, Korea. His research interests include enterprise engineering, business process management, enterprise architecture, and virtual enterprise.

Kwangsoo Kim is a professor in the Department of Industrial and Management Engineering at Pohang University of Science and Technology, Korea. He holds BS and MS degrees from Seoul National University, Korea, and a PhD degree from University of Central Florida. His teaching and research interests are focused on real-time and virtual enterprise, with emphasis on enterprise architecture, semantics & ontology, business process management, and Web services.

Tae-Young Kim received his BS degree (1998) and MS degree (2000) from Pohang University of Science and Technology, Korea, and is currently a PhD student at the same university. His main research interests are in the fields of enterprise engineering, virtual enterprise, business process management, enterprise architecture, and ontology engineering.

John S. "Stan" Kirk is the deputy director, Division of Information Systems for the National Science Foundation in Arlington, Virginia. Dr. Kirk has over 20 years of experience providing leadership and direction in developing, acquiring, implementing, and managing information technology programs and policies at the enterprise level. His focus has been in providing day-to-day operational leadership and the long-range planning required for building and maintaining successful information management operations. He received a MS in computer systems management and a BS in information systems management, both from the University of Maryland University College. Kirk is a member of the Federal Information Technology Review Board and the Senior Executive Service.

Chris Lawrence is business architecture consultant and has designed and implemented solutions in the UK, U.S., and Southern Africa over a 25-year career in financial services IT. He has addressed conferences in the UK and U.S. specializing in the area where process architecture meets holistic delivery and transition methodologies. In 1996, he left England for Cape Town to co-found Global Edge, a strategic business-enablement competency employing a version of Sungard's *Amarta* architecture to support financial services group Old Mutual's international expansion. His book *Make Work Make Sense* (Future Managers, 2005) is based on the process-architectural delivery methodology he developed for Global Edge. Dr. Lawrence studied philosophy at Cambridge and London.

John Leaney has been researching and developing techniques for architecture-focussed management, design, and measurement of computer-based systems for over 17 years. His recent consulting experience includes the measurement, assessment, and risk evaluation of the new combat system for the Royal Australian Navy, which was completed in the year 2000. For the past eight years, he has been the leader of the architecture-based engineering research group at the University of Technology, Sydney (UTS). Leaney has authored or co-authored over 70 papers and reports and six hypothetical-style videos.

Jeong-Soo Lee is in the unified course of the master's and the doctor's at Pohang University of Science and Technology, Korea. He obtained his BS degrees from the same university (2003). His research interests are focused on enterprise architecture, ontology engineering, and real-time enterprise.

Sunjae Lee is a PhD student at Pohang University of Science and Technology, Korea. He received his BS and MS degrees from the same university (1999 and 2001). His research activities focus on the role of process states in the area of business process management and Web service management.

Sebastiano Lombardo holds an MSc from NTNU, Trondheim, Norway and a master of management from BI Executive School, Oslo Norway. He worked as a scientist at SINTEF, the Norwegian Foundation for Industrial and Technology Research. He is currently a Business development manager at PERA Innovation ltd. Dr. Lombardo's main fields of research are innovation processes and business development, his interests also include change management and organizational development, with particular attention to learning mechanisms and cross-cultural challenges.

Daniel Lübke worked as a software developer, coach, and trainer within various projects and received his diploma degree at the Technical University of Clausthal (Germany) in the area of business informatics. Currently he is research assistant and PhD student at the Software Engineering group at University Hannover. His research interests include service-oriented architectures (SOA) and agile methods.

Dat C. Ma is a PhD student within the School of Information Technology and Electrical Engineering at the University of Queensland. His thesis is concerned with the investigation of data and process flow in rule-based messaging systems for collaborative processes. The research is focused on the designing, modelling, enactment, verification, and validation aspects of collaborative processes. Before doing his PhD, Dr. Ma received a bachelor of engineering degree from Ho Chi Minh City University of Technology, Vietnam (1993), and completed a master degree in information technology at Queensland University of Technology, Australia (2002).

Raghunath Mahapatra is currently working as a manager in Ernst & Young India. He has over 15 years of experience of working in government, public sector, and private sector organizations advising them on process reengineering, ERP as a change enabler and tool for organization restructuring, integration of processes for convergent citizen services delivery amongst others. His focus area is tools for organizations' process reengineering and bringing governance focus to public sector organizations. He has presented and published papers on e-governance and its effectiveness.

John Mo obtained his PhD from Loughborough University in manufacturing engineering (1989). He is currently team leader of Manufacturing Systems in the Division of Manufacturing and Infrastructure Technology, CSIRO. His expertise includes computer integration manufacturing, enterprise architecture methodology, data communication, process modelling, and robotics. In his 10 years in CSIRO, he led several large-scale international projects involving multi-disciplinary teams in the development of advanced manufacturing systems and the integration of manufacturing facilities using the internet, wireless, and RFID technologies. Prior to joining CSIRO, he was course leader of Master of Manufacturing Engineering course in RMIT University, Australia.

Dave Nicholson is a director at the MITRE Corporation in McLean, Virginia. He spent over 20 years in army research, development, and acquisition program management, and for the last 10 years has been leading architecture efforts with MITRE. Dr. Nicholson is a graduate of the United States Military Academy and received MS degrees from the Naval Post Graduate School in electrical engineering and from Stevens Institute of Technology in technology management. He is currently the project director of MITRE support to the U.S. Air Force Office of Warfighting Integration and CIO.

Ovidiu Noran has received his PhD in enterprise architecture from Griffith University, studying a meta-methodology for the creation and operation of collaborative networked organisations. He also holds an engineering degree in building services and automation and a master degree in information and communication technology. Dr. Noran is active as an engineer and enterprise architecture/management consultant and is currently lecturing in the enterprise architecture, e-commerce, and software engineering domains at Griffith University. He is a member of professional bodies (e.g., Engineers Australia, Australian Institute of Management) and standardization committees such as ISO/IEC SC7/WG7 (Software Engineering / Life cycle Management) and ISO TC184 SC5/WG1 (industrial automation).

Tim O'Neill holds a bachelor of engineering degree in computer systems and a PhD from the University of Technology, Sydney (UTS). Currently he is a research fellow in the UTS Institute for Information and Communication Technologies (IICT) and for the last three years has been the CEO of Avolution Pty Ltd. In the last 10 years, Dr. O'Neill has published over 20 internationally refereed papers and consulted on large systems engineering projects in all sectors in Australia and overseas. He is currently undertaking multi-disciplinary, qualitative, and quantitative research and consulting for large-scale, complex enterprises and systems on behalf of UTS and Avolution Pty Ltd.

Maria E. Orlowska's contributions in the database systems field appear in over 200 published research papers in peer reviewed international journals and conferences. Twenty-five PhD students have successfully completed their studies under her supervision, and to date, she has served on the Program Committees of 128 international conferences. Her research covers a diverse range of considerations, from pure theoretical and fundamental contributions to applied and experimental computing issues. She gained her PhD (computer science) (1981) from the Institute of Applied Mathematics, Technical

University of Warsaw, and was awarded the Polish Ministry of Education Award for best thesis in the computer science area. She gained a DSc (computer science) (2004) from The University of Queensland, Australia. Since September 1990, Maria has held a tenured position as professor of information systems in the School of Information Technology and Electrical Engineering, The University of Queensland, and is currently the head of the school's research division of data & knowledge engineering. From July 1992, she acted as the distributed databases unit leader, and until 2004, the leader of the Workflow Technology Group for the cooperative Research Centre for Distributed Systems Technology Pty Ltd (DSTC). In August 2004, she was awarded an innovative Commonwealth funded network grant for a period of 5 years, and is now acting as network convener for the ARC Research Network in Enterprise Information Infrastructure. From March 2002 until December 2004, Orlowska was a board member of the Australian Research Council (ARC), and also acted on the Expert Advisory Committee for ARC Mathematics, Information, and Communication Sciences. Also in 2004, she acted as chair of the ARC Linkage Infrastructure Equipment and Facilities (LIEF) panel at the national level. In March 2003, she was made a Fellow of the Australian Academy of Science.

Sinnakkrishnan Perumal is a doctoral candidate at Indian Institute of Management Calcutta, Kolkata, India. Before pursuing his doctoral studies, he worked as a software engineer in WIPRO Technologies Ltd., Bangalore, India for about four years. His doctoral research is in the area of business process management, in particular it is on workflow verification. Recently, he has published a book chapter on workflow verification in the book, *Workflow Handbook 2005*. His other research interests include e-governance and artificial intelligence systems like heuristic search methods, neural networks, fuzzy logic, and genetic algorithms.

Tan Eng Pheng is currently the cluster director in charge of promoting IT-enabled business transformation in manufacturing, logistic, finance, and tourism sectors at the Infocomm Development Authority of Singapore. Prior to assuming his current appointment in November 2005, he was the director of the e-Government Planning and Management Division in the Government Chief Information Office. In that capacity, he coordinated the development of the Singapore e-Government Action Plan, a multi-year strategic plan, which spells out the major thrusts of e-government initiatives in the whole Singapore public sector. In FY 2003-2005, the Plan had a budget of S$1.3 billion. Dr. Pheng also spearheaded the development and implementation of Infocomm policies, technical standards, and architecture for the public sector. These included the formulation of a service-wide technical architecture to facilitate systems interoperability and information exchange across more than 60 government agencies in 2003, and the initiation of the Singapore Government Enterprise Architecture development in 2005. During Oct 2004 to Sep 2005, Pheng also served as project director of an IDA-private sector consortium, which successfully formulated a national level strategic IT plan for another country.

Steven J. Ring is a principal information engineer at the MITRE Corporation in Bedford, MA. He has over three decades of experience including technical and managerial roles in commercial/military product development and integration. Mr. Ring received his BEE from Cleveland State University and MS in systems engineering from Case Institute of Technology. He has focused on applying information and knowledge-based repository technology to DOD architecture development and integration in support of interoperability and simulation based acquisition. He has contributed in the areas of techniques, methodologies, and tools for integrating, analyzing, and validating both static and dynamic DOD architecture models. Mr. Ring is currently examining how architecture analysis can support portfolio management investment decision-making and is also involved with the next generation of DoDAF (v2.0).

Phil Robinson is Lonsdale Systems' principal trainer and consultant. Dr. Robinson has worked with information technology, in a variety of roles since 1975. He has been involved in the planning, analysis and implementation of a diverse range of business, scientific, and technical information systems. Dr. Robinson is an experienced workshop facilitator and has led numerous workshops in the course of his consulting assignments. He has extensive training experience, earning a reputation as a lucid and knowledgeable presenter. Dr. Robinson has presented training courses for clients in Australia, Malaysia, Philippines, Thailand, Hong Kong, Singapore, and Indonesia. As well as presenting courses, he has authored numerous courses for industry and three University units. He has also had two books published on programming Apple computers. The books were published in a number of countries including the USA, UK, and as translations in Germany and France. More recently, he co-authored two award-winning articles describing an original organizational theory. Dr. Robinson was subsequently appointed to the editorial board of the UK journal that published the articles.

Shazia W. Sadiq is a senior lecturer in the School of Information Technology and Electrical Engineering at The University of Queensland, Brisbane, Australia. She is part of the Data and Knowledge Engineering research group and is involved in teaching and research in databases and information systems. Sadiq holds a PhD from the University of Queensland in information systems and a master's degree in computer science from the Asian Institute of Technology, Bangkok, Thailand. Her research focus is on innovative technology solutions for business process management. Dr. Sadiq has contributed widely to the body of knowledge in the field of dynamic workflows, has published several papers on this topic, and serves on several program committees on related areas.

Roger Sliva has been serving in the Nevada State government as an IT professional and practitioner for over 11 years including two years as the state's only enterprise architect. He received a BA degree from the University of California, Riverside.

Michel Spadoni obtained his PhD degree in automatic control from University of Metz (1987). Since 1988, he has been an associate professor at Ecole Nationale d'Ingénieurs de Metz (ENIM) and a member of the Laboratory for Industrial and Mechanical Engineering (LGIPM – EA: 3096). His research interests include representation and exploitation of knowledge and the know-how in manufacturing engineering and production management. He is a member of EEA (Electronic, Electrotechnic, and Automatic) Club and of WSEAS (World Scientific Engineering Academy and Society) Working Group on Computer Science.

Steven Thornton (PMP, CUA), an Information Technology (IT) Architect and Certified Usability Analyst (CUA), graduated West Point in 1994. He served in the United States Army until 1999 in various roles, including platoon leader, battery executive officer, and deputy joint operations officer. He joined Nextel Communications in 1999 as an IT project manager and later worked as the content manager for Nextel.com and as the senior manger for corporate communications for the Nextel intranet. Since 2003, he has worked as an IT Architect on contract to the National Institutes of Health (NIH) enterprise architecture team. At NIH he helped build the enterprisearchitecture.nih.gov website and assists with other enterprise architecture program requirements.

Gail L. Verley implemented the enterprise architecture (EA) program for the FDIC and with the support of the FDIC's CIO Council the development and publication of the first IT Strategic Plan. Under her leadership, the EA program introduced an enterprise application integration strategy, developed an EA repository for business decision-making, instituted an EA governance model, and published articles, reference material, and standards through an e-mail publication and internal Web site. Dr. Verley played a major role in FDIC receiving the 2004 Zachman Institute EA Excellence Award for FDIC's target conceptual data architecture and governance model. Dr. Verley's career in the bank regulatory arena began at the Federal Savings and Loan Insurance Corporation (FSLIC) (1981) where she held the position of assistant director of Field Operations. She received her bachelor's degree in education from Shippensburg State University (1977) and her master's degree in public administration from the American University (1980).

Zachary B. Wheeler is a principal of SDDM Technology located in the District of Columbia and a graduate of Howard University. Mr. Wheeler specializes in process and work flow improvement and has a strong propend of software reusability. He has developed a keen interest in Web services and SOA and their integration into process reengineering. He recently published *Using SOA and Web Services to Improve Business Process Flow*, in the 2005 Workflow Handbook by the Workflow Management Coalition. Mr. Wheeler would like to thank Dr. Faith Hayes for her assistance in content organization.

P.M. (Nel) Wognum has been an assistant professor in the Department of Operations, Organisation, and Human Resources Management of the Faculty of Business, Public Administration, and Technology of the University of Twente in The Netherlands since 1996. She received a master's degree in computer science (1986) and a PhD in knowledge systems (1990). She has worked as an assistant professor in the Department of Computer Science in the Knowledge-Based Systems Group from 1990 to 1996. Her main area of research is concurrent engineering in (networks of) industries with a focus on the interaction between (information) technology and organisation. She has coordinated the research work in the IST project BEST (Better Enterprise SysTem implementation) resulting in a tool to assess readiness of an organisation to start an enterprise system implementation project. Although she currently entered early retirement, she continues her research and is involved in the AsiaLink project Mi-EIS and the international MBA programme of the University of Twente and Hunan University in China.

Index